Adulthood and Aging

An Interdisciplinary, Developmental View

Adulthood and Aging

An Interdisciplinary, Developmental View

John Wiley & Sons, Inc.
New York   London
Sydney   Toronto

Douglas C. Kimmel

*Department of Psychology,
City College
City University of New York*

To Ron
and all who grow older

Library of Congress Cataloging in Publication Data:

Kimmel, Douglas C
  Adulthood and aging.

  Includes bibliographies.
  1. Adulthood. 2. Aging. I. Title.

[DNLM: 1. Aging. WT104 K49a 1974]
BF724.5.K55   155.6   73-13557
ISBN 0-471-47700-1

Printed in the United States of America

10 9 8 7 6 5 4 3 2

Preface

Adults control the political and economic power in society. They produce, reproduce, and reach the apex of their abilities. They achieve success, they fail, and they grow old. Yet these important years of the life span have seldom received the detailed attention that they deserve. This book begins where child and adolescent development books end, and it continues the study of human development from young adulthood to old age and death.

In addition to focusing on adulthood and aging, this book is unique in at least three other ways. First, it applies the *developmental approach* as a systematic framework for viewing these adult years. Second, it attempts to bring an *interdisciplinary perspective* to the study of adult development by emphasizing the interaction of psychological, social, and physiological aspects; thus, the central theoretical framework is the interactionist perspective. Finally, the book includes six *case examples*—interludes between the chapters—as a challenge and an opportunity to bridge the gap between theoretical concepts and actual adults who are living competent and varied lives in the real world.

Since I usually dislike textbooks, I have tried to write a nontext that will not only be a useful introduction to an emerging field but will also raise the level of awareness about this period of life and about the problems of growing old in society. I have also attempted to contribute some new ideas, to encourage thinking, and to raise important questions. Since I am only 30, my perspective is the same as the perspective of a person at the beginning of his journey through adulthood, but I am very curious about what lies ahead. Hopefully this perspective has compensated somewhat for my lack of firsthand experience and years of research.

The approach and much of the information I present reflects my study of human development at the University of Chicago. I am deeply indebted to Bernice L. Neugarten, whose course in adult development provided the initial outline for my conceptualization of the study of adulthood, and to the other faculty members of the Committee on Human Development. A considerable proportion of the useful information in this book is a direct result of their research and insight. I also thank the other pioneers in the field whose research and teaching has created the study of adult development and aging. And I am grateful to my students, who helped me to improve mimeographed versions of these chapters, and to my colleagues at City College who read, criticized, and used portions of the manuscript in their own classes and who encouraged me along the way. Vern L. Bengston, Jacqueline M. Falk, Marjorie Fiske Lowenthal, and William Kessen also made useful suggestions to various portions of the manuscript, and I thank them for their help and encouragement. Also, the six persons who opened themselves to my questions in the interviews and shared part of their life with me deserve thanks (Harry Charner requested to be mentioned by name). Finally, I am grateful to Ronald Schwizer, who provided invaluable help in transcribing the interviews, preparing illustrations, and proofreading, and to Roxanne Dodds and Frank Eng for their assistance with bibliographic work.

I feel that adulthood and aging will continue to emerge as a field of study, and I hope that this book will be useful in a variety of contexts. For example, it might be a basic source in undergraduate courses in psychology, sociology, and in interdisciplinary programs. Graduate courses in fields such as geriatric social work, nursing, geropsychology, social gerontology, and life span or human development may also find this book useful. I use it in conjunction with readings in fiction (such as *Death of a Salesman*) or biographies for my undergraduate psychology course. Other faculty members, especially at the graduate level, might wish to use a supplementary book of readings (such as *Middle Age and Aging*, which contains many of the references used here). Some instructors might wish to emphasize field experience—for example, students working as volunteers in senior citizen centers, nursing homes, chronic disease hospitals, or simply interviewing adults of varying ages. In any case, I hope that this book is good reading, and that it encourages continued growth of the knowledge about adulthood and aging.

New York, N.Y., 1973   DOUGLAS KIMMEL

Contents

Credits

Credits

Frontispiece — Degas: Old Italian Woman (Metropolitan Museum of Art, Bequest of Charles Goldman, 1980)

Chapter 1 — Ellenville Milestone on the Albany Post Road (Courtesy of The Historical Society, New York City)

Chapter 2 — James Carl Jones, Dladimr (Anders Collection)

Chapter 3 — Michelangelo: David (Alinari/Scala)

Chapter 4 — Rodin: The Kiss (Alinari/Scala)

Chapter 5 — Munch: Family Group (Munch Museum of Modern Art)

Chapter 6 — Young Man with a Pick (Metropolitan Museum of Art, gift of Edward H. Harkness, 1918)

Chapter 7 — Halt! (Little Dance) (Metropolitan Museum of Art, purchase, 1981)

Chapter 8 — Cross section of coronary arteries (National Institute of Health)

Chapter 9 — Dying man (Copyright © 1963 by Charles Harbour, Aba num Photos Inc., all rights reserved)

Chapter 10 — Senior Power (Courtesy of Senior Ghisw of Greater New York)

introduction
The Developmental Approach

Each of us is like every other person, like many other persons, and like no other person.[1] There is something that is uniquely me, distinct even from my identical twin; there is something about me that is rather similar to others of my age, my culture, and my education; and there is something about all of us that is similar, regardless of race, sex, or culture.

These assertions indicate the complexity inherent in understanding adulthood because we are interested in grasping the similarities and the differences between such diverse people as Charles De Gaulle, Charles Smith (who runs the corner filling station), and Margaret Chase Smith (former senator from Maine). How can this be done? How can we understand the complexity of a man such as Martin Luther King or the dancer Rudolf Nureyev, while at the same time increasing our understanding of Mary Hall (business executive and housewife) and Herb Brown (steel worker and father)? More immediately, how can we gain a greater understanding and appreciation of our unfolding lives and the lives of the people we live with and the people we pass on the street? What framework, what point of view will help to reveal the pattern in the complex fabric of adulthood?

Let us focus our sights so that we see clearly certain similarities of these diverse people; at the same time let us allow their individual differences to momentarily fade so that our gaze is not distracted from the differences that are more systematic—such as age differences. Let us focus, for example, on the age differences between a man of 40 and a man of 18 or on the differences between a woman of 60 and a woman of 25. If we can see such differences clearly, then we can also see in what ways women of 60 are similar to young women, and in what ways they are

[1] First stated, I believe, by Kluckhohn and Murray (1953).

1

different from young women but similar to other women of the same age. We can then bring the uniquely individual differences back into focus to produce a richer and more complete picture than when only the similarities or only the idiosyncratic differences are seen.

This complex task is the intellectual adventure offered by the developmental approach to adulthood in this book. This approach provides the important perspective of *time* and *age* that allows us to explore similarities and differences as they vary systematically and in orderly progressions with age during adulthood. Our aim is to discover some of the regularities in human life, to explore some of the steps along the journey from puberty to death, and to gain a greater understanding of where we are going and how we arrived at where we are today.

DEVELOPMENTAL APPROACH

The developmental framework employed here is a point of view with the following characteristics: (1) we are interested in human growth, behavior, and change; (2) we are interested in normal, everyday individuals rather than just individuals who find their way into a mental hospital or a psychotherapist's office; and (3) we are interested in the progression of life as a continuous process of change, sequential development, and continuity from birth to death.

We choose to focus on the adult years of the life span, and our first assumption is that people continue to grow, to change, and to develop after the onset of adolescence. We do not agree that personality is fixed in childhood and stable after adolescence; instead, we are interested in how continuous personality seems to be throughout an individual's life; and we wonder what brings about the changes and what brings the continuity of personality. This question arises and is discussed in each of the following chapters, so it provides a central thread in our examination of change and continuity and of antecedent-consequent relationships in adulthood.

A second assumption in our developmental approach is that adulthood can be seen as a sequential, orderly progression. Yet we wonder what makes it orderly—what are the factors that regulate this orderly progression? In development during childhood we know that biological maturation plays a central role in regulating the timing of the child's development, but what factors would play such a role in adulthood? Certainly there is a qualitative difference between the milestones in child development (such as weaning, walking, talking, and toilet training) and the milestones of adulthood (such as marriage, parenthood, retirement, and widowhood). Yet in both cases the milestones suggest a sequential order to the life span and bring changes in a wide range of experiences that have effects on such important psychological characteristics as personality and self-concept. So when we apply the developmental approach to adulthood, we do so to understand the process of continuity and change throughout the entire life span.

A third assumption is that the developmental study of adulthood is not a simple extension of child development; that is, many of the important issues in child development—such as learning language, achieving in school, or establishing independence from parents—do not remain as important in adulthood; instead, new issues—which may not have been at all relevant during childhood—become important concerns. Consider, for example, whether occupational success in adulthood is related to intelligence (IQ) or school performance. Certainly, the relationship between IQ and school performance is important during childhood and adolescence. But neither IQ nor school grades have much of a direct relationship to adult success in an occupation (Hoyt, 1965). Instead, success in an occupation reflects such variables as experience, career goals, emotional satisfaction, skill, and monetary reward. In an important sense, the cognitive, affective, and sexual developments of early adolescence greatly expand the individual's ability to think abstractly, to interpret feelings, and to interact with others. As a result, development during adulthood—as well as the framework that may be used to study it—is significantly different from development during childhood.

Thus, to understand adult development, we need to focus on *adult* issues and to consider the processes of both change and consistency as individuals progress through sequential milestones during the adult years.

INDIVIDUAL DIFFERENCES

In our developmental framework, we will focus heavily on the effects of normative or typical milestones and developmental changes during the adult years in order to better understand how these events and changes affect an individual in society. To be sure, individual differences—and differences between societies—are so marked that they may sometimes seem more striking than developmental differences between persons of different ages. However, individual differences reflect not only the person's uniqueness and the effects of their society but also the person's unique interaction with sequential developmental changes. That is, one's personality (or sociocultural environment) affects one's response to being a mother, to retiring from work, or to being a grandparent. And these developmental events may affect specific individuals in different ways. Thus the developmental approach provides us with a framework for examining the interaction of personality (or sex role or environment) with an individual's normative developmental changes. Obviously it makes a difference whether a person is black, lives in India, or is poor; but the question that the developmental approach raises is: How do these characteristics interact with an individual's developmental progression through the adult years?

Our approach will be to underplay individual variation and to emphasize the developmental theme. We argue that when the developmental theme is understood, one may then bring in the individual variations and examine a specific individual in a specific place at a specific time in life; however, if we do not understand the theme clearly, individual variations may be a confusing "noise" of idiosyncratic differences that make little sense.

There will be several "interludes" of individual case histories interspersed between some of the chapters in this book. We see these interludes as examples of individual variation in which both the general developmental theme as well as the interaction of this theme with idiosyncratic differences stand out. The interludes (and other persons we see around us) challenge our ability to understand the developmental theme in the midst of its variations; yet if we can understand the theme, the variations can be better understood.

At times it may seem that individual variation is being underemphasized. Or it may seem that social class or cultural variations on these developmental themes are also underemphasized in order to emphasize the developmental aspects. This is not done to deny their importance but, instead, to provide a more general framework for viewing the effects of these differences. However, individual variation should remain constantly in the back of one's mind and frequently be brought into focus to see how it interacts with the developmental progression we will be emphasizing here. Indeed, much of the currently exciting developmental research is examining the impact of ethnic and social class variations on the developmental progression during the adult years.

INTERDISCIPLINARY ASPECTS

Our focus on human growth and development demands our consideration of the insights provided by all of the scientific disciplines that study human behavior. This characteristic of the developmental approach is as valid for adulthood as for childhood because, when we discuss the various factors that play a role in development, we quickly realize that cultural and historical factors are relevant, as are social, biological, and psychological factors. Indeed, since we are focusing our attention on the human organism as it progresses across a span of time, we are impressed with the importance of the *interaction* of many factors representing various disciplines; but the human organism is a unity, and the study of that unity brings these separate disciplines together in a new and profound way. Thus we pick freely from the various sciences because we know that the human organism itself develops in exactly this interdisciplinary, interactive way. As a result, we will attempt to understand *adulthood* instead of the psychology, sociology, or physiology of adults.

PLAN OF THE BOOK

The indisciplinary and developmental approach that we have selected for our study of adulthood leads us to focus simultaneously on the developmental progression from young adulthood to old age and on the social, personality, and physiological processes during the adult years. We begin with a discussion of developmental theory and research approaches to the adult years of the life span that provides an overview of the central themes of the book. The second chapter—social-psychological processes of development—presents a theoretical framework or point of view for understanding the important effects of social factors on adult development and serves as a major unifying theoretical perspective for the book.

Chapter 3 focuses on young adulthood and begins the discussion of the major issues, turning points, and crises of the adult years. This developmental progression is carried on implicitly through the remainder of the chapters. Chapter 4 discusses the differences and similarities between men and women in adulthood and considers the effects of these differences on developmental issues during the adult years. This chapter builds upon the discussion of young adulthood and sets the stage for the discussion of the middle and late years of life.

Chapters 5 and 6 deal with the major involvements of adults during the middle years of the life span: the family and one's occupation. The important issues of increased leisure, forced retirement, and the similarities and differences between single (unmarried or previously married) and married adults are also included in these chapters.

Chapters 7 and 8 focus implicitly on the changes during the second half of life with a discussion of personality processes and changes during adulthood and a discussion of physiological and intellectual processes in human aging.

Chapter 9 deals with death and bereavement, two relatively "taboo" topics in our society that have recently begun to receive a great deal of attention in research and in the popular media. Certainly our rapidly improving medical ability to keep persons alive is raising important and difficult ethical and humanistic questions. Similar questions are raised by our society's general attitude toward and treatment of the elderly— the topic of Chapter 10. What is the current condition of the aged in the United States, and what changes are likely to take place for this minority of two million persons in the future? We conclude with an outline of some of the rapidly growing fields that are open to persons seeking an occupation (either professionally or as a volunteer) that deals with the needs of the aged.

Six case examples are inserted between some of these chapters. While they do not represent "typical" adults (whatever that might be), they do represent a variety of adults who are currently at different points in the adult life-span. They are presented in chronological order (ages 27, 34, 48, 65, 75, and 89) and are placed after the chapters that deal with their respective issues. It is hoped that the cases will bring some of the concepts in the chapters to life and will also provide an opportunity to test how well these concepts apply to actual persons in the real world.

References

Hoyt, D. P. 1965. The Relationship Between College Grades and Adult Achievement: A Review of the Literature. *ACT Research Reports*, No. 7, September, 1965. Iowa City, Iowa: American College Testing Program.

Kluckhohn, Clyde, and Murray, Henry A. 1953. Personality Formation: The Determinants. In Clyde Kluckhohn and Henry A. Murray (Eds.), *Personality in Nature, Society and Culture.* (2nd ed.) New York: Alfred A. Knopf.

one
Adulthood: Developmental Theory and Research

When does a person become an adult? At what point in the life span should we begin our investigation of adulthood? Does it begin when a person becomes biologically mature and able to have children? Is there some social milestone that marks the beginning of adulthood in our society—such as moving away from the parent's home or getting married? Or is it marked by some kind of psychological maturity, perhaps a feeling of independence and responsibility? Or does adulthood begin when others begin to treat an individual as an adult, or when the person feels like an adult and expects others to respect this sense of being an adult?

There is no obvious definition of the point when adulthood begins. In our society, adolescence seems to gradually fade into "young adulthood" and, at some point, full adulthood begins. But since there are many different indications of adulthood—biological maturity, psychological maturity, social milestones (such as working full time, marriage, and parenthood), and "perceived" maturity (seen by oneself and by others)—it is impossible to say that all 18-year-olds (or even all 35-year-olds) are necessarily "adult." For example, one 35-year-old may be psychologically 35 (is responsible, looks toward the future, and has resolved the issues of adolescence) but is socially 18 (still in school, living at home, and unmarried) and may be biologically 65 (suffering arthritis or heart trouble).

Thus, chronological age by itself may not be a very meaningful indicator of the beginning of adulthood, "middle age," or of "old age." Perhaps the most meaningful index of the beginning of adulthood is the individual's perceived age: "How old do you feel?" This index would typically reflect the person's chronological age as well as his social and biological age. One person might feel, act, and look like an adult (and others would respond to that person as an adult) at the age of 16; another person might not feel like a full adult until he finished graduate school at the age of 30.

However, chronological age may be a useful index for measuring change with time and for studying progressive and sequential changes during the course of a human life. Sometimes age indicates that several social milestones have been passed; it may indicate a greater amount of "wear and tear" resulting from the simple fact of living longer; it may reflect an accumulation of experience, biological change, or a different perspective on life because of a lengthening past and a shortening future. Thus, age is a convenient index of a host of variables; and changes with age, differences between people of different ages, and the process of aging are of particular interest in the developmental study of adulthood.

In this chapter we will examine the meaning of age from a developmental perspective. We will begin with a close look at the human life cycle and the way in which social and biological factors interact with age to mark developmental milestones and to "time" development. We will also consider some of the theories of adult development that suggest that this adult part of the life span is marked by developmental changes. Next, since an individual's life cycle is located at a particular historical time, we will examine the intersection of the individual and the historical time lines since it makes some difference whether an individual is 20 years old in 1975 or in 1935; or does it? Finally, we will discuss the ways in which developmental research is conducted since it makes considerable difference whether we are discussing age differences between different people (such as oneself and one's parents) or age changes in the same person at different times (such as oneself today and oneself in 30 years); it is not necessarily true that in 30 years we will be just like our parents —or is it?

CONCEPT OF THE LIFE CYCLE

Developmental studies have one central concern: *age*. But age is merely a measure of the number of revolutions that the earth has made around the sun since a person's birth. Thus it is an index of a host of other variables and is frequently only an approximate and convenient index of sequential progression. However, changes with age, differences between people of different ages, and the process of aging are of particular interest in human development. Many of these age-related changes or differences are defined by the society in which the individual lives; as we will see, this is particularly true for adults. But biological changes and changes that occur in the process of human development in any culture also play an important role in development; this is certainly true in childhood, but it is also true in the adult years.

To illustrate the importance of the index of age, consider the human lifeline (Figure 1.1). Every individual has such a lifeline, beginning with

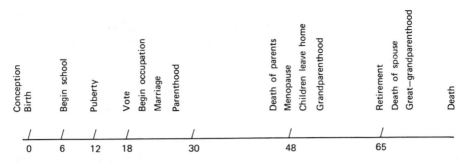

Figure 1.1
The human lifeline. Ages of important events are approximate since there are considerable individual and sex differences in the ages and the order of these milestones.

conception and ending with death. And we intuitively know that a person at one point in his life (for example, at age 45) not only is different from a person currently at a different point (age 18 or 75) but also is different from what he was like when he was younger. Think back yourself for a moment to the changes you have experienced since entering college; and think back further to the first day of high school; there has certainly been development (progression and change) since then.

This lifeline is a schematic representation of the human life cycle and emphasizes the progressive and sequential aspects of the entire span of human life. On this lifeline, certain ages are noted for special age-related events in our society. Obviously, the end points are set by biological and physiological variables; and biological growth plays an initially central but decreasingly important role as we scan the lifeline from conception to birth, from birth through puberty, and from puberty through middle age, and so on. But what variables determine the significance of events on the lifeline that are not biological? What do these milestones represent?

One useful analogy is to think of the lifeline as a representation of a journey with a number of interesting places and crucial junctions along the way. Some years ago when travel was slower, roads were commonly marked with *milestones* or mileposts to mark off each mile traveled. These milestones were important because the traveler was progressing toward a goal through time, and his progress was measured by the number of miles traveled in a unit of time (such as a day). Not surprisingly, humans tend to mark off their progress through their life cycle in a very similar way. We are consciously aware of our progress during the past year, and we have a sense of moving too slowly or very quickly along the path toward our goal based on a measure of time. So the notion of milestones in human development is an appropriate concept, because when we think of the life cycle we mark it off with developmental milestones and, in fact, often celebrate these milestones (such as graduation, marriage, or retirement). Let us then look at some of these milestones.

The age of 5 or 6 is significant, for example, because it is the milestone that marks the child's entrance into school and begins a long period of formal training in our culture. This event is, primarily, socially determined by the age at which a child is accepted into kindergarten or elementary school. The next major age-related event after the start of school is the onset of puberty, about age 12. Although our Western cultures ordinarily do not celebrate puberty as a *rite of passage*, anthropological reports of other cultures point out that initiation rites at puberty were very important in their society, marking the end of childhood and the beginning of adulthood. In some Indian tribes, for example, the young male passed through a series of tests of his courage and endurance that culminated in a celebration of his new status as a warrior. Celebrations such as bar mitzvahs and confirmations in Western religions have some elements in common with these puberty rites; and fraternity or sorority initiations, although they may occur several years after puberty, also involve some of the components of this rite of passage. Perhaps, in our society, the award of a driver's license is emotionally similar to a rite of passage because the child of the moment before has then received the keys to the symbol of adult technology and responsibility. However, the main event in our society signaled by puberty itself is the beginning of *adolescence* and the entry into what many consider to be a youth culture. Adolescence, in many ways, serves as an extended period of *moratorium* between childhood and adulthood and, as such, precludes a clear transition point between childhood and adulthood.

Continuing up the lifeline, the next important age-related event in our society occurs at the age of 18. Many social and legal rights and privileges are awarded on the eighteenth birthday: the driver's license, voting rights, selective service registration, criminal trial as an adult, and the right to drink liquor. Some states distribute these rights over two or three ages (such as a driver's license at 16 and the right to drink at 21), but there is a growing emphasis on the age of 18 as a socially defined turning point in the life cycle that, in many ways, marks the beginning of adulthood in a social and legal sense. Of course, another major event that occurs at 18 for a growing number of young people is the completion of high school and, for a large number, the entrance into college. Frequently this involves leaving home for the first time and a sudden increase in self-reliance. For the young adults who begin work or marry at the end of high school, the age of 18 may signal the beginning of full participation in society as an adult, since one useful definition of the beginning of adulthood is the shift in roles brought about by entrance into the work and family cycles. For the persons who enter college, however, the period of moratorium is extended, often for 4 years and, frequently, for 6 to 10 years if graduate degrees are sought. For this group the moratorium between childhood and full participation in adult roles may last 15 years or even longer.

Although the twenty-first year has traditionally been a significant age in our society, the recent lowering of the age for voting and drinking has tended to decrease the age of 21 as a significant milestone and, as we just suggested, the entrance into adulthood is characterized more exactly by the shift in roles—from student to employee and from single person to husband or wife—than it is by a particular age. This observation foreshadows a difficulty in discussing the remainder of the lifeline, because what is the next significant age-related event after 18 or 21?

Sometimes the age of 30 is suggested as the age that begins middle age and the "downhill slide," as well as the age, that the popular media frequently reminds us, past which one cannot be trusted. We will return to this latter point in a moment when we discuss the "generation gap"; but the age of 30 seems to be a relatively inconsequential milestone. We have noticed that somewhere during the late twenties, when we ask friends how old they are, they tend to have to calculate their age, subtracting in their mind the year of birth from the current year and correcting for the birthday that has not yet passed; in contrast, younger respondents seem instantly aware of their age, perhaps because of the greater amount of *age grading* during the school years. Also, the age of 30 does not seem to mark the beginning of middle age. About 80 percent of a middle-age sample (Neugarten, Moore, and Lowe, 1965) see "middle age" as beginning at age 40 and lasting to age 50, while the decades of the thirties and forties are the ages when both men and women are seen by these respondents to have the most responsibilities and to accomplish the most; the "prime of life" for a man is generally seen to be between the age of 35 and 50 for these respondents. And, since physiological decline has been found to be highly dependent on the presence of mild disease instead of on age alone (Birren, Butler, Greenhouse, Sokoloff, and Yarrow, 1963), the "downhill slide" is likely to reflect the lack of exercise and sedentary life-style characteristic of middle age, rather than middle age itself.

There are, of course, many exciting things going on around the age of 30 and during the middle years of adulthood: marriage, parenthood, occupational advancement, child rearing, and launching the children from the home. In addition, the death of one's own parents often occurs during this period. And during this long age-span the individual makes much of his contribution to society and to the producing economy. It is, in fact, only this segment of the population (from the beginning of work to retirement) who are supporting the children, students, part of the elderly population, and the various levels of governmental service. Although these developmental milestones during the middle years are not rigidly related to age, they usually remain progressive and sequential and are partly governed by social expectations about the "proper time" to marry, to change occupations, or to become grandparents (and so on). In addition, adults seem to have an intuitive sense of a distinct middle-age period that is qualitatively different from other age periods (Neugarten, 1967).

Although the decades after adolescence are marked by few events that are precisely related to age in our society, there are two outstanding age-related events in middle adulthood: menopause and retirement. Menopause, the cessation of the menses and the decline in production of sex hormones, occurs in women between the ages of 45 and 50 (on the average); it is, of course, physiologically determined, but we do not yet know precisely what causes it to occur. Retirement, in contrast, is socially determined and is quite a recently established milestone that was set at age 65 as part of the Social Security legislation in 1935 (actually, the age of 65 was first set as the age for retirement by Bismarck in Germany in 1882; the age was adopted for the United States during the Depression partly because it seemed that young men supporting families should have a higher priority for the scarce jobs than older persons). This socially established retirement age calls attention to the increased longevity of the average adult in this country. Of course, persons "retired" before 1935, but they often did so because of incapacitating illness or death prior to the age of 65. Life expectancy at birth in 1900 was about 50 years; in 1969, it was about 70 years, and the longer life expectancy of women was becoming more exaggerated (Figure 1.2). Most of this increase in the average length of life has resulted from medical advances that have decreased childhood mortality; however, a 15-year-old could expect to live to age 66 in 1900 and to age 78 in 1971; and life expectancy for persons aged 65 has increased about three years since 1900. Thus today nearly everyone may expect to live beyond retirement age, but there is also a current trend toward lowering the age for retirement. These combined trends are effectively creating a long postretirement period of life for a growing number of healthy old persons.

The later years of life may be seen as initiated by this milestone (and rite of passage) of retirement; and because of the growing number of persons surviving to this postfamily, postwork period, these years are growing in social importance today. This period is typically characterized by a sudden drop in income (often to less than one-half of the preretirement income), by the sudden increase in free time and time to spend with the spouse, and by an eventual decline in physical health. The death of one's spouse (especially for women, who usually live longer than men) and the death of one's friends are milestones that may precede one's own death. And death is, of course, the final point on an individual's lifeline. However, there is some interesting evidence that death is a significant

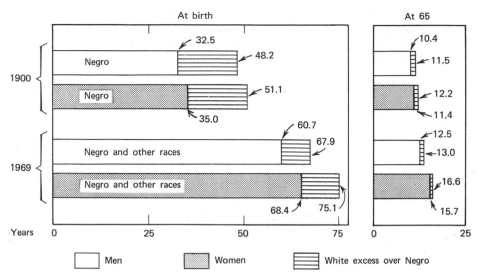

Figure 1.2

Life expectancy at birth and at age 65 by race and sex in 1900 and 1969 in the United States. Most of the increase is the result of reduced childhood mortality; the increases for older persons are less dramatic. (Source. U.S. Bureau of the Census. Some Demographic Aspects of Aging in the United States. Current Population Reports, Series P-23, No. 43. Washington, D.C.: U.S. Government Printing Office, 1973, Table 13.)

developmental event in the sense that nearness to death seems to become a relevant measure of time in old age, perhaps more relevant than chronological age. This research (Lieberman, 1965) suggests that psychological changes occur as death becomes more imminent. Also, the perception of being near the end of one's life may bring a tendency to look back over one's life and to evaluate the meaningfulness of one's encounter with history.

THEORIES OF THE LIFE CYCLE

Philosophers, writers, and social scientists have suggested a variety of views on the nature of the human life cycle. One of the most common views is the analogy between the seasons of the year and the stages of life: spring is the time of growth and coming into bloom; summer is the time of maturity and greatest productivity; autumn is the time of harvest and culmination, when the seeds are sown for new generations; and winter is the time of decline and death. Each season is beautiful in its own right, yet each is unique; there is a definite progression from one season to the next; and one complete cycle prepares the way for the next. Of course, this analogy is too simple to describe human development; but in a poetic way it captures much of the essence of the various developmental theories: development is progressive, sequential, and follows the same pattern generation after generation; it is also circular in the sense that as each generation matures, it nurtures the next generation.

Another poetic, but more satirical view of human development as a series of seven stages was offered by Shakespeare.

> All the world's a stage,
> And all the men and women merely players.
> They have their exits and their entrances,
> And one man in his time plays many parts,
> His acts being seven ages. At first the infant,
> Mewling and puking in the nurse's arms.
> And then the whining schoolboy, with his satchel
> And shining morning face, creeping like snail
> Unwillingly to school. And then the lover,
> Sighing like furnace, with a woful ballad
> Made to his mistress' eyebrow. Then a soldier,
> Full of strange oaths, and bearded like the pard,
> Jealous in honor, sudden and quick in quarrel,
> Seeking the bubble reputation
> Even in the cannon's mouth. And then the justice,
> In fair round belly with good capon lin'd,
> With eyes severe, and beard of formal cut,
> Full of wise saws and modern instances;
> And so he plays his part. The sixth age shifts
> Into the lean and slipper'd pantaloon,
> With spectacles on nose and pouch on side,
> His youthful hose, well sav'd, a world too wide
> For his shrunk shank; and his big manly voice,
> Turning again toward childish treble, pipes
> And whistles in his sound. Last scene of all,
> That ends this strange eventful history,
> Is second childishness and mere oblivion,
> Sans teeth, sans eyes, sans taste, sans everything.
>
> *As You Like It*, Act II, scene vii

Perhaps Shakespeare paints a rather cynical view of human development (and speaks only of men, not women); but the seven stages are quite similar to the ones currently used: infancy, childhood, adolescence, young adulthood, middle age, old age, and senescence. And while we might quibble with Shakespeare's description of these seven stages, there is a sense in which social science is still attempting to *describe* the progressive and sequential changes of the life cycle. We have made little progress in proposing a theory of *why* these changes occur in this order, or how much of the development results from social factors, biological factors, or psychological factors; and we are not certain whether these changes occur in individuals in *every* culture, or whether we have been able to describe only the *interaction* of culture, biology, and psychological development.

However, a few theoretical models of adult development have been suggested, and we will discuss three of the most prominent: the theories proposed by Bühler, Jung, and Erikson. These theories tend to be "arm-chair" theories; that is, they are based on inferences drawn from clinical or empirical observations, but none has been rigorously tested and supported by empirical research. Yet they suggest important dimensions of the life cycle and call attention to potentially salient turning points during the adult years. Hopefully, future research will indicate which theory or combination of theories is most appropriate and will suggest refinements or new theories of adult development that will be appropriate for describing the process of adult development in all social classes and in all cultures (or will at least indicate the ways in which variables such as social class and culture influence development).

Bühler's Theory of the Course of Human Life

Charlotte Bühler and her students studied the course of human life from biographies and autobiographies collected in the 1930s in Vienna; they developed a methodology for analyzing these biographies to reveal an orderly progression of phases on the basis of changes in events, attitudes, and accomplishments during the life cycle.

They were also interested in examining the parallel between the course of life revealed in the biographies and the biological course of life. They noted five biological phases: (1) progressive growth—up to age 15; (2) continued growth combined with the ability to reproduce sexually—age 15-25; (3) stability of growth—age 25-45; (4) loss of sexual reproductive ability—age 45-65; and (5) regressive growth and biological decline—age 65 on (Bühler, 1968).

Based on their studies of 400 biographies, they proposed five phases of life that correspond to these five biological phases.

Age	Phase
0–15	Child at home; prior to self-determination of goals.
15–25	Preparatory expansion and experimental self-determination of goals.
25–45	Culmination: definite and specific self-determination of goals.
45–65	Self-assessment of the results of striving for these goals.
65 up	"Experience of fulfillment or failure, with the remaining years spent in either continuance of previous activities or a return to the need-satisfying orientations of childhood" (Horner, 1968, p. 65).

It may be assumed that the ages are intended to be approximate and reflect such social age-related events as retirement (at age 65). Frenkel, one of Bühler's students, describes the developmental progression as follows:

> The young person just passed through childhood—the first phase of life—makes the first plans about his life and his first decisions in adolescence or shortly afterwards. Here begins the second phase of experience. It is characterized first through the fact that the young person wishes to acquire contact with reality. He experiments with people and professions. An "expansion" of his person takes place. Also characteristic for him is the temporary nature of his attitudes as to what his life calling will be. . . .
>
> . . . At the end of the second phase . . . the individuals have become clear as to their definite attitude toward life. . . . During the third phase, vitality is still at its high point, while direction and specification are now also present, so that very often this time is found to be the culmination period for subjective experiences.
>
> The transition to the fourth phase very often is introduced by a crisis, since at this point the unfolding of the individual powers has come to a standstill, and much has to be given up which depended upon physical aptitude or was connected with the biological needs. Contrary to the descent of the biological curve and the experiences which are connected with that, we find here an ascending scale by virtue of new interest in the results and productivity of life. . . .
>
> Finally, in the fifth phase we find more strongly mentioned age, premonitions of death, complaints of lonesomeness, and often those in this phase are occupied with religious questions. This last period contains experiences of a retrospective nature and considerations about the future, that is, about oncoming death and one's past life. The balance-sheet of life is drawn up, so to speak (Frenkel, 1936).[1]

In general, this view emphasizes the parallel between the biological process of growth, stability, and decline and the psychosocial process of expansion, culmination, and contraction in activities and accomplishments. Often the biological curve is ahead of the individual's psychosocial curve; this is especially true when a reliance on mental abilities allows a person to continue a high degree of productivity for several years after his physical powers have begun to decline. Also there is considerable individual variation since one person may become highly productive rather late in life and reach the psychosocial culmination phase several years after reaching the biological culmination period.

---

[1] Reprinted with permission from *Character and Personality* (now *Journal of Personality*), copyright by the Duke University Press.

Recent formulations of this theory (Bühler, 1968) emphasize an individual's process of setting goals for his life. Thus, this developmental sequence is also seen to reflect different perspectives in an individual's *goal setting* at different phases in the life cycle. For example, goals become gradually established during the first two decades of life, which ideally lead to self-fulfillment during the culmination period; some zestful persons may reexamine these goals and strive for new goals during the fourth phase but, for most individuals, the goals probably shift to stability and retirement in the second half of life. A study by Kuhlen and Johnson (1952) illustrates the shift in goals during the middle years for a group of public school teachers (Figure 1.3). These data indicate marked sex-differences as well as age differences—for example, in the goal "to get different job or promotion in education."

Kuhlen (1964) has elaborated on this growth, culmination, and contraction theory is a slightly different way. He proposed that the growth-expansion motives (such as achievement, power, creativity, and self-actualization) dominate an individual's behavior during the first half of life; however, these motives may change during a person's life because they have been relatively satisfied (for example, the need for success or for sex), and because the person moves into new social positions (such as becoming a mother or the president of a company). In addition, Kuhlen suggests that with advancing age there is ". . . a shift from active direct gratifications of needs to gratifications obtained in more indirect and vicarious fashion" (ibid.). Thus the human life cycle may be characterized by a "curve of expansion and contraction."

In the second half of life, anxiety and threat become more important sources of motivation in Kuhlen's model. This may begin in middle age when the individual senses that the process of expansion is coming to an end and when he begins to be affected by irreversible losses (such as physical illness, death of friends, or loss of job opportunities). Kuhlen cites several studies that indicate that, with advancing age, people are less happy, see themselves more negatively, and experience a loss of self-confidence; there is also a marked increase in symptoms of anxiety among older persons. These data also indicate that aging has less marked (or slower) effects on women and persons in the higher social classes compared with men and persons in the lower classes.

In sum, this view of adult development suggests that the life cycle may be seen in terms of two general tendencies—growth-expansion and contraction. Somewhere, during the middle of life, there would thus seem to be a major turning point between these two contradictory tendencies. Bühler sees the turning point during the period of self-assessment following the culmination phase of midlife (about age 40-45). Kuhlen sees the turning point less clearly defined; it may result from a satisfaction of the earlier growth-expansion motives that allows the emergence of other

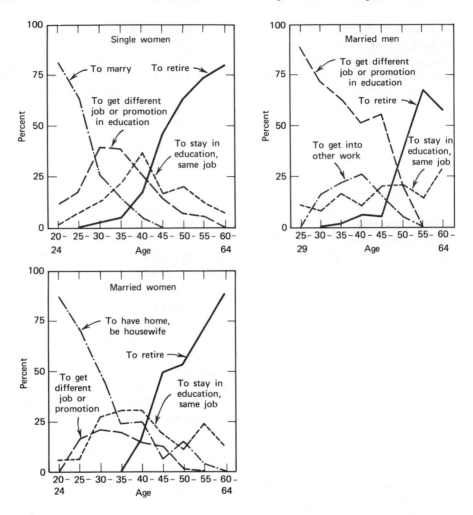

Figure 1.3

Changes in goals with increasing adult age of public school teachers to the question: "What would you most like to be doing ten years from now?" (Source. Kuhlen and Johnson, 1952. Reprinted with permission from the Journal of Consulting Psychology, copyright © 1952 by the American Psychological Association.)

motives; it may result from physical or social losses, from the sense of being "locked into" a situation, or even from the changing time perspective that results from having lived over half of one's life. Probably, it results from the interaction of social, biological, and psychological factors, which may affect men and women differently, and which may affect persons of different social classes in different ways. However, as important as this shift in goal-setting (or in motivation) may be, Bühler concluded from her studies that the individual's assessment of whether he

did or did not reach fulfillment was more critical in old-age maladjust-
ment than biological decline and insecurity. So while avoiding or coping with anxiety and threat may be more salient concerns during the
second half of life (and growth-expansion motives may be more salient
during the first half of life), the person's own sense of having realized his
goals and reached a sense of fulfillment may be the crucial final result of
lifelong goal setting and striving.

Jung's Concept of the Stages of Life

While Bühler's view of the life span grew out of a systematic study of
biographies, and Kuhlen's concepts are based on considerable empirical
research, Jung's view of the stages of life is based primarily on his clinical work and his theory of psychology. He begins his discussion of the
stages of life with *youth*, the period extending from after puberty to the
middle years (age 35-40). Jung was interested in problems of the psyche,
and although it may seem strange that he does not include childhood, he
argues that while the child may *be* a problem to parents, educators and
doctors, the normal child does not *have* problems of his own—only the
adult "can have doubts about himself" (Jung, 1933).

The period of youth involves giving up the dream of childhood, dealing
with the sexual instinct and feelings of inferiority, and in general, widening the horizon of life. The next important change begins between 35
and 40:

> At first it is not a conscious and striking change; it is rather a matter
> of indirect signs of a change which seems to take its rise in the uncon-
> scious. Often it is something like a slow change in a person's char-
> acter; in another case certain traits may come to light which had
> disappeared since childhood; or again, one's previous inclinations
> and interests begin to weaken and others take their place. Con-
> versely—and this happens very frequently—one's cherished convic-
> tions and principles, especially the moral ones, begin to harden and
> to grow increasingly rigid until, somewhere around the age of fifty,
> a period of intolerance and fanaticism is reached. It is as if the
> existence of these principles were endangered and it were therefore
> necessary to emphasize them all the more (Jung, 1933, pp. 12-13).

He sees neurotic disturbances during the adult years as an indication
that the person is attempting to carry the "psychology of the youthful
phase" into these middle years—just as neurotic disturbances in youth
reflect an inability to leave childhood behind. In old age Jung sees some
"deep-seated and peculiar changes within the psyche" (p. 14). There is a
tendency for persons to change into their opposites, especially in the
psychic realm. For example, he suggests that older men become more

"feminine" and older women become more "masculine"; and he points out "an inexorable inner process" that "enforces the contraction of life" (we will discuss these points in detail in Chapter 7). In general, he argues that "we cannot live the afternoon of life according to the programme of life's morning; for what was great in the morning will be little at evening, and what in the morning was true will at evening have become a lie" (p. 17).

There must be some purpose in human life continuing into the late years, such as the caring of children; but what is the purpose of life after this has been accomplished? Is the purpose to compete with the young, as so often happens in our society? Jung points out that in most primitive societies the old people are the sources of wisdom, the "guardians of the mysteries and the laws . . . [in which] the cultural heritage of the tribe is expressed" (p. 18). In contrast, we no longer have any clear sense of meaning or purpose in old age. Thus we try to hang on to the first half of life, clinging to youth instead of looking forward. Jung argues that many people reach old age with unsatisfied demands, but it is "fatal" for such persons to look back. It is essential for them to have a goal in the future. This suggests that the reason that all the great religions hold out the hope of an afterlife is to make it possible for man to live the second half of life with as much purpose as the first half. Jung recognizes that modern man has become accustomed to disbelieve in life after death, or at least to question it, and that we cannot know whether there is an afterlife. But he argues that "an old man who cannot bid farewell to life appears as feeble and sickly as a young man who is unable to embrace it" (p. 20). He feels it is psychologically positive "to discover in death a goal towards which one can strive, and that shrinking away from it is something unhealthy and abnormal which robs the second half of life of its purpose" (p. 20). He suggests that in the second half of life the individual's attention turns inward, and that this inner exploration may help the individual to find a meaning and wholeness in his life that makes it possible for him to accept death.

Erikson's Eight Ages of Man

Like Jung, Erikson's theory of human development is based primarily on his clinical impressions and on his theoretical (Freudian) view of psychology. However, his eight ages of man (Erikson, 1963, 1968) represent a series of crucial turning points stretching from birth to death and thus are somewhat more comprehensive than any of the views presented so far. Nonetheless, his stages emphasize childhood development, and the first five stages are largely expansions of Freud's stages of childhood development. Although we will focus only on the later stages that deal with youth and adulthood, the earlier stages, in his view, are the building blocks upon which success or failure in the later stages depends. Each stage presents a new challenge, a new point of "turbulence" in the "stream of life" that must be negotiated successfully; following our metaphor, if one's raft is severely damaged during one of the early turning points, the later turbulent points will be more difficult to negotiate. In this sense, Erikson's framework provides one view of the "river of life" and its major turning points and forks, so that we might have a sense of what the crucial challenges are for the individual at various points along the stream.

The use of this river metaphor seems appropriate on two levels: first, it expresses the sequential, progressive course of an individual through the eight turning points; and second, it suggests that this framework may be a simplified overview, from a great height as it were, of the general course of the life cycle. The theory is quite difficult to test empirically, and when it has been examined it has not borne up well (e.g., Gruen, 1964); yet it provides useful insights into the central issues of human development and, especially when expanded and refined (as we will indicate later), seems to provide a useful *descriptive* framework for understanding some general issues and changes during the adult years.

Identity versus Identity (Role) Confusion. Erikson's fifth stage begins with the onset of puberty and the increasing social necessity to find one's role in life as a sexual, productive, responsible adult with a reasonably consistent set of attitudes and values about oneself. This stage tends to be resolved about the time one's schooling is completed, an occupation begun, and a marriage partner secured. That is, many important components of one's identity tend to be resolved around the same time, but there is no one clearly defined event that marks the transition into the next stage. Indeed, there is a sense in which these adult stages overlap or even occur simultaneously in many ways. However, these identity issues are assumed to be most pronounced during this stage, although components of it may be altered throughout the rest of life. If one does not resolve this crisis in a positive way, then "identity confusion" may result—a lack of certainty about the role one is playing in the scheme of life. The resolution of this turning point (or identity crisis) may be a consciously deliberated concern, perhaps partly reflecting the adolescent's newly acquired ability to think abstractly (the stage of "formal operations" in Piaget's scheme of cognitive development). At the same time, however, much of the resolution of this crisis involves emotional issues that may be relatively hidden beneath the surface of conscious awareness.

Intimacy versus Isolation. Although the capacity for sexual intimacy begins during adolescence, the individual does not become capable of a fully intimate relationship until the identity crisis is fairly well resolved. That is, one must have a sense of who one is before one can fuse that identity with another in full appreciation of the other's uniqueness and humanness; earlier attempts at intimacy are frequently attempts to try to define oneself through a romantic relationship with another.

Sexual intimacy is only part of what I have in mind, for it is obvious that sexual intimacies often precede the capacity to develop a true and mutual psychosocial intimacy with another person, be it in friendship, in erotic encounters, or in joint inspiration. The youth who is not sure of his identity shies away from interpersonal intimacy or throws himself into acts of intimacy which are "promiscuous" without true fusion or real self-abandon.

Where a youth does not accomplish such intimate relationships with others—and, I would add, with his own inner resources—in late adolescence or early adulthood, he may settle for highly stereotyped interpersonal relations and come to retain a deep *sense of isolation* (Erikson, 1968, pp. 135-136).

Generativity versus Stagnation. This seventh stage of life may be the longest, because it refers to producing something that will outlive oneself, usually through parenthood and in occupational achievements. It is the stage during which nearly all of one's productivity takes place and extends from young adulthood until old age; it also plays a large part in achieving a sense of fulfillment in life. The negative resolution in this stage is a sense of stagnation—boredom, impoverishment, and perhaps an overconcern with one's physical or psychological decline.

Integrity versus Despair. The final stage is brought on by an increasing awareness of the finitude of life and of one's closeness to death. Frequently it may be triggered by retirement or a decline in health. The crucial task during this stage is to evaluate one's life and accomplishments and to affirm that one's life has been a meaningful adventure in history. The accomplishments during the earlier stages play an important role in the resolution of this crisis, because a sense of integrity is the final fulfillment of the previous seven stages, and one's physical or mental offspring provide a continuity of life with the newborn generations. The negative resolution of this turning point is a sense of despair—an existential sense of total meaninglessness, a feeling that one's entire life was wasted or should have been different than it was.

Expansion and Refinement of Erikson's Theory. It may be noted that the last two of Erikson's stages encompass all of the middle and late years of the life cycle, and there is a sense in which the basic issue of generativity may be resolved 40 or 50 years before the life cycle ends. For these reasons, Peck (1955) attempted to define the crucial issues of middle age and old age more precisely; he sees seven central issues in these two periods.

The challenges in middle age are: (1) *Valuing wisdom versus valuing physical powers.* That is, there is a transition point during the forties when persons who cling to physical powers become more and more depressed as these powers decline, but persons who shift to using their mental abilities as a primary resource seem to age more successfully. (2) *Socializing versus sexualizing in human relationships.* If men and women are redefined as individuals and companions with the sexual element playing a lessening role, then interpersonal relationships may take on a greater depth of understanding and enhance the marital relationship during the period when the children are leaving the home. (3) *Cathectic flexibility versus cathectic impoverishment.* A shift in emotional (cathectic) openness is suggested here so that as parents die, old circles of friends are broken up, and children leave home, individuals are able to reach out and take advantage of their widening circle of possible friends (who may represent as large and as varied a group as they will ever know), and to take advantage of new emotional ties with their children's family. (4) *Mental flexibility versus mental rigidity.* Is one able to continue to be open to new experiences and new interpretations, or do past experiences dictate a set of inflexible rules that close off the person to the task of seeking new or different answers to current problems?

In old age, Peck sees the following three issues as central. (1) *Ego differentiation versus work-role preoccupation.* The task here is to establish a varied range of valued activities so that loss of one's occupation (at retirement) or one's accustomed roles (as when the children leave home) allows other meaningful activities that will provide a sense of satisfaction. (2) *Body transcendence versus body preoccupation.* Nearly all old people suffer illness and growing amounts of pain or discomfort, yet some persons remain able to enjoy life immensely, finding more comfort in human interaction or creative activities that allow them to transcend the frailty of their own aging bodies in a sense. (3) *Ego transcendence versus ego preoccupation.* Through children, through contributions to the culture, and through friendships, human beings can extend the significance of their actions beyond their lifetime; death is inevitable (and the full impact of this fact may be realized in old age for the first time), but a person might be able to find a gratifying meaning for his life in the future potential of his family, his ideas, or future generations of the human species.

Conclusions

These theories of development during adulthood provide a number of useful outlines for understanding the sequential progression of the human life cycle. They indicate some of the ways in which persons in the second half of life might be expected to differ from persons in the early years of adulthood. And they sensitize us to some of the normative crisis points or central issues during the adult years. These concepts also suggest a possible midlife crisis when the growth and expansion trends of the earlier years gradually give way to a contraction of social participation and productivity in the later years. Thus, these theoretical perspectives help us to understand some of the broad outlines of the human life cycle and suggest a number of questions for further exploration.

However, these theories tend to be not only too general but also too idealistic. That is, they do not give very much indication of the ways in which cultural differences, sex differences, or social class differences interact with this general developmental progression; and they describe a process of development that leads toward the ideal of "human fulfill-ment" or "successful aging" as defined in the middle class in our society. For other persons, fulfillment or successful aging may mean physical sur-vival and providing one's offspring with at least a reasonable chance for survival; for others, aging means illness, poverty, and isolation with little opportunity for fulfillment or success. Since many aged persons in our society are currently living in poverty, fearing crime and mugging, and dreading an incapacitating illness resulting in a slow painful death, these theories may not be wholly relevant to the lives of many aging persons. Systematic research on the effects of social class, ethnic background, and male-female differences on adult development are currently underway, but the results are not yet available. Until these effects are better under-stood, we can only caution against accepting these rather speculative theories of the life cycle as applying to *all* persons in *all* conditions of life.

This criticism of these theories leads us to raise two important ques-tions, which we will discuss in the remainder of this chapter. First, if we accept these developmental theories as useful general guidelines for understanding the human life cycle, does it not make an important dif-ference whether that life cycle begins in 1850 or 1900 or 1950? That is, what is the effect of the intersection of an individual's life cycle with historical time?

Second, since theory is based upon and tested by empirical research so that theory and research must go hand in hand, how does a develop-mental researcher study the course of human development? For example, would we learn the same things about adult development if we were to study young people and their parents as we would if we were to study the same group of young people when they were 20 and study them again when they were 40? Probably not—unless children grow up to be very much like their parents.

INDIVIDUAL LIFE CYCLES AND HISTORICAL TIME

An individual's developmental progression through the life cycle is only one source of age-related change. We have outlined some of the central biological and social age-related events that influence and serve to "time" the individual's progression through the life span; and we have discussed the theoretical changes that occur with age. But the historical time line that intersects with a person's lifeline is another age-related dimension that affects the individual's progression through his life cycle.

Recalling the lifeline described above (Figure 1.1), we will now intersect it with the historical time line at a moment in 1975 (Figure 1.4). Persons age 65 in 1975 were born in 1910 during a period in the United States of peace and isolation from world conflicts. They were at the forefront of the industrial expansion and westward migration. Obviously, a great deal has changed since then. Average length of education has increased by several years, and the tasks of living in society have become more and more complex. For example, the elderly frequently have a difficult time understanding computer cards or forms required for Medicare.

If you are in college today, your parents were probably born between the end of World War I and the early years of the Great Depression. They learned the interdependence of the nations of the world, but, most of all, they learned that economic security and material possessions may evaporate for reasons beyond their control. Your parents probably went to school during the Depression and their early socialization experiences, which influence later attitudes and values, took place during this period of inadequate material resources. And they lived through World War II, perhaps fought in it, when the security of the United States was felt to be directly threatened, and the material products of the expanding economy continued to be in short supply.

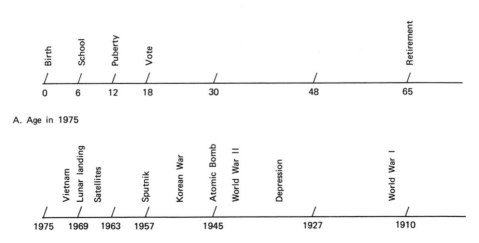

Figure 1.4
Intersection of individual lifeline (A) with historical time line in 1975 (B).

With the atomic bomb came the end of the war and the beginning of the "atomic age." Everyone born after the mid-1940s has experienced not only the economic growth of the country and the increased abundance of the middle class but has also experienced the omnipresent threat of nuclear war. More recently, we have learned of other possible means of annihilation: overpopulation and pollution. We have lived through historical experiences unprecedented in their immediacy resulting from the development of television and news coverage via satellite. The post-Sputnik world not only has experienced an increase in technology and an amazing shrinkage in the effective size of the world but also has focused its attention beyond the earth. In addition, we have experienced a missile crisis, at least three major assassinations, and the longest war in our history.

There can be no doubt that there have been great historical changes during the course of the lives of individuals currently living, and that the pace of these changes is rapid and escalating. For example, if you have not studied the "new math" now being taught in elementary school, you have probably been confounded by the simplest addition problems "to the base of seven." And we can confidently predict that one important aspect of growing older in our society will continue to be increasing complexity in the tasks and skills required of the adult. Speculate for a moment about the complexity involved in adjusting to a computer-based system of universal credit cards where money is no longer used; or about the possibility of spending the first year of your retirement vacationing on the moon!

Such cultural-historical experiences have an effect on the attitudes, values, and world view of individuals living through them. And they have a differential effect on individuals of different ages. For example, the direct experience of a historical event, such as the bombing of Britain or the Great Depression, will have a far more profound personal and psychological effect than merely hearing or reading about the event. Thus, individuals born after World War II, for example, could not have been influenced by the Great Depression in the same way their parents were. This generational effect of historical events may also operate on one rather select segment of the population more strongly than on older or younger population segments. That is, Sputnik had a clear effect on the career direction of many young people who were, at that time, deciding on a career and went into engineering or science as a result of the national emphasis on a competitive space program. The result was that young engineers and scientists were eventually overproduced and were not able to be absorbed into the job market. More recent events such as the moon exploration and the Vietnam war may also have important differential effects on persons of differing ages. In general, such historical events help to establish attitudes, values, and a personal world view that are more enduring than the historical conditions that brought them about.

There is also another kind of historical effect following an event. This is illustrated by the direct connection between the end of World War II and the increased proportion of young people in the United States today. Nearly twice as many people reached the age of 18 in 1965 as reached the age of 18 in 1950: 2 million in 1950, 2½ million in 1960, and 3¾ million in 1965. If we refer back to the intersection of individual and historical time lines (Figure 1.4) we note that an 18-year-old in 1965 would have been born in 1947 and conceived in 1946—the end of World War II. What occurred was that fathers came home from the war in 1945-1946 and began raising families at about the same time; in addition, few infants died in early childhood because of such medical advances as sulfa and penicillin. This bulge in the population slowly tapered off until 1965 when the rate of new births decreased, probably as a result of birth control and family planning; recently the birth rate has dropped to the point where there will be no growth of the population if that rate is maintained (at just slightly over two children per couple).

However, the postwar population bulge (or "explosion") will continue to move through the lifeline (the leading edge of this bulge would be 29 in 1975) and has brought a wide range of effects including overcrowded schools and a lowering of the average age in the United States. It will have another profound effect when these young people begin having children of their own and schools will again be crowded. In addition, since they would be expected to live longer than in the past, the young people will eventually swell the ranks of the aged. Although only about 10 percent of the population is currently over age 65, if the current drop in birth rates continues, the proportion of the population over 65 will soon exceed 10 percent.

Example: The Generation Gap

A great deal of attention has been focused on the "generation gap." This phenomenon, if it actually exists, is an interesting example of the inter-action of individual life cycles with the historical time line.

Assuming that the "generation gap" consists of differing values, atti-tudes, and life styles between young people and persons in their parent's generation, there are two differing interpretations that are possible: developmental and historical.

From a developmental perspective, this difference results from the differing stages in the life cycle of young persons and their parents. Young persons are involved in resolving the identity issues of "Who am I," and "How do I link up with society?" In Erikson's (1968) view, this involves a period of questioning society's values and a partial rejection of parental values in order to develop one's own system of values and attitudes. Even Aristotle, writing 2300 years ago, noted this tendency of the young.

> The young are prone to desire and ready to carry any desire they may have formed into action. Of bodily desires it is the sexual to which they are the most disposed to give way, and in regard to sexual desire they exercise no self-restraint. They are changeful too, and fickle in their desires, which are as transitory as they are vehement. ... They are passionate, irascible, and apt to be carried away by their impulses....They have high aspirations; for they have never yet been humiliated by the experience of life, but are unacquainted with the limiting force of circumstances.... Again, in their actions they prefer honor to expediency.... If the young commit a fault, it is always on the side of excess and exaggeration....They regard themselves as omniscient and are positive in their assertions; this is, in fact, the reason of their carrying everything too far (cited in Conger, 1971, p. 1119).

In contrast, parents tend to be in a developmental period that is concerned primarily with transmitting the values of society, with providing economic and emotional stability, and with the concerns of leaving one's mark on the world (generativity versus stagnation in Erikson's model). It seems evident that a conflict between these generations is built into the human condition as Mannheim (1952) has argued. From this perspective, the generation gap is as old as human history. And it is predicted that when these young people move into later developmental periods and are faced with the tasks of raising children, producing in society, and earning a stable income, these responsibilities and their changed perspective on life will result in values that are more similar (but not identical) to their parents' values; they will find a gap in values between themselves and their children.

This process of conflict between generations may be one mechanism of social change through successive generations and may be particularly important during periods of rapid social change when the elders are not able to fully prepare the youth for the new and more complex society that is developing. The greater the speed of social change, the greater the importance of this readjustment between successive generations. Currently this period of youth has been stretched out so that it now extends into the mid-twenties for many young people. This provides more time to question and to evaluate society and social values from a position of (often) economic security, personal freedom, and intellectual inquiry. It also provides growing numbers of young people who are attending college (around eight million today) with an *age-segregated environment*. This means that there is little contact with people of grandparental age, almost no contact with children, and only scheduled contact with people of parental age (such as teachers and professors—an atypical type of adult). One result of such an environment is to stimulate the growth of shared values and attitudes among college-age young people through mutual socialization by peers rather than the more traditional intergenerational socialization. The result is what may be termed a *de-facto* youth culture.

These historical factors that intersect with the period of youth—the prolonged moratorium between childhood and adulthood, the age-segregated communities where as many as 50,000 students may live in immediate proximity with one another, the affluence of many young people comparison with the economic insecurity of their elders' youth, and the massive number of young people in the postwar population bulge—may all be seen as important historical factors that may have intensified this developmental period of generational conflict into a much more striking conflict that was picked up by popular media as the "generation gap." Thus we cannot fully understand the developmental phenomenon without also considering the intersection of the developmental period with the historical period. But also, in order to understand a phenomenon such as the conflict between generations, we need to be able to separate the developmental (age) factors from the historical factors.

An alternate explanation of the generation gap has been suggested by Margaret Mead (1970); this explanation emphasizes the historical changes instead of the developmental factors. Mead argues that young people are living in a radically different historical time brought about by the end of World War II and the atomic bomb, which ushered in major changes resulting in a *cultural discontinuity*. Thus the values and attitudes of young people are different from those of their parents, because their parents grew up in a different world from the one in which young people are living (with the threat of nuclear annihilation, satellites, computers, threats of pollution and overpopulation, and a new sense of a worldwide community of mankind). She feels that this cultural discontinuity will move through the life cycle so that, in 1985, it will exist between persons who are 41 and those over 55, and so on. This prediction is in direct conflict with the developmental prediction that the "gap" will remain between young and middle-aged persons forever; it is only exaggerated now because of these historical factors.

Implications

This example of the generation gap suggests that age differences may be very difficult to understand and to interpret. On one hand they mean that one person (age 45) is at a different point in the life cycle than another person (age 18); but they also mean that the older person has lived through a different historical time span than the younger person (everything that occurred during the first 27 years of the older person's life could not have been directly experienced by the younger person). Thus, research on age differences must take the interaction of these developmental (age) and historical (time) factors into account.

Or suppose we wanted to test these two opposing hypotheses about the generation gap. The developmental prediction is that the generation gap will remain associated primarily with the identity-formation period in adolescence and young adulthood so that individuals will pass through this period in successive generations and then adopt values and attitudes similar to their parents' attitudes and values. The cultural discontinuity prediction is that the generation gap will move with the individuals as they age so that persons on either side of the gap will still differ even in 20 years. We may speculate about the outcome in perhaps, 20 years, but only empirical research will provide a definitive answer. An ideal research methodology would follow individuals on either side of this supposed gap over a period of several years; if they remain markedly different in attitudes and values, then we accept the cultural discontinuity hypothesis; if they become essentially similar, then we accept the developmental hypothesis.

DEVELOPMENTAL RESEARCH METHODOLOGY

The discussion of theoretical models of the life span and the example of the generation gap concluded with the need to actually find out what is happening in the real world. Our speculations may be interesting, but they do not increase our understanding of the human life cycle very much. However, these theoretical models, and the developmental approach in general, suggest research strategies for the study of adults that are far less obvious in other frameworks (in psychology or sociology, for example). That is, the central focus in developmental research is a systematic emphasis on *age* or change over *time*. Thus, the developmental approach might lead one to investigate the way in which biological or sociological or psychological processes change with age or with time during an individual's life span. Or the developmental approach might lead one to investigate the interaction of biological, sociological, cultural, and psychological processes on an individual during a particular developmental phase (such as the effects of personality, social isolation, decrease in income, and disease on the occurrence of mental illness in the post-retirement years).

Problems With Age as a Research Variable

In the preceding discussion of the life cycle we have been concerned with age as an *index of change*. For example, there are apparent age differences between 20-year-olds and 40-year-olds, including such factors as greater occupational achievement, greater family responsibility, and greater past experience for the 40-year-old group. Presumably these differences are not *caused* by age; instead, they are the result of the interaction of social, biological, and psychological changes in addition to having lived longer and accumulated more experience.

Thus, age is most clearly seen as an index intervening between a set of explanatory variables (such as biological changes or social influences) and a set of consequent variables (such as attitudes or personality processes). In other words, age *per se* is not a very meaningful explanatory variable because (as we pointed out earlier) it is only an index of the length of time an individual has been alive, an index defined by the number of revolutions the earth has made around the sun.

Therefore, when we find age changes or age differences, it is important to keep in mind that these findings only point to changes that occur with age but do not indicate the possible causes of these changes. Consider the generation gap once again: there would be a measurable age difference in attitudes and values expected between a sample of 20-year-olds and a sample of 40-year-olds; but once such a difference is found, the causes of the difference still remain obscure. Although our methodology can be refined to isolate some of the variables (whether this difference is cultural or developmental, for example), we are still faced with a number of complex interacting variables (such as changes in child-rearing practices, education, economic security, and technology).

One attempt to get behind the index of age in order to isolate the actual causes of age-related changes has been suggested by Baltes and Goulet (1971). They propose that *age simulation* may be used systematically to manipulate the conditions under which age differences are found. For example, if we find that 65-year-old men perform less well in a dart-throwing experiment than 20-year-old men, we have no idea what may have caused this age difference. But if we manipulate the amount of light so that the 20-year-olds perform as poorly as the 65-year-olds when the light is very dim, but the 65-year-olds perform as well as the 20-year-olds when the lighting is increased, then we know that this age difference reflects differences in perceptual ability and indicates that the older men require more light to see as well as the younger men. Alternatively, it might be that lighting makes no difference, but when the older men are allowed to stand closer to the board, they score as well as the younger men, suggesting that physical strength is the important factor; thus we might simulate these age differences (i.e., experimentally cause the young men to perform like the old men and vice versa) by varying the distance the dart must be thrown. Again, it might be that if the older men are allowed to practice for an hour, they do as well as the young men, suggesting that the age difference really involves practice effects. This age-simulation methodology thus allows an investigator to experimentally manipulate the factors that might reasonably be thought to affect the performance and to identify the factors that are responsible for the age differences that may be found.

Cross-Sectional and Longitudinal Research Strategies

In order to investigate the factors that cause the age differences, it is obviously important to identify the changes that occur with age. The most apparent—and the easiest—way to find age differences is to gather a sample of persons of differing ages, give them questionnaires, tests, or interviews that are appropriate for the question being studied, and to compare the results. Such studies are called *cross-sectional* studies, since they are based on a cross section of ages at one point in time. The differences that are found in this way are called *age differences*.

A second approach to studying the index of age is a *longitudinal* study. In this strategy, a group of subjects is selected, appropriate for the question being studied, and is given a series of questionnaires, tests, or interviews *periodically over several years* (an easy way to remember this is that *long*itudinal studies take a *long* time). For example, a group of persons would be studied when they were 20, again when they were 40, and again at age 60. These results would then be compared and any differences would be called *age changes*, since they represent changes within individuals over time; thus they allow the examination of individual differences and the ways in which different individuals change with age.

There are three central difficulties with longitudinal studies, however, which have limited their use in adult development (although there are several studies that have been carried out in child development, few have been continued into the adult years). One difficulty is that they obviously require a long time and are thus quite expensive; also, the study may outlive the investigators, and longitudinal studies typically involve a great amount of travel and effort to contact each subject at the next test interval. Nonetheless, longitudinal approaches are often superior to cross-sectional studies, because they reflect individual differences and may include a large number of measures of other age-related explanatory variables (such as medical history, past experiences, or family history) that are useful in determining the causes of the particular age changes that are being studied.

A second difficulty is that the measures that the researcher is using in a longitudinal study may be relevant at one age (in childhood or adolescence) but not at a later age (adulthood or old age), since the important issues for an individual's life vary as he progresses through his lifeline. In addition, as science progresses, new techniques become available to measure the variables of interest. As a result, a well-designed longitudinal study begun in 1930 may have focused on issues and relied on measures no longer relevant to either the subjects who are now 45 or to the social scientists who might prefer data on adjustment to menopause over data on the effect of early child-rearing practices. However, the longitudinal studies that were begun during the 1930s are beginning to provide some useful data on adulthood.

A third difficulty with longitudinal studies is that, because of the long time span involved, subjects may die or drop out of the sample before the study is completed. And these dropout rates may be relevant to the variables being investigated. For example, subjects with lower intelligence may drop out of longitudinal studies more frequently than those of higher intelligence; if one variable in the study is intelligence, this selective dropout rate would tend to increase the average intelligence in the sample over time and thus distort any age changes that might be found.

One solution to this dilemma is the use of *longitudinal sequences* (Baltes, 1968) in which a group of subjects is followed for a few years, possibly over a period of time that might represent a developmental turning point (such as marriage, parenthood, menopause, or retirement). In this way it is possible to assess longitudinal change (and individual differences) without committing the subjects and the investigator to a lifelong study.

Age and Cohort Effects

Since the bulk of data about adulthood and old age are based on cross-sectional studies, it is important to take a closer look at the implications of the differences between cross-sectional and longitudinal studies and to examine the difficulties implicit in cross-sectional studies.

A cross-sectional study is illustrated by any of the vertical columns in Figure 1.5; for example, C, G, K, N, and P. It is apparent that a study based on such a sample will provide information on age differences in

	Year Measured			
Year Born	1950	1960	1970	1980
1900	(A) 50	(B) 60	(C) 70	(D) 80
1910	(E) 40	(F) 50	(G) 60	(H) 70
1920	(I) 30	(J) 40	(K) 50	(L) 60
1930		(M) 30	(N) 40	(O) 50
1940			(P) 30	(Q) 40
1950				(R) 30

Figure 1.5
Illustration of hypothetical cross-sectional and longitudinal studies, showing that chronological age reflects the interaction of year of birth and year of measurement.

1970. And the problems encountered in a longitudinal study will be minimized by the collection of all the data for the study at one time-point. However, it is important to note that the difference between the groups of subjects is not only age but is also their *year of birth* (or cohort). That is, a 70-year-old in 1970 was born in 1900, but a 40-year-old was born in 1930.

Previously, we discussed the importance of social, historical, and cultural changes for the individual's development through his lifeline. Now it may be seen that a cross-sectional study does not separate the cultural-historical factors from the age differences. That is, *age* and *year of birth* are confounded in a cross-sectional study, and the effects of one cannot be separated from the effects of the other. Thus, age differences may be partly or entirely due to cultural or social differences. For example, the combined effect of improvement in medical care and nutrition, increased education, and the effects of the Depression and World War II may explain any differences found among the five samples in the 1970 cross-sectional study (C, G, K, N, and P); hence the age differences may be associated primarily with the year of the individual's birth rather than with actual age-related factors. The effects of "year of birth" are called *cohort effects*, since a cohort is a group of individuals born at about the same time.

In contrast, longitudinal studies (such as A, B, C, and D) hold the year of birth constant so that whatever effects might be caused by cultural-historical changes are not a factor confounding the age changes in the study. However, these longitudinal studies also confound two variables: *age* and *year of measurement*. Thus, a change such as a sudden decrease in cigarette smoking in the population generally between 1960 and 1980 may counteract the age-related decrease in lung capacity expected with advancing age and would thus tend to conceal a possible relationship between lung capacity and age; there might also be effects on other related physiological measurements.

In general, however, longitudinal studies are preferred over cross-sectional studies, because environmental changes between test points are less likely to be overlooked than cohort differences, since these cohort differences are likely to involve highly influential cultural-historical factors that are very difficult to isolate and to accurately assess for their impact on the measures of interest. One way to assess the influence of these confounding variables of year of birth and year of measurement is to compare subjects of the same age (for example, A, F, K, and O). Although this will provide an estimate of the effects of these social-historical variables, it is a less-interesting study, since age does not vary.

Perhaps ideal developmental studies would involve all three types of strategies and follow the entire schedule shown in Figure 1.5; Schaie (1965) terms this approach *cross-sequential* and has proposed a sophisticated statistical procedure for separating the effects of age and cohort. This combined methodology would allow the samples to be followed longitudinally but, since a cross-sectional sample would also be available at each test point, it allows the speedy recovery of cross-sectional age differences and provides a means to compare each sample with others of the same age at different historical times.

Practically, however, this type of study not only involves a long period of time but also involves a large sample of subjects and great expense. A more practical solution is to begin with a cross-sectional sample and to follow them over a predetermined length of time (as in the longitudinal sequence design described above).

Example: Change in Intelligence with Age

An important illustration of the differences between longitudinal and cross-sectional studies, and of the influence of cultural-historical factors in contaminating the cross-sectional findings, is the change in performance on intelligence tests with age.

Longitudinal studies are just beginning to yield data on adult intelligence (up to about age 50) that suggest that performance increases less and less rapidly, until it reaches a plateau between the ages of 25 and 30. It then declines slightly with age for subjects of average intelligence but is maintained or increases slightly for initially more able subjects at least to age 50 (Botwinick, 1967). However, cross-sectional studies have repeatedly shown that performance on intelligence tests begins to drop at age 30 and continues to decline markedly through the rest of adulthood. These comparisons are shown in Figure 1.6.

How do we explain this obvious discrepancy? Can we assume that either result is accurate? What factors have to be considered? Suppose we consider the cohort effects first; let us graph the average length of education completed for subjects in each group and compare this graph with the change in intelligence (Figure 1.7). It appears that the differing amounts of education (a cohort effect) explain much of the decline found in cross-sectional studies. Added factors may be the amount of time between the end of school and the test point (the longer the time, the lower the performance) or the decreasing relevance of intelligence test questions as individuals grow older. Thus, we may conclude that the cross-sectional result *underestimates* the level of intelligence in the later years under current social and educational conditions, and so it overestimates the amount of decline in intelligence with age.

But what about the longitudinal studies; are they more accurate? There are at least two factors that indicate that the longitudinal result *overestimates* the level of intelligence in later years: the selective dropout rate raises the average score, since the more highly intelligent are less

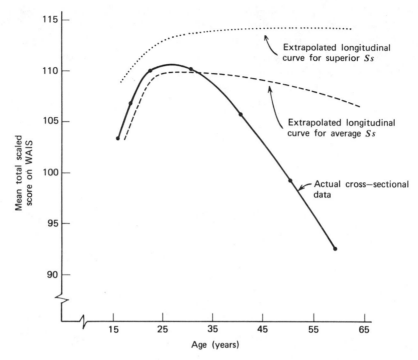

Figure 1.6

Comparison of actual cross-sectional data from the Wechsler Adult Intelligence Scale and curves extrapolated from longitudinal data of changes in intellectual performance with age. (Source. WAIS data from Wechsler, David. Manual for the Adult Intelligence Scale. New York: The Psychological Corporation, 1955, Table 10. Adapted and reproduced with permission. Copyright © by The Psychological Corporation.)

likely to drop out; and the experience of taking the test repeatedly, even at five-year intervals, is likely to have some positive test experience effect.

We may then conclude that the change in intelligence with age is neither the drastic decline indicated in cross-sectional data nor a continual gradual increase shown for the highly intelligent subjects in longitudinal data. Instead, it is bounded by the cross-sectional data at the bottom and by the longitudinal data for average subjects on the top and actually lies somewhere in between these two boundaries.

Implications

The developmental approach provides some unique perspectives on the adult years of the life span, because it is concerned with changes that occur with age. It strives to understand age changes in persons of all social classes, cultures, and conditions of life. Yet it is apparent that these age changes interact with individual variation, social and cultural

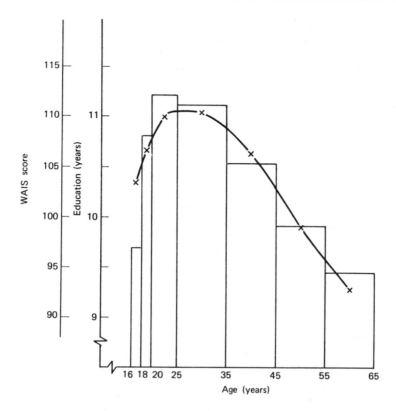

Figure 1.7
Comparison of cross-sectional measure of intellectual performance by age with the average education of the subjects. Vertical bar represents years of education for each panel of subjects; "X" represents average WAIS total score for that same panel. (Based on Wechsler, David. Manual for the Adult Intelligence Scale. New York: The Psychological Corporation, 1955, Tables 5 and 10. Adapted and reproduced with permission. Copyright © 1955 by The Psychological Corporation.)

factors, and with historical change. We have discussed some of the age changes that theoretical frameworks have suggested and have pointed out the important interaction between historical changes and these developmental changes. In general, the task of developmental research is to attempt to disentangle the developmental processes from the historical changes.

However, since our task in the following chapters is to understand adulthood—primarily in our society in the 1970s—we will need to examine not only the developmental changes but also the interacting effects of historical changes. To take an obvious example, the woman's liberation movement, the declining birth rate, and increasing longevity are modifying the timing of developmental milestones in the lives of many women who enter a second (occupational) career after raising a family, have a long postparental period of marriage, and not only have grandchildren but may have great-grandchildren while they are still strong and healthy. Because the effect of social factors is so thoroughly intertwined with developmental factors we will turn to a discussion of the psychosocial processes of development in the next chapter.

References

Baltes, Paul B. 1968. Longitudinal and Cross-Sectional Sequences in the Study of Age and Generation Effects. *Human Development, 11*(3), 145–171.

Baltes, Paul B., and Goulet, L. R. 1971. Exploration of Developmental Variables by Manipulation and Simulation of Age Differences in Behavior. *Human Development, 14*(3), 149–170.

Birren, James E.; Butler, Robert N.; Greenhouse, Samuel W.; Sokoloff, Louis; and Yarrow, Marian R. (Eds.) **1963.** *Human Aging: A Biological and Behavioral Study.* Publication No. (HSM) 71–9051. Washington, D.C.: U.S. Government Printing Office.

Botwinick, Jack. 1967. *Cognitive Processes in Maturity and Old Age.* New York: Springer.

Bühler, Charlotte. 1968. The Developmental Structure of Goal Setting in Group and Individual Studies. In Charlotte Bühler and Fred Massarik (Eds.), *The Course of Human Life.* New York: Springer.

Conger, John Janeway. 1971. A World They Never Knew: The Family and Social Change. *Daedalus, 100*(4), 1105–1138.

Erikson, Erik H. 1963. *Childhood and Society.* (2nd ed.) New York: W. W. Norton.

Erikson, Erik H. 1968. *Identity: Youth and Crisis.* New York: W. W. Norton.

*****Frenkel, Else. 1936.** Studies in Biographical Psychology. *Character and Personality, 5*, 1–34.

Gruen, Walter. 1964. A Study of Erikson's Theory of Ego Development. In Bernice L. Neugarten and Associates (Eds.), *Personality in Middle and Late Life.* New York: Atherton Press.

Horner, Althea J. 1968. The Evolution of Goals in the Life of Clarence Darrow. In Charlotte Bühler and Fred Massarik (Eds.), *The Course of Human Life.* New York: Springer.

Jung, Carl G. 1933. The Stages of Life. (Translated by R. F. C. Hull.) In Joseph Campbell, *The Portable Jung.* New York: Viking, 1971.

*****Kuhlen, Raymond G. 1964.** Developmental Changes in Motivation During the Adult Years. In James E. Birren (Ed.), *Relations of Development and Aging.* Springfield, Ill.: Charles C Thomas.

Kuhlen, Raymond G., and Johnson, G. H. 1952. Changes in Goals with Increasing Adult Age. *Journal of Consulting Psychology, 16*(1), 1–4.

*Lieberman, Morton A. 1965. Psychological Correlates of Impending Death: Some Preliminary Observations. *Journal of Gerontology, 20*(2), 181–190.

Mannheim, Karl. 1952. The Problem of Generations. In P. Kecskemeti (Ed.), *Essays on the Sociology of Knowledge.* New York: Oxford University Press.

Mead, Margaret. 1970. *Culture and Commitment: A Study of the Generation Gap.* New York: Doubleday.

*Neugarten, Bernice L.; Moore, Joan W.; and Lowe, John C. 1965. Age Norms, Age Constraints, and Adult Socialization. *American Journal of Sociology, 70*(6), 710–717.

*Neugarten, Bernice L. 1967. The Awareness of Middle Age. In Roger Owen (Ed.), *Middle Age.* London: British Broadcasting Corporation.

*Peck, Robert C. 1955. Psychological Developments in the Second Half of Life. In John E. Anderson (Ed.), *Psychological Aspects of Aging.* Proceedings of a Conference on Planning Research, Bethesda, Maryland, April 24–27, 1955. Washington, D.C.: American Psychological Association, 1956.

Schaie, K. Warner. 1965. A General Model for the Study of Developmental Problems. *Psychological Bulletin, 64*(2), 92–107.

* References marked with an asterisk appear in Bernice L. Neugarten (Ed.), *Middle Age and Aging.* Chicago: University of Chicago Press, 1968.

two
Psychosocial Processes of Development: Stability and Change over Time

It is a common observation that individuals change in important ways during the adult years; yet at the same time they also remain relatively consistent as they pass through the milestones of adulthood. If we were to attend our high-school reunion in a few years, we would notice this simultaneous change and consistency. One old friend might have become a successful businessman and gained a sense of competence and power that contrasts with his happy-go-lucky attitude in high school; yet he would also be recognizably similar to the boy we knew years ago. Another old friend may have changed from the prom queen we remember to a brilliant research chemist; but she is still the outgoing, popular, and engaging person we remember. How does this happen? It is such a common phenomenon that we seldom examine it closely. However, it is puzzling. How do persons change, and how do they remain fairly consistent even if they have also changed considerably?

In the first chapter we presented an overview of the human life cycle and suggested some of the age-related changes that occur. This chapter will focus on the processes by which age changes occur in adulthood. We will pay particular attention to three central questions posed by the developmental study of adulthood: (1) What are the processes by which individuals change; and what processes are involved in the stability of individuals over long periods of time? (2) Is there any age-related sequence to these changes so that the adult years may be conceptualized as a sequential and progressive period of life; in addition, if there is a sequence, what serves as *timing* factors to order the developmental changes during adulthood? (3) What is the effect of *experience* on the individual—because it is this diffuse variable of "experience" that most

Photo at left: "All the world's a stage, and all the men and women merely players."
—*Shakespeare.*

43

clearly accumulates with age; moreover, what is the process by which experience affects the individual?

Our approach to these questions and to the processes of development in adulthood is a social-psychological one. That is, we see the adult as an individual in interaction with others in society, and we feel that this interaction process is central to an understanding of the processes by which age-related changes occur in adulthood. Thus, the processes of change, stability, timing of development, and the accumulation of experience seem to be best understood in terms of the individual interacting with others in social interaction.

At the same time, we expect that physiological changes (such as changes in hormonal production, blood chemistry, or neural conductivity) also play an important role in producing developmental change and stability during adulthood. However, we currently know relatively little about the effects of age-related physiological changes on normal persons. Although we expect that eventual research will provide a great deal of information about these physiological processes of developmental change, we are currently able to draw only upon the effects of such major physiological changes as menopause or disease (see Chapters 4 and 8, respectively), and we are left with the tentative conclusion that biological factors provide a great deal of latitude for the impact of social-psychological processes on development in adulthood. Thus it appears that as individuals move through their lifeline, the biological factors that played an initially large part in determining the rate and order of change decline in relative importance after the early years of childhood; and after puberty social factors come to play an important role in the regulation of developmental change.

Our conceptual model of adulthood emphasizes the view that the *interaction* of the various factors is central (rather than any one factor alone); thus, even when physiological factors are more fully understood, they will probably be most profitably seen as one set of factors interacting with the social-psychological processes that we will discuss in this chapter. Our model also emphasizes the view that the individual is *active* in this complex pattern of interactions instead of a passive respondent to social, cultural, or biological changes. We view adults as actively selecting many aspects of their physical and social environment and being affected by their assimilation of that environmental experience. We also see adults as actively affecting their social and physical environment and being changed in that experience. Moreover, we view the human individual as a social being with a mind and a self that are brought about by the active interaction between the individual and society.

Our social-psychological framework for viewing the process of adult development is based on this interactive social process as analyzed by G. H. Mead (1934). In the following section we will introduce some of

Mead's concepts and discuss the three questions of change and consistency, experience, and timing in adulthood. The remainder of this chapter will be devoted to more contemporary social-psychological concepts such as roles, norms, and the process of socialization as they apply to the adult years.

SYMBOLIC INTERACTION AND ADULTHOOD: G. H. MEAD

Mead argued that man evolved as a social being and that man has evolved the capacity to *interact* with others through the use of shared symbols. Because this evolved human ability was central to his thinking, Mead's approach to social-psychology is called *symbolic interaction*. He argued that an individual's self arises out of this process of symbolic interaction and that it consists of two simultaneous aspects: the *I* and the *me*. He focused on the process of human functioning in a social community and saw the individual as an active agent instead of a passive recipient of external stimuli—in fact, the individual responds selectively to external stimuli and interprets them symbolically with reference to his *self*. Thus, Mead's approach is particularly useful for understanding the ways in which adults function in a highly complex social world and is also a useful approach for understanding the processes of development in the adult years.

We will discuss these concepts in detail, but first let us introduce the man whose ideas we are using. George Herbert Mead was born in 1863 and, in 1894, joined the Department of Philosophy at the University of Chicago where he remained until his death in 1931. According to Strauss (1964), William James had been one of Mead's teachers, and at Chicago he was a colleague of John Dewey and W. I. Thomas at the time when the Chicago School of Sociology was evolving among a star-studded faculty at the University. Mead's scholarly writing was devoted primarily to philosophical and psychological issues; he was 40 before his first major paper appeared, and he had not published a single book when he died at the age of 68. Strauss notes that "he had published few major papers for someone who would gain recognition posthumously as one of the most brilliantly original of American pragmatists" (Strauss, 1964, p. vii). However, sociologists at the University discovered Mead's unique insights a decade before his death, and graduate students "flocked to his classes" (ibid.). After his death these students published their collected notes as well as his own notes and unpublished writings in books such as *Mind, Self, and Society*. These Chicago sociologists succeeded in carrying his ideas into the mainstream of sociology by 1939. His influence has not been a particularly dominant one since World War II, but there are many contemporary concepts that have grown out of his insights, and the symbolic interaction approach remains a current sociological framework. His insights have been useful in analyzing family interaction (see Chapter 5), and we will use his framework extensively throughout our discussion of adulthood.

Perhaps Mead's approach may best be seen as a framework or perspective for understanding human interaction. It is a theory that describes human functioning in society and provides useful concepts for conceptualizing the processes of social interaction. It is not the kind of theory that allows us to predict behavior; but it helps us to understand it better.

The Self

A central concept in Mead's analysis is the *self*, which he viewed as a product of the evolutionary development of man in society. The self is probably a uniquely human characteristic that man acquired as he evolved the capacity to interact with other humans in social settings through the use of symbolic communication and language. The self is different from the physiological organism. It is not present at birth; it develops in each individual through the process of social experience and social communication; and it continues developing throughout one's life. Thus the self is a *process* that is continually developing and changing.

One aspect of the self consists of the way we see ourselves and the way others see us. This aspect of the self is the *me* or the *social self*. This is the aspect of the self that is seen by others when they interact with us; and it is the aspect of others we see when we interact with them. For example, in sensitivity groups there is a procedure called "feedback," which consists of telling another person how we see him. In Mead's terms, this involves describing the other person's *me*. In this process the individual is told how others see him, and he compares their perceptions with the way in which he sees himself. Of course, different people will see him differently, or people will see him differently in different situations, or they will see him differently at different times in his life. So the self is not a "thing" with concrete unalterable properties (like a table or a chair); it is a dynamic aspect of an individual that develops and changes and is responded to subjectively by other people and by oneself.

Taking the Attitude of the "Other." The self arises through the process of symbolic interaction between an individual and others in society. Just as the "feedback" in a sensitivity group provides an individual with some insight into his *self*, social interaction in general allows the individual to see himself as others see him. When he interacts with other persons, he may take the attitude of the other person toward himself and try to imagine how he appears to them. Often the other people will tell him how he appears to them (as in the feedback technique in sensitivity groups); but frequently he must try to understand their perceptions of himself by interpreting their gestures or facial expressions or by sensing whether their reaction to him is consistent with the reaction he expected. One example of a man who suddenly realized he was middle aged illustrates the way in which taking the attitude of the other toward oneself may bring about a significant change in the way one sees oneself.

> ... the realization suddenly struck me that I had become, perhaps not an old fogy but surely a middle-aged fogy.... For the train was filled with college boys returning from vacation.... They cruised up and down the aisles, pretending to be tipsy ... boisterous, but not obnoxious; looking for fun, but not for trouble.... Yet most of the adult passengers were annoyed with them, including myself. I sat there, feeling a little like Eliot's Prufrock, "so meticulously composed, buttoned-up, bespectacled, mouth thinly set" . . . Squaresville (Harris, 1965; cited in Neugarten, 1967).

He seems to have looked at himself from the point of view of another—perhaps a college student, perhaps an adult passenger, or possibly just imagined how he looked as if he were watching himself from across the aisle—and from that perspective realized that his *self* looked like a "middle-aged fogy."

We may take the attitude of the "other" toward ourselves when we are alone by looking in a mirror and seeing how we look to others or by imagining how someone else might see us. We may take the attitude of a particular "other" when we are interacting with them—for example, when a man is arguing with his wife and tries to see her perspective on the issue by imagining how she sees him and is interpreting his comments. Or we may take the attitude of others in general (Mead refers to this as the *generalized other*) by imagining how others would respond to us if we were to get a divorce or if we were to leave our job and join a farming commune.

Although taking the attitude of the other toward ourself is crucial for the development and change of the self, we probably do not use this process very often in ordinary social interaction. It is most useful when an individual is trying to understand or define or examine his *self*, or when the ordinary interaction process breaks down because the other people are not responding to the person the way he expects they should. For example, if a teacher is having difficulty explaining a concept to his class, he may try to take the attitude of the students toward the concept and ask them to describe what is confusing, or to put himself in their place and try to guess why they are having difficulty. Similarly, if he wishes to improve his teaching, he may ask for "feedback" from the class and try to imagine how his teaching looks from the student's perspective. This process of taking the attitude of the other is quite useful when one is trying to understand another (as in close friendships or in

psychotherapy), and examples may be found in all kinds of social interactions. However, typical social interactions tend to be habituated and
only occasionally involve taking the role of the other—for example,
"How are you?" "Fine; how are you?" (habituated) "Awful!" (unexpected). One may then respond automatically, "That's too bad" or take
the time to find out what that surprising response means from the point
of view of the other person.

Significant Symbols. The process of taking the role of the other, and the
development of the self, requires communication between the persons
involved in social interaction. This important process of communication
is based on the exchange of *significant symbols*—that is, symbols (gestures, words, and so on) that call up the same inner response in oneself
that they call up in others. For example, if Mary says that Joe is "fat and
ugly," she knows what is meant because she can take Joe's attitude and
can imagine how he will interpret her comment (based on how she would
interpret it if someone were to say it to her); and Joe knows what she
means too. Or if Mary is told she is intelligent and beautiful, her interpretation of what is meant depends on her sense of the attitude of the
speaker toward her—is this comment made by someone who can judge
these qualities; is there a sexual interest being communicated that makes
the comment less "objective" than it might otherwise be? Thus, in order
to fully understand the meaning of a significant symbol, one must take
the attitude of the other and try to perceive the meaning that symbol has
for the other person.

   Since language consists of a set of agreed-on significant symbols whose
meaning is generally shared, these symbols can be exchanged without
continually requiring one to consciously take the attitude of the other.
But this process is implicit in all communication, and when the symbol
is not a meaningful one, or its meaning is not fully understood, then one
must take the attitude of the other in order to clarify the meaning.

   Significant symbols exist when the meaning of the symbol is shared by
oneself and by the others involved in the interaction. When an individual speaks, he responds to the significant symbols that he utters in the
same manner in which others respond to these symbols; conversely, he
responds to the symbols used by others in the same manner in which
the other is responding. That is, when we talk we hear ourselves say the
words and respond to them as if they were said by another person so we
know what they mean to another person; or when we make a gesture
(or communicate through "body language") we understand the meaning
of that gesture insofar as we can see ourselves making the gesture and
respond to it as others respond to it.

   Perhaps this concept of a significant symbol may be further clarified
by briefly referring to a formulation of the internal process that gives

meaning to significant symbols. Gendlin (1964), in discussing the broader concept of psychological experiencing, presents the concept of *felt meaning*.

> ... At first it may seem that experiencing is simply the inward sense of our body, its tension, or its well-being. Yet, upon further reflection, we can notice that only in this direct sensing do we have the meanings of what we say and think. For, without our "feel" of the meaning, verbal symbols are only noises (or sound images of noises).
>
> For example, someone listens to you speak, and then says: "Pardon me, but I don't grasp what you mean." If you would like to restate what you meant in different words, you will notice that you must inwardly attend to your direct referent, your *felt* meaning. Only in this way can you arrive at different words with which to restate it.
>
> In fact, we employ explicit symbols only for very small portions of what we think. We have most of it in the form of *felt* meanings (Gendlin, 1964, p. 112).

Another example of the link between these felt meanings and verbal symbols is the process of trying to remember the right word to say the feeling that is "on the tip of my tongue." In such a situation I am searching for the significant symbol that calls up the exact felt meaning I wish to express; when I arrive at the correct word, I "know" it is right because that word (or significant symbol) calls up the same felt meaning in me that I felt but could not express in words before. However, for that word to be a significant symbol, it must call up the same felt meaning in you as it does in me; so it is possible for you to actually suggest the right word to me if I can give you enough clues as to what my felt meaning is.

In addition, when listening to others, the felt meanings that their symbols call up in us are affected by many subtle characteristics in addition to the words used such as intonation, sentence position, facial expression, our belief in the speaker's sincerity, and our knowledge of the speaker. In that sense, we take the attitude of the speaker in order to try to accurately understand the felt meaning of what he is saying.

Development of the Self. Mead argued that the self develops through the interaction with others with whom one shares significant symbols. The child gradually develops a self by taking the attitude of the other toward himself; that is, he begins to react to himself as others react to him. The reactions of *significant others* (i.e., persons whom an individual values, such as one's parents or role models) are particularly important for the development and change of the self in childhood and even in adulthood. As the child develops, he begins to be able to take the attitude of several others at once (as when he is playing baseball and must be aware of the positions and expectations of all of his teammates on the field). Finally, he is able to take the attitude of the *generalized other* toward himself; that is, he is able to perceive how others in general (or "society") would react to him. Possibly after adolescence when the child achieves the ability to think abstractly he would be able to take the attitude of this abstract, generalized other.

The Self in Adulthood. This ability to take the abstract attitude of the generalized other toward oneself, and the ability to take the attitude of other individuals toward the abstract characteristics of the social order (such as religion, morality, or politics), may be seen as a central hallmark of the process of symbolic interaction in adulthood. In Mead's formulation, it is not sufficient for an individual to merely be able to take the attitudes of other individuals toward himself, he must also be able to take their attitudes toward the various aspects of their shared social activity if the self is to develop to its fullest extent. That is, the complex cooperative processes of human society are possible only insofar as every individual is able to take the attitude of all other individuals who are involved in these social processes and is able to direct his own behavior accordingly. For example, a young mother needs to be able to take the attitude of her husband, her parents, her children, and society in general toward herself as a wife and mother. But she, ideally, should also be able to take the attitude of teachers toward her children, the attitude of the other parents (and the police and city council) toward the conditions of her neighborhood, and the attitude of federal and state politicians about day-care centers and transportation, and so on. She must be able to do this if she is going to be able to participate in these complex social activities. Thus the complex and differentiated self in adulthood requires the individual to be able to take the attitude of a wide range of persons in society toward those social activities in which they are engaged.

To take another example, a successful lawyer has mastered a large set of significant symbols within the realm of legal terminology. Ideally, he is adept at taking the attitude of the prosecutor (if he is the defense lawyer) and can anticipate the behavior and tactics of his opponent. He is also able to take the attitude of the defendant, as well as the attitude of the judge and the attitude of the jury toward his client, toward himself, and toward the trial as a whole. His skill is shown by his ability to convey a set of felt meanings by the use of significant symbols to the judge and jury that will convince them of his client's innocence. His success in convincing them will depend to a large extent on his ability to understand their attitude toward the defendant, the trial, the legal process, and social politics in general. Thus, the jurors are selected by the lawyers on the basis of the lawyer's perception of the prospective juror's attitudes in all of these areas.

The Self and Mind. Mead saw a close relationship between the functionings of the mind (i.e., rational thought) and the self. And our discussion has implicitly assumed that the individual is a rational, thinking person who can reason, understand, and anticipate future consequences. Since an individual's self develops through the process of taking the attitude of the other toward oneself, the rational process of perceiving and understanding the meaning of the attitude of the other is clearly involved in the development of the self. Memory, foresight, the ability to understand language and to communicate, as well as thinking, planning, and creating are all processes that are involved in the functioning of the self. Consider the rational processes that are involved in the example of the successful lawyer—whether he is trying to take the attitude of the others, trying to present a convincing argument, or trying to express a social self that is perceived as being honest and believable, his rational mind is at work. The self cannot be understood apart from the functioning of the mind.

Self-Consciousness. One important manifestation of these rational abilities is self-consciousness. Mead does not use this term in its ordinary sense. It is the process by which an individual becomes aware of his *self* and is able to reflect on it. For example, when a man has just made a complete mess out of a social interaction, he may spend some time examining himself to try to understand what he did wrong and why his behaviors or his words were so misinterpreted by the others. He may take the attitude of the others toward himself and try to see himself as they saw him. He may look at himself in the mirror as if he were another person and talk with himself in an introspective fashion about the interaction and the implications it may have for his *self*.

This process of self-consciousness occurs when one's self becomes an object to oneself. It frequently occurs when the significant symbols one is using (or hearing) do not call up the same response in the other person that they call up in oneself; that is, it often occurs when habituated responses, gestures, and acts do not work in the present situation. For example, if a man is trying to pick up a woman in a singles bar, and he responded to her initially encouraging gestures by beginning his habituated "pick up line," and she suddenly slaps him or walks away, he is left in a quandary. He must engage in a moment of self-consciousness to determine what went wrong. Perhaps after several moments of reflecting on his *self* as the object he presented to her, he may realize that he forgot to take off his wedding ring, or that he inadvertently suggested that she might accept some money (which in her eyes meant that he thought she was a prostitute). Perhaps he made a slip of the tongue that he only barely noticed, but which he may now ponder in a moment of self-consciousness. Another example might be a professor who is in the midst of a lecture she has given several times when a student asks one of those unanticipated questions that cause her to stop and think back over what she was saying. She becomes self-conscious for a moment as she searches for the source of the confusion and then tries to restate her misunderstood point. Moments of self-consciousness are also present for the example of the successful lawyer described above. He self-consciously selects the impression he is trying to convey in the courtroom and attempts to influence the perceptions of his client held by the others in the social interaction. In introspective moments of self-consciousness he may also reflect on the morality or the political consequences of his behavior; and he may reflect on the future consequences or past experiences that pertain to the particular case. And when he meets with his colleagues or has dinner with his wife he is also engaging in social behavior that is characterized by these processes of symbolic interaction. If his wife should decide to divorce him, or if he enters psychotherapy or joins a sensitivity group, he will again probably have moments of self-consciousness as he tries to see himself as others see him and tries to integrate these perceptions with his feelings about himself. These moments of self-consciousness are one of the main sources of change in the self. They include the abilities to take the attitude of the other, to communicate with oneself and with others with significant symbols, and the interaction of the mind and the self. They may occur in moments of introspection or in extended interactions in which one is attempting to understand a social interaction that has gone awry for some reason.

An example from a middle-aged respondent illustrates this process of self-consciousness.

"I used to think that all of us in the office were contemporaries, for we all had similar career interests. But one day we were talking about old movies and we realized that the younger ones had never seen a Shirley Temple film or an Our Gang comedy . . . Then it struck me with a blow that I was older than they. I had never been so conscious of it before" (Neugarten, 1967).[1]

The I and the Me

Mead conceptualized the self as a process that consists of two distinct but simultaneous aspects: the *I* and the *me*. Up to this point we have focused on the *me* or the "social self." The *me* comes about through taking the attitudes of others toward oneself. It is the objectified aspect of the self which is presented to others and which we see when we take their attitude toward our *self*. The *me* is what one sees when he interacts with another person; it is what one sees when he looks in the mirror. An individual has several *me*s at any time—there is the physical *me*, the *me* in this particular interaction (patient, understanding, and warm), the *me* as a parent, the *me* as a child, the *me* as a graduate student, and so on.

[1] All quotations from Neugarten (1967) are reprinted with permission.

In contemporary terminology many of the *mes* that make up the self are called *roles* (defined on page 66); hence the social self consists of a combination of roles and all of the other characteristics that an individual sees when he interacts with another person. In general, the *me* aspect of the self consists of all the characteristics of the individual that may be seen and described as if they were objects that have labels and can be described. Paraphrasing the play *David and Lisa*, anything you see when you look at me is a *me*.

The *I* is logically involved in the self, however, since an objective self formed through taking the attitude of others presupposes a subjective aspect of the self that reacts to the *me* and that responds to the *me* presented by others in interaction. This aspect of the self, the *I*, is a fleeting, momentary, process self; it can never be observed or objectified because it exists only in moment-to-moment consciousness; it exists only in process. In some ways it resembles the "stream of consciousness" that James discussed—it is moment-by-moment awareness, everchanging, and existing only in process. Because it is process (rather than content), it is most easily identified by the "ing" ending on words that describe its functioning: experiencing, reacting, reflecting, feeling, responding, interpreting, and so on.

Since the *I* is responding to a situation in the immediate present experience, it is always uncertain, unpredictable and, hence, introduces the possibility of novelty and of change. "The possibilities of the 'I' belong to that which is actually going on, taking place, and it is in some sense the most fascinating part of our experience. It is there that novelty arises . . ." (Mead, 1934, p. 237).

The *I* exists only in the present moment since it is ongoing, moment-by-moment experiencing; we are always feeling, responding, experiencing (and so on) in this present moment. If we wish to focus on these feelings, or examine our response, we are trying to grasp the *I* of the past moment and make it a *me* so that we may label, examine, and talk about *it* (as an object). That is, the *I* of the past moment may become part of the *me* in the present when we make that past experiencing the object of our present experiencing. For example, if Jan wishes to examine how he felt when his girl friend told him she was pregnant because he has to decide whether he should marry her, he may try to focus on those feelings[2] he was experiencing when she first told him. He may try to reexperience those feelings and examine them for clues to his question. He is treating those past feelings as a *me* (objectified aspect of the self) and his *I* is experiencing those feelings, reacting to them, labeling them, watching them change into new feelings, and so on. When Jan examines this process in a few minutes, his *I* will again experience that whole process as if it

[2] This concept has been developed by Gendlin (1964).

were a *me* and he may interpret his feelings to indicate that he was scared but also thrilled about being a father; he doesn't feel quite ready but thinks that he can be ready for marriage in a few months. These are past *I*s that he is treating as *me*s; he is describing his *self*. Suddenly he feels very good and relieved; his *I* of that moment is experiencing his reaction to this conclusion and a moment later his *I* is feeling that he made the right decision. Our self is made of these kinds of moment-by-moment interactions between the *I* and the *me* aspects of the self. When this kind of *I*-*me* interaction does not occur, something is amiss. Perhaps the individual's experiencing (the *I*) is split off from the individual's perception of himself or other people's perception of him (his *me*) as in some forms of schizophrenia. Probably a corpse is the only human form of a pure *me* with no experiencing at all; perhaps only a person completely "tripped out" on LSD is pure *I*—only experiencing with no awareness of the *me*. Most of us have a reasonable amount of interaction between our experiencing and our perception of ourselves (that is, interaction between the *I* and the *me* aspects of the self). As Mead phrased it:

> I talk to myself, and I remember what I said and perhaps the emotional content that went with it. The "I" of this moment is present in the "me" of the next moment. There again I cannot turn around quick enough to catch myself. I become a "me" insofar as I remember what I said. . . . It is because of the "I" that we say we are never fully aware of what we are, that we surprise ourselves by our own action (Mead, 1934, p. 229).

The concept of the *I* serves a number of important functions, not the least of which is to clearly alert students of adulthood to the process nature of the self. That is, the self is an ongoing, changing, active, processing characteristic of the human individual. Later, when we discuss such factors in adult development as shifts in roles, it will be important to recall that it is the *I* that is selecting, interpreting, and integrating these roles (or *me*s). The self, in Mead's view, does not consist of a set of roles or even a set of self-concepts alone; instead, the self consists of both the self that can be seen (the *me*) and the experiencing self (the *I*).

This concludes our discussion of some of the central concepts in Mead's thinking about the self. We will now discuss some of the specific ways in which these concepts help to clarify the processes of development in adulthood. We are particularly interested in how adulthood is timed—that is, how do people know that they are "middle aged," too old to do something (like change jobs or wear a two-piece bathing suit), or too young to do something (like move into a retirement community). We are also interested in the process by which experience affects development and the process by which change and consistency come about during the adult years. Each of these questions will be discussed.

Timing in Adult Development

In our view, development in adulthood is not regulated primarily by biological factors, as is early childhood development, nor is it timed primarily by social events such as marriage or retirement. Instead, it is regulated and timed by the individual's subjective sense of himself as he actively assimilates and integrates the age-related biological and social events. That is, as one passes through such social events as graduation, first job, parenthood, retirement, and death of one's spouse, one responds to these events, and the *I* is experiencing one's inner reactions to them as well as one's perception of other's reactions to the self. These events bring changes in the *I*'s experiencing and in the *me*; and thus the self is changed.

For example, a shift in roles from "wife" to "mother" brings changes in the *me*. The woman sees herself differently and others see her differently. Her *I*'s experiencing also changes because she is experiencing the changed perceptions of her *me* and is also experiencing the internal physiological changes associated with pregnancy. Her *I* is also integrating her memory of her past *me*s, her perception of her present *me*s, and is anticipating the future consequences of having children and raising them to maturity. Clearly, her rational mind, her objective aspect of the self (the *me*), and her experiencing aspect of the self (the *I*) are all interacting to make this event a milestone, or a *timing event* in her life.

Such timing events are related to age largely because the events themselves are related to age in our society. Grandparenthood, menopause, retirement, the children leaving home, and widowhood are similar age-related events that serve as timing events for most adults. They are timing events because the individual experiences them as marking an age-related change—"I am getting older." Biological changes and the accumulation of experience are also age-related and may play a similar role in bringing about an age-related change in the self. For example, the loss of hair, increase in wrinkles, decline in strength, gray hair, or an increase in weight would each affect the way in which one sees oneself when one takes the attitude of the other toward oneself.

However, the concept of *timing* we are using here refers not so much to the continual and subtle changes in the self over time but, instead, it refers to the occasional, *self-conscious*, realization that one's *me* has changed in an age-related way. It may occur in a formal event such as retirement, or it may occur in an informal moment of self-consciousness and introspection as in the examples of the middle-aged man sitting on a train or talking about old movies, cited above. Neugarten (1967) quotes another example of the reaction to suddenly becoming aware that one is middle aged:

> "When I see a pretty girl on the stage or in the movies—we used to say 'a cute chick'—and when I realize, 'My God, she's about the age

of my son,' it's a real shock. It makes me realize that I'm middle-aged."

In such moments of self-consciousness, transformation of the *me* is possible, and one's conception of oneself may change markedly through a series of such events. In these moments the functioning of the *I* is apparent as the person reflects on his *me* or on the attitudes of other persons toward himself. For example, one salient aspect of a person's *me* is age; it influences the way a person sees himself and the way in which others see him. Thus, when one takes the attitude of the other toward oneself, one may note that young people are holding doors open or giving up their seats on the bus, which indicates that they see one as getting old. If one realizes that others see him as "middle aged" or "old," this realization leads to a changed perception of oneself.

Timing events, then, are subjective experiences, moments of self-consciousness, in which the *I* reacts to the newly perceived *me* as now different from past *me*s because one is now older. The newly perceived *me* results from taking the attitude of the other in a situation where the previous, habituated *me* is disconfirmed.

Effect of Accumulated Experience

For the individual's self, *experience* consists of habituated reactions and memories of previous *I*s and previous *me*s. In any situation one can call upon such memories and habits to decide on the *me* to present in that situation. For example, a business executive may "know" that the best way for him to deal with his subordinates is to be firm and distant because in the past his employers were always firm and distant, and once when he tried to be warm and friendly, he lost control of the office and was nearly fired. He may also "know" that the best *me* to present to his wife is the supportive, understanding, and not too-dominant side of his *self* (because she "needs to feel important and loved"): he discovered this when she found out he was having an affair, and he has been very careful to try to meet her needs because he does "need" her too. He also has habituated *me*s that he presents (for better or worse) to his children, his golf partners, his parents, and his in-laws. These *me*s have been built up over time and generally work fairly well. He knows what to expect from the others in the interaction; and they know what to expect from him. If he finds that they don't work, he will probably work out a better set of *me*s for that situation and will learn from that *experience*—he will then be able to present this *me* in a future situation and be able to interact better because he has had that previous experience.

In general, as a person ages he gains increased knowledge of what responses lead to which outcomes in a wide variety of situations. Much of this knowledge is reduced to automatic (non-self-conscious) habits. For example, driving on a crowded expressway is largely an habituated behavior, but when something out of the ordinary occurs (such as ice on the road or an accident ahead), we drive more self-consciously and pay more attention to what we are doing and the consequences it may have. Similarly, in social situations, we typically interact in habituated ways unless something unexpected happens and then we become self-conscious (in Mead's sense) and try to solve the interactional difficulty. The greater the amount of experience in similar situations, the more readily an habituated *me* is called up for the response. If that *me* is inappropriate for the social interaction, then self-consciousness is required to select a more appropriate *me*. This self-consciousness may result in a timing event, or in an insightful solution to the problem. The new *me* that results may be remembered to be called up again in a future situation. It is this phenomenon of remembered and practiced *mes* accumulating with age that is called "experience." The *I* is closely involved, of course, because the *I* is experiencing the memory of that old *me* that did not work, is selecting an innovative new *me*, and then is experiencing the satisfaction of the successful resolution of the problem by the new *me*.

One of Neugarten's (1967) successful middle-aged business executives provides a vivid example of the meaning of experience:

"I know now exactly what I can do best, and how to make the best use of my time . . . I know how to delegate authority, but also what decisions to make myself . . . I know how to buffer myself from troublesome people . . . one well-placed telephone call will get me what I need. It takes time to learn how to cut through the red tape and how to get the organization to work for me . . . All this is what makes the difference between me and a young man, and it's all this that gives me the advantage."

We suggest that there are at least three types of experience that are particularly important for the complex symbolic interaction processes that characterize adulthood. (1) *Situation experience.* The person gains a greater range of past situations from which he can draw possible responses for the present situation. (2) *Interaction experience.* The person becomes increasingly adept at taking the attitude of the other and at interpreting the significant symbols being used in the present interaction. (3) *Self experience.* The person becomes increasingly adept at seeing himself from the point of view of the other and at integrating this awareness in the present moment with the memories of this awareness in past situations; that is, he has a greater amount of self-conscious experience of himself.

These forms of experience each accumulate with age so that an older person would have greater amounts of situation, interaction, and self experience compared with a younger person. This is not necessarily to imply that an older person would have greater insight into himself, or greater introspective abilities than a young person, for many of these experiences may be carried on in the present by habituated responses. But the older person would clearly have the potential to benefit from the greater range of experiences of himself in a larger number of situations in comparison with a young person.

Concluding her report on "The Awareness of Middle Age," Neugarten (1967) states:

> In pondering the data on these men and women, we have been impressed with the central importance of what might be called the executive processes of personality in middle age: self-awareness, selectivity, manipulation and control of the environment, mastery, competence, the wide array of cognitive strategies.
>
> We are impressed, too, with reflection as a striking characteristic of the mental life of middle-aged persons: the stock-taking, the heightened introspection, and above all, the structuring and restructuring of experience—that is, the conscious processing of new information in the light of what óne has already learned; and turning one's proficiency to the achiévement of desired ends.

In this description of the complex functioning of these economically successful middle-aged men and women, we see the self—the *I* and the *me*—and self-consciousness very much involved in these "executive processes of personality" and in the process of "reflection" as well. Certainly, the self's ability to profit from experience is also at work.

Change and Consistency in Adulthood

The issue of change and consistency in adulthood is a complex matter. On one level, we recognize that an individual we have not seen for several years is rather different (in appearance, in the self and, perhaps, in personality) from when we last saw her; yet she is also rather similar to our memories of her, and we usually have little difficulty in resuming an old friendship and catching up on the changes that have taken place. On another level, we note that some of the changes we see in her may be the result of actual changes in her, but some of them may be the result of changes in us. That is, we may have changed so that our *I* notes and responds to different aspects of her *self* (as when we see something new in a painting or film or scene we have not seen for years, but which has remained unchanged). On yet another level, it may be that our friend is presenting a different set of *mes* to us than she did before—*mes* that were present in the past but were never revealed to us.

Nonetheless, we recognize that our friend has had several years of *experience*, and she has probably had some *timing events* since we last saw her. She may have married, published several books, and become a highly respected judge in the intervening years. Such age-related changes will undoubtedly affect not only our perception of our friend but will also affect her *self*. However, we would also expect a certain amount of consistency as well. How do we explain these interrelated processes of change and consistency?

Change. In general, change comes about as the *I* selects a new *me* in its spontaneous response to situations. For example, when a clinical psychology student first walks onto a ward in a mental hospital at the beginning of his internship, he needs to develop a *me* that is appropriate in that situation. Since this is his first experience in a situation like that, he will probably develop a relatively new *me*, and his self will change somewhat in the process. Most change of this type is relatively gradual and often occurs in an evolutionary kind of process in which the *I* selects a response (a *me*) to which the *I* reacts, and to which others react, and the *I* may modify the response again, and so on. The clinical psychologist, for example, might try out a *me* that is criticized by the other staff members, that does not suit him, or that does not work with the patients; so he modifies it and tries again. All the while, the *I* is experiencing, reacting, and modifying the *me*.

These new behaviors are deliberately selected by the rational mind as the best possible response to the situation. They emerge from past experience, but could not be precisely predicted in advance because the *I* may be spontaneous and innovative in finding solutions to present problems, especially when the future consequences of those solutions cannot be predicted in advance. Thus, an entirely new *me* may arise in a new situation where there are no habituated responses that are appropriate, and one must become self-conscious. Or a new *me* may arise as an active effort to respond in new ways to old situations or in an effort to present new aspects of the self in various situations. One middle-aged woman in Neugarten's (1967) study described a change she found in middle age:

> "I discovered these last few years that I was old enough to admit to myself the things I could do well and to start doing them. I didn't think like this before . . . It's a great new feeling."

Thus, change in the self occurs when the situation prompts the *I* to select a new *me* that is then integrated into the range of *me*s that make up the social self, or when the *I* selects a new response in an old situation and that new *me* is integrated into the self, or when one self-consciously modifies the self as in the examples of timing events we discussed earlier. From this point of view, there is little difficulty in explaining change in the self. Instead, the difficulty appears to be in explaining the consistency in adulthood.

Consistency. Just as the *I* and the *me* are simultaneous aspects of the self, so are change and consistency simultaneous processes of the self. There are at least three factors that bring about a fairly high degree of consistency over time. One factor is memory. The *I* may reexperience past *I*s and *me*s, and the process of self-consciousness allows the individual to integrate these past selves into a coherent, consistent whole. That is, self-consciousness enables the individual to contemplate himself as a whole, and his ability to see himself from the perspective of other individuals (and from the perspective of the generalized other) makes it possible for him to consciously integrate and unify the various aspects of his *self*. For example, a physician may perform surgery, conduct research, direct a hospital staff, attend a concert, interact with his wife, play baseball with his children, and help his parents with their income tax. All of these *me*s are unified into a coherent whole, however, for he is able to integrate the attitudes of all these different people toward his *self*. He is also able to integrate his *self* at the present moment with the various *me*s he has had in the past and with the *me*s he envisions for the future. He is able to see his *self* in all of these activities. Thus the process of self-consciousness not only allows an individual to modify his *me* when necessary or desired but also to maintain a reasonably continuous self and to present consistent *me*s in a range of different social situations.

A second factor bringing consistency is the tendency for the situations in which one finds oneself to be relatively consistent. This results partly from an individual's self-selection of situations so that a person typically does not find himself in an entirely new or unexpected situation. This tendency to select familiar situations reduces the confusion that would result from continually finding new *me*s that are appropriate for each new situation. The consistency of situations is also enhanced by an individual's tendency to perceive situations selectively. That is, persons typically see a new situation in terms of the situations with which they are familiar and may misperceive or even distort the new situation to avoid the confusion of dealing with the complexity of a new situation.

A third factor leading to consistency of the self is an individual's tendency to respond in habituated ways in various situations unless there is a breakdown of the interaction, and one must then search out a new *me* to facilitate the interaction. However, most social interactions proceed in relatively habituated patterns of communication and only occasionally evoke self-consciousness.

"I know what will work in most situations, and what will not. I am well beyond the trial and error stage of youth. I now have a set of guidelines ... And I am practised" (Neugarten, 1967).

Thus, for at least these three reasons, individuals tend to be relatively consistent over time (and to be seen by others as fairly consistent). But this explanation of consistency is somewhat different from the explanation suggested by theories of personality where much of an individual's consistency results from personality characteristics that were formed in childhood (see Chapter 7). Instead, we suggest that the consistency of an individual during adulthood is brought about by memory, habituated responses, selective perceptions, and situational consistency. This is a clearly social-psychological view that deemphasizes the determining role of childhood factors (except as these factors are carried to the present *I* and *me* through memory or habituated responses).

In addition, if we shift the focus of the discussion from the individual to the social situation, we note that situational consistency and change is probably at least as important for change and consistency in adulthood as are individual factors. Becker (1964) has argued that:

> Situational adjustment produces change; the person shifts his behavior with each shift in the situation. Commitment produces stability; the person subordinates immediate situational interests to goals that lie outside the situation. But a stable situation can evoke a well-adjusted pattern of behavior which itself becomes valuable to the person.

Conclusion

Up to this point we have presented some social-psychological concepts that help to illuminate the process of developmental change in adulthood. In the remainder of this chapter we will present other social-psychological concepts, such as roles, norms, and socialization, which have grown out of the work of Mead and other sociologists. The meaning of these concepts will flow from the basic concepts of the self and the *I* and *me* we have dealt with so far in this chapter. The following discussion will be somewhat less theoretical than has been the case up to this point. We will also shortly return to research data.

SOCIAL TIMING FACTORS: NORMS, STATUS, AND ROLES

The discussion of Mead's approach to social interaction focused on the individual in the interaction. To expand this perspective, we shift our focus to the social side of the interaction. That is, we will examine the ways in which society affects the individual in age-related ways as he takes the attitude of the generalized other (i.e., society or his social community or "others in general") toward himself.

Age Norms

Norms are a set of expectations about behavior that people carry in their heads and use to regulate their own behavior and to respond to other's behavior. That is, norms are the attitudes of the generalized other and affect our behavior as we take the attitude of the generalized other toward ourselves in any social situation. Norms are linked to social *sanctions*; sanctions are the pressures brought to bear on an individual who violates the norms or expectations. Thus, norms exert some degree of *constraint* on an individual's behavior so that he chooses to do one thing and not do something else when the first choice is expected and the second is a violation of expectations. For example, social norms prescribe the expected behavior of persons in such socially defined positions as policeman, mother, student, and doctor; and there are informal as well as legal social sanctions that are used to maintain the expected behavior.

Similarly, individuals have expectations for what behavior is appropriate at different ages. We are all aware of these expectations, these *age norms*, and frequently our behavior and our responses to others are affected by them. We may note that we respond differently to a young person in "hippie" clothes than we would to a similarly dressed middle-aged person; or that we ordinarily respond differently to a young person than we do to a middle-aged person or an elderly individual. In addition, we are unlikely to see a 65-year-old woman wearing a two-piece bathing suit on the beach and, if we do see such a woman, we would think her behavior rather improper. On the other hand, if we see a 35-year-old woman dressed like an aged grandmother, we are just as likely to think that her behavior is inappropriate. Neugarten, Moore, and Lowe (1965) inquired about various age-related characteristics in a middle-class, middle-aged sample and found a high degree of consensus about the ages that the respondents associated with each characteristic (Table 2.1). For example, 80 percent of the men and 90 percent of the women felt that the 20-25 age range is the best time for a man to marry. The authors report that this consensus about age norms is not limited to persons residing in a particular part of the country, white persons, or middle-aged persons. The same set of questions was asked of other middle-class respondents aged 20-30 who lived in a midwestern city, a group of Negro men and women aged 40-60, and a group of persons aged 70-80 in a New England community. Essentially the same patterns of age norms were found for each group of respondents.

Since these age norms involve the individual's perceptions of what is appropriate and inappropriate behavior at different ages, it is also possible to measure the amount of *constraint* that age norms exert. For example: Is it appropriate for a woman to wear a two-piece bathing

Table 2.1 Consensus in a Middle-Class, Middle-Aged Sample Regarding Various Age-Related Characteristics

	Age Range Designated as Appropriate or Expected	Percent Who Concur	
		Men (N=50)	Women (N=43)
Best age for a man to marry	20–25	80	90
Best age for a woman to marry	19–24	85	90
When most people should become grandparents	45–50	84	79
Best age for most people to finish school and go to work	20–22	86	82
When most men should be settled on a career	24–26	74	64
When most men hold their top jobs	45–50	71	58
When most people should be ready to retire	60–65	83	86
A young man	18–22	84	83
A middle-aged man	40–50	86	75
An old man	65–75	75	57
A young woman	18–24	89	88
A middle-aged woman	40–50	87	77
An old woman	60–75	83	87
When a man has the most responsibilities	35–50	79	75
When a man accomplishes most	40–50	82	71
The prime of life for a man	35–50	86	80
When a woman has the most responsibilities	25–40	93	91
When a woman accomplishes most	30–45	94	92
A good-looking woman	20–35	92	82

Source. Neugarten et al. (1965), Table 1. Reprinted with permission from the *American Journal of Sociology*, copyright © 1965 by the University of Chicago.

suit on the beach (a) when she is 18? (b) when she is 30? (c) when she is 45? (Neugarten et al., 1965). If the answer is "yes" to all three ages, there is no age constraint reflected. If the answer is "yes" to only one, then the degree of constraint is fairly high. In this manner, age constraint can be measured for individuals of different ages and also for the individual's perception of "other's views" (that is, their perception of the generalized other).

Neugarten et al. (1965) found that individual's age constraint was fairly low for young people's personal opinions but increased for older respondents. At the same time, the perceptions of other people's opinions in terms of age constraint were rather high for young respondents but were somewhat lower for older respondents. Personal opinions and other's opinions nearly converged for the sample aged 65+ (Figure 2.1). These findings indicate that while young people feel "others" think age is important, they do not feel much age constraint themselves; however, the older respondents (age 65+) feel that age is moderately important in determining appropriate behavior, and that "others" place about the same amount of importance on it as they do themselves. Note, however, that these data are from a cross-sectional study; thus, respondents born at the turn of the century may place more emphasis on age as an important variable for regulating behavior than respondents born in 1940, because of cultural changes rather than age-related factors. However, all

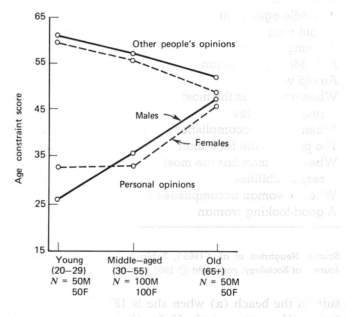

Figure 2.1
Perception of age constraints in adulthood, by age and sex. (Source. Neugarten et al., 1965, Figure 1. Reprinted with permission from the American Journal of Sociology, copyright © 1965 by the University of Chicago.)

age groups indicate that age determines what behavior is appropriate, at least in the eyes of other people.

Age-Status Systems

In addition to socially defined age norms that indicate appropriate *behavior* on the basis of age, there is also an age-related status system in many cultures whereby one's social *position* and *status* is based at least partly on the person's age. That is, an age-status system in a society awards the rights, duties, and privileges to individuals differentially on the basis of age.

There is some degree of *age grading* in our social structure, so that status and power are awarded to individuals in part because of their age, but it is not nearly as tight a system as the age grading in elementary school where children pass from grade to grade as they age. However, some American Indian tribes, for example, placed their greatest status on the aged, especially the aged man, who was often their chief or medicine man. There is a certain logic to such a structure, since if a man were to live to an old age he had to be a successful warrior, strong and healthy, and adept at avoiding the various pitfalls that might have resulted in his earlier death. Other cultures, particularly preindustrial and Oriental societies, are thought to have fairly rigid age-status systems in which the aged are accorded high status.

In our society the aged tend to have fairly low social status and, although there are many exceptions, old persons have often lost the power and responsibility they possessed in their prime. In our society, individuals seldom reach positions of power simply because they are aged. Even in the seniority system in Congress, both skill and age are required since there is the requirement not only for long service but also for continual reelection by the voters. However, skill alone does not automatically bring high status either, since "experience" is usually also required and, of course, accumulates with age.

Currently one of the serious problems in our society is the precarious economic and social position of many elderly, retired persons (see Chapter 10). Not only are they in positions of low social status, but also many are living in isolation and at subsistence levels of income. Thus, where there are age-status systems in the United States, they do not seem to apply after retirement. And, in general, age-status systems may be less important in our society than socioeconomic status that reflects the status of one's parents, one's education and occupation, and is manifested by one's style of life, power in the community, and geographic neighborhood in the city (cf. Coleman and Neugarten, 1971).

Age-Sex Roles

The concept of *role* is related to both the individual's social position and to the norms of the society. A role is the *behavior* that is expected from a person occupying a social position. The norms prescribe that expected role behavior. Since many social positions have role behaviors associated with them, the social position is often called a role. For example, the role of "mother" involves some very clear expectations and behaviors for the appropriate enactment of that role. It may be contrasted with the role of "wife" that she also plays or with the role of "business executive" that she may also play. In the symbolic interaction framework, the role is a *me* that the individual presents in a social interaction; it arises from taking the attitude of the other (or generalized other) toward one's own behavior. However, a *me* is not always a role; it may be any characteristic of the self that may be seen by others. A *me* may reveal a feeling such as "depressed" or "anxious," or it may be an attitude such as "honest" or "punctual"; but a role is always a *me*. One plays many roles during the day (that is, presents many *me*s), and it is the task of the *I* to select and integrate these various *me*s into a sense of self.

Perhaps we play roles because it would be much too complicated to self-consciously work out moment-to-moment behavior without being able to rely on the partial scripts that accompany a role. Consider the chaos that would result if teachers, students, policemen, and doctors (and so on) forgot how to play their roles—how to teach, how to act in classes, and so on. Social interaction would become incredibly chaotic!

Individuals have a fair amount of latitude in how they ad-lib their roles, and we probably all play our roles in slightly idiosyncratic ways; but if one steps too far out of line, one feels some degree of social constraint. For example, a shopper in a large department store is playing the role of "customer"; he is greeted by a person playing the role of "salesclerk." As long as each of them plays his role, they can interact and complete the transaction quickly and easily. If the shopper changes his role, for example by trying to sell a watch to the salesclerk, there is an abrupt shift and some interactional discomfort. Or if the shopper violates the expectations of his role, such as by offering to pay less for the item than the price marked, the salesclerk may give a response that means, "Get with it; that's not the way to play your role!" If the customer persists in playing his role incorrectly and, for example, pays the clerk $10 for a $15 pair of slacks and walks out of the store, he is likely to feel the social constraint of the store security guard.

Since roles involve norms, they also differ in their expectations at different ages; in addition, since roles are related to social position, they may begin, change, and end at certain ages. For example, at marriage there is a shift in role to that of husband or wife; at the birth of the first child there is a new role added, that of parent—mother or father. Such role change through the lifeline, in which new roles are added and old ones are dropped, makes it possible to view the life cycle in terms of social roles and the milestones in adulthood as the addition or change in roles. For example, when we discuss the family, we will examine the social timing for the adult as measured by role changes: unmarried, wife, mother, working mother, working grandmother, retired grandmother, and widow. Similarly, we may examine a man's life cycle in terms of his roles: student, married student, working father, working grandfather, retired grandfather, and widower. However, at the same time that an individual has one set of roles in the family he also has a number of other roles in his various activities and interactions. Thus, as roles shift they may change in a number of areas at once or change slowly over a longer period of time. Also, the range of roles may change with cultural changes such as the current phenomenon of women entering the work force today in much greater numbers than a century ago.

The Social Clock

The interaction of age norms, age constraints, age-status systems, and age-related roles produces a phenomenon that Neugarten (1968) calls the *social clock*. This concept is sometimes mentioned by middle-aged people themselves as an internal sense of social timing that acts as a *prod* to speed up accomplishment of a goal, or as a *brake* to slow down one's progress through the social events of the lifeline. The sense of regulation comes from the self—from the internalized perception of social norms, expectations, and roles. These concepts act as timing cues that give an individual the idea that it is time to take that European trip before he is too old to enjoy it (or too old to think that he *should* take a long trip), or when it is time to go back to school to study painting "now that my children are on their own."

This internalized social clock is one of the major sources of timing in adulthood; that is, it regulates the sequential progression of an individual through the age-related milestones and events of the adult years. The norms and expectations of society (the generalized other) set off internal processes in the individual when he takes the attitude of the generalized other toward himself, which result in changes in behavior that are, then, age-related. Extending the analogy slightly, we say that there is a social "Big Ben" (the age norms), and we set our individual watches (internalized age norms) to Big Ben. Of course, some of our watches keep better time than others, so there is some variation in the timing of major milestones, but most of us have a reasonably good sense of "the right time" to marry, change jobs, or become a parent, and so on. One example of this social clock indicating that it is time to change jobs is given by one of Neugarten's (1967) middle-aged respondents:

> "I moved at age forty-five from a large corporation to a law firm. I got out at the last possible moment, because after forty-five it is too difficult to find the job you want. If you haven't made it by then, you had better make it fast, or you are stuck."

The process by which these social norms, roles, and expectations are translated into age-related behavior is the process of socialization, to which we turn our attention in the final section of this chapter.

SOCIALIZATION IN ADULTHOOD

Socialization is the process by which an individual learns to perform his various social roles adequately; it is the process by which norms, values, and expectations are transmitted from one generation to the next. In the symbolic interaction framework, socialization involves the basic social process of taking the attitude of the other (or generalized other) toward oneself. In addition, it involves taking the attitude of the other toward the entire range of social objects. Much of this process, as well as the learning of the significant symbols required for the process to occur, undoubtedly occurs according to complex principles of learning theory such as the modification of behavior on the basis of the consequences of that behavior. However, because of the selective, innovative processes of the *I*, this socialization process is not a passive molding of an unformed, socially dangerous child but, instead, is a complementary fitting together of two active social processes—the individual and his social community— ideally maximizing the potential of both. That is, the socialization process is active and reciprocal so that both the *socializee* and the *socializing agent* are being socialized by each other in the process.

The Socialization Process

Until recently it was felt that socialization was primarily, if not exclusively, limited to childhood and early adolescence; so the idea that adults are also socialized by the persons with whom they interact is relatively new. However, the process of socialization does not differ much for children and for adults. It involves a relationship with a *significant other*. As these individuals interact, usually in an emotional relationship of some salience, they influence one another and provide feedback to one another through the symbolic interaction process. This feedback functions to build up a set of mutual expectations for each other's behavior. These mutual expectations contain the role prescriptions, the norms, and the values that the agent attempts to transmit. He, in turn, responds to the behavior and to the expectations of the socializee and may modify his own expectations or provide corrective feedback to the socializee.

It may be that this interaction occurs whenever two people are interacting in a relationship with some emotional involvement; it is a broad, general view of the socialization process. However, it also pertains to such specific situations as the situations in which the socializing agent is informally conveying information or formally "teaching"; it pertains to the transmission of values and moral views, to ways of interacting with others, or to operating a piece of complicated machinery. That is, the degree of formality or informality varies and the content varies, but the relationship, the mutual influence, and the centrality of a salient relationship between the two interacting individuals does not vary.

However, as the individual develops from childhood into adulthood, certain parameters of the socialization process may change. For example, as the child gains the cognitive capacity to think abstractly, to conceptualize situations that are not concretely present, and to take a more objective view of his own behavior, he also gains the cognitive ability to expand his set of significant others from people immediately present (his parents, teachers, and peers) to people who are not now living or concretely present, such as historical figures, religious deities, or deceased parents and grandparents. This ability continues through adulthood so that an individual may base his central values and expectations for himself on the remembered or imagined expectations of these not currently present significant others. Perhaps this ability plays a part, for example, in the often noted increase in religious fervor during adolescence.

In addition, the young adult has a wider range of social interactions than was true for the child, and this social world continues to broaden in adulthood. That is, the range of significant others who are physically present increases, and with it there is an increase in the range of individuals whom one may choose to interact with. Thus, there is greater freedom to select one's significant others—one's socializing agents—during adulthood than is true in childhood. However, allowing for the increased intellectual ability of the adult and the different kinds of roles that the adult is socializing himself into, the process of socialization remains essentially unchanged from childhood.

Anticipatory Socialization and Resocialization

The general process of socialization may be subdivided into more specific types of socialization experience. Two of the most common types are anticipatory socialization and resocialization. *Anticipatory socialization* is the process of preparation for a change in role or status. It involves exploring the new norms and expectations that will be associated with the new role or status once the transition is made. It involves an element of practice and of trying out a new role before the actual shift takes place. Examples of this process include the college student choosing a career— imagining what it might be like, talking to persons in that career, and perhaps trying it out in a summer job, or a medical student in his first year who is given a "black bag," wears a white lab coat, and begins to play the role of "doctor" before he has his M.D. Later in life, a mother may return to school or begin preparing herself in other ways for returning to work several years before her children leave home, and she actually enters her field of special interest. Similarly, the father may begin exploring new interests and preparing for his retired status several years before it actually occurs. Or the family may begin reading different magazines and driving a different kind of car in preparation for the next promotion and a move to another neighborhood. In such cases there is a period of anticipation of the new roles or status and preliminary socialization into them before they are actually achieved.

Resocialization, in contrast, takes place when the role or status is actually begun. The amount of resocialization, or reorganization of one's expectations about oneself, depends on the amount of difference between the previous role and the new one. It may involve learning a new skill when one's job is replaced by a machine; or it may involve learning the role of grandparent when one's first grandchild is born. Adulthood involves a series of resocialization experiences, and many of the changes that occur during the adult years involve or reflect socialization experiences.

Adult Socialization: Stability and Change

Once again we turn to the question of change and consistency in adulthood. Previously we considered the issue of change and consistency as simultaneous processes for the individual's self, the *I* and the *me*. Now we complete the discussion by focusing on social situations that are likely to bring about change; conversely, the general stability of social situations is, largely, responsible for the consistency of an individual through adulthood (Becker, 1964). Thus, changes in situations lead the individual to appropriate socialization experiences that bring about changes in the self (i.e., in the set of *me*s and even in the *I*'s response to those *me*s). However, in each socialization situation the individual carries part of his old self along with the new part of the self into his new situation. For example, the husband who becomes a father changes somewhat as a result of the socialization into his new role; but many of his other *me*s are not affected and are reintegrated into his integrated sense of self. Thus, there is simultaneous continuity and change within each individual's self.

Brim (1968) has suggested a number of situations in adulthood that typically lead to socialization experiences; we will discuss each of them.

Demands of Self or Others. From time to time an individual may feel that he is not living the kind of life he wishes to live or doing the kind of things he wishes to do; conversely, others may feel that about him. As a result he may change somewhat through informal socialization, or he may seek out a socialization experience to bring about the desired changes. For some people, this experience may be psychotherapy; for others, it may be a shift in reference group to bring about the desired change in roles and expectations about himself (an example would be an executive who seeks out other people interested in new life styles and finally moves to a commune); for others it may involve finding a new reference group (or spouse, perhaps) whose norms and expectations are compatible with his own so that he changes relatively little. Insofar as there is change, however, socialization will be involved since there will be new norms, values, and expectations about himself and about his own behavior that he will learn. Even the changes that result from the individual's internal social clock (by which age norms exert constraint on him to behave differently) lead him to learn the appropriate expectations for "people of his age." In general, an individual seeks formal and informal socialization experiences when he feels that a change is in order.

Role or Status Change. Social situations may change as a result of age-related changes such as the shift in roles from "single" to "wife" to "mother." Or they may change from one's growing seniority on the job that brings shifts in role and status. In any case, there would be new expectations and norms to learn that would involve anticipatory socialization and resocialization; perhaps it would even involve a kind of radical resocialization if the shift is from, for example, "junkie" to "ex-addict" where there is a major shift in self-conception and a clear dichotomy between the previous role and the new role. One characteristic of role or status change is that the conflicts that result between the new role and previously held roles must be resolved; for example, the young husband may have some role conflict between his previous role of "swinging bachelor" and his present role of "husband" in his interactions with his unmarried friends. A second characteristic of such socialization is that the individual will need some support in the new role, that is, someone (the socializing agents) to whom he can turn for encouragement and for help in working out his new role; for the young husband these socializing agents would probably include his spouse, parents, and friends. Third, this process of socialization is likely to take place in informal ways; usually one's colleagues, neighbors, and relatives provide most of the socialization and do so subtly and informally. Only when there are distinct skills to be learned is the socialization formal, requiring education or reading.

Occupational Shift or Entry. A frequent cause of resocialization are changes in occupation or role in the occupation. A major change or even a promotion brings with it the necessity for developing new skills, for playing new roles, for forming new relationships, and for changing the level of aspiration. Thus, the man promoted from a machinist to a foreman has to develop some managerial skills, relate in different ways with the men in the shop and with the upper levels of management, and be more concerned with efficiency and productivity than with his skill on the machine (cf. Lieberman, 1956). Similarly, a woman who shifts from the role of housewife to novelist will find herself being socialized along the same dimensions as she learns the role and norms that now apply for writing and publishing books; if she is very successful she may also have to learn the skills of appearing on TV interviews.

Changes in the Family. During the course of the family cycle there are a number of role shifts that take place. In addition, there are mutual expectations that are set up by the husband and wife about each other's behavior; and the spouses function as very important socializing agents for one another. For example, the periods of courtship, engagement, and the first years of marriage involve a great deal of mutual socialization as the couple match their expectations with each other and reach working agreements on a great range of behaviors such as housework, sexual behavior, food preferences, entertainment, desire for children, brand of toothpaste, handling of finances, and so on. Then the birth of the first child brings a shift from previous roles of husband and wife to mother and father. This change not only brings about the socialization into their new roles as parents but also intensifies the mutual socialization for their ongoing relationship. The baby, of course, also has some "expectations" —in the form of immediate and imperative needs—that influence the parent's expectations about their own behavior. As the children grow, they begin exerting an ever-increasing socializing influence on the parents. Although the parents may be the primary socializing agents for the children, the interaction is never only one way, and children's expectations ordinarily influence parent's expectations as well. Finally, as the children begin leaving home and the parents again resume a dyadic relationship, additional socialization may be needed to again match their expectations for one another. In addition, there may be some personality changes as well as biological changes which occur in the later years, so expected behaviors may change over time. Of course, divorce, wherever it may occur in the family cycle, brings with it a marked change in role and status. Again, there is socialization involved in learning to play the role of a divorcee; a new marriage brings another attempt at resocialization. Similarly, with the death of one's spouse there is a change of role and the need for some additional socialization to learn the norms and expectations for the role of widow or widower.

Geographic Mobility. Another socialization situation in adulthood may be brought about by physically moving from one community to another. This may result from a promotion and increase in status so that a new home is possible; or it may result from a promotion combined with a transfer. In the latter case, the shift in occupational role is combined with geographical transfer (often to preclude conflict with previous roles on the job). This brings the necessity for the wife and children to become resocialized into the new community; and it may be an abrupt shift in role and status for the wife if she is not also moving upward at about the same speed as her husband, and if she has not been able to anticipate the new role and status demands. A similar kind of situational change, but necessarily more intense, results from immigration. Frequently the socialization process resulting from this type of change continues up to the second or third generation since the tendency is to decrease the disparity between the previous community and the present one by living in an ethnic community.

Downward Mobility. Finally, another change that brings about a need for adult socialization is a decline in status or in the number of roles. Although this is essentially the same process as upward mobility in terms of the demands for socialization, it is, unfortunately, a shift to a lower status. It is rather common for the aged to need to adjust to a lower standard of living after retirement (although this does not necessarily involve a loss of social status). Downward mobility may also occur in a period of national economic decline or as a result of an individual's emotional or social problems, such as alcoholism or mental illness. Accepting a lower status job because of overcompetition in one's field of training or because one was fired from a better job may also bring downward mobility. Similarly, divorce or widowhood may bring a decrease in income or in social status that leads to resocialization into the norms and expectations for the new position of widowhood or divorced and the new style of life. Again, the process of socialization is one aspect of the adjustment to such changed role and status demands.

Conclusion

The adult is an active participant in social interactions. He is affected by these interactions, and he plays an important role in affecting others. During the adult years he typically reaches his zenith of social power and responsibility; he also reaches his maximum number and range of social interactions. These varied interactions are a primary source of the change and the consistency of his *self*. We have examined the process by which individuals change while they simultaneously remain consistent; and we have discussed the ways in which social situations bring change and consistency to an active participating individual. Yet, as much as a person may change in socialization experiences, there is part of his old self that he carries into his new role, insuring a degree of consistency along with a degree of flexibility.

Some of the changes that occur in adulthood seem to be sequential changes, regulated primarily by the age norms in our society. Thus, part of the timing of adult development appears to result from the "social clock"; part of the timing also seems to result from various timing events that occur in moments of self-consciousness.

Experience clearly accumulates with age and seems to be an important dimension of the meaning of "maturity." We examined the meaning of this phenomenon and suggested that it affects the process of development by providing a greater range of situations, interactions, and self-conscious moments that are available to the individual's self in social interactions.

Many of these concepts are illustrated in the case examples, the first of which may be found after the next chapter. At the least, one may note the moments of self-consciousness and the effects of various socialization experiences on each of the individuals. And one case or another illustrates each of the changes we have outlined leading to socialization experiences —geographic mobility, changes in the family, demands of self and others, and so on.

But before formally introducing a case, we will begin a discussion of the first part of adulthood—or the last part of the transition from adolescence into adulthood—we call it "young adulthood." From this point on, we will progressively move through the lifeline until Chapter 9, where we discuss death and bereavement.

References

*Becker, Howard S. 1964. Personal Change in Adult Life. *Sociometry*, 27(1), 40–53.

Brim, Orville G., Jr. 1968. Adult Socialization. In John A. Clausen (Ed.), *Socialization and Society*. Boston: Little, Brown.

Coleman, Richard P., and Neugarten, Bernice L. 1971. *Social Status in the City*. San Francisco: Jossey-Bass.

Gendlin, Eugene T. 1964. A Theory of Personality Change. In Philip Worchel and Donn Byrne (Eds.), *Personality Change*. New York: Wiley.

Harris, Sidney J. 1965. Strictly Personal. *Chicago Daily News*, May 11, 1965.

Lieberman, Seymour. 1956. The Effects of Changes in Roles on the Attitudes of Role Occupants. *Human Relations*, 9(4), 385–402.

Mead, George Herbert. 1934. Mind, Self, and Society. In Anselm Strauss (Ed.), *George Herbert Mead: On Social Psychology*. Chicago: University of Chicago Press, 1964. (Originally published: *Mind, Self, and Society*. Charles W. Morris, Ed.)

*Neugarten, Bernice L. 1967. The Awareness of Middle Age. In Roger Owen (Ed.), *Middle Age*. London: British Broadcasting Corporation.

*Neugarten, Bernice L. 1968. Adult Personality: Toward a Psychology of the Life Cycle. In Edgar Vinacke (Ed.), *Readings in General Psychology*. New York: American Book Co.

*Neugarten, Bernice L.; Moore, Joan W.; and Lowe, John C. 1965. Age Norms, Age Constraints, and Adult Socialization. *American Journal of Sociology*, 70(6), 710–717.

Strauss, Anselm. (Ed.) 1964. *George Herbert Mead: On Social Psychology*. Chicago: University of Chicago Press.

* References marked with an asterisk appear in Bernice L. Neugarten (Ed.), *Middle Age and Aging*. Chicago: University of Chicago Press, 1968.

three
Young
Adulthood:
Identity
and
Intimacy

It is puzzling: young people appear to be growing up much faster today and taking a longer time to do it. On the one hand, many young adults are deeply involved with political, ecological, and social issues that are far more "mature" than the issues that preoccupied young people a decade or two ago. And the age at which one first becomes aware of such social complexities as drug use, alternate life styles, racism, and poverty appears to be decreasing—at least in the middle class. Yet, on the other hand, the length of time spent between the last days of childhood and full self-supporting independence in adulthood is growing longer. Today a high school education is almost mandatory and even college diplomas are no longer an assurance of unlimited occupational opportunity. Thus, the complexity of the issues faced in young adulthood seems to be growing and, at the same time, the number of years spent dealing with these issues is also growing. Of course, these phenomena partly reflect the complexity of our society; but they also involve the developmental tasks inherent in the transition from childhood to adulthood in any society (such as socialization into adult roles and the establishment of a relatively enduring sense of identity that is integrated with the social matrix of the culture).

However great the differences among various societies, there is one focal point within the life span of an individual which in most known societies is to some extent emphasized: the period of youth, of transition from childhood to full adult status, or full membership in the society. In this period the individual is no longer a child (especially from the physical and sexual point of view) but is ready to undertake many attributes of an adult and to fulfill adult roles. But he is not yet fully acknowledged as an adult, a full member of the society. Rather, he is being "prepared," or is preparing himself for such adulthood (Eisenstadt, 1961, p. 32).

This chapter will focus on the developmental issues of this period of transition into full adulthood and will discuss some of the salient concerns of this period in American society. However, this period of transition is very difficult to conceptualize because it seems to consist of two or three different periods. That is, early adolescence (from puberty to 15 or 16) is clearly very different from later adolescence (from 16 to 18 or so), and there may be a new phase of this transitional period emerging in our society: young adulthood.

The term "young adulthood" probably conveys a reasonably clear picture of the span of time we have in mind. For example, in the last chapter we presented some data from a study of age norms; one finding was that most middle-aged respondents felt that the ages that best described a "young man" or a "young woman" were 18-22 and 18-25, respectively (Neugarten, Moore, and Lowe, 1965). These are approximately the ages we think of as well. We mean "after adolescence" and "before adulthood." On one hand there is more stability than in early adolescence (since many of the basic identity issues have been dealt with); on the other hand there is not yet the full adoption of occupational, marital, and parental roles characteristic of normative adulthood in our society. That is, the 19-year-old young adult is different from a 14-year-old adolescent and, typically, also differs from a 24-year-old parent.

However, this period of young adulthood is a relatively uncharted phase of the lifeline. It seems to be an emerging period of the life span in our society, and not everyone may experience it or there may be many varieties of the young adulthood experience. For example, it may be that this stage is most applicable to young people in college—about one-third of white persons and about one-fifth of black persons between 18 and 21 were attending college in 1972 (U.S. Bureau of the Census, 1973). The transition from adolescence to full adulthood may be more direct for young people who marry and begin working after high school, since they may work out their occupational and marital identity "on the job" so to speak. Nonetheless, another group of young people such as unmarried men and women who join the armed forces or go to work after high school and postpone marriage and parenthood, and young people who cannot find jobs may also experience a kind of young adulthood—that is, an extended period of transition where they are certainly not adolescents but also have not fully assumed the typical adult roles in society.

In this chapter we will explore this uncharted period of life and will suggest some of the characteristics, challenges, and potentials that seem to be involved in this part of the transition from adolescence to adulthood in our present society. We will begin by discussing some of the characteristics of this period, the cultural factors that have played a part in creating it in our society, and two diverse styles of young adulthood. We will then examine some of the central developmental issues and potential growth trends that arise during young adulthood and we will explore some of the current issues that are involved in young adulthood in the 1970s. We will conclude by tying the major themes of young adulthood together with a symbolic-interactional analysis of the process by which young adults deal with the central developmental issues of young adulthood: identity and intimacy.

YOUNG ADULTHOOD IN AMERICAN SOCIETY

Perhaps the most striking characteristic of young adulthood in America today is the somewhat artificial way in which it was created as a stage in human development.

> Puberty is a biological fact, but youth is a social one. There is no biological imperative to reinforce the idea that for several years after puberty young persons should continue to be segregated from adults and prevented from assuming adult sexual, economic, and social roles. By age 18, at the latest, virtually everyone is physiologically adult, having reached sexual maturity and the peak of physical and mental capacity. Thus, the segregation and categorization of young people is unknown in many cultures; furthermore, it is a very recent development in western civilization (Flacks, 1971, p. 9).

A number of social, economic, and technological factors have combined to bring about an extended period of transition from childhood to adulthood. Aries (1962) points out that in the Middle Ages children moved into the world of adults as soon as they could manage on their own (as early as 6 or 7); with the Industrial Revolution and the eventual laws against child labor a period of apprenticeship developed and evolved into a period of adolescence. However, the view of children as "little adults," and the absence of a period of adolescence among the poor, is suggested as late as the nineteenth century by such writers as Dickens. Certainly, Little Nell or David Copperfield thought and acted like adults and had no period of moratorium to resolve their identity crises. But as industrialization increased, greater education and skill became necessary to perform the tasks of the new occupations, and the principle of compulsory education was extended to all children after 1900.

Social Characteristics of Young Adults

Within the last 50 years our society has grown increasingly complex and the demands for greater education have increased enormously. In 1972 80 percent of all persons 25-29 years old had completed four years of high school or more (19 percent had completed four years of college or more);

this represents a dramatic increase from the 38 percent who completed four years of high school or more in 1940 (Figure 3.1). The increase has been equally dramatic for Negroes and other nonwhite races—the percentage of persons between 25 and 29 who completed four years of high school or more increased from 12 percent in 1940 to 67 percent in 1972, and the percentage who completed four years of college or more increased from 1.6 percent in 1940 to 11.6 percent in 1972. The percentage of high school graduates who went on to college increased by about 10 percent between 1960 and 1972; in 1972, 53 percent of the men and 42 percent of the women who graduated from high school went on to college. Over half (57 percent) of the white students enrolled in college grew up in

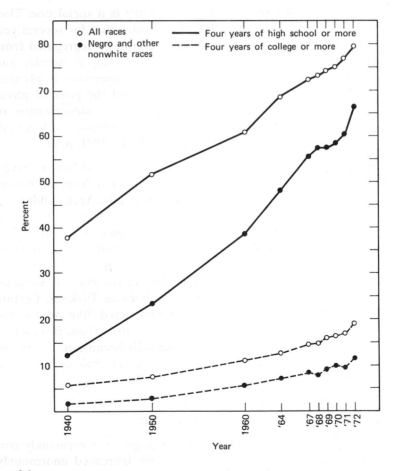

Figure 3.1
Level of school completed by persons 25 to 29 years old, 1940 to 1972. (Source. *U.S. Bureau of the Census, 1973, Table 18.*)

families in which the head of the family had not attended college (and 20 percent came from families in which the head of the family had not completed high school); among Negro persons in college the corresponding percentages were 78 percent and 56 percent in 1971 (U.S. Bureau of the Census, 1973).

A slightly higher percentage of young adults were single in 1972 than in 1960. In 1972, two-thirds of white men and three-fourths of black men between 18 and 24 were single (for women the percentages were 47 and 58, respectively). They are highly mobile persons—44 percent of the persons between 22 and 24 moved between 1970 and 1971 (this does not include those who move away from home to attend college). They are less likely to vote than older persons—50 percent of those between 18 and 24 reported they voted in 1972 compared with 66 percent of those over 25; white young people were more likely to report they voted (52 percent) compared with black young people (35 percent).

Among young people attending college, about 6.6 million in 1972, 40 percent were living with parents or other relatives; 29 percent were living in college housing, and 18 percent lived in their own household in 1971. Older college students (between 22 and 24) were more likely to have their own household (47 percent), yet 26 percent lived with parents or relatives.

Less than half of all persons between 16 and 24 were enrolled in school in 1971 (43 percent); about one-third were employed and about 5 percent were in the armed forces. The largest proportion of unemployed men and women is in the late-teenage group—in 1970, 13.7 percent of white men, 13.3 percent of white women, 24.9 percent of black men, and 34.4 percent of black women between the ages of 16 and 19 were unemployed (U.S. Bureau of Labor Statistics, 1971).

Obviously the labor market could not absorb the large number of young people currently attending school, and prolonged education is one way to reduce the number of potential workers when increasing automation and productivity per man-hour of work are reducing the number of workers needed to maintain high levels of production (earlier retirement and shorter work weeks also serve this function; see Chapter 6).

Interaction of Cohort and Developmental Factors

As the postwar "baby boom" moved through the lifeline, the median age of the population declined a year and a half from 1960 to 1972; it was 28 in 1972. The number of young people of college age (18-21) is expected to increase to 16.8 million persons in 1980; in 1970 it was 14.6 million. College enrollment has almost doubled between 1964 and 1972, and the enrollment of black persons in college has jumped by 211 percent; in 1972 black persons comprised 9 percent of all college students (and about 11 percent of the total population). Women were also more likely to attend college in 1972 than in 1962 and in 1972 comprised 42 percent of all college students.

These cohort-historical changes in our society—the increased proportion of young people, increased college attendance, and decreased participation in the labor force during young adulthood—interact with the developmental changes that arise during young adulthood. In a sense, these factors have played an important role in lengthening the period of transition into full adulthood today. They clearly illustrate the important interaction between the cohort factors and developmental changes that we discussed in Chapter 1. Similar cohort factors are seen in the so-called "sexual revolution" and in the current concern over the use of drugs by young people.

Several other factors are involved in creating this prolonged period of transition and reflect the interaction of these cohort and developmental factors. First, as society becomes more complex, and as the speed of social change becomes more rapid, the family becomes unable to adequately prepare the offspring for future roles. Other institutions (such as education) are similarly unable to fulfill this function adequately, and the young person is thrown onto his own resources and onto his peer group for finding ways to assume the adult roles. Margaret Mead (1970) described this phenomenon as characteristic of "cofigurative cultures" in which the young must "develop appropriate styles of behavior for which there are no parental models" (p. 46). Yet, she sees our society moving toward a "prefigurative culture" in which "it will be the child—and not the parent and grandparent—that represents what is to come" (p. 68) and in which "the young ... can lead their elders in the direction of the unknown" (p. 73). A second factor in these changes is that the adult roles, the range of choice between roles and life styles, and society itself are becoming more complex and diversified. For example, the number of occupations in our society is enormous and increasing (over 35,000 separate titles are listed in the third edition of the *Dictionary of Occupational Titles*); and if such movements as Women's Lib and Gay Lib have a social impact in modifying sex-role prescriptions, sex-roles and acceptable life styles may become more varied and more a matter of individual choice. A third factor is that in our society democratic values, emphasis on freedom of choice, and stress on individuality further increase the complexity of the tasks in adolescence. That is, there is more encouragement and ability to choose the direction of one's life than would be tolerated in a totalitarian society. A fourth factor, especially among middle-class parents, is that there is a growing permissiveness toward postponing job and marriage commitments through the age of (even) 30, as long as one is in school. Thus, many young adults are able, with social approval, to postpone the tasks of adulthood, to experiment, and to work out their own transition from childhood through a complex series of "choices" into adulthood.

Hence, the longer period of transition—and the consequent "creation" of a period of young adulthood in our society—seems to be a realistic social development to cope with these varied social and economic changes; it provides more time to make the necessary complex linkages into adult society, to acquire the necessary education, and to postpone entry into the job market. The difficulties that are, perhaps, the unintended consequences of this social adjustment are widely discussed— particularly premarital sexuality, political activism, alienation, and drug use. In a sense, they may be seen as largely a result of these social changes we have outlined in combination with the sexual and intellectual maturity of young adults, the relative leisure of college students and unemployed young people, the affluence of middle-class young people, and the social-political characteristics of our current society.

Given the complexity of young adulthood in our society, how do young people negotiate this transitional period? Most do, of course, but the process is undoubtedly very different for affluent college students and for young persons living in an urban ghetto. We will take a look at both of these different groups.

Youth into Maturity—A Study of Affluent College Students

Rachel Cox (1970) studied the progress of 63 young men and women who were elected to the student council at three "high-level liberal arts colleges"; they were selected as subjects because they were considered to be functioning "successfully." Her study is a report of the interviews conducted 10 years after the initial study of these young people as college undergraduates. Most of the subjects would be classified as "adults" at the follow-up interview. They ranged in age from 30 to 36; 95 percent were economically self-supporting, 93.6 percent were married, and all were functioning in their chosen roles.

The transition was not always a smooth one, but nearly all of the respondents coped with it very well. However, the 10-year period involved pain, disillusionment, and discouragment for a considerable number of the respondents. The deaths of loved ones, the trials and errors involved in finding and settling on a job, and the ups and downs of marriage seemed to have a greater impact on these young people than their high level of successful functioning and emotional maturity in college would have indicated. Their capacity to cope with these crises was often put to the test; but several other respondents experienced very smooth transitions and sometimes raised the question about how well they might be able to cope with unhappiness or disappointment.

Emotional Stress. Fifty-eight of the 63 subjects (92.1 percent) were judged to be "unquestionably within the normal range" of mental health at the time of the revisit; none of the subjects was described as psychotic or neurotically disabled. However, at least 10 subjects had experienced "periods of profound disheartenment" (4 of them verged on a mild depression), one reported experiencing extreme anxiety, and one had attempted suicide and two others had briefly considered it. Thirteen respondents were disturbed by serious problems in their marriages. The most frequently reported stresses during the 10 years ranged from shattered love affairs and problems in career development to relations with parents and financial pressures (Table 3.1). In general these difficulties indicate the range of tasks that are involved in the transition during young adulthood: establishment of a self separate from the parents, selection of a way of life and of making a living, and developing a solid intimate relationship.

Education and Work. At the 10-year interview, two-thirds of the men and a quarter of the women had achieved postbaccalaureate degrees. The men were working in the professions and in executive positions in business and were generally seen to be above average in effectiveness. Fourteen (39 percent) had pondered changing their career and 4 had started over; 5 remained undecided and the remaining 5 were progressing in a related but more congenial field. Since many of the men acquired postgraduate training, they postponed their start in a vocation; however, 11 of these men married before they began their careers.

Table 3.1 Most Frequently Reported Stresses Between College and Ten-Year Follow-Up Interview ($N = 63$)

	Frequency
Shattered love affair	25
Career development slow or disappointing	24
Parents' marriage broken by divorce or marked by conflict	24
Harassed by indecision about whether vocational choice is good	23
Long-continued financial dependence on parents after college	22
Relation to mother too close emotionally, too dominated by her, or too distant	22
Neuroticism in parent	19
Relation to father too close emotionally, too dominated by him, or too distant	19
Financial pressures (regardless of income level)	19
Financial stringency or insecurity in parental home	16

Source. Cox (1970), p. 73. Reprinted with permission of the publisher, Mental Health Materials Center.

The women in the study (which took place during the 1950s and early 1960s) conformed predominately to the socially accepted career pattern for women at that time. Most worked after college until their first pregnancy was advanced and then devoted themselves to homemaking and child rearing. They reported that their education was not being wasted and that they were content with their maternal and wifely roles. While 4 of the 23 married women were working outside their homes, all of the unmarried women were involved in work they felt was worthwhile. However, they also shared the attitudes of their married counterparts that the homemaker-mother role was the preferred one.

Marriage and Parenthood. Fifty-eight of the 66 respondents were married at the 10-year follow-up. Eighty percent of the marriages were judged to be satisfying marriages that provided the partners with warmth and contentment. Only eight marriages were judged to be unhappy although five subjects had divorced (a ratio considerably lower than 1 out of 4 in the general population), and three subjects had subsequently remarried. There was a significant relationship between the rating of the respondent's marital happiness and both the length of courtship and the age of the respondent at marriage (Table 3.2). In general, courtships of less than 12 months were associated with the happiest third of marriages (however, four out of the five divorces were in marriages with a courtship of less than one year); and marriages between the ages of 23 and 25

Table 3.2 The Relation Between Happiness of Subjects' Marriage, Length of Courtship, and Age at Marriage

| | Marital Happiness | | | |
	Highest Third (N=19)	Middle Third (N=18)	Lowest Third (N=19)	Total (N=56)
Length of Courtship				
Up to 12 months	15**	5	9	29
More than 12 months	4	14	9	27
Age at Marriage				
Before 23	1*	3	8	12
Age 23–25	13	15	7	35
After 25	5	0	4	9

* $p < .05$ by chi-square test
** $p < .01$ by chi-square test
Source. Adapted from Cox (1970), Tables 24 and 25. Reprinted with permission of the publisher, Mental Health Materials Center.

(as compared with before 23 or after 25) were happier and also more frequent for these respondents.

Fifty-four of the respondents were parents. They were judged to be generally very good parents, and even when their parental functioning was least ideal the difficulty often arose from the father's extended absence from the home because of his deep involvement in developing a career.

Relation to Own Parents. Since college graduation the respondents dispersed across the country, and a few moved to other countries. Very few lived within one day of automobile travel of their parents except for respondents living in the same metropolitan area. Ten of the respondents maintained only minimal contact with their parents and were described as involved in some kind of continuing conflict with their parents, which made contacts difficult. At the other extreme, 23 respondents seemed to sincerely enjoy their parents and responded to them positively either in spite of their failings or because of their good qualities. Surprisingly, for 11 of these 23 respondents close to their parents, the death of a parent had occurred since graduation from college (there were only three other deaths reported for the rest of the sample); and serious illness or other practical difficulties occurred for the parent, child, or both in five additional cases. Perhaps, Cox suggests, these misfortunes may have played a role in bringing about the closer relationship between parent and young adult.

In general, the respondents are self-supporting—63 percent had been supporting themselves for at least five years, but 14 percent remained significantly dependent on parental finances. In addition, 22 percent had resumed extended residence with the parents at some time during the 10-year period—for either financial or emotional reasons on one side or the other.

Conclusion. In many respects these respondents typify the normative expectations in society for the transition during young adulthood. They were select students at the beginning of the study (in the late 1940s) and the vast majority married, had children, and became self-supporting. The transition was not without some emotional stress and upset but, for most, the path was well-worn and well-marked by social expectations. Many young people are probably following similar paths today, even if they are not quite as economically secure as these respondents. The central tasks of establishing a practical style of independent life away from the parents, developing a long-term relationship with a spouse, beginning a career, and having children are probably still the dominant themes and potential crisis points of young adulthood for many persons. However, various alternate life styles and life plans are being explored by some young people today, and those paths are not so well-marked by social expectations. And some young people do not know the affluence or comfortable environment of the young adults that Cox studied. We might expect that many of the same themes would be involved—establishing an occupational identity, finding sexual and emotional companionship, and developing an autonomous and independent style of life. But we wonder whether Cox would have found similar patterns of adjustment and assimilation into adult society if she had studied young adults who moved into communes or who lived in urban ghettos. Such studies would be fascinating because it is not clear how different the outcome would be or what the nature of the differences might be.

Young Adulthood in an Urban Ghetto—A Firsthand Report

In contrast to the upper-middle-class young adults that Cox studied, a firsthand essay on young adulthood in black America from the perspective of a black undergraduate points out some of the contours of young adulthood in an urban ghetto.

In Black communities dating and courtship begins earlier; perhaps due to close proximity of living conditions, curiosity develops earlier. . . . I tend to agree that most mate selection is based on homogamy. Blacks are concentrated in one area of any city; there is little social mobility and chances of meeting others from varied socioeconomic classes, national origins, or educational backgrounds are restricted. Therefore, mate selection from common backgrounds is almost forced. What spurs dating? Usually it is romance. The romantic concept in Western culture includes two people falling in love, dating, moonlit walks, proms, picnics and finally the ritual of engagement. Blacks don't identify with this simply because it doesn't exist for them. It is difficult to be romantic walking down a garbage-strewn, crime-ridden area of the city. Proms are hampered by gang wars and fights. A simple act such as holding hands is difficult because the boyfriend always has to keep one hand on his pocket knife, ready to ward off attackers. That dreamy period of enchanted love and romance is destroyed. Instead, all too often courtship leads to physical fulfillments. Pregnancy occurs and young girls find themselves in awkward situations. . . . The young fathers are not yet mature enough to handle the situation and often leave the girl to bear the burden. The entire rituals of engagement and marriage ceremonies die just as a teen-age girl's dreams do. . . .

Blacks, in order to survive, take on responsibilities early in life and they enter adulthood long before marriage. Once married they are never as secure as the average middle-class family, financially. This necessitates both partners working and makes it difficult for young couples to relax and have a chance to get used to each other. The unemployed male, feeling useless and unable to fulfill his role as husband, leaves. Other couples, realizing that they can't afford to live independently, move in with one partner's parent(s). This causes a host of problems including overcrowding, lack of privacy, in-law expectations, etc. Failure in stability and economic security can lead to divorce or separation (Phyllis Cooper, 1971. Unpublished essay, City College of the City University of New York).

The contrast between young adulthood in these different social classes and environments is striking. Where one group follows the idealized norms of dating and eventually mating with relative ease and success, the other group is also striving to survive and to retain a sense of dignity and self-respect. Where one group is highly educated and faced with difficult choices about vocations, graduate school, and career development, the other group of young adults is faced with high unemployment (24.9 percent for men and 34.4 percent for women in 1971), a struggle for economic survival, and marriages fraught with perils. The social norms and the social clock we discussed in Chapter 2 are operating for both groups, but the meaning of a successful transition through young adulthood is clearly much different for these two groups. Yet the social norms, as transmitted through TV and the popular media, indicate that white middle-class success is the only (or the best) kind of success. Perhaps, for these young people that Cooper describes, the period of young adulthood does not really exist; they move from adolescence into adulthood after graduating or dropping out of high school and their identity is formed on the street in a contest for survival, status among their peers, and a source of income (legal or illegal). Sometimes their identity is forged in jail cells where the *me* of a successful criminal is socialized into them by the prison environment and other prisoners. Sometimes it is forged into a *me* as a drug addict when the pain of searching for the hoped-for identity is blocked at every turn by a racist society that tolerates and perpetuates poverty.

Or possibly the period of young adulthood is extended throughout much of the rest of life for some persons living in urban ghettos. Perhaps the task of developing a secure identity and sense of self that can be hooked up with society during young adulthood can never be fully achieved if one's education, background, and environment provide few possible ways to integrate one's sense of self with the roles offered by society. Certainly some of these young people find adult roles that they can move into. Many find jobs, marry, and raise families with surprising success (considering the hardships involved). Other young people find illegal social roles that provide a viable way of establishing an identity and perhaps even a viable way of achieving financial success. Still others, for a complex variety of reasons, develop a set of *me*s and a set of skills that allows them to enter college and perhaps to experience the kind of young adulthood characteristic of college students.

At present, our knowledge of the variety of styles of young adulthood is sketchy, and considerable research is badly needed if we are to fully understand this period of young adulthood in all of its many forms. In the next section we will discuss the central characteristics of the period of young adulthood—at least among college students (whom social scientists understand best). Although many of these characteristics may be applicable to many young adults, the question of how widely appropriate they are remains open.

CENTRAL CHARACTERISTICS OF YOUNG ADULTHOOD

The central characteristics of young adulthood may be traced back to the earlier issues of adolescence and to the level of intellectual maturity that is generally attained about the time of puberty. In Piaget's framework (cf. Piaget, 1972), the period of *formal operations* is the highest stage in a progressive, sequential development of intelligence and is reached around the age of 12 to 15. With formal operations, the adolescent can, for the first time, think abstractly, consider hypothetical possibilities, and reason using all possible logical operations. This implies that he can understand, question, and formulate ideologies; he can ponder the meaning of his life in the scheme of the universe; he can find logical flaws in political systems or institutions or in parental reasoning; and he can identify with historical or distant role-models. He is intellectually equipped (unlike a younger child) to earnestly raise the *identity* questions and to begin to develop a coherent, unified sense of self—as a person, as a member of a society, and as a creature in the universe. He is cognitively prepared to begin choosing an occupation, an abstract set of moral values, a political philosophy, and a view of himself in the world. He is intellectually capable of learning the scientific method and the complex skills he may need in an occupation. He is fully able to view himself abstractly "from the point of view of the other" (in G. H. Mead's terms) and to analyze social interaction. And he is able to begin integrating his sense of who he is—sexually, morally, politically, and socially—into an abstract *sense of identity* whose hallmarks are *continuity, wholeness,* and *integration* (Erikson, 1968). Thus, much of Erikson's concept of identity (as discussed in Chapter 1) is uniquely characteristic of adolescence because the adolescent's level of cognitive development is sufficiently complex to deal with those identity issues.

That he is intellectually capable of the task does not mean that the adolescent resolves these issues on wholly intellectual grounds or resolves them rapidly, however. To the contrary, the central issues are psychological and social in nature, largely colored by culture (but possibly universal in basic form), that involve intellect, emotion, and social interaction simultaneously. In our society these issues are worked through rather slowly; but by the time the adolescent reaches young adulthood these issues are nearing resolution. Specifically, the young adult would be engaged in the final working out of his identity and would be coming near to having a firm sense of who he is within and across his various social roles; perhaps the central issues in this later stage of identity would primarily concern the relation between the individual and the social system—"How do I fit the sense of who I am into my sense of what my society is all about?" Although this developing sense of identity would not remain unchanged throughout the rest of his life, it would not likely be as wholly in flux as it has been in the recent past. In addition, the beginnings of the Intimacy versus Isolation crisis would be emerging for the young adult. That is, the interactions with others would be tending toward an exploration of intimate relationships for their own sake instead of primarily as attempts to firm up or discover one's own identity.

One useful formulation of the central issues of young adulthood is proposed by White (1966) based on case studies of college students. He proposes five *growth trends* that describe at least some of the important issues and direction of growth during these final years of transition into adulthood. In his work, White describes not only the direction of these growth trends, such as toward increased "stabilization of ego identity," but also describes some aspects of the process by which these trends come about. His observations are drawn from a sample of college students, so we may hesitate to generalize from his work to all young people. Yet, his work clearly points out plausible developmental changes and calls out the need for additional observation and research to discover whether these trends are appropriate descriptions of the central issues of young adulthood more generally.

Stabilization of Ego Identity

The first growth trend that White discusses is a movement toward a stable ego identity. By "identity" he is, like Erikson, referring to "the self or person one feels oneself to be." Thus, the sense of identity is becoming "not only more sharp and clear, but also more consistent and free from transient influences." Not only is there a greater perception of oneself as having a clearly defined self, distinct from others, but also that sense of self tends not to fluctuate as much as during the early stages of identity resolution in adolescence.

The process by which this clarity and stability of identity comes about will be discussed in more detail in the final section of this chapter. But White's view is that it results partly from the adoption and commitment to social roles that are relatively enduring and characteristic of adult life. That is, a measure of stability results from the external stability and social support for well-defined roles, including sex roles and occupational roles. As commitments to these roles are made (reflecting increased clarity of some aspects of identity in itself), these roles lead to increasing selectivity of experience so that social reinforcement and social interactions tend to confirm the developing sense of identity. Other identities, which earlier might have seemed attractive, become less appealing as the experience reinforces the chosen roles and aspects of the identity. Also, as participation in adult roles becomes deeper, the young adult makes decisions about the style of his participation and decisions about the combinations of roles he is playing. And these decisions form aspects of his solidifying sense of identity as well. Probably also important are the rewards he is receiving for his roles and identity. That is, the student who is developing a sense of identity as a psychologist, for example, will stabilize that identity as he gets more and more experience in that role, as he begins to resolve the ways in which *he* will be a psychologist, and as he gets positive reinforcement from others for his role performance, role choice, and potential in that role. Of course, a lack of satisfactions or rewards in a role as the experience becomes more concentrated and selective would likely raise serious questions about stabilizing his identity in those directions.

Another factor involved in this stabilization of identity is the tendency for individuals to be consistent, or at least to feel that they are being consistent. Festinger (1957) has argued that inconsistency, or *cognitive dissonance*, is unpleasant at least if it is very intense, and that an individuals will attempt to change their beliefs or behaviors so that they feel they are being consistent. This tendency toward consistency is probably an important motivating factor in the stabilization of ego identity as well since it would incline individuals toward consistency in their sense of identity—not only day by day, but also within their set of beliefs, attitudes, and behavior.

Freeing of Personal Relationships

A second growth trend White notes in young adulthood is that relationships become "increasingly responsive to the other person's real nature." That is, the interpersonal relationships become more a relationship with a unique person who is appreciated in his uniqueness, and less a relationship with the projection of one's own fantasies, needs, and search for a sense of identity. Certainly, the relationship with one's parents is an important example of this trend because often the young adult is surprised to discover that he is relating to his parents as a friend, relative, or colleague instead of a person trying to break ties of dependency and assert his own individuality.

Some of the factors involved in this shift include the progressive stabilization of identity and also the selection and concentration of relationships during this period; that is, as one's sense of identity stabilizes, one's experiences in general (and interpersonal relationships as well) become more selective and are explored in more depth. Erikson argues that in order to relate freely with another person as a unique person, one needs to have a fairly firm sense of who he is in the relationship. And this factor of increased sense of identity, along with the increased duration and greater selectivity involved in establishing relationships in young adulthood, contributes to the exploration of the unique personhood of others from the firm basis of knowing who one is oneself. Another interesting point White makes here is the importance of unexpected interactions. For example, when we are surprised by something another does, we are suddenly more attuned to the uniqueness of that person; similarly, when we have an interaction with someone who is unexpectedly different from us (or an unexpected interaction with someone who differs from us), we tend to become more aware and sensitized to differences and important personal uniquenesses in persons. In terms of G. H. Mead's concepts (presented in Chapter 2), these unexpected interactions are one means by which "self-consciousness" (in Mead's sense) may come about; this process of self-consciousness is probably very much involved in the deepening of personal relationships as well as in the stabilization of identity in young adulthood (we will expand this point later).

Deepening of Interests

This third growth trend pertains to activities that interest or engage a person. White sees an important trend in the direction of deeper engagement by some interest, or more whole-hearted engagement in some interest during young adulthood. The trend is away from fleeting involvements that end when the immediate rewards cease or when curiosity is satisfied. And it is toward commitments in vocations or avocations that involve one in depth and are pursued for sufficient time to allow real accomplishment. There is a growing command over the sphere of the interest, whether it is an interest in sports or in some academic or scientific field. Another characteristic is that the person experiences rewards for doing the activity for its own sake. For example, writing may be interesting because of the satisfactions derived from self-expression and the act of writing itself, rather than from rewards that may accrue; or the satisfactions in skiing are from the growing skill and excitement and enjoyment of the sport in its own right.

The process here is that first a person undertakes some activity that, in some sense, intrigues the individual; second, satisfying consequences follow from the activity; third, feelings of competence and skill also follow, which are themselves satisfying; and fourth, these feelings lead to even greater interest and deeper involvement. Such deepening of interest undoubtedly contributes as well to the stabilization of identity and may play an important part in, for example, vocational choice. Or it may increase the freeing and deepening of personal relationships as one becomes more and more fascinated by another person. In general, it provides a growing sense of competence.

Humanizing of Values

Studies of moral development (Kohlberg, 1964; Piaget, 1932) have indicated the potential for a high level of abstract moral philosophy developing in young adults. Such attitudes as "the greatest good for the greatest number" are seldom held by preadolescents when asked to make moral judgments. And the current interest among some young adults for political change based on their sense of incongruity between the moral philosophy and daily practice of our society seems to attest to the capacity for high-level moral thinking during this period of young adulthood (Smith, 1969). This ability to formulate abstract moral philosophies probably continues throughout adulthood, although there is the possibility that societies generally function at less-abstract levels, and thus persons in the society may operate at less-abstract levels than their capability indicates. But for young adults, this ability is a new achievement in their individual history; and so there is a trend toward humanizing values and giving a deep human meaning to values (rather than, for example, "It's all right as long as you don't get caught" or "Bad actions are always punished in the end"). In part, young adults are bringing their own experiences to bear on the value system and are making their own personal system of values, again reflecting the developing clarity and stability of identity. And they are creating their value system out of their growing understanding and synthesis of their own feelings and responses to those persons with whom they are beginning to relate more freely and more deeply. Thus, they are responding with more empathy to the needs of others while at the same time they are creating their own unifying philosophy of life. These processes ideally would work together toward the potential for more humanized values.

Expansion of Caring

This fifth growth trend partly reflects the humanizing of values, but it carries this trend into actual feelings for the situations of others. This trend is toward a growing empathy with others and deep caring and concern for their feelings. It does not apply simply to one who is deeply loved but, instead, to the deep caring for the poor, the oppressed, or persons in mental or physical pain. It is an outgoing concern for persons who hurt and whose pain hurts us. Examples of this caring trend in young adulthood might include the involvement of the young in the civil rights movement, in the Peace Corps, and in VISTA.

Conclusion

This set of growth potentials derived from case histories, and the intensive study of many young adults, sheds some light on the central issues and characteristics of young adulthood. They parallel but also fill in more detail in Erikson's analysis of identity and intimacy crises. In many respects these growth trends are potential characteristics of the latter half of adolescence and the first years of adulthood in any society. In our society these potentials seem to develop during the period we are calling young adulthood. However, not all young adults seem to carry these potentials to their ideal fulfillment, and they may characterize the actual behavior of only a few young adults. Only additional research can reveal the extent of their occurrence. Certainly, each refers to a *potential* for growth that may progress much further in some young adults than in others. For example, the expansion of caring is likely to differ in content, if not in degree, for young adults of different economic and educational backgrounds.

In the next section we will shift our focus from the general characteristics of young adulthood to some of the issues that are currently associated with it in our society.

CURRENT ISSUES IN YOUNG ADULTHOOD

We have discussed some of the social characteristics of young adulthood in our society and have sketched the contours of the developmental progression through young adulthood in two widely diverse groups of young people: affluent college students and persons in an urban ghetto. And we have discussed the psychosocial characteristics and potentials that arise during this young adulthood period. We have suggested that the young adult is typically concerned with the final steps of identity resolution (in Erikson's model of development)—the linkage between his identity and society—and also with the first steps of intimacy resolution—the beginning explorations of others as unique sexual human beings. These developmental issues seem to be intensified in our society at present by the lengthening of adolescence to form this young adult period we are discussing and by a range of other educational, sexual, and social changes.

My students have told me that the central concerns for them include seeking their identity in terms of a career and in terms of social participation in adult roles, seeking a mate, and seeking and deciding upon a meaningful life style and circle of friends who support their life style. It includes a broadening of social contacts and a vulnerability to social pressure. It also involves feelings of an impending loss of freedom and increased responsibility once college is completed and jobs and marriages are begun; this implies that one must accept the future consequences of one's actions and choices in a way never before quite realized. Young adulthood also means that other people react to one as an adult and one reacts to oneself as an adult—that is, the self takes on the characteristics of an adult, and this represents a substantial change from the self that one is accustomed to.

In less-complex societies, or in times of less-rapid social change, these concerns might well occur in adolescence; they would not necessarily indicate an emerging stage of life intervening between adolescence and adulthood—as we have been suggesting in our discussion of young adulthood. Keniston (1968) has argued that this new stage of life that he calls "youth" (or young adulthood in our terms) seems to characterize at least some young people who have a firm sense of identity but who are unable to hook this sense of identity up with adult roles and responsibilities. He saw this stage of youth vividly expressed among a group of young political radicals he studied in 1967, but it is not at all clear that other, more typical, young people experience such a stage. In any event, his conception of the central developmental issue of this period seems to incorporate much of the current challenge associated with young adulthood in our society. He calls this developmental issue *individuation versus alienation.*

> The achievement of youth is an enduring ability to acknowledge both self and society, personality and social process, without denying the claims of either. Men and women sometimes achieve with each other a mutuality in which the individuality of each is the precondition for loving the other and being able to join together. So in youth, acknowledging the independent reality and the separate claims of both self and society is a precondition for achieving a defined relationship in which both coexist as separate yet interlocked entities.... The essence of youthful failure is a kind of alienation either from self or society—a denial of the reality and importance of the self, or a repudiation of the existence and importance of social reality (Keniston, 1968, p. 270).

Individuation versus Alienation

This developmental issue of individuation versus alienation parallels Erikson's developmental turning points, but it focuses on the later aspects of the identity issue (now that I know who I am, how do I align myself

Table 3.3   Important Concerns Mentioned by College Students (1969)

$(N = 2500)$

40 Percent or over		39.9 to 30.0 Percent	
Education	45.8	Sexuality	36.6
Vietnam	44.1	Self-identity	32.4
		Draft	30.4

with society?) and the beginning of the intimacy issue (how do I relate as a unique person to another unique person?). This theme may be involved in a variety of the important concerns in young adulthood. For example, a recent study by Thornburg (1971) found that "sexuality" and "self-identity" were important concerns mentioned by about one-third of 2500 respondents at five universities; only "education" and "Vietnam" were mentioned by more students (Table 3.3). Interestingly, such popular topics as "drugs," "marriage," and the "generation gap" were mentioned as important concerns by less than 20 percent of the respondents.

Sexuality concerns in young adulthood may reflect the individuation issue insofar as the individual has a firm sense of sexual identity but feels that socially defined norms about sexual behavior or sex roles and stereotypes do not define the manner in which his or her sexuality may best be expressed. For example, a young woman may not be comfortable with a sex role that defines her as a sexual object, a housewife, and a mother; a young man may not be comfortable with the masculine role of aggressive, nonemotional, and competitive breadwinner for his wife and children. As these young people strive to align their identity with these social roles, they will ideally develop an individuated sense of themselves and of their roles; at worst, they will feel alienated from themselves or from the rest of society. Similarly, as they strive to align their sense of who they are with the expectations and requirements of society they ideally

Table 3.3   (continued)

29.9 to 20.0 Percent		19.9 to 10.0 Percent	
Occupations	28.5	Future	18.9
Competition	27.5	Cultural norms	18.7
Civil rights	27.4	Parental approval	18.1
Religion	23.8	Drugs	16.5
Activism	22.6	Marriage	15.8
Politics	21.9	Individuality	13.4
Economic stability	21.8	Violence	13.3
Social identity	21.7	Generation gap	12.5
Morality	21.5	Emancipation	10.6
Peer approval	21.1	World affairs	10.4
Social approval	21.0		

Source. Thornburg (1971), p. 331. Reprinted with permission from Contemporary Adolescence: Readings, copyright © 1971 by Wadsworth Publishing Company, Inc. Reprinted by permission of the publisher, Brooks/Cole Publishing Company, Monterey, California

create an individuated "fit" between their sense of who they are and their occupational, marital, parental, and political roles in society. However, again the danger may be a sense of alienation from oneself or from society if some reasonable "fit" cannot be achieved.

In striving for a sense of individuation, the young adult ideally searches both inside himself and outside in his social world. Goethals and Klos (1970) suggest three styles of identity-seeking: turning inward in an introspective attempt to find one's individuated identity, turning outward in an attempt to define oneself by involvement in a cause or by an external identity (such as a black person or a medical student), or by a combination of the two simultaneously. The "turning inward" style brings with it the danger of alienating oneself from the social world; the "turning outward" style brings the danger of alienating oneself from one's inner feelings and experiencing. In G. H. Mead's framework, the first involves the risk of too much emphasis on the I, and the second involves the risk of too much emphasis on the me. Overconformity, even to a political movement or to the demands of an occupational identity, may lead to a sense of self that is alienated to some degree from one's inner processing, experiencing I. Somehow, both processes need to be involved simultaneously in this process of individuation.

There is a sense in which three issues that have recently received national attention—alienation, political activism, and drug use—may also be related to the difficulties posed by the individuation versus alienation issue in young adulthood. Keniston (1965) described the extremely alienated youth he observed and studied in the 1950s, a period many observers felt was characterized by apathetic and conforming college students. Shortly after Keniston's work, the Civil Rights struggle began attracting national attention and many young adults became deeply involved in the movement and with one another (quite different from an alienated response). The organization of the Students for a Democratic Society followed and the decade of the 1960s was largely colored by an activist approach to the Civil Rights and, later, to the Vietnam issues. During the late 1960s, the use of drugs (especially marijuana and LSD) among young people began receiving national attention. The "hang-loose ethic" (Suchman, 1968) and the emphasis on intensifying and deepening one's own inner resources through the use of drugs represent a third type of response, differing from both alienation and activism, yet also related to the individuation issue. Although it would obviously be an oversimplification to reduce these three different and complex phenomena to a single theme, there is a sense in which they reflect, in part, an unwillingness or an inability to align with social institutions and to find one's own individual place in society. That is, they may be largely symptoms of the difficulty involved in the linkage between the individual and society, reflecting dissatisfaction with the present social order, individual developmental histories, and difficulties inherent in the transition process itself in our "electronic" society.

This basic issue of "linkage" is particularly clear in the data Keniston (1965) gathered from 12 young men who were selected from a large group of undergraduate men on the basis of extremely high scores on psychological measures of alienation. Two central characteristics of these young men were their rejection of American society and a lack of a coherent sense of identity. These extreme cases of alienation were seen to be stuck in their transition into adulthood by a rejection of conventional adult society on the one side, and by a fragmented sense of identity on the other side; hence the task of aligning their identity to social institutions was a nearly impossible one for them. The reasons for their difficulty were similarly two-sided—their individual histories indicated a great deal of potential anger at both parents and the alienating characteristics of our technological society. In general, these alienated young adults of the 1950s were estranged from their peers as well as from themselves and society in a time when college students were seen by many observers as generally unconcerned with value questions, complacent, and status oriented (cf. Goldsen, Rosenberg, Williams, and Suchman, 1960).

Perhaps the social components of this extreme alienation were harbingers of the later upsurge of student activism. That is, possibly young adults who, like the alienated, found fault with society (but who differed in their personal histories and sense of identity from the alienated) were

drawn together in the Civil Rights movement and later student movements; they developed a committed, active stance to changing the society
that the alienated students rejected in total. But if the alienated young
adults may be characterized by "dropping out" of a society that cannot
be changed, and the activist is identified by his commitment to changing
that society, then there is a problem of "linkage" for both groups.

Flacks (1967) studied student political activists in the 1960s and concluded that activists tend to come from upper-status families, they are
more "radical" than their parents, but their parents are much more
liberal than others of their status, and activism is related to a complex
of values that are shared by both the students and their parents. For
example, activist students were less likely to approve of "bombing of
North Vietnam" than their fathers; but both groups were less likely to
approve than nonactivist students and their fathers (Table 3.4). In general,
student activists were seen as having the "most socially fortunate upbring-
ings," to be concerned with "living out expressed but unimplemented
parental values," and to come from families that were "unusually equali-
tarian, permissive, 'democratic,' and highly individuated" (Keniston, 1967,
pp. 117-120). The problem of "linkage" for them was implementing the
values that they shared with their parents, but they felt they could do this

Table 3.4   Students' and Fathers' Attitudes on Current Issues (1965)

Issue	Activists		Nonactivists	
	Students (N=34)	Fathers (N=30)	Students (N=37)	Fathers (N=30)
Percent who approve:				
Bombing of North Vietnam	9	27	73	80
American troops in Dominican Republic	6	33	65	50
Student participation in protest demonstrations	100	80	61	37
Civil disobedience in civil rights protests	97	57	28	23
Congressional investigations of "un-American activities"	3	7	73	57
Lyndon Johnson	35	77	81	83
Barry Goldwater	0	7	35	20
Full socialization of industry	62	23	5	10
Socialization of the medical profession	94	43	30	27

Source. Flacks (1967), p. 67. Reprinted with permission.

only if society were changed. Thus, perhaps the activist's wrestling with the problem of individuation versus alienation led him to turn outward to change the society he could not accept, rather than to turn inward or to drop out.

There may be a similar "linkage" issue involved, at least in part, in the "rioting" of black young adults in the 1960s. After all, how does one link up with the white middle-class values that are pervasive in our society if one cannot get as high paying a job or as good an education or as good housing? Unless one's identity is that of a "second-class citizen," how can a person align his identity with second-class roles in adult society?

As this is being written (in the spring of 1973), activism on college campuses and in urban ghettos seems to have declined markedly, at least in visibility and violence. Perhaps the decline in student activism is the result of a combination of the partial success in shifting public opinion and changing the public policy on Vietnam, the relative lack of widespread social impact (at least in bringing the kinds of changes the activists sought), and the discovery of the potential violence that is close to the surface on both sides of the conflict produced by active protest. We wonder whether this type of activism is dormant, awaiting a salient issue, or whether this outward focus has shifted to an inner focus. That is, perhaps those young adults who are most troubled by the problem of linking one's individual identity to the social order have turned inward in terms of concern with sex-role stereotypes, intellectual pursuits, and expanding inner experience (possibly with the use of drugs).

In any event, we will shift to a discussion of two of the most widely discussed current issues in young adulthood: drug use and sexuality. Both issues involve the individuation versus alienation focus to some extent, but both are also considerably wider in scope. Certainly, both issues point out the effect of cohort-historical changes on the nature of the issues that are involved in a developmental period such as young adulthood.

Drug Use in Young Adulthood

Few topics have received as much current attention as drugs. There seems to be little doubt that the use of marijuana has increased markedly in the last decade, and the use of tobacco and alcohol does not seem to have declined. Hallucinogenic drugs like mescalin and LSD are undoubtedly still being used by a small minority of young adults, but the attention they received in the 1960s has been largely replaced by the attention given to heroin (and even more recently to methadone), which seems to have "graduated" from the urban ghettos where it has been present for years to middle-class neighborhoods and schools.

There is a sense in which drug use in young adulthood may be a form of an active search for individuation and for meaning through intense personal experiencing. Keniston (1966) points out that this search for meaning through inner experience partly reflects the intense competition in undergraduate education (often resulting from competition for graduate school) and a trend toward "psychological numbing" as a result of stimulus overload in our noisy, overlighted, transistorized society. These trends may combine, in his view, to encourage—for a minority of students—experimentation with ways of finding a personal sense of meaning in inner experience through the use of psychoactive drugs. However, there are a number of possible reasons for the use of drugs in our society. One is that some drugs (such as alcohol or tobacco) may be associated with being an adult in our society and are used partly out of conformity to social norms. Some drugs (such as illegal ones) may be a manifestation of a subcultural, possibly rebellious way of life characterized not only by drug taking, but also by a "hang-loose" ethic (Suchman, 1968). And some drugs may be taken as an attempt to reduce anxiety or other unpleasant feelings or as an attempt to escape from some kind of painful reality. One prevailing theme in our society may also enhance the general tendency to use drugs of some kind—this is the theme that says: "All human frailties, from difficulties in heterosexual relations to a dislike of one's grandchildren, can be corrected by buying a bottle or a tube or a spray can." Unfortunately, many serious problems can not be solved so easily, despite our medical technology.

Thus, it is not particularly surprising that nearly all college students use drugs of one kind or another (including alcohol). A large-scale study of drug use among undergraduates in randomly selected classes at 10 campuses of a "large middle-Atlantic state university" in 1969 found that alcohol was used by 91 percent of the respondents, marijuana by 23 percent, amphetamines by 10 percent, opium by 6 percent, and LSD by 4 percent (Milman and Anker, 1971). In general, they found that the prevalence of illegal drugs was essentially parallel regardless of other characteristics of the respondents (such as "relationship with parents," "heterosexual activity," or "history of psychiatric difficulty"). This suggests that the particular drug used does not reflect an individual's idiosyncratic psychosocial history but, instead, reflects his tendency to use drugs in general and the prevalence of each drug in his social environment. They also found that "emotional instability" (history of psychiatric difficulty, negative mood, poor relationship with parents, and homosexual experience) was related to a high incidence of illegal drug usage (for all of the drugs); that drug use is much more common among those whose friends also use drugs; and that drug use is related to "rebellion or resistance to authority" (independent residence, living with a partner of the opposite sex, greater heterosexual experience, lack of religious practice, cutting classes, and poor relationship with parents). In sum, there was considerable evidence that the use of any illegal drug in college was associated with a life style that is different from the dominant culture. This is quite similar to the conclusion reached by Suchman (1968) with regard to marijuana use in a study of undergraduate and graduate students at a large West Coast university:

> Among students, this sub-culture is strongly characterized by a "hang-loose" ethic which attempts to cut itself loose from the traditional "establishment" and to develop freedom from conformity and the search for new experiences. This culture becomes expressed in such behaviors as attending "happenings," reading underground newspapers, participating in mass protests, avoiding the draft, engaging in sexual intercourse and, very much to the point of this report, smoking marijuana. Such use of marijuana constitutes an important means both of attaining "freedom" from the pressures of society and of expressing antagonism toward the "unfair" laws and restrictions of that society (Suchman, 1968, p. 154).

In that sense, drug use may reflect in part an aspect of the individuation versus alienation issue—an attempt to establish an individualized sense of identity that is not based on, or fully engaged with, cultural norms.

A further examination of these data (Milman and Su, 1973) focusing on the characteristics of heavy users (three times a week or more) of alcohol and marijuana (21 percent for alcohol, 4 percent for marijuana) lends some support to this notion. For example, they found a declining use of marijuana with age (which may partly reflect cohort-historical factors) but an increasing use of alcohol with age; a significant correlation between poorer relationships with parents and heavy marijuana use, a lesser correlation with heavy alcohol use; a significant correlation between emotional instability (negative mood or history of psychiatric difficulties) and heavy marijuana use but not with heavy alcohol use; and a negative relationship between dating and heavy marijuana use, while the opposite was true for heavy alcohol use. Taken together, these data suggest that heavy marijuana use may reflect some difficulty in the individuation versus alienation conflict in young adulthood. Other cultural factors seem to be involved also. For example, the heavy marijuana user is more likely to be Jewish, while the heavy alcohol user is more likely to be Catholic; the heavy alcohol user is more likely to have a less-educated father than the heavy marijuana user; and the heavy marijuana user is more likely than the heavy alcohol user to have friends who use drugs. The two groups overlap somewhat also. Both heavy-user groups were likely to have greater heterosexual and homosexual experience, lower grades, and to cut more classes than the light users.

In sum, drug use among young people in college is a complex phenomenon reflecting our drug-oriented society, the pressures and challenges of young adulthood, and the individual's psychosocial history and environment. In part, subcultural factors seem to be important since marijuana (and the other illegal drugs these studies explored) are not socially sanctioned and thus may be taken as one element of an anti-establishment reaction to the young adulthood question of "How do I hook my identity up with society?" The heavy marijuana user seems to be more alienated or "rebellious" than the heavy alcohol user on the basis of poorer relations with parents, emotional instability, and not dating (the connection with being Jewish or having a well-educated father is not obvious)—as well as by the choice of an illegal drug. But both the heavy marijuana and heavy alcohol user seem to be having difficulty in school and having greater sexual experience; this may indicate that marijuana and alcohol are being used heavily because of anxiety in these central developmental tasks of young adulthood for college students, or that these characteristics reflect differing versions of the "hang-loose" ethic (one for students from well-educated Jewish families, the other for students from less-educated Catholic families).

Drug use among young adults who are not college students is probably both similar and different. Some recent attention has been given to assembly-line workers who use drugs to dull the boredom of the work. And it would seem that heroin use among the poor may be least partly an attempt to escape from the painful reality of poverty and unemployment. Certainly narcotic drugs such as heroin differ in effect as well as in cause from the drugs we have discussed here. However, the concern with drugs (other than alcohol) is one which most young people did not have to deal with a decade ago and which may make the period of young adulthood a bit more difficult now than it was then.

Sexuality in Young Adulthood

Another topic that has received considerable attention—and that clearly applies to more than a minority of young adults—is sexuality. Certainly one of the difficult aspects of adolescence and young adulthood in our society is the implicit social expectation that the period between puberty and marriage is a sexual moratorium. That is, young women never think of or desire sex; and young men may think of sex but limit their "activities" to occasional nocturnal emissions. Insofar as that social expectation exists, it seems to be quite different from reality. "Over 95 percent of the adolescent males are regularly active [primarily through masturbation] by 15 years of age. . . . Considering the active, single males in the population, the maximum mean frequencies are almost 3.4 per week. . . . This rate is reached between adolescence and 20 years of age" (Kinsey, Pomeroy, and Martin, 1948, p. 219). Yet astonishingly, a recent survey of 2000 medical students (Lief, 1972) is reported to have found that "about 20 percent of respondents said masturbation is etiologically related to mental illness" (30 percent said, also incorrectly, that impotence is universal in men over 70).

> Masturbation is for most adolescent boys the major sexual activity, and they engage in it fairly frequently. It is an extremely positive and gratifying experience to them. Such an introduction to sexuality can lead to a capacity for detached sex activity—activity whose only sustaining motive is sexual. This may be the hallmark of male sexuality in our society (Simon and Gagnon, 1969, p. 13).

According to the Kinsey data, the peak of sexual activity is reached somewhat later for women (age 26-40), is largely affected by marriage, and consists primarily of marital intercourse (Kinsey, Pomeroy, Martin, Gebhard and Associates, 1953). Probably such differences in sexual behavior between men and women result from cultural pressures and differing sexual physiology (we will discuss this in detail in Chapter 4).

These sex differences as well as sexual activity have probably changed since their study was completed. A recent nationwide survey of adolescent sexual behavior (Sorensen, 1973) found that sexual intercourse was reported by about half of their respondents 13 to 19—59 percent for boys and 45 percent for girls. By age 19 only about 5 percent of their respondents reported that they had not had any sexual contact other than kissing that involved pleasurable physical reactions. About 37 percent of respondents with intercourse experience and 28 percent of the virgins reported that they felt guilty sometimes. Over two-thirds of the boys 16 to 19 and 42 percent of the girls reported that they masturbated. Thus, it seems clear that there is considerable sexual activity among contemporary adolescents—although these percentages may be inflated (e.g., for sexual activity) or deflated (e.g., for masturbation and guilt) because they are self-reports.

This increase in sexual activity among adolescents undoubtedly carries over into young adulthood. However, it may complicate the young adult period since as sexual activity is increasing, the average age at marriage is also increasing (since the mid-1950s). And marriage may be especially likely to be postponed among those young people who most clearly are in the period we describe as young adult (most of the subjects in the Cox (1970) study married around the age of 24; and Keniston's (1968) study of young radicals found that his respondents were postponing marriage along with other adult commitments). In addition, the development of contraceptive pills, and a gradual change in sexual mores in our society have resulted in what has been termed, probably incorrectly, a "sexual revolution." But this change in itself presents some additional difficulties for the young adult: "Do I adhere to more tradtional norms or to the most contemporary ones?" Thus, as greater freedom of choice becomes involved in premarital sexual relations, more decisions have to be made by the individual couple, and decisions are always more difficult than obedience to a rigid standard. At the same time, the growing freedom allows the individual to more fully meet his individual needs (and hence to reduce the personal anguish that adherence to a rigid standard may involve). But there is a tension between the difficulty of choosing one's own sexual standards on one hand and the suffering of being confined by rigid standards that are inappropriate for a given individual on the other. For example, "gay liberation" may be a positive social development for a young homosexual who is allowed a greater feeling of personal acceptance and self-worth than would have been typical a decade ago; however, it may complicate the choice of sexual pattern among young adults who previously would not have considered homosexuality as a viable life style.

Several studies indicate an evolution of sexual mores toward greater acceptance of premarital sex (especially among women), although other countries are even more accepting of sexuality (and still others less accepting, presumably). One such study (Christensen and Gregg, 1970) found little change between 1958 and 1968 in the number of men having premarital sex at two universities in the United States, but they also found an increase in Denmark to a rate almost twice as high as in the United States; in both countries there was an increase in premarital sexual activity among female college students, but the rate in Denmark rose to about three times the rate in the U. S. samples (Table 3.5). The major change for both men and women seems to be that they are more accepting of their premarital sexual behavior in 1968 compared with a decade earlier (Table 3.6). Perhaps men are tending to have premarital sex more with dates rather than with a few "easy" dates or prostitutes

Table 3.5 Percentage of College Students in the United States and Denmark Having Premarital Sex Relations, 1958 and 1968

	1958	1968
Male College Students		
U.S. Intermountain College	39 (94)[a]	37 (115)[a]
U.S. Midwestern College	51 (213)	50 (245)
Danish	64 (149)	95 (134)
Female College Students		
U.S. Intermountain College	10 (74)	32 (105)
U.S. Midwestern College	21 (142)	34 (238)
Danish	60 (86)	97 (61)

[a] Number of respondents shown in parentheses.
Source. Adapted from Christensen and Gregg (1970). Reprinted with permission.

Table 3.6   Percentage of Midwestern College Students Who Had Had
            Premarital Intercourse and Did *Not* Approve of It

	1958	*1968*
Men	35 (213)[a]	18 (245)[a]
Women	59 (142)	22 (238)

[a] Number of respondents shown in parentheses.
Source. Adapted from Christensen and Gregg (1970). Reprinted with permission.

since the female college student rate of premarital sex is increasing while
the male rate remains about the same. This is another clear example of
the cohort changes discussed in Chapter 1.

However, there is probably more change involved in the sexual aspects
of young adulthood than just sexual behavior. A recent study at Harvard
found changes in sexual behavior over the last few years, but the study
also found changes in attitudes toward intimacy and nature of intimate
relationships.

It is clear that both current freshmen and seniors at Harvard are
experiencing much more sexual intimacy than those of a decade
ago. . . . The changes during the undergraduate years toward increased sexual intimacy are steady and very large for all samples. . . .

It seems that the revolution in sexual behavior means that many
emotionally involved couples do not stop short of intercourse—a
relatively small movement from petting to climax that was very frequently the terminus of the sexual relationships ten years ago. . . .

Both attitudes toward women and dating habits have changed considerably in the past decade, but our evidence does not suggest the
sexual revolution that has been publicized. The Harvard men of the
'70s are much more interested in the *companion* pattern of dating,
characterized by an intense emotional relationship with a woman
that, although containing a sexual component, is similar to a same-sex
peer relationship. Girls are sought as friends in their own right rather
than partners for recreation or status achievements (Vreeland, 1972,
pp. 9-10).

There are two crucial consequences of this increased frequency of
sexual activity in young adulthood that deserve brief comment: the
increased possibility of pregnancy and of venereal disease. With regard
to pregnancy, the obvious facts of the matter may be stated simply: if
one engages in sexual intercourse, one must either expect a child, plan an
abortion, or use a contraceptive. Surprisingly, only a small majority of the

adolescent boys and girls in the Sorensen (1973) study reported that they use contraceptives "sometimes." At the time of first intercourse, 55 percent reported that they and their partner did not use any contraceptive method. One-third of the girls said they used birth control pills, and this was the most frequent type of contraceptive. Withdrawal of the penis was the second most popular "contraception method"—used by 17 percent. An equal number said they "trusted to luck that I wouldn't become pregnant." Nearly one-third of the nonvirgin boys and one-quarter of the nonvirgin girls 16-19 said that in case of pregnancy they would prefer an abortion; over one-third of these girls would prefer to have the baby and get married. Twenty-eight percent of the nonvirgin girls 16-19 have been pregnant; 16 percent of the nonvirgin boys have made a girl pregnant.

However, even if effective contraception were used, contraceptives (with the exception of the condom) do nothing to protect against venereal disease. Currently syphilis and gonorrhea are becoming more and more prevalent.

> The fact is that the entire nation is in the grip of a VD epidemic of unparalleled proportions—and no one at any level of society is immune. . . .
>
> As infectious diseases, syphilis and gonorrhea are outranked in incidence only by the common cold. . . .
>
> VD is particularly rampant among young Americans. At least one in five persons with gonorrhea is under 20. . . . "The probability that a person will acquire VD by the time he's 25," says Dr. Walter Smartt, chief of the Los Angeles County Venereal Disease Control Division, "is about 50 percent." . . .
>
> What makes this . . . state of affairs hard to comprehend is the simple fact that both syphilis and gonorrhea can be cured with penicillin and other antibiotics (*Newsweek*, 1972, p. 46).

Indeed, it seems that growing into adulthood is happening faster today but taking a longer time. If one were able to marry at the age of 16, or if puberty occurred at 18, then the sexual standards of abstinence or only masturbation before marriage would be considerably more feasible. But with the lengthening of adolescence (or the creation of a new stage of young adulthood) combined with—or helping to bring about—an evolution of sexual norms, the sexual aspect of young adulthood can be difficult. Somehow the young person in his process of individuation also has to resolve his individual answers to what he is going to do with his sexual identity. Perhaps the individual task of individuation that Keniston sees evolving is paralleled by an evolving social pluralism in which the individual has greater freedom in the ways in which he may hook up with society—such as in marriage or in some alternate life style. But the pluralism of choices brings with it a growing responsibility to make choices and to take the responsibility for those choices. Indeed, these changes clearly represent the interaction of these cohort-historical and developmental factors that we indicated in Chapter 1 are crucial to an understanding of adult development.

To conclude this chapter we will return to the symbolic interaction concepts from Chapter 2 and apply them to analyze the processes of development we have discussed in this chapter.

IDENTITY AND INTIMACY: SYMBOLIC INTERACTION APPROACH

The central theme in our discussion of young adulthood has been the issue of the identity crisis, and we have dealt with a number of facets of this psychosocial turning point characteristic of adolescence and young adulthood. But up to this point we have been primarily discussing the *content* of the identity issues; that is, it involves working out a viable sense of who one is—as a sexual being, as a social being, as an independent, unique person, and as an individual with a place in society. We have not dealt with the *process* by which an individual develops a sense of identity—that is, a sense of wholeness; a sense of continuity between past, present, and future; and a sense of integration and continuity across various social situations. Now let us discuss an exploration of the process of identity formation in adolescence and (as in Chapter 2) draw upon symbolic interaction theory for some insights into the process by which a relatively enduring sense of identity comes about. We will also argue (in agreement with Erikson) that a relatively firm sense of identity is a prerequisite for the beginnings of true intimacy and will present an analysis of basic issues of intimacy and of the transition from identity to intimacy issues in the symbolic interaction framework.

First, however, let us briefly summarize the central issues in the identity crisis by referring to Erikson:

> As technological advances put more and more time between early school life and the young person's final access to specialized work, the stage of adolescing becomes an even more marked and conscious period and, as it has always been in some cultures in some periods, almost a way of life between childhood and adulthood. Thus in the later school years young people, beset with the physiological revolution of their genital maturation and the uncertainty of the adult roles ahead, seem much concerned with faddish attempts at establishing an adolescent subculture with what looks like a final rather than a transitory or, in fact, initial identity formation. They are sometimes morbidly, often curiously, preoccupied with what they appear to be

in the eyes of others as compared with what they feel they are, and with the question of how to connect the roles and skills cultivated earlier with the ideal prototypes of the day. In their search for a new sense of continuity and sameness, which must now include sexual maturity, some adolescents have to come to grips again with crises of earlier years before they can install lasting idols and ideals as guardians of a final identity. They need, above all, a moratorium for the integration of the identity elements (Erikson, 1968, p. 128).

Thus the process of identity formation is one of social interaction by which the individual takes the role of the other toward himself and takes the role of the "generalized other" (society) toward himself in a particularly self-conscious period. In a sense one of the main characteristics of adolescence is this self-consciousness and concern with seeing oneself from the point of view of others. And this process of being self-conscious is, of course, central to G. H. Mead's formulation of social interaction and the development of the self.

> Self-consciousness involves the individual's becoming an object to himself by taking the attitudes of other individuals toward himself within an organized setting of social relationships (Mead, 1934, p. 245).

We see three aspects of the process of identity formation that are particularly salient and that may be explicated by the symbolic interaction theory. (1) Identity formation occurs during a period of heightened self-consciousness and reflexive introspection; this is characterized by the process of taking the role of others toward oneself. (2) Identity formation involves the synthesis of a wide range of roles or social selves or *mes* into a unified sense of self; the unity or sense of wholeness of this self is a result of the integrative function of the *I*. Erikson makes this point very well (although he arrived at it through ego psychology rather than through social psychology).

> What the "I" reflects on when it sees or contemplates the body, the personality, and the roles to which it is attached for life—not knowing where it was before or will be after—are the various selves which make up our composite Self (Erikson, 1968, p. 217).

(3) Identity formation involves sensing a continuity between past *mes*, present *mes*, and future *mes*; again, the continuity and integration is the result of an active, creative *I* that draws upon memory (for past *mes*), upon the view of oneself from the point of view of others (for present *mes*), and upon the imagined view of one's future self from the point of view of others (for future *mes* and "senses" the integration and continuity of these *mes*.

Thus it is not surprising that adolescents are frequently characterized as being "self conscious," or that they place a great emphasis on the response of others such as the peer group, or that they seem overly conforming at some times and overly defiant at others. With the beginnings of adolescence they become intellectually capable of taking the attitude of others toward themselves in highly complex and abstract ways; they are also able to take the attitudes of an abstract, "generalized other," toward themselves or to guide their behavior by the criteria of a "distant drummer." They now have the intellectual capacity to interact with others in the complex, abstract, symbolic terms of adult social interaction; they are able to hypothesize, to experiment, and to conform or deviate in order to observe the response of others and of "society." The aim of this process is to "decide" who one is—based on the responses of others to the various selves that are presented and based on one's own feelings about oneself.

The process is complex; yet, by young adulthood, through a series of progressive refinements, one arrives at a sense of who one is, which is reaffirmed by the important others in one's relevant social world. Part of this refinement comes about through progressive selection and limiting of the range of experience so that the developing sense of self is reaffirmed by one's experiences (stepping outside that range of experience is commonly called "culture shock"); however, one's sense of self is also broadened or reaffirmed by surprising encounters with different experiences. These experiences bring about a renewed self-consciousness, which may challenge the previous sense of continuity and integration or may solidify that sense by finding a fit between one's self and the new experience. As one reaches a sense of self (or identity) that provides "a feeling of being at home in one's body, a sense of 'knowing where one is going,' and an inner assuredness of anticipated recognition from those who count" (Erikson, 1968, p. 165), one feels at home in his range of experiences and is able to deal with unexpected ones by momentary self-consciousness that does not disrupt the sense of continuity and integration. This is approaching the optimal sense of identity; yet one's identity is never rigidly fixed or determined, for socialization into new roles, moments of self-conscious introspection, and increased responsiveness to the needs of others continue to interact with one's sense of identity throughout life.

However, once the sense of self has sufficiently developed so that there is a core self that is uniquely one's own self, then one can begin interacting with others in more intimate social interactions without fear of losing one's self in the other. That is, once there is a firm sense of "I", the possibility of an "I-Thou" or "I-I" relationship becomes an enticing possibility. Previously one took the role of another toward himself for increased understanding and clearer perception of himself; now, in intimate relations, one takes the role of the other for a better understanding of the other. Previously, one attempted to evaluate his *me* from the point of view of the other; now one attempts to reach the *I* of the other for the sake of the mysteries that lie within the other. Only when one is less-deeply involved in defining oneself can one fully relate to another and try to see the world (rather than just oneself) from the perspective of the other.

Perhaps the symbolic interaction process involved in identity formation and also (but in a somewhat different way) in intimate relationships may be illustrated most clearly in the current practice of sensitivity groups. In such groups, members are often encouraged to "provide feedback" to one another; this process is identical with the more general process of taking the attitude of others toward oneself—except in groups it is made explicit. One may utilize this "feedback" to assess the "self" he is present-ing or the "role" he is playing; this is another way of saying that he is self-conscious and explicitly receiving symbolic information about the *me*s he is presenting. This process is often useful in clarifying or working-through one's self-concept and is an explicit example of the more general way that the various components (*me*s) of the identity are defined and evaluated. Thus, it is not surprising that such groups and the use of "feedback" in the groups is useful and rather popular among young adults. It is useful in that the "feedback" can be "checked out" with others in the groups, and one's own distorted perceptions of oneself (based perhaps on biased and selected audiences) may be disconfirmed and possibly changed.

Another aspect of such groups is to encourage "honest" interaction, and is thought to lead to feelings of closeness or intimacy. Often these warm feelings result from group consensus (in which the group defines itself as a warm, intimate group and is thus defined as such by the members); but they may also result from some earnest attempt to understand and appreciate the other. That is, unlike "feedback," where the attempt is to clarify one's self, understanding is an attempt to clarify the other and to try to respond (with one's own *I*) to the other's *me* with as little inter-ference from one's own *me* as possible. The movement is toward an *I-I* relationship; this may be one reason the usefulness of symbols (lan-guage) declines and members may attempt to communicate feelings "nonverbally"; symbols are necessary for creating and maintaining the *me*s and for developing a sense of self, but may hinder *I-I* interactions.

In sum, the process involved in the identity stage may be seen as one in which the *I* succeeds in bringing a sense of consistency, continuity, and wholeness out of the mass of *me*s that others respond to in social interaction. Perhaps the motivation for this process comes, as White (1966) suggests, from striving for self-consistency and competence. How-ever, it seems that this integration could not arise in the sense of a fully formed identity prior to the development of intellectual mastery of abstract thought and that the sexual maturation occurring at puberty also would play an unquestionably important role in presenting radically different *me*s from any that were experienced before. In addition, the *me*s that developed in childhood and gave rise to the rudimentary sense of self prior to adolescence were limited in complexity, abstractness, and future-orientation due to absence of the ability to think in terms of possibilities (i.e., Formal Operations). Finally, the eventual development of a smoothly functioning *I-me* interaction in the young adult, with a firm sense of wholeness across the various *me*s, would set the stage for a new aim of social interaction—intimacy. That is, once the identity issue is fairly well resolved, one can relate with others in an attempt not to better see and integrate oneself (although that may happen as a useful by-product) but to know and sense (with one's *I*) the uniqueness of the other as a social self (their *me*s) and, perhaps catch a fleeting glimpse of their *I* at work in its spontaneity and creativity.

These processes of identity, intimacy, and individuation that have been major themes in this chapter will be major concepts to bring with us to the first of the case example interludes that follow. It illustrates a number of the issues we have considered in these first three chapters, and more. However, we will not attempt to integrate these interludes with the chapters either here or in the later chapters. Rather, this is the task and challenge that we wish to share because it seems that an important part of the learning process is being able to bridge the gap between theoretical concepts and real persons living their complex lives in a variety of ways. If these chapters have done their work, the interludes will be illuminated and will challenge us to apply our concepts to them and, in turn, the concepts may be illuminated. Following the interlude, the next chapter will discuss the important topic of the complex similarities and differences between men and women.

References

Aries, Philippe. 1962. *Centuries of Childhood.* New York: Vintage.

Christensen, Harold T., and Gregg, Christiana F. 1970. Changing Sex Norms in America and Scandinavia. *Journal of Marriage and the Family,* 32(4), 616–627.

Cox, Rachel Dunaway. 1970. *Youth into Maturity: A Study of Men and Women in the First Ten Years After College.* New York: Mental Health Materials Center.

Eisenstadt, S. N. 1961. Archetypal Patterns of Youth. In Erik H. Erikson (Ed.), *The Challenge of Youth.* Garden City, N.Y.: Doubleday (Anchor), 1965.

Erikson, Erik H. 1968. *Identity: Youth and Crisis.* New York: W. W. Norton.

Festinger, Leon. 1957. *A Theory of Cognitive Dissonance.* Evanston, Ill.: Row, Peterson.

Flacks, Richard. 1967. The Liberated Generation: An Exploration of the Roots of Student Protest. *Journal of Social Issues, 23*(3), 52–75.

Flacks, Richard. 1971. *Youth and Social Change.* Chicago: Markham Publishing Co.

Goethals, George W., and Klos, Dennis S. 1970. *Experiencing Youth.* Boston: Little, Brown.

Goldsen, Rose; Rosenberg, Morris; Williams, Robin; and Suchman, Edward. 1960. *What College Students Think.* Princeton, N.J.: Van Nostrand.

Keniston, Kenneth. 1965. *The Uncommitted: Alienated Youth in American Society.* New York: Harcourt, Brace and World.

Keniston, Kenneth. 1966. Drug Use and Student Values. Paper presented at National Association of Student Personnel Administrators' Drug Education Conference, Washington, D.C. In Richard E. Horman and Allan M. Fox (Eds.), *Drug Awareness: Key Documents on LSD, Marijuana and the Drug Culture.* New York: Avon Books, 1970.

Keniston, Kenneth. 1967. The Sources of Student Dissent. *Journal of Social Issues, 23*(3), 108–137.

Keniston, Kenneth. 1968. *Young Radicals: Notes on Committed Youth.* New York: Harcourt, Brace and World.

Kinsey, Alfred C.; Pomeroy, Wardell B.; and Martin, Clyde E. 1948. *Sexual Behavior in the Human Male.* Philadelphia: Saunders.

Kinsey, Alfred C.; Pomeroy, Wardell B.; Martin, Clyde E.; Gebhard, Paul H.; and Associates. 1953. *Sexual Behavior in the Human Female.* Philadelphia: Saunders.

Kohlberg, Lawrence. 1964. Development of Moral Character and Moral Ideology. In Martin L. Hoffman and Lois Wladis Hoffman (Eds.), *Review of Child Development Research.* New York: Russell Sage Foundation.

Lief, Harold. 1972. Note on research in progress. *Behavior Today, 3*(2), 2.

Mead, George Herbert. 1934. Mind, Self, and Society. In Anselm Strauss (Ed.), *George Herbert Mead: On Social Psychology.* Chicago: University of Chicago Press, 1964. (Originally published: *Mind, Self, and Society.* Charles W. Morris, Ed.)

Mead, Margaret. 1970. *Culture and Commitment: A Study of the Generation Gap.* New York: Doubleday.

Milman, Doris H., and Anker, Jeffrey L. 1971. Patterns of Drug Usage Among University Students: IV. Use of Marihuana, Amphetamines, Opium, and LSD by Undergraduates. *Journal of the American College Health Association, 20*(2), 96–105.

Milman, Doris H., and Su, Wen-Huey. 1973. Patterns of Drug Usage Among University Students: V. Heavy Use of Marihuana and Alcohol by Undergraduates. *Journal of the American College Health Association, 21*(3), 181–187.

Neugarten, Bernice L.; Moore, Joan W.; and Lowe, John C. 1965. Age Norms, Age Constraints, and Adult Socialization. *American Journal of Sociology, 70*(6), 710–717.

Newsweek. 1972. VD: The Epidemic. January 24, 1972, 46 ff.

Piaget, Jean. 1932. *The Moral Judgment of the Child.* New York: Harcourt, Brace and World.

Piaget, Jean. 1972. Intellectual Evolution from Adolescence to Adulthood. *Human Development, 15,* 1–12.

Simon, William, and Gagnon, John. 1969. Psychosexual Development. *Transaction, 6*(5), 9–17.

Smith, M. Brewster. 1969. *Social Psychology and Human Values.* Chicago: Aldine.

Sorensen, Robert C. 1973. *The Sorensen Report: Adolescent Sexuality in Contemporary America.* Cleveland, Ohio: World Publishing Co.

Suchman, Edward A. 1968. The "Hang-Loose" Ethic and the Spirit of Drug Use. *Journal of Health and Social Behavior, 9*(2), 146–155.

Thornburg, Hershel D. 1971. Student Assessment of Contemporary Issues. In Hershel D. Thornburg (Ed.), *Contemporary Adolescence: Readings.* Belmont, California: Brooks/Cole.

U.S. Bureau of the Census. 1973. Characteristics of American Youth: 1972. *Current Population Reports,* Series P-23, No. 44. Washington, D.C.: U.S. Government Printing Office.

U.S. Bureau of Labor Statistics. 1971. Employment and Unemployment in 1970. *Special Labor Force Report,* No. 129. Washington, D.C.: U.S. Government Printing Office.

Vreeland, Rebecca S. 1972. Sex at Harvard. *Sexual Behavior, 2*(2), 4–10.

White, Robert W. 1966. *Lives in Progress.* (2nd ed.) New York: Holt, Rinehart and Winston.

Interlude
George, Age 27

George is the first of six case examples to be presented in this book; taken together, these examples represent a series of views of the life span from early adulthood to old age. Each is an edited transcript of an interview that lasted one to two hours; interviews were conducted by the author during the spring of 1973. The respondents—George, age 27; Theresa, age 34; Murray, age 48; Joan, age 67; Henry, age 75; and Mrs. K., age 89—were contacted through friends of the author. They do not represent "typical" adults—whatever that might mean—instead, they were selected to represent a range of adults—in age, social class, and life style. One respondent lives in a nursing home; another lives in Harlem and has five grandchildren; one man is a successful modern dancer, another is a successful executive, and another is a waiter looking forward to retirement; the sixth respondent is a young working mother.

The interview was designed to explore the major milestones and crisis points during the respondent's adult life. Questions about the family, the occupation, thoughts about the future, and reflections about the past were central issues that were explored. The questions are indicated by italics in the text; the respondent's own words are used throughout with a minimum of editing or grammatical correction. All of the names have been changed and basic identifying names and places have been changed in order to insure anonymity.

One important characteristic of these interviews is that the respondents knew how they were to be used. Thus, the information is censored by the respondent to the extent that each tended to present his or her life in a relatively positive light under these conditions. To be sure, negative aspects and crises are discussed also but, in general, these interviews are revealing the more integrated, better understood, and socially acceptable aspects of their lives. Of course, this is a characteristic of well-functioning persons who have a reasonably good understanding of their strengths and shortcomings and who do not dwell on their failures or weaknesses. However, one should read these cases with a healthy mixture of skepticism and openness. While there is probably much under the surface that is less positive, the strengths and ability to cope with mistakes, conflicts, and flaws are as important for understanding human functioning as any "deeper" conflicts and frustrations may be. In short, these are *developmental* interviews that are exploring the contours and milestones of human life; they are not clinical interviews attempting to uncover neurotic or unconscious psychodynamic conflicts.

George is a 27-year-old man who moved to New York to join a dance company after graduating from college. He makes no secret of his homosexual life style and has been living with his lover (Rick) for several years. By almost any standards he is successful and has a promising career ahead; he is comfortable with his life style and, as he puts it, they live very well. His parents have accepted his homosexuality and his lover and take considerable pride in his accomplishments. Yet he feels unfulfilled in an important way that seems to be puzzling and disturbing to him.

This case raises a number of questions. What does it mean to be a "normal" adult? Why did the milestones and crisis points he selected to discuss stand out in his memory? In what ways has his "gay" life style affected the developmental milestones of young adulthood? Was his decision to become a dancer a usual example of vocational choice? How has he changed in the last few years; this is, what effect has "experience" had on him? Are there any examples of some of White's Growth Trends in his comments (such as "deepening of interests" or "humanizing of values")? Does he seem to have resolved Erikson's identity and intimacy (and generativity?) issues? What do you think the future might hold for him?

As you look back over your life, what are some of the milestones that stand out? In terms of just profession, in terms of personal life? Do you want specifics? *Yes. What made me choose my profession? Was that a milestone?* It certainly was. I became a dancer out of the blue, literally—overnight. It wasn't my first dance class as such that made me become a dancer, because, although I enjoyed it very much, I knew I loved to dance. I've known that all my life. I had never seen dancers performing to even know there was such a thing as dance, other than ballet. I remember seeing [a famous dancer] on stage, watching him perform. I can even picture one thing that he did that just so struck me, absolutely hit me, and was such a fabulous thing to be able to do. I said "I want to do that." *Do you remember the time that you saw him do that?* I remember the exact moment. I can see it right now, I can picture it happening again ... the exact moment in a particular dance—it was one particular solo that I remember as breathtaking. *And that was the turning point for you?* I look back and that's what I remember, so that's a milestone for me, what one would have to call a milestone. . . .

Other milestones. I don't know, they just flow in.... Probably teachers I consider milestones in shaping my personality. My speech teacher in high school
was very elemental in how I think today. He was a superb teacher, ultra-
conservative. His political views just turn my stomach, but he was such a
fabulous teacher that as a teacher he could overcome some of these ... well,
almost fascistic views. He was just a great teacher. He developed many things
that I didn't know existed as such. The drama department was nothing in high
school. He was a vital force, a vital person. And an English teacher ... as I
struggled to find my own identity as a homosexual, besides my identity as a
person, as George. Just this little thing she did that made me realize that
homosexuals as a class can be accepted by respected people. She called me in
quite late in the semester just for a little talk. She was having some terrible
times of her own, in terms of her lover of some 40 years, who I assume was
her lover, a woman who lived with her for 40 years, who was dying of cancer.
This was a very traumatic period for her. And she called me in and she said,
"George, I just want you to know that I understand." She didn't say understand what. "And as far as your English grade, don't worry about it. I understand you're having problems and you'll have many more. This is some way
I can help you. But you don't have to worry about your English grade." And
that was it. She never said what or anything else, but of course I understood
and she understood. I'm a sentimental slob and, of course, tears and all of
that, but it was just a beautiful moment to know that there was.... It was the
first time I was confronted, outside of a doctor situation. I did have psychiatric
care in school. Here was someone who was not ... I was not talking to in a
medical way which is ugh, dry ... even when you're probing inner problems,
and because, I guess the way I think—I become so clinical as a person probing
these problems and so far outside of them that I never feel a sense of satisfaction or of real searching, as I did with this teacher.

Anyway, other milestones. Oh, I'm sure I have some. Oh! Telling my folks
I was gay was a milestone. Partly because of the way they responded (laughs).
When did that happen? I was a junior in college. It was at the breakfast table,
where in our family "great events" occur. 'Cause that's where most of the talking happens. And I finally just said, "Mom, Dad, I have something I just have
to say, have to tell you." I told them I was gay. They both sighed, the two
biggest sighs of relief you ever heard. And I was perplexed until they explained
that they'd known for years. They never said how they'd known, I've never
asked. And they just knew some day that I would tell them, and they just
hoped that I would express my trust that they felt I had in them—which I do—
could express it enough to say, "Folks, I am different than what we consider a
norm," and that about the way I said it. What could they say besides "Whew!
Golly, you finally trusted us enough to tell us," and they were so pleased. That
began a great chapter in our parent-child relationship. I still am their child.
I love being their son, not a child, well yes, child, meaning offspring, not meaning adolescent.

Okay. More milestones. Can you think of some other areas maybe that would
interest you? Or that would be relevant? Or that would help me remember?
What about more recent milestones? Like coming to New York? Well, coming
to New York wasn't really a milestone for me because that was so planned, so

matter-of-fact that I was going to do it that it wasn't really a milestone. Let me see. My life has been going so according to schedule lately, and so very planned. My working life I mean. *You planned everything out at some point back?* It seems to have evolved that way, you know. Because I'm going in the direction with goals, specific goals in mind and I'm going that way and nothing has really detoured me off. My traveling has been very exciting. I wouldn't call any of it a milestone because I think of a milestone as changing, as a point where I can say from here on there is a real change. Richard, in a way maybe, I could call a milestone, meeting him and settling down with him; that's something I always wanted; even though maybe other people wouldn't interpret it that way, I've always been a very settled down kind of person. And we've just integrated our lives together, so it didn't really change my life or his, I don't believe. Other than it fulfilled for each of us something we needed and wanted. But again not a milestone. *It sounds like in a very real sense, once you made the decision to become a dancer, then somehow the rest of it is kind of an unfolding and fairly continuous.* Oh, yes; very much, very much kind of an unfolding kind of thing. I went ahead and graduated from college, came to New York, studied, moved into the dance company and, have been working ever since as a dancer. Now I have started for the past year and a half getting jobs of my own, teaching dance last summer; and I have two offers to do teaching this coming summer, both for one-month periods. That would be two months of very well-paid teaching I might add, and do very well for myself in terms of building my own career. It's still all part of an unfolding. I live well now, very well.

As you look back over your life have you changed much do you think, or has it been pretty similar all the way through? I was going to say I haven't changed. That's silly, of course I've changed. I've changed a lot. But to me, I'm still just me. And that me has always been here and present. Just different facets of it are more evident now as opposed to other facets which were more evident then, which I'm sure are still part of me, and could in the future be shown again. I have not changed as a person. Because people are such complex beings, like great crystal, the different sides are shown at different times, and at different angles, and because of different presences and outside influences, different things are seen. If nothing but green lights are shining on something, it's going to appear green, no matter what color it is. It's going to be changed. And yet it itself is not changed. It is still whatever it is. Take away the green lights and it's still there. So, I have not changed. I may appear different and seem to show different things.

We've been talking about milestones. What about crisis points? Have there been any crisis points that stand out? Yes, I've had a lot of crises. Do you want some of them? *Yes.* Well, younger crises, the natural crises of growing up, going through puberty, adolescence. I was a very nervous child. I'm still highly strung, but I just express it in very different ways. *Adolescence was a difficult time for you?* Oh, terrible. But, it is for everyone. I just probably expressed it more obviously than most children do. Through eighth, ninth, tenth, eleventh, twelfth [grades] and the first year of college I had my annual spring nervous breakdown, for which I had to be shuttled off for a time. Because it might have built to the point where I couldn't, in the course of my everyday things, I could not handle myself. *What do you mean by "shuttled off"?* Well, sometimes it just meant going home for a few days, staying away from everyone. The last couple of years of high school and the first year of college it meant running off to the hospital. I just became that bad. So, just getting out of my mainstream, away from my peer group, which is for me where the real pressures are. The people I work with now is where the real pressures are. *Was that partly because of your homosexuality?* I thought so at the time. I look back now and I say maybe it is, or was; maybe it was because I was gay; but it was because I felt so extraordinarily different, and was treated as someone very very different, and because I had some very sick high school and junior high counselors. I know now; then I didn't know. I trusted them and they simply could not cope with it. I'm an open person. I tell people how I feel. In eighth grade I said, "I'm in love with that boy" and my counselor simply could not cope with it. He didn't know what to do so it turned out he did all the wrong things. He said, "No, you're not," and such other stupid things, or "That's wrong." So my feelings of being different were constantly being reinforced by the very people who should have been helping me. *You say "different." What do you mean "different"?* How was I different? How do I consider myself different? *I gather that was more than just being gay.* Well, we don't know what being gay means as an adolescent, I don't think. We're all growing up and we're all changing. I didn't seem to be changing the way I saw the people around me changing. I always felt, especially from my male peers, that I was not like them. I didn't know why. And I was angry because I wasn't like them. Sometimes this anger was in terms of fighting and I would fight. Sometimes it was in terms of crying. I was extremely high strung, emotional; I'm still emotional. I'll cry. I did just Monday night, after talking to Mom. Just knowing what pain she was in talking to her on the phone [in the hospital]—she could hardly communicate—it just killed me. Tears just streamed down my face. I couldn't control it. Other boys were not so emotional. And so, I was ridiculed. And ridicule at 15 is tough, very tough.

Any other crises? Any other crises. Ah, I should go back to my building of my personality, because of my strong Christian background, I think I have a double set of morals inside of me that is constantly having trouble. I do not even understand them both. One comes from life as I lived it so far, and one comes from the morals that I've been taught. Maybe we all have these, probably. *Somehow these Christian values are in conflict with the values that you live with day by day.* Right. And to add on to that, the ideas and values that I live with day by day I consider correct. How can they both be correct? I don't know. This is my problem. And I admit this, because I have said to myself many times, if I did not truly believe what I was doing was correct, I wouldn't be doing it. And yet, at the same time, I will acknowledge to myself that I believe this, whatever it is, is wrong or not right, and yet I'm doing it. I don't know how to justify that and I don't know if I can. These are the kinds of philosophical questions one justifies, maybe never. *Is a lot of the content of this conflict sexual?* Part of it is. Like, just today I read something in the Post that deeply disturbed me...a Catholic priest saying that one cannot be a Christian and be a homosexual. That's intellectually sick, but inside me, I say maybe he's right. Yet, I know he's not right, and yet I can still believe he could be right. You know, there's an example of what I mean. *Can you think of another kind of example that is not sexual?* Yeah...abortion. I do not believe in abortion, and yet there are arguments that I have to agree with *for* abortion. How can this be resolved, because I can argue both sides and believe both sides? Absolutely believe them. And that is not compartmental thinking. *You really believe both and are caught in between.* Right, I truly believe both sides are correct.

Have there been any crisis points in your relationship with your family? Not really. Some childish things. Nothing really recently. I've never run away from my family or anything like that as a child. *You said at one point when we didn't have the recorder on that your mother was in the hospital.* Yeah, she is. *Is this a serious matter?* It's not, now, as it's turned out thank goodness. Oh, I see what you mean, a crisis in those terms. No, there's not even been any in those terms, no. Were my Mom and Dad, and they're not young, to die, that could be critical to me, I believe. Not permanently hurt, or upset by it, but I would be truly hurt because I love them as human beings, I want them to be around, to enjoy them. It's such a very selfish thing to be saying, but it would be such a personal loss; the reason I can say that is because I know how fully they've both lived, and that in terms of them, there's no loss. They could both have died tomorrow, and they have lived very full lives. I think their lives may have been fulfilled a long time ago, and this is just all the frosting on the cake. I know a few young people who are such good people that their lives are fulfilled and that everything they do, the goals they reach, their quests and so forth are just growing beyond them. A tree can be a tree at two foot high, and can be a whole tree, and there it is...but if it grows to be 50 feet high it's just all grand and fabulous. *Is that somehow the way it is for you? Do you feel that way about yourself?* I'd like to think it were true, but it's not, no I'm not.

Before you changed [the topic] I was going to say that I have a romantic ideal in my psychic sexual fulfillment that I do not have. And I have had about three maybe four boys, and I knew that they were my desired sexual outlet, who, in my eyes, could have been the fulfillment of that psychic sexual need. And, as yet, it still goes unfulfilled. And whether it even can be fulfilled, I don't know. And whether any of these boys could have fulfilled it I've no way of knowing. I just know that there are people who I have said to myself or even to them, "I love you," and it has not gone beyond. It has not been a fulfillment of that "I love you." *It never turned into a relationship?* Right. *So then your relationship with Rick is not one of these?* No, it's not, because my relationship with Rick is very fulfilled. I wouldn't give it up for anything. I have questioned it before. But I've only questioned it because I think it's healthy to question. I would not give it up for any of these ["ideal" boys] because this is something I truly need, want, have found, and am not going to let go of. So, I truly love Rick. But this thing, whatever it is in my head that I call a need; right now I call it a need for Bill or before him it was another Bill. Whatever that is in me, I don't know. I guess I'll have to find out, if I ever do. Don't people as they all grow older have unanswered questions, about themselves, about their living? It is almost accepted there will be unanswered questions in my life. I won't know everything. I'll see through the glass darkly and it gets clearer, but will never be gone.

How long have you and Rick been together? Five years last November, and this is February . . . a long time. *Have there been any crisis points in that relationship?* Oh, yes, several (laughter). *Do you regard it as a marriage?* I suppose so. I look on it as very similar to the relationship that my parents have. Because we're two people who want to live together and are greater because we're together; and that's perhaps, what a marriage is. *Have there been some crisis points?* Yes, there have been crises. For example, when we first got together we were still discovering each other, and I'm sure you know that one doesn't understand someone else immediately. We must all make concessions. That's a good word, it doesn't have to be a bad word. All have to make concessions if we are going to live with someone else. None of us can perfectly fit into someone else's life; such a thing doesn't exist. It takes you a while to find out how you must act or react to someone else before you can be together. Now, considering this I was talking about earlier—I don't know if I'll ever find [that "need"] fulfilled, like for example [with] Bill. Richard has had some real troubles because he feels that maybe somehow he's to blame for not "fulfilling" me. I, of course, say that's silly, because I don't even know if I can be fulfilled; how could you blame yourself for not fulfilling me? Then, maybe I am fulfilled, and this other is a manifestation of some other problem. It has nothing to do with *fulfillment* as such. These are all possibilities that a person must face in their own lives. So, this has been a crisis a couple times—where he has felt outrageous jealousy, what I consider outrageous jealousy, and then self-pity after thinking about it because he felt that he was inadequate. So, this has been a crisis. But, there have been no others as such. We hardly even argue anymore. We do get mad at one another and it's usually silly; but we forgive so quickly anymore, so easily. I'm glad, and I think he's glad that we both know that we can get mad at one another and just get outraged and throw things, and be furious, and even shout and it doesn't matter. That's very important to both of us because we're both volatile people; and to know that we don't have to be anything else or anybody else when we come into this house. When we come home we can be ourselves; we can be angry, we can literally take out our day's frustrations on each other, which we do do, both of us. The night before last, both of us had horrible, frustrating, interminably long days. And we both came home at different times, outraged, and we both took it out on the other one (laughter). But that really didn't matter, you know; we were cuddling and having a good time.

How long did you know him before you decided to move in with him? The whole thing was so gradual that it's really hard to tell. There's no date I can list of having moved in because I had two apartments; I lived here sort of and still had my other apartment. Some nights I slept there; eventually I slept here more than there, and then eventually I sublet that one out and eventually got rid of that one completely and then only lived here; but this was all so gradual that there's no way to say. I knew when I met him that I was interested. Here's a point that I think is very interesting. He is more like my best friends that I went to college with than any of my previous lovers ever were. He is more like the people I wanted to spend time with than the people I spent [time] in bed with, which is an interesting point. I knew he was bright and that probably attracted me to him more than anything else, because he's just so exceptionally bright. That's very important to me.

I gather that neither of you have any children. No. *Do you resent that?* No,

I don't. That's interesting timing on that question, because just a couple days ago I was reading about adoption. And also, someone else had been talking about a way man is immortal is by having children. And I tried to think about that; what that meant to me. I said maybe I should worry about that. I'm a good worrier. Maybe I should think about that too. Would I some day worry about my own immortality and would not having a son make that hard for me. Well, I thought and I said, "What about the people who do not have children and who adopt?" I know from experience that they consider them their children every bit as much. And yet, if they were to think about it intellectually, I'm sure they would have to say, "No, I'm not passing myself on." And so I say this doesn't really interest me—having children—I don't particularly want children. I know that I will probably do a great deal of teaching in my life and I can be a grander father to more people that way. Already, the list of people, young men in general, even young ladies who have written to me after I've been somewhere teaching and said, "You have changed my life." And that, you know ... how much greater father can I ever be than to have people tell you that you've changed their lives. Just a couple days ago I got a letter from a boy in Iowa who, after seeing me and talking with me in class—this was his first dance class ever—he's changed his whole life. He's come out, told his family. I was the first homosexual he met who was proud; not proud to be gay, that's so dumb—who was *proud* and who was a homosexual. Because I must make a distinction between saying I am not ashamed of being gay, and I am proud of being gay. I'm not proud of being gay any more than a heterosexual is proud of being heterosexual. But I am not ashamed of being gay any more than a heterosexual is ashamed of being heterosexual. There is a big, big difference there that I think is very important, [in contrast] to the idea currently in vogue that I'm gay and I'm proud that I'm gay. I think that's silly. They're making the wrong thing important in their lives. So, this young man has dropped out of school, applied to another school which has a big dance department; it's in the West; he'll be going to study dance. He's been accepted there already. It really changed his life. [I've received] several page letters. This has happened to me several times. And I couldn't feel more of a father than that. I wouldn't want to be. I'm not interested in bringing more children into the world; we've got enough and therefore I can, as a father, in terms of a father, in the old Biblical sense of a father, I can father people. I'll be doing more than most people do.

In terms of your occupation as a dancer, have there been any milestones or crisis points? Oh, I've almost quit several times if that's what you mean. I almost quit the company I'm currently in. But that's, that's still in grappling with knowing the situation I am in is not perfect, and I must be continually aware that I have to be there—this may sound crass and I don't mean it to sound crass—to get out of it what I can get out of it. Now I'm *giving* a hell of a lot too. So, that's why it's not crass to be getting out of it what I can get out of it, because I'm also giving every bit as much as I'm getting out of it. But I am there to get out of it what I can. And so, sometimes a really bad situation will arise; some personal thing with the director, some impossible tour situation—because touring can be impossible. And I'll say, "What am I doing? Why am I doing this? I'm not enjoying this. I've got to get out," and then I say, "No; my greater goals are more important and are satisfied better and can be reached better by staying." So I stay, although that's how I get over these kinds of crises. One of the most exciting personal things that happened to me arose out of my being a dancer besides the applause—which is the greatest thing in the world for me—was meeting Mr. and Mrs. Shah, the Shah of Iran, which was so exciting. I am excited by great people and I really felt I was in the presence of two great people when I met them. I am middle class, bourgeois, mid-America . . . I shouldn't . . . forget that. That is my background. I think it's important I remember that this is from where I came. I've been lucky. I just this morning made a list of countries I've been to—twenty-five of them. That's pretty impressive. And, it's unusual for someone from my circumstances and background. And in that way I can appreciate it even more because I say say, "This is unusual. I have gone beyond myself in some way." In some ways I am a better person for it. How could a son of a multimillionaire be proud at my age of having traveled all over the world when he can do it at will?

Thinking back to when you first came to New York and started dancing with the company, how was that? Was that a crisis point in some way? Well, it was planned. It was all planned. I just did it. It was exciting. I loved it all. I was thrilled by everything. Golly, eager? Was I eager!

How did you come to the point of deciding that you were going to come to New York and be a dancer? I was always going to come to New York as long as I can remember. Some day I was going to go to New York. For many years I said that I was going to come to New York and be an actor. Practically, I never said that. I said things like, in ninth grade, you know, it's time to make a report on what you're going to be when you grow up, and I said I was going to be an accountant; and another time I was going to be something else, because I always thought of myself as a very practical person. But I always said to myself, "Someday I'm going to go to New York and be an actor." So that's how I got to college, thinking in those terms. Then I discovered dance. For me this somehow seemed even better, and even greater; I could see more fulfillment, and as it turned out that's where it looks like I belonged. And so I did come to New York, not as an actor; I came as a dancer.

How does your future look in terms of your career as a dancer? How do you see it developing? Well, if we only knew what lies ahead. I know what I want, I know what my goals are, and I know that's what I'm striving for. I value myself as an artist and a dancer, they are two very different things, which gets back to some basic philosophy of what a performer is. Is the performer an artist or is the performer a craftsman? Just to make things simple, I'll say the performer is a craftsman for me and I value myself as an artist. And therefore, I have to do my art; my art is theater. And so I'm working toward that goal. I'm a dancer; I work all the time to get better, to become continually a better technician and a better performer or craftsman, and I'm also learning the art of dance. I practice it as a craftsman with increasing craft ability, knowing that I also have artistic abilities. How good they are? All I can say is that what I have done so far artistically has been successful. I just hope that by continuing that I'll be more successful. That's what I'm working toward—which may mean my own company or maybe being part of another company. Maybe it will eventually lead its way from dance as such. *What are your career goals?* I don't know what it is specifically. I know that it will be in the theater. It may not even be as a performer. I don't know. I'll find out what peaks I can reach as a performer. And there's the age variable. One gets better as they get older. It's through sheer doing that one gets better. So, for my age I will be able to judge my peak as an artist. But, I don't know if it will even be in dance; it might be in some other form of theater. I don't know.

Has the way people reacted to you changed over the years? I'm still different. I still feel very different, and think I am treated as such. People are not ready for candid observation and conversation. People are not ready to be touched. If I want to touch someone I do; I get in trouble with it sometimes—male or female. Or, to say, "I love you" or to say, "I want to go to bed with you," or to say any everyday little thing, they're not ready for that kind of candidness, and I am. I am that way and I don't think it's wrong. If I thought it was wrong, I would have stopped it. So I will continue doing it, even though it offends people. I will say, "Okay, I'll watch myself under certain circumstances." If I think there will be long-range problems by my being candid or being open, or being too emotional, then I say, "Okay, George, don't. This is the time to say no."...I am still different, and I'm treated differently; but now I kind of like being different because I have met enough people to whom that differentness was not bad, it was exciting, and I found out that the people to whom it seemed exciting were more the people I liked, were more the kind of people I was interested in. And the people who found it offensive were the people I didn't care about anyway. *So it's not so much that the people respond to you differently in general, but that you've found more people who respond to you the way you want them to respond.* Yeah, it's one of the reasons I probably love New York City. It's a huge city and I love big cities. I'm excited by them. I'm excited by many people. For me maybe it takes many people to find the few I want to call my peers, that I want to be my associates.

Would you say that you've got a pretty firm sense of who you are right now? Do you know who you are? Oh, that's a hard one. Let me think....I know *exactly* who I am. *Who are you?* I'm George and my friends all know. That's all I can say. I am complex. I am simple. I'm emotional. I'm volatile. Creative. I'm an S.O.B. I have a nasty temper at times. I love sex. I love giving; I love receiving. I love beautiful things, and I even like some ugly things. I think I'm open. I don't have a closed mind, and yet I know that at times I will absolutely shut everyone and everything off because I think they're wrong, which is a closed mind, as closed as you can be. So I know that's part of me too. I'm opinionated. I'm educated. All those opinions mean things to me. Do I think I'm right? Darn right I think I'm right! If I didn't think I was right I would do different things and say different things. Am I always right? Oh, no! I'm not always right. That's been obvious through my life. But when I did it I thought I was right, or I wouldn't have done it, whatever it is at the time. *Have you always felt that way about yourself, that you really knew who you were? Or was there some time when you began to get more of a sense of really knowing who you were?* Probably always thought I knew who I was, but I can look back and say I hadn't the foggiest idea who I was when I was 15, 16, 17, 18,

...19,...20,...21. And I'm sure at 35 I'll say, "George, you had no idea really what you were at 27." Now I think I do. That's what I hope maturing is; that's what I hope wisdom is—all of which I want. I'm not mature. God knows I'm not mature (laughter), but it's not bad to be immature because when I'm mature I'll probably be dead (laughter). Because maturing means "full," "the end," maturing is the top, and I hope I don't reach the peak until I'm gone. I want to reach the peak on my death bed.

Do you sometimes think about death? I guess. Death's death. Someday, maybe soon, maybe not. It doesn't matter. It really doesn't. I have wanted to die, so I guess then it mattered. I have enjoyed myself so much that I don't think I want to die right now, because it's so fabulous; but, at the same time I've said, "Maybe this would be a good time." But, I'm going to die; I hope it's not painful for someone else. Or I hope it's as painless as it can be. Death always seems to cause pain to the living. I assume mine will, because I know there are people who care. I know Rick cares. If I were to die tomorrow he would be very very hurt. My family would be very hurt. But, this is why, even though I thought about suicide because I was suffering a pain which I don't understand, I said, "Well, when I die I want to hurt as few people as possible. And if I die now by killing myself it would probably hurt as many people as possible, so I don't want to die." But...I'm not dead yet. So, that's about it. *Do you sometimes look over your life and review where you've been, what you've done?* I love memories, if that's what you mean? I value memories greatly. I have such fabulous memories! They are very important to me. ...I love to go over them, I love to reexperience. My life has been exciting! And sometimes exciting-bad. And even then it was exciting. I wouldn't trade it. That doesn't mean it couldn't have been different or couldn't have been better, and even maybe wished it had been better, but the whole thing I wouldn't trade. I value my past.

Is sex as important to you now as it used to be? Yes. *More, about the same?* About the same. I don't have as much, yet it's still very, very important. Seriously important, not frivolously. I love sex. I love to talk about it. I love to do it, even though I don't do it much, because it is so much a part of every person. It is a great expression of giving and taking between two or more people. And sometimes, just one—giving yourself—because I enjoy masturbation, too...I enjoy, fantasizing. Oh, my fantasies when I masturbate are extraordinary, they're beautiful. If you wanted to find a fault you could probably say I fantasize too much in my life. That's probably my greatest fault, as I see it. One of the things I would change is, perhaps, I would be more real—fantasize less. Although I enjoy my fantasies, so I doubt that I will. *Why are you having sex less now than you used to?* Partly because I know I can get it when I want it. So, the urge to be constantly in there fighting for it—it's hard work—sex can be hard work too. You go in there and prove yourself, which all of us, I think, tend to do, especially in more frivolous circumstances. I know that if I see a boy I want sexually, I can probably have him 99 times out of 100, straight or gay. I don't have to prove that anymore. So, I'll see a pretty boy and say, "Oooh, I'll have to go to bed with him," and I just don't put out the effort that it might take, because I have lots of things to do, and the rewards of just having conquered someone are not always equal to the effort involved. I know I could probably do it, and I have lots of other things to do, and I do the other things. *How about your relationship with Rick in terms of sex; are you having less sex now than you once did?* Oh, yes. We don't have sex very often. *Why is that?* Well, I'm not really sure. I know it's probably a good thing, but once again, we don't have to perform for one another. We both work extraordinary hours, we're tired, so when we have it it's because we want it, and for no other reason. Oh, there are some times when one of us wants it and I know we just do it for the other one, just to please the other one. I've been too tired and Rick has really wanted sex, and I say "Oh, okay." I hope he doesn't ... well, intellectually we both know we do that, but I hope he doesn't know when it has happened, because I want to please him and I know it wouldn't please him if he thought I were doing it out of obligation. And, the same for him. I know he's done it for me. I don't know when ... I have no particular times in mind. I have sometimes known afterwards when he's told me, like the next day ... "Oh, I really didn't want to ... I was so tired last night. I hope it wasn't too bad."

In general, in your life, do you have a sense of being particularly productive, of leaving or having left your mark? Yes, I think it's obvious by the things I've said. *I guess you've also said this before, but has life been a meaningful adventure for you?* Very. Yes, I've also said that, yeah. *You are pleased with how it's been?* Pleased, not satisfied, pleased. *What are some of the things you'd like to change?* About my life? I would like to understand why I think I love Bill. I'd like to understand that ... or why I think I need him, and need him to love me, because I don't understand that. I would like to learn a better way of being candid without insulting and hurting, which sometimes I do. But it is usually of more value for me to be honest than not to hurt. So sometimes I'll say things that other people will say, "You shouldn't have said that," and I'll say, "It needed to be done. Somebody had to say it." *Finally, would you say that your life is different now than it was a year or two ago? Have you changed? Are you different now than you were a year or two ago?* No, I'm not different at all. I know more. I have a greater understanding of some things; not as great as it will be next year. I hope it's better next year. I hope I understand more. I have to grow in wisdom. I want to be wise, truly wise; what I consider wise. I want to be generous. I can be more generous. *What would you like to be doing in five years?* Exactly what I'm doing right now ... getting ready for another New York season ... whatever that may mean. That could mean a hundred things.

four
Male
and
Female in
Adulthood

Few areas of psychosocial inquiry are currently as controversial as the study of sex differences; and perhaps one's bias is least easy to detect in this field because sex differences are so familiar and so well-recognized (both physically and stereotypically). Also, it is impossible (in our view) to discuss sex differences without confronting the essentially political issue of sex discrimination, whereby the differences between the sexes are not only facts but have political and economic consequences as well. Equally controversial, however, is the origin of these differences; that is, it is impossible to discuss sex differences without dealing in some way with the controversy of "nature" versus "nurture" or "heredity" versus "environment." And as if all of this did not present enough difficulty for one chapter, we must also point out that the research on sex differences (and on the "psychology of women") as well as the Women's Liberation movement are focusing attention, challenging old assumptions, and rapidly producing new data and new theories on the nature, origin, and meaning of sex differences. At the same time, our society is evolving toward increased flexibility of sex roles and greater equality of economic participation (at least on the surface and in legislation). Thus, our discussion of sex differences in adulthood may best be seen as a description of how things appear at the moment in a field of seeming constant motion. Nonetheless, as difficult as it may be to describe this field-in-motion, it is probably many more times difficult to work out one's individual sense of what it means, personally, to be a man or a woman when everyone is writing, studying, and debating about it. Perhaps our discussion may add some light, if not many final answers, to this current and important topic (both personally and intellectually).

This chapter, then, explores the complex question of what difference it makes whether one is a man or a woman during the adult years from a perspective of interacting physiological, social, and psychological factors. To be sure, our understanding of this complex area is only beginning to develop, and new data are constantly being discovered. Nonetheless, it is apparent that an individual's gender (male or female) is an important characteristic—physiologically, socially, and psychologically—and it influences the individual in countless ways. For example, an individual's gender is apparent from a wide variety of cues, and it plays an important role in most social interactions; that is, one's gender implies that certain roles and behaviors are appropriate while others are not, depending on the gender of the other actors and on the nature of the social situation. Thus, in our society, two women or a man and a woman may embrace and kiss in greeting, but two men typically do not; women are allowed to cry, but men are expected not to; men may be physically aggressive with one another, but not with women; and women are typically not physically aggressive with one another; and so on. In many ways sex functions as a similar kind of social cue as age, and these two social cues operate in combination so that the kind of age-sex roles or age-sex statuses we discussed in Chapter 2 typically function as important social frameworks for behavior. Also, individuals usually react differently to men and women and also tend to expect different behavior from men and women. This leads, of course, to smooth social interaction (since appropriate expectations facilitate the interactions). But it may also lead to the kind of discrimination pointed out by the various Women's Liberation groups— that is, those situations where men and women are constrained to play roles that do not meet the individual's needs, or where women are expected to perform less rewarding roles than men, or are expected to perform the same roles with less reward. Certainly, social-cultural factors are involved in these manifestations of sex differences; however, physiological factors and psychological characteristics undoubtedly interact with social-cultural norms and expectations as well.

In our view, sex differences at any given time and in any particular society may best be seen as the result of the interaction of physiological and social factors; and each factor is influenced to some degree by the other. Were there no physiological differences between men and women, and were there no social distinctions made between the behavior expected of men and women, then sex differences would be essentially individual differences. However, in our society there are pervasive and subtle sex-related norms and expectations; also there are considerable physiological differences between men and women that we will discuss in some detail. As a result of the interaction of these factors, men and women differ in their internal experience, in their external experience, and in their psychological makeup. At the same time, men and women are probably at least as similar as they are different and there is considerable individual variation. In a sense our society has tended to stress and perhaps amplify the differences between men and women; another society might stress and amplify the similarities. In either case, men and women need not be assumed to be opposites: active versus passive, rational versus emotional, independent versus dependent, and so on. Instead of this commonly assumed oppositeness, we would stress both the similarities and the differences. For example, a well-adjusted man or woman may be high on both "masculine" and "feminine" qualities if both sets of characteristics consist of similar and different personality traits and are not assumed to be opposite to one another. Similarly, one woman may be less "feminine" than another, but need not be any more "masculine"; and a man may be highly "masculine" while also relatively high (or low) on "feminine" qualities. As long as it is clear that "masculine" is not necessarily the opposite of "feminine," both sets of personality characteristics may involve positive, adaptive, and different qualities.

In sum, we feel that less confusion results if it is kept in mind that men and women are probably as similar as they are different; they share many of the basic human characteristics of individuals in our society, and they share many of the same social values and attitudes. The two differences we will discuss in this chapter are physiological differences and differences that result from the interaction of physiological, social, and psychological factors. The goal of our discussion is to examine these differences—and the similarities—and to explore the effects they have on the progression of the adult life cycle for men and women. We will begin with the discussion of physiological similarities and differences.

PHYSIOLOGICAL DIFFERENCES BETWEEN MEN AND WOMEN

Perhaps one of the reasons male and female characteristics are generally assumed to be opposite and mutually exclusive is that most persons are indeed *either* a male or a female. Very few persons have physiological characteristics of both sexes; nearly always the internal and external genital organs, the hormones, and the chromosomes are in agreement with one another as well as with the sex the child was assigned by society. Hampson and Hampson (1961) studied a group of hermaphrodites (persons with one or more characteristics of both sexes) and found that *assigned sex* (by parents and society in general) before the age of 2½ years was nearly always the gender role (or psychological sex) adopted by the child. Many of these children were characterized by underdeveloped male genitalia and female chromosomal or hormonal reversals, but were raised as males, and chose at puberty to remain males; surgical and hormonal treatment during adolescence helped reduce the contradiction between the various aspects of sex characteristics. This study suggests that physiological sex differences, while usually either all male or all

female, are considerably more complex than the obvious anatomical differences. Thus, to understand the nature and origin of physiological sex
differences we must begin at the beginning.

Prenatal Differentiation

When a sperm fertilizes an egg, the chromosomes that determine the sex
of the offspring usually form either an XY pair (producing a male) or an
XX pair (producing a female); the ratio of XX to XY is estimated to be
as high as 150:100. There is also a slight excess of male births—the ratio
is about 106:100 and 103:100 for American white and black populations,
respectively (Harrison, Weiner, Tanner, and Barnicot, 1964). The rate of
prenatal and childhood survival gives an edge to girls so that the excess
of male births leads to an approximately equal number of men and
women during the childbearing years; thereafter women outnumber men
of the same age (Figure 4.1). The Y chromosome seems to be so powerful
in producing a male that even when there is an extra chromosome and

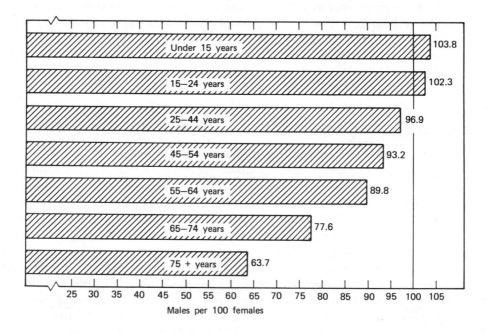

Figure 4.1
*Sex ratio by age in the United States, 1970 (males per 100 females). (Source. U.S. Bureau of
the Census. Some Demographic Aspects of Aging in the United States. Current Population
Reports, Series P-23, No. 43. Washington, D.C.: U.S. Government Printing Office,1973, Table 6.)*

the configuration is XXY, the offspring is a nearly normal male (often with small testes and an inability to produce sperm). Another atypical configuration is XYY and some recent evidence indicates that such males are overrepresented among prison populations (Hook and Kim, 1971; Price, Strong, Whatmore, and McClemont, 1966).

There is a sense in which the female form is the basic one and the male form is a differentiation of the female form that would develop in the absence of an androgenic hormone (similar in chemical composition to the male hormone testosterone). About the seventh week after conception, the genes on the Y chromosome (in males) cause the gonad in the developing embryo to become recognizably a testis, that, about the twelfth week, begins to produce this androgenic hormone. This hormone causes the genitalia to form a penis and scrotum out of the same organs that would otherwise become the clitoris, labia minor, and labia major; one set of internal ducts (Wolffian) develops into a system of sperm ducts in the male while another set of ducts (Müllerian) develops into the vagina, uterus, and oviducts in females (Harrison, et al., 1964). Thus, the male becomes differentiated by the action of a self-produced androgenic hormone during this critical period of prenatal development and, in the absence of this hormone, the female form develops.

It would seem plausible that the presence or absence of androgens would have other effects on the developing embryo in addition to producing the male or female genital structures; however, we currently lack data on these other possible effects in humans. Harris (1964) argued that the *hypothalamus*, which plays an important role in regulating the female sex cycle, and perhaps other aspects of the central nervous system are also differentiated into male and female forms before birth because of the effects of these hormones (that, of course, continue to affect the central nervous system throughout adulthood). Several studies have found characteristic male and female behaviors in young rhesus monkeys and have also found that the behavior of females becomes more like the behavior of males when androgens were injected into their mothers when the young monkey was an embryo (cf. Young, Goy, and Phoenix, 1964). Other studies with animals have found that prenatal or after-birth injections of androgen to females lead to a permanent impairment of the post-pubertal sexual cycle (Money, 1965), and the female's sexual behavior is also affected (Levine and Mullins, 1966; Young et al., 1964).

While we would not expect such complex human behavior as "masculine" or "feminine" social behavior or sexual behavior to be directly affected by prenatal presence or absence of androgens—as seems to be the case for rhesus monkeys and rats—we would expect the different internal biochemical environment for infant boys and girls to make some difference. That is, it would seem that the internal differences—different hormones for certain, perhaps differences in the hypothalamus and, possibly, other central nervous system differences—would interact with the more well-known differences in the external (social) environment to produce the sex differences throughout the life span. While it is not likely that complex patterns of behavior are biochemically determined, it is quite plausible that the *predisposition* to respond or be influenced in differing ways to differing social stimuli may be biochemically affected by hereditary and hormonal factors.

For example, the level of male aggressiveness and dominance in monkeys seems to be related to levels of testosterone in the blood plasma. In one study, when male monkeys were placed in a high-dominance situation (in which only females were present), the level of plasma testosterone was found to increase nearly four times over the previous level; but when the male was then placed with more dominant males and subjected to defeat, testosterone levels were found to fall sharply (Rose, Gordon, and Bernstein, 1972). The link between testosterone and aggression in human males is less clear. Kreuz and Rose (1972) found no connection between the amount of fighting among a group of young male prisoners or the level of hostility on psychological tests and testosterone levels. However, they did find that the 10 prisoners with a history of violent and aggressive crimes in adolescence had significantly higher levels of testosterone than the other 11 prisoners. And a study by Persky, Smith, and Basu (1971) did find a positive correlation between the level of testosterone and amount of self-reported aggressiveness for young men (age 17-28) but not for older men (age 31-66). Obviously, additional research is needed to clarify these conflicting results. However, part of the difficulty in establishing a link between testosterone and aggression in humans results from the complexity inherent in defining "aggression" in humans since the mode (verbal, physical, indirect, and so on) is largely under conscious control, regardless of hormonal level.

Although our understanding of the interaction between physiological (e.g., hormonal) factors and human behavior is only beginning to develop, the complexity of that interaction is certainly becoming clear. For example, a recent study by Kolodny, Masters, Hendryx, and Toro (1971) found a significantly lower level of testosterone in the blood plasma of predominately or exclusively homosexual men (who had volunteered for the study from a local gay activist organization) compared with a sample of heterosexual men or those homosexual men who were equally homosexual and heterosexual or predominately heterosexual. In addition, they found a significant correlation between the number of viable sperm in the semen and the degree of homosexuality among the homosexual men; similarly, the sperm count and level of plasma testosterone were significantly correlated. At first glance, these data might suggest that biochemical factors produce the complex social behavior of homosexuality. However, the authors conclude that it is equally likely that the lower plasma testosterone levels "... could be the secondary result of a primary homo-sexual psychosocial orientation . . . relayed through the hypothalamus from higher cortical centers" (Kolodny et al., 1971, p. 1174).

It might be noted that this research on levels of plasma testosterone has only recently been possible because of a refinement in the laboratory techniques required for the precise analyses used in the studies; thus as such new techniques are applied to this complex area of the interrelation between physiological and psychosocial factors, we may expect further fascinating findings about these complex interactions. For example, we know that animals subjected to stress or to "crowding" in their cages have enlarged adrenal glands (Christian, 1955), but we do not know what effect that may have. And we know that electrical stimulation of specific areas of the brain produces such complex behavior as aggression in ani-mals (Delgado, 1969), but we do not know the connection between brain stimulation and hormone production and psychosocial behavior.

In sum, while the necessary data about the nature of physiological dif-ferences between men and women as a result of prenatal sex-differentia-tion are yet to be discovered, it seems reasonable to expect that there are some differences in the functioning of the central nervous system that may imply important predispositions to respond to the external environ-ment in sex-differing ways. In addition, we know that men and women have differing internal biochemical environments; and it is reasonable to expect that these differences (especially in hormones) interact with psy-chosocial factors to produce, at least, predispositions toward sex-differing social behavior. To be sure, the internal (physiological) environment and the external (psychosocial) environment interact, and neither is "all important." Instead, it seems that each may affect the other. However, there are additional dimensions to the physiological differences between men and women—manifested in adulthood but defined in this prenatal critical period; the two most apparent differences are the female sex cycle and differences in sexual anatomy. We will discuss each one, keeping in mind possible psychological implications of these biological and physio-logical sex differences.

Sex Cycles and Mood Shifts

Until recently it was thought that one basic difference between men and women is that women have a monthly menstrual cycle, which involves periodic shifts in hormonal levels, periodic times of fertility, and monthly menstruation, while men are constantly able to produce sperm and were thought to produce hormones at constant rates. To be sure, women's menstrual cycle is a uniquely female characteristic; but recent evidence has suggested that men may also experience cyclic fluctuations in hor-mone production. For example, Exley and Corker (1966), in a study of four men over a period of 47 days, found an 8-to-10-day cycle in the fluctuating level of chemicals in male urine that results from testosterone production (probably from the testes). Recently developed techniques of measuring testosterone levels in the blood are currently being used in at least one large-scale study to identify the nature of these cycles. If these findings indeed confirm the presence of male cycles, they may shed considerable light on the similarities and differences of the hypothalamus (up to this point thought to function cyclically in women but not in men) and hormonal functions in men and women.

In women, the sex cycle is a complex process involving the interaction of the hypothalamus, pituitary, ovaries, and uterus. One complete cycle lasts about 28 days and is repeated fairly continuously from puberty until menopause. Two major hormones—*estrogen* and *progesterone*—play a central role and fluctuate cyclically during the 28 days. Two gonadratropic hormones, follicle-stimulating hormone (FSH) and luteinizing hormone (LH) are produced by the pituitary gland and interact with the level of estrogen and progesterone in a complex feedback process to regulate the cycle. Estrogen is at a low level during and immediately following menstruation; it peaks about the time of ovulation, declines and peaks again about the 22nd day of the cycle, and then declines rapidly a few days before menstruation (Figure 4.2). Progesterone rises after ovulation and peaks about the 22nd day; it declines along with estrogen before menstruation. FSH and LH also fluctuate, but it seems that the effects of changes in levels of estrogen and progesterone are more important.

Several studies have found a shift in various psychological measures reflecting the woman's mood and sense of well-being during the menstrual cycle. Frank (1931) termed these mood changes that occur after the twenty-second day "premenstrual tension." Benedek (1959) reported a nearly total absence of anxiety-related themes during the ovulation phase but found a high degree of feelings of anxiety and depression, fears of mutilation and death, and sexual fantasies during the premenstrual phase. In a study of 465 women, Coppen and Kessel (1963) found that depression and irritability were typically more severe before menstruation (when both estrogen and progesterone levels are declining rapidly) than during menstruation. Gottschalk, Kaplan, Gleser, and Winget (1962) and Ivey and Bardwick (1968) found a decrease in levels of anxiety and hostility, and high levels of self-esteem at ovulation (when estrogen is high) and a significant increase in anxiety, hostility, and depression during the premenstrual period (when estrogen and progesterone are low).

In the Ivey and Bardwick (1968) study, 26 "normal female college students" were asked to tell of an experience they had had. The level of anxiety (based on scores of the reported experience on the Gottschalk Verbal Anxiety Scale) was found to be significantly higher just before menstruation than at ovulation. However, there was no difference in anxiety scores between two successive ovulation phases, nor between two

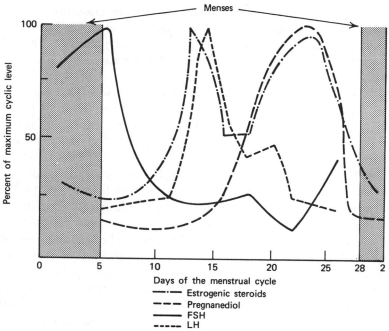

Figure 4.2
Variations in urinary gonadal and pituitary hormone secretion rates during the menstrual cycle. Hormone secretion rates are expressed as a percentage of the maximal cyclic level. Pregnanediol is a metabolite derived in part from progesterone and is assayed in order to estimate progesterone levels. (Source. Barkwick, 1971, Figure 3. Reprinted with permission of Harper & Row, Publishers, Inc. Copyright © 1971 by Judith M. Bardwick.)

premenstrual phases—which indicates a clear pattern of fluctuation. One theme of the stories that typically characterized the ovulation phase were feelings of self-satisfaction either about success, or about being able to cope successfully: "... so I was elected chairman. I had to establish with them the fact that I knew what I was doing. I remember one particularly problematic meeting, and afterwards, L. came up to me and said, 'you really handled the meeting well.' In the end it came out the sort of thing that really bolstered my confidence in myself" (Bardwick, 1971, p. 31).[1]

The same girl, premenstrually, expressed strikingly different feelings: "They had to teach me how to water ski. I was so clumsy it was really embarrassing 'cause it was kind of like saying to yourself you can't do it and the people were about to lose patience with me" (ibid). Another example at premenstruation expressing anxiety about death: "I'll tell you about the death of my poor dog M. ... Oh, another memorable event, my grandparents died in a plane crash. That was my first contact with death

[1] All quotations from Bardwick (1971) are reprinted with permission of Harper & Row, Inc. from *Psychology of Women*, copyright © 1971 by Judith M. Bardwick.

and it was very traumatic for me.... Then my grandfather died" (ibid., p. 32). In contrast, at ovulation, the same girl said, "Well, we just went to Jamaica and it was fantastic, the island is so lush and green and the water is so blue ... the place is so fertile and the natives are just so friendly" (ibid.).

One striking confirmation of their findings was that one respondent told of an experience that was scored quite high on anxiety although it was told at the time that ovulation would be expected; she began to menstruate the next day, two weeks early. More systematic confirmation was provided in a later study by Paige (1971) that compared women on two different types of contraceptive pill. One type, the combination pill, prevents ovulation by providing constantly high levels of both estrogen and progesterone so that there is no cyclic fluctuation. For these women, there was no significant change in levels of anxiety or hostility during what would otherwise be their monthly cycle. The second group of women were taking a sequential pill that consisted of 15 days of estrogen pills, followed by 5 days of estrogen and progesterone pills, and 7 days off (essentially duplicating the ordinary cyclic fluctuations). This group on the sequential pill was found to differ from the group on the combination (noncyclic) pill. They showed the same signs of anxiety when both estrogen and progesterone were low as women in a third group who were not taking any pill. This evidence suggests a causal link between fluctuations of the female sex hormones and shifts in mood.

In sum, these data lead to the tentative conclusion that declining or low levels of estrogen and progesterone are associated with negative emotions such as anxiety and hostility, while high levels of estrogen are associated with positive moods such as high self-esteem and feelings of well-being. Although these data are not sufficient to infer a causal relationship or even to pinpoint the specific hormonal changes involved or the ways in which the moods are affected, these initial data are highly suggestive. Bardwick concludes:

> As psychologists we would expect to find strong individual differences in reactions during the menstrual cycle. Instead, in almost all of our subjects we found the consistent and significant mood swings characteristic of a particular menstrual phase. These physical changes, probably endocrine changes, so influence psychological behavior that in spite of individual personality differences, even in normal subjects, psychological behavior seems predictable on the basis of menstrual cycle phase alone. Women may cope or not cope, become anxious, hostile, or depressive, appear healthy or neurotic, due as much to menstrual cycle phase as to core psychological characteristics (Bardwick, 1971, pp. 32-33).

To be sure, not all women report such mood shifts during their monthly cycle. Moos (1968) found that between 30 and 50 percent of 839 "normal young married women" reported cyclic symptoms of mood swings in irritability, tension, and depression. This suggests that many women, perhaps most, either do not experience marked mood changes, are not aware of them as cyclic changes, or successfully cope with them so that they are of minor importance. Certainly, we would expect that personality factors, satisfaction with one's various roles, and general coping ability would be as important in determining the effect of these shifts in hormone levels as the physiological changes themselves. Indeed, we again argue that the effects of physiological sex differences are most usefully seen as an interaction of biological, psychological, and social factors. One woman may feel little change in mood—or little negative effect of the mood shift— because she is involved in ego-satisfying projects. Another may automatically anticipate or adjust to the changes by scheduling her activities to minimize the effects of negative moods and to maximize the effects of positive moods. Most probably continue functioning without major change, just as all of us do on days when we "get up on the wrong side of the bed" or are dealing with other factors that decrease or enhance our feelings of competence and well-being.

The recent findings of male hormone cycles may indicate some cyclical variations in men's moods also. Ramey (1972) reports that a private transport company in Japan has adjusted bus routes and schedules to maximize efficiency and to minimize accidents among its male drivers on the basis of "the time of month for each worker." She also reports that a study made over 40 years ago of male factory workers found that their emotions varied on a near-monthly cycle. "Low periods were characterized by apathy, indifference, or a tendency to magnify minor problems out of all proportion. High periods were often marked by a feeling of well-being, energy, a lower body weight, and a decreased need for sleep" (Ramey, 1972, p. 11).

It seems clear that considerably more research needs to be done on the nature and the implications of these male and female sex cycles and on the interaction of the differing male and female sex hormones with psychosocial factors. While men and women differ in the levels of various hormones and perhaps in other biochemical ways as well, there may be important similarities in sex cycles that are only beginning to be understood. However, these data are more suggestive than conclusive at this point and current large-scale research on male cycles may shed considerable light on these issues in the next few years.

Menopause: When the Cycle Stops

Technically, the term *menopause* refers to the cessation of the menses; the term *climacterium* refers to the loss of reproductive ability. In women they are two sides of the same coin since when the menstrual cycle ends, reproductive ability also comes to an end. In men, there is no *menopause* (since there are no menses), but there probably is a climacterium late in life when fertile sperm are no longer produced. A related change with advancing age is the change in hormone production. With menopause, both estrogen and progesterone are no longer produced by the ovaries, and the level of these hormones drops markedly. In men the level of testosterone declines gradually with age, eventually reaching a very low level; however, fertility and the production of testosterone are separate phenomena, and some rather old men have fathered children, despite a presumably low level of testosterone. In addition, for both men and women, the ability to engage in satisfying sexual relations is unrelated to either hormone levels or to fertility. Thus, men and women are typically capable of continued sexual intercourse following menopause; and indeed, since there is no longer a need to worry about conception, sexuality may be enhanced (see Chapter 5).

Menopause typically occurs between the ages of 45 and 50. Although it is not clear why menopause occurs, it appears that the ovaries stop responding to the FSH produced by the pituitary; they do not respond by bringing an egg to maturity and do not produce estrogen. Thus the cycle ceases to operate. The onset may not be sudden, but may be preceded by a period of irregular cycles and menses. But eventually, fertility, the production of estrogen and progesterone, menstruation, and the cycle itself cease. An artificial menopause, usually caused by the surgical removal of the uterus and ovaries (hysterectomy), would have similar effects. However, since it is typically performed because of a medical problem, women may react to it differently than to normal menopause.

The frequency and severity of menopausal symptoms in the general population are not known. Yet a range of symptoms is commonly thought to be associated with it. These include physical symptoms such as hot flashes and breast pains, psychosomatic symptoms such as dizzy spells, headaches, and heart palpitations. Women sometimes are seen to become intolerant, hypochondriacal, depressed, or anxious. These symptoms occur in some women before menopause actually occurs; for others they may occur at the same time as the cessation of the menses or even several years later. Other women seem to remain entirely free of such symptoms (Neugarten, 1967a). The extreme symptoms often reported in medical literature and popular books are probably biased by the fact that women who are experiencing extreme symptoms would be the ones most likely to come to a physician's attention. Nonetheless, the decline in estrogen and progesterone production, and the increase in the gonadatropic hormone (FSH), may have immediate as well as long-term effects.

The range of menopausal symptoms, from hot flashes to loss of elasticity of the skin and changes in the breasts and genitals, may be treated with tablets or injections of artificial estrogen. Masters and Johnson (1970) point out that such sex-steroid replacement is often "...indicated in order to enable most women [in the 50-70 year age group] to continue to function effectively as interested and interesting sexual partners" (p. 342). Wilson (1966) reports that "nearly total avoidance of all menopausal symptoms was achieved" through estrogen treatment; and Kantor, Michael, Boulas, Shore, and Ludvigson (1966) found that 50 women (age 60-91) given estrogens showed a significant improvement in two out of three cases. And Neugarten (1967a) points out the importance of informing women and their physicians about the benefits of estrogen replacement, especially for the average woman in her late forties.

One empirical study of menopausal symptoms (Neugarten, Wood, Kraines, and Loomis, 1963) found that about one-half of their middle-class sample agreed that menopause is a disagreeable, depressing, disturbing, troublesome, unpleasant event; and one-half disagreed (Table 4.1). However, *middle-aged* women (over 45) were more likely than younger women to see positive changes after menopause has passed. Middle-aged women are also more likely than younger women to feel that menopause creates no major change in life, that the woman has a relative degree of control over the symptoms, and that they need not inevitably experience a crisis. Some women, particularly those with higher educational levels, felt that menopause was of little social-psychological importance:

"Why make any fuss about it?"

"I just made up my mind I'd walk right through it, and I did . . ."

"I saw women complaining, and I thought I would never be so ridiculous. I would just sit there and perspire, if I had to. At times you do feel terribly warm. I would sit and feel the water on my head, and wonder how red I looked. But I wouldn't worry about it, because it is a natural thing, and why get worried about it? I remember one time, in the kitchen, I had a terrific hot flush . . . I went to look at myself in the mirror. I didn't even look red, so I thought, 'All right . . . the next time I'll just sit there, and who will notice? And if someone notices, I won't even care . . .' "

Others confessed to considerable fear:

"I would think of my mother and the trouble she went through; and I wondered if I would come through it whole or in pieces . . ."

"I knew two women who had nervous breakdowns, and I worried about losing my mind . . ."

"I thought menopause would be the beginning of the end . . . gradual senility closing over, like the darkness . . ."

"I was afraid we couldn't have sexual relations after the menopause —and my husband thought so, too . . ."

Table 4.1 Attitudes Toward Menopause: By Age

Illustrative Items	Percentage Who Agree,[a] in Age Groups			
	A 21–30 (N=50)	B 31–44 (N=52)	C 45–55 (N=100)	D 56–65 (N=65)
"Negative Affect":				
Menopause is an unpleasant experience for a woman	56	44	58	55
Women should expect some trouble during the menopause	60	46	59	58
In truth, just about every woman is depressed about the change of life	48	29	40	28
"Post-Menopausal Recovery":				
Women generally feel better after the menopause than they have for years	32*	20*	68	67
A woman gets more confidence in herself after the change of life	12*	21*	52	42
After the change of life, a woman feels freer to do things for herself	16*	24*	74	65
Many women think menopause is the best thing that ever happened to them	14*	31	46	40
"Extent of Continuity":				
Going through the menopause really does not change a woman in any important way	58*	55*	74	83
"Control of Symptoms":				
Women who have trouble with the menopause are usually those who have nothing to do with their time	58	50*	71	70

Women who have trouble in the menopause are those who are expecting it	48*	56*	76	63
"Psychological Losses":				
Women worry about losing their minds during the menopause	28*	35	51	24*
A woman is concerned about how her husband will feel toward her after the menopause	58*	44	41	21*
"Unpredictability":				
A woman in menopause is apt to do crazy things she herself does not understand	40	56	53	40
Menopause is a mysterious thing which most women don't understand	46	46	59	46
"Sexuality":				
If the truth were really known, most women would like to have themselves a fling at this time in their lives	8*	33	32	24
After the menopause, a woman is more interested in sex than she was before	14*	27	35	21

[a] Subjects who checked "agree strongly" or "agree to some extent" are grouped together.

* The difference between this percentage and the percentage of Group C is significant at the .05 level or above.

Source. Neugarten et al. (1963). Reprinted with permission from *Vita Humana* (now *Human Development*), published by S. Karger, Basel.

"When I think of how I used to worry! You wish someone would tell you—but you're too embarrassed to ask anyone . . ."(Neugarten, et al., 1963).

In the broader social-psychological context, menopause may be seen as a developmental turning point; thus, it is important to note that it typically occurs in combination with one's children leaving home, fears about old age, and concerns about the health of one's husband (see Chapter 5). The 100 women between 45 and 55 in Neugarten's (1967a) sample indicated that of all the changes and fears of middle age, menopause does not rank very high (Table 4.2)—the greatest concern was widowhood. The most common complaints about being middle-aged were "getting older," "lack of energy," and "poor health or illness"; only a few women related these changes to menopause. Three-fourths of the women reported the "best thing" about menopause was either not worrying about pregnancy or not having to bother with menstruation; the worst things were not knowing what to expect, the pain and discomfort, and the indication of getting older. Four percent reported that the inability to have children or loss of sexual enjoyment was the "worst thing"; and three percent reported greater sexual enjoyment as the "best thing" about menopause. Most felt menopause has no effect on sexual relations or on physical and mental health; one-half felt that it has a negative effect on a woman's appearance, however. Individual differences in coping ability were also evident as some respondents indicated great discomfort but discounted the importance of menopause, while others did the opposite. In general, the respondents were eager to discuss menopause since there are apparently few social supports for menopausal women (as compared with the many such supports for pregnant women); and they frequently indicated an interest in more information about this seemingly taboo topic. These respondents also indicated that there is a social expectation for a crisis at menopause since they generally felt that "other women" see it more negatively than they see it themselves.

In summary, menopause is a biological change that may have important psychological implications for the individual woman. Not only does one's body cease functioning cyclically and the hormonal balance change but also one is relieved of the possibility of pregnancy. In addition, many "old wives" tales exist that say that menopause is inevitably unpleasant, and that it is a sign of old age. Neugarten has speculated that the severity of symptoms may be related to previous coping patterns with such psychosexual events as the first pregnancy, and to such psychological variables as the overall anxiety level and general sense of satisfaction. Adequate information—particularly about estrogen replacement—is also important. Thus this event is an important developmental turning point since it involves not only biological and phychological variables but also may mark the perceived beginning of "old age" and a general shift in life

Table 4.2 Attitudes Toward Menopause Among White Mothers 45–55
($N = 100$)

	Percent
The worst thing about middle age	
Losing your husband	52
Getting older	18
Cancer	16
Children leaving home	9
Menopause	4
Change in sexual feelings and behavior	1
What I dislike most about being middle-aged	
Getting older	35
Lack of energy	21
Poor health or illness	15
Feeling useless	2
None of these	27
The best thing about the menopause	
Not having to worry about getting pregnant	30
Not having to bother with menstruation	44
Better relationship with husband	11
Greater enjoyment of sex life	3
None of these	12
The worst thing about the menopause	
Not knowing what to expect	26
The discomfort and pain	19
Sign of getting older	17
Loss of enjoyment in sexual relations	4
Not being able to have more children	4
None of these	30
How menopause affects a woman's appearance	
Negative changes	50
No effect	43
Positive changes	1
No response	6
How menopause affects a woman's physical and emotional health	
Negative changes	32
No effect	58
Positive change or improvement	10
How menopause affects a woman's sexual relations	
Sexual relations become more important	18
No effect	65
Sexual relations become less important	17

Source. Neugarten (1967a), p. 44. Reprinted with permission from *Psychology Today* Magazine, copyright © 1967 by Communications/Research/Machines, Inc.

stages; it may also coincide with the woman's return to the work force after raising a family. And it may be a particularly difficult crisis for some women because so many factors are involved at once. However, as one woman phrased it: "Yes, the change of life is an unpleasant time. No one enjoys the hot flushes, the headaches, or the nervous tension. Sometimes it's even a little frightening. But I've gone through changes before, and I can weather another one. Besides, it's only a temporary condition" (Neugarten et al., 1963).

Differences and Similarities in Sexuality

Perhaps genital anatomy is the most apparent physiological difference between men and women. Certainly, the complementarity of sexual organs and the insertion of the penis into the vagina is, so far at least, necessary for the survival of our species. Surprisingly, however, until recently little was known about the precise similarities and differences in the functioning of male and female genitalia. Of course, the physical structure of the genitals and the physiology of the male's ejaculation has been known for some time; but the physiology of the female's orgasm—what causes it, how it is similar to and different from the male's orgasm, and what the connection is between the vaginal and the clitoral aspects of the orgasm—has been little understood. However, the recent research by Masters and Johnson (1966, 1970) produced a marked improvement in our knowledge about sexual physiology. For example, they report that male and female orgasms are physiologically similar, disregarding (of course) the anatomic differences. That is, the orgasm is initiated by similar muscles and involves a similar reflex mechanism in the responding muscles; the muscle contractions produce the expulsion of blood from the erectile chambers in men *and* in women (men have three chambers in the shaft of the penis that fill with blood to produce the erection; women have five such "erectile bodies") and indirectly also produce the ejaculation of semen in men and contractions of the lower vagina in women (Sherfey, 1972, p. 94). In addition, the female's orgasm results from congestion of blood in these erectile tissues in a manner akin to the male's erection, and the "actual orgasmic experiences are initiated in both sexes by similar muscle components" (Masters and Johnson, 1963, p. 90). In both men and women the sexual response cycle may be divided into four stages (somewhat less well-defined in men than in women). Phase I (excitation) occurs more rapidly in men than women and is characterized by the erection in men and by the rapid production of lubricating fluid in the vagina, increased diameter of the clitoris, and increased blood congestion in the labia major and labia minor in women; nipple erection occurred in all women and in about one-third of the men studied. Phase II (plateau) is marked by a high degree of blood congestion and sexual tension in the entire pelvic area for both men and women; there is a sexual flush of the chest, neck, and forehead in either sex and, in women, it frequently includes the lower abdomen, thighs, and lower back; it was noted in about 75 percent of the women and 25 percent of the men studied. The orgasmic phase (Phase III) occurs in two stages for men— the first part involves slight contractions of all the involved organs and is experienced as a sign of imminent ejaculation; the second part is the actual ejaculation produced by the same contracting muscles as are involved in the female's orgasm; the initial contractions occur at intervals of 8/10 of a second (the same as in women) for two or three expulsive efforts and then slow in spacing and in expulsive force. The female orgasm occurs in one longer stage. It is characterized by contractions of the uterus, vagina, and labia minor providing the sensation of pelvic visceral contractions associated with the orgasm. In both sexes there are contractions of the rectal sphincter muscles (intervals of 8/10 of a second), contractions of other body (skeletal) muscles, rapid and shallow breathing (hyperventilation), and rapid heart rates (100 to 160 beats per minute); a "sweating reaction" develops in 30-40 percent of either sex—usually on the soles of the feet and palms of the hands for men, but more widely distributed over the back, thighs, and chest for women. Phase IV (resolution) is a lengthy process of decreasing congestion of the many blood vessels involved in the sexual response cycle; this usually proceeds more slowly in women than in men.

Despite the many similarities in the sexual response cycle of men and women, there are marked differences as well. Most notable are the "refractory period" characteristic of the male's cycle and the ability of the woman to have repeated orgasms. That is, after completing the orgasm, the male requires a period of return to the plateau stage before another orgasm can be achieved; this period is relatively short in young men (the highest frequency was three in a 10-minute period) but typically requires complete resolution and a new response cycle in men over the age of 30. Women, however, are usually able to experience successive (or multiple) orgasms without loss of sexual tension below the plateau level; more than 50 percent of the female sample was capable of immediate return to the orgasmic experience.

If a female who is capable of having regular orgasms is properly stimulated within a short period after her first climax, she will in most instances be capable of having a second, third, fourth, and even a fifth and sixth orgasm before she is fully satiated. As contrasted with the male's usual inability to have more than one orgasm in a short period, many females, especially when clitorally stimulated, can regularly have five or six full orgasms within a matter of minutes (Masters and Johnson, 1961, p. 792).

Other notable differences include first, the male's ability to continue the orgasmic response, once begun, even in the event of distracting external stimuli or the cessation of stimulation; but the female's orgasmic response ceases when the stimulation ceases and is ended by external distractions. Second, the greater response time in the female pattern so that the excitement phase, which may last only seconds in men, may last from several minutes to hours in women (since the vasocongestive process is more generalized and takes longer to develop). Third, orgasmic responses are experienced by essentially all young men (peaking in frequency between puberty and age 20 according to the Kinsey data), but become most frequent among women during the adult years (ages 26-40). One part of the reason for this is that childbirth involves a "flooding" of the body with hormones (estrogen and progesterone) that Sherfey (1972) argues produces a "sudden and enormous growth and vascularization of the pelvic structures as great as or greater, I believe, than the pubertal transformation" (p. 127). She argues that this "pregnancy effect" combined with increased sexual experience is "much more" responsible for the increased capacity for regular and multiple orgasms (at the time the husband's sexual capacity may be declining) than any "recovery from neurotic fears or inhibitions" (p. 134). That is, after the birth of the second or third child and several years of sexual experience, the woman's capacity for orgasm is likely to increase to its peak, while the man's capacity peaks much earlier; yet, advancing age does not set any limits to sexual orgasm as long as there is continued sexual experience. Fourth, while there is variation in intensity of orgasm between individuals (both men and women) and between orgasms for the same individual, but apparently little difference between intensity between men and women, sexual arousal tends to occur more readily during the premenstrual phase of the woman's sex cycle. Kinsey, Pomeroy, Martin, Gebhard, and Associates (1953) noted that about 90 percent of American women prefer sexual relations during this luteal period (or last 14 days). Sherfey (1972) reports that

> ... During the luteal phase, the majority of women have a greater spontaneous interest in sexual matters, experience a greater desire to initiate love-making, find an increased ease in reaching the plateau phase of arousal, have a more copious transudate of a different, slightly "slippery" consistency, and achieve multiple orgasms with greater ease. This facilitation of sexual responsivity is due primarily to the higher base line of pelvic congestion and edema [accumulation of fluid] characteristic of the premenstrual phase and, in part, to the increased influences in support of a possible pregnancy at this time (pp. 96-97).

The possible evolutionary significance of these characteristics is apparent: increased interest in sexuality between ovulation and menstruation increases the chances of a pregnancy. Also, the increased sexual satisfaction following childbirth enhances the chances of one woman giving birth to several children, thereby increasing the survival chances of the species.

One of the most important findings of the Masters and Johnson research is that there is no difference, physiologically, between an orgasm reached through vaginal or clitoral stimulation and that, indeed, clitoral stimulation is always achieved during intercourse. That is, there is no vaginal orgasm without a clitoral orgasm since the orgasmic reaction includes all of the pelvic sex organs and is identical regardless of the mode or area of stimulation. While they found that the lower third of the vagina is an erotic zone during intercourse, its sensitivity is about equal to that of the clitoral shaft, but the clitoral glans is much more sensitive. During vaginal intercourse, the vaginal passageway narrows because of the increased accumulation of blood in the many veins; this leads to greater stimulation of the penis; the penile thrusts increase the stimulation on the tighter vaginal walls and also create simultaneous stimulation of the labia minor, the clitoral shaft, and glans as an integrated unit. The clitoral glans seems to be the most important source of stimulation.

> In by far the majority of instances, [the glans is] the indispensable initiator of the orgasmic reaction. With these observations, the evidence seems overwhelming: *it is a physical impossibility to separate the clitoral from the vaginal orgasm as demanded by psychoanalytic theory* (Sherfey, 1972, p. 85).

The implications of these findings about the sexual functioning of men and women are currently having important theoretical and practical influences—such as the debate in psychoanalytic circles about Freud's equation of vaginal sexuality with mature psychosexual development,[2] and the recent proliferation of clinics dealing with practical techniques of therapy with persons experiencing some kind of sexual dysfunction. For our purposes, however, the important implications are that men and women are at once physiologically similar and different in terms of sexual functioning. Certainly, an understanding of the differences may enhance sexual relations, but the striking data on the similarities clearly suggest that adult men and women have a great deal in common that may aid in understanding and communicating with one's partner; neither men nor women can ever really know what the experience of the other is like, but they can discuss it, if they will, so that the sexual relationship is a fully integrated aspect of their total relationship.

---

[2] The debate about whether a so-called "clitoral orgasm" is less mature than a "vaginal orgasm" postulated by Freud is too complex and tangential for a discussion here; see Sherfey (1972) and Bardwick (1971) for an introductory overview and for more basic references.

It is far too easy to generalize from the anatomical differences or from the physiological differences to personality and social differences between men and women. For example, Sherfey (1972) suggests that the woman's capacity for multiple orgasms ("satiation in insatiation") is an important factor in the social subjugation of women in monogamous, maternal roles in which they are dependent on their husband's (less insatiable) sexual desires; the relevance of this point for modern society and the implica-'tions of this sex difference in sexuality are highly complex questions, however, and easy generalizations, while fascinating, are likely to be too simple. Similarly, it is too simple to generalize from women's sexual "receptivity" and men's "activity" to such psychological differences as "passivity-activity" or "dependence-independence." Certainly, the human organism (as well as the sexual act) is more complex than such generalizations would suggest.

In sum, it is clear that there are anatomical sex differences that may contribute important psychosocial elements to one's identity; but the Masters and Johnson research also clearly indicates that these differences are intertwined with physiological similarities. This suggests that there is considerable latitude for cultural interpretations and exaggerations of physiological sex differences. While it seems likely that a wide variety of cultural patterns may be reinforced by these sex differences (including female-dominant societies where one woman has many husbands and male-dominant societies in which the man literally owns the woman), our growing understanding of physiological differences also suggests that men and women have a great deal in common that would allow both to transcend rigid sex-role constraints. Thus, while hormonal differences, different roles in procreation, and possibly different sex cycles distinguish men from women, the interaction of these physiological aspects with social-cultural and psychological-developmental factors together produce the sex differences that currently exist in our society. As Bardwick (1971) suggests, the cultural patterns probably both reflect and modify the implications of these physiological differences. To be sure, one does not begin life without physiological sex characteristics; but the meaning and importance of these differences depends largely on the social context into which one is born. So let us now turn to a closer examination of the interaction of these factors.

INTERACTION OF PHYSIOLOGICAL, PSYCHOLOGICAL, AND SOCIAL SEX DIFFERENCES

Although basic physiological differences are little affected by cultural or psychological factors, it is clear that sex differences (and similarities) are very much affected by society (through differential socialization of boys and girls) and by individual developmental progression. That is, all women experience relatively similar internal environments (such as fluctuations in levels of estrogen and progestorone), menstruation, pregnancy, and menopause; but the psychological meaning of these sex-related experiences differs from individual to individual; and the culture interprets and defines these experiences—and indeed, the entire meaning of being male or female—in differing ways. For example, Margaret Mead (1949), in her classic study, *Male and Female*, describes the great impact of culture:

> In every known society, mankind has elaborated the biological division of labour into forms often very remotely related to the original biological differences that provided the original clues. Upon the contrast in bodily form and function, men have built analogies between sun and moon, night and day, goodness and evil, strength and tenderness, steadfastness and fickleness, endurance and vulnerability. Sometimes one quality has been assigned to one sex, sometimes to the other. Now it is boys who are thought of as infinitely vulnerable and in need of special cherishing care, now it is girls. In some societies it is girls for whom parents must collect a dowry or make husband-catching magic, in others the parental worry is over the difficulty of marrying off the boys. Some peoples think of women as too weak to work out of doors, others regard women as the appropriate bearers of heavy burdens, "because their heads are stronger than men's." The periodicities of female reproductive functions have appealed to some peoples as making women the natural sources of magical or religious power, to others as directly antithetical to those powers; some religions, including our European traditional religions, have assigned women an inferior role in the religious hierarchy, others have built their whole symbolic relationship with the supernatural world upon male imitations of the natural functions of women. In some cultures women are regarded as sieves through which the best-guarded secrets will sift; in others it is the men who are the gossips. Whether we deal with small matters or with large, with the frivolities of ornament and cosmetics or the sanctities of man's place in the universe, we find this great variety of ways, often flatly contradictory one to the other, in which the roles of the two sexes have been patterned.
>
> But we always find the patterning. We know of no culture that has said, articulately, that there is no difference between men and women except in the way they contribute to the creation of the next generation; that otherwise in all respects they are simply human beings with varying gifts, no one of which can be exclusively assigned to either sex. We find no culture in which it has been thought that all identified traits—stupidity and brilliance, beauty and ugliness, friend-

liness and hostility, initiative and responsiveness, courage and patience and industry—are merely human traits. However differently
the traits have been assigned, some to one sex, some to the other,
and some to both, however arbitrary the assignment must be seen to
be (for surely it cannot be true that women's heads are both absolutely weaker—for carrying loads—and absolutely stronger—for carrying loads—than men's), although the division has been arbitrary, it
has always been there in every society of which we have any knowledge (Mead, 1949, pp. 7-8).[3]

In our view, what it means to be a woman (or a man) is a product of
the interaction of at least three interrelated processes: one's inner
(physiological) environment, one's social-cultural environment, and one's
(psychological) developmental progression from birth on. That is, in our
view, sex differences in adulthood are not the result of socialization alone,
nor of physiological factors alone, nor of psychological factors alone
(although each is certainly important). Instead, sex differences result
from the interaction of the inner and outer experience of being a male
or a female in a social network (family and society) from birth until
death. And all individuals forge their own sense of maleness or female-
ness out of this interaction of experiences as they progress through the
differing developmental experiences of boys and girls (which includes
differing oedipal conflicts and differing identification processes).[4]

Three manifestations of the interaction of these factors are differences
in the self, in personality patterns, and in the impact of these sex differences during adult years for men and women in our society. Let us first
discuss the differences in the self.

The Social Self: Male and Female

In many ways, one's gender functions as a label that is applied to oneself;
thus one's gender is a salient aspect of the self and may be seen as one
of the most important *me*s in a person's collection of *me*s. As we noted
in Chapter 3, the sexual *me* is one of the major components of an individual's identity, and the changes brought about in that aspect of the self
at puberty is a crucial part of the identity conflict: "Who am I as a
sexual person?" "What does it mean to be male or female?" "How do I
integrate the little boy/girl I was with the man/woman I have become
and the adult/parent/spouse I will become?"

[3] Reprinted with permission from *Male and Female*, copyright © 1949, 1967 by Margaret Mead.

[4] This topic of differing developmental processes in childhood is too complex and
beyond the scope of this chapter for discussion here; see Bardwick (1971), Chapter 1,
and Maccoby (1966) for an introduction to the area.

Such questions are at the core of the identity issue in adolescence and young adulthood and, in the symbolic interaction framework, one works through such issues by taking the role of others toward oneself (as a man or a woman), by reflexively looking at oneself as if one were someone else viewing oneself, and by integrating the various *me*s that one sees in such moments of self-consciousness into a coherent concept of the self. Simultaneously, the *I* is experiencing one's bodily feelings of being a male/female, feelings of being a sexual person, feelings of guilt, anxiety, and pleasure associated with sexual experiences, feelings one has as a man or woman in social interactions with other men and women, and such inner experiences as mood shifts and other feelings that may result from hormonal sex differences. From such *I-me* interactions, one evolves a concept of oneself over a long period of time, beginning in early childhood and continuing into adulthood.

In general, an individual's gender affects the self in two ways. First, part of our collection of *me*s includes a *me* that is a man or a woman; we clearly perceive and experience this *me*, and others also perceive it and respond to us accordingly. Second, many of our other *me*s are also permeated by those qualities that are typically called "masculine" or "feminine." Thus, an individual's *me*s are affected by the social sex-roles in the society; one's *me*s as a student, as a teacher, as a lover, and as a parent (and so on) are expected to be consistent with one's gender and, when they are not, social pressure may be brought to bear to encourage conformity of all of one's *me*s to the *me* specified by one's gender. This is one example of *role conflict* in which one's roles (*me*s) do not mesh well with one another; that is, when one takes the attitude of the other toward oneself, there is an inconsistency felt by the *I* and the offending *me* may be altered or this felt inconsistency may be managed internally by several coping or defensive mechanisms. For example, if one's *I* experiences a conflict between a *me* as a lover and the *me* as a man, serious questions of consistency may be experienced; or, if one experiences a conflict between the *me* as a lawyer and the *me* as a woman, the inconsistency (or role conflict) will be felt. However, such perceived inconsistencies (from the point of view of the other) may be outweighed by the feeling of consistency—for example between one's *me* as a man and one's *me* as a father who takes a paternity leave from work to care for his newborn infant; one's feeling of consistency between the *me* as a woman and the *me* as a business executive; or one's *me* as a man and as a homosexual lover. In such cases the self is consistent (as the *I* experiences it), and the inconsistency is between this sense of consistency and the perception of significant or generalized others who perceive an inconsistency. To resolve such conflict, one may attempt to change one's significant others to find persons whose perceptions concur with one's own perceptions of consistency; or one may (perhaps simultaneously) attempt to change the perceptions of these others to convince them that, indeed, these various *me*s are essentially consistent; or one may modify his set of *me*s to conform more closely to the perception of these others. Probably all of these processes occur in varying degrees at the same time. And it is of such processes that the evolution of an individual's self is made; it is from such unique combinations of *me*s that individualized selves and individual differences arise. And it is in the midst of such perceptions of inconsistency that the creative characteristic of the *I* may be most important, since new *me*s and new combinations of *me*s may always be produced to promote a sense of unity and coherence to the self.

In general, the content of the male or female *me* and the connotations of "masculine" and "feminine" are primarily produced by the continuing socialization processes begun at birth. As we discussed in Chapter 2, this process of socialization is the main mechanism by which cultural transmission of roles and norms takes place. It includes the subtle impact of "pink or blue" clothes (and so on) for the baby, encouragement of sex-typed behaviors, discouragement of sex-inappropriate behaviors ("girls don't fight; boys don't cry"), and standards of acceptable sexual behavior in adolescence. Typically, boys are responded to differently by significant others than girls; and as the self develops, the attitude of the generalized other is taken toward oneself, and the child learns that his gender *me* is linked to a range of sex-appropriate behaviors in society generally. To be sure, the content of this socialization differs from one culture to another. And it does not operate in a vacuum since the physiological differences undoubtedly interact with the socialization process; for example, it it likely that socialization not only modifies physiological predispositions (perhaps greater aggressiveness and activity in males) but also reflects these differences (by allowing greater physical aggression and activity for boys).

By adolescence, the content of culturally prescribed sex-roles is clearly understood, and the task becomes one of establishing a firm individual sense of one's sex- and sexual-role. Adult parental and occupational role behaviors also involve socialization, of course, and typically confirm and strengthen one's gender identity (or possibly put it to the test). However, with advancing age and completion of the tasks of child rearing, the meaning and importance of one's gender may change so that, on one hand, sex-roles become less salient in the perception of one's *me* and, on the other hand, greater tolerance is allowed for both men and women in the range of acceptable sex-role behavior—for example, retired men and women may play a number of roles that are more similar than different such as "grandparent." At the same time, with greater social and personal experience, one's set of *me*s would be likely to have evolved in such a way as to have resolved the feelings of inconsistency between the gender *me* and one's other *me*s. In addition, social expectations about role behavior change during the life span so that, for example, an old man would no longer be expected (or expect himself) to have an athletic *me* and could feel quite "male" sitting and watching younger persons playing football; and an old woman might not feel at all inconsistent in her set of *me*s if she took over the family business when her husband became too sick to manage it; but similar behavior at younger ages would tend to "raise the generalized other's eyebrow," so to speak.

Thus, one important way in which an individual's gender influences the person in adulthood is in terms of the self, role behaviors, social expectations, and one's experience of oneself as a sexual being. Let us expand on this latter point since it is reasonable to expect that the sex-differing hormones would affect one's experience of oneself, and the cycling of hormone production as well as menstruation in women would be likely to influence one's experience of being a woman. Bardwick (1971), for example, points out the ambivalence expressed by many young women about being a woman because it is associated with both pleasure and with pain and bleeding; being a woman involves both the gift and joy of producing a child and "the curse." Men, however, typically experience their maleness unambivalently as a source of pride and pleasure. Similarly, the experiences of pregnancy and of menopause are likely to markedly influence a woman's experience of herself. For example, since during pregnancy both estrogen and progestorone are at high levels, it may be expected that this period would be characterized by high self-esteem and low levels of anxiety (Bardwick is currently studying this hypothesis). In addition, the nurturing of a life (that, in our society, partly represents the fulfillment of a woman's identity) would be expected to be a major developmental turning point, and significant others would typically respond with support and encouragement, further enhancing self-esteem. Thus, both the *me* and the *I* would be likely to be positively affected (if the pregnancy is, in fact, desired). Certainly, the man's *me* changes when he becomes a father, but the experience of the changes (for his *I*) may well be less intense and different than for the woman. Similarly, in menopause, the change in the *I* ("hot flush," unpredictable feelings, and so on) and *me* ("I'm growing old," and so on) may be quite marked for some women, but the man does not face a similar event; instead, he may face impotence at some point that drastically affects his *me* as a man (i.e., one who can have an erection).

Thus, through a complex interaction of physiological and social influences, children develop into male or female adults; and they develop along somewhat different paths because they are boys or girls. They develop a sense of self (and, later, an identity) that is "male" or "female," and they experience adulthood in differing ways. Of course, the meaning of these differences, and the extent that the differences are emphasized or differentially rewarded, is largely a matter of the society (culture). But, in our society, these interacting differences seem clearly to produce some general sex differences—for example, in personality—that we now discuss.

Personality Differences

Certainly there are stereotyped differences that are generally thought to characterize the personality of men and women. These stereotypes usually portray men and women as *opposite* (although that assumption need not be made, and its denial may shed some light on similarities and the overlapping humanness of both sexes). For example, Rosenkrantz, Vogel, Bee, Broverman, and Broverman (1968) found that 41 items were agreed on by at least 75 percent of a college sample as either "masculine" or "feminine" (Table 4.3); in each case the items are opposite each other. In a recent report of this data Broverman, Vogel, Broverman, Clarkson, and Rosenkrantz (1972) conclude:

> Our research demonstrates the contemporary existence of clearly defined sex-role stereotypes for men and women.... Women are perceived as relatively less competent, less independent, less objective, and less logical than men; men are perceived as lacking interpersonal sensitivity, warmth, and expressiveness in comparison to women. Moreover, stereotypically masculine traits are more often perceived to be desirable than are stereotypically feminine characteristics.
>
> ... The stereotypic differences between men and women described above appear to be accepted by a large segment of our society. Thus college students portray the ideal woman as less competent than the ideal man, and mental health professionals tend to see mature healthy women as more submissive, less independent, etc., than either mature healthy men, or adults, sex unspecified. To the extent that these results reflect societal standards of sex-role behavior, women are clearly put in a double bind by the fact that different standards exist for women than for adults. If women adopt the behaviors specified as desirable for adults, they risk censure for their failure to be appropriately feminine; but if they adopt the behaviors that are designated as feminine, they are necessarily deficient with respect to the general standards for adult behavior (Broverman et al., 1972, p. 75).

Such stereotypes are very difficult to separate from more "real" sex differences between the personalities of men and women, precisely because the stereotypes tend to be internalized by the individual as guides for one's behavior and feelings. As Broverman et al. phrase it:

> Most importantly, both men and women incorporate both the positive and negative traits of the appropriate stereotype into their self-concepts. Since more feminine traits are negatively valued than are

Table 4.3 Stereotypic Sex-Role Items (Responses from 74 College Men and 80 College Women)

Competency Cluster: Masculine pole is more desirable	
Feminine	*Masculine*
Not at all aggressive	Very aggressive
Not at all independent	Very independent
Very emotional	Not at all emotional
Does not hide emotions at all	Almost always hides emotions
Very subjective	Very objective
Very easily influenced	Not at all easily influenced
Very submissive	Very dominant
Dislikes math and science very much	Likes math and science very much
Very excitable in a minor crisis	Not at all excitable in a minor crisis
Very passive	Very active
Not at all competitive	Very competitive
Very illogical	Very logical
Very home oriented	Very worldly
Not at all skilled in business	Very skilled in business
Very sneaky	Very direct
Does not know the way of the world	Knows the way of the world
Feelings easily hurt	Feelings not easily hurt
Not at all adventurous	Very adventurous
Has difficulty making decisions	Can make decisions easily
Cries very easily	Never cries
Almost never acts as a leader	Almost always acts as a leader
Not at all self-confident	Very self-confident
Very uncomfortable about being aggressive	Not at all uncomfortable about being aggressive
Not at all ambitious	Very ambitious
Unable to separate feelings from ideas	Easily able to separate feelings from ideas
Very dependent	Not at all dependent
Very conceited about appearance	Never conceited about appearance
Thinks women are always superior to men	Thinks men are always superior to women
Does not talk freely about sex with men	Talks freely about sex with men

Warmth-Expressiveness Cluster: Feminine pole is more desirable	
Feminine	*Masculine*
Doesn't use harsh language at all	Uses very harsh language
Very talkative	Not at all talkative
Very tactful	Very blunt
Very gentle	Very rough
Very aware of feelings of others	Not at all aware of feelings of others
Very religious	Not at all religious
Very interested in own appearance	Not at all interested in own appearance
Very neat in habits	Very sloppy in habits
Very quiet	Very loud
Very strong need for security	Very little need for security
Enjoys art and literature	Does not enjoy art and literature at all
Easily expresses tender feelings	Does not express tender feelings at all easily

Source. Broverman et al. (1972), p. 63. Reprinted with permission.

masculine traits, women tend to have more negative self-concepts than do men. The tendency for women to denigrate themselves in this manner can be seen as evidence of the powerful social pressures to conform to the sex-role standards of the society (ibid.).

Thus, these stereotypes are not only internalized to some degree through the socialization processes, but also influence levels of self-esteem for men and women. One side of this self-esteem coin is: "Am I really feminine/masculine?" The other side is: "Is a woman (or women's activities and characteristics) valued as much by the social-economic system as a man?" Obviously, self-esteem is likely to be a personality characteristic differing between men and women, and we will discuss it in more detail in a moment.

Sex stereotypes also affect one's personality characteristics since, as a result of socialization, men and women tend to develop differing degrees of aggressiveness, dependency, social sensitivity, and so on as well as differing patterns of social rewards (such as achievement or being highly popular). But we would also expect that physiological and developmental factors are involved in addition to these socialization pressures. That is, while social stereotypes and even the level and sources of self-esteem may be largely socially determined, personality characteristics also result from differing childhood development (such as patterns of identification with the same- and cross-sex parent) and physiological factors.

While it would be impossible to review all of the data that have been collected on sex differences in personality, there are several themes that stand out and that seem important for understanding adult men and women. One of these differences is in the dimension of *self-esteem* and the different sources of esteem that seem to be salient for men and women. A second is the *fear of success* that seems to occur in young women but not in men. A third theme is the different types of *motivation* that are salient for men and for women. And a fourth dimension is the constellation of *personality traits* that seem to differ for men and women. All of these themes are complexly interwoven in their effect on personality, and it is difficult to attempt to separate them, but it is even more difficult to discuss them all at once; thus, let us attempt to maintain a sense of their interaction as we explore each theme.

Self-Esteem. A few years ago Simone de Beauvoir (1953) described the "problem" of women from an existential framework. She analyzed the role of woman as an *object*, by which she meant more than a "sex object" (although it is only quite recently that men have been used as sex objects in magazine pictures designed for women). She argued that men function as a *subject*—active, manipulating, controlling, and generally taking an active stance toward the world of objects that includes women. Women, however, are looked at, manipulated, controlled, and generally passive—

like objects. Certainly this view is partly a stereotype, but when we examine the sources of self-esteem for women and men, women tend to be prized for how they appear to others (i.e., as "objects") while men are prized for what they accomplish (i.e., as "subjects"). For example, Bardwick (1971), based on her review of the psychological literature, asserts that

> Women ... tend to esteem themselves only insofar as they are esteemed by those they love and respect. Unlike the man, who is considered successful when he has achieved within his occupation, the woman who achieves is generally not considered successful unless she also has a husband and children (p. 158).

That is, there appears to be a greater importance placed on external or interpersonal sources of esteem among typical women and, consequently, less emphasis placed on internal standards of success. This difference need not be inherently negative toward women's self-esteem except that in our society, accomplishment tends to be valued as a source of esteem. That is, male-type, objective accomplishment is prized (and rewarded monetarily) while interpersonal success is less rewarded, and the woman's apparently major source of esteem turns out to be "second rate." In addition, stereotypes about the lesser value of women decrease the value of being a woman in one's own eyes and in the eyes of others. One recent study (Pheterson, Kiesler, and Goldberg, 1971) found that 120 women rated a series of abstract paintings higher if they were told that the artist's name was male (such as *David* Smith) than when told it was female (*Jane* Jones); another study (MacBrayer, 1960) found that females perceive males significantly more favorably than males perceive females. In sum, it appears that women tend to have lower levels of self-esteem and self-confidence than men partly because their sources of esteem seem to differ and partly because male sources of esteem and males generally are more highly valued.

Fear of Success. Horner (1968) found that a motive to avoid success was much more common among women college students than among men; in one study where respondents were asked to tell a story that began: "After first-term finals, Anne (if a woman subject; "John" if a man) found herself at the top of her medical-school class . . ."; only 9 percent of the men indicated any fear of this success, while two-thirds of the women did so ($N = 88$ and 90). Subsequent studies on various young adult samples have found this "fear of success" in 45 to 88 percent of the women (Table 4.4). In one sample fear of success was scored for 47 percent of the men and 88 percent of the women (a statistically significant difference), but it was a very different kind of fear for men than for women:

Most of the men who responded with the expectation of negative

Table 4.4 Incidence of Fear of Success Imagery in Samples Tested, 1964–1970

Study	Year Data Gathered	Nature of the Sample	Total N	Subjects Showing the Response TAT Format (Standard Verbal Cue)	
				N	Percent
Horner, 1968	1964	*College Freshmen & Sophomores*	178		
		Males	88	8	9.1
		Females	90	59	65.5
Horner & Rhoem, 1968	1967	*All Female*			
		Junior high (7th grade)	19	9	47.0
		Senior high (11th grade)	15	9	60.0
		College undergraduates	27	22	81.0
		Secretaries	15	13	86.6
		Students at an Eastern University			
Schwenn, 1970	1969	Female juniors[a]	16	12	75.0
Horner, 1970b	1969	Female juniors/seniors	45	38	84.4
		Same subjects[a]	45	34	75.5
		Female law school students	15	13	86.6
Watson, 1970	1970	Female summer school students	37	24	65.0
Prescott, 1971	1970	Male freshmen	36	17	47.2
		Female freshmen	34	30	88.2
		Same females 3 months later	34	29	85.3

[a] Questionnaire format employed.
Source. Horner (1972), p. 160. Reprinted with permission.

consequences because of success were not concerned about their masculinity but were instead likely to have expressed existential concerns
about finding a "non-materialistic happiness and satisfaction in life."
These concerns, which reflect changing attitudes toward traditional
kinds of success or achievement in our society, played little, if any,
part in the female stories. Most of the women who were high in fear
of success imagery continued to be concerned about the discrepancy
between success in the situation described and feminine identity
(Horner, 1972, pp. 163-164).

Unusual excellence in women was clearly associated for them with
the loss of femininity, social rejection, personal or societal destruction, or some combination of the above. Their responses were filled
with negative consequences and affect, righteous indignation, withdrawal rather than enhanced striving, concern, or even an inability to
accept the information presented in the cue. There was a typical
story, for example, in which Anne deliberately lowers her academic
standing the next term and does all she subtly can to help Carl, whose
grades come up. She soon drops out of med-school, they marry, and
Carl goes on in school while she raises their family (ibid., pp. 162-
163).

Horner also had the subjects perform tasks in competitive and noncom-
petitive situations with both men and women; she found that two-thirds
of the men did better in competitive conditions, while only one-third of
the women did so. She concluded: "The results suggest that women,
especially those high in the motive to avoid success, will explore their
intellectual potential to full measure only when they are in a noncom-
petitive setting and least of all when competing against men" (Horner,
1968, p. 11). Thus, these data suggest that striving for socially valued types
of esteem (such as achievement, success, and accomplishment) may be
threatening for many young women as it may interfere with winning
affection, approval, and social success. And the data are remarkably consistent in finding women to be more socially conscious or more dependent on receiving esteem from others than is true for men (Oetzel, 1966).
This seems to imply, on one hand, that in our contemporary society,
femininity may conflict with achieving socially rewarded "success"; and,
on the other hand, it suggests that men and women may be motivated
by differing goals (such as "achievement success" for men and "affiliation
success" for women). Let us explore this point further.

Achievement and Affiliation Motivations. McClelland, Atkinson, Clark, and
Lowell (1953) defined a concept that they called *achievement motivation*
as a propensity to compete in situations where there are standards of
excellence. It is generally assumed that this motive is internalized so that

a high degree of achievement motivation may be characteristic of a particular individual. Also it is assumed that this motive to achieve is independent of (i.e., not related to) another motive, *affiliation motivation*. In brief, a person high on achievement motivation would strive because of the internal standard of excellence and would gain satisfaction from producing successful accomplishment; a person high on affiliation motivation would strive for esteem from others. Certainly, any person would respond to either type of motivation, but it is typically found that women are characteristically higher on affiliation motives than men (Oetzel, 1966; Walberg, 1969). And it was the lack of clear achievement motivation in women that led Horner to develop her theory about a motive to avoid success that seems to function as a competing motive to achievement motivation in women but not in men. For example, Hoffman (1972) concludes her review of research on achievement motivation in childhood by pointing out that "the data suggest that they [females] have higher affiliative needs and that achievement behavior is motivated by a desire to please. If their achievement behavior comes into conflict with affiliation, achievement is likely to be sacrificed or anxiety may result" (p. 149). In contrast, men are more readily motivated by internal standards of excellence and competition, which are reinforced by the social role for men, and by our highly achievement-oriented society. This suggests that "achievement" may mean different types of accomplishment for men and women. Veroff (1969) has suggested that in girls, external support is of critical importance for achievement, while for boys, achievement is stimulated by internal standards of excellence. And Bardwick (1971) has hypothesized that although the motives for achievement and affiliation are independent of each other in men, they are combined for women so that women strive for "affiliative-achievement" and are motivated to achieve success in interpersonal relationships and in the affiliative role with husband and children. However, there is some interesting data that suggest that (at least among college-educated women) "male-type" achievement motivation (measured from stories told after looking at Thematic Apperception Test cards) increases among women who have been out of college for 15 years (Baruch, 1966); while longitudinal data are crucial to confirm this hypothesis, it may be that the success in family roles and changes in one's self-concept decrease the fear of success motivation and allow women to respond to achievement needs without conflict with their feminine self-concept and needs for affiliation. To be sure, this difference in motivation between men and women (as well as achievement motivation in general) is primarily a cultural characteristic. A recent study comparing American and Danish adolescents found a much higher emphasis on affiliative concerns for the Danish adolescent than for the American, and that achievement was emphasized much more by adolescents in the United States than in Denmark (Kandel and Lesser, 1972).

Personality Characteristics. As with differences in levels of self-esteem, fear of success, and achievement motivation, sex differences in personality characteristics are undoubtedly the result of the interaction of physiological, psychological, and social-cultural factors. For example, one series of studies by Witkin, Dyk, Faterson, Goodenough, and Karp (1962) found sex differences in a type of *cognitive style* called "field independence/dependence." In one experiment, the subject sits in a dark room and watches an illuminated rod and frame; the task is to tell the experimenter when the rod is vertical although both the frame and the subject's chair may be tilted so that inner cues of verticality must be used instead of perceptual cues alone. They found that women tend to perceive the rod as vertical in terms of the frame, while men tend to disregard the "field" and to judge verticality on the basis of internal cues of uprightness. Several related experiments suggest the conclusion that women tend to be more field dependent than men; in this sense, men tend to be more independent and analytical while women are more subjective and dependent on cues from the environment. Is it plausible that these differences result from socialization alone, or are they more likely the result of the interaction of social, developmental, and physiological factors? In general, girls are found to be more socially sensitive and dependent in nearly all studies (Oetzel, 1966). And young women seem to have a better memory for names and faces than young men do (Kaess and Witryol, 1955). Several studies have also indicated that girls are more dependent, suggestible, and more conforming than boys (Maccoby, 1966), suggesting a greater passivity among women than men. Social factors are clearly involved in this. Perhaps the pattern is that some basic predispositions (such as greater reliance on external rather than internal stimuli or some kind of social sensitivity) is enhanced and built upon by social and developmental factors into a distinct—almost stereotypic—difference: passive-dependent women and aggressive-independent men. For men, the aggressiveness may reflect the presence of testosterone but again, this is overlaid by a thick coating of social and developmental pressures so that men are found to be more aggressive than women in all types of aggression except verbal, where women occasionally score higher than men (Oetzel, 1966).

Sex differences have also been found in *ego style*. Gutmann (1968) observed that men and women respond differently to the presentation of TAT cards when they were asked to look at the card and tell a story about it.

> Men tended to approach the cards as a task or as a puzzle, while women . . . responded to the cards as if they actually were vivid, exciting or troubling events, rather than representations of such events. . . .
>
> Most interesting was that women seemed to find this rather bound-

aryless mode congenial and perhaps even adaptive. Men who demonstrated an unboundaried approach to the TAT showed up as neurotic by other independent measures. But women who featured the unboundaried TAT approach achieved higher scores on life satisfaction and morale than did their more contained and boundaried sisters. That is, the women whose ego style resembled the normative male style was more apt than either the typical man *or* the typical woman to be anxious, depressed, neurotic (Gutmann, 1968).

In some ways these observations parallel the findings of greater field dependence in women. But they also suggest that, at least in the current realities of our society, these sex differences may be positive qualities related to satisfaction and morale. That is, personality qualities on which women may excel need not be considered negative; they may be "healthy" and competent personality styles, such as passivity or dependency.

In women, healthy dependence means a sensitivity to the needs of persons who are important to them, which allows appropriate nurturant or supportive behaviors (Bardwick, 1971, p. 115).

Passivity in the sense of indrawing, of elaborating and evolving a rich, empathic, intuitive inner life—in contrast with activity directed outward—may be a necessary part of the personality equipment of healthy women. It is also probable that this tendency is a preferred coping technique at particular times such as during pregnancy or in those years when one is nurturing very young children (ibid., p. 125).

And what of men? Is there "healthy aggression" for them? Probably, but might they not also be capable of "healthy dependence" or "passivity"; and might women not also be capable of "healthy aggression" and so on? Certainly, not all women are passive and not all men are aggressive; but at this point in time in our society these characteristics seem to stand out as differential aspects of femininity and masculinity.

Implications. These data indicate that the general outlines of male and female stereotypes in our society are borne out by studies of sex differences in personality. However, it is probable that these sex differences are a joint product of social role prescriptions (including the stereotypes) and physiological and psychological factors. While we do not yet have very satisfactory data about the nature or implications of these biological differences, it would seem that they are much more subtle than the obvious differences in genital structure or the active/passive roles in sexual intercourse (which, of course, are as much a result of social norms as of genital differences). Yet, given the current realities of socialization processes and the development of sex-role identities in our society, these personality differences seem to be the present reality and are therefore important to note. However, it is important to consider that individual differences are likely to be large and equally important. Moreover, social class differences (as well as differences between subcultures within American society) are likely to be marked. For example, sex roles of low-income black men and women appear to differ markedly from the ones we have discussed here in that the woman often has primary responsibility for the income and stability of the family, and the man has considerable difficulty developing a masculine self-image due to discrimination and lack of opportunity for achievement. Also, current Women's Liberation movements are likely to have some effect on roles and sex-discrimination—at least among the better educated women who probably already have greater role freedom and greater opportunity for choosing a life style that is personally satisfying.

Sex Differences Through the Life Cycle

While much attention has been focused on personality differences between men and women, perhaps an even more important consideration is the differing developmental progression for men and women through the adult years in our present society. Although there are differences in childhood and in early development, we will begin our summary of some of these differences in adolescence when sexuality becomes explicitly important.[5] Adolescent boys typically value men, want to become a man, and feel no conflict between their sexuality and being a man; girls, however, often feel ambivalent about their sexuality as the physical changes are linked with blood and pain and may bring fears of being entered by a man and being pregnant while, at the same time, these changes mark the beginning of womanhood. For girls, the conflicts between achievement and affiliation, between doing well and being attractive, and between being feminine and being a sex object come to the fore. Certainly boys have conflicts about whether they are adequately masculine; but being popular, masculine, and successful do not contradict each other. In late adolescence (and young adulthood), young men come to grips with their identity and, again, the links between masculinity and vocational and academic success do not conflict but together form a major part of the man's sex identity. For young women, it is assumed that their identity involves being a wife and mother, regardless of whatever else they may do. Somehow this conflict between being "traditionally feminine" and also productively involved in a vocation or a profession needs to be resolved, and even today this seems not to be an easy task. Fear of success, fear of losing affiliative satisfactions, and fear of failure, as well as anxiety seem to be some of the responses to this conflict. How-

[5] This discussion is based on Bardwick's (1971, pp. 207-216) excellent summary.

ever, Gump (1972) found that most women believe it is possible to be a wife and mother while also being involved in extrafamilial interests, and respondents high on a measure of "ego strength" (purposiveness, resourcefulness, and self-direction) were actively pursuing both goals rather than "traditional" goals of only wife and mother roles.

While marriage is an important milestone for a man, it is typically merged with an enduring vocational commitment and is an additional manifestation, but not a definition, of his masculinity. For a woman, marriage may mark the resolution of her identity crisis (perhaps symbolized by her change of name).

> Because of their investment in the relationship, because of their history of assessing themselves by others' responses, and because they really do perceive reality in interpersonal terms, they overwhelmingly define and evaluate identity and femininity within the context of this relationship (Bardwick, 1971, p. 211).

We will discuss the family and occupation during the middle years in Chapters 5 and 6; however, a brief overview of the sex differences is appropriate here. Bardwick suggests that the birth of the first child is the greatest developmental task for a women. While the father takes pride and is psychologically invested in his child, the mother's femininity is fulfilled—she has produced a "real achievement"—and her needs for affiliative satisfaction shift to encompass the child in addition to her husband. "Pregnancy and early maternity may be 'peak' experiences, the emotion felt toward the child, largely joy" (ibid., pp. 211-212). However, maternity is an ambivalent and difficult role. Not only is child rearing difficult and complex but the energy required by this task leaves little for occupational investment, and there are a host of normative behaviors (such as participation in the PTA) that are expected of mothers. Educated women may fear that they are losing their intellectual abilities while doing routine, repetitive household tasks. Or the mother who is also working may feel anxious about not depriving her children, husband, and herself of their rightful "feminine" attention. Seldom do these issues pose conflicts with a man's occupational role or his sense of masculinity.

If the marriage breaks up, although divorce is usually a devastating experience for both partners, it may be particularly traumatic for the woman. It is a personal crisis for both persons, but it is also a failure of "affiliation achievement" for the woman and is likely to bring up questions of identity that may have been passed over as she shifted her identity (and dependency?) from daughter to wife. She must cope with a double or triple crisis, often with the added burden of children while the man can rely on his occupational identity and may find dating and remarriage easier.

If the marriage is a good one, it is probably 10 to 15 years old during the partners' thirties, and the woman's level of sexual satisfaction has probably developed fully while the man's sexual desire may be declining partly because he is highly involved in his occupation. The wife-mother may feel "trapped" at home while the husband-father is exposed to a potentially more "exciting" world, and he may continue growing at a faster rate than his wife.

The forties brings menopause, the launching of the children from the home, and the awareness of middle age. These changes may involve redefinitions of the self, awareness of one's own mortality, and a kind of mourning process for the women when the children leave home. Neugarten (1967b) found that middle-aged women tend to associate "middle age" with the launching of their children. Even unmarried women often time the beginning of middle age by the family they might have had. Men, in contrast, are more likely to time the beginning of middle age by cues from the occupation or from physical decline and the illness or death of friends.

"It was the sudden heart attack in a friend that made the difference. I realized that I could no longer count on my body as I used to do . . ." (Neugarten, 1967b).

Neugarten reports that women become concerned over the health of their husbands at this time and while men are feeling increased physical vulnerability, women tend to engage in what she terms "rehearsal for widowhood." Also, women are likely to feel a sense of increased freedom at this point and may also gain a new degree of self-understanding.

Aging also differs between men and women. Certainly, death rates and suicide rates are higher for men than women at all ages; but women can almost always expect to live longer and healthier lives (from childhood on) than men and to live out the late years of their lives with other women far exceeding men in their circle of friends.

Popular writers such as Sontag (1972) and Beauvoir (1972) have recently called attention to the "double standard of aging"—which may have far more impact than simply living longer. For example, insofar as women receive considerable esteem for their physical appearance, when advancing age reduces their attractiveness (in our "youth-oriented" society), their self-concept and self-esteem are diminished in ways that do not occur for men (especially "successful" men). Similarly, while older men receive social approval for marrying or dating younger women, older women are seldom likely to date younger men (although in some countries older women are felt to be appropriate initial sexual partners for young men since they have had more experience). Thus, older women who divorce or are widowed are usually less able to find suitable marriage partners than is the case for older men. However, as we will discuss in Chapter 7, sex differences seem to decrease in salience with advancing age; for example, it is likely that a grandfather will be around the house and will be willing to play with young children as readily as will the grandmother. Thus, while aging may affect women more severely and earlier than men in terms of the self-concept and self-esteem, there is also a sense in which sex differences and sex-role stereotypes become less salient among older persons.

SEX DISCRIMINATION IN FACT AND THEORY

There is hardly a characteristic of an individual that is more apparent or more universally noted by others in social interaction than the individual's gender. Certainly, racial characteristics (such as skin color), socioeconomic status, age, physical disability, and flagrant expressions of social or psychological deviance may be equally noticeable; but there is a sense in which these bases of discrimination become less salient as individual personal relationships deepen and other aspects of the individual's uniqueness become more important. However, this does not seem to be the case with gender differences; the salience of the differences between men and women tends not to decrease (and may, in some ways, increase) with deeper social involvement. That is, while increased social contact and "integration" may decrease the importance of skin color or age or physical handicaps, "integration" of the sexes has not made gender a nonsalient dimension of a person. Not only does an individual's gender affect the responses of the persons *she* casually passes on the street, but also it permeates nearly all interpersonal relationships. And obviously, this type of "discrimination" is necessary for heterosexuality to be more than a chance occurrence and, in this sense, is necessary for the survival of the human species.

In general, any dimension that is regarded as *salient* about a person may be the basis of discrimination—some of the most typical are race, religion, gender, and age. We tend to wonder what cues are used to distinguish between Protestants and Catholics in a country such as Northern Ireland because, in our country, this dimension is not salient; yet, if eye or hair color were defined as salient characteristics about an individual, it would follow that even these items could be used as the basis for discrimination.

Although the origin and dynamics of prejudice are complex, it seems clear that when some characteristic is deemed significant, it can become the basis of discrimination and prejudice. However, reducing the salience of gender as a basis for discrimination may take either of two forms, which are essentially political decisions: (1) To assume that whatever sex differences may exist are not relevant to full participation in socioeconomic positions, and that only individual differences, apart from gender, should be considered; or (2) To enhance the importance and status of socioeconomic positions for which women are likely to be more competent than men. Perhaps both may occur simultaneously. The first position implies that traditionally male positions and abilities will continue to be rewarded, and those women who develop the "masculine" qualities of aggressiveness, achievement motivation, objectivity, and so on will excel. The second position implies that areas of competence may differ for men and women, and only when such abilities as interpersonal sensitivity, subjectivity, and nurturance, for example, are equally valued with the "masculine" abilities will some semblance of equality exist. As Bardwick phrases it:

> Women are able to successfully compete in the masculine occupational world to the extent that they can bring "masculine" personality qualities to the role: objectivity and not subjectivity, assertion and not passivity, achievement motivation and not fears of success or commitment or ambition and drive. By temperament and socialization, relatively few women have these personality qualities. Success can be achieved by a greater number of women in less masculine occupations—those that professionalize interpersonal communication, subjectivity, empathy and nurturance—not simply because these are traditionally feminine fields but because the personality qualities women bring to these fields aid them in achieving (Bardwick, 1971, pp. 162-163).

This does *not* mean that women are better suited to cleaning house, typing letters, and answering the telephone than men; but it may mean that hiring women for executive and professional positions may also bring skills in which men typically do not excel into the position; and these new skills should be rewarded as highly as the more traditional masculine skills.

However, we presently lack clear data on the implications of many of these sex differences; and indeed, these differences involve a large measure of socialization in addition to the physiological differences. Thus, it is clear that what a society would offer men and women in a minimal discrimination situation (perhaps best approximated in Scandinavian and Communist countries) is quite different from the current situation in our country. For example, the percentage of women in medical, legal, and engineering professions is considerably lower in the United States than in other countries, and the percentage in education is somewhat higher (Table 4.5); but it seems clear that these differences reflect differing social systems and do not necessarily indicate "natural" inclinations of either men or women, if there is such a thing. In the United States, the percentage of women in various professions and trades has changed relatively little since 1950 (Table 4.6), so there seems little indication of a

Table 4.5   Percentage of Women in the Medical, Legal, Engineering, and
            Higher Education Professions in Various Countries (Middle
            1960s)

Country	Medical	Legal	Engineering	Higher Education
USSR	76	38	37	36
Great Britain	25	4	0.06	15
France	22	19	3.7	20
West Germany	20	5	1	6
Austria	18	7	NAa	12
Sweden	13	6.7	NAa	11
USA	6	3	0.07	22

a NA: data not available.

Source. Sullerot, Evelyne. *Women, Society and Change.* (Translated by M. S. Archer.)
New York: McGraw-Hill (World University Library), 1971, Tables 5.6, 5.7, 5.8, and 5.10.
Reprinted with permission.

Table 4.6   Percentage of Women in Various Occupations 1950 and 1970

	1950	1970
Nurses	97.6	97.3
Secretaries, typists	94.6	96.6
Telephone operators	95.8	94.5
Bank tellers	44.6	86.2
Retail clerks	48.9	56.5
Editors, reporters	32.1	40.6
Postmasters	44.9	31.8
Bakers	11.6	30.0
Buyers	24.6	29.8
Teachers, college	22.4	28.6
Bus drivers	2.9	28.0
Accountants	14.9	26.2
Bartenders	6.4	21.1
Doctors	6.7	9.3
Lawyers, judges	4.1	4.9
Architects	3.8	3.6
Clergy	4.4	2.9
Electricians	0.6	1.9
Engineers	1.3	1.6
Auto mechanics	0.6	1.4

Source. *Economic Report of the President.* Washington, D.C.: U.S. Government Printing
Office, 1973, Table 33, adapted.

general trend away from sex-typed occupations—as a result of either discrimination or preference.

The central thrust of arguments about sex discrimination in employment is that currently, and with little realistic basis, women are markedly underrepresented in many occupations for which they might be personally and intellectually qualified and are paid less than men for the same work. And the gap between the income of working men and women is *increasing* because of the faster gains of men (Figure 4.3). Even in professions such as psychology where women's talents should favor employment, there are clear signs of greater unemployment among women than men, perhaps largely the result of women being "laid off" first when the

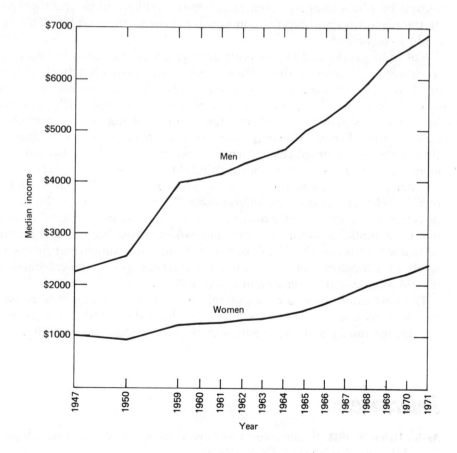

Figure 4.3
Median income in dollars for men and women in the United States, 1947–1971. (Source. U.S. Bureau of the Census. Money Income in 1971 of Families and Persons in the United States. Current Population Reports, Series P-60, No. 85. Washington, D.C.: U.S. Government Printing Office, 1972, Table 47.)

job market began to shrink (Astin, 1972). And certainly there are ample data that women are being discriminated against in employment. For example, studies conducted at various universities in recent years generally find that fewer women are granted tenure, women receive less salary, are underrepresented in many fields (compared with the number of qualified persons), are given less prestigious positions, take longer for promotion, or do not have as much administrative power as men; even when two equally qualified applicants are being considered, men are generally favored over women (cf. Lewin and Duchan, 1971). Women also suffer a "double standard" in getting credit, borrowing money, or buying stock (*Newsweek*, 1972). And Chesler (1972) has documented the psychological "double standard" by which women are more likely to be in therapy or mental hospitals than men, but men are more likely to be the therapist or the person responsible for committing them to the hospital. This list could go on and on.

Not to be overlooked in this issue are the discriminations that men are subjected to because of their gender. Some are relatively trivial such as not being able to show affection toward other men or not being able to show emotion and cry openly. But others are more serious such as having little chance of gaining custody of children or receiving alimony and child support after divorce. However, more important perhaps is the range of similarities—in human characteristics, potentials, and needs—between men and women. While one approach might be to ignore sex differences, another possible approach might be to allow greater individual flexibility in role behaviors and social interactions. To some observers this latter direction is the one along which our society is evolving. This, of course, will have implications for both men and women. Possibly the next decade or two will bring not only increased opportunity for women but increased levels of self-esteem, and perhaps even changes in the typical developmental progression for women in adulthood.

The next interlude is·a case example of a young working mother who has dealt with a number of the issues we have discussed. Then we will discuss the family and single adults during the middle years of life.

References

Astin, Helen S. 1972. Employment and Career Status of Women Psychologists. *American Psychologist,* 27(5), 371–381.

Bardwick, Judith M. 1971. *Psychology of Women.* New York: Harper & Row.

Baruch, Rhoda. 1966. *The Interruption and Resumption of Women's Careers.* Cambridge, Mass.: Harvard Studies in Career Development, No. 50.

Beauvoir, Simone de. 1953. *The Second Sex.* (Translated by H. M. Parshley.) New York: Alfred Knopf.

Beauvoir, Simone de. 1972. *The Coming of Age.* (Translated by Patrick O'Brian.) New York: G. P. Putnam and Sons.

Benedek, Therese F. 1959. Sexual Functions in Women and Their Disturbance. In S. Arieti (Ed.), *American Handbook of Psychiatry.* New York: Basic Books.

Broverman, Inge K.; Vogel, Susan Raymond; Broverman, Donald M.; Clarkson, Frank E.; and Rosenkrantz, Paul S. 1972. Sex Role Stereotypes: A Current Appraisal. *Journal of Social Issues, 28*(2), 59–78.

Chesler, Phyllis. 1972. *Women and Madness.* New York: Doubleday.

Christian, J. J. 1955. Effects of Population Size on the Adrenal Glands and Reproductive Organs of Male Mice in Populations of Fixed Size. *American Journal of Physiology, 182*(2), 292–300.

Coppen, Alec, and Kessel, Neil. 1963. Menstruation and Personality. *British Journal of Psychiatry, 109*(463), 711–721.

Delgado, Jose M. R. 1969. *Physical Control of the Mind.* New York: Harper & Row.

Exley, D., and Corker, C. S. 1966. The Human Male Cycle of Urinary Oestrone and 17- Oxosteroids. *Journal of Endocrinology, 35*(1), 83–99.

Frank, R. T. 1931. The Hormonal Causes of Premenstrual Tension. *Archives of Neurology and Psychiatry, 26,* 1053.

Gottschalk, L. A.; Kaplan, S.; Gleser, G. D.; and Winget, C. M. 1962. Variations in Magnitude of Emotion: A Method Applied to Anxiety and Hostility During Phases of the Menstrual Cycle. *Psychosomatic Medicine, 24*(3), 300–311.

Gump, Janice Porter. 1972. Sex-Role Attitudes and Psychological Well-Being. *Journal of Social Issues, 28*(2), 79–92.

Gutmann, David L. 1968. Female Ego Styles and Generational Conflict. Paper presented at the Midwestern Psychological Association, Chicago, May, 1968. In Judith M. Bardwick et al. (Eds.), *Feminine Personality and Conflict.* Belmont, California: Brooks/Cole, 1970.

Hampson, J. S., and Hampson, J. G. 1961. The Ontogenesis of Sexual Behavior in Man. In W. C. Young (Ed.), *Sex and Internal Secretions.* Vol. 2. Baltimore: Williams and Wilkins.

Harris, Geoffrey W. 1964. Sex Hormones, Brain Development and Brain Function. *Endocrinology, 75*(4), 627–648.

Harrison, G. A.; Weiner, J. S.; Tanner, J. M.; and Barnicot, N. A. 1964. *Human Biology.* New York: Oxford University Press.

Hoffman, Lois Wladis. 1972. Early Childhood Experiences and Women's Achievement Motives. *Journal of Social Issues, 28*(2), 129–155.

Hook, E. B., and Kim, D. S. 1971. Height and Antisocial Behavior in XY and XYY Boys. *Science, 172*(3980), 284–286.

Horner, Matina S. 1968. A Psychological Barrier to Achievement in Women— The Motive to Avoid Success. Symposium presentation at the Midwestern Psychological Association, Chicago, May, 1968. Cited in Bardwick (1971).

Horner, Matina S. 1972. Toward an Understanding of Achievement Related Conflicts in Women. *Journal of Social Issues, 28*(2), 157–176.

Ivey, Melville E., and Bardwick, Judith M. 1968. Patterns of Affective Fluctuation in the Menstrual Cycle. *Psychosomatic Medicine, 30*(3), 336–345.

Kaess, Walter A., and Witryol, Sam L. 1955. Memory for Names and Faces: A Characteristic of Social Intelligence? *Journal of Applied Psychology, 39,* 457–462.

Kandel, Denise B., and Lesser, Gerald S. 1972. *Youth in Two Worlds.* San Francisco: Jossey-Bass.

Kantor, H. L.; Michael, C. M.; Boulas, S. H.; Shore, H.; and Ludvigson, H. W. 1966. The Administration of Estrogens to Older Women, a Psychometric Evaluation. *Proceedings of the 7th International Congress of Gerontology.*

Kinsey, Alfred C.; Pomeroy, Wardell B.; Martin, Clyde E.; Gebhard, Paul H.; and Associates. 1953. *Sexual Behavior in the Human Female.* Philadelphia: Saunders.

Kolodny, Robert C.; Masters, William H.; Hendryx, Julie; and Toro, Gelson. 1971. Plasma Testosterone and Semen Analysis in Male Homosexuals. *New England Journal of Medicine, 285,* 1170–1174.

Kreuz, Leo E., and Rose, Robert M. 1972. Assessment of Aggressive Behavior and Plasma Testosterone in a Young Criminal Population. *Psychosomatic Medicine, 34*(4), 321–332.

Levine, S. N., and Mullins, R. F., Jr. 1966. Hormonal Influences on Brain Organization in Infant Rats. *Science, 152*(3729), 1585–1592.

Lewin, Arie Y., and Duchan, Linda. 1971. Women in Academia. *Science, 173,* 892–895.

MacBrayer, Caroline T. 1960. Differences in Perception of the Opposite Sex by Males and Females. *Journal of Social Psychology, 52,* 309–314.

Maccoby, Eleanor E. 1966. Sex-Differences in Intellectual Functioning. In Eleanor E. Maccoby (Ed.), *Development of Sex-Differences.* Stanford, California: Stanford University Press.

Masters, William H., and Johnson, Virginia E. 1961. Orgasm, Anatomy of the Female. In Albert Ellis and Albert A. Abarbanel (Eds.), *Encyclopedia of Sexual Behavior.* Vol. 2. New York: Hawthorn.

Masters, William H., and Johnson, Virginia E. 1963. The Sexual Response Cycle of the Human Male. I. Gross Anatomic Considerations. *Western Journal of Surgery, Obstetrics, and Gynecology, 71,* 85–95.

Masters, William H., and Johnson, Virginia E. 1966. *Human Sexual Response.* Boston: Little, Brown.

Masters, Wiliam H., and Johnson, Virginia E. 1970. *Human Sexual Inadequacy.* Boston: Little, Brown.

McClelland, D. C.; Atkinson, J. W.; Clark, R. A.; and Lowell, E. L. 1953. *The Achievement Motive.* New York: Appleton.

Mead, Margaret. 1949. *Male and Female.* New York: William Morrow (Apollo ed., 1967).

Money, J. 1965. Psychosexual Differentiation. In J. Money (Ed.), *Sex Research: New Developments.* New York: Holt, Rinehart and Winston.

Moos, Rudolf H. 1968. The Development of a Menstrual Distress Questionnaire. *Psychosomatic Medicine, 30*(6), 853–867.

Neugarten, Bernice L. 1967a. A New Look at Menopause. *Psychology Today, 1*(7), 42–45, 67–69, 71.

*Neugarten, Bernice L. 1967b. The Awareness of Middle Age. In Roger Owen (Ed.), *Middle Age*. London: British Broadcasting Corporation.

*Neugarten, Bernice L.; Wood, Vivian; Kraines, Ruth J.; and Loomis, Barbara. 1963. Women's Attitudes Toward the Menopause. *Vita Humana, 6*(3), 140–151.

Newsweek. 1972. Finance: Who Gets the Credit? August 21, 1972, 69–72.

Oetzel, R. 1966. Annotated Bibliography. In Eleanor E. Maccoby (Ed.), *Development of Sex-Differences*. Stanford, California: Stanford University Press.

Paige, Karen E. 1971. The Effects of Oral Contraceptives on Affective Fluctuations Associated with the Menstrual Cycle. *Psychosomatic Medicine, 33,* 515–537.

Persky, Harold; Smith, Keith D.; and Basu, Gopal K. 1971. Relation of Psychologic Measures of Aggression and Hostility to Testosterone Production in Man. *Psychosomatic Medicine, 33*(3), 265–277.

Pheterson, Gail L.; Kiesler, Sara B.; and Goldberg, Philip A. 1971. Evaluation of the Performance of Women as a Function of Their Sex, Achievement, and Personal History. *Journal of Personality and Social Psychology, 19*(1), 114–118.

Price, W. H.; Strong, J. A.; Whatmore, P. B.; and McClemont, W. F. 1966. Criminal Patients with XYY Sex-Chromosome Complement. *Lancet, 1*(7436), 565–566.

Ramey, Estelle. 1972. Men's Cycles. *Ms.,* Spring, 1972, 8ff.

Rose, Robert M.; Gordon, Thomas P.; and Bernstein, Irwin S. 1972. Plasma Testosterone Levels in the Male Rhesus: Influences of Sexual and Social Stimuli. *Science, 178*(4061), 643–645.

Rosenkrantz, Paul S.; Vogel, Susan Raymond; Bee, Helen; Broverman, Inge K.; and Broverman, Donald M. 1968. Sex-Role Stereotypes and Self-Concepts in College Students. *Journal of Consulting and Clinical Psychology, 32*(3), 287–295.

Sherfey, Mary Jane. 1972. *The Nature and Evolution of Female Sexuality*. New York: Random House.

Sontag, Susan. 1972. The Double Standard of Aging. *Saturday Review of the Society,* September 23, 1972, 29–38.

Veroff, J. 1969. Social Comparison and the Development of Achievement Motivation. In Charles Smith (Ed.), *Achievement Related Motives in Children*. New York: Russell Sage Foundation.

Walberg, H. J. 1969. Physics, Femininity and Creativity. *Developmental Psychology, 1*(1), 47–54.

Wilson, Robert A. 1966. *Feminine Forever*. New York: M. Evans and Company.

Witkin, H. A.; Dyk, R. B.; Faterson, H. F.; Goodenough, D. R.; and Karp, S. A. 1962. *Psychological Differentiation*. New York: Wiley.

Young, W. C.; Goy, R. W.; and Phoenix, C. H. 1964. Hormones and Sexual Behavior. *Science, 143*(3603), 212–218.

* References marked with an asterisk appear in Bernice L. Neugarten (Ed.), *Middle Age and Aging*. Chicago: University of Chicago Press, 1968.

Interlude
Theresa, Age 34

Theresa is a 34-year-old woman who moved to New York to pursue a career as a laboratory technician. She worked for nine years until her first son was born; when he was five she returned to work and is doing what seems to be important research. However, she returned to her career almost accidentally and is now thinking of eventually having a second child and working for her husband (Al) in his free-lance business. She seemed rather unsatisfied staying home when her son (Jan) was young, but even now does not seem entirely clear about how to be a mother, a wife and also to have a satisfying career.

Several questions are raised in this case example. How important is her career to her? What are the important satisfactions in her life? In what ways does it make a difference that she is a woman in terms of her milestones, satisfactions, and goals in life? What would her life have been if she had not returned to work? Is she different from other women in that way? In what ways has she changed in the last few years? How do you think things will work out in the future for her?

What are some of the milestones that stand out in your memory as you look back over your life? Well, the first thing that I think of ... when I was in fourth grade we were asked to write a theme on my ambition. I had no idea what I wanted to be. And my mother first brought up the subject of what I eventually ended up doing ... medical technology. And she told me when she was young she wanted to work in a laboratory and work with animals and work in a health field. And so I wrote my theme about being a laboratory technician and from that time on every time somebody asked me what I was going to be, this was it. And I did, I just went right on.

Another milestone was ... well, I guess that's not really a milestone ... my mother has a blood disease, and because of her connections with a blood specialist I eventually got into the field of hematology and that's something I enjoy doing. When I returned to work this time I didn't go into hematology, though; I went into cancer research. It's also very interesting. In a way it's allied to hematology, blood diseases like leukemia are cancer. *Were there any particular reasons you changed?* Only because there was an availability. In fact, I wasn't even going to go back to work. A friend of mine heard about an opening ... some doctors needed a technician very badly, so she called me up and asked me if I wanted to come in. And, Jan is getting on three-and-a-half and he's going to start nursery school and I've a pretty easy routine around here; I thought it might be stimulating; and I'm glad it worked out. I was getting pretty bored, I think—addicted to the afternoon movies, the soap operas, you know, that rut that I didn't want to be in. *How long ago was it that you went back?* Last October [five months ago].

Are there any other milestones that stand out to you? I guess another milestone was moving to New York because I met my husband. *You met him in New York?*

Right. A mutual friend who was our best man, came to New York and visited me and asked if I'd like to come with him. He had to visit a friend of his, and then I met Al. We didn't start dating right away. We eventually had our first date back in Hartford when we were both home for Thanksgiving. Another milestone? It's hard, you know, when you think back for milestones you can't think. *Anything more recently?* More recently. Not really. I guess my husband's business probably is a milestone. I'm getting ... I feel like I'm getting out of the sciences and into the arts, because I do work with him. I help him with some editing, and practically every aspect of his business we consult together, and I find that very interesting. *Are there any milestones in terms of your career? Your occupation?* I guess so. I went from an $80-a-week technician when I started out in my home town to a research assistant for my mother's blood specialist and then I came to New York and became supervisor of hematology at _____. And when I got married and we moved to _____, I started to work at _____ because it was more convenient, and I did some pediatric hematology, and now I'm back in the research field. It's been a progressive rise up the ladder, so to speak.

Would you say that being married or the birth of your child was a milestone? Oh, yes. It was. Getting married for me was especially a milestone. We have a mixed marriage [religions] and you know, we had so many hurdles to overcome before we actually got to say "I do" so to speak; that was a big accomplishment. And our son was a big thing too. He was a planned child, and we looked forward with great anticipation. My husband took some courses [in natural childbirth] with me. We went through the Lamaze Method. He was present when Jan was delivered, and he was present in the labor room and everything. At first he didn't want any part of it. He didn't want to look at blood or anything and can't stand hospitals. But he rallied and really came through very nicely and I think he was glad to have been there. This was something very big. It's a long wait, you know, to have a child. You build up to a certain point. We were delighted with him. He's shaping up.

What about crisis points? Have there been any crises? Oh, yeah. There have been crises. Well, I guess we had a crisis over our marriage. When I moved to

New York there was a crisis. When I left home [in a nearby suburb] and moved to Hartford there was another crisis with my family. As far as personal crises—I like to think of myself as a fairly stable, fairly calm, fairly relaxed, easy-going individual, so I usually don't get too upset about things. My parents are both alive, so there have been no crises over death. I did lose my grandmother when I was living in Hartford, and although this didn't really wreak havoc with my life, you know, it left a fairly marked scar, 'cause I was very close to her. She's the only grandparent I knew. All the others died before I knew them. I got through college pretty easily, there was no problem there. I guess there weren't too many crises.

No real crisis points in your marriage? No, no, we have a pretty good life. Of course, occasionally, we have a little blow-up, but we get along well, I think.

What about in terms of your job? Any crisis points there? There was a crisis with Jan. When I first returned to work; actually I started working on a part-time basis before October—Saturdays and Sundays from four to midnight. I was getting a little bit bored around the house and I thought maybe I'll try working part-time and see what happens, because I didn't know if I could handle everything. At first, Jan didn't really understand what was happening, Mommy was going to work. But when he got to realize that on certain nights I wasn't putting him to bed, he got very upset about this, and the days that I had to go to work would reach an absolute tantrum on his part. And especially if my husband were working on the same night. So, eventually, I got to bribing Jan with certain things. "When mommy goes to work I'll bring you something back." Sometimes it would be a candy bar, a package of M & Ms, or something. And he got to associate my going to work with something nice would come to him the next day, so that's a pacifier. And then, when I found out about the full-time job, we enrolled him in nursery school and he was ecstatic. He was going to go to school like the big kids. It was just wonderful, until the first week. The second week of putting him on the bus was such an emotional thing. I'd put him on the bus and he'd cry, cry, cry. So I talked to the teachers at school and they said that's very strange because when he gets to school, he's very happy; he's a very well-adjusted child; he mixes with the other children; he loves being there; he loves to do things; he does whatever they tell him. So we had another period the second week of school where he went from this real enthusiasm about going to this reluctance to go; finally in the third week he got on the bus with a smile and a wave again. There were times when he did not want me to go to work, he wanted me to come to school with him, or he did not want to go to school, he wanted to stay home with me, and I'd explain that mommy wasn't going to be home, "Mommy's going to work." And "Why do you have to work? Why can't you stay with me?" Finally now he's pretty well over this. Saturdays and Sundays come and he says, "Why can't I go to school today?" Occasionally he'll ask me if I can be home to meet his bus. My husband usually meets his bus about four-thirty and then they come and pick me up. I try to get out once in a while early so that I can be there. It seems to please him. And, another thing that makes him happy is that my husband or I will go to school at four o'clock and pick him up instead of letting him take the bus home. *What were your feelings about leaving him like that?* It tore the heart out of me when he started to cry. It was very important that he did have some contact with other children because right now he is our only child and there are no other children in the building his age. There's one little boy but he doesn't really enjoy playing with him. Most of his contact has been with older children. Now he does have children of his own age and he refers to his friends at school as "my friends."

How do you feel about working? Very good. For sanity reasons I wanted to go back. I think I was getting in a terrible rut. I feel I'm now being stimulated again. We talk about someday having another child. I just have this feeling, you know, how soon after we have this second child can I go back to work again? Because I just don't want to get into the same rut, but I have a feeling that I probably won't go back to work again, that I'll do work at home with my husband, which is all right, as long as I'm not with that boob tube [TV] on all the day. That gets very bad. I guess I have always looked forward to the day I'd be married and home with a child and I didn't have to do anything. Well, I had three years of this and, you know, it was just too much. You don't need that. *You couldn't stand that any longer.* Right. I think that I could probably have filled my days more efficiently, but, you know, you grow up in the middle America society thinking the epitome of life is to get married, have a family and stay home, and take care of your family. But that's just not it. You've got to have other things to fill your days. Before I went to work I started to do some paintings and some crewel. I do sew, so I've always done a bit of that, but I find now working with my husband, working, and helping my son, I'm doing more things now than I ever did and I seem to have just as much free time. You know, just on the go, I don't watch television as much; I don't get to read much either. I'm out every day. I get out early in the morning. When you're home you . . . well, maybe I'll get the house picked up and get dressed, then you find that it's eleven o'clock before you're dressed. You know, we have another cup of coffee, and then you get a phone call, and don't get dressed until one, and if it's summertime you don't get out to the park until two, then the baby has to have a nap, and you're in until four. It's really bad.

How did you happen to take the career route rather than just be the mother that middle America entices you to be? I don't know. I guess . . .well, probably it was financial. We had just started business and my husband's brother is a Ph.D. in finances and he came over from Chicago on his way to Hartford last summer and Al says please look at the books and tell me what's happening here; and he said, "Believe it or not, your trouble isn't financial." It was just that we're having growing pains. So he said the best thing you could do is send Theresa out to work. So I said, "I don't want to go out to work. Are you kidding? I've got things to do here." And, finally, I started to think about it and I said well, maybe that wouldn't be such a bad idea. So, all things considered, the best thing is to find something suitable. And a friend of mine had heard about this opening. So I guess if the need had not been financial, I probably would still be sitting home. *So in a sense it's almost accidental.* It's accidental, but it's probably the best thing that ever happened. *Yet you had a career before Jan was born.* Right. Well, I had worked. I graduated in 1960 and Jan was born in '69, so I had been working for nine years already. You know, I felt that this is almost a decade of work and that's enough. I had also worked while I was in college because I lived right near a hospital and I was doing weekend technology work, which was good because it pointed out to me that I was on the right track. I was getting into something that I would enjoy doing later. This was something my mother encouraged me to do, because I guess she knew a lot of people that graduated, and then they found when they went into their field they finally hated it. So, she said . . . even in high school: "If you think you're going to want to work in a hospital you should go down and see if you can get a job there to try the atmosphere." So I did. I started in my senior year and kept the job all through college. *Did you do graduate work in this?* No, I didn't. I didn't feel it was necessary because, you know, that middle America bit, I said some day I'm going to be home . . . I didn't want to make a full-time career for the rest of my life. *How does it look to you now? Do you think that you will?* No. I think I'll be working, but . . . I think there's more of a need here. I do his [Al's] bookkeeping, I write out all the checks for the employees. I do all his typing. You know, I never meant to be a secretary or bookkeeper, but I think it's better. He really can't afford to hire anybody right now and we're in at the beginning of it together so that as it grows I can grow with it. And I think in a way I like this. I don't want to feel too much apart from my husband; I don't want to feel that I don't really know what he's talking about. I just want to be able to communicate with him. I was in the sciences and he's in the arts; you know, I just don't want there to be a distance there. The other nice thing about working for him is that I guess it is not quite as regimented as being some place at nine o'clock and being there 'til five. You know, if my husband is my boss, then he's not really. I don't have to impress him.

I guess it's almost obvious in the way you've answered the questions so far, about how he feels about your working. He was negative also. He didn't want me to have to go to work. In fact, just the other day he said, "I wish you didn't have to go to work." I guess he's seeing that I'm enjoying it. He always felt that, you know, it was his place to support the family, and by the fact of my working, he gets a little feeling that he is not quite able to do it, which isn't right at all, because he's always been able to do it, and it's just been that, you know, he started a business and he's got to work very hard to have it grow. If I can help out, well, I'm glad to.

I'm curious what your feelings are about women's lib. Well, I've been liberated, I guess. I've never run into any discrimination problems, so I can't feel very sympathetic towards women's lib. I feel, however, that they're doing something very good and that equality in wages . . . I believe that this should be— equal money for equal work. However, I feel some of their, well, getting into a men's bar is absolutely ridiculous! I believe that there should be places where men can go and women can go. Why does it always have to be integrated? I don't really approve of that. I think the work they're trying to do for the overpopulation is very good. I think the work they're trying to do for day care is very good. They've got some very good things. I think that if women want to work, they should be able to have good care for their children. A lot can go out and do what they want to do, but I can't agree with everything. *I get the feeling from you that you don't feel that either motherhood or having a career is the necessary way of life for a woman.* Well, some people are just not meant to be mothers. Some people are getting married today, and just not having children, which is very fine, if they don't feel cut out to have children. I think they should do what's best for them. *The two can merge and being a career person doesn't necessarily mean being full time in some occupation completely separate from the husband, it can be almost like a partner.* Right. Another thing about work too, when I first started to go back my feeling was that I didn't want anything that was going to take too much time away from me at home. I didn't want to have to come home and think about the work that I was doing. I felt that I don't want to have anything that is going to infringe on my time with my family. And so, that's why I took this weekend evening job, because it was purely routine...absolutely nothing to think about when I got home. And yet, now that I'm in research, I do come home and you know, there'll probably be a time during the evening when I'll think I know a way to do something and I'll go in the next day and try it out. So, I do think about it...it's not really infringing as much as I thought it would be. I think the thing that I had feared was when I was supervisor at _____, I used to have to often come home with paper work that I couldn't get to; and absolutely none of that I wanted here. Now whatever I take home is up here [gesturing toward head].

If I would ask you who you are, how would you answer? Who I am? I don't like to think of myself as a woman, because a woman has always been to me an older person and I like to think of myself as young. I'm 34 and somebody asked me the other day how old I was and I said "[19]38 from [19]72...." I don't think in terms of age. I feel young and I like to think of myself as young. I don't think numbers are significant. Who I am. I guess primarily I'm a mother because I can feel so much emotion for my son. I also feel emotion for other parents, you know when you see something on television in the news about some tragedy—I never used to feel this way before—I feel emotional. I'm a wife. I care about my home and care about my family. I want to do things for my husband and child. And I guess naturally, I'm in a career which I care very much about also. It's something that means a lot to me also—cancer research. I feel that I can probably make a significant contribution. Cancer means—to me—something that will probably strike in our family, because it's been coming from all angles in our family. My grandfather died of it. My husband's mother had a form of cancer. My mother's blood disease was a benign type of cancer. I just feel that, you know, it's doomed that it's going to happen to us; if I can help by working now, maybe help science discover more about, not how to cure it, but how to prevent it and treat it, maybe I can be doing something for my family, which makes it all worthwhile. *It sounds like very exciting work for you. Very meaningful.* I'm happy doing this. I find it stimulating, challenging, rewarding.

Do you feel you have a firmer sense of identity now than you had before? Oh, yes, much so. *How has that changed? How has that firmer sense come about?* Well, it's come about by my life being full again. By being very active, getting me out of the house, getting me to do more things. I guess I'm stronger emotionally; stronger about wanting to get things done. Before I might have said well, I have this and this to do, I'm home ad infinitum and so I'll get it done, some day, but now I say I have these things to do and I assign a day to them in order to get them done. I make up a little schedule. I really live by a schedule. It's the only way you can fit everything in when you're so busy. We're working now to move out of an apartment into a house, because one little room for my husband's business is not adequate, so we're considering getting a two-family house where we can have some help on some income coming in, to help pay off the mortgage, where he can have an entire basement to set up as his studio. We have goals.

Would you say that you've changed very much over the past few years? I don't know if I've changed *very* much. I've probably become more mature. I probably worry a lot more. I think mothers do. *What do you mean, "more mature"?* I always used to think of myself as ... not really silly, but I used to take things lightly. I was probably more daring. You know, now I worry about going too fast in a car. Before, I would speed to get there faster. I think I take the business of running a house a lot more seriously, more maturely. Certainly, when you have a child you have to become more mature. I think one thing is I can probably handle situations better now. My husband would sometimes say, "I guess I'm not a good father. I don't know the proper things to do." But this is something you learn, you know; I've learned. When my son doesn't want to do something that I feel he has to do, what is the best way of getting him to do it? And so I've learned these little tricks to get him to do what I want him to do. My husband hasn't learned them because, you know, he hasn't had to deal with him as much. And so, I've been passing these little tricks along to him. I guess that's maturity too.

What other ways have you changed? I think in my relationship with my husband too, I've become more mature. I know that in our early courtship and marriage, if he were away from me, it really bothered me a lot. It's just growing used to each other a little bit. If I have to go to Hartford for a weekend, you know, I don't feel falling apart as we leave one another. I can take it easier. *Any other ways that you've changed in the last few years?* Not really; I guess the biggest change in our lives in the last few years is having a child, and trying to do what's best for our son. Seeing that he gets a liberal enough upbringing. You know, just enough discipline.

Was giving birth to him a big event for you? Oh, yes. It really was. I don't know how old I was—I must have been a teen-ager probably—sixteen or seventeen. I had seen a movie and I believe it was called "The Case of Dr. Laurent." And for some reason the interpretation from the French, the word "strange" was put before "case ..." "The Strange Case of Dr. Laurent." And a couple of girlfriends and I had gone to see this movie. We knew nothing about it, and we got there and found out that it was a movie on natural childbirth. It was playing at the local cinema, so it wasn't anything educational at all. This girl had, through breathing, delivered her child without pain, and I'd never forgotten this. I guess it must have made some impression on me. And when I did become pregnant, I had since been hearing more things about what they call the Lamaze Method and I started to investigate. We got involved in a course on breathing. And the big thing was that I had heard from so many people that childbirth is the most terrifying of all pains, and that what you go through—you curse your husband, you say that you're not going to have any more children, and then, you know, a couple years later you have another child. So, it can't be all that bad, but everybody says "Well, you forget pain. You don't remember pain." Well, I just did not want to be in this position of coming to pain. I wanted to be in control, so we took this course, and were very pleased with the outcome of it. You know, I felt on top of everything. We had a very good experience. Now, everybody that I find out is pregnant I recommend the Lamaze Method to. It worked for us. We were both there and we saw our son being born and it was a very rich experience.

Has your outlook on life in general changed in the last few years? Yes, it has. Again, I think because of our child. I have this overwhelming drive to preserve myself. Before, I didn't care if ... I didn't care when death came. I never thought about it, you know ... death, it has to be part of life, so when it comes it comes. Now ... I think part of it may be the violence that is so prevalent. You hear about it constantly. I worry more about living. I'm very happy; I don't want to die and I want to protect myself.

Has your marriage changed in any way? Your relation with your husband in the last few years? We've been married five years. I think the only way it possibly has changed is for the better. I think that it's nurturing. I think we're helping each other a lot. We had been dating for over three years before we got married and so we didn't enter a marriage as strangers. We knew each other very well. And, in spite of it, the first year was a big adjustment. Some friends of ours had said that the first year of marriage the word "divorce" flies around so much because there is such an adjustment. You have two virtual strangers coming together—you know, he puts his dirty socks by the bed, she hangs her stockings in the bath tub—all these things that you have to work out and adjust to. It's a big thing. *So the first year was pretty difficult.* The first year, I don't think was as difficult for us as it was for some of our friends. We'd lived together for a while before we were married. We sort of got some of the wrinkles ironed out. We also knew each other for three years. I knew his hangups and he knew mine before we got married. Knowing them we went into marriage not wanting to change one another, but willing to accept each other's idiosyncracies. You know, you cope—you just have to understand. Somebody wise made the best statement I ever heard: "If you are willing to each give into your mariage, feel that you're giving more; if you can always go through your marriage giving the most of yourself; if each one does that, you're always giving and you're not wanting to take all the time, you'll have a good marriage," and I think we give a lot.

Has sex become more important, less important or about the same in your marriage? I think it's less important. I think that probably in the beginning it's something new. It's probably the thing that brings you closer together as your marriage gets older. It becomes less important because there's other things that you do together. Unfortunately we don't get to do too many social things because we're too busy, but whenever we do it, it seems to be enough. It's not that driving need that there used to be in our early marriage. I guess it's still fairly important, but I guess it's not quite as imperative, so to speak.

Have your relations with your parents changed in the last few years? Yeah, I guess. I feel that I'm not quite as close to my father as I used to be and would like to be. It's probably that we don't get to see each other too often.

You know, when you think about going home once a month for a weekend after I've spent a lifetime with people, you only see them for ... twenty-four days a year. I find that I don't know what to say to him any more, outside of his work ... What do you talk about? I think that I'm in a different world now. I feel that they're not really into our world. It's just, you know, we have this gap. I can talk to them about Jan. They can talk to me about the other grand-children. My mother and I talk about what's going on in the family—who's doing what. It's not that I have trouble talking, I just feel that I don't have as much to say as I would like to. I'd like to be able to talk more to him [father]. *Is your relationship now different from, say, when you were a teen-ager?* Oh, yes. Heavens! There's a great deal of difference. My mother was very strict and my father tended to be more liberal. As a teen-ager growing up I hated to ask my mother for permission to do anything. I'd much rather ask my father. I resented very much that lack of freedom that I grew up with. A lot of my friends had a lot more freedom, and this was, you know [a source of] ... good arguments; [I was] really rebellious. *I take it that there was a fair amount of tension between you and at least your mother then?* Yes, terrific tension when I was a teen-ager. As I grew older, when I left home to go to Hartford—I don't know how I got away. I really don't know how I got away. I must have been very strong. I'm sure there must have been arguments, but I must have mentally blocked them out. When I moved to New York I came home and announced ... I think this is what I said, "They need me in New York!" (laughter) You know, I don't know how they ever fell for this stuff. "There's a job and they need a hematology supervisor and I must go." I drove off in my Volkswagen into the sunset; my mother's standing at the door say-ing, "This is terrible! This is a terrible way to go!" But I went and I got there. It was always my mother I had to work the hardest to get to do what I wanted to do, but we're very good friends now. And once we got married, once all the hurdles were over, you know, and I finally settled down—after she came to New York and saw where we were living and saw our furniture and saw that we did have substantial material things—she stopped pressuring me. We're very close now.

Has the way other people think of you changed over the years? The way other people think of me? I guess I care about what people think of me. Some people can just go on in life. It bothers me. It bothers me if I'm not well-accepted. That doesn't bother me as much now, where as a child in grammar school ... I was part of a popular group, but I never felt that I was completely accepted. But today I am more accepted for myself. I still worry what the neighbors think ... that sort of thing. I try to keep up appearances.

Would you say that you married at about the right time? Or early or late? No, we married about the right time. I was 29, I think, I'm not sure any more. I had traveled what I thought was fairly extensively. Probably not as exten-sively as some people, but I had gone to Europe once. I've gone cross-country. I went to a couple of islands. And, you know, I enjoyed being single. I worked what I thought was sufficiently. There was nothing left that I wanted to do. Like a lot of kids get married at 17 and 18 and that's it. They get nowhere. I think I got married at the right age. Maybe a year or two years earlier would have been okay, too. But I don't feel that it was too late. Certainly not

too early. *Did you feel much pressure to get married earlier?* Oh, yes. My
mother was always urging a little bit. She didn't like the fact that I was single
and living in an apartment. That's not the way she was brought up. She probably would have been happy if I had stayed at home and gotten married a
couple of years after I got out of college, but I enjoyed it very much.

Would you say that you have a pretty firm sense of who you are? Yes. I'm
not confused about my personality. I don't try to fool myself in being something I'm not. The only thing that I hope is that I can "grow up" to be as
gracious as some of the more mature women I see today. You know, you
learn things as you go through life. You learn things like tact; you learn things
about being kind to people, which, I think, as a teen-ager . . . you just don't
consider. I think about them more now. You know, I feel it's important to be
charitable. I think if every woman could learn to be gracious, if every person
could be gracious, if every man . . . Graciousness is a composite of everything
I'd like to be. *How long have you felt that you had a firm sense of who you
were?* I guess most of my life. Maybe not most of my life; well, at least since
probably the middle of college. I guess in high school you don't think about
that too much. Maybe it's become more important that I was aware of who
I was since maybe the last five years or so. So much of your youth is finding
out where you're going, what you're going to do and getting there. I think once
you get there—like, I probably got there after I got married—the rest of your
life becomes pretty much a straight course. You find your mate and start your
family and you go in one direction. I guess, getting married [was the point]
now that I think about it.

Do you sometimes look back over your life and review what's happened?
Yes. I think about things I would have done differently . . . ways I would have
handled situations differently. I think if my mother had been different, probably things would have been a lot different too. Maybe not, maybe I don't
resent the strictness as much now as I did then. You know . . . when you want
to do something and you can't do it you're very upset about it. It's probably
very good for you.

Do you sometimes think about death? I think I mentioned that I think about
it with great trepidation. I didn't mind it before, but I mind it now. I don't
want my husband to die, I don't want my son to die, I don't want me to die.
As far as my parents now, I love them very much; I know they are getting
older, you know; I'm more willing to accept the fact that maybe in this decade,
maybe in the next decade, they'll go. This is a fact that I can accept, whereas—
this is something too when I was not married and I didn't have a child—I just
couldn't conceive of my parents dying. I didn't want them to die. I knew that
I'd get very, very upset if they died. Now, I feel that I could accept it. So, I
guess I've got my own family too—it's not as important.

How does the future look to you in terms of your life? It's good. We have
dreams. We have dreams about a home in the country and a prosperous business. I think the business is getting good. As far as a dream house in the
country, I don't know. We obviously dream too hard. But if you don't have
something to aim for, what are you going to work for?

I gather that you'd say that you have a very intimate relationship. Yeah, we
do. We have a good understanding of one another. It's good. If lovers can be

friends, that's important; and I think we're friends. Anybody can be a relation, but to be a friend is to know somebody, and we know each other. It's
nice. *Do you feel pretty productive in your life now?* Yeah, I do. And again,
it's all since I returned to work. I'm doing a lot; I'm doing a lot more and I
enjoy it. I enjoy being busy. I thought I was going to enjoy just having lots
of leisure time, but I don't. I'm not cut from that mold, and the busier I can
be, it seems, the better I function.

Do you have any sense of leaving your mark? I guess I'm leaving my mark.
I'm not a radical. I don't feel that I got to go around and change everything,
leave my mark in that way, but I guess, you know, in very quiet, subtle ways
I do leave my mark. *Is that important to you?* No, no. Not especially. I just
get along and get things done. I know that . . . maybe it sounds vain but once
I've been somewhere, like once I've worked somewhere, I must have left some
impressions there. One thing my boss said to me a couple of weeks ago:
"Whenever you take your vacation, I'm going to take mine," because . . . you
know, I'm getting so much work done that if he stays and I'm away, that
he's going to have all the work to do and he'll never get it done. I just feel
that after I'm gone I think he's going to have a difficult time finding someone
as efficient, as vain as it may sound. You know, I think this is how I leave
my mark, but it's not important.

What kind of things are important for right now? I guess they're all material things. Getting a flourishing business, getting a house, having one more
child. I think those would have to be the three important things. Getting my
son into a good school is really important, too. That's just about it. As far as
material possessions, the house is the only real thing.

Would you say that your life has been a meaningful adventure? Yes. I think
so. I feel sorry that it didn't start becoming more meaningful earlier. But, I
guess . . . you just can't have a more meaningful life too early. I'd say that my
life has probably become more meaningful again in the last five years. It
seems to me, since I've been married that things have had a definite purpose.
Before that, you know, you're just running from here to there; you're unset-
tled. Now I feel this is home, because for many years I would always refer to
home as my parents' house, and now I refer to my own home as home. And
like, thoughts are channeled here.

*Are you looking toward the future mostly, or thinking about the past, or
just concerned with the present?* I'm more concerned with the future. Well, I
guess I'm concerned with the present in order to get to the future. Yeah, I
don't really think about what's gone past. I never cry over spilt milk, but I
care about the present . . . whether we're going to survive in the jungle long
enough to get to the future. *But the future is important for you now.* Yes, it's
important. I guess it's important that I get my home in the country and I get
my children, well, raised without getting them hung up on drugs and, you
know, without having them travel with some wild crowd—protecting them in
this world is important.

five
Families
and
Singles

Adults are highly complex human beings, and they live in a highly complex society that offers a range of possible life styles and institutional involvements. Yet, nearly all adults invest a great deal of time and emotional energy in one of these social institutions—the family. Sometimes families provide deeply meaningful intimate relationships and significant opportunities for personal growth and fulfillment. Occasionally they provide some of the greatest emotional upsets and potentials for violence. For example, homicide rates indicate that most people are killed by family members, the problem of "battered" children is receiving increasing attention, and police approach all family disputes with great caution. Still other families provide little more than comfortable bedrooms and dining facilities. But, by and large, adults marry, have children, launch them into their own families, and grow old along with their mate.

However, some adults do not marry, and others do not remain married. We are curious about the characteristics, life styles, and developmental milestones of the single adults in our society. We are also curious about some of the emerging family styles since there seems to be a great variety of family life styles that are possible in our complex, pluralistic society.

Still, regardless of the style these intimate personal relationships may take, they obviously are only part of the significant involvements during the middle years. That is, they interact with the satisfactions, challenges, and frustrations involved in the occupation (which we will discuss in the next chapter). These are the issues that Erikson described by the terms Intimacy versus Isolation—where the task is to achieve a truly intimate relationship—and Generativity versus Stagnation—where the task is to gain a sense of productive accomplishment through one's occupation or

Photo at left: *Family Group* (1945-1949) by Henry Moore, bronze (cast 1950), 59¼" high. Collection, The Museum of Modern Art, New York. A. Conger Goodyear Fund.

as a parent so that there will be something one has done that will outlive oneself. These are philosophic ideals, of course, and many people may be too busy caring for the family and earning a living to consider these issues very seriously. Yet, there is a sense in which they describe the challenge and potential satisfactions of these middle years rather clearly.

In this chapter we examine this long span of adulthood from the perspective of the family because it is clear that family involvements change over time, family roles shift, and the family has a development of its own that we may call the *family cycle*. These family events and the progression through the family cycle provide important clues to the changes, timing events, and the progression of the adult years. Of course, these family commitments and changes occur simultaneously with occupational involvements and changes. Therefore, it is important to be aware that each theme is being played simultaneously while we begin discussing the middle years with an examination of the family and unmarried life styles.

We will focus on three aspects of the family because it would certainly not be appropriate to attempt a discussion of the entire field of marriage and family life. First we will explore the kind of families that currently exist in our society and some experimental family styles. Second, we will view the family from the symbolic interaction perspective as a unity of interacting personalities. And third, we will summarize the major events in the family cycle and some of the crisis points that result. Then we will discuss unmarried adults since we are curious about the ways in which their lives and life styles are similar and different in comparison with the married majority. Throughout this discussion we will also note the continuing importance of sexuality through the adult years because sexual desire and capability does not cease with the birth of the last child, at menopause, nor necessarily at widowhood; and we may assume that sexuality has a similarly long life for single adults as well.

THE FAMILY: EXTENDED, NUCLEAR, AND COMMUNAL

Most of the families in our society seem to be *nuclear families* in that they are made up of a mother, a father, and their children. However, these nuclear family units have a variety of ties with other members of their family—that is, with their *extended family*. Although the young couple typically establishes a home away from the parents, family ties generally remain intact, and even if the family units are separated by a considerable physical distance, they keep in contact by telephone, airplane, and automobile. Sussman and Burchinal (1962) report that, in general, nuclear family units retain close ties with other family units in a kin network and that mutual aid and social interaction are frequent. Financial help, as well as help by providing services (house cleaning, baby sitting, and shopping, for example) frequently occur between generations of the family so that parents help the newly married couple, and later the younger couple help their parents after retirement or during illnesses. A recent study of three-generation families (children, parents, and grandparents) found that the youngest generation is *least likely* to say that young people and their parents should each go their own way and *most likely* to feel a responsibility for keeping in touch with their parents (Hill, 1971). Thus it seems that although families appear to exist as isolated nuclear units, there is also an interlocking family network that provides at least some help and support for each family unit. Sussman and Burchinal (1962) term this family structure a *modified extended family* (after Litwak, 1960). It differs from the extended family that was prevalent in Europe, and it differs also from the isolated nuclear family since the family units maintain their interrelations between siblings and across generations while also maintaining much autonomy and mobility.

However, there are a wide variety of family structures and a wide variety of family styles within the modified extended family structure. For example, minority families and families living in poverty would be likely to have to maintain intergenerational ties in order to help one another through periods of hardship and, in general, to survive in a hostile environment. The extended family might have to provide shelter or food to those unable to work or unable to live in an unheated tenement. Grandmothers who can no longer work may be able to care for the children of their daughters (or daughters-in-law) who can work. Men unable to find work because of discrimination or past history may be hired by a relative. And the extended family also serves as an anchor point for one's sense of identity, especially for minority groups. At the other extreme, some nuclear families may have little contact with extended kin because of some family dispute—such as marrying out of one's race or religion— severing the ties that might otherwise have existed for that couple. Or a couple might choose to isolate themselves from the extended family because of some long-standing personality clash or for any number of reasons.

Families differ in other ways than the degree of intergenerational contact, of course. For example, some families have only one parent living with the children—either because of divorce, widowhood, or desertion. Other families have "extra" people in the family—an aged parent, a housekeeper, or an unmarried relative, and so on. And some families may be incredibly complex since they reflect the effects of divorce and remarriage. Thus, one "nuclear" family may consist of parts of two previous families living together during the week as a single family; but on weekends the members shift and visit their parents as if they were members of an extended family. If the relationships with the various sets of grandparents (at least six grandparents, perhaps eight or more) are included, the family structure becomes very complex indeed.

In sum, there are a variety of family styles in our society, even considering only the styles that are, essentially, extended nuclear families. But since family structure seems to reflect and adapt to the social conditions of the society in which it exists, there is no reason to assume that all of the possible family styles have been developed. At present it would seem that the extended nuclear family, for all of its shortcomings and potential pitfalls, is reasonably well suited to our society. It seems to provide a variety of alternative forms, allows geographic mobility, provides a means for transmitting values and attitudes across generations, and ideally provides a set of emotional relationships that sustain and support individuals and buffer them against the strains and crises of our fast-paced technological society. However, it does not always work very well, and it is probably continuing to evolve into new family styles that may, for example, allow women who wish to make child rearing a career and women who wish to enter a career outside the home the freedom to make that choice. In addition, day-care centers, "foster grandparent" programs, and changing sex-role stereotypes may allow adults who do not have young children of their own to have contact with children and to participate in child rearing in a variety of settings. Thus, men and women of all ages who otherwise could not find work, but are very good at caring for children, might be able to provide a range of valuable services in day-care centers, elementary schools, and hospitals for disturbed or retarded children and allow mothers (or fathers and grandmothers) to enter other jobs when they no longer have to care for their own children during the day. And, of course, the current decline in birth rate will mean smaller families and fewer years spent caring for young children than has been the case in the past.

Thus it would seem that the extended nuclear family is probably capable of evolving with the demands of society into further modified forms. However, some young people (and others not so young) are experimenting with different styles of family life, such as the communal family. Although there have been a number of communal family experiments in America— such as the Oneida commune (cf. Kanter, 1970)—perhaps the most familiar example of communal family living is in the kibbutzim (collective settlements) in Israel. Talmon (1961) described the main features of these settlements as:

> ... common ownership of property except for a few personal belongings and communal organization of production and consumption on an equalitarian basis. All income goes into the common treasury, each member getting a very small annual allowance for personal expenses. The community is run as a single economic unit and as a single household (Talmon, 1961).

Obviously, the family structure and parent-child relations are also modified in such situations. In the kibbutzim that Talmon studied, the children are socialized primarily by peers, specialized nurses, instructors, and teachers. This leaves very few primary familial roles to the parents. However, the family is a primary source of intimate relations for both parents and children, and only in the family do they receive love and care that does not have to be shared with several others. In addition, since all family members live in relative proximity, the three generations interact frequently and casually. As the grandparents grow older, their needs are met by communal institutions and by their children and grandchildren.

Undoubtedly there is considerable variation among the different kibbutzim, and communal life is not the typical pattern of life in Israel. Rabkin and Rabkin (1969) report that although there are over 200 such communal settlements in Israel, their total membership is only three percent of the country's population; nonetheless they have contributed a disproportionate number of the nation's military and political leaders. In many ways these settlements are an attempt to develop a utopian community free of the double standard for men and women and different from traditional Jewish family structure.

There have been attempts at establishing such utopian communal settlements in this country as well. Kanter (1970) studied nineteenth-century communes and reports that the Oneida community, for example, separated the parents and children in different dwelling units and raised the children communally; they would visit their parents frequently but the community's life was the focus of their lives. Kanter was particularly interested in the variables that differed between successful and unsuccessful communities as an historical guide to predicting the success of contemporary communtal experiments. She identified 9 successful groups and 21 unsuccessful ones and examined the ways in which they handled the basic issues involved in maintaining a viable group structure such as property, work, sexual relations, membership, and group solidarity. In general, the highly structured groups survived more often. On this basis she argued that today's "growth and learning" communities (such as Synanon or Esalen)—communities that create a family-like feeling, use mutual criticism and ritual, organize work communally, have stringent entrance requirements, and often develop strong values and charismatic leaders— are more likely to survive than "anarchistic" communes that lack such organization. From a developmental perspective we might add that a commune of several generations (children and parents of varying ages as well as grandparent figures) would seem to be considerably richer and also more stable than a commune consisting only of young parents and children, for example.

Whether the communal family will be an important style of family life in the future is, of course, a totally open question. Other alternate family styles such as "swinging" or "swapping," "living together" (unmarried), or "serial monogamy" (through successive divorces and remarriages) as well as homosexual "marriages" may be other alternate family styles that might evolve from (or into) nuclear family styles. And many young people are experimenting with communal arrangements in a variety of differing styles. Perhaps the seeming rise in pluralism in our society where a variety of life styles coexist side by side will lead to an increased prevalence and stability of a variety of family structures. Or perhaps the basic family pattern that has existed for centuries will continue to evolve and survive. In any event, the isolation between family units living side by side, the current concern with population growth and effective contraception, and the expanding consciousness of women's roles are likely to have some effects on the family structure. Margaret Mead, in a speech on future families, makes this point well (with her characteristic mix of insight and overstatement).

> One of the things the communes are emphasizing is a lot of people sharing child-care, sharing bringing up the children again, so the children have more security. . . .
>
> It will take quite a little while, because it means building new houses, on the whole—new kinds of apartments, closer together, places where you don't have to drive 15 miles to use somebody else's washing machine when yours breaks, and where people can get together more closely. We won't have this right away—but we're going to have it.
>
> It means places where all the people can live somewhere near young people, and places where young married couples with children will be cherished and cared for and flanked on all sides by people who don't have children at the moment. Maybe they've had them before; maybe they haven't had them yet; maybe they don't want any. But it'll be a place where they, also, can find children, and won't be banished from children as they are at present. . . .
>
> With the population explosion, the pressure on women to marry is going to be reduced, and the pressure to be mothers is going to be enormously reduced. . . .
>
> Twenty years from now, we'll have many fewer families, but children will still be brought up in families because we don't know how to bring them up any other way (Mead, 1971, pp. 52-53).

THE FAMILY: A UNITY OF INTERACTING PERSONALITIES

Let us consider the family structure most prevalent today—the modified extended family—and discuss the *internal* characteristics of this family. Our aim will be to view the family as a functioning unit in which the adults and children interact with one another and consequently affect one another. We will argue that the family is an interacting system so that a dysfunction in any one aspect of the family will be felt in all other aspects of the system. And we will argue that it is not meaningful to view the mother or the father or any of the children separately when seeking to understand *the family* because the whole of the family is different from the sum of its parts.

This view of the family—"a unity of interacting personalities" (Burgess, 1926)—grows out of the symbolic interaction approach since the meaning of the interaction between family members is contained in the interaction itself rather than in the parts the family members play in the interaction. For example, a father's drunkenness or his permissiveness may mean something very different in the family interaction from its meaning apart from the family. That is, each family member responds to that behavior, it has a history within the family, it influences the family system as a whole, and it affects each member's perception of the family. Thus, our attempt is to get into the "psychosocial interior" of the family (Hess and Handel, 1959) and to see adults as participating members of family systems.

One example of this approach is the relatively recent development of family therapy as an important treatment modality for disturbed family members. An underlying assumption in family therapy is that the "patient" is really the "identified patient"; he is the one most obviously expressing the pain that is actually shared by all interacting family members (Satir, 1964). That is, an individual's disturbance is primarily a manifestation of the disturbed family in which he is living and of a dysfunctional family interaction. There is something going wrong in that family indicating that the entire family needs to meet together with a therapist. One example of this might be a child who is "scapegoated" and assigned the family role of "problem child" so the parents can focus their anxiety on him rather than on the unsatisfying and conflictual marriage that is too threatening for either of them to face (Vogel and Bell, 1960). Another example might be the "psychotic mother" who is periodically hospitalized and serves as the family scapegoat so that the father's shaky sense of adequacy may be maintained, and he does not have to face the conflicts within himself and within the family that, were he to actually face them, might lead to his own psychosis.

While this discussion of family therapy is very brief, it should be pointed out that the assumptions underlying family therapy and its practice are relatively new and, at least on the surface, contradict some aspects of older conceptions of psychopathology: that an individual problem involves individual dynamics and requires individual therapy. However, individual therapists often find that the progress of their patients is impeded and frustrated by their families and that, even in the best cases, the families have some difficulty in adjusting to the changes brought about by an individual's psychotherapy. This occurrence helped stimulate the growth of family therapy and suggests the significance of the interaction within families. In addition, family therapy need not deny the internal dynamic causes of an individual's dysfunction (in fact, through family therapy the seriously disturbed individual may be located, since he is often not the original "identified patient," and may then be seen in individual therapy). Actually, instead of denying individual causes of individual pathology, this view provides a framework for understanding the peculiar family interaction often seen in families of schizophrenics even in the event that a physiological-chemical cause for schizophrenia is discovered. That is, it need not be assumed that the family interaction *causes* the disorder, only that they are interrelated. Thus, if a person's chemistry causes him to think and behave in a bizarre manner, it would be expected that his family would be upset by this occurrence and over a period of time might come to manifest this peculiar pattern of interaction (called "schizophrenigenic," meaning "causing schizophrenia"). It should not matter what sets off the dysfunctional interaction in the family; but once it begins, every member in an intense family interaction will have to deal with the dysfunction in some way, and that dysfunction is likely to be felt in all aspects of the family interaction.

The central point is that the family is a unity of interacting personalities. A disruption in any of these personalities, in their relationships, or in their interaction in the family system will disrupt other aspects of the family system. One study by the author attempted to test this hypothesis in a sample of families with school-age children who had not sought therapeutic help (Kimmel, 1970). We measured the quality of the marital relationship, the parent's perception of the child's behavior, and the parent's perception of the family unit. We found that a dysfunction in the marital relationship (low marital satisfaction) was related to a dysfunction in the child's behavior (high degree of aggressiveness), and that both measures of family dysfunction were related to negative perceptions of the family unit. Thus, these data support the concept that families function as interacting systems, and that a dysfunction in one aspect of the system is related to dysfunctions in other aspects of the system. To be sure, additional research is needed to verify this hypothesis using a wider variety of measures of the family system; but these data suggest that the basic hypothesis is tenable.

One important corollary of this view is that individual family member's perceptions of these various family aspects are likely to be more salient for understanding the family system than an outside observer's view of the same family variables would be (for this reason we used the report of the mother and the father in the study cited above). For example, one child in a family may perceive the family functioning in a way different from his siblings for a number of reasons. The result may be that he is adversely affected by the family interaction, while his brothers and sisters —who live in the same family but perceive it differently—would not be adversely affected or would be affected in different ways.

Ferdinand van der Veen has developed a construct that he terms the "Family Concept" to explore and measure the ways in which individual family members perceive their family unit. The idea is that family members have concepts of their *family* just as they have concepts of their *self*, and that the family concept may be measured in the same way that the self concept has been measured. For example, "We are an affectionate family," "We have very good times together," or "We resent each other's friends" are items that may be rated on a continuum from "most like our family" to "least like our family." In one study using this measure, Novak and van der Veen (1970) explored the central question of how the same family can produce emotionally disturbed adolescents *and* normal siblings. They measured the family concept held by the disturbed and the normal adolescent and found that the adolescents differed despite the fact they were both talking about the same family. The family concepts held by the normal siblings were also compared with the concepts held by adolescents who did not have a disturbed sibling (a group of "normal controls"). Not only did the degree of "adjustment" and "satisfaction" indicated by the family concepts differ between the groups (disturbed siblings were lower on both than their normal siblings or the normal controls) but also the content of the family concept differed.

> . . . The disturbed children perceive emotional dependence in the family, their siblings view the family as competent and task-oriented, while the normal controls see it as a source of positive experience with good interpersonal relationships. The siblings, therefore, clearly differed from the normal controls in not stressing the positive interpersonal aspect of family life, but they also avoid the emotional dependent features associated with the disturbed child's view. It may be important for the normal sibling in the disturbed family to stay away from personal involvement and to instead be oriented toward adequacy and achievement, to doing well. He may avoid problems by avoiding feelings, by filling a social role, and by gaining satisfaction from accomplishment rather than intimacy (Novak and van der Veen, 1970, pp. 168-169).

This perspective on families as interacting systems in which an individual's subjective perception of the family and his role in the family interaction are perhaps more crucial than other family characteristics helps to clarify a major difficulty in understanding the role of the family in psychopathology. A review of the research on child pathology and family variables from 1925 to 1965 pointed out that the same kind of families that produce psychotic children—mothers who are dominant, overprotective, overpossessive, and yet unconsciously rejecting; fathers who are passive; and considerable family disharmony—also produce neurotic children, children with behavior disorders, and normal children (Frank, 1965). Perhaps the family is not as important a source of psychopathology as has been assumed. Or, a more likely possibility is the one we are suggesting here: the subjective effects of an individual's participation in the family interaction, the way he perceives the family, and the role he plays in the family interaction are crucial variables that these studies have overlooked. In addition, physiological factors and factors outside the family may also be involved in both psychopathology and in disordered patterns of family interaction.

This complex interactive view of the family is an important framework for discussing the family cycle and the changes that it marks off in adult development for two reasons. First, it sensitizes us to the possibility that the meaning of family events, crises, and disorders may exist in the minds of the family members and in the family interaction of the whole family unit. Thus, the meaning of a family event, such as the children leaving home, may differ markedly from family to family, may differ for the husband and the wife and, if it involves a family crisis, the whole family is involved in differing ways. For example, if the oldest daughter wants to leave and travel around Europe for a year, she is affecting the entire family system, and the pressure on her to leave or to stay reflects the role that she and all of the other family members play in the family interaction. And second, this view suggests the organismic quality of family functioning in which the father, mother, children, and other relatives play important interacting parts. The parents are not only socializing their children; children also socialize their parents. The grandparents and other significant relatives, although they may be geographically distant, may play important family roles as well. For example, a crisis in the life of a grandparent (such as a serious illness or admission to a nursing home) may disrupt family interaction, and everyone may benefit from some brief family counseling to alleviate the guilt or anxiety that might disrupt the whole family system. And fathers play a role in the family that is, at least, as important as the role played by the mother. For example, Barry (1970) reviewed the literature on marital adjustment and concluded:

> Factors pertaining to the husband appear to be crucial to marital success.... It would appear—to generalize a bit—that a solid male identification, established through affectional ties with the father and buttressed by academic and/or occupational success and the esteem of his wife, is strongly related to happiness in marriage for the couple (Barry, 1970, p. 47).

In sum, the family—whether it is an extended nuclear family or even a communal family—is a complex system of interacting personalities. We suggest that it can best be understood as a unity in which the whole is different from the sum of its parts and as a system that is perceived differently by each interacting member. This point of view has implications for psychotherapy, for the origin of psychopathology, and for the meaning of events in the family cycle.

THE FAMILY CYCLE

The preceding discussions have dealt with the structure of the family in our society, with some changes in that structure over the past several decades, with some possible future trends, and with an analysis of the functioning of the family system. Let us build on that background in this final section on the family with a presentation of a developmental view of the family. Consider, for example, the important ways in which the family is involved in the milestones that generally mark the transition from childhood to adulthood. Three out of the four milestones marking this transition involve the family directly (the one exception is the beginning of full-time work). The first milestone is the individual leaving the family in which he was raised (the family of *orientation*). The second milestone (which may follow immediately or occur several years later) is marriage. This transition, plus the third family-related milestone—the birth of the first child—marks the full entrance into adult roles and status as well as the beginning of the family of *procreation*. Thus, the passage of these milestones marks, in a normative sense, the transition into adulthood in our society. This does not mean that a couple without children, unmarried adults, or adults living with their parents are not "adult"; but, in general, these family milestones serve to socially and psychologically mark the transition from childhood to adulthood.

Of course, this interaction of family events with adult development does not end with the birth of the first child; it continues through the developmental progression of the *family cycle*. This family cycle consists of the major milestones in the life of the family: marriage, birth of the first child, birth of the last child, the last child leaving home (the "empty nest"), and widowhood. These milestones suggest a framework for examining the differing demands and possibilities that are present for the adult at various times in the cycle of the family.

However, the events that make up this family cycle reflect cultural factors and social change. This is another important example of the effect of cultural-historical factors on the developmental progression through the life span (which we discussed in Chapter 1). That is, the average age for the family events from marriage to the launching of the last child has decreased since 1890 while the average age at widowhood has increased (Figure 5.1). Thus, the parental years of the family cycle have *speeded up* as a result of the combined effects of earlier marriages (up to the mid 1950s; the age at first marriage has increased slightly since then), smaller families, and the earlier departure of the children from the family. However, the length of time between the launching of the last child and widowhood has increased so that the postparental years of the family cycle (which did not exist at all, on the average, in 1890) have been steadily lengthening and are expected to continue growing longer. These

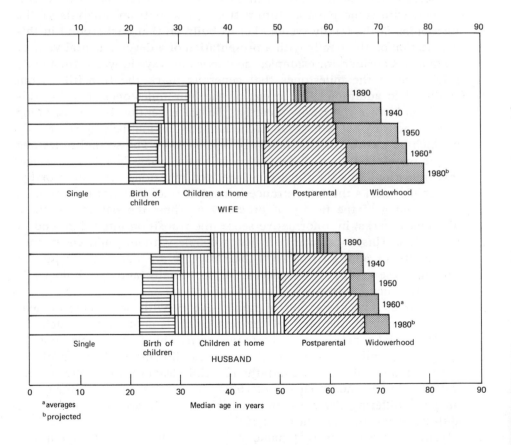

Figure 5.1

Median age of husband and wife at critical stages of the family cycle. Length of the life span is the average life expectancy at age 20. Note that although the projections for 1980 indicate otherwise, the median age of first marriage has been rising since the mid-1950s; in 1972 it was 20.9 for women and 23.3 for men. (Source. Adapted from Duvall, 1971, Table 41–1. Reprinted with permission of J. B. Lippincott Company. Copyright © 1971.)

historical changes in the family cycle have changed the family cycle considerably. They have brought about "middle-aged grandparents," an increase in four-generation families (that is, great-grandparents), the long postparental period for the couple, and an increase in the freedom of middle-aged women to enter the work force full time earlier and to work longer.

In addition, the events of the family cycle also call our attention to the social and psychological effects of these family cycle events on the individual. For example, the birth of the first child not only brings a shift in role from "spouse" to "parent" (with the consequent shift in norms and expectations), but may also bring a shift in self-conception and motivation as well as a possible reawakening of unresolved childhood conflicts in the parents.

Thus, the milestones of the family cycle suggest a progressive development of the family through a series of sequential phases. The division of these phases within the general guidelines of the family cycle is somewhat arbitrary, so we will use a slight modification of the schemes suggested by Hill (1965) and by Duvall (1971). That is, we will discuss the family in each of the following phases: premarriage, establishment, new parents, preschool family, school-age family, family with adolescents, family as "launching center," postparental family, and the aging family. Of course, families with more than one child will find themselves in two or more of these phases at once; in general, we will focus principally on the family's first experience in each phase (i.e., with the oldest child). It is also important to note that these events in the family cycle may be only one major influence on adult change and development since the occupational cycle (to be discussed in Chapter 6) would also be likely to play an important role in the middle years of adulthood.

Premarriage

For the most part, marriages occur as a result of a process of mate selection involving dating, courtship and, usually, a formal ceremony of marriage. Currently the process of mate selection is one of relatively free selection of one potential mate from a limited group of possible individuals. Most mate selection is made on the basis of *homogamy*, that is, on a similarity of age, race, religion, ethnic origin, social class, education, and even personality. An opposing theory—*complementarity*—argues that mates are chosen with different and complementary characteristics (especially personality). However, most studies have shown that complementary needs and dispositions are usually not the case, and that similarity is more frequent (Barry, 1970). The explanation of this process of homogamous choice may be that marriage between two relatively similar individuals will involve less conflict of expectations and will ease the process of mutual socialization during dating and courtship (and, of course, also during the early years of marriage). There are also social pressures and parental interest, if not involvement, in the selection of one's mate that also tend to favor homogamy.

However, the question of mate selection jumps ahead of a prior question that has seldom been considered by research: the question of why individuals marry. Certainly there is great social pressure to marry in this country. At least 90 percent of all Americans marry at some time in their life; this is a higher proportion than is found in other Western countries and clearly represents a significant social expectation. The "social clock" indicates the expected time for an individual to marry. One's friends, family, and employer expect one to marry. One's psychosocial development points toward an intimate relationship and a desire for offspring that strongly imply marriage in our society. And then there are the factors of sexual attraction and, most important (at least according to the romantic myth), *love*.

Interestingly, psychology and sociology books do not often deal very directly with love. McCurdy (1961), in a text on personality, suggests that the shyness of psychologists about love is related to their restraint in dealing with religion. He goes on to point out the irony of discussing sex with complete candor but hesitating to give much attention to religion or to love. One notable exception is Maslow (1955), who distinguishes between D-love (deficiency love) and B-love (love for the being of another person). D-love (selfish love, *need* for love) involves loving the other to make up for a deficiency within oneself. In contrast, B-love is generous, therapeutic, and mystical; it is nonpossessive, does not diminish from being gratified, and is not tainted with anxiety or hostility.

> B-love, in a profound but testable sense, creates the partner. It gives him a self-image, it gives him self-acceptance, a feeling of love-worthiness and respect-worthiness, all of which permit him to grow (Maslow, 1955, p. 28).

One of the most interesting discussions of love is the analysis of the romantic myth in Western culture by Rougemont (1956). He argues that the quest for a perfect love is a culturally transmitted ideal that can be traced back to a heresy in the early Christian church. The most poignant example of this mythical romantic ideal is the Tristan and Isolde legend, in which ideal love is one that is prevented from being consummated except in the eternity of death. This romantic myth is also portrayed in the story of Romeo and Juliet as well as in countless current stories and movies. The essential ingredients are two passionate lovers who are drawn together but, for some unalterable reason, are unable to grow old together in mutual love. Thus, he argues, the image of love that is prevalent in our society leads us to seek passionate attachments that, in their fulfillment, sow the seeds of their own destruction. The enchantment of "affairs" is thus heightened, while the fulfillment of this love in marriage is negated.

> Romance feeds on obstacles, short excitations, and partings; marriage, on the contrary, is made up of wont, daily propinquity, growing accustomed to one another. Romance calls for "the far-away love" of the troubadours; marriage, for love of "one's neighbour." Where, then, a couple have married in obedience to a romance, it is natural that the first time a conflict of temperament or of taste becomes manifest the parties should each ask themselves: "Why did I marry?" And it is no less natural that, obsessed by the universal propaganda in favour of romance, each should seize the first occasion to fall in love with somebody else (Rougemont, 1956, pp. 292-293).

He goes on to argue that *"to be in love* is not necessarily *to love.* To be in love is a state; to love, an act" (p. 310). The heresy, from a Christian point of view, is to view love as a sentiment instead of as an act that is the result of a decision.

The meaning of this active love toward God is for theologians to debate; but the meaning of active love toward one's neighbor (or toward one's spouse) is appropriate for psychologists to consider. Recall Maslow's definition of B-love: "creates the partner...gives him...permits him to grow." This is an active definition, not a description of a sentiment. And this also applies to marriage. That is, married love undoubtedly involves a sentiment of love that is probably similar to the sentiment of romantic love; but also married love ideally involves the active love of one's most intimate of neighbors—one's spouse. Thus the decision to marry is ideally not based only on romantic love, as historical and contemporary Western mythology would suggest, but is also based on a decision to love that must always have an arbitrary element and that involves undertaking to bear the consequences of that decision whether the consequences turn out to be happy or unhappy.

Assuming that the couple has decided to love, to marry, and to raise children, they begin the family cycle, and we will sketch some of the characteristics of family development that they might anticipate. We begin with the event of marriage and the establishment phase of the family cycle and follow the family up to the death of one of the spouses in old age. Along the way we will point out some of the crisis points and some of the interesting data related to each phase. Because this discussion will be quite brief, we cannot attempt to consider the many variations in the family that result from social class, ethnic background, or differences in family style. But let us be clear at the outset that there are many possible variations from the typical middle-class family cycle we are outlining.

Establishment

This phase begins at marriage and continues through the initial period of marriage until the first child is born; it is characterized by the couple functioning as a dyad. The process of mutual socialization is undoubtedly of great importance during this phase as the couple seeks to fulfill their new roles with one another, with parents, and with society in general. To aid in this respect, the event of marriage serves as a rite of passage between past roles and future roles so that at least the entrance into these new roles is clearly defined.

One of the early tasks in this phase is to develop mutually satisfying patterns of sexual interaction and patterns of living intimately with another person; in many ways the traditional honeymoon allows a period of privacy during which time the couple can begin working out these new patterns and role relationships. Other important tasks during this phase include the resolution of conflicts between the couple (such as whether to squeeze or roll the toothpaste tube as well as more serious conflicts); the development of styles of conflict resolution, decision-making, and social interaction; the development of role patterns within the family; and the division of family responsibilities.

However, romanticized ideas about marriage and about one's mate may lead to disenchantment fairly early in the marriage. This disenchantment, combined with failure in mutual socialization, probably plays an important role in early divorce. Data from a 1967 nationwide survey indicate that the probability of divorce is relatively high and rises rapidly during the early years of marriage, reaching an overall peak after two to four years of marriage (possibly coinciding with the birth of children); the probability of divorce then declines with the length of the marriage (Figure 5.2). Men who marry before the age of 20 (women marry two years younger than men, on the average) have the highest rate of divorce throughout their marriages—for example, they are four times more likely to divorce at the beginning of marriage (or after 15 years of marriage) than men who married between 25 and 29.

Sexual intercourse is also at a high point during the early family stages and declines fairly steadily with age according to the Kinsey data (Figure 5.3). The parallel frequency and decline with age for married men and women seems to reflect the male's pattern of sexuality since the frequency of orgasm declines similarly for both married and single men while the pattern for single women changes little with age. Indeed, the frequency of total outlet is highest for women between the ages of 31 and 35 and the percentage of women reaching orgasm increases up to age 40 (Kinsey, Pomeroy, Martin, Gebhard, and Associates, 1953). According to their data, sexual capacity for men reaches its peak at different ages de-

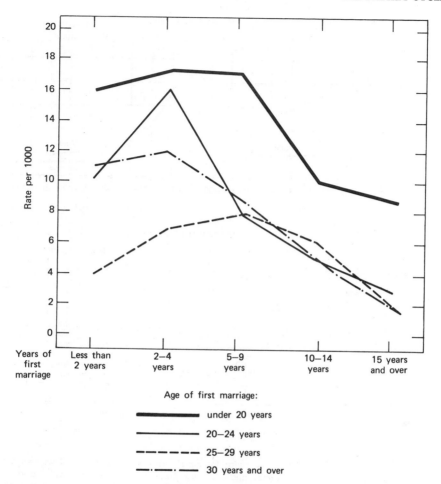

Figure 5.2
Probabilities of divorce per 1000 white males by age at first marriage and duration of first marriage, 1960–1966. (Source. Duvall, 1971, Chart 16–6. Reprinted with permission of J. B. Lippincott Company. Copyright © 1971.)

pending on which measure is used. For example, a man's capacity for multiple orgasms is highest between adolescence and age 15; his mean frequency of total outlet is highest between 21 and 30 (reflecting the degree of opportunity since *active* single or married men peak between adolescence and age 20); and his frequency of morning erection is highest between 31 and 35 (Kinsey, Pomeroy, and Martin, 1948).

The final task of this establishment phase is planning for children, which involves a process of anticipatory socialization for the next milestone: parenthood.

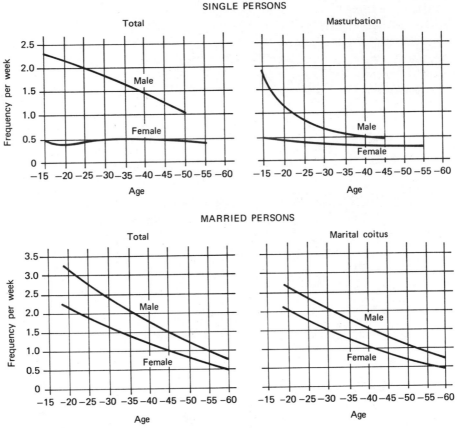

Figure 5.3
Comparison of patterns of sexual activity for single and married men and women by age: median frequencies of all orgasms and orgasms resulting from masturbation and marital coitus. (Source. *Adapted from Kinsey et al., 1953. Figures 144–147. Reprinted with permission.*)

New Parents

This phase begins with pregnancy and the birth of the first child. It involves a major shift in roles from wife and husband to mother and father. In addition to the resocialization involved in that role shift (or addition of a new role to one's set of roles), the couple needs to adjust to the presence of a third family member. Up to this point the couple has probably established a fairly stable relationship. The addition of a third person, who is also a demanding, dependent infant, may bring some upset to the couple's relationship and may involve some jealousy or anger at the disruption. For example, the father may feel that his wife cares more about their child than about him; and in some sense this might be realistic and accurate, and he will have to deal with it. Or the mother may feel "tied down" to the child and the home while her husband is outside in the "exciting" world. And indeed the infant does not wait patiently to be fed or cared for—even if the parents are in the midst of intercourse.

One study by LeMasters (1957) focused on this period of family life in 46 families. He found that 83 percent of the parents reported a "severe" or "extensive" crisis with the birth of their first child. This high percentage indicates widespread upset during this period, and LeMasters explored further to discover what contributed to this upset. He found that the crisis was not the result of an unwanted child since most of the births had been "planned." It was not the result of unhappy marriages since 89 percent of the marriages were rated as of "good quality." Finally, it was not related to poor personality adjustment since all the parents were rated as "above average" on adjustment. LeMasters did find, however, that there had been little preparation for the couple's new role as parents—little anticipatory socialization. Instead, most parents who suffered a crisis had "romanticized" parenthood, and thus their expectations were disconfirmed when the child turned out to be demanding and to upset their routine. In addition, he found that the couple's previous experience with crises and their previous organization of roles were related to the absence of a severe crisis; apparently their ability to adjust quickly to this new experience was a crucial factor. Further, LeMasters found that mothers with professional training and with extensive work experience *all* suffered "extensive" or "severe" crises with the birth of their first child. In all cases they gave up their work, an act that probably intensified their role shift and brought about an even greater change in self-concept, which was an added upset to be resolved.

These findings indicate that the role shift at parenthood is a crucial turning point that involves considerable potential for emotional crisis. One additional factor that may add to the potential crisis (combined with the change in family structure and the shift in roles) is that the advent of parenthood is the final step into adulthood and into adult responsibilities and obligations. The early increase in divorce rates may also reflect this potential crisis point. In any event, the importance of parenthood as a developmental milestone seems apparent, and it deserves a great deal more research.

Family with Preschool Children

The oldest child in the family is now between the ages of three and six. There may be younger siblings in the family by this time, but we will focus on the family's first experience with each of the phases. This is not to suggest that the birth of the second child, for example, is necessarily a repetition of an event with little additional importance, or that a family is not involved in the issues of several phases at the same time. But our discussion must be less complex than the families we are describing.

Some of the central tasks of this family phase include maintaining an intimate relationship with one's spouse, providing space and financial resources for the expanding family, and raising the children. The task of child rearing may receive quite a lot of attention because it involves nurturing, socialization, and providing opportunities for the child's maximum emotional and psychological growth. According to psychoanalytic theory, the child is developing rapidly and progressing through a series of psychosexual stages. Benedek (1952) suggests that the child's development may also cause the parents to re-work their resolution of these psychosexual stages at the same time. In addition, the parents need to develop effective and comfortable styles of parenting that allow them to interact with their children as fully human beings and to allow for themselves to change at the same time their children are growing and changing. For example, the process of socialization—by which the parents teach their children the norms, values, and expectations of society—is a mutual process that also allows the parents to be socialized by their children. This mutual socialization process is especially clear when the children become adolescents. But through this complex process of learning how to be a parent for this particular child, and fitting that *me* as a parent together with one's other *me*s into a coherent sense of self, both the children and the parents ideally grow in their own ways. Sometimes parents become anxious about how to raise their children "correctly." Of course, this is a realistic concern and there probably are some ways that are "better" in some sense than others. But, in general, children are rather hardy creatures and manage to grow and develop surprisingly well, even in relatively difficult circumstances. After all, if children had to have perfect parents, few of us would be functioning today! Perhaps the best guide is for parents to develop a style of parenting that is comfortable for them and comfortable and realistic for the child; yet the more one knows about children, the more comfortable and realistic one can be.

Family with School-age Children

The fourth family phase begins when the oldest child enters school full time. One frequent change during this period is the mother returning to work. Considering only married women who are living with their husbands, the percentage of white women working in 1970 was 28 percent for those with children under 6 and 48 percent for those with children between 6 and 17; for nonwhite women the increase was only slightly smaller—47 percent with preschool children and 63 percent with school-age children. Economic factors seem to be involved in white preschool mothers working since over half again as many women with children under 6 were working if their husband's income was under $10,000, compared with those whose husband earned over $10,000. The husband's income was less related to the proportion of mothers working in nonwhite families or in white families with no children under 6 at home (Table 5.1). The largest percentage of working women is during the establishment phase (no children, wife 16-34) and during the postparental phase (no children under 18, wife 35-54). The percentages of working women are increasing rapidly; the figures are about 4 percent higher in 1970 than in 1967 for all groups except the oldest.

Hoffman (1963) studied the effect of maternal employment on the mother-child relationship. She found that the attitudes of the mother about working were related more to the reactions of the child to the mother and to the mother's behavior toward the child than to whether the mother worked or not. That is, working mothers who liked working related positively with their children and avoided inconveniencing the child with housework; the children were not aggressive or hostile. Mothers who worked but disliked it were less involved with their child altogether, and the child was judged to be assertive and hostile toward

Table 5.1   Percentage of Wives Working by Age, Age of Children, and Husband's Income, March 1970

Age of Wife and Children		Income of Husband				
	Total	Under $3000	$3000 to $4999	$5000 to $6999	$7000 to $9999	$10,000 and over
ALL PERSONS						
No children under 18						
Wife 16–34 years	69.0	63.2	68.2	71.9	70.3	70.0
Children under 6 years	30.3	31.7	37.5	36.0	33.4	21.4
Children 6-17 years	49.2	54.7	53.7	54.4	54.7	41.9
No children under 18						
Wife 35–54 years	54.5	57.0	59.0	59.0	55.8	48.9
No children under 18						
Wife 55 years +	24.7	20.7	20.8	29.3	30.9	27.1
WHITE PERSONS						
Children under 6 years	28.4	29.7	34.5	34.5	31.5	20.4
Children 6–17 years	48.1	53.6	51.4	53.6	54.1	41.2
NEGRO AND OTHER RACES						
Children under 6 years	46.9	37.6	47.9	44.6	55.1	46.2
Children 6–17 years	62.6	59.3	62.6	61.0	62.5	71.8

Source. U.S. Bureau of Labor Statistics. Marital and Family Characteristics of Workers. Special Labor Force Report, No. 130. Washington, D.C.: U.S. Government Printing Office, 1971, Table J.

the mother. Thus, the mother's comfort and lack of negative feelings about working seems to be more important than whether she works or not. The same may be true for nonworking mothers if they have negative feelings about not working or feel "trapped" in the house.

Family with Adolescents

The next phase begins with the oldest child reaching puberty. Hill (1965) suggests that this may be a period of relative equilibrium in the family's economic growth and expansion. The family is usually at its maximal size, and all members are living at home. Some of the issues in this period center on the career choices for the children, their selection of a college, dating, the beginning of mate selection, sexuality, the gradual increase in independence and mobility (including use of the family car), the current concern with drug abuse, and the more traditional concern with alcohol abuse. These concerns often bring periodic family crises in which the parents as well as the adolescents are likely to be affected and to change.

At this point in the family, the "generation gap" may be quite apparent. It is a complex phenomenon as we discussed in Chapter 1. But in the context of the family, it also represents a *lineage gap* between two successive generations of the family (Bengston, 1971). Typically this lineage gap is smaller than the "cohort gap" between generations in the broader society since family members tend to be more similar to one another in general. For example, a nationwide study of young people 18-24 in 1968 found that less than one-fourth of the respondents felt there was a "very great" difference between their values and their parents' values (Table 5.2). Also, the young people felt a sense of solidarity with both their family and their own generation. As might be expected, young adults who were not attending college or were attending college with "practical" goals ("For me college is mainly a practical matter...") felt fewer differences between themselves and their parents than "forerunner" students ("I'm concerned with the intangible benefits of college such as the opportunity to change things rather than make out well in the existing system"). The "practical" students were a slight majority (58 percent), but *Fortune* called the others "forerunners" because they felt this group was likely to become more prevalent.

This lineage gap reflects the difficulties inherent in the socialization and cultural transmission functions of the family. And because family members have different perspectives on the family and different investments in the continuity of family values, the lineage gap is seen differently by young people, parents, and grandparents. That is, young people have an interest in perceiving greater differences between generations, while par-

Table 5.2   Young Adults' Values and Identifications With Their Families
and Peers, in Percent (Nationwide Sample, 18-24, 1968)

	No College	Practical College[a]	Fore-runner College[b]
Differences between parents and your values:			
Very great	15	11	24
Moderate	41	49	51
Slight	44	40	25
Identification and sense of solidarity with:			
Family	82	78	65
Own generation	60	65	68

[a] Students concerned with practical benefits of college.
[b] Students concerned with intangible benefits of college.
Source. Fortune-Yankelovich Survey. What They Believe. Fortune, January, 1969, 70-71, 179-181. Reprinted with permission.

ents (and especially grandparents) have a "developmental stake" in minimizing differences they perceive between generations (Bengston, 1971).

Family as Launching Center

This phase refers to the departure of the children from their family—either into families of their own at marriage or into separate living arrangements. It involves the parents' "letting go" of their children, launching them into the world, and the concomitant increase in the independence and autonomy on the part of the children. Although the effect of the launching of their children on the parents would be an interesting developmental study, we know of no such research. The process would probably involve some degree of upset and conflict for the parents, particularly for the mother if she has centered her time and interest on the family up to that point. The launching of the children would then involve a considerable role shift for her. In addition, this event frequently coincides with the mother's climacterium (menopause) between the ages of 45 and 50 since the parental phase of the family cycle has speeded up in this century. This biological change combined with the "empty nest" would suggest that this phase is likely to be a potential crisis point in the family cycle for women. In addition, the husband would be likely to be working very hard to attain the pinnacle of his career and consequently may be somewhat more distant and preoccupied with his occupation during this phase of the family cycle (when he is 45-55). The interaction of these various factors for the husband and the wife might well intensify the potential for psychological upset and crisis.

Another related factor is that many women report an increase in sexual interest at this time, either resulting from a fear of losing sexual satisfaction with menopause (which does not in fact occur) or out of relief at not having to worry about the possibility of pregnancy. Their husbands, on the contrary, may feel less interest in sexual intimacy at this time due to their preoccupation with vocational goals and may experience impotence (the inability to have an erection during intercourse). Masters and Johnson (1970) point out that the incidence of sexual inadequacy increases sharply after age 50 for men. They cite six general reasons for this increase: (1) monotony of a repetitious sexual relationship; (2) preoccupation with the career or economic pursuits; (3) mental or physical fatigue; (4) overindulgence in food or drink; (5) physical and mental infirmities of either the individual or his spouse; and (6) fear of performance associated with or resulting from any of the other categories. However, although the aging man may note some physiological changes such as delayed erective time, reduction in the volume of seminal fluid, or decreased ejaculatory pressure, Masters and Johnson stress that he does not ordinarily lose his physiological ability to attain an erection. Thus, most of the impotence in middle and late life is a secondary result of these six factors.

Postparental Family

The family phase following the departure of the last child is often a time of life characterized by high economic productivity (at least in the middle class), by independence and freedom, and by a high degree of marital happiness. Although one study (Pineo, 1961) found that marital satisfaction drops gradually from the first years of marriage through the 20 to 25 years of child rearing, Deutscher (1964) found that reported marital satisfaction was as high for *postparental* couples as for any of the preceding periods. Rollins and Feldman (1970) substantiated the findings that marital satisfaction declines to a low point during the launching stage and then increases in the postparental stage to quite high levels of satisfaction for the aging couple (Table 5.3). However, couples whose satisfaction was very low may have divorced so that these data may partly reflect a process of selection of durable marriages.

Two major changes typically occur in the extended family during this postparental period. First, sometime during these middle years of the life span, the couple is typically faced with providing some form of care for their aging parents. And eventually they will have to deal with their feel-

Table 5.3 Marital Satisfaction by Present Stage of the Family Cycle (Percent)

Stage of Family	Husbands Degree Satisfied			Wives Degree Satisfied			Each Sample N
	Very	Quite	Less	Very	Quite	Less	N
Establishment	55	39	6	74	22	4	51
New parents	69	23	8	76	18	6	51
Preschool children	61	31	8	50	33	17	82
School-age children	39	45	16	35	44	21	244
Adolescent children	44	41	15	17	38	15	227
Launching center	9	25	66	8	16	76	64
Postparental	24	13	63	17	13	70	30
Aging family	66	30	4	82	14	4	50
Total of all stages	44	37	19	45	33	22	799

Source. Adapted from Rollins and Feldman (1970), p. 24. Reprinted with permission.

ings of mourning upon the death of their parents. Certainly the death of one's parents would seem to be an event of great importance during this phase of the family cycle—and for adulthood in general. Yet there have been few studies on the effect of the death of one's parents on adults. Perhaps this topic may be too threatening for middle-aged social scientists to investigate (see Chapter 9).

Second, at the other end of the generation continuum, the parents probably become grandparents. This involves a shift in roles and may also bring a sudden realization of one's advancing age. However, with the speeding up of the family cycle, grandparenthood may occur during the decade of the forties when the couple is still middle aged. So this shift in roles may involve taking on a relatively new role—a "middle-aged grandparent."

Neugarten and Weinstein (1964) explored the satisfactions and the styles of grandparenthood among middle-class respondents in their fifties and sixties. They found that the majority of grandparents felt comfort, satisfaction, and pleasure in the role; but about one-third felt some discomfort or disappointment in the role of grandparent (Table 5.4). The meaning of the role varied considerably among the respondents. Some felt it provided a sense of biological renewal ("It's through my grandchildren that I feel young again") or biological continuity ("It's carrying on the family line"). Others felt it provided a source of emotional self-

Table 5.4   Ease of Role Performance, Significance of Role, and Style of
            Grandparenting

	Grandmothers (N=70) N	Grandfathers (N=70) N
A. Ease of role performance:		
(1) Comfortable-pleasant	41	43
(2) Difficulty-discomfort	25	20
(Insufficient data)	4	7
Total	70	70
B. Significance of the grandparent role:		
(1) Biological renewal and/or continuity	29	16
(2) Emotional self-fulfillment	13	19
(3) Resource person to child	3	8
(4) Vicarious achievement through child	3	3
(5) Remote: little effect on the self	19	20
(Insufficient data)	3	4
Total	70	70
C. Style of grandparenting:		
(1) The formal	22	23
(2) The fun-seeking	20	17
(3) The parent surrogate	10	0
(4) The reservoir of family wisdom	1	4
(5) The distant figure	13	20
(Insufficient data)	4	6
Total	70	70

Source. Neugarten and Weinstein (1964), Table 1. Reprinted with permission.

fulfillment ("I can do for my grandchildren things I could never do for
my own kids. I was too busy with my business to enjoy my kids, but my
grandchildren are different. Now I have the time to be with them" [all
quotes are from Neugarten and Weinstein, 1964]). Others felt they served
as a resource person to their grandchildren, and still others felt they were
able to achieve something through their grandchildren that they (and
their children) were not able to achieve. A substantial number felt

remote from their grandchildren ("It's great to be a grandmother, of course—but I don't have much time" [ibid.]).

Neugarten and Weinstein also identified five different styles of grand-parenting. Three are fairly traditional grandparent roles: the "formal," who leave parenting to the parent but like to offer special favors to the grandchild; the "surrogate parent," usually the grandmother, who assumes parental responsibility for the child at the invitation of the parent; and the "reservoir of family wisdom," who maintains his authority and sees himself as the dispenser of special wisdom or skills (it was usually the grandfather, but this type was not very frequent). Two of the grand-parenting styles seem to be emerging in our society as new roles for grandparents: the "fun seeker," who joins the child in activities to have fun, to enjoy leisure, and tends to ignore authority issues; and the "distant figure," who is present only on special occasions and has only fleeting contact with the grandchild. Neugarten and Weinstein found that those two new roles were significantly more common among younger grandparents (under 65) while the most traditional role ("formal") was more frequent among older grandparents. Also, the two emerging roles seem to be neuter roles—that is, the "fun seeker" and the "distant figure" are neither "masculine" nor "feminine" roles. Thus, the increase in middle-age grandparents may be changing the meaning of grandparent-hood, and new styles of grandparenting may be emerging in our society.

The Aging Family

The onset of this final period of the family cycle is marked by the retire-ment of the husband. If the wife has worked, she probably retires at about the same time. This period brings a major role shift for the hus-band and frequently involves a major milestone for him (we will discuss this in Chapter 6). One factor involved in retirement, in addition to the substantial change in demands, responsibilities, and allocation of time, is the sharp decline in income. Often this necessitates some decline in the family's standard of living since the income is cut by one-third to one-half at retirement (Maddox, 1966). The economic difficulty typically worsens as the aging couple's health begins to fail. Often extended family help patterns reverse at this time so that the young families (which the old couple once helped) now begin giving economic and service aid to their parents. This phase of the family cycle may also involve a change of resi-dence from the family home (which is now almost empty and too much to take care of) to an apartment or a retirement community—at least for couples who have the economic freedom to move.

Because of the speeding up of the family cycle, and increasing longevity, this family period also brings the possibility of great-grandparenthood and the emotional satisfaction of being at the top of a four-generation

family. A cross-national study of older persons in 1962 (Shanas, Townsend, Wedderburn, Friis, Milhøj, and Stehouwer, 1968) found that 40 percent of persons over 65 in their United States sample had great-grandchildren; 23 percent in Denmark and 22 percent in Britain were also at
the top of four-generation families. In Britain, the average woman became a grandmother at 54 and a great-grandmother at 72; men averaged
three years later (Townsend, 1966). This change has a wide range of
effects on the structure of the extended family. For example, the grandparents may have to divide their time and energy between caring for
their aged parents and providing attention to their adult children and
their grandchildren. And one person may have 20 to 30 grandchildren
and great-grandchildren spread across the country in a complex extended
family network.

In addition, the growing longevity and earlier retirement trends in our
society allow the possibility for a second career for many retired couples
who are dedicating their time-tested talents to dealing with social and
political issues. At the other extreme are the disadvantaged elderly who
find the complex and rapidly changing society very difficult to compre-
hend and who need help in dealing with an abundance of computer cards,
forms for rent reduction and for Medicare, and with information about
special privileges for "senior citizens."

Finally, the capacity for satisfying sexual relations continues into the
decades of (at least) the seventies and eighties for healthy couples. Masters and Johnson (1966) report:

> The most important factor in the maintenance of effective sexuality
> for the aging male is consistency of active sexual expression.
> When the male is stimulated to high sexual output during his forma-
> tive years and a similar tenor of activity is established for the 31-
> 40-year age range, his middle-aged and involutional years usually are
> marked by constantly recurring physiologic evidence of maintained
> sexuality. Certainly it is true for the male geriatric sample that those
> men currently interested in relatively high levels of sexual expression
> report similar activity levels from their formative years. It does not
> appear to matter what manner of sexual expression has been em-
> ployed, as long as high levels of activity were maintained (pp. 262-
> 263).

They report a similar indefinite ability for sexual expression among
women.

> In brief, significant sexual capacity and effective sexual perform-
> ance are not confined to the human female's premenopausal years.
> Generally, the intensity of physiologic reaction and duration of ana-
> tomic response to effective sexual stimulation are reduced ... with the
> advancing years. ... Regardless of involutional changes in the repro-

ductive organs, the aging human female is fully capable of sexual performance at orgasmic response levels, particularly if she is exposed to regularity of effective sexual stimulation (p. 238).

In short, there is no time limit drawn by the advancing years to female sexuality (p. 247).

Masters and Johnson (1970) also report that although many women may benefit from the administration of hormones after menopause, the physical changes following menopause do not necessarily interfere with sexual enjoyment, especially if sexual activities are reasonably frequent.

Probably the main factors involved in limiting sexual activity for the aging person are male attrition (resulting from greater longevity for women), which leaves the woman without a sexual partner and with little chance of finding another partner (Newman and Nichols, 1960), the possibility that the man may lose his ability to have an erection because of sexual abstinence in his later years (e.g., when he or his wife is hospitalized), and social norms that imply that sexuality is only for "dirty" old men and women.

Conclusion

We have presented an overview of the family cycle in rather generalized terms. Our intent has been to view the family developmentally, as a sequential series of phases. But we have not dealt with the variety of family styles that exist, nor with the families in differing social classes or with differing ethnic or racial backgrounds. Any of these topics could readily fill an entire book. However, the family cycle we have described is probably a pervasive stereotype in our society that influences these other family styles and even single adult life styles.

We have also pointed out the major crisis points in the family cycle—particularly parenthood, the empty nest, and retirement. We did this because we are interested in the adults in the family and in the crises they face. We are also interested in the ways in which this family cycle intersects with the occupational cycle, to be discussed in the next chapter, and in the ways in which they both influence the milestones and timing of adult development. For example, we see the social clock at work, timing the "right" time to get married, to have the last child, to enter the work force (for the mother), to launch the children, and to move out of the family home. The process of adult socialization is also clearly involved in the many role shifts that occur during the family cycle. Of course, many other factors are also involved, just as these events may have wide-ranging psychological and emotional meaning for each individual couple. Certainly each individual progresses through his family cycle in slightly different ways and these individual differences may seem more clear now that the typical family cycle has been outlined.

In sum, we have examined the family in a way that we feel aids our understanding of the whole time span of adulthood. We will now turn to single adults and attempt to gain a greater understanding of adulthood and its diversity by exploring some aspects of their lives.

SINGLES: THE UNMARRIED AND THE PREVIOUSLY MARRIED

Although marriage is typical in our society, there are a numerically sizable minority of the population who are not married at any census point. For example, in 1972 about 2.9 million men and 5.1 million women in the United States (over 14) were listed as separated or divorced; this does not include those who were divorced and remarried by the census date. Another 1.8 million men and 9.6 million women were recorded as widowed. And 3.2 million men and 2.8 million women over the age of 30 were single (U. S. Bureau of the Census, 1972, Table 1).

We would expect that there is at least as much diversity among these single and previously married adults as there is among their married counterparts. That is, their life styles may be found to consist of distinct qualities that differentiate them from married life styles in more important ways than the simple lack of marriage. For example, the life style of celibate priests and nuns is probably more influenced by their commitment to the church and by their religious vows than it is by the simple lack of marriage. Similarly, a homosexual's life style may differ from the life style of a heterosexual more because of a difference in sexual orientation than because of the absence of marriage. At present there are relatively few data on single adults except for census data and spotty data on some single life styles. However, we will attempt to sketch some rough outlines of single life styles because we are interested in single adults since there is relatively little known about singles in adulthood (except that they are not married), and we expect that knowing more about their life styles will increase our understanding of adulthood. One central developmental question in this regard is: What are the milestones that mark the developmental progression through the adult years for single people? We currently lack the data to answer this; but perhaps the milestones primarily involve only the occupation, or perhaps they are based on the person's love affairs, or possibly they reflect the family cycle that singles would be going through if they were married even though it does not fit their own lives very well. Certainly, such events as divorce or widowhood would be plausible milestones in the lives of previously married adults; the death of one's parents would be expected to be important for all single adults; and the beginning and development of long-term homosexual or heterosexual relationships would probably be a source of important milestones for some single adults (who are "single" only in a legal sense). However, having acknowledged the need for much more research in this area, let us investigate some data on single adults, beginning with divorced and separated adults.

Divorced and Separated Persons

Termination of a marriage, either by divorce or by separation, results from a variety of causes both personal and social. On one hand, divorce is more common among persons poorly prepared for marriage, among those who married to escape their parents, and among the couples who cannot tolerate differences; it is more common among children of divorced or unhappy parents, among childless marriages, and among pregnant brides (Duvall, 1971). On the other hand, divorce rates reflect a range of social factors such as education, race, income, age, and religion. Previously we noted that there are higher probabilities of divorce among

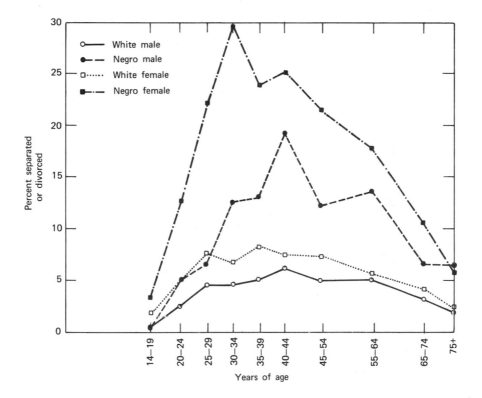

Figure 5.4
Percent separated or divorced by age, sex, and race in the United States, 1972. Combined rates for "Negro and other races" are slightly lower than the data for Negroes presented. (Source. U.S. Bureau of the Census, 1972, Table 1.)

those couples who marry in their teens. Census data also indicate that higher family income and higher levels of education increase the likelihood of both partners marrying only once. And the percentage divorced or separated is higher for Negro than for white persons and higher for women than for men (Figure 5.4).

The rate of divorce also reflects social factors such as national prosperity (when divorce rates increase) and the relaxation of social pressure against divorce. The divorce rate has been increasing since the 1960s in this country; but the rate in 1969 (13.4 per 1000 married women) is lower than the rate after World War II (Figure 5.5). In 1972 there were 52 divorced persons for every 1000 intact marriages, which is a substantial increase from 26 per 1000 intact marriages in 1960; however, this increase may reflect not only the rising divorce rate but also indicates a tendency for divorced persons to remain divorced (that is, to not remarry) as quickly in the 1970s as they did in the 1950s. Thus the rising divorce rate, or the growing proportion of divorced persons, does not necessarily indicate that marriage is any more "risky" now than it was in the past. And indeed, census data do not say anything about the prospects of an individual marriage. Yet these data do indicate that the number of divorced persons is growing in our country.

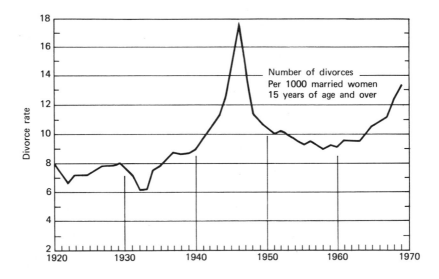

Figure 5.5
Divorce rates in the United States, 1920–1969. (Source. Adapted from Duvall, 1971, Chart 3–1. Reprinted with permission of J. B. Lippincott Company. Copyright © 1971.)

In 1972 there were 3.2 million persons who were separated and 4.8 million who were divorced at the time the census was taken. Higher proportions of women and nonwhite persons were in these groups and nearly 40 percent of all *separated* persons were Negro (U. S. Bureau of the Census, 1972, Table 1). Income data indicate that separation often functions as a poor man's divorce since it is much more common among low-income persons (Carter and Glick, 1970, p. 320). Census data also indicate a trend toward earlier first divorces and separations; in 1971 the median age (half were older, half younger) was 31.6 for first divorce and 28.7 for separation after the first marriage.

Census data provide a few clues about the life style of divorced persons (Table 5.5). In 1972 the vast majority were living in homes or apartments and were recorded as "Head of Household." About half of the men were living alone ("Primary Individual"), while about half of the women especially during middle age were living with their children ("Head of Primary Family"). Older divorced persons were generally living alone. Younger divorced men and women were frequently living with their parents ("Not Head of Household in Families").

These clues from the census data provide useful basic information but do not provide an adequate sense of what it means to be a divorced person. For an individual, divorce involves a process of resocialization and typically leads to rediscovering the art of dating and eventually to remarriage. Yet divorce may also reflect emotional or physical difficulties —or the divorced life style may lead to such difficulties.

Change in Status and Resocialization. Just as marriage involves a change in social role and status from "single" to "married," so does the process of divorce—which is often a lengthy one—also involve a marked change in role and in status. This change is not only shifting to a single life again but also involves reformulating the whole range of social ties—to one's ex-spouse, to one's children, to one's relatives, and to one's friends. Unlike marriage, divorce is not an institutionalized status passage in which the new roles are prescribed by social norms. Instead, one has to reformulate all these roles with little outside support and with almost no normative guidelines. Often there is a feeling of failure involved in terminating a marriage, and one's married friends are apt to feel somewhat divided and threatened in their loyalties to the divorced couple. Legal aspects of the process are often difficult and provide more chance for expressing anger than for smoothly meeting responsibilities and dividing up joint possessions. The long-term family upset that frequently precedes divorce increases the difficulty of reformulating new role relationships and of explaining the new relationships to the children. The process often involves a complex tangle of emotions and adjustments to new situations; feelings of love and hate, of mourning and relief, of failure and a new beginning all alternate while one attempts to adjust to sleeping alone,

Table 5.5 Divorced Persons by Family Status, Age, and Sex (March 1972)

Subject	Total, 14 Years and Over	Age (Years)						
		14 to 24	25 to 34	35 to 44	45 to 54	55 to 64	65 to 74	75+
WOMEN (in thousands)	3055	254	666	689	711	443	219	73[a]
Percent	100.0	100.0	100.0	100.0	100.0	100.0	100.0	—
Head of household	79.3	50.2	76.7	84.9	85.8	81.0	79.8	—
Head of primary family	48.2	40.9	64.2	71.6	45.9	19.7	9.5	—
Primary individual	31.1	9.3	12.5	13.3	39.9	61.3	70.3	—
Living alone	29.6	5.3	11.7	12.5	38.6	58.5	69.6	—
With nonrelatives	1.5	4.0	0.9	0.8	1.2	2.9	0.6	—
Not head of household	20.7	49.8	23.3	15.1	14.2	19.0	20.2	—
In families	17.2	45.0	19.0	13.0	11.2	15.6	13.8	—
Secondary individual	3.6	4.8	4.2	2.1	3.1	3.4	6.4	—
MEN (in thousands)	1781	103	372	451	390	321	112	33[a]
Percent	100.0	100.0	100.0	100.0	100.0	100.0	100.0	—
Head of household	63.3	29.0	49.9	54.7	73.3	77.8	93.1	—
Head of primary family	12.0	6.9	5.2	12.2	22.7	12.0	5.1	—
Primary individual	51.3	22.1	44.7	42.5	50.5	65.7	88.0	—
Living alone	47.0	16.7	37.3	39.9	45.8	63.2	84.0	—
With nonrelatives	4.3	5.4	7.4	2.6	4.7	2.5	3.9	—
Not head of household	36.7	71.0	50.1	45.3	26.7	22.2	6.9	—
In families	25.0	50.7	35.7	31.9	17.0	13.1	4.3	—
Secondary individual	11.6	20.3	14.4	13.4	9.7	9.2	2.6	—

[a] Number too small to calculate percentages by living arrangements.

Source. U.S. Bureau of the Census (1972), Table 6.

eating in restaurants (especially for men), and dividing up treasured joint possessions; loneliness is frequently a major reaction.

Some time after the divorce, propelled by loneliness, sexual desire, or other important realistic needs, a divorced person generally meets other divorced individuals, and they may play an important role in the resocialization process. In a sense, there is a kind of subcultural support that is provided by divorced friends and by more structured groups such as Parents Without Partners, travel and ski clubs, and other special interest groups. Hunt (1966) reports that the "formerly married" subculture involves a body of rules of behavior, subcultural norms and expectations, and subtle styles of communicating one's availability and interest at social gatherings. Thus, social contacts and dating (often including sex) provide much of the support for the resocialization process, assist the adjustment to lost roles (such as having been a father), and provide some relief for loneliness and sexual desire.

Dating. Most divorced persons eventually remarry, and the rate of marriage is higher for divorced persons (with the exception of widowers) than for single persons at all ages (Figure 5.6). Dating is the usual course to remarriage, but it not only involves redeveloping dating skills that have not been used for several years (and questions about one's current dating skills and assets) but also involves meeting potential dates. Goode

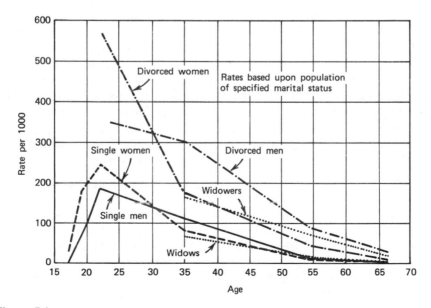

Figure 5.6
First marriage and remarriage rates by age at marriage, 1963. (Source. Carter and Glick, 1970, Figure 3.3; from National Center for Health Statistics. Reprinted with permission.)

(1956) found that one-third of a divorced sample reported that friends were a primary source of new contacts; relatives were most helpful in providing new contacts for one-sixth; and one-fourth of divorced women indicated their job was the most important source. Church activities, community work, informal cocktail parties, and clubs or organizations as well as resort hotels and cruises are other potential sources of dating contacts. Less-acceptable possibilities for many formerly married persons include singles bars, open parties (advertised in "underground" newspapers), matrimonial agencies, and dating services using computer matching.

Although dating probably provides an important means of rediscovering one's value as a person and repairing one's damaged "ego" (as well as firming up one's sense of identity), dating is undoubtedly more difficult for divorced persons, especially those with custody of small children, than it is for other single adults. Children not only make the arrangements for going out more difficult (baby sitters, meals, and so on), but also ask potentially embarrassing questions or volunteer potentially embarrassing information and preferences. In addition, sexual relations are more complicated and potentially embarrassing with children waiting at home or sleeping in another room. However, based on a survey and his interviews, Hunt (1966) reported that five out of six formerly married persons began intercourse within the first year after divorce, and most had relations with more than one partner. Gebhard (1970) reported that a sizeable majority of divorced women in the Kinsey study reported postmarital intercourse (Table 5.6). Hunt differentiates between "abstainers" who tend to be relieved at not being expected to engage in sex after the divorce, "users" who tend to form liaisons with casual sex and less emphasis on love, at least at first (this group made up most of his respondents), and "addicts" who seemed to be habituated to casual sex. He argues that casual sex among formerly married persons helps to restore confidence and to overcome one's fears of trusting deep emotional feelings that have so grievously betrayed the person; but the progression back to marriage probably includes at least one serious love affair.

Remarriage. Glick (1949) reported that 75 percent of divorced persons remarried within five years, and that divorced persons married other divorced individuals about 60 percent of the time. Hunt (1966) calculates that about 60 percent of these remarriages last until death, although some become chronic repeaters. Locke (1951) found that 75 percent of remarried couples rated their remarriage as "happy" or "very happy"; and 90 percent considered their second marriage much better than their first one. However satisfying the remarriage, the 60 percent of divorced persons with children often remain involved with their former spouse through child support and alimony payments; about half of the remaining 40 percent without children remain involved with alimony, according to

Table 5.6   Age-Specific Incidence of Postmarital Coitus (Females) and Average (Mean) Frequency of Postmarital Coitus Among Widowed or Divorced Females with Such Coitus

		Divorced			Widowed	
Age-Period	N	Percent with Coitus	Frequency per Week	N	Percent with Coitus	Frequency per Week
21–25	177	73.4	1.36	19	42.1	a
26–30	236	70.3	1.36	42	54.8	0.85
31–35	207	78.3	1.23	53	47.2	0.78
36–40	154	77.9	1.40	53	35.8	0.69
41–45	118	68.6	1.01	49	34.7	0.39
46–50	61	59.0	0.88	49	26.5	a
51–55	33	39.4	a	38	26.3	a
56–60	14	42.9	a	34	23.5	a

a The number of cases is less than 15 so no calculation is feasible.

Source. Adapted from Gebhard (1970), p. 94, Tables 1 and 2. Reprinted with permission of Doubleday & Company, Inc. from Divorce and After, copyright © 1968, 1970 by P. Bohannan.

Hunt (1966); only two states allow temporary alimony and child support, and in some states even remarriage of the person receiving alimony does not automatically terminate legal responsibility and another court appearance is necessary.

Mental and Physical Health. Separated and divorced persons seem to be more vulnerable to mental and physical illness than married persons. For example, separated and divorced persons were residents of mental hospitals in 1960 at higher rates than married or widowed persons but at lower rates than unmarried persons (Table 5.7); however, one study found that the rate for first admissions to mental hospitals was higher for divorced persons than for any other group, at least over age 55 (Locke, Kramer, and Pasamanick, 1960). Also, death rates are lower for married than for unmarried (widowed, divorced, or single) men and women. In general, death rates for women are markedly lower than for men, and death rates for white persons are lower than for nonwhite persons regardless of marital status; however, widowed men and women have the highest death rates for nonwhite persons, and divorced men and women have the highest death rates for white persons (Figure 5.7). In 1960 divorced persons had the highest death rates (among white persons 15-64) for the following causes of death: tuberculosis (for men), cirrhosis of the liver, pneumonia (for men), homicide, accidental falls (for men), suicide (for women), and syphilis (Carter and Glick, 1970, Table 11.12).

These data on mental and physical health probably indicate the effects

226 Families and Singles

Table 5.7 Mental Hospital Residence Rate per 10,000 Population 14 Years Old and Over, by Marital Status and Sex, Standardized for Age (United States, 1960)

| | Mental Hospital Rate Standardized for Age | | |
| | Men | Women | Women as Percent |
Marital Status	Rate	Rate	of Men
Total, 14 and over	61	42	69
Married[a]	18	23	128
Widowed	94	47	50
Divorced	188	105	56
Separated	169	132	78
Single	405	214	53

[a] Married, not separated.

Source. Adapted from Carter and Glick (1970), p. 338, Table 11.7 (from U.S. Bureau of the Census). Reprinted with permission.

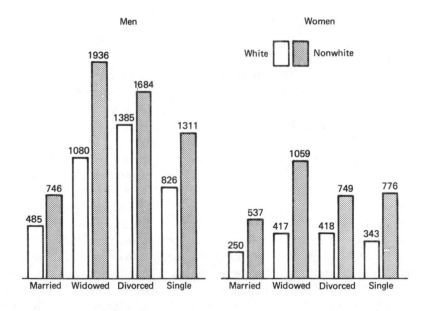

Figure 5.7
Death rate per 100,000 persons 15 to 64 years old by marital status, standardized for age in the United States, 1959–1961. (Source. Carter and Glick, 1970, Figure 11.1; from National Center for Health Statistics. Reprinted with permission.)

of stress caused by the divorce and the ensuing unmarried life style (e.g. homicide, cirrhosis of the liver, and syphilis). However, they also reflect characteristics of persons who do not eventually *remarry*. That is, those who remarry (and thus are not listed in the census as divorced or single, for example) tend to be persons in better mental and physical health.

Widowed Persons

Marriages inevitably end in either divorce or widowhood for one spouse or the other (unless both spouses die simultaneously in an accident, for example). Because of the lengthening of the life span since 1900, there were markedly fewer women widowed before the age of 45 and considerably more widowed after the age of 55 in 1964 than there were around 1900 (Figure 5.8). The rising length of life also implies that widowed persons who do not remarry spend a greater number of years in widowhood than a person widowed at the same age a decade or two ago.

In 1972 there were 1.8 million widowed men and 9.6 million widowed women in the United States; most of these persons (1.4 million men and 6.3 million women) were over the age of 65 and there is, not surprisingly,

Figure 5.8
Age distribution of new widows in the United States, 1900 and 1964. Includes allowance for deaths of husbands in the armed forces overseas during 1964. (Source. Adapted and reprinted with permission from Jacobson, Paul H. The Changing Role of Mortality in American Family Life. Lex et Scientia, 1966, 3(2), p. 121.)

a dramatic increase with age in the percentage of persons widowed (Figure 5.9). Women outnumber men who are widowed by more than five to one because of the longer average length of life for women, the tendency of women to marry older men, and the higher remarriage rate of widowed men (who tend to marry younger women). Because of higher mortality rates and lower remarriage rates, widowed persons constituted a larger proportion of Negro adults than white adults.

About 80 percent of all widowed persons were heads of households in 1972, and well over half of those under 55 lived with their children (U. S. Bureau of the Census, 1972, Table 6). However, the majority of widowed

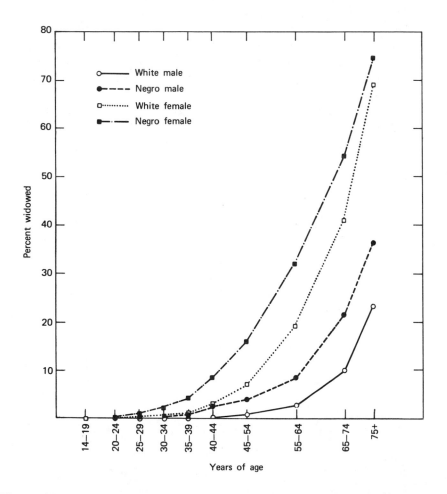

Figure 5.9
Percent widowed by age, sex, and race in the United States, 1972. Combined rates for "Negro and other races" are the same or slightly lower (up to the age of 75) compared with the data for Negroes presented. (Source: U.S. Bureau of the Census, 1972, Table 1).

persons are over 65. In 1971 about 14 percent of all widowed persons over 65 lived in institutions. Of the widowed persons over 65 not living in institutions in 1972, more than three-fourths were heads of households and, of this number, about 80 percent lived alone. Over 90 percent of noninstitutionalized widowed persons over 65 who did not maintain their own household lived with relatives (U.S. Bureau of the Census, 1972, p. 2). Carter and Glick (1970) report that older widowed persons were more likely to live with a daughter than a son (in 1960), but a larger proportion of widowed sons than daughters lived with their parents. White persons living in central cities (where there is often a "deteriorating" older neighborhood) had a relatively high percentage of widowed persons in 1960 (ibid.).

Death rates for widowed persons are highest for nonwhite men and women and are higher than all but divorced white men and women (Figure 5.7). Again, cause of death provides some clues to the physical and emotional health of widowed persons. They have higher death rates from accidental fire or explosion, accidental falls (for women), suicide (for men), and motor vehicle accidents than any other group (Carter and Glick, 1970, Table 11.12). These causes of death that are more common among the widowed suggest a greater prevalence of personal problems and less available help or resources to deal with them than is the case for married (and to a lesser extent, for single or divorced) persons. In this context we might note that suicide (which among women is the most common cause of death for the divorced person) is one of the few causes of death that is higher for white than for nonwhite persons of every marital status and is considerably higher for men than for women (see Chapter 7). Widowed persons were more likely to be living in mental hospitals than married persons, but were less likely to be mental hospital residents than other single or previously married persons (Table 5.7).

We will discuss widowhood and bereavement in more detail in Chapter 9; now we will only point out some of the more salient aspects of the widowed life style. In some respects, particularly for younger widowed persons, many of the characteristics of the formerly married life style discussed in the preceding section are applicable. Many widowed persons remarry, although their remarriage rate is about one-half the rate for divorced persons (Figure 5.6). The vast differential between the number of widowed men and women makes it difficult for women to find new marriage partners, especially at older ages; and even younger widowed individuals may be more reluctant to remarry because of enduring love for the deceased spouse. However, we would expect that the process of resocialization into the role of widowed would be an important transition—more structured than for the divorced, perhaps; but more direct grief and mourning would be involved, and the emotional reactions of failure and love-hate ambivalence would probably be less prominent. Loneliness would be a central experience for most and, for some (especially younger persons), the resocialization process would involve new friends, some dating, and some participation in the formerly married subculture. There seems to be a generally low degree of social tolerance (particularly among family members) for aged widowed persons forming sexual and social liaisons as younger formerly marrieds do, and remarriage after age 65 is not widely encouraged either. Thus, the aged widows (most are women) tend to live alone in relative isolation; loneliness and the management of health problems are the major burdens.

Unmarried Persons

Although current population trends suggest that an overwhelming proportion of the population (96-97 percent) will eventually marry (Carter and Glick, 1970), there has been an increase in the percent of single persons under the age of 35 since 1960; the percentage among men increased about 5 percentage points between 1960 and 1972 and it increased about 7 percentage points among women (Table 5.8). Most of this rise is among men between 20 and 23 and among women between 19 and 23, so it may indicate that more and more young persons are waiting a few years to marry or that this particular cohort may not marry at the same high rates as older cohorts (the ones over 30 in 1972).

In 1972 there were 1.4 million single men and 0.9 million single women between the ages of 25 and 29; there were 3.2 million single men and 2.8 million single women over the age of 30. Of course, the percentage of single persons declines dramatically with age. However, there were higher proportions of single Negro men than white men at every age up to 65; this is true for women up to the age of 55 (Figure 5.10).

Carter and Glick (1970) report that most persons who will eventually marry do so by the age of 40 (about the age the graphs level off in Figure 5.10). Men who do not marry tend to have lower occupation and income levels than men who eventually marry, and almost none of the middle-aged men with high incomes (over $10,000 in 1960) had never married. Women with incomes between $5000 and $10,000 and women with high levels of education were more likely to be unmarried (in 1960). It may be that men tend to marry women of lower socioeconomic status, with poorer men and better educated women less likely to marry, or the better educated women with higher incomes might have attained these characteristics in order to be self-supporting.

Although it is not known how many single persons do not marry out of preference, the proportion is probably not very high since there is considerable social pressure to marry. However, the number of persons who choose to remain single may be growing along with the percentage of

Table 5.8   Percent Single by Age and Sex (1972 and 1960)

	Male			Female		
Age	1972	1960	Change[a]	1972	1960	Change[a]
Total, 14 years and over	28.6	25.0	3.6	22.2	19.0	3.2
Under 35 years	55.3	50.7	4.6	44.6	37.6	7.0
35 years and over	6.2	7.8	−1.6	5.2	7.2	−2.0
14 to 17 years	99.5	99.0	0.5	97.3	94.6	2.7
18 years	95.6	94.6	1.0	83.0	75.6	7.4
19 years	87.9	87.1	0.8	70.7	59.7	11.0
20 to 24 years	56.9	53.1	3.8	36.4	28.4	·8.0
20 years	79.5	75.8	3.7	59.0	46.0	13.0
21 years	67.9	63.4	4.5	44.3	34.6	9.7
22 years	58.2	51.6	6.6	36.3	25.6	10.7
23 years	45.8	40.5	5.3	25.3	19.4	5.9
24 years	33.7	33.4	0.3	17.4	15.7	1.7
25 to 29 years	19.3	20.8	−1.5	12.4	10.5	1.9
25 years	26.8	27.9	−1.1	17.5	13.1	4.4
26 years	22.5	23.5	−1.0	13.9	11.4	2.5
27 years	17.2	19.8	−2.6	11.3	10.2	1.1
28 years	17.7	17.5	0.2	9.5	9.2	0.3
29 years	10.7	16.0	−5.3	8.2	8.7	−0.5
30 to 34 years	12.4	11.9	0.5	6.7	6.9	−0.2
35 to 39 years	9.1	8.8	0.3	4.5	6.1	−1.6
40 to 44 years	7.4	7.3	0.1	4.5	6.1	−1.6
45 to 54 years	5.5	7.4	−1.9	4.2	7.0	−2.8
55 to 64 years	5.1	8.0	−2.9	5.5	8.0	−2.5
65 years and over	5.5	7.7	−2.2	6.6	8.5	−1.9

[a] Differences shown were derived by using rounded percentages for 1972 and 1960.
Source. U.S. Bureau of the Census (1972), Table E.

single persons in their early twenties. In 1960 only a small fraction (5 percent) of unmarried women and even fewer men were residents of religious "group quarters"; a similarly small fraction lived in institutions, mainly mental hospitals (Carter and Glick, 1970). Thus, the reasons the vast majority of single persons do not marry are unclear; they probably include personal preference, emotional instability, lack of opportunity, economic insecurity, homosexuality, and jobs that require continual travel.

In 1972 the vast majority of young single persons—as well as over half

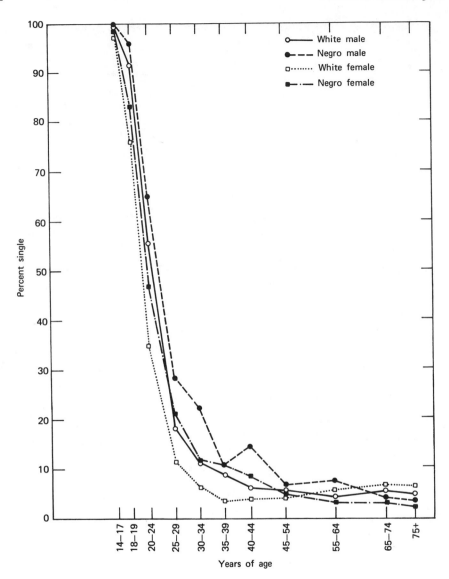

Figure 5.10
Percent single by age, sex, and race in the United States, 1972. Combined rates for men of "Negro and other races" are somewhat higher than for data for Negro men presented, especially at older ages; rates for women of "Negro and other races" are slightly lower than the data for Negro women presented. (Source. U.S. Bureau of the Census, 1972, Table 1.)

of the single men and about 43 percent of single women between the ages of 35 and 44—were living "in families," probably with parents (Table 5.9). A substantial proportion (22 to 59 percent for men and 24 to 50 percent for women) were living alone; these percentages increased

Table 5.9 Single Persons by Family Status, Age, and Sex (March 1972)

Subject	Total 14 Years and Over	Age (Years)						
		14 to 24	25 to 34	35 to 44	45 to 54	55 to 64	65 to 74	75 and Over
WOMEN (in thousands)	17,649	13,981	1321	522	514	550	470	292
Percent	100.0	100.0	100.0	100.0	100.0	100.0	100.0	100.0
Head of household	14.4	4.9	42.5	47.5	52.7	57.6	60.0	63.8
Head of primary family	3.8	1.4	10.9	17.2	14.5	14.2	11.9	12.5
Primary individual	10.6	3.4	31.6	30.3	38.2	43.4	48.1	51.3
Living alone	8.7	2.2	24.4	26.6	35.3	41.4	45.3	49.8
With nonrelatives	1.8	1.2	7.1	3.7	2.9	2.0	2.8	1.6
Not head of household	85.6	95.1	57.5	52.5	47.3	42.4	40.0	36.2
In families	80.8	91.7	46.4	42.8	38.6	35.0	28.4	28.2
Secondary individual	4.7	3.4	11.2	9.7	8.7	7.3	11.5	8.0
MEN (in thousands)	20,759	16,227	2108	903	613	452	314	141
Percent	100.0	100.0	100.0	100.0	100.0	100.0	100.0	100.0
Head of household	12.6	4.3	32.3	32.6	51.0	66.1	73.1	79.5
Head of primary family	1.9	0.4	3.4	5.6	11.0	16.7	12.7	17.7
Primary individual	10.8	3.9	28.8	26.9	40.0	49.4	60.4	61.8
Living alone	8.3	2.2	22.1	24.0	34.8	46.5	57.6	58.7
With nonrelatives	2.5	1.8	6.8	3.0	5.2	2.9	2.8	3.1
Not head of household	87.4	95.7	67.7	67.4	49.0	33.9	26.9	20.5
In families	82.0	92.2	55.8	54.1	37.6	20.7	19.8	12.0
Secondary individual	5.3	3.5	11.9	13.3	11.4	13.2	7.0	8.5

Source. U.S. Bureau of the Census (1972), Table 6.

with age for both men and women. About 7 percent of men and women between 25 and 34 were living with a roommate or other nonrelative. About half of the older single persons were living alone, but more than one-fourth of older women lived with relatives. In 1960 about 12 percent of single men and women over 75 lived in homes for the aged, compared with about 7 percent for widowed persons over 75 (Carter and Glick, 1970).

Data on causes of death indicate that single women are more likely to die from tuberculosis or pneumonia than either married or previously married women; there is no cause of death for which single men are more vulnerable than other groups (Carter and Glick, 1970, Table 11.12). Single persons had higher death rates than married persons, but these rates were lower than the rates for previously married persons (Figure 5.7). Similarly, suicide rates are higher for single than for married persons, but they are lower than for previously married persons. However, single persons were considerably more likely to be residents of mental hospitals than married or previously married persons in 1960 (Table 5.7). In 1960 single persons were overrepresented in large urban areas, but currently there seems to be an increase in the number of singles living in the suburbs (Malcolm, 1972).

In general it would seem that there are at least three identifiable subgroups of unmarried adults: the so-called "swinging singles" who tend to be younger and more avidly seeking marriage than the middle-aged singles described above; the so-called "gay singles" who have sexual and emotional relationships with others of the same sex and sometimes seek long-term or marriagelike relationships; and the singles who cannot find someone to marry or choose not to marry. This latter group is so diverse as to defy discussion beyond the demographic description presented above; but we will briefly discuss the other two types of single life that are available, particularly in large cities.

"Swinging Singles." The stereotype of unmarried adults tends to be that they are carefree and unencumbered by the burdens of family responsibilities; that the women work until they catch a husband and the men read *Playboy*; and that they are able to engage in sexual relations and develop tastes and life styles with relative freedom. However, there is very little data available on unmarried, heterosexual, marriage-prone adults. One study currently in progress (Starr and Carns, 1972) is exploring Chicago's singles community; they are interviewing only college graduates in their early to midtwenties. They report that, unlike some cities and even some suburbs, Chicago has no "singles only" buildings, and even one complex that is called "swingle's city" near the singles bars has only a minority of single residents under 25. They found that there is relatively little socializing with other residents of the apartment building and, contrary to media impressions, their "typical" graduates (who often moved to the city without expectations about the city's social life) frequent singles bars one or two nights a week (or less) and go less often the longer they have lived in the city; by the age of 25 the "typical" female has little use for the singles bars—males tend to frequent them for a longer time. Many of the more popular bars are noisy and crowded especially on weekends, and many are arranged to discourage sitting and to allow for nonverbal and (later) verbal contact. One of my students (Kaplan, unpublished) is studying men in singles bars in New York. He reports that the bartender often functions to introduce patrons and works hard to learn the names of regular patrons for that purpose and to talk with them when they come in to socialize. At least three types of male patrons are common: the neighborhood type who comes in to see friends and to have a drink or two; the out-of-town businessman who wants to meet a potential date; and the weekend single who hopes to meet a date, often with marriage as only a vague possibility. Thus, singles bars function as social centers, with the bartender an important participant, and as places for meeting potential dates or sexual partners; in addition, they may offer a re-creation of college-type environments for casual evenings and for meeting friends and dates. Most singles, however, probably only go to such bars infrequently. Starr and Carns (1972) report that most of their sample of singles do not establish dating relationships in bars, in the apartment building, in organizations, or in "singles only" dances. Instead, most dates arise from contacts at work—usually co-workers are not dated, but they arrange dates in a friend-of-a-friend pattern. In fact, they conclude, the popular image of "swinging singles" is a misnomer, for these singles are persons coping with the same kinds of problems everyone else is and are not living lives of "wild abandon."

"Gay Singles." Homosexual men and women lead many different styles of life; some are politically active in "gay liberation," others attempt to deny their sexuality, some form long-term homosexual relationships, others probably marry heterosexually, and many have short-term affairs. Curiously, the description of "gay" bars by such studies of homosexual life as the one Hoffman (1968) has conducted indicates that there is considerable similarity between singles bars and gay bars—with the exception that gay bars tend to function more blatantly as a "sexual marketplace" and participation socially types one as a "deviant."

> The gay bar has almost become a social institution in America. It is the central public place around which gay life revolves and is to be found in all large and medium-sized cities across the country....
>
> Perhaps the most important fact about a gay bar is that it is a sexual marketplace. That is, men go there for the purpose of seeking sexual partners.... [A]lthough homosexuals also go there to drink and to socialize, the search for sexual experience is in some sense the core of the interaction in the bar.... The gay bar plays a central role in the life of very many homosexuals—one which is much more

important than the role played by straight bars in the life of all but a
few heterosexuals. This is connected intimately with the use of the
gay bar as a sexual marketplace and, of course, with the fact that
homosexuals, as homosexuals, have really no place else where they
can congregate without disclosing to the straight world that they are
homosexual (Hoffman, 1968, pp. 50-51).

Hoffman also points out that lesbians tend to have fewer bars of their
own and to use the bars in a different way; they tend to become acquainted with one another socially, then to go on dates, and to leave the
sexual involvement for a later stage in their relationship.

The social stigma attached to homosexuality undoubtedly has an important influence on homosexual life styles since there are few social
supports for long-term relationships, and social norms devalue the integrity of such relationships and even the value of the individuals. For
example, while the early years of marriage for a heterosexual couple
may not be strewn with roses, the marital bond is supported and
strengthened by social roles, norms, and by such significant others as
one's parents and friends. The contrary is often true for homosexual
couples, for there is no socially acceptable role they can adopt; and in
fact, they may not even be certain that a paired relationship is the best
one for a homosexual to adopt (it may be appropriate only for heterosexual couples expecting children). Thus there are a wide variety of
homosexual life styles (as there are heterosexual life styles) including
durable relationships lasting several decades.

While we cannot attempt a discussion of the psychosocial factors associated with homosexuality, a recent review of psychological research on
homosexuality and psychological functioning concluded:

> The results of the empirical research studies ... are, on the whole,
> positive about the relationship between homosexuality and psycho-
> logical functioning. They demonstrate that most of the homosexually
> oriented individuals evaluated in the studies function as well as
> comparable groups of heterosexually oriented individuals; that their
> functioning typically could be characterized as normal; and that, in
> some cases, their functioning even approximates that [ideal] of self-
> actualizing people (Freedman, 1971, p. 87).

Conclusion

Although nearly all people seem to try their hand at beginning a family,
most people, if given the chance, would join in the continuing debate
about whether the family is a valuable institution and whether it is vital,
changing, or dying. Certainly, families are very complex social systems
that provide some of the most deeply satisfying rewards, frustrations,
and challenges during the adult years. Yet they are probably not suited

to all individuals and the population explosion combined with an apparently greater tolerance and interest in experimental life styles may lead to a decrease in the percentage of adults who live in families. The divorce rate might also decrease if there were less social pressure for everyone to marry, regardless of whether they are suited for marriage or not. But, predictions aside, it is apparent that adults currently live out their lives in a wide variety of styles. Some may be fairly isolated, but most have important intimate relationships for longer or shorter periods of time. These relationships are typically significant for understanding and timing the developmental progression through the middle and late years of life.

In the next chapter we turn to the other important sphere of emotional and physical investment—the occupation. The task for the student of adulthood is to attempt to integrate these two spheres and to try to grasp the complex ways in which they interact to produce the tempo, challenges, satisfactions, and disappointments during the middle years of adult life.

References

Barry, William A. 1970. Marriage Research and Conflict: An Integrative Review. *Psychological Bulletin, 73*(1), 41–54.

Benedek, Therese. 1952. *Psychosexual Functions in Women.* New York: Ronald Press.

Bengston, Vern L. 1971. Inter-Age Perceptions and the Generation Gap. *Gerontologist, 11*(4, Part 2), 85–89.

Burgess, Ernest W. 1926. The Family as a Unity of Interacting Personalities. *Family, 7,* 3–9.

Carter, Hugh, and Glick, Paul C. 1970. *Marriage and Divorce: A Social and Economic Study.* Cambridge, Mass.: Harvard University Press.

*Deutscher, Irwin. 1964.** The Quality of Postparental Life. *Journal of Marriage and the Family, 26*(1), 263–268.

Duvall, Evelyn Millis. 1971. *Family Development.* (4th ed.) Philadelphia: Lippincott.

Frank, George H. 1965. The Role of the Family in the Development of Psychopathology. *Psychological Bulletin, 64*(3), 191–205.

Freedman, Mark. 1971. *Homosexuality and Psychological Functioning.* Belmont, Calif.: Brooks/Cole.

Gebhard, Paul. 1970. Postmarital Coitus Among Widows and Divorcees. In Paul Bohannan (Ed.), *Divorce and After.* Garden City, N.Y.: Doubleday.

Glick, Paul C. 1949. First Marriages and Remarriages. *American Sociological Review, 14,* 726–734.

Goode, William J. 1956. *After Divorce.* Glencoe, Ill.: Free Press.

Hess, Robert D., and Handel, Gerald. 1959. *Family Worlds: A Psychosocial Approach to Family Life.* Chicago: University of Chicago Press.

*Hill, Reuben. 1965. Decision Making and the Family Life Cycle. In Ethel Shanas and Gordon F. Streib (Eds.), *Social Structure and the Family: Generational Relations.* Englewood Cliffs, N.J.: Prentice-Hall.

Hill, Reuben. 1971. *Family Development in Three Generations.* Cambridge, Mass.: Schenkman Publishing Co.

Hoffman, Lois Wladis. 1963. Effects of Maternal Employment on the Child. In Marvin B. Sussman (Ed.), *Sourcebook in Marriage and the Family.* (2nd ed.) Boston: Houghton-Mifflin.

Hoffman, Martin. 1968. *The Gay World.* New York: Basic Books (Bantam).

Hunt, Morton M. 1966. *The World of the Formerly Married.* New York: McGraw-Hill.

Kanter, Rosabeth Moss. 1970. Communes. *Psychology Today, 4*(2), 53–57, 78, 88.

Kimmel, Douglas C. 1970. Interacting Family Components: An Analysis of the Inter-relationship Between Child Behavior, Marital Adjustment, and Family Perceptions. Unpublished doctoral dissertation, University of Chicago.

Kinsey, Alfred C.; Pomeroy, Wardell B.; and Martin, Clyde E. 1948. *Sexual Behavior in the Human Male.* Philadelphia: Saunders.

Kinsey, Alfred C.; Pomeroy, Wardell B.; Martin, Clyde E.; Gebhard, Paul H.; and Associates. 1953. *Sexual Behavior in the Human Female.* Philadelphia: Saunders.

LeMasters, E. E. 1957. Parenthood as Crisis. *Marriage and Family Living, 19*(4), 352–355.

Litwak, Eugene. 1960. Geographic Mobility and Extended Family Cohesion. *American Sociological Review, 25*(3), 385–394.

Locke, Ben Z.; Kramer, Morton; and Pasamanick, Benjamin. 1960. Mental Diseases of the Senium at Mid-century: First Admissions to Ohio State Public Mental Hospitals. *American Journal of Public Health. 50*(7), 998–1012.

Locke, Harvey J. 1951. *Predicting Adjustment in Marriage.* New York: Henry Holt.

*Maddox, George L. 1966. Retirement as a Social Event in the United States. In John C. McKinney and Frank T. deVyver (Eds.), *Aging and Social Policy.* New York: Appleton-Century-Crofts.

Malcolm, Andrew H. 1972. Singles Seek Better Life in the Suburbs. *New York Times,* May 8, 1972, 1.

Maslow, Abraham. 1955. Deficiency Motivation and Growth Motivation. In Marshall R. Jones (Ed.), *Nebraska Symposium on Motivation.* Lincoln: University of Nebraska Press.

**Masters, William H., and Johnson, Virginia E. 1966. *Human Sexual Response.* Boston: Little, Brown.

Masters, William H., and Johnson, Virginia E. 1970. *Human Sexual Inadequacy.* Boston: Little, Brown.

McCurdy, Harold G. 1961. *The Personal World.* New York: Harcourt, Brace and World.

Mead, Margaret. 1971. Future Family. *Trans-Action, 8*(11), 50–53.

*Neugarten, Bernice L., and Weinstein, Karol K. 1964. The Changing American Grandparent. *Journal of Marriage and the Family, 26*(2), 199–204.

Newman, Gustave, and Nichols, Claude R. 1960. Sexual Activities and Attitudes in Older Persons. *Journal of the American Medical Association, 173,* 33–35.

Novak, Arthur L., and van der Veen, Ferdinand. 1970. Family Concepts and Emotional Disturbance in the Families of Disturbed Adolescents with Normal Siblings. *Family Process, 9*(2), 157–171.

*Pineo, Peter C. 1961. Disenchantment in the Later Years of Marriage. *Marriage and Family Living, 23,* 3–11.

Rabkin, Leslie Y., and Rabkin, Karen. 1969. Children of the Kibbutz. *Psychology Today, 3*(4), 40–46, 72.

Rollins, Boyd C., and Feldman, Harold. 1970. Marital Satisfaction Over the Family Life Cycle. *Journal of Marriage and the Family, 32*(1), 20–28.

Rougemont, Denis de. 1956. *Love in the Western World.* (Rev. ed.) (Translated by Montgomery Belgion.) New York: Pantheon.

Satir, Virginia. 1964. *Conjoint Family Therapy: A Guide to Theory and Technique.* Palo Alto, Calif.: Science and Behavior Books.

*Shanas, Ethel; Townsend, Peter; Wedderburn, Dorothy; Friis, Hennig; Milhøj, Poul; and Stehouwer, Jan. 1968. *Older People in Three Industrial Societies.* New York: Atherton Press.

Starr, Joyce R., and Carns, Donald E. 1972. Singles in the City. *Society, 9*(4), 43–48.

*Sussman, Marvin B., and Burchinal, Lee. 1962. Kin Family Network: Unheralded Structure in Current Conceptualizations of Family Functioning. *Marriage and Family Living, 24*(3), 231–240.

*Talmon, Yonina. 1961. Aging in Israel, a Planned Society. *American Journal of Sociology, 67*(3), 284–295.

*Townsend, Peter. 1966. The Emergence of the Four-Generation Family in Industrial Society. *Proceedings of the 7th International Congress of Gerontology, Vienna, 8,* 555–558.

U.S. Bureau of the Census. 1972. Marital Status and Living Arrangements: March 1972. *Current Population Reports,* Series P-20, No. 242. Washington, D.C.: U.S. Government Printing Office.

Vogel, Ezra F., and Bell, Norman W. 1960. The Emotionally Disturbed Child as a Family Scapegoat. *Psychoanalysis and the Psychoanalytic Review, 47*(2), 21–42.

* References marked with an asterisk appear in Bernice L. Neugarten (Ed.), *Middle Age and Aging.* Chicago: University of Chicago Press, 1968.
** Reference marked with a double asterisk has relevant selections in *Middle Age and Aging.*

six
Work,
Retirement,
and
Leisure

"Freud was once asked what he thought a normal person should be able to do well. The questioner probably expected a complicated, 'deep' answer. But Freud simply said, *'Lieben und arbeiten'* ('to love and to work')" (Erikson, 1968, p. 136).

Certainly these two aspects of human life are central during most of the years of adulthood; they encompass Erikson's stages of Intimacy versus Isolation and Generativity versus Stagnation; this lengthy period of generativity (that includes not only productivity and creativity in work but also the production and caring for offspring) extends from the resolution of the identity crisis to the beginnings of the final stage in Erikson's framework—Integrity versus Despair.

In the last chapter we discussed the first part of Freud's response, "to love"; here we turn our attention to the occupation, the job, or the career that occupies approximately 40 hours a week (but often up to twice that many hours) for 30 to 45 or more years of the life cycle. Perhaps such a large amount of time is a sufficient reason to take a careful look at the interaction between the occupation and the person during his middle years. But we are also interested in the interaction between the occupation and the family and in the role that the occupation plays in the final resolution of the identity crisis. We are interested in the process of occupational choice and in the process of socialization by which the individual is prepared for his occupation and comes to accept the roles and status that the occupation entails. We are also interested in the end point of the occupational cycle, retirement, and in the use of nonworking time (leisure) since these issues are becoming more and more important in society today.

In regard to retirement, more people are living past 65 today than ever before and this trend will undoubtedly continue (Figure 6.1). Thus, more

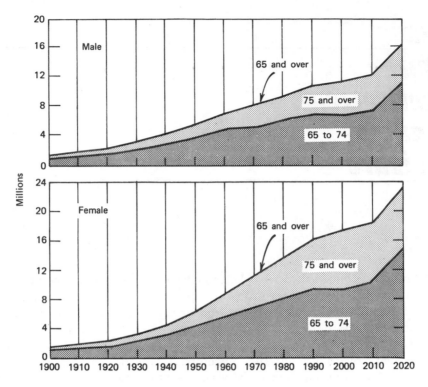

Figure 6.1
Growth of population FE *years and over, 1900 to 2020. (Source: U.S. Bureau of the Census, 1973, cover.)*

people are able to work up to the age of retirement and often beyond; consequently, more people are retiring and are living in retirement for a greater number of years or are entering a new career late in life. One effect of greater longevity has been to increase the significance of retirement as a developmental milestone; we will examine this milestone in detail in a later section of this chapter.

In regard to leisure, technological advances such as automation and computers have increased the amount of productivity for each man hour of work. The result of this growth has been a growing trend to reduce the effective size (number of man hours) of the work force. There are a number of ways this may be done and most have been utilized to some degree: longer preemployment training keeps large numbers of young people off the labor market; longer vacations, shorter work weeks, and shorter work days reduces the number of hours a person works; earlier retirement shortens the total number of years of work; and, of course, increased unemployment is a temporary means of reducing the work force. This trend toward shortening the amount of time an individual spends working during his lifetime is likely to continue, resulting in an extension in the amount of time potentially devoted to leisure; we will discuss this relatively new phenomenon in the final section of this chapter. But first, let us look at the concept of work itself.

WORK AND THE LIFE CYCLE

Neugarten and Moore (1968) point out a number of characteristics of the work cycle in the United States today; for example, the proportion of young women in the labor force has been increasing while the proportion of young men working has been decreasing in recent years. In 1971 the percentage of women working dropped after the age of 25, probably coinciding with the birth of the first child. Women may reenter the labor force after the children are in school (or sooner if child care is available), or they may wait until the children have left home before returning to work. Thus, there is a gradual rise in the percentage of women in the labor force between the ages of 30 and 50, with a high percentage of working women in their late forties (Figure 6.2). In addition, there have been marked changes in the characteristics of women who work since 1900: in 1890, 13 percent of the women who worked were married; in 1970 it was 58 percent. In 1940 only one out of ten female workers had children under 18; in 1970, it was one out of three (Neugarten and Moore, 1968; U.S. Bureau of Labor Statistics, 1971). Also for women today, the trend is to enter the work force earlier and to work considerably longer than was true in 1900.

The opposite pattern is true for males. They tend to enter the work force later and to retire earlier than was true in 1900 (however, because of longevity and better health, the average length of working life lengthened from 31 to 42 years between 1900 and 1966).

Identity and Generativity

Particularly for men, but for growing numbers of women as well, the occupation involves a great investment of time, emotional energy, and commitment. Often the man is particularly engaged in his occupation during the middle years of the family cycle while the woman is expected to be highly involved in the home and family. These intense involvements mark the final resolution of the identity crisis for both men and women. Success and satisfaction in the occupation and family reaffirm the individual's sense of identity and also provide social recognition for that identity. Clearly, the job is a salient aspect of a person's identity, ranking in importance along with his name, sex, and citizenship. Although this

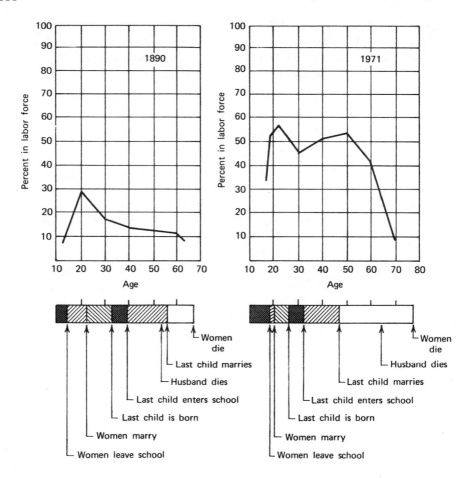

Figure 6.2

Work in relation to significant stages in the lives of women. (Source. Adapted from Neugarten and Moore, 1968, Figure 2. Reprinted with permission from Middle Age and Aging, *Bernice L. Neugarten (Ed.), copyright © 1968 by the University of Chicago. Upper right-hand portion of figure has been revised based on labor-force data taken from U.S. Bureau of Labor Statistics.* Handbook of Labor Statistics, *1972, Bulletin 1735. Washington, D.C.: U.S. Government Printing Office, 1972, Table 3.)*

close tie between the identity and the occupation may be more true for those in the professions ("I am a lawyer . . . doctor . . . psychologist . . ."), we know that certain occupational characteristics (such as "blue collar" or "white collar") are reflected in attitudes, values, and politics; in addition, the occupation reflects such factors as social class and amount of education.

Entry into the adult occupational and parenthood roles also marks the beginning of the Erikson stage of Generativity versus Stagnation. Thus, success and a profound sense of satisfaction in one's job (or in rearing children and managing a home) not only brings the resolution of the identity crisis but also leads to a sense of generativity.

Conversely, frustration and lack of a sense of fulfillment in the occupational roles (including the role of housewife-mother) would imply a sense of stagnation and possibly an emotional upset that may, somewhat awkwardly, be termed a "generativity crisis." Perhaps this crisis is an accurate description of the difficulties and frustrations experienced by some American housewives who, seeking to avoid the emotional discomfort of a sense of stagnation, turn to alcohol or pills. Thus, this emotional crisis may have some elements in common with the earlier identity crisis, but it would follow from its occurrence during the generativity stage that the issue is less "who am I," than "what am I doing."

Occupation and Family

The profound sense of satisfaction and accomplishment or of frustration and incompetence also influences other important aspects of an individual's life—specifically, the other salient aspect during the middle years—the family. The interaction between the family and the occupation is best seen as a system of mutually interacting factors that add to or compensate for dissatisfactions in either sphere. That is, a frustrating job, in depersonalizing surroundings, with no opportunity for a sense of pride or accomplishment promotes the importance of the family (and of leisure time) as a source of satisfaction and feelings of competence. The strain that may result as the frustrations are transferred from the work place to the family is likely to counteract the person's needs, however, by adding to family tension and thus enlarging the degree of frustration felt not only by the worker but by the entire family. In addition, the requirement that the family provide satisfactions of such a degree as to compensate for the lack of satisfaction in the occupation is likely to overburden the family and to snowball into a family crisis reflecting, in this example, job frustration.

In the other direction, an unsatisfying family interaction and marital disharmony may shift the burden to the job as the primary source of satisfactions and rewards. Thus, the occupation may be used as an effective escape from the frustrations of family life, leading the person to acquire a second job, work longer hours, spend evenings entertaining clients or be out of town as a substitute source of satisfactions. Sometimes, also, the family and the job are competing in their demands for the individual's time and loyalty. For example, the young executive or professional may be called upon to sacrifice a part of his (her) family life in order to obtain advancement or to establish a career that may, of course, produce family tension.

Factors in Occupational Choice

In the preceding discussion, we presented an overview of the central role played by the occupation during the middle years of the life cycle. Let us now look at more specific aspects of the occupation and consider the process by which a person is matched with an occupation.

One aspect of that process is the person's occupational choice. At the same time, however, a reciprocal consideration is the individual's socialization into the occupation by the training requirement or preparation (anticipatory socialization) and by the role demands of the job itself (resocialization). Thus, the individual and the occupation are fitted together not only by the individual's selection of the occupation to meet his requirements but also by the socialization process required by the new occupational roles and expectations. In addition, part of the earlier socialization process in childhood and adolescence serves to prepare the individual for eventual occupational requirements and roles. Although this "personnel office" model is an oversimplification of the socialization process, it calls attention to the ways in which schools and other socializing agents influence later occupational choice. For example, Cicourel and Kitsuse (1968) point out the way in which high schools define "academic careers" and "delinquent careers" for their students and type the students according to "college preparatory" or "vocational" goals; this social typing defines many of the academic, cultural, and social experiences available and expected for each type of student.

Thus, the process of "occupational choice" in reality begins many years before an actual job is selected; and the factors that are involved in this "choice" do not usually include the (impossible) task of deciding among the thousands of possible occupations. Instead, background factors (reflecting the effects of early socialization), role models, experience, interests, and personality are some of the important factors that influence the selection of an occupation. We will discuss each factor here and later discuss the resocialization of the individual upon entry into his occupation to complete the reciprocal view of the matching process.

Background Factors. Social class, ethnic origin, intelligence, sex, and race tend to operate in complex and often illegal ways to limit the range of occupations open to an individual. Many times a person may find a way to open the door to an occupation and be less bound by these background factors than his peers, but a simple survey of occupations indicates that some are disproportionately Jewish, white, male, black, or poor. Education, discrimination, and contacts in a particular occupation are some of the ways in which these background factors operate for or against an individual's movement into an occupation. In general, these factors operate similar to the way that they do in the choice of a marital partner: by setting general boundaries within which one searches for his occupation (or his mate). However, since many occupations require specialized training or specific education, they are effectively unavailable to persons lacking those requirements. Thus, the occupational decision is usually between accepting a job at one's present level of preparation or getting more preparation that will allow entrance into a new range of possible occupations. The boundaries thus created are often unfair to particular groups of people (notably the poor, the black, and the Chicano), particularly when individuals are unable to acquire the necessary skills at a later point because their prerequisites were denied in childhood and in adolescence by the socialization process and these background characteristics. However, there are two ways in which these boundaries are typically overcome in childhood and adolescence: (1) by selecting a role model in an occupation outside the usual range or (2) by having a particular kind of experience different from the usual range of experiences for individuals of similar background factors. Clearly, these solutions avoid the social problem involved in institutionalized racism in its subtle and overt forms; and that problem must be faced and dealt with; yet our analysis here is intended to be general enough to also include persons who strive to move into an occupation out of the usual realm for their family and peers but who are not held back by racism.

Role Models. Frequently one selects his occupation on the basis of an identification with someone in that occupation. Often this role model is a relative; and in more traditional societies one frequently followed in his father's or uncle's footsteps. Some still do. However, the selection of and identification with a role model who does not share one's background is one powerful way to move into an occupation outside the common experience of one's peers. An example of this process is given by Brown (1965) in *Manchild in the Promised Land* in which one staff member in a school for boys had a lasting effect on him and his subsequent involvement in getting an education. Thus, a laborer's son or daughter may aspire to become a teacher or a doctor because of early role models and later find another role model who leads the person to a career in biochemistry, for example.

Experience. Similarly, an individual may choose a job on the basis of an experience he has had. A man may become a policeman because he saw his older brother killed in a gang war; or a fireman chooses his occupation because his grandmother's house was destroyed by fire. Again, he may move out of the range of jobs common to his peers because he has had, or was uniquely responsive to, a particular experience; for example, he may decide to become a child psychologist because of a chance opportunity to be a counselor in a day camp one summer.

We illustrate the influence of experience and role models on occupational choice with some data from a recent study of mental health professionals. Henry, Sims, and Spray (1971) found that different influences led to the initial interest in medicine, psychology, or social work among psychotherapists trained in these respective professions.

> Comparatively speaking, both psychiatrists and psychoanalysts, but especially analysts, were directed toward the general field of medicine primarily through "familial dynamics"—either by way of identification with a relative (most frequently a parent) who was a doctor, or through the setting of the goal of becoming a doctor by a parent (who was not in medicine). In short, the influences on psychiatrists and psychoanalysts operated early, consisted of persons rather than experiences, and were expressed through close relationships.
>
> In contradistinction, clinical psychologists and psychiatric social workers were directed to their general fields at a later time and essentially equally by persons and experiences. For psychologists the most important person was the teacher, the most important experiences were training and reading, and the most important mode of influence was intellectual stimulation. For social workers the key figure was the nonrelated professional social worker, the crucial experience was the job, and the chief modes of influence were exposure to the field and the opportunity to recognize their ability and pleasure with the work (Henry, Sims, and Spray, 1971, pp. 111-112).

It is interesting to note that, for these psychotherapists, a second specialized occupational choice was also made, usually at a later point. That is, after deciding on medicine, psychology, or social work, they later decided to specialize in psychoanalysis or psychiatry, clinical psychology, and psychiatric social work, respectively. The influences for this specialized decision were generally drawn from within the profession (the influence of the parent is largely replaced by the influence of peers while teachers, supervisors, and experiences are also important influences).

Interests. Of course, the individual's interests, preferences, and values play a large part in his choice of an occupation, at least insofar as he has an actual choice to make. In the case of psychotherapists, individuals in either of the professional disciplines would tend to be drawn to psychotherapy by similar interests (for example, understanding and helping people); but, conversely, these interests could be satisfied in several different occupations and professions. In general, a person's interests, values, and preferences partly reflect his experiences and the effect of role models; they would also reflect his unique range of past accomplishments, talents, and abilities as well as his sense of who he is and what he wants to do with his life.

Personality. In addition, occupational choice often reflects a "fit" in some sense between the person and his job. A number of studies have sought to identify the personality characteristics of adults in various occupations in order to specify the way in which personality factors correspond with the pattern of attributes and roles involved in various occupations (e.g., Roe, 1961). One interesting example of this correspondence between an occupation and certain personality characteristics is a study by Henry (1965) of professional actors. He expected that a group of actors would show many signs of "identity confusion," the negative side of Erikson's identity stage. The reasoning was that actors, whose occupation consists of the portrayal of roles, would be attempting to compensate for a basic confusion about their own identity by taking on the roles of others. It was found that, indeed, this group of professional actors was lower on a measure of identity than comparison groups of nonactors; that the lower the identity score (that is, the more identity confusion), the more likely the actor was to be successful as an actor; and that identity scores rose during the several weeks of play rehearsal preceding the opening performance. These findings suggest that, at least for actors, the occupation may serve as a source of satisfaction of (or compensation for) certain personality factors. It is also interesting that for this group of actors, most chose acting as their career because the very first time they played a part in a play, they felt that they wanted to be actors; it is as if the choice was so good for them they could almost hear it "click" the very first time.

Patterns of Careers

As may by now be obvious, when we attempt to discuss the interaction between the occupation and the individual, we conjure up different ideas of the occupation itself. For example, when we think of a pattern of consistent socialization through a long training period, or a job whose demands for advancement may interfere with family life, we think of a career in which there are distinct steps in the pattern of advancement. The kind of occupation we imagine when we think of a frustrating, depersonalized job, however, tends to be that of a routine job on an assembly line.

Thus it seems that there are vast differences between certain occupations and indeed, between various patterns of occupations. First consider the *career* in which there are well-defined steps of advancement, a hierarchical progression (or ladder), up which one moves if he is successful. This pattern, then, is one of vertical movement up the status ladder; it is a pattern of orderly progression, often within the same company over a period of years. Then consider a *disorderly work history* in which there is no pattern to the sequence of jobs an individual holds; there is neither a vertical progression in functionally related jobs providing increased status nor a horizontal progression of functionally related jobs with increased status (e.g., apprentice, journeyman, and foreman). Wilensky (1961) defines these criteria as one way of exploring the obvious differences in types of work histories. He found that at most, one-third of the "middle mass" (persons who ˙are economically secure but not upper middle class) have work histories that may be characterized as orderly careers. Thus, the majority of those working are not involved in long-term career aspirations and in progressing up a status ladder but, instead, are likely to move up primarily on the basis of seniority with little increased responsibility or status on the job. In addition, Wilensky found that these two patterns were reflected in greater community involvement and in overlapping patterns of social participation on and off the job for the orderly group compared to the disorderly group.

> Men who have predictable careers for at least a fifth of their worklives belong to more organizations, attend more meetings, and average more hours in organizational activity. Their attachments to the local community are also stronger—indicated by support of local schools and, to a lesser extent, by contributions to church and charity. . . .
> . . . If we give a man some college, put him on a stable career ladder, and top it off with a nice family income, he will get into the community act. Give a man less than high school, a thoroughly unpredictable sequence of jobs, a family income of five to eight thousand and it is very likely that his ties to the community will be few and weak (Wilensky, 1961).

Finally, he suggests that the pattern of the work history (orderly or disorderly) has more impact on a man's social life than any of the work positions that he may have picked up and dropped along the way.

These findings point to an important variable for understanding the role of the occupation, although there are several other factors that are also significant for the understanding of the interaction between the person and the occupation. These factors include motivation (money, sustenance, status, service, creativity, and so on) and sources of satisfaction (money, helping, status, skill, accomplishment, fame, and so on). Thus, potentially orderly careers such as physician, machinist, and engineer are characterized by a number of differing factors (such as motivations and satisfactions) that distinguish one from the other despite the orderly progression common to all of them. Such differences between specific orderly careers are as important as the similarities between them.

In addition, a third type of career progression may be suggested as an important variation of the orderly career; this type is a pattern in which the individual changes occupations in a relatively sudden and major way. Perhaps he does this out of frustration in an attempt to find a more satisfying career, or he does this from a position of success and accomplishment in an attempt to find new challenges. On one hand, this pattern differs from the disorderly pattern because there would be only one or two such shifts in an otherwise orderly career. On the other hand, the shift itself distinguishes this pattern from a strictly orderly career. Examples of this pattern include the business executive who switches to government service or the priest who enters a secular career. We expect that such individuals are better able to take risks, to face insecurity, and to deal with challenges than the individual who remains in a single, orderly career. In addition, this shift would highlight a crisis point in the individual's career development. It is to such crisis points in occupational development that we now turn.

The Occupational Cycle: Crisis Points

When we view occupations from a developmental perspective, we are sensitized to potential *turning points* or *crisis points* in the progression of the occupational cycle. These points are more easily identifiable in orderly careers since they entail a clear progression; the disorderly pattern, by definition, is not characterized by predictable crisis points in quite the same way because each break and new start in a disorderly history involves a crisis of some sort—that is, a period of readjustment and resocialization to the demands of the new job. Similarly, in a disorderly work pattern, when the individual is no longer able to find another similar job either because of his age or because his job has been automated, he may face a crisis similar to that brought about by forced retirement in an orderly career; however, in this case, he would face it before retirement age and may face it with a sense of failure at not being able to find another job.

Retirement, of course, is one major developmental turning point in the occupational cycle. It is a crisis point, in this sense, whether it results from an inability to find a job or is the next and final step in the career progression. However, because of the importance of retirement as a major shift in the life cycle, it will be discussed in detail in a later section of this chapter.

Instead, let us consider the earlier turning point of *entry into the occupation*. This point marks the conclusion of a process of occupational choice and is also one of the milestones marking the beginning of adulthood. The individual, having learned and practiced many of the roles involved in his new job during the period of anticipatory socialization, now actually enters the job for the first time. He is confronted by the *real* demands of the job, the *real* expectations, and the *real* rewards. Probably, these factors will differ from what he expected; and he will experience some conflict between the idealism of his earlier expectations and the actuality of the job. Consider, for example, a psychiatric social work student meeting his first patient in a mental hospital as a social work intern. He may not have been in a hospital ward before and certainly was never there as a staff social worker before; he needs to define the situation and to define his role in it; usually role models and resocialization by other staff members help him with these tasks during the first few weeks of the entry period. But during the first few months, he may begin to realize that his skills, the state of psychological knowledge, and the resources of the hospital are less than ideal, and that the needs of the patients are often greater than the resources available. He begins to feel that he may not be as helpful as he hoped he would be; perhaps he will not be able to solve the problems he sees around him because there is not enough time, enough staff, or enough money to provide effective treatment within the walls of the hospital, let alone to do preventive or after-discharge work in the community. Thus, while his idealism may persist, he must readjust his expectations to the real demands of the actual situation. He may become frustrated and angry, he may become "radicalized" and begin working to change the situation, or he may decide to become the most effective social worker he can be and to do his job with as much innovation and enthusiasm as possible.

In a similar way, a policeman, a farmer, and a factory worker are resocialized by the demands of their new jobs and go through a period of "adjustment" and potential emotional upset during the first weeks or months in their first full-time job. "Bootcamp" for army inductees would be a more extreme example of this resocialization process because although the same process is involved, the situation is full time, more intense, and less consistent with the inductee's previous roles and identity (Janowitz, 1965).

From a symbolic interaction perspective, the individual is developing a new *me* during this period of resocialization into the occupation. He is taking the attitude of the others (employer, co-workers, and customers) toward himself and learning the role behavior that is expected. At the same time, he sees himself and reacts to himself in this role. This process, which G. H. Mead called *self-consciousness*, allows him to analyze the correspondence between his *I*'s inner feelings about his *me* in the occupation and the way he sees himself behaving. For example, the social work intern we discussed above might feel some inconsistency between his behavior and his expectations about himself. His *I* might experience this inconsistency, and he might attempt to find a *me* that fits his expectations and the demands of the situation. It is apparent that the greater the extent of this inconsistency, the greater the difficulty he will have in finding a *me* or set of *me*s that satisfies the *I*'s perception of both his *self* in that situation and the expectations from the point of view of the significant others in that situation. In addition, the greater the salience of that particular *me* to his *self*, the greater weight the inconsistency will have in the *I*'s experiencing of his *self* in that situation. If he feels that his occupational *me* is relatively unimportant—he is just working to make money or having a *me* that is seen as a "good Joe" is more important than the *me* as a "good worker"—then the inconsistency will be equally trivial. On the other hand, if his occupational *me* is a cornerstone of his sense of identity—as a "doctor," a "psychologist," or an "artist"—then when his *I* perceives that *me* as unsatisfying, or if his *I* perceives others' attitudes toward his *me* as unfavorable, the crisis may be much more serious. An extreme example would be "malpractice" or "prostituting oneself as an artist in order to make money."

Even if there is no particular inconsistency which is upsetting, the shift in the self involves the *I*'s integrating this new *me* into the array of other *me*s and attending to the expectations of a new group of significant other people. Thus, during this initial period of entry and socialization into the occupation, the individual may find himself readjusting aspects of his *self* as he encounters the actual demands of the job and his ability to deal effectively with them. The point of occupational entry, therefore, is a crucial point not only because it marks the transition into adult status and a shift in roles but also because it may involve a major shift in one's *self* and the emotional crisis that such a shift entails.

A second typical crisis point during the occupational cycle occurs in the middle years of the occupation. This turning point contains elements similar to the crisis at the entry point in that it involves readjusting one's goals and idealistic hopes to what, at this stage, is perceived as one's realistic future possibilities in light of how much time is left in the occupation. An example might be the university professor, hoping to be famous in his field and to contribute great books, who decides, at the age of 50, that he had better begin on his first book if he is ever to write any! This crisis differs from the earlier occupational crisis, however, because it involves what may be called the *career clock*. This "clock" is similar to the "social clock"; it is the individual's subjective sense of being "on time" or "behind time" in his career development. During the middle years (approximately 40 to 55), a person typically becomes aware of the number of years left before retirement and of the speed with which he is attaining his own goals. If he is markedly "behind time," or if his goals are unrealistic, he begins to adjust his goals to be more consistent with what is likely to actually be feasible; he may also decide to change jobs before it is too late.

Men perceive a close relationship between life-line and career-line. Middle age is the time to take stock. Any disparity noted between career-expectations and career achievements—that is, whether one is "on time" or "late" in reaching career goals—adds to the heightened awareness of age. One 47-year-old lawyer said, "I moved at age forty-five from a large corporation to a law firm. I got out at the last possible moment, because after forty-five it is too difficult to find the job you want. If you haven't made it by then, you had better make it fast, or you are stuck" (Neugarten, 1967).

In addition to the growing introspection involved in this period of stock taking and reassessment of career goals, Neugarten also found a sense of mastery, competence, and control in her sample of middle-aged business executives. Often successful men at this point in their career report a highly developed decision-making ability, built from experience in similar situations over a period of years; a prevailing theme is a sense of "maximum capacity and ability to handle a highly complex environment and a highly differentiated self. Very few express a wish to be young again" (Neugarten, 1967).

Once again, we see the changes in the self very much involved in these events of the middle years of the occupational cycle. There is the effect of experience very much in evidence, as we discussed in Chapter 2. And there is the *I*'s ability to take the attitude of the generalized other involved in the career clock—noting when it is the "right time" to change jobs or obtain a promotion if one is to reach one's goals. But also, the process of selecting another job, or gaining the training and resocialization involved in a promotion such as from machinist to shop foreman, involves changes in the *me* and the active processes of the *I* in selecting and integrating these changes in the self. In general, every step up a career ladder, or every job change that involves any resocialization, as well as every promotion that also involves moving to a new community involves changes in the self. And the *I* and *me* aspects of the self are always involved in these changes.

Of course, the career clock may also be involved in timing the milestones of career development (such as promotions and major advances); but it is less clear whether the career clock is a meaningful concept for understanding disorderly patterns of work history or whether its usefulness is limited to orderly careers. We might speculate that the awareness of age and of having little time left to work would increase for individuals with disorderly patterns during this middle-age period as well. The possibility of acquiring another job if one is laid off becomes more and more difficult as one approaches retirement age since employers are hesitant to hire a man who may need to be retrained and who may receive a company pension but can only work for 10 or 15 years. Thus the potential for an emotional crisis during this middle period of the occupation may be at least as great for the disorderly pattern as it is for the orderly career.

RETIREMENT: A MAJOR MILESTONE

Retirement is a major turning point in adult development since it is the social milestone marking the shift from the middle years to old age. It may be seen as a transition point, similar to the transition point at puberty, but reflecting the increased importance of social factors in adulthood over the biological factors that are so important in the younger years. Retirement, also, marks the end of work and the beginning of a period of relative leisure. Thus there are three relatively distinct aspects to the phenomenon of retirement: retirement as an event, the retired status, and the process of retiring (Carp, 1966). Each will be discussed, with the retirement process receiving the greatest attention.

First, retirement is partly an *event* that marks a transition point. Due primarily to Social Security legislation in the 1930s, retirement is usually placed at age 65; however, as a result of increased productivity, the age of retirement is decreasing and, in some occupations, is being set as low as 30 years of continuous service. In other occupations, notably the professions and political office, retirement may not be mandatory and some individuals continue to work into their seventies or eighties; others who have retired often secure another job or continue working part-time. However, because of the rising life expectancy in the United States, most individuals reach retirement age and, in greater numbers, pass into a period of retirement (that is lasting longer as life expectancy increases). In 1971, 26 percent of men over 65 were working (compared with 46 percent in 1950); about 10 percent of women over 65 were working and these rates have not declined since 1950 (U. S. Bureau of the Census, 1973). This transition point, as a rite of passage from one social position to another, may be celebrated publicly with a banquet and a token of appreciation. The event may even be noted in the trade or union journal. But, more often than not, retirement occurs unceremoniously and is not noted as an item of public interest. Thus, retirement tends to be a social event without a precise social meaning; instead, its meaning must be understood within the social life-space of the individual (Maddox, 1966).

Second, retirement may be considered a *status*. Following the event of retirement, the individual passes into a new social position with its own unique roles, expectations, and responsibilities. This shift generally involves a reduction in the number of roles played and a decline in the standard of living. For example, the median income for families with the head of the family over 65 was one-half of the median income for all families in 1970; 12 percent of these white families and 33 percent of these Negro families were below the poverty level (U. S. Bureau of the Census, 1973). Thus, to some degree, the shift to a retired status is a negative change in social position, despite the decreased role demands and increased leisure (which are potentially positive changes). However, as the number of retired persons continues to rise (from 9 million in 1940 to 20.2 million in 1970 to a projected 29 million in 2000), and as the amount of time spent in retirement lengthens (resulting from the combined effect of earlier retirement and longevity), it is likely that the retired status may become more positive and evolve a more rewarding set of role definitions than the definitions that presently exist (Miller, 1965). That is, as our society places more value on leisure roles for persons of all ages, and as retired persons develop a variety of roles that provide meaningful service to the community and utilize their time-tested talents (in day-care centers, aiding minority businessmen, working with schools or hospitals, and so on), the social position of retired persons is likely to rise.

Third, retirement may be considered as a *process*: the process of anticipating the new status as one approaches retirement and the conscious and unconscious working-through of the conflicts and resocializations involved in the change in status. This view of retirement suggests the importance of other biological, social, and psychological factors that may be occurring during the same time as the retirement process since an understanding of the process involves not only the influence of the event itself but also characteristics of the individual and his situation, as well as characteristics of the new status into which he is moving. Thus, let us discuss some of the interrelated aspects of the retirement process.

Biological Factors

Although the biological changes associated with aging and with disease will be discussed in much greater detail in Chapter 8, it is important to consider some of the effects of physical health on the retirement process. The most obvious of these factors is whether poor health is the cause of retirement. Probably as many as one-half of the current retirees retire because of poor health (Maddox, 1966). The *1963 Social Security Survey of the Aged* found that

> Only 28 percent of the wage and salary workers aged 65 and over retired for such voluntary reasons as desire for leisure, being needed at home, or dissatisfaction with their job. The rest had retired for such compelling reasons as poor health, a compulsory retirement age, or being laid off. . . .
>
> More than half the retirees were not well enough to get another job; 11 percent were well enough to work and interested in working but could not find suitable employment (Epstein and Murray, 1967).

An extreme example of retirement hindered by health would be the person so incapacitated by poor health that he could neither find a part-time job nor enjoy travel and recreation during retirement. More usually, retirement for health reasons indicates an inability to continue the old kind of work full time but may allow a reasonably full participation in other activities at least during the early years of retirement.

Clearly, biological decline is a major factor in the person's ability to find sufficient satisfactions in retirement; and disease is the major factor in biological decline associated with age (Birren, Butler, Greenhouse, Sokoloff, and Yarrow, 1963). If there is no disease, there are relatively few changes with age, although decrements in vision, hearing, and trust in one's body are frequently reported even in the absence of disease. Thus, when we consider the biological changes that would affect retirement, we are speaking almost entirely of disease and poor health because when even a subclinical degree of disease is present, a wide array of functions begin showing a marked decrement. For example, the onset of mental illness after retirement is frequently preceded by a physical impairment and is thought to be more highly related to the effects of disease and to consequent social isolation than to retirement itself (Lowenthal, 1964). Similarly, depression may occur following retirement, but this is usually transitory and does not require treatment or hospitalization unlike the severe depression that may occur several years later after the onset of physical disease (Spence, 1966). Thus, disease is a biological factor of crucial importance since one's physical health may influence the satisfactions, the roles one plays, and the status one receives in retirement, and it may affect the way the retired person perceives himself. That is, if he requires constant care or is physically dependent on mechanical or pharmacological aids, his feeling of independence, competence, meaningfulness, and self-esteem are likely to be difficult to maintain.

In the future, medical progress will likely achieve an actual separation between the time of onset of disease and retirement so that these events will not be interrelated. Only a generation ago, retirement was far less prevalent because many persons died before reaching retirement age. So perhaps in another generation, retirement will seldom be influenced by disease and failing health in the way in which it often is today.

Social-Cultural Factors

The meaning of retirement for the individual is also affected, to a large degree, by social variables and by the cultural definition of the meaning of retirement. For example, since retirement is an abrupt shift in roles, whether this shift is *voluntary* (i.e., selected by his own choice because he wanted to do something other than work and was able to do so) or whether it is *forced* by a mandatory retirement age is likely to have a differential effect on the meaning of retirement for the individual. The meaning of this shift in roles is also affected by the characteristics of the retired status and the range of social roles that are associated with it. That is, does the retired person choose the retired status because it is desired, or is he forced into a status of a "nonperson" who is socially defined as worthless and useless? What roles is he expected to play according to the age norms of the society? How meaningful are those roles for him? How much status do they provide? Is he able to maintain a decent income, or is he forced to live at a standard below the federally-defined poverty level?

A major study of retirement—the Cornell Study of Occupational Retirement (Streib and Schneider, 1971)—explored these questions in a longitudinal study of persons nearing retirement age in the 1950s. They obtained a group of 1486 men and 483 women living in the 48 continental states; the respondents represented a wide variety of occupations and all social classes except the lowest. While their respondents were not entirely representative of all retiring persons in the country, the longitudinal design allowed them to explore important aspects of the process of retirement.

In general, they found that both men and women with higher incomes, education, and higher status occupations continued working longer than others, and that persons who indicated they were "willing to retire" did, in fact, retire earlier than persons who were "reluctant to retire." Somewhat more surprising, however, they found that women tended to be less willing to retire than men, and that single or married women tended to retire earlier than widowed or divorced women. These complex patterns reinforce the idea that retirement can be understood only in terms of the life-space of the individual. Apparently, since the women generally had more education and a higher proportion in professional occupations than the men in their study, they were less eager to retire. Single or married women could plan for retirement better than divorced or widowed women, so they were more likely to retire earlier than divorced or widowed women.

Over half of the respondents reported a drop in income—about a 50 percent reduction from preretirement levels on the average for the entire group. Yet, the group reporting a decline in income was about twice as large as the group that reported that their postretirement income was "inadequate." Thus, a sizable majority say that their income is sufficient to meet their needs—however, most have not had to face the economic drain of physical illness, which is likely to occur in their later years of retirement. Perhaps a cohort-historical factor is also operating in their perception of having an adequate income since they lived through the Depression and may well be more economically secure than they were earlier in their lives.

Contrary to the notion that retirement is equated with "old age" in the minds of retiring persons, there was no indication of any age-related change in the self at the point of retirement beyond that which occurred in persons of the same age who did not retire at that point. Although there was an increase in feelings of "uselessness" at the point of retirement for some persons, over three-fourths did not report feelings of uselessness. There was a tendency for persons who continued working to feel more useful than those who retired, but this may reflect part of the reason they continued working. There was no difference between feelings of "satisfaction with life" for persons who retired and persons who did not, nor was there any consistent change in psychological health for persons who retired.

Those respondents who retired earlier tended to be more satisfied with retirement than the respondents who retired later, but the respondent's prior attitudes about retirement ("willingness to retire") seemed more important for satisfaction in retirement than whether the retirement was "voluntary" or "forced" by administrative regulations (and, as noted above, was associated with earlier retirement).

In sum, there was little evidence of a wide range of negative consequences that are typically thought to be associated with retirement in the data provided by these respondents.

> The cessation of the work role results in a sharp reduction in income, but there is no significant increase in "worry" about money in the impact year of retirement. There is no sharp decline in health, feelings of usefulness, or satisfaction in life after retirement. Neither do respondents suddenly think of themselves as "old" when they stop working (Streib and Schneider, 1971, p. 163).

Instead, retired persons seem to adapt to the changed role requirements and to tolerate the negative aspects that may be associated with the retired status in our society in much the same way that they probably adapted to the earlier changes they experienced. It may be that the changes associated with retirement are different from the changes associated with earlier milestones (such as puberty, entry into the occupation, or grandparenthood) but are not necessarily more devastating. After all, retired persons are "survivors" in an important sense—they have survived all kinds of social changes, milestones, crisis points, and personal difficulties earlier in their lives so that retirement—like menopause —is only another of the transitions that survivors cope with. Also, persons who are willing to retire and look forward to it may find a number of positive satisfactions in it. One of their respondents said:

> I take it easy. But I keep busy—a man has to do something. I cut the grass, and pull the weeds. I monkey around—keep reading. I like to read the Reader's Digest. I take a walk—go one and a half miles. Then sometimes I go fishing with a couple of fishing partners—I went

three times this year to an inland lake. I watch the ball games every
night on TV. I walk over to my daughters' houses three or four times
a week and see them and their families. We all go on picnics sometimes (Streib and Schneider, 1971, p. 113).

Of course, there may be important changes in this retirement process
that make it more traumatic for some individuals. For example, if retirement is the final step in a progressive, sequential career line in which the
individual retires with a sense of completion, it may be more satisfying
than if it occurs in a disorderly work pattern by the inability to find
another job once the last one is lost. In the latter case, retirement may
be an experience of great frustration, without a clear event or period of
transition, without a sense of completion, and possibly at an early age.
However, if one is leaving an unsatisfying job and can find more satisfying pursuits in retirement, it may be a positive transition.

The interaction of retirement and the family relationships is also important. For example, if the spouse is living, retirement will thrust the
couple into a more intense, full-time relationship than they have probably
experienced for many years. Although Deutscher (1964) reported that
these postparental years are very happy years for couples in general, it
may also be a difficult period for some. In either case, C. S. Lewis in
The Screwtape Letters is probably accurate in noting that "when two
humans have lived together for many years, it usually happens that each
has tones of voice and expressions of face which are almost unendurably
irritating to the other" (Lewis, 1943). An additional family issue for the
retiring man is that he is leaving his world of work and is entering and
spending much of his time in what has been his wife's realm—at least in the
tradition family pattern. Is she going to be willing to share her domestic
roles and duties with him and will he accept them as meaningful for himself? Alternatively, if the wife continues working after the husband retires
(or retains a range of community activities), the shifts in family roles
for both spouses may provide an added source of potential upset to this
developmental turning point.

One of the most important implications of studies on retirement is the
importance of preretirement planning—or anticipatory socialization for
the new set of roles that one will occupy when the work roles are no
longer present. This planning probably involves many aspects, such as
developing a reliable source of income after retirement, anticipating the
kinds of roles and activities that would be desirable and are available in
the family and community, developing a few interests that may deepen
into satisfying leisure pursuits (and possibly provide a new circle of
friends to help replace those one is leaving at the job), and generally
raising one's level of consciousness about retirement. Since this process
takes some time, it may well begin approximately when the midlife occu-

pational crisis (that we discussed earlier) is resolved—around 40-55. In particular, in view of the current minimal levels of Social Security ($156 for an individual and $271 for a couple was the average monthly payment in 1972) and the lack of protection for pensions (for example, if the company files bankruptcy or if one cannot qualify for one's pension if one changes jobs), financial planning is clearly important at least a decade or two before retirement.

In sum, retirement is a major social shift for an individual, but it does not necessarily involve a major psychosocial crisis. It clearly involves a process of anticipation and adjustment but, in general, the meaning of retirement for the individual reflects a complex array of social and cultural factors that reflect his unique life situation and also his perception of the social meaning of retirement. Let us now turn our attention to the more personal perceptions of retirement and consider some of the psychological factors involved in the retirement process.

Psychological Factors

In the Erikson framework, retirement marks the transition between Generativity versus Stagnation and the crisis of Integrity versus Despair. Thus, the evaluation of one's contribution in the occupation and in the family gains importance as a crucial issue at the point of retirement. The sense of satisfaction, the sense of having produced meaningful products, and the sense of accomplishment in the occupation (as well as in the family) are therefore important attributes to bring to the next stage of life. Conversely, a sense of stagnation and of frustration will increase the difficulty of this next stage. But, of course, the possibility for generativity does not end at retirement, particularly with the current lengthening of the retirement period; nor is the issue of integrity suddenly salient only after retirement. Instead, these two stages of the life cycle, and the intimacy stage as well, overlap and are probably as simultaneous as they are distinct; only the relative emphasis of the crucial issue distinguishes each stage from the others.

Yet, some of the other events that are occurring at about the same time as retirement increase the importance of the issue involved in Integrity versus Despair. The events leading to increased introspection and reminiscence include the increased awareness of death as something personally relevant (some friends have died, one's spouse may be ill or deceased, and one's health may be failing); the fact that the sphere of meaningful personal interactions may be decreasing and the sphere of physical life-space may be shrinking; the fact that there may be a change in residence (to an apartment or a retirement community); and the task of establishing new social relationships and adjusting to unfamiliar surroundings.

In addition, there may be extended periods of mourning over the loss of a friend or spouse, reawakening old memories and leading to a reevaluation of one's life. This introspective process may be called the life review (Butler, 1963) and will be discussed in detail in Chapter 9.

With retirement there is also a shift away from a complex world in which one has played an important, decision-making part to a smaller, less complex leisure life without the same kind of important tasks to deal with; there are obvious occupational differences in this consideration, however. But what a change it must be for a man such as Lyndon Johnson or Charles De Gaulle to suddenly find himself retired!

Certainly, one important factor in the smoothness of the shift at retirement is the extent of planning and preparation that preceded it. But there also seem to be personality characteristics associated with successful retirement. Reichard, Livson, and Peterson (1962) reported that three personality types were associated with good adjustment to retirement, and two types were found in their group of retired men who adjusted poorly.

The largest group identified among the well adjusted we called the "mature." These men moved easily into old age. Relatively free of neurotic conflict, they were able to accept themselves realistically and to find genuine satisfaction in activities and personal relationships. Feeling their lives had been rewarding, they were able to grow old without regret for the past or loss in the present. They took old age for granted and made the best of it. A second group, whom we labeled the "rocking-chair men" because of their general passivity, welcomed the opportunity to be free of responsibility and to indulge their passive needs in old age. For these men, old age brought satisfactions that compensated for its disadvantages. A third well-adjusted group consisted of persons who maintained a highly developed but smoothly functioning system of defenses against anxiety. Unable to face passivity or helplessness in old age, they warded off their dread of physical decline by keeping active. Their strong defenses protected them from their fear of growing old. We called them the "armored."

Among those who were poorly adjusted to aging, the largest group of individuals we called the "angry men." Bitter over having failed to achieve their goals earlier in life, they blamed others for their disappointments and were unable to reconcile themselves to growing old. A second group of maladjusted men also looked back on their past lives with a sense of disappointment and failure, but unlike the angry men they turned their resentment inward, blaming themselves for their misfortunes. These men tended to be depressed as they approached old age. Growing old underscored their feelings of inadequacy and worthlessness. We called this group the "self-haters."

With the exception of the mature group, many of whom had had difficulties in personal adjustment when they were younger, these personality types appeared to have been relatively stable throughout life. Poor adjustment to aging among the angry men and the self-haters seemed to stem from lifelong personality problems. Similarly, the histories of the armored and rocking-chair groups suggest that their personalities had changed very little throughout their lives (Reichard, Livson, and Peterson, 1962, pp. 170-171).[1]

These data suggest that an individual's style of personality is relatively enduring and that it affects one's ability to adjust to a developmental turning point such as retirement. The data also suggest that retirement may have different meanings for persons with differing personalities and that a satisfying retirement for some (for example, the "rocking chair" group) may be quite unpleasant for others (the "armored" who seemed to have to keep active). We will discuss personality and the relationship between personality and life satisfaction among the aged in Chapter 7, but this study sensitizes us to the variety of ways in which individuals differ and to the importance these personality differences may have. In general, it might be noted that retired persons differ from one another at least as much as younger persons differ from one another. Thus, the personal needs, goals, satisfactions, and coping abilities differ among retired persons just as they do among all persons. Persons involved in planning for the retired should therefore note that a satisfying life style for one retired person is not necessarily satisfying for another. This implies that the individual's needs, interests, and personality should be considered, respected, and allowed to maximize the variety of roles and styles of retired persons. Ideally, the retired person is able to strive for his most fully human potentials in an environment that supports and encourages his freedom and growth.

Conclusion

It should by now be apparent that when a complex social, cultural, and psychological event (with biological factors also relevant) is studied from an interdisciplinary, developmental perspective, much of the complexity is included in the analysis. We may only conclude that each set of factors is of major importance, although no single factor alone (such as personality or physical health) is sufficient to understand a complex event such as retirement. Instead, we need to gather much more data and to study the process of retirement comprehensively across time and across a num-

[1] Reprinted with permission.

ber of different situations (such as voluntary or forced, orderly career or disorderly work history, and men or women) in order to gain a richer understanding of the process of retirement as it occurs over a period of perhaps 15 or 20 years. For example, it seems that a kind of "disengagement" occurs in which the individual and the social system mutually release and disengage from one another (Cumming and Henry, 1961); but some research has shown that this pattern may not be the ideal outcome, although it may accurately describe at least part of the retirement process. We will defer this discussion to the next chapter on personality where we will also take a closer look at the question of consistency of personality. But let us now conclude this chapter by returning to the social-cultural sphere and taking a look at the role of leisure in America and the relationship it has to work and retirement.

CHANGING LEISURE VALUES

One of the results of the increased productivity of the work force (resulting from automation and other technology) is that there is an increasing amount of nonworking time becoming available in our society. For example, Kreps (1966) estimated that men born in 1960 will have nine more years of nonworking time than men born in 1900. She has projected several possible uses of nonworking time from 1965 to 1985 if the per capita gross national product were to remain constant (Table 6.1). In this extreme case, the amount of nonworking time would be sufficient to allow

Table 6.1   Alternative Uses of Potential Nonworking Time

| | | | | Education and Training | |
Year	Retirement Age	Length of Workweek (hours)	Vacation Time (weeks)	Labor force Retrained[a] (percent)	Years of Extended Education
1965	65 or over	40	3	—	—
1966	65	39	4	2.9	1.2
1967	63	38	7	5.0	2.4
1968	61	36	7	8.7	3.4
1969	59	36	8	11.1	4.2
1970	57	34	10	13.8	5.1
1975	50	30	16	26.2	9.4
1980	44	25	21	37.2	13.8
1985	38	22	25	45.2	17.5

[a] Figures are in addition to the number of workers now trained in public and private programs.
Source. Adapted from Kreps (1966), Table 1.

retirement at age 38, a work-week of 22 hours, or 25 weeks of vacation time a year in 1985! If the nonworking time were invested in education and retraining of the labor force, nearly half of the labor force could be in training each year, or the average amount of lifetime education could be extended by 17.5 years! However, the most likely prospect would be increases in the per capita gross national product as well as some combination of these alternate uses of nonworking time. Thus, shorter work-weeks, longer vacations, periodic "sabbatical leaves" for education and retraining, and earlier retirement may all occur together—and may characterize the future work-life of today's young people. Even today with a 40-hour work-week, some occupations are experimenting with four 10-hour work days. Consider for a minute: this is still a 40-hour week, but if it edges down to four 9-hour days, which are essentially 3½ 10-hour days, the amount of working time would *equal* the amount of nonworking time—3½ days of each a week—in addition to the other 14 hours each day for sleeping, eating, and recreation that is "pure gravy" not counted in the 3½ 10-hour days of nonworking time each week!

The obvious question is what will all of this nonworking time mean to individuals in our society? And what will it mean for society? Does it mean additional time to watch television, more time for travel, or increased time for socializing with friends? Will it mean more time spent in education, participating in the arts, or in community service? As the amount of nonworking time increases, these decisions will be made as each person decides how he will spend his time. But society is also involved because it would seem that the socially defined meaning of non-working time will be involved in the individual's decision. That is, will this nonworking time be a valuable blessing that allows individuals to spend their time in ways that, in the past, were only possible for a few upper-class persons who led a life of leisure? Or will it be a time that is irrelevant to social values so that "wasting time" will no longer have negative connotations? Or perhaps it may be seen as a negative, unproductive time that is best used by getting a part-time job or developing an interest in some hobby or activity to prevent idleness and boredom?

It may be apparent that social values are intertwined with the meaning of nonworking time. For example, what is the meaning of *leisure*? Is non-working time the same as leisure time? Is *free time* the same as leisure time? The literature on leisure emphasizes that leisure is very difficult to define. Suppose a professor is reading a scientific book when he is at home and "not working." Or suppose a business executive goes out to play golf on Saturday morning because he knows a business contact will be there. And consider the salesman who "entertains" a customer with dinner and an evening in a night club. Are these examples of leisure—or of some other kind of job-related time? A worker in a plant may come home and watch TV because he is too exhausted from the job and the drive home to do anything else—is this leisure?

Kelly (1972) has proposed one useful model for conceptualizing leisure along two dimensions: the amount of choice the individual has in undertaking the activity and the relation of the activity to work (Figure 6.3). This model suggests that there are three differing types of leisure and one type of nonworking time that is not leisure (Type 4—preparation and recuperation). Type 1, *unconditional* leisure, is chosen freely and is unrelated to one's work. It is a kind of ideal leisure that Aristotle and, more recently, deGrazia (1964) regarded as the only pure type of leisure. For Aristotle it meant enjoyment of music and contemplation. More generally, it would be the kind of activity that is freely chosen and undertaken for its own sake alone. Thus, it could consist of any activity that one chooses for the enjoyment of the activity but is not related to one's work. If one were to ski in one's leisure, this would be Type 1 leisure only if one went skiing for its own sake, not to become a ski instructor and not to escape from the frustrations of one's occupation. If one went camping, hiking, hunting, or traveling for its own sake, it would be unconditional leisure; if one went away to escape the telephone and the pressures of the job, it would not be Type 1 in this model. Thus, the meaning of the activity—whether it was related to the job—and the freedom of its choice are crucial to whether or not it is unconditional leisure.

The second type of leisure in Kelly's model is *coordinated* activity. This is also freely chosen but is related to the occupation in some way. It is

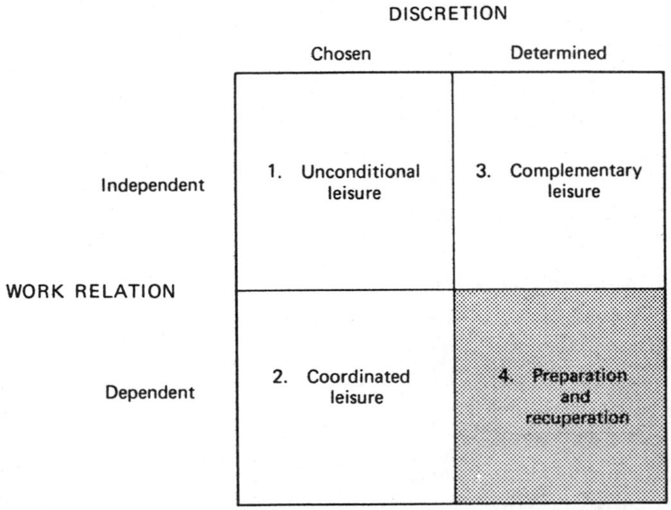

Figure 6.3
Nonworking time classified by degree of choice in activity and relation of activity to work.
(Source. Kelly, 1972, Figure 3. Reprinted with permission.)

not required (like the salesman who entertains a customer as a requirement of his job) but is related to one's work. The professor who reads a
scientific journal in his leisure would be a clear example; or the machinist who uses his skills in his home shop to make something he wishes to
make would be another example of coordinated leisure. The meaning and
the intent of the activity is crucial in deciding whether the activity is
freely chosen coordinated leisure. For example, if a businessman went to
the golf course for the sake of playing golf, this would be Type 1 leisure;
if he went in order to meet a business associate for business purposes,
the activity would be considered coordinated leisure (Type 2) because it
is freely chosen activity but connected to his work activity.

The third type of leisure in this model is *complementary* activity which
is not freely chosen in a strict sense, and is not directly related to one's
work. It is complementary to one's work role in the sense that it reflects
the role expectations associated with one's occupation—such as participation in voluntary organizations (e.g., unions, professional associations,
or civic clubs) or participation in community activities (such as a school
board) that may be expected of a person in certain occupations. This style
of leisure may reflect one's occupation in less-direct ways as well. For
example, it may be activity that is sought as a diversion or an antidote to
one's work—such as a factory worker who seeks outdoor leisure activity
because he is "locked up inside all day" (and not as an end in itself as in
the "pure" Type 1 style). Or complementary leisure may reflect one's
socioeconomic status, education, and desire to move up in socioeconomic
status; since these factors relate to one's occupation, Kelly's model proposes that leisure activity determined by these occupation-related variables is also complementary leisure (Type 3).

Nonleisure use of free time in his model is activity that is related to the
occupation and is not freely chosen. For example, the person who is too
exhausted by working to do anything except watch TV, the salesman who
has to entertain clients, and the teacher who is preparing for tomorrow's
class are not engaging in leisure activities during their free time. In general, these activities involve *preparation and recuperation* (Type 4) directly related to and determined by one's occupation.

Two characteristics of leisure in our society stand out in this model.
First is the observation that any number of activities may be leisure activities, depending on the reason they are undertaken and the meaning they
have for the individual. An activity, such as watching TV may be Type 1
leisure for one person who is doing it for its own sake; it could be Type 2
for another person who is a TV producer but is watching it because he
wants to. It would be a Type 3 activity for a person who is watching the
program because he is expected to by his co-workers (for example) who
will discuss it tomorrow; it would be a Type 4 activity for the person
who is too tired from working to do anything else. And, for the techni-

cian at the TV station, he is watching it because it is his *job*. The second implication of this model is that leisure is intimately associated with work. Whether leisure is defined as time spent not working, or is analyzed in more detail as in Kelly's model, it is clear that work and leisure are interdependent in our society.

This interdependence between work and leisure probably reflects the high degree of work preoccupation in our society. That is, to a large extent an individual's meaningful activity is his job—it provides monetary "reward" that provides food, shelter, and the necessities of life; it also provides an important aspect of his identity and his socioeconomic status. It also defines the time that is nonworking time (potential leisure time) and affects the nature and meaning of his leisure activities (in Kelly's Type 2 and Type 3). Thus, leisure tends to be seen in the negative context of "time not working" rather than as a potentially positive experience in its own right. Perhaps this concept of leisure is partly a manifestation of the Protestant Ethic in which work was not only seen as good, but was also a path toward eternal salvation, while idleness was seen as sinful and the road to eternal damnation. According to that ethic, working (and having money) was one of the most important characteristics of a person.

The moral value of work may have diminished in our society today, but the belief that work is important remains high. For example, Pfeiffer and Davis (1971) found that about 90 percent of the men and 80 percent of the women in their sample of middle-class persons (age 46-71) would still work if they did not have to work for a living. The respondents also reported they derived more satisfaction from work than from leisure activities (only 7 to 28 percent derived more satisfaction from leisure). Only a few wanted more free time (about 25 percent); and those who were working said they had "more fun" recently than those who were not working. Pfeiffer and Davis concluded that these respondents indicated clearly that our society is a work-oriented, not a leisure-oriented society. It is especially interesting that in the cohort that will soon have much more free time (those 61-65), 89 percent of the men and 79 percent of the women said they would still work if they did not have to work for a living. And only 20 percent of the men and 22 percent of the women in this cohort felt that leisure provided more satisfaction than work. It would seem that these respondents are approaching a period of increased leisure with little orientation to leisure as a positive activity in its own right.

The high degree of work orientation in our society is somewhat surprising since the actual amount of "free time" per week actually exceeds the amount of work time. Robinson and Converse (1972) reported on their survey of the amount of time spent in various activities in 8 European countries, the Soviet Union, and the United States in 1965-1966. The number of hours per day spent working ranged from 5.6 in Bulgaria to 3.7 in West Germany. The number of hours of free time per day ranged from 5.1 in the United States and one town in Yugoslavia to 3.2 in Hungary. Time spent sleeping (about 8 hours in all countries) was the only activity that consumed more time than work or free time. In four countries (United States, Belgium, West Germany, and Yugoslavia) the amount of free time exceeded the amount of work time per day (averaged over the seven-day week, of course). In the United States there was about one more hour of free time than work time (Table 6.2).

Table 6.2 Number of Hours per Day Spent in Work and Free Time in 13 Survey Sites

Site	Work Hours/Day	Free Time Hours/Day[a]
United States (Cities 50,000)	3.8	5.0
United States (Jackson, Mich.)	4.1	5.1
France (6 Cities)	4.2	3.9
Belgium (425 Cities)	4.3	5.0
West Germany (100 Districts)	3.7	4.4
West Germany (Osnabruck)	3.7	4.9
Hungary (Gyor)	5.4	3.2
Poland (Torun)	4.9	4.4
Yugoslavia (Maribor)	4.3	3.6
Yugoslavia (Kragujevac)	4.0	5.1
Bulgaria (Kazanlik)	5.6	3.6
Russia (Pskov)	5.4	4.1
Czechoslovakia (Olomouc)	4.9	3.9

[a] Includes time spent in resting, education, organizations, radio, television, reading, social life, conversation, walking, sports, various leisure, and amusements.
Source. Robinson and Converse (1972), Table 1, adapted. Reprinted with permission from The Human Meaning of Social Change by Angus Campbell and Philip E. Converse (Eds.), copyright © 1972 by Russell Sage Foundation.

As the amount of nonworking time increases in the future, will it bring a shift in the social meaning of leisure time—or will we retain our apparent work orientation in spite of an increasing excess of free time over work time? It seems that social attitudes about leisure are at the heart of this question. One interesting study of leisure attitudes compared a group of intellectually elite persons (members of the Mensa society whose criterion for membership is an IQ score higher than 98 percent of the general population) with a sample of adults working full time (Neulinger and Raps, 1972). The Mensa subjects differed from the other respondents on several attitudes toward leisure. They had a higher affinity for leisure and preferred more vacation time than the other adults. The Mensa subjects had a more positive conception of leisure, viewed leisure as more "honest" than work, and generally had more positive attitudes toward leisure than the other group of adults. While it is not surprising that an elite group of persons would have greater affinity for leisure than more ordinary persons (they also had high income and education levels), we wonder whether a greater affinity for leisure might be a desirable social goal and one that might be taught.

In terms of recreation and leisure planning, the most important point may well be to teach people how to cope with free time, not by filling up free time with a string of compulsively carried out activities, but by developing attitudes which will permit a person to be with himself, perhaps by himself, in a truly leisurely manner. As we have been taught to work, not just by acquiring certain skills but by acquiring the "right" work attitude, so perhaps must we now learn how *to leisure* by acquiring the "right" leisure attitude (Neulinger and Raps, 1972, p. 206).

The anticipated increase in leisure time will interact with the family and with the occupation. That is, individuals now have the possibility of an additional source of satisfaction and meaning in their lives beyond that which is provided by the job or the family. A large part of this new leisure time may initially be taken up with families, with community participation in athletics, social, or cultural activities, and with hobbies or recreation. However, not everyone may find satisfaction in these leisure activities, particularly as the amount of free time continues to grow. Instead, the frustrations of an increasingly automated, routine job, poverty, or an unsatisfying family life may only be compounded by excessive free time. More optimistically, it may be that greater leisure will lead to new forms of community and new styles of community participation such as block clubs, T-groups, and voluntary organizations to improve the quality of life—including schools, natural resources, and the world of work. The essential question is whether the increase in leisure time will become a source of growth and fulfillment that allows individuals to actualize their human potentials to the fullest. The challenge implicit in that question is whether we will be able to develop meaningful styles of leisure in our society and whether these will be available to all persons or only to those who also have good jobs and good educations.

Perhaps Freud's answer to the question of what a normal person should be able to do well may need to be extended slightly today: the normal person should be able to love, to work, and *to leisure.*

We will now turn to a case example of a successful middle-aged executive. Many of the issues and concepts we have discussed about the family and the occupation may be seen in this interlude. In the next chapter we will discuss personality changes and continuity throughout the life span and begin to shift our focus to the later years of adulthood.

References

Birren, James E.; Butler, Robert N.; Greenhouse, Samuel W.; Sokoloff, Louis; and Yarrow, Marian R. (Eds.) **1963.** *Human Aging: A Biological and Behavioral Study.* Publication No. (HSM) 71-9051. Washington, D.C.: U.S. Government Printing Office.

Brown, Claude. 1965. *Manchild in the Promised Land.* New York: Macmillan.

*****Butler, Robert N. 1963.** The Life Review: An Interpretation of Reminiscence in the Aged. *Psychiatry, 26*(1), 65–76.

Carp, Frances M. 1966. Background and Statement of Purpose. In Frances M. Carp (Ed.), *The Retirement Process.* U.S. Department of Health, Education and Welfare. PHS Publication No. 1778. Washington, D.C.: U.S. Government Printing Office.

Cicourel, Aaron V., and Kitsuse, John I. 1968. The Social Organization of the High School and Deviant Adolescent Careers. In Earl Rubington and Martin S. Weinberg (Eds.), *Deviance: The Interactionist Perspective.* New York: Macmillan.

Cumming, Elaine, and Henry, William E. 1961. *Growing Old: The Process of Disengagement.* New York: Basic Books.

*****Deutscher, Irwin. 1964.** The Quality of Postparental Life. *Journal of Marriage and the Family, 26*(1), 263–268.

*****Epstein, Lenore A., and Murray, Janet H. 1967.** *The Aged Population of the U.S.: The 1963 Social Security Survey of the Aged.* Department of Health, Education and Welfare Research Report No. 19. Washington, D.C.: U.S. Government Printing Office.

Erikson, Erik H. 1968. *Identity: Youth and Crisis.* New York: W. W. Norton.

Grazia, Sebastian de. 1964. *Of Time, Work, and Leisure.* Garden City. N.Y.: Doubleday.

Henry, William E. 1965. Identity and Diffusion in Professional Actors. Paper presented at the meeting of the American Psychological Association, September, 1965.

Henry, William E.; Sims, John H.; and Spray, S. Lee. 1971. *The Fifth Profession: Becoming a Psychotherapist.* San Francisco: Jossey-Bass.

Janowitz, Morris. 1965. *Sociology and the Military Establishment.* (Rev. ed.) New York: Russell Sage Foundation.

Kelly, John R. 1972. Work and Leisure: A Simplified Paradigm. *Journal of Leisure Research,* 4(1), 50–62.

Kreps, Juanita M. 1966. The Allocation of Leisure to Retirement. In Frances M. Carp (Ed.), *The Retirement Process.* U.S. Department of Health, Education and Welfare. PHS Publication No. 1778. Washington, D.C.: U.S. Government Printing Office.

Lewis, C. S. 1943. *The Screwtape Letters.* New York: Macmillan.

*Lowenthal, Marjorie Fiske. 1964. Social Isolation and Mental Illness in Old Age. *American Sociological Review,* 29(1), 54–70.

*Maddox, George L. 1966. Retirement as a Social Event in the United States. In John C. McKinney and Frank T. deVyver (Eds.), *Aging and Social Policy.* New York: Appleton-Century-Crofts.

*Miller, Stephen J. 1965. The Social Dilemma of the Aging Leisure Participant. In Arnold M. Rose and Warren A. Peterson (Eds.), *Older People and Their Social World: The Subculture of the Aging.* Philadelphia: F. A. Davis.

*Neugarten, Bernice L. 1967. The Awareness of Middle Age. In Roger Owen (Ed.), *Middle Age.* London: British Broadcasting Corporation.

*Neugarten, Bernice L., and Moore, Joan W. 1968. The Changing Age-Status System. In Bernice L. Neugarten (Ed.), *Middle Age and Aging.* Chicago: University of Chicago Press.

Neulinger, John, and Raps, Charles S. 1972. Leisure Attitudes of an Intellectual Elite. *Journal of Leisure Research,* 4(3), 196–207.

Pfeiffer, Eric, and Davis, Glenn C. 1971. The Use of Leisure Time in Middle Life. *Gerontologist,* 11(3, Part 1), 187–195.

**Reichard, Suzanne; Livson, Florine; and Peterson, Paul G. 1962. *Aging and Personality.* New York: Wiley.

Robinson, John P., and Converse, Philip E. 1972. Social Change Reflected in the Use of Time. In Angus Campbell and Philip E. Converse (Eds.), *The Human Meaning of Social Change.* New York: Russell Sage Foundation.

Roe, Anne. 1961. The Psychology of the Scientist. *Science,* 134, 456–459.

Spence, Donald L. 1966. Patterns of Retirement in San Francisco. In Frances M. Carp (Ed.), *The Retirement Process.* U.S. Department of Health, Education and Welfare. PHS Publication No. 1778. Washington, D.C.: U.S. Government Printing Office.

Streib, Gordon F., and Schneider, Clement J. 1971. *Retirement in American Society: Impact and Process.* Ithaca, N.Y.: Cornell University Press.

U.S. Bureau of Labor Statistics. 1971. Marital and Family Characteristics of *Workers,* March 1970. *Special Labor Force Report,* No. 130. Washington, D.C.: U.S. Government Printing Office.

U.S. Bureau of the Census. 1973. Some Demographic Aspects of Aging in the United States. *Current Population Reports*, Series P-23, No. 43. Washington, D.C.: U.S. Government Printing Office.

*****Wilensky, Harold L. 1961.** Orderly Careers and Social Participation: The Impact of Work History on Social Integration in the Middle Mass. *American Sociological Review, 26*(4), 521–539.

* References marked with an asterisk appear in Bernice L. Neugarten (Ed.), *Middle Age and Aging*. Chicago: University of Chicago Press, 1968.
** Reference marked with a double asterisk has relevant selections in *Middle Age and Aging*.

Interlude
Murray, Age 48

The serious problems in life . . . are never fully solved. If ever they
should appear to be so it is a sure sign that something has been lost.
The meaning and purpose of a problem seem to lie not in its solution
but in our working at it incessantly (Jung, 1933, p. 11).[1]

Murray is a 48-year-old successful vice-president in a large organization. As he quickly points out in the interview, he has just published a
book, teaches in a university, and lectures around the country. He is a
man of many abilities and much energy; yet there is a sense in which he
feels insecure and unfulfilled. Although George said it explicitly and
Theresa implied it, Murray seems to be the person who is most clearly
working at a problem that perhaps will never be fully solved. He has had
serious problems with his marriage, problems with his son, and leaves
the impression of having escaped into his work where he feels confident
and secure, yet also strangely vulnerable.

Several intriguing questions are raised by this case example. How satisfied is he (actually) in his job? Why does the need for security remain so
important? What is happening in his relationship with his son? Why did
so many turning points occur when he was 28 (a major milestone for
him)? What happened in his marriage and in his attempts to fit his job
and family together? How did his work life and the rest of his life get
so split off from one another? How does his future look? Are his future
goals and plans for retirement realistic; or are they typical for a middle-
aged person? Is he leaving his mark (in Erikson's sense of generativity)?
Are his feelings about death realistic, or is the thought rather frightening
to him; why?

[1] See references for Chapter 7.

What are some of the milestones in your life? As you look back over it, what are some of the events that stand out? Let me start from the present and go backwards. I wrote a book which came out last week. That probably is one of the most important things that's happened to me in my life. Going back from there, I was given an award this last year for outstanding contributions to literature in my field. That was an important milestone; one coming on top of the other. Over the last five years, I have been the president of _____. That was a milestone. One of the more important things that happened to me was finally getting the recognition in the company and becoming vice-president. That's a milestone for several reasons. I'll never forget that day, when the board passed on that. *Was it celebrated in some way, that event?* Yes, it was celebrated. My wife and I celebrated it. It was celebrated with friends as well; it was important. It really didn't change my role in the company, but it meant something to me. I can't really document what it meant, because it didn't change my salary; it didn't change the respect I receive from my peers; it didn't change my national reputation or my business reputation, but it had some effect on me. I considered it quite a moment. I suppose these are the most important things in my work career.

My social life, my life as a husband and a father has had many milestones, some good and some bad. I'm going through a very important trying time now. My son left college after two years, settled in Europe for a while, and is trying to get himself out of Casablanca today. My son is my only child, so a great deal of my life has been affected by my son. My life with my wife has had many milestones, most of them not happy ones; so, that is another area. There are pockets. The third pocket of my life is my academic life, which I find probably the most rewarding of all my pockets. I'm an associate professor at _____ College in the Graduate Program. This has been the unique part of my life, because it's almost without any relationship to superiors. It's a very independent kind of existence. I find my life very free in the school. Another part of my life which is really tied into my academic life is the lectures I give around the country, and that's probably—with the lectures in the classroom— the most rewarding of all my endeavors.

Let me go back a minute and pick up on some of these. You mentioned the book that you've just published. I had published 50 articles before that, and I started together with a young member of the faculty to get this book out and we got it out in a year's time. It's being well received, and it's a damn good book. I think basically the real rewards I get out of life are tied in to the recognition I get outside in the field. Inside it's a real fight. It's a very, very complicated environment.... It's trying.

Probably the turning point of my life has been not to be an entrepreneur and work for a living. I love to live well, and I'm always tempted to parlay my success into something other than working for a living; but I do not do it. Probably because I'm a Depression child. And that's another part of my life, a milestone in my life, growing up as a young boy in the Depression years in more or less a limited-income family. I wouldn't say poverty, but a limited-income family. The second milestone in my life was the War, World War II, which was the first time I was away from home; and the constant knowledge that you might be killed. I got married when I was very young—21—right after

I was discharged from the service. Another milestone was deciding that I
didn't want to be an accountant after graduating as an accountant and starting a career in my present field. So these are the milestones; I never put
them together.

What was it about the Depression that made that a milestone for you? Well,
the struggle, to see my parents struggling, my father being out of work for
almost two years; my mother having to work and be away. The whole era
where ... and it's very vivid ... where small things were very important. Where
certainly no one ever thought of luxuries. I think while I was living through
it I didn't realize how my parents were sheltering me from it. The impact was
later. It became more obvious as I got more affluent. We talked about it and
reflected upon the little things that were so important then, that are so
unimportant now. I never, never took a train or a trolley to school. I walked
to school and that was several miles. One would never spend a nickel to do
that. That was no sacrifice. Based upon that experience during the Depression,
I find money to be very important as a base of security, and I'm not willing
to gamble with it. That's what I came out of the Depression with. *That's what
you meant earlier when instead of an entrepreneur, you don't risk?* That's
right. No risk. I have to know what's going to be ahead for me in the next
year, and that's why the relationship, employee to employer is more satisfactory in that area. The more interesting facet of that is that it's probably the
most unsatisfactory part of my life, inasmuch as I have a hard time accepting the superiors who are not really my superior intellectually or otherwise.
And I find that in order to exist you must supress that feeling and in an
organization such as ours you deal with many many powerful people. And you
walk a tightrope.

Let me tell you something that just, you know, popped in and out of my
head. I never had this feeling of desire for security until in the midst of my
career there was a milestone. I was 28 years old. I had a fairly nice job, and
I lost the job because the place was in deep financial trouble. At the very
moment my wife gave birth to our first and only child after six years of marriage where both of us worked and made comfortable salaries; we found ourselves—she not working—with the child; me not working with no savings, and
I did not handle that situation well. I was out of work for eight weeks and it
seemed like eight years. [I was] very frightened, extremely frightened. And
that fear has really permeated the years subsequent to that. Up to that time
I don't think I really thought about the Depression. I didn't think about security. I was happy go lucky. That changed my life, and that made me want to
be in a very secure situation, and altered my later life. Now, 20 years later,
where I have a national reputation, and I probably would have a job the day
I was fired from this job or quit this job, that still gnaws at me. That has
affected my ability to gamble, and yet I'm certainly not famous for my reserved
attitude. I'm very outspoken, and that's a form of gambling. So, I don't know
how you put it together. I haven't thought about it enough.

*It sounds like there are some ways in which you are reserved in the sense
of not taking financial risks, but other kinds of ways in which you really let
it hang out.* You're on an interesting point in this interview—many milestones
all within the same week span—book coming out, my son on his way back

from Europe, and I just decided to buy a country home. I've never been a homeowner. I've committed myself to a country home, an economic commitment I've never made in my life. I've been very cautious. For a man in my income level, as of this moment I have no, well, minor outstanding debt . . . minor. That's how cautious I am about that. And yet, I've taken that step. I thought that that's a major commitment, financial commitment. So, I don't know, that's certainly a milestone. What brought about that shift in terms of buying a country home? I suppose there are several things. One, I would like to have the comfort of a retreat like that. Two, I hope it will affect my son's desire to stay home, rather than float around the world; it might be this country home which is a little remoter than living in the city would help that. Third, economically I feel that it is feasible, and that I've been too cautious, and fourth, I think it's a good investment. [Telephone rings; call about son's arriving flight from Casablanca.]

I gather that was about your son. Yeah. That has dominated much of my life in the last 20 years. *You mentioned him earlier as a milestone.* Oh yeah. *In what sense? Can you say more about him?* Our whole relationship, my wife's and mine, is built around a deep concern about our son and investment in our son, emotionally an investment, probably far beyond what a psychiatrist would permit as normal. It's not unusual. It's not unusual in a Jewish family, okay. It's not unusual with an only son, an only child, and it's not unusual based upon my wife's background, which was abject poverty, an orphan at thirteen; and not unusual since we were both planning on not having a family when we had a family, although we were married six years without one. So we are . . . our son has a great deal to do with our moods, and with our satisfactions. We're highly protective. . . . so when I consider it a milestone, it is a very important part of my life. I define milestones as important parts . . . . negative, positive, or anything that changes your life. I consider my son as something that has had a deep effect on my life. *I gather both positive and negative?* Yeah. Yeah, both.

Have there been some crisis points in that relationship? Very, very many. And crisis points in my marriage as well. Crisis points, with anyone who has had a 20-year-old son, of the same type—directionless kind of existence, underachiever. I don't like the word, but basically what I'm saying is a lack of motivation . . . the drug scene . . . terrible crisis one time. We got a call from Canada that he was in jail; and going up there to get him out. *How did you feel about that?* I was . . . first of all, my wife almost cracked up. She's very . . . she gets very uptight. She's having a tough day today. She doesn't know . . . because he called us yesterday saying he couldn't get out of Casablanca and now we're hoping he's on one of these two planes. Ah, I felt the way I usually feel when there's a crisis with my son; I get very, very worried, but basically I attempt to handle it the same way I have success with handling my business life. I tend to get overpowering at that point with my wife, and that may be a mistake. I take charge, which I normally don't do. My wife is in charge in the house. My wife is in charge with my son. I quickly started the checklist and within hours I had a lawyer specializing in this, who I picked up at three in the morning; went down to the airport, had the tickets arranged, had several thousands dollars in cash in my pocket, got on the plane, got there;

he got back on the plane with us within two hours. It's very interesting as I reflect back. I never was that kind of individual while my father was alive. And my relationship with my father was interesting. My father used to be an arranger. He was a bright guy but he wasn't an intelligent guy, and he was the arranger. And I did very well as a young man, everything was arranged. When I was in trouble, he would arrange things. I wasn't famous for being an arranger; in fact, most of my life 'til the last 10 years, I avoided problems. Now I've become an arranger. You asked me how I felt and I felt very troubled, deeply disturbed, but didn't get my mind off of what I had to do. I knew what I had to do. And nothing would stop me from doing it. Without a doubt, nothing would stop me, and it didn't stop me. *It sounds like a lot of the skills you use here on your job are relevant there.* Exactly. Exactly. That's the way I operate. It's successful in my job. I have not been successful in my marriage, so that . . . that's another area. At times I get too short-tempered about that kind of problem and I may operate too quickly, because basically I tend to want to do it myself. *I'm getting a sense that you would like a lot more out of this relationship with your son than you're getting.* Oh, sure I would. Sure. But I think every father would. My son's not going to follow in my footsteps and that's good. I didn't want him to. And he's not going to do what I want him to do. I have to come to accept that. Certainly I have disappointments, but I have a lot of satisfactions. He's a brilliant boy. He's starting to challenge my own sense of intelligence and that I like. I would like to see him less concerned with the occult and more concerned with day to day happenings. I am not a father who is interested in seeing him join the establishment as it's defined, but in some ways . . . yes, compromise. I don't think he has a sense of compromise yet, but he's only 20. I'm not sure I had it. At 20 I was dodging bullets. *You were doing what?* Dodging bullets. It was a favorite pastime of my generation.

You fought in the Second War? Yeah, I was in the Navy. It wasn't really that bad. *But you indicated that it was one of the milestones for you.* Oh, yes . . . it was a milestone, being away from the protected environment very young, naive, traveling around the world for better or worse. That's certainly a milestone. And, wondering if your ship is going to get hit or not by a submarine. That's a milestone. Getting by it was a milestone also.

I think I changed the direction of my life, and I did it rather than having it done for me. I decided that I didn't want to go on to accounting. I went on to evening school to do my graduate work in education, which I thought I wanted to do, and then got involved in industry and decided that the _____ field was a good field, and just by making the decision got into the field, which is very interesting. That I did myself. I had no preparation for it, and made a career out of it, and reached the point where I am considered the dean of my field; so that was an important turn in my life. Much has come from that decision. *It took you several years to reach that decision?* Oh, yeah, I didn't know what I wanted to do. I was just floating around, doing the best I could, like most people do, until I was 28. You do the best you can. *That was the time when you lost the job?* Right. *And your son was born?* Yeah. *And you made the decision to get into your present field?* Right. And I did it. I was in industry for many years and moved into my present specialty. That's another milestone. It afforded me an opportunity to make out of myself what I am now. It was a burgeoning industry, as far as my field of specialty. That was a little fortuitous also. After being with a firm for a long time, I took a job in Illinois because I had that feeling from the last time of being out of work, and I didn't want to go through it again, so I took the first job that was offered to me, and it was offered to me before my last check, and I made sure that I was set. And I moved to Chicago and my wife didn't want to move there. And we had a very difficult six months. She insisted that we come back to New York and, fortuitously, there was a job opening at this company. It changed my whole life. That was not planned. It was still in my same field that I planned on staying in, but not in the same industry, and that changed everything. *It was almost accidental that you wound up in this position?* Oh, very, very much so. But in reviewing it, it wasn't accidental that I made out of it what it turned out to be. That was me. No one could take that away from me. I had come to the company knowing that they had very little here, and it was not very difficult for me to look like a genius by rediscovering the wheel. I'll be very, very frank about it. Here I am with a bag of tricks . . . really a great magician . . . coming into a situation where all the tricks were perfect, useful. That was magnificent . . . unbelievable! I don't know how many men get that opportunity in their lifetime. That was unbelievable! Before I knew it, there was an industry-wide problem and I was an industry spokesman, and from there on in it was all very easy, to the point where anything I wrote would be published. It was just great! Not very many people find themselves.

That didn't make me happy, though. . . . Satisfaction with your job and over-all happiness with your life are usually two different departments. One may have an effect on the other. I have an extreme satisfaction . . . I *had* extreme satisfaction from my job, tremendous recognition. I did not have that kind of satisfaction from my life, in the main. I've come to grips with that in the last two years. I think I have more of an understanding of the satisfaction I've had in the past, but during that time my life was work oriented. This was my total satisfaction. Certainly not satisfaction in my social life.

So your personal life was very different, very much less satisfying? Yes. *What was happening there?* Marital problems that are not untypical of affluent, middle class people who have some satisfaction in their life and tremendous exposure to a different world. *Exposure to a different world?* Yeah, rather than the limited world of your home and your neighborhood. Yeah, my wife is in a terrible disadvantage. Women's lib . . . there's a lot of nonsense in it, but there's a lot of meat, and the whole business of being tied down to the home, although I think that's also a choice a person makes. Geographic exposure . . . a man's a successful executive like myself who travels around and is exposed to the academic world, is exposed to a work area that's large and interesting has so many more contacts and so many more opportunities for satisfaction and for exploration, that it's definitely a threat when the woman is not exposed to anything other than the family and the home. And that caused a great deal of difficulty in my marriage. *What was some of that difficulty about?* Women. My exposure to many women, who happen to have the same drive I have. My feeling of lack of freedom, which has always been a pervasive feeling, that I was always tied down economically. You see that business from the Depression . . . although I didn't want to be tied down economically. I was frightened of economic responsibility. I always had it. So my hedge against it was a secure job, and yet innately what I wanted was freedom. I didn't want a secure job. I wanted to be able to not worry about economic pressures that most men do. When women's lib talks about exchanging roles with men, I wonder if they talk about or consider the economic pressures that are on most men in our society. Some real and some not real; but they are just as real if the person thinks the pressure is upon him. And most men do think that the economic pressure is upon them. *Were there other ways you felt tied down?* Oh, sure. I wanted to be a jet setter. I always had that feeling of being able to enjoy, always wanting to enjoy. I suppose you kind of do that as a couple as well, so a lot of it is rationalization. An individual says he is tied down, but most people tie themselves down. I realized that a couple of years ago. It was not in my stars, but in myself that the problem lay. I'm coming to peace with myself on that.

Did you always feel this way in your marriage, or was there some point when it became a really definite feeling? When I was 28 and my son was born. That's probably the single most important milestone in my life. Because a lot turns on that. The feeling of the pressure of the responsibility of a child. My wife's own feeling about this. She was very, very hysterical about being a mother. Once it happened she became the ultra mother, the most mother. I suppose that was a guilt reaction, but all this happened then . . . the feeling of being tied in. That eight-week period of being unemployed had a tremendous . . . this is where . . . see, look at the economic responsibility that's on my shoulders, that I didn't want. My parents shielded me from the economic responsibility during the whole Depression. This is a direct relationship, my feeling about the need for freedom. How did I define that? Was I talking about girls? Yes I was talking about girls. Was I talking about traveling? Yes, I was talking about traveling. But when you got to the core of it I was talking about no need to provide for anybody but myself. That's what I wanted when all this pressed in on me, and had an effect on me for a period of 10 years, 15 years. *What kind of an effect?* That I tended to run away from the responsibilities at home. And became more responsible on the job, but less responsible at home. That business that happened with my son was atypical. The pressure was on me, and I had to deal with it. Usually I walked away from those problems. Those were my wife's problems . . . taking care of my son.

How did she feel about this? Terrible. We had a terrible relationship. It culminated in our splitting up and going back together again. But it was all a function of my feeling of wanting less responsibility at home and more responsibilities at work. I never ran away from responsibilities at work. Figure that out. *So you did split up at one point.* Yeah. *How long ago was that?* Two years ago. *And you've recently gotten back together?* No, right away. It was a very short split. It was only two weeks that I was away, and we've restructured our lives since then. It's been satisfactory. *What do you mean you restructured your lives?* Well, there are a lot of things that bothered me in our relationship. We moved into the city. We started to do more things together. I made an investment, which I hadn't done in the past. Let me give you a mind picture. I'm like a balloon. I tend to fly with the air currents. That's been the opposite of my life in the business world. There I'm like a lead balloon—really anchored.

And I tend to fly around from experience to experience and not make an investment; and you could be married a long time and never make an investment,
you know. The fact that you see people celebrating their fiftieth anniversary
together, their twenty-fifth anniversary together, doesn't tell you whether
they've been together, really together. I find that many marriages are two
separate lives that meet in the night. On the other hand, one of the problems
I've had with marriage is that I find it didn't afford enough freedom, and I'm
more and more enchanted with the writings on the open marriage concept...
not that I practice it. I practiced a one-way open marriage for 15 years, 10
years, I should say. So we start to restructure our lives. I did, it's never too
late.

It sounds like you've decided to stay together. Yeah. Without a doubt. *Why is
that?* Well, there are many factors. One is that I, for some reason, find divorce
impossible to think of, and that deep-seated problem that I went through with
a psychiatrist when we broke up for a period of time after that. It's my own
feeling that I don't want to hurt people. That's interesting, because I'm in a
business where you have to be real rough sometimes. But I don't see it the
same way. I have a strong feeling of my responsibility for other people, and
yet I don't. It's really a contradiction... that I really want to escape that. I've
always felt I didn't want the responsibility... I always take on the responsibility. Being the arranger is part of that. I find this drive that I can't stop to be
the responsible person. That's the way we even manage the house. I take care
of the complete finances. I pay all the bills. You know, it's the kind of thing...
it's almost male chauvinism. But it's this... the two forces that are constantly
at fight with each other. One is the force that gnaws at me... that I don't want
responsibility. The other is constantly taking responsibility... feeling responsible. Therefore, divorce is something that I can advise other people about if I
think it's appropriate, but I could never take it into my own life. *You could
never take that step.* Yes, it's impossible. You can't kid yourself about it. You
can pretend about it, but it's just not my makeup. I feel like I would be
deserting my family, and you always, there's always a rationalization for it,
but... there's always a good reason why you do it, but basically it's that sense
of responsibility that I'm driven to. I always feel that I don't want to hurt
anybody.

Have there been any crisis points in your relations with your parents? No.
My parents were my children for a long time. Again I took the responsibility.
My father always arranged things when I was younger, then, as soon as I got
out and made something of myself in the business world, I became the arranger for my parents, and they depended on me. And I did it with great
relish. When my father died I had my mother still alive, and I take care of her.
I arrange everything for her. So, there have been no crisis points with my
parents. My mother tends to be irresponsible. When you're 75 you can be irresponsible, too. I don't mind it. I don't mind taking that responsibility. *Was it a
crisis point at all when your father died?* No... a very sad point. It becomes
sadder by the year because I reflect back more and more on it. It's funny
about sons... although if my son treated me like I treated my father I would
be ecstatic but, in reflecting back, I think I should have been closer to my
father. *How long ago did he die?* Seven years now. Seven years.

Have your relations with your parents changed over the years? No! They were always childlike, whoever assumed the role of the child in the relationship. It was always me the child and then, finally, they became the child. No, it didn't change. I never discussed important matters with my parents ... of intellectual or philosophical importance that my son discusses with me now ... challenges me on. My father and mother thought that the sun rose on me, the sun set around me, and that I could do no wrong. They were very good to me. Whether it was because I never rocked the boat in exchange or not, I don't want to challenge. I closet that. It has been suggested to me that it was easier for them to be good to me than to face up to the problems. I can't deal with that. I had a good relationship with my parents.

Have there been any crisis points in your job? Oh, many. I have a terrible, terrible reaction to doing something wrong. And there's a depression that comes over me when I think I made a mistake. At my company I took on ... or someone took me on, in a fight that I was unequal to. Now I'm the middleweight champion, not the heavyweight champion, and the heavyweight champion took me on, and I didn't talk for two days ... I couldn't speak. I ran away and didn't want to speak to anybody about it. That was a real crisis. *I take it you lost the battle.* No, I won the battle. *You won the battle?* Yeah, isn't that funny? I won the battle, but inside I had the feeling of having lost, of having been bested. In fact I not only won, I won the battle for the industry, inasmuch as what came out of it was very important for the industry. And that guy became a very close friend of mine, a very close backer. I won the battle, but it was very, very traumatic for me. *Traumatic in what sense?* I felt crushed that I was being singled out individually, and singled out for making an error. By the way, I didn't make an error then ... you see, I started the story off by telling you that there are times I made errors. This was not an error, but it was considered as an error by some. I have a hard time when people criticize me. ... It's strange. I would love to have the ability to be thick skinned. People think I am, but I'm very thin skinned, extremely thin skinned. That was the time where I needed a thick skin, and I was very thin skinned. He hit me hard and I thought he was unfair. I didn't do well emotionally. I've reached a level of acceptance and respect that when somebody doesn't give me acceptance and respect, I get childish about it. I sulk. I've got to be able to be like an actor who's got to be able to take a bad review. I haven't been able to take bad reviews too well, even when they were deserved.

In what ways have you changed on the job? What effect has the experience that you've had made? Well, let's first get out of the way the fact that I've become a true expert rather than a magician based upon a bag of tricks. After the years of dealing with the problems, I'm an expert in them. I have the confidence. I know my job. I am the best person I know in my job! So, that gives me a lot of confidence. That's how I've changed, and I've developed that over the years. Number two, I suppose the feeling of that whole thing about the outside of the organization. I've changed inasmuch as I expect less from the inside of the company and expect more and get more outside again, within the parameter of my business life. I'm talking about the respect of my peers outside. That's not a new change, but it's something that has developed over the years. I think I'm less defensive than I was. With all I told you, I think I do better at taking a bad review. I'm willing to say, "That's the way the cookie crumbles." I get a lot of comfort when I'm able to do that, because I know that that's a different person than the person I've been all my life. I think I churn up inside less—that's another thing—because I have so many outlets now. If I'm unhappy over what happened today at the job, tonight I'll be writing something; the next day I'm lecturing at _____. I've got that. So I have a lot of escape valves. And maybe they're not as haphazard as one may think. Maybe I put them there, because I'm worried about the repetition of that time when I had no escape valves. I've got lots of escape valves! The final escape valve for me is when I'll have enough money where I won't even need an escape valve. But I've never done anything about that. *In terms of building up money faster or something?* Yeah. We live extremely well! We live an upper middle class existence ... within our means, but right up to the extent of our means. We never want for anything. We're opera goers, ballet goers, concert goers, Europe goers ... we've done well by ourselves in that area.

How does your job future look to you? What do you see ahead for yourself? I see myself retiring in this job. Normal retiring age is 65 and I'm 48 now, so I see myself retiring in 17 years. I see myself continuing to teach during this period of time, continuing to write, and continuing to have outside activities. So, it's really a repetition of what I've had in the last few years, only with new challenges, variations on the challenge. I don't see myself outside of this job. *Does that mean after retirement?* Oh, after retirement? No. I want to get to retirement. I hope that within this period of time I'll be able to manage an early retirement. I would love to retire at age 55. I don't think it's realistic, but certainly no later than age 60. If I could manage a reduced retirement at age 55, I would certainly grab it. What do I see myself doing? Just what I told you ... teaching, consulting, lecturing ... that's my life ... and writing more. *So it would be retirement from the job and not from all your other activities?* That's right. That would be the only retirement. The activities that I have outside the job are great, and I would love to be freed from the job with the same nice salary and be able to do the others. *Do you see yourself retiring from your other activities of teaching or writing?* Oh, yeah ... I could ... in fact I would see probably the first year that I retire, traveling around the world. I could do that. I would have no trouble, because I could keep myself busy; I would not be moping around. I would love the freedom. I would retire to my country home and retire on and off. When I say I would continue to do the other things, I would continue them, but not on a full-time basis. I want the freedom of retirement. I want the freedom of not having to work this week, you see. I look towards that. I don't look towards it to play golf or to settle in some retirement community ... God I wouldn't ... I would die ... I look to it, towards the freedom it affords me to do whatever I want to do.

How do you see your personal life developing in the future? Do you think there will be more satisfaction there? Yeah, I think so. I'm optimistic. I think there is a ... my friends would say a ... good prognosis for my marriage. That's an area I've changed sharply in the last two years. Every problem doesn't make me say, "Let's fly away."

Has your outlook on life changed much over the years? Yeah, I think it has. I've been what might be considered a radical-liberal all my life and I think I am as close to being a conservative as possible now, so I would say that was a sharp change, and that's recently. *What brought that about?* I'm tired of violence. I'm tired of rationalizing the act on the basis of a cause. I think they're two separate things. I think the cause is important, and that causes, the root causes, should be remedied, but on the other hand, that's where my former philosophy stopped, and my new philosophy incorporates dealing with the acts as well. A crime is a crime no matter what the cause. I'm tired of violence. So, that . . . and I suppose, now your getting to a more basic cause . . . my affluence is threatened by the radicalism, so I'm not going to kid myself about it. I've got it. I got it the hard way.

Would you say that you have a pretty firm sense of who you are? I've always had a firm sense of who I am. My problem was, was I happy with who I am? I'm getting a lot happier with it. But I knew who I was and what my limitations were, what my strong suit was for a long time. When I say a long time I mean for ten years or so. That's a long time. *Before then you didn't have quite a . . .* No, I wasn't sure, I wasn't sure. I also think I have a firm understanding and realization of where I'm going, and where I'm not going. I've got a good thing going. I don't use the word "happiness." That's from my other life. Happiness equals good times equals excitement.

Do you sometimes look back over your life and kind of review it? Yes, I sometimes do that. I don't dwell on it. I like to review my life. I like to go back and think about things that happened to me, both pleasant and unpleasant. I do it every so often. I'm not afraid of doing it, but I don't dwell on it, and . . . I rarely have the feeling I would like to be seventeen or eighteen again.

I must say that I don't think of myself as destructible. I think I'm going to live forever. That's a nice feeling. I'm not worried. Maybe in about 10 years from now I'll start worrying about dying. I'm still not at the point where I'm worried about dying. Then, when you worry about that, you look back on your life more. No, I'm still looking ahead. I really think I have 20 productive years ahead of doing something and then maybe the kind of retirement where you sit around and contemplate your navel. I've got 20 years. I've got a lifetime ahead of me. *Do you sometimes think about death?* Death? Yeah, I think about it sometimes. In fact, recently I have prepared my will. I never had one. I think about it—not oppressively. When I say I think I'm indestructible, that's nonsense. I mean, I don't think about death as imminent. I think of it as a possibility, and it's not a . . . it's not within the context of my life right now. As I said before, it may be five years from now or ten years from now. On and off it appears. I was thinking of death a great deal two years ago when I had this great difficulty at home. *You mean in terms of possible suicide?* Just about death. Just about it being an easy way. Now I don't. I think of life more than I think about death. Much more. There's so much more of life right now. I'm very excited about what's ahead of me, you know, in the next year, with my country home, my son coming home, my book. There's a lot of exciting things ahead, so I've got a lot . . . it's not going to be a dull year. I say it's more of the same of what I'm doing, but it's always a variation on a theme. So it's a very exciting period ahead, very exciting.

Is sex as important to you now as it used to be? No. *In what way?* Well, it was very important to me. I don't know if you decide this or it happens to you, but it's just something that takes a back seat in my life now. It took a front seat for much of my life. *What do mean that it takes a back seat now?* Oh, I'm not as hung up about the whole thing. Which I was in the past. Hung up inasmuch as I used to sleep around a great deal. I think I've come to some kind of understanding of that. Maybe it's accepting less. But in any case, it's an acceptance, and I'm not willing to rock the boat. I'm accepting it, and I'm not willing to go into the psychological roots of my acceptance. There's no question about it. It's a compromise. *What about sex with your wife?* That's what I'm talking about as well. It's a compromise. *A compromise in what sense?* I expect less. I give less too. I've always given less at home, but now every time I'm unhappy about my sex life, I don't run out and satisfy myself in a relationship. My relationships were always permanent relationships. When I say "sleep around," that's a very poor term. Always that sense of responsibility. They were long-term relationships—a strange phenomenon—my analyst enjoyed that. You see, I see a difference between a guy who sleeps around, and a guy who has a permanent mistress. Within the context of my stupid kind of morality, one is quite different from the other.

Would you say that you're having a close, intimate relationship now with someone? No. Other than my wife. *With your wife?* Yeah. I think we're close now. Closer than we've ever been. Extremely close now. More understanding on my part. *Was it very intimate earlier; for example, after your marriage?* No, we were children ... absolute children ... playing house. There should be a law. One big game. No responsibilities. *From the very beginning?* From the very beginning. Until my son was born. Then all of a sudden we found ourselves with responsibilities. It was a very free life. That's what it was. It was just an extension of our childhood. I came right out of the service ... not even finished with college ... and got married. My wife worked while I went to college. It was like being home with mama. The same thing, no difference. Just moved from one place to the other; in fact, we lived at home for a while, at my house for a while. No difference. Same kind of life. No responsibilities. My only responsibilities were getting good marks at school. That was very important. That had carried over from being at home with my mother and then later with my wife.

Would you say that you are different now than you were a few years ago? Oh, it's like day and night. Oh, sure. *In what ways?* I tend, as I said before, and I'm very happy when it happens, to be reserved at times where I never was reserved, number one. Number two, I tend to accept more often than I have in the past, a bad review. Number three, I'm not looking for the excitement of the good life, the jet-set life, as I did in the past. And I could find happiness in a very comfortable relationship at home. That's very important. That's really the one thing that I needed to stabilize my life.

Do you have a sense now of leaving your mark: somehow being productive? Yeah. I think my obituary would interest me if I was reading it to someone else. Let me put it that dramatically. Yeah, my obituary would interest me now, if I read it in today's paper to somebody else. I think I will have left my mark. I will have left my mark with this book. This book will be around long after I expire, and with all I'm going to do after this. I set the standards. I've legitimized my profession in this industry. That's a deep mark. And in teaching I've left my ... we didn't talk about it much, but of all the things I do, I teach with the best. I'm just alive in that classroom. I didn't even talk about it; that really is the thing that I do well. So, I've left my mark. I've left my mark now if I stop now. I'm not going to stop now. There's a lot more to do. Yeah, I'll leave my mark. They won't say, "He was a nice guy," like they did when my father died, with all of the accomplishments and say he was a nice guy. A lot of people will say I was a nice guy, but that won't be my accomplishment. I will have accomplished something.

seven
Personality
Processes
and
Psychopathology

At a common-sense level we probably all assume that the human adult is a complex creature who possesses a unique and relatively stable *personality*. For example, some adults seem to be particularly daring, bold, and extroverted; others seem to be quiet, conservative, and introverted; and still others impress us with their enthusiasm, their gregariousness, or their dependability (and so on). Each of us, it would seem, has an individual style, a uniqueness, a characteristic set of attributes that distinguish us from others and also help to make us recognizably similar in different situations and at different times over the years. Such assumptions are clearly useful since most people are rather consistent from day to day (and those who are not tend to be labeled "mentally ill"). Moreover, the existence of relatively stable personalities is clearly a necessary assumption for human interaction to proceed smoothly. Consider the chaos that would result if we all woke up each morning with a new personality: one's cheerful, cooperative wife today might be a demanding tyrant tomorrow; the capable efficient boss of yesterday might be an indecisive guilt-ridden neurotic today and a dictator tomorrow; the calm, reliable newscaster last night might become a biased bigot the next morning; and one's trusted friends, the national leaders, and the corner druggist might all become totally unpredictable. In such a situation, human interaction as we know it would become, at least, unpredictable and immensely difficult; at worst, it would be totally impossible. If we could not rely on some kind of predictability of the personality characteristics of oneself and of others, we would be as unable to interact with each other in meaningful ways as would be the case (pointed out in Chapter 2) if we all stopped playing social roles; in either case, each interaction would have to begin anew without the great advantage of prior experience and a set of expectations. It would be an impossibly confusing world indeed!

Thus, the concept of *personality* provides two important insights into human behavior: it allows us to examine individual differences in the ways in which they respond to similar situations; and it provides a system by which individual behavior remains fairly consistent across differing situations and over a number of years. In a sense, personality represents a kind of "fit" between the individual and his environment; it reflects his unique adaptation to his past experiences and colors his responses to his present social and physical environment. That is, personality is generally assumed to reflect previous experiences (particularly in childhood) and to be manifested in the individual's unique reactions to various kinds of situations. For example, a person who was trained to be independent and to strive for a high degree of achievement (in order to win his parents' praise in childhood) would be expected to respond in independent and achievement-oriented ways in adolescence, young adulthood, and adulthood. In this sense, personality is seen as an internal kind of gyro or "inertial navigation system"; it is set in motion and then resists change while it provides a stable framework within which the individual responds to his present situations. Thus, an individual's unique inner dynamics are seen as fairly consistent once they are formed and an individual's personality is assumed to be revealed in his response to various kinds of situations—by his personality *style*, his personality *traits*, or by his personality *type*, for example. In this manner an individual's uniqueness is seen in his unique set of personality characteristics (traits, styles, and dynamics, for example) that are sufficiently stable across different situations (school, work, family, and old age) to make up an identifiable personality that is generally consistent.

However, we intuitively know that people do change—they do not respond to every different situation in the same way, they change (hopefully) in psychotherapy, and they may change as they accumulate new roles and new experiences as they move through the decades of adulthood. So we wonder how consistent individuals actually are in different situations and at different times in their lives. We touched on this point in Chapter 2 in terms of the *self* that, we argued, changes with new roles and experiences while it also remains consistent through the memory of past *I*s and *me*s, through habitual reactions to generally similar situations, and through selection and selective perception of situations so that these situations remain generally similar. However, personality, as psychologists conceive of the concept, is not identical to the concept of the self since personality is a kind of internal predisposition to respond in predictable ways to a variety of different situations. Perhaps the self may be seen as functioning at the core of personality; that is, our *I* experiences our personality (and the personality characteristics of others), and our personality characteristics resemble *me*s (I am "hostile," "dependent," or "passive," and so on). Yet, personality also involves motives (such as a need for achievement or for affiliation, as discussed in Chapter 4) and internal predispositions to respond in individual ways to external situations. Thus the relationship between the self and personality is rather complex. And the relationship between personality and the external situations is also complex. For example, an individual's personality is thought to reflect his childhood experiences (perhaps including his cultural and national heritage); but once formed, personality is thought to reflect inner dynamics rather than external situations. Nonetheless, it seems that personality is intermeshed with external situations; as Murphy (1968) has pointed out: "... there is never ... a sharp distinction between you and your environment.... The situation around you makes a continuing impress upon you; changing, modulating, remaking you" (p. 33).

All of these points taken together suggest that personality is a rather complex but important area in understanding adulthood. Questions of personality consistency and change, the interaction of the self, personality, and the environment, and the nature of personality change during the adult years are both puzzling and significant questions. In this chapter we will discuss the data on personality continuity and conclude that personality is perhaps best seen as an interacting system of physiological processes, cognitive processes, and the physical-social environment with the self processes (the interaction of the *I* and *me*) functioning at the core of the personality system. We will then propose a conceptual model of this personality system that will be useful in interpreting the data on personality change in adulthood. After presenting the data on adult personality, we will discuss dysfunctions in the personality system, briefly discuss psychopathology (particularly in the later years of life), and suggest some modest ways of helping in cases of psychological dysfunction (or "mental illness").

CONTINUITY AND CHANGE IN PERSONALITY: DATA AND CONFLICTING MODELS

Throughout our discussions of young adulthood and the family and occupation in middle adulthood, we have suggested numerous ways in which an individual's personality would be likely to change—in the resolution of the identity conflict, in parenthood, in occupational socialization, and in widowhood, to mention a few. Yet, the standard view of personality would predict that individuals are not totally changed, and perhaps not changed in important ways, by such events. This raises several interesting questions: does personality remain fairly consistent over 10 or 20 or more years? What aspects of personality are highly consistent? What are the processes which bring about this consistency? And, conversely, how much change is there in personality and in what aspects of it?

Data on Personality Continuity

Mischel (1968) reviewed studies of personality continuity and observed that studies that measured *self-description of personality* found considerable stability. For example, Byrne (1966) reports that trait self-descriptions on several personality questionnaires show considerable stability. Similar findings of considerable stability for self-descriptions of personality were reported by Kelly (1955) over a 20-year test-retest interval. And Woodruff and Birren (1972) found no statistically significant age changes in the scores of 85 respondents on a measure of self-adjustment over a 25-year age-span; that is, there was no significant difference in the way in which they described themselves in 1944 (at average age 19.5) and their self-descriptions in 1969 (at average age 44.5). However, they also found that their respondents' *retrospective* descriptions of themselves in 1969 (as they thought they had answered in 1944) were markedly different (lower in personal and social adjustment) from the *actual* score in 1944 (Figure 7.1). Apparently, these respondents tended to perceive that they had changed (and in positive ways) since young adulthood, although this change was not objectively present. Thus, perhaps persons tend to subjectively feel that they have changed, although they also tend to describe themselves in highly similar ways over a period of 25 years.

Another aspect of personality that Mischel concluded is particularly stable is *cognitive style.* For example, field dependence-independence (mentioned in Chapter 4 as differing between men and women) has been found to be highly consistent over time (correlations as high as .92 over a few years and .66 over 14 years); however, it is also highly correlated with some measures of intelligence (Witkin, Goodenough, and Karp, 1967). Hence, the stability of the cognitive-style aspect of personality may result in part from the stability of intellectual processes.

Mischel also points out that self-defined typologies of ourselves and of the world are highly stable across situations and over time. That is, the *personal constructs* one uses in describing oneself or others are quite resistant to change. "Studies of the self-concept, of impression formation in person perception and in clinical judgment, of cognitive sets guiding selective attention—all these phenomena and many more document the consistency and tenacious continuity of many human construction systems" (Mischel, 1969). Certainly cognitive and intellectual processes are implicated in these construct systems, and together they may provide much of the continuity we see in personality. That is to say that much of the continuity we *see* may be in the eye of the beholder, and much of

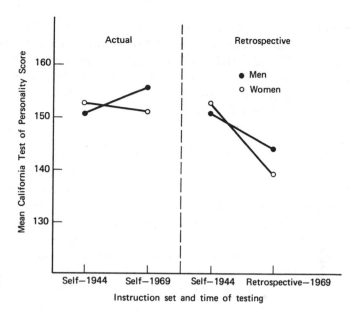

Figure 7.1
California test of personality scores in 1944 and 1969 for the 1924 cohort in the actual and retrospective condition. (Source. Adapted from Woodruff and Birren, 1972, p. 255. Reprinted with permission from Developmental Psychology, copyright © 1972 by the American Psychological Association.)

that continuity results from our own relatively stable construct systems and cognitive processes. Mischel (1969) refers to this selective perception of continuity as the mind functioning as "a reducing valve" decreasing the complexity of the real world through such mechanisms as construct systems (perhaps for the sake of stable social interactions).

In sum, the clearest evidence of personality continuity is found in respondents' self-descriptions and in their cognitive styles; their personal categories also seem to be relatively stable, perhaps increasing the stability of self-descriptions; and stability of intellectual functioning may be implicated in the stability of both cognitive styles and personal categories. But what about the stability of more psychodynamic personality characteristics, such as measures of aggressiveness or dependency or honesty?

In general the correlations over time between such personality traits as attitudes toward authority or dependency or aggressiveness are moderate but are often statistically significant (Skolnick, 1966a, 1966b). That is, these correlations indicate a degree of stability greater than would be expected by chance; but they generally only account for between 10 and 25 percent of the total variation in the personality characteristic (the amount of variance is approximately equal to the square of the correlation coefficient). For example, data from the Fels Longitudinal Study suggest consistency from childhood into young adulthood on achievement, sex-typed activity, and spontaneity; however, dependency of girls between ages 6 and 10 correlated only .30 with later dependence on family, and there was no correlation for boys (Kagan and Moss, 1962). Thus it appears that while personality (as rated or judged by others) is not random by any means, it is not highly consistent either. Part of the difficulty in this area is that these personality traits are measured by judges or raters rather than by the individual himself (as in the self-descriptions); thus, we are not tapping the individual's cognitive constructs about himself but are attempting to infer personal traits from his behavior. And it appears that personality traits are judged to be most similar for an individual when the situations in which they are judged are most similar (Mischel, 1968). That is, one interpretation of these modest correlations (which sometimes reach as high as .60-.70 for achievement orientation in the Fels study) is that both the individual and the situation are contributing to the behavior that is being rated.

Similar moderate correlations between personality characteristics are also found between identical twins, which indicates that a genetic factor may be contributing to personality characteristics (Thompson, 1968). Moreover, the correlations between identical twins (Mz, or monozygotic) are generally somewhat higher than for fraternal twins (Dz, or dizygotic) and are about the same magnitude as the correlations for the stability of the personality characteristics over 20 years (Table 7.1). Gottschaldt (1960) examined the consistency of a number of personality characteristics from adolescence to adulthood among twin pairs and found that age seemed to increase the importance of the genetic factor in these characteristics. So it appears that genetic factors may play a role in at

Table 7.1 Similarities in Personality Traits Between Monozygotic and Dizygotic Twin Pairs

	Mz	Dz	
		Like Sex	Unlike Sex
Neuroticism	.63	.32	.18
Self-sufficiency	.44	−.14	.12
Introversion	.50	.40	.18
Dominance	.71	.34	.18
Self-confidence	.58	.20	.07
Sociability	.57	.41	.39

Source. Carter, H. D. Twin Similarities in Emotional Traits. *Character and Personality*, 1935, 4, 61-78. Reprinted with permission of the Duke University Press.

least some personality characteristics, and that this genetic factor may be partly responsible for the consistency of an individual's personality over time. Of course, intellectual processes have long been felt to be partly genetic in origin, so that their contribution to personality stability may also reflect hereditary factors.

Summarizing briefly, these data indicate that personality traits that show greatest stability over time are traits that involve cognitive processes—self-defined typologies of ourselves and of the world—and cognitive styles (Mischel, 1969). Other aspects of personality (such as traits that are based on ratings or interpretations of projective tests rather than on self-descriptions) yield much less convincing evidence of consistency over time—significantly more consistency than would be expected by chance, but consistency explains only a modest amount of the variance—and the magnitude of the effect is about as high as the effect of genetic factors shown in twin studies.

However, if we view personality as an interactional system—that is, located in the interaction between the individual and the situation and as a joint product of the individual and the situation—then these data on personality consistency are quite meaningful. They suggest that there is a degree of continuity in this interactional system, jointly produced by the individual's predispositions and by the situation. Kurt Lewin (1935) made a similar point: "a person's behavior in any situation is jointly determined by the characteristics of that situation, as he perceives them, and by the particular behavioral dispositions of which he is possessed at that time (cited in Carson, 1969, p. 9). Thus, both change and consistency may occur simultaneously in personality and, to a large extent, which aspect of personality one observes is determined by the lenses one uses—if one looks for continuity (as with Freudian lenses), it will be observed; if one seeks change (as in the behaviorist framework), it also can be found.

Conflicting Models of Personality

Personality theory has generally adopted the consistency view—that personality consists of "contents" that are "inside" somewhere and exert an influence on behavior across all situations. Gendlin (1964) suggests that personality is most clearly manifested when one would be expected not to behave as he does (because of situational factors), so his inappropriate aggressiveness or dependency (or whatever) indicates his personality. He also points out the difficulty of explaining personality change within this type of content model of personality. That is, this consistency model does not allow us to explain how change in the personality comes about.

An alternate model, emphasizing change, is best represented by the social and the behavioral view of personality; in both frameworks the concept of personality is largely irrelevant since all of the important parameters of behavior may be found outside the organism. For example, in the social model, personality consists of an individual's unique collection of roles, and these roles are maintained by social sanctions and social expectations and are transmitted to the individual through socialization. Thus, in social behaviorism, an individual's *me*s (roles and other social behaviors) are maintained by the social and interpersonal consequences of his behavior—if the *me* fits the expectations of others, it is reinforced; if it is not appropriate to the situation, then the behavior is eventually shaped to the expected or appropriate behavior. Clearly, change is easily explained and consistency is less relevant. Notably, personality seems to vanish in this model into a collection of roles (Heine, 1971). For example, one need not know a policeman's personality to know that he will, if necessary, risk his life to save you; or that a well-trained soldier will bomb civilians in Vietnam; or that a clinical psychologist will spend a great deal of time and effort attempting to help a patient whom he would ignore if he were to have first encountered that person on a bus quietly talking to himself. It seems that role theory is quite powerful in explaining behavior—particularly if other social variables such as age, sex, occupation, race, and religion are also considered.

A similar "change model" is psychological behaviorism in which, again, personality appears to vanish. In this view, behavior is maintained by the consequences of that behavior, so that (as in social behaviorism) behaviors that are reinforced in some way will be maintained. In order to change the behavior one need know nothing about personality except the technological question of what rewards are reinforcing to the individual; then the appropriate rewards (consequences) are linked to the desired behavior.

Thus it seems clear that in these models situational factors have an important influence on behavior and, by inference, on personality consistency. However, we do not take this argument of situational influence to rule out the importance of internal factors. Instead, recalling Lewin's statement, behavior in any situation is *jointly determined* by the situation (as the individual perceives it) and by the individual's predispositions at that time. That is, the situation itself is filtered through the person's selective perception and is often chosen by the person in the first place. In addition, such internal processes as physiological functioning, hormone balance, and activation levels are probably closely interrelated both with the way in which the situation is perceived and with the individual's predisposition to respond.

For example, the data from Kolodny, Masters, Hendryx, and Toro (1971) that we presented in Chapter 4 on lower levels of testosterone in the blood of homosexual males compared to heterosexual males indicate that such complex physiological processes are interrelated with personality (or at least with exclusive homosexual behavior). The relationship may be a causal one—either from personality to physiology or from physiology to personality—or it may be a complex interaction involving other factors as well. Other studies such as the ones reported by Bardwick (1971) on the relationship between the female sex cycle and mood, or by Luce (1971) on the effects of the disruption of body time by long-distance jet travel across time zones, also indicate the possible ways in which physiological and personality processes may be interrelated. In addition, the effect of genetics on personality is not to be discounted. Ellefson (1968) reports that many observers of primates see "personality" differences between individual animals and note modal differences in temperaments among species that may be related to ecological differences in their physical environment. Also we know that selective breeding of animals produces many different characteristics, some of which may be considered to be "personality," for example in dogs (Freedman, 1958) or in rats (cf. Broadhurst and Eysenck, 1965). However, a great deal of research must be done before we have much of an understanding of the complex interactions of genetic predispositions, physiological processes, and personality.

Interacting Aspects of the Personality System

Taken together, the data on personality continuity and the differing views of personality that we have briefly presented leave us with the impression that personality is a very complex field of inquiry indeed. A basic distinction about personality views was suggested by Allport (1962): some views consider man as a "reactive being" (the behavioral view in our discussion); other views consider him as a "reactive being in depth" (the consistency view in our discussion); and still others see him as a "being-in-process-of-becoming." Allport favors the latter view, and we tend to agree. While we do not deny the insights of other views, we see man's personality as structure (consistency) and process (change), as both reacting to the immediate situation and reflecting past experience, and as planning for and being affected by expectations of future situations.

We also see personality existing only in the interaction of the diverse aspects that we have presented—the psychological, situational, behavioral, and physiological—and as our interactionist point of view implies, these aspects can be fully understood not in isolation but only in light of the whole. That is, we see individual personalities intermeshed in countless social interactions, affected by countless environmental factors, and carrying their own physiological-perceptual-conceptual systems around with them. Sullivan once defined the personality system in a similar way: *"Personality is the relatively enduring pattern of recurrent interpersonal situations which characterize a human life"* (Sullivan, 1953, pp. 110-111).

In the midst of these mutually interacting processes the human organism functions in equally complex cognitive and affective ways. For example, Carson (1969) has described the intricate ways in which one plans, processes information, utilizes feedback mechanisms, and generates decisions as to future operations. He discusses an exchange view of interpersonal transactions in which the outcome is negotiated on the basis of costs and rewards involved in reaching the end result. And he suggests that individuals develop a personal *style* that, once it is established, tends to be maintained; this stability partly results from reflected appraisals (i.e., taking the role) of others; and it may also result from the relatively enduring characteristics of cognitive styles and personal constructs. Such styles are interpersonal in nature, often developed through contractual arrangements with particular others and thus tend to be defined by the interaction rather than by the individual in isolation. Perhaps these styles reflect the current "fit" between the individual and his social and physical environment in all of the complexity that each interacting aspect involves.

There is much in personality we have not touched upon—needs, motives, dynamic conflicts, and basic strivings of mankind (to mention a few). While each may be important in particular frameworks, for our purposes we will call attention only to motivation, since such a concept suggests some possible answers to the ultimate question: why? Why do individuals play roles? make plans? seek outcomes with a greater reward than cost? allow themselves to be socialized? and so on. Many motives have been suggested (achievement, curiosity, avoidance of pain, and so on), but the motives that are most consistent with our man-in-process-of-becoming are the motive toward *self-actualization* (Maslow, 1950) and the motive toward *competence* (White, 1959). Put simply, the motive for self-actualization is the tendency of the human organism to strive to realize its fullest potential in a particular social environment by seeking to "... develop all its capacities in ways which serve to maintain or enhance the organism" (Rogers, 1959, p. 196); and, "Competence denotes the desire of the person to involve himself in effective interaction with the environment" (Kroll, Dinklage, Lee, Morley, and Wilson, 1970, p. 30). Undoubtedly, the manisfestation of these motives is likely to differ at different points in adult life; however, we are suggesting that they combine to describe the goals of the person interacting with the social and physical environment—in terms of negotiating interpersonal styles, or in terms of exploiting and repairing the physical environment.

Let us conclude this complex section with a brief list of the concepts we have suggested and that we will pull together in the next section. First, there are the interacting aspects of personality: personal styles, social roles, and physiological processes; these aspects are, to some degree, "internal" in the sense that we carry them around. Second, there are the external aspects: social situations, consequences of behavior, and the network of social interactions. Third, the interaction of these aspects

—or the self, in Mead's terms—is the crux of personality. Fourth, personality strives toward self-actualization and toward competence within this interacting social matrix. Fifth, personality changes while retaining its continuity at the same time. Sixth, personality is oriented toward the future and is affected by the consequences of its manifestations in the present; it is also related to the past but is not determined by it. And, finally, personality as a unity is different from the sum of these various parts; this is a basic principle of interacting aspects but is particularly important with regard to personality because of the innovative and creative action of the *I* (in Mead's sense) that is at the experiential core of this model of personality. It should be apparent that each of these seven statements is a descriptive assertion, which combined provide (we feel) a useful, although complex model of personality in adulthood. Some of these assertions may be empirically testable but, at this point, they represent a framework within which to view the complex personality of adults. Let us assemble these assertions together into a model in a beginning attempt to answer one of Neugarten's provocative questions:

What terms shall we use to describe the strategies with which such a person [a business executive, age 50, who makes a thousand decisions in the course of a day] manages his time, buffers himself from certain stimuli, makes elaborate plans and schedules, sheds some of his "load" by delegating some tasks to other people over whom he has certain forms of control, accepts other tasks as being singularly appropriate to his own competencies and responsibilities, and, in the same 24-hour period, succeeds in satisfying his emotional and sexual and aesthetic needs? (Neugarten, 1968).

TOWARD A CONCEPTUALIZATION OF PERSONALITY IN ADULTHOOD

We view personality as a complex system that involves both the unique individual and his unique social environment. That is, personality is the "fit" between the individual and his social environment. The personality system consists of the characteristics of that "fit" and the dynamic processes by which that "fit" comes about. Consider as an example a living organism (such as a flower). Let us assume that "flowerness" is a characteristic of that organism that is its "personality." Now, obviously the flower exists only because it fits in with its environmental niche; otherwise it would die. And we can describe the "personality" of the flower either by its characteristic—"flowerness"—or by the dynamic processes that are involved in the flowering of the flower. The same is true with personality. We can look at the *"contents"* of the personality system —personality traits, personal styles, and even social roles—and we can describe them. Or we can look at the *processes* of the personality—the dynamic interaction between the person and his environment. Thus, the personality system consists of both content aspects and process aspects. These aspects exist and function simultaneously and—as noted earlier— what we see depends on the lenses with which we view the personality system.

The personality system, since it represents the fit between the individual and his unique social niche, is both relatively stable and continuous as well as relatively flexible and changeable. That is, it can change while remaining fairly consistent at the same time. This ability of the personality system to change while it also remains continuous is an important ability since we feel that the personality is not fixed and stable during the adult years. Instead, like the self that we discussed in Chapter 2, the personality system is always open to change but is also relatively consistent over time.

As may be apparent, there are considerable similarities between our conception of the personality and our conception of the self. Both are dynamic, interacting systems that are made up of process and content aspects (in the self, these aspects are the *I* and the *me*, respectively). However, we mean something different by personality than we mean by the self. That is, the personality system is the fit between the individual and the environment, while the self (system) is the interaction between the individual's experiencing (the *I*) and the individual's perception of himself (the *me*). These two concepts fit together in our model in that we see the self as functioning at the core of the personality system. In other words, the personality system is the fit between the individual's *self* and the environment.

The model of the interacting personality system that we are proposing is diagrammed in Figure 7.2. At the core is the self with its two interacting aspects: the *I* and the *me*. Part of the self—as well as part of the personality system—is "private" in the sense that it is internal, inaccessible to view by others, and able to be examined only by its secondary effects. For example, the *I* processes, memory, thinking (cognitive processes), physiological processes (such as levels of hormones), and hereditary factors (such as intelligence) are seen as private aspects of the personality system. In general, they cannot be observed or measured directly, only their external manifestations may be public. In contrast, part of the self and part of the personality system is "public" in the sense that they are revealed in varying degrees in social interactions. There seem to be several variations or "layers" in the degree to which the various aspects of the personality system are relatively public or relatively private. In the diagram it may be noted that the most public aspects of the personality system are the external social situations in which the individual finds himself—that is, the external social environment. It is involved in the personality system since changes in the external social (or physical) environment affect the fit between the individual and his environment.

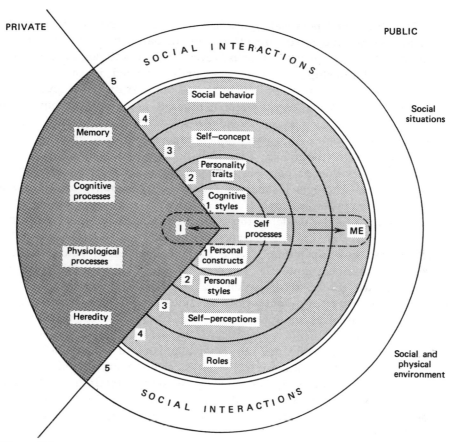

Figure 7.2
Interacting aspects of the personality system.

Such changes may bring about an adjustment of the personality as the dynamic personality system evolves toward a new fit with its changed niche.

The aspects of the personality system that are diagrammed in between the private and the public extremes of the personality system in Figure 7.2 are the various personality aspects that most clearly represent the dynamic fit between the individual's self and the external environment. They are diagrammed (somewhat arbitrarily) along the private-to-public continuum and also along the continuum from relatively stable to relatively changeable (based on the data presented earlier in this chapter). Thus, social interactions are highly public and fairly changeable. Cognitive styles and personal constructs are rather private and relatively stable aspects of the personality system.

Other aspects of the personality system, in our view, include social behavior and social roles, which tend to be relatively public (Level 4). The individual's self-concept or self-perceptions (Level 3) and his personality traits and personal styles (Level 2) are a mixture of public and private. Traits and styles are often seen in daily interactions, but they may also be fairly private—that is, revealed on psychological tests or in intimate relationships but not necessarily revealed in ordinary interactions. The most private aspects of the personality system (Level 1), but aspects that still may be directly expressed in external behavior, are cognitive styles (such as the "field dependence/independence" that we discussed in Chapter 4 and mentioned earlier in this chapter) and personal constructs (the unique ways in which we understand and perceive the world and other people). Note that these (Level 1) characteristics are also the ones found to be most stable of all personality characteristics in the data we presented earlier.

At the core of the model is the self: the interacting *I* and *me* aspects. It is apparent that the *I* is private but that the *me* is public. In fact, as we pointed out in Chapter 2, the *me* includes social roles, or social behaviors. And certainly the self-concept and self-perception are *me*s (the way we see ourselves when we take the attitude of the other). Even personality traits and personal styles can be *me*s when they are aspects of ourselves that others see and react to in social interaction (and we may see them when we take the attitude of the other toward ourselves). Thus, while the self is at the core of our model, the *me* aspect of the self extends up to the physical boundary of the interacting organism (up to Level 5) and encompasses the first four levels of the public component of the personality system. We will discuss the implications of this when we discuss the content and process aspects of personality in detail.

Let us conclude the description of the model by noting that some of these aspects of the personality system may not be fully recognized or "known" by the individual. That is, there may well be some social behaviors, roles, self-perceptions, personality traits, or cognitive styles (and so on) that the individual is only dimly aware or totally unaware of. Similarly, some of the internal aspects—such as memory or physiological processes (and so on)—may be unavailable to the individual's experiencing for some reason. This is not to say that they are necessarily "repressed" (in a psychoanalytic sense) but simply that they are unknown or unrecognized or unexperienced aspects of the personality system. However, we know that these unknown aspects may influence the personality system and daily behavior just as those aspects that are recognized may influence them.

Content and Process Aspects of the Personality System

Although this model may seem very complex, the phenomenon of personality interacting with a complicated social environment in adulthood is also quite complex. For example, adults experience a wide range of internal and external experiences during their life. They experience various feelings and moods; they experience their reactions to themselves and to others; and they experience a variety of social situations. The aspect of the personality system that is experiencing, reacting, feeling, and observing is the *I*. It is at the core of the personality system and is a purely *process* aspect that provides the continuing possibility of innovative change—for the self (as we pointed out in Chapter 2) or for the personality system. In addition, the physiological processes and the cognitive processes in the personality system are process aspects that bring the continuing possibility of change to the personality system. And the dynamic, interacting nature of the personality system itself is a process conception of personality. Thus, our personality model conceptualizes the personality system as a continually processing, dynamic, changeable system that is continually fitting the changing individual and the changing social environment together. This is not to imply that the individual is "molded" to fit the environment; certainly the individual also molds the environment and perceives (or misperceives) the environment as he participates in this process of fitting himself and his environment together.

We suggested earlier that two of the motivating forces in the personality system are striving for *competence* and striving for *self-actualization*. This means that the personality system operates in its dynamic, processing manner of fitting the individual and his environment together to achieve a sense of competence in that environment. If one does not fit in with one's environmental niche (which he has partially selected and created), then one is not likely to feel very competent and one's personality system will likely evolve toward a fit that provides greater feelings of competence. Similarly, we assume that one strives for self-actualization in the sense of realizing one's fullest human potentials. But if one does not fit in with one's niche (if the niche is too "small" or "dehumanizing," for example), the personality system will evolve toward a new fit or find another niche that allows greater potential for self-actualization. Probably these idealistic goals of competence and self-actualization are not very fully realized in general. But it seems reasonable that the personality system represents the individual's best efforts to fit himself with his environmental niche in a competent, self-actualizing manner.

In addition to these process aspects of personality, the personality system also includes a number of *content* aspects. That is, the aspects of the system that are objectifiable, that can be seen or measured, and that are indistinguishable from the *me* are the content aspects of the personality system. For example, roles, personality traits, the self-concept, self-perceptions, and personal styles all have an element of content to them. They are seen when individuals interact; we talk about them and measure them; and we see them in ourselves. They have a tendency to seem like "things" that we carry around inside—for example, "aggressive-ness," "dependency," "inferiority," or all of the roles that we play. In this sense, personality traits and social roles have an important common element—they are both *me*s. And these content aspects of the personality tend to be relatively stable (although the aspects on Level 4—social behavior and roles—change far more readily than those on Level 1 or 2—e.g., personality traits or cognitive styles). They tend to be stable pre-cisely because they are not process aspects—they are not continually fresh and thus changeable. Instead, they tend to become habituated and reinforced by their success in fitting the individual with his environment in ways that are relatively competent.

In sum, we see personality as a complex, dynamic system that simul-taneously consists of process aspects and content aspects. In a sense, whether we see the process of fitting or the content of that fit between the individual and his niche depends on the what we are looking for. Similarly, this personality system allows both change and consistency simultaneously—and what we see depends, again, on the lenses we use when we look at the individual in interaction with his environment.

Consistency and Change in the Personality System

When personality is seen in terms of an interacting system, we note that a change in any aspect of that system will bring a change to the entire system. This point is parallel to the discussion of the family (system) as a unity of interacting personalities in Chapter 5.

For example, changes in the external aspects of the system (social sit-uations or the environment) tend to bring about changes in social inter-actions (Level 5 in Figure 7.2) that lead to changes in social behavior and roles (Level 4). These role changes tend to affect one's self-perception and self-concept (Level 3) and may even have some effect on personality traits or personal styles (Level 2). Cognitive styles and personal con-structs (Level 1), which show the least change with time, may also be affected—the degree probably depends on the extent of change in the social situation (which varies from a trivial change through ordinary changes such as marriage or a new job to a major change such as being placed in a concentration camp). This process is essentially the process of socialization (discussed in Chapter 2) cast in a different model. Simi-larly, changes in the entire system may result from changes in any other aspect. That is, changes in physiological processes—such as disease or more subtle changes—may bring a change to the entire system. In gen-eral, since the personality system is a dynamic process, any change in any of the aspects (roles, self-perceptions, cognitive processes, and so on) may bring about a new fit between the individual and his environment.

At the same time, there is considerable stability in the personality system. The more private aspects of the personality system (Levels 1 to 3) and the content aspects of the system tend to change least, as we have noted. And even social roles (Level 4) and social situations tend to be fairly stable through much of adulthood. These external consistencies tend to reinforce the consistency of the personality system over time. Thus, the personality system is characterized by simultaneous consistency and change throughout the life span. Let us consider some of the developmental changes we would expect in the personality system during adulthood.

Developmental Changes in the Personality System

We would suggest that during young adulthood the personality system is characterized by a *centrifugal* tendency that propels the individual from the self out into the external social world. This results from the necessity to master new roles and to develop new personal styles and new self-concepts to maximize the fit of the individual with his expanding social environment. Kuhlen (1964) describes this period as one of "growth-expansion" in which striving for achievement, power, self-actualization, and competence predominate. Social relationships are also expanding in addition to the number of roles and social responsibilities. There may be a tendency for young people to place more emphasis on the more external (i.e., social) aspects of behavior and to conform to the social norms of their associates. Also, they may tend to feel some tension between the inner aspects of the personality (nearest the self) and the more external aspects (such as roles) as if the centrifugal movement were denying the importance of the inner aspects (such as the *I*). This process (and tension) is probably central to the individuation versus alienation issue we discussed in Chapter 3.

During the middle years of adulthood there seems to be a balance of sorts in the personality system. On one hand, the individual's social world is no longer expanding rapidly, and he has developed ways of dealing competently with it (through situation experience, as discussed in Chapter 2). On the other hand, he has also had greater self-experience and may have learned relatively comfortable ways of integrating the internal and external aspects of the personality system. In the ideal case, this leads to a smoothly functioning, competent fit between the individual and the environment that also allows some striving for the goal of self-actualization. The potential for rigidity and a tendency to resist change to this balanced system may also occur during this period.

With advancing age there seems to be a kind of *centripetal* tendency in the personality system in which the importance of the external social situation becomes less salient and the internal processes become more salient. That is, as the number and variety of roles, social behavior, and

social interactions (Levels 4 and 5) decrease in frequency or in importance, the more internal aspects of the personality (such as personality
traits) seem to be more clearly revealed. In addition, the feelings of
competence that may have been experienced during the middle years,
combined with the increased realization of a finite amount of time left
to live, may shift the focus for self-actualization inward. The theories
proposed by Bühler and Jung (which we discussed in Chapter 1) reached
a similar conclusion about these changes during the life span. For
example:

> Ageing people should know that their lives are not mounting and
> expanding, but that an inexorable inner process enforces the con-
> traction of life. For a young person it is almost a sin, or at least a
> danger, to be too preoccupied with himself; but for the ageing person
> it is a duty and a necessity to devote serious attention to himself.
> After having lavished its light upon the world, the sun withdraws its
> rays in order to illuminate itself (Jung, 1933, p. 17).

In the next section we will discuss the empirical studies of personality
change with advancing age. In general, they substantiate Jung's observations and are the basis for our own speculations presented above.

DATA ON PERSONALITY IN ADULTHOOD

Certainly, we would expect that there would be personality change with
age for specific individuals; but the data presently available suggest that
the general developmental change in personality is a shift toward a kind
of contraction or centripetal development or increased internalization
within the personality system for typical adults beginning, apparently,
about age 50. For example, Riley, Foner, and Associates (1968) reviewed
several studies of personality change in old age and reported that old
people have been found to be more rigid than young people and less
disposed to adapt to changing stimuli; their attitudes indicate a higher
degree of dogmatism, a greater intolerance of ambiguity, and less susceptibility to social pressure. They are also reported to be more passive
(i.e., conforming and accommodating), more preoccupied with their own
emotions, physical functions and inner-world orientation, and more
introverted than young people. Although cross-sectional (cohort) factors
may be important considerations in addition to age-related changes—such
as in some data on increased "conservatism" or higher political interest
and voting habits among the aged—these findings suggest a decrease in
the salience of outer situational factors and an increase in the importance
of inner processes in the personality system with advancing age. Certainly, physiological factors such as a decline in vision, hearing, excitation

levels of the central nervous system, and changes in intellectual processes with age are probably important interrelated factors (in addition to a decline in social role participation and inner psychological changes) for explaining these age-related personality changes. Once again, the interaction of the various factors involved in the personality system is crucial; and each of the interrelated aspects may play an important role in changes of the personality system.

One of the major studies of personality change and continuity in adulthood was conducted by a group from the Committee on Human Development at the University of Chicago. We will discuss this study in detail because it attempted to investigate developmental change in personality structure; that is, instead of studying changes in specific personality characteristics (as did the studies in the preceding paragraph), the researchers sought to investigate age-related changes in the total personality system. While a major shortcoming of the study is the absence of data on physiological and health factors, in many ways this study is a classic because it is one of the few large-scale studies of "normal" community residents, and it contains both cross-sectional and longitudinal data on personality change in adults. Some of the major publications based on these data are Cumming and Henry (1961), Havighurst, Neugarten, and Tobin (1963), and Neugarten and Associates (1964). They obtained a sample of nearly 700 respondents between the ages of 40 and 90 who were in relatively good health and who were living in homes or apartments (not in institutions) in Kansas City in the mid-1950s. Respondents were selected on the basis of age, sex, and economic status and were interviewed repeatedly over a period of up to seven years. The studies found three age-related personality changes: a shift in sex-role perceptions, a personality shift toward "increased interiority," and a shift in the coping styles of personality. In addition, they found a number of personality aspects that did not change with age. Thus, there are data on both change and on consistency in personality; and many of these findings have been supported in other smaller studies of adult personality. Let us begin our discussion of these data with the findings of consistency; we will then deal with the specific age-related changes that were also found.

Consistency of Adaptive Personality Characteristics

Since *age* was a major variable in the Kansas City studies, one of the central findings was that some personality characteristics did not change with age of the respondent while other personality aspects did change. Those characteristics that did *not* change seemed to share a common theme—they dealt with "adaptive, goal directed, and purposive qualities of personality" that Neugarten (1964) describes as "socioadaptational" characteristics of personality. That is, general adaptation (based on interview data), adaptive characteristics of the personality (such as integrity or adjustment or cognitive competence based on responses to projective tests), and general personality structure (based on personality tests) differed between individuals regardless of their chronological age. For example, they administered a personality test that, when the results were analyzed, yielded four general personality types: "integrated," "defended," "passive-dependent," and "unintegrated." However, there were no consistent age differences among the respondents in each of these types. Similar data were obtained in another study on a different sample conducted by Reichard, Livson, and Peterson (1962) where they found no clear age differences among their five personality types (which were discussed in Chapter 6: "mature," "rocking-chair men," "armored," "angry men," and "self-haters"); instead, these personality patterns seemed to be consistent patterns of adaptation in the histories of the men in their sample. Other data on "adjustment" to aging found no age-related differences in a sample of healthy old men (Butler, 1963a). Indeed, in that study (to be discussed in more detail in Chapter 8), *disease* was identified as a far more important variable than chronological age. Another study, based on the Kansas City samples, found no relationship between age and a measure of "life satisfaction"—which is, again, a measure of adaptive adjustment to aging (Havighurst et al., 1963).

Thus, the data seem to indicate that there is little predictable change in these socioadaptational characteristics of personality with advancing age. We interpret this finding as indicating that the *content* aspects of personality (i.e., personal styles, personality traits, and other *me* aspects) remain generally consistent during middle and old age; and that these objectifiable, relatively external aspects of personality are generally stable during adulthood. In addition, these data imply that the adaptive interaction between the person and his social environment remains fairly stable (that is, an old person seems to adapt and interact with the environment with as much satisfaction as a middle-aged person) so that—at least for generally healthy adults—there are a variety of ways in which a relatively stable personality (in terms of content) can adjust and adapt to changes in roles and status while remaining generally stable. Neugarten summarizes this conclusion in the following way:

> In a sense, the self becomes institutionalized with the passage of time. Not only do certain personality processes become stabilized and provide continuity, but the individual builds around him a network of social relationships which he comes to depend on for emotional support and responsiveness and which maintain him in many subtle ways....
>
> ...Behavior in a normal old person is more consistent and more predictable than in a younger one—...as individuals age, they be-

come increasingly like themselves—and, on the other hand, . . . the personality structure stands more clearly revealed in an old than in a younger person (Neugarten, 1964, p. 198).

Thus, the content aspects of personality seem to be relatively stable over time. For example, a slightly hostile middle-aged person is likely to become more clearly hostile as an old person; and a passive or dependent young person would be likely to remain passive into old age. In this sense, these personality "contents" remain relatively consistent, even when we might expect them to change due to situational changes such as role, status, and other changes associated with aging. However, the data from the Kansas City studies also found important age-related changes in personality that seem to involve changes in the *process* aspects of personality. Perhaps these changes in personality processes, in conjunction with stability in highly important interpersonal and social commitments (despite role changes in the family and occupational cycles), allow the general stability of salient personality "contents" and general personal satisfaction and adaptation. Let us examine these changes in personality processes, and then we will examine the important role played by stability in social and interpersonal commitments for aging individuals.

Change in Personality Processes with Age

Three sets of data in the Kansas City studies indicate related changes in personality processes with age. In general, this change is one of "increased interiority of the personality" (Neugarten, 1968), which seems to begin in middle age in a tendency toward increased self-reflection and introspection (in the decade of the fifties for most persons); it becomes more marked in later life, perhaps leading to the reminiscence characteristic of many aged persons (Butler, 1963b; this reminiscence and the "life-review process" will be discussed in detail in Chapter 9). Two of these studies (each of which we will discuss) suggest this increased interiority; one study found a decrease in "ego energy" with age, and the second found a shift in "ego style" with age. A third study found a shift in sex-role perceptions and a growing responsiveness to inner impulses with age. Each of these studies was based on data from projective tests (in which pictures were presented to the respondents who were then asked to tell a story about the picture and to describe the characters) and each dealt with "intrapsychic" processes of personality in contrast with the "socioadaptational" and content aspects of personality discussed above.

Decrease in Ego Energy. Rosen and Neugarten (1964) analyzed the responses of Kansas City respondents to five of the pictures in the Thematic Apperception Test (TAT) on four measures of "ego energy": introduction of nonpictured characters into the story told about the card, introduction of conflict into the story, extent of vigorous activity ascribed to the characters, and the intensity of emotion (affect) described for the characters. It was assumed that each of these four variables tapped the amount of psychic energy that the respondent devoted to the task of making up a story about the picture presented; hence, low ratings suggest that the respondent invested little energy in the task. Their data show a consistent decline with age on all four measures; differences between age groups were statistically reliable. Although these findings were obtained from a cross-sectional sample, since many of the respondents were interviewed subsequently it was also possible to obtain longitudinal data on these dimensions. Lubin (1964) administered the same TAT cards to 93 of the subjects five years later. He found a significant decline on a combined measure of ego energy over the five-year test-retest interval. Thus, these findings add considerable support to the notion that ego energy, which is available for tasks in the outer world, does decline with advancing age. "The implication is that the older person tends to respond to inner rather than to outer stimuli, to withdraw emotional investments, to give up self-assertiveness, and to avoid rather than to embrace challenge" (Rosen and Neugarten, 1964, p. 99).

Shift in Ego Style. A change with age that is closely related to the decrease in available ego energy is a shift in ego style from active mastery to passive mastery and magical mastery styles. Gutmann (1964), again using TAT responses, rated the stories on these three ego mastery styles separately for males and females. The three mastery types were seen as points on a continuum of ego strength in which "active mastery represents the most vigorous, effective style of ego functioning and magical mastery represents stress-laden, maladaptive ego functioning" (Gutmann, 1964, p. 119). The data show a shift with age toward passive and magical mastery styles for both males and females (Figure 7.3). In subsequent studies of these same dimensions of ego style, Gutmann studied aging men in various different cultures including subsistence corn farmers in a remote Mexican province (Gutmann, 1967) and American Indians (Krohn and Gutmann, 1971). Similar shifts from active mastery to passive and magical mastery styles were found in these widely differing cultures, which suggests a developmental shift in personality processes with age that is not related to the culture in which the individual grows old.

Shift in Sex-Role Perceptions. In a third study Neugarten and Gutmann (1958) asked respondents to describe each of four figures shown on a TAT card prepared especially for this study (Figure 7.4). The descriptions given by older respondents (age 55-70) differed significantly from descriptions given by younger respondents (age 40-54) when describing the old man and the old woman in the picture. The most striking differences

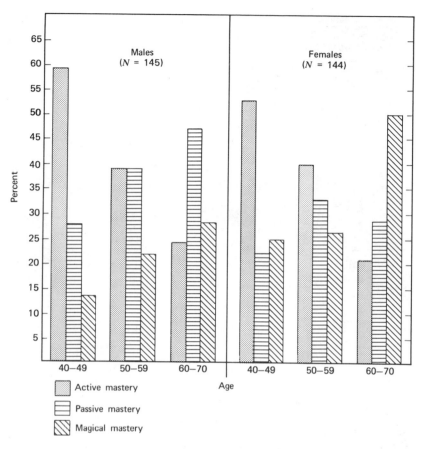

Figure 7.3
Percent of respondents exhibiting active, passive, and magical mastery styles by age and sex. By the chi-square test, the distribution of active, passive, and magical mastery totals by age groups is significantly different from chance at the .02 level. (Source. Adapted from Gutmann, 1964, Tables 6.1 and 6.2. Reprinted with permission of the Aldine Publishing Company.)

(which were statistically significant) were that the perception of the old man shifted in the direction of increasing submissiveness when seen by older respondents (both males and females) as compared with younger respondents; and the old woman's role shifted from a subordinate to an authoritative position when seen by older respondents as compared to younger ones. Essentially the same findings were obtained in a later study by Singer (1963) for a different sample of 47 old men. Although these projective data (in which the respondent is describing figures in a picture instead of his own behavior) must be interpreted with caution in terms of actual changes in sex-role behavior among older persons, it was striking that the old man and old women were consistently seen as

Figure 7.4
TAT picture designed for the Kansas City Study of Adult Life. (Source. Neugarten and Gutmann, 1958, Figure 1. Copyright by the Committee on Human Development, University of Chicago. Reprinted with permission.)

playing reversed roles in regard to authority in the family by the older respondents as compared with younger respondents; the old woman was seen as dominant and the old man was seen as submissive, regardless of other qualities attributed to them. In addition to this role shift, these data also imply personality changes.

For example, women, as they age, seem to become more tolerant of their own aggressive, egocentric impulses; while men, as they age, [seem to become more tolerant] of their own nurturant and affiliative impulses. To take another example, with increasing age in both men and women, ego qualities in the personality seem to become more constricted—more detached from the mastery of affairs and less in control of impulse life (Neugarten and Gutmann, 1958, p. 89).

This empirical finding is especially striking because it substantiates Jung's clinical observations three decades earlier:

Man's values, and even his body, do tend to change into their opposites.

We might compare masculinity and feminity and their psychic components to a definite store of substances of which, in the first half of life, unequal use is made. A man consumes his large supply of masculine substance and has left over only the smaller amount of feminine substance, which must now be put to use. Conversely, the woman allows her hitherto unused supply of masculinity to become active.

This change is even more noticeable in the psychic realm than in the physical. . . . Very often these changes are accompanied by all sorts of catastrophes in marriage, for it is not hard to imagine what will happen when the husband discovers his tender feelings and the wife her sharpness of mind (Jung, 1933, p. 16).

It might also be noted that their finding of increased interiority of the personality with age also substantiates Jung's observations on the contraction of life noted above.

Conclusions. Although the shift in sex-role perceptions may be partly a reflection of the decreased authority of men in the home after retirement, or (alternatively) may reflect physiological changes in hormone levels (decreased levels of sex hormones in both men and women at that age), these three studies seem to have a common theme of *increased interiority*. That is, in terms of personality *processes*, there seems to be a shift with advancing age toward a decreased concern with external social and environmental constraints toward an increased focus upon internal interests and inner dynamics. Neugarten summarizes these findings in the following words:

To recapitulate some of these findings, forty-year-olds seem to see the environment as one that rewards boldness and risk-taking and to see themselves possessing energy congruent with the opportunities presented in the outer world. Sixty-year-olds seem to see the environment as complex and dangerous, no longer to be reformed in line with one's own wishes, and to see the self as conforming and accommodating to outer-world demands. This change has been described by one of the present investigators as a movement from active to passive mastery. . . .

Different modes of dealing with impulse life seem to become salient with increasing age. Preoccupation with the inner life becomes greater; emotional cathexes toward persons and objects in the outer world seem to decrease; the readiness to attribute activity and affect to persons in the environment is reduced; there is a movement away from outer-world to inner-world orientations. . . .

There is a constriction in the ability to integrate wide ranges of stimuli and in the willingness to deal with complicated and challenging situations. . . .

. . . Older men and women, in verbalizing their opinions in more dogmatic terms than younger persons, in failing to clarify past-present or cause-effect relationships, in using idiosyncratic and eccentric methods of communication, gave evidence of lessened sensitivity to the reactions of others and a lessened sense of relatedness to others. . . .

. . . Older people seem to move toward more eccentric, self-preoccupied positions and to attend increasingly to the control and the satisfaction of personal needs (Neugarten, 1964, pp. 189-190).

Such shifts in personality processes suggest a lessening concern with some kinds of external involvements, perhaps as a result of physiological changes (such as decreased vision, hearing, and a general slowing down —to be discussed in Chapter 8), perhaps as a result of physical illness and impaired ability to interact with a complex environment, and perhaps because of decreased participation in a wide range of social roles. This interiority may also reflect developmental processes. That is, as we suggested earlier, the development of the personality system may progress from a period of maximal expansion (learning new roles, developing new *mes*, and attending to feedback from others about the "rules of the game") in young adulthood through a period of relative balance between internal processes and external demands in middle age to an increasing focus on internal processes in old age. This view, relating these data to our model of personality, is also consistent with the basic concepts of *disengagement theory* that we now discuss.

Disengagement and Successful Aging

Cumming and Henry (1961) proposed the theory of disengagement on the basis of initial cross-sectional data from the Kansas City studies. In those data it was clear that there was a marked decline in the amount of social interaction, present role activity, ego investment in present roles, and changes in role activity with age (Table 7.2). On that basis it was hypothesized that the decrease in role activity and decrease in ego energy (described above) were interrelated in such a manner that they represented a process of normal and successful aging called *disengagement*. Specifically, it was hypothesized that as individuals age they simultaneously are released from social roles and withdraw psychological energy from social ties. Events such as widowhood and retirement are seen as society's "permission to disengage," which leads to a reduction in the number and variety. of social roles and to more freedom from social norms. Ideal aging, in this view, results from the *mutual* disengagement of the individual and society at the same time; if the person disengages too early, or if society disengages him before he is also prepared to decrease his psychic investment in social interaction, the disengagement process will be dysfunctional and the individual's morale will suffer.

Although these predictions seem plausible, the theory prompted a great deal of debate (which lasted nearly a decade; e.g., Maddox, 1963, 1966, 1970) partly because it contradicted a more "common-sense" view of successful aging that has been called "activity theory." The activity view predicts that an aging person's morale will be high as long as he is able to keep active (that is, as long as he does *not* disengage), despite the various role reductions he may experience. Thus, in order to retain a high degree of satisfaction, the successfully aging person, in this view, needs to replace lost roles and activities with new ones (such as hobbies).

Table 7.2   Age Differences in Social Participation by Sex

	MEN		WOMEN	
	54–69 (N = 41)	70–94 (N = 31)	54–69 (N = 36)	70–94 (N = 51)
Social interaction	2.6	2.2	2.8	2.4*
Amount of present role activity	44.6	38.9*	46.5	36.1**
Investment in present roles	34.2	26.5**	37.9	28.4**
Change in role activity since age 60 (or in last 10 years)	−1.8	−6.6**	−2.2	−7.7**

* p.<.05
** p. <.01

Source. Adapted from Havighurst et al. (1963), Table 2. Reprinted with permission from *Middle Age and Aging*, Bernice L. Neugarten (Ed.), copyright © 1968 by the University of Chicago.

Clearly, there is a contradiction between these two views; and fortunately, both views are stated in ways that allow for empirical studies to determine which one is more accurate.

Havighurst et al. (1963) and Neugarten, Havighurst, and Tobin (1965) explored these theories with later longitudinal data from the Kansas City studies and concluded that the disengagement theory was deficient in two major respects. First, while the longitudinal data indicated that the *process of disengagement* does occur—there was a drop (between 1957 and 1962) in ego energy for each age group as noted above, and a consistent decline in three measures of role activity for all age groups during the same period—they concluded that *psychological disengagement* preceded the decrease in social role activity by about 10 years; that is, psychological disengagement was high for respondents in their fifties and social disengagement was high in the sixties and seventies. Thus, while disengagement does occur, psychological and social disengagement do not seem to be mutual processes. Second, they found that a measure of life satisfaction (LSR) not only did not decrease with age (as some might expect) but was generally higher for respondents who had greater amounts of activity. Hence, respondents over 70 who seemed to be aging most successfully (in terms of LSR) were those who were *not* disengaged. Only 7 out of 34 respondents with high LSR had a low degree of role activity (Table 7.3). However, personality characteristics were found

Table 7.3　Personality Type in Relation to Activity and Life Satisfaction (N = 59)

Personality Type	Role Activity	Life Statisfaction		
		High	Medium	Low
Integrated	High	9	2	
	Medium	5		
	Low	3		
Armored-defended	High	5		
	Medium	6	1	
	Low	2	1	1
Passive-dependent	High		1	
	Medium	1	4	
	Low	2	3	2
Unintegrated	High		2	1
	Medium	1		
	Low		2	5
	Total	34	16	9

Source. Neugarten et al. (1965), Table 1. Reprinted with permission.

to be involved also. That is, respondents who were high on the "integrated" type of personality had high LSR whether they were active *or* disengaged; respondents who were seen as "unintegrated" were medium or low on LSR whether active or disengaged. "Armored-defended" types who were high or medium in activity were high on LSR; those low on activity were medium on LSR. "Passive-dependent" types tended to be medium on LSR regardless of their degree of activity. Thus, personality characteristics seem to be pivotal dimensions for whether successful aging is one of maintained activity or gradual disengagement from activity and social involvement.

People, as they grow old, seem to be neither at the mercy of the social environment nor at the mercy of some set of intrinsic processes—in either instance, inexorable changes that they cannot influence. On the contrary, the individual seems to continue to make his own "impress" upon the wide range of social and biological changes. He continues to exercise choice and to select from the environment in accordance with his own long-established needs. He ages according to a pattern that has a long history and that maintains itself, with adaptation, to the end of life (Neugarten et al., 1965).

Thus, it seems that while general developmental changes such as the increased interiority of the personality (psychological "disengagement") and social disengagement may be typical for older individuals, their personality and their active *I* continues to reveal individuality and to influence their own interaction with the physical and social environment. That is, old persons, while they may show some similar developmental changes, remain (and perhaps become even more) like themselves and thus are no more like "older people" than a young person is like other members of his cohort. However, there may also be losses of significant persons who have supported an important aspect of the individual's self-esteem and personality organization with age. One of the most important of these losses (and one of the most important resources) for the aged is a close and trusted friend.

Importance of a "Confidant"

Lowenthal and Haven (1968) found that the presence of an intimate relationship—being able to confide in someone or talk to them about yourself or about your problems—is highly important for older people (as it probably is for all of us). They found, in a study of 280 persons aged 60 and older who were living in the community, that the presence of such a *confidant* serves as a "buffer" against losses such as loss of role or a decline in social interaction. That is, those respondents who had a stable intimate relationship were less likely to be depressed (and more

likely to be satisfied) than respondents without a confidant, even if their
level of social interaction or their level of role status had decreased. This
intimate relationship even seemed able to buffer these respondents
against such significant losses as retirement and widowhood (Table 7.4).
In fact, a slightly higher percentage of respondents were "satisfied" even
though widowed if they had a confidant than if they were married but
had no confidant. Similarly, a retired respondent with a confidant was as
likely to be satisfied as a respondent who was still working but had no
confidant. In addition, psychiatrists' ratings (for a subsample of 112)
of the mental health of the respondents also showed the importance of a
stable intimate relationship; that is, while the presence of a confidant
was only slightly related to psychiatric status, 80 percent of the respond-

Table 7.4 Effect of Widowhood, Retirement, and Physical Illness on
Morale in the Presence and Absence of a Confidant (Age
60+)

	Morale	
	Satisfied	Depressed
	Percent	Percent
Widowed within 7 years:		
Has confidant	55	45
No confidant	(27)[a]	(73)
Married:		
Has confidant	65	35
No confidant	(47)	(53)
Retired within 7 years:		
Has confidant	50	50
No confidant	(36)	(64)
Not retired:		
Has confidant	70	30
No confidant	50	50
Serious physical illness within 2 years:		
Has confidant	(16)	(84)
No confidant	(13)	(87)
No serious illness:		
Has confidant	64	36
No confidant	42	58

[a] Percentages are placed in parentheses when the numbers on which they are based are
under 20 ($N=14$–19).
Source. Lowenthal and Haven (1968), Table 5. Reprinted with permission.

ents who maintained the *same* confidant during the past year were rated "unimpaired" (compared with 20 percent rated "impaired"). Thus, the maintenance of a stable intimate relationship seems to serve an important function in protecting the individual's morale and mental stability against the various social losses that are associated with aging and with social disengagement.

However, as shown in Table 7.4, a confidant does not seem to buffer the individual against the psychological effects of physical illness. It appears that physiological decline, and particularly the onset of disease, is a process of such significance to the total organism that even the apparently powerful buffer provided by a confidant is unable to prevent the loss of morale. The overpowering impact of disease will be a central theme in Chapter 8 because more than any of the social and psychological changes which are associated with aging, *disease* seems to be the most important factor in a wide range of social and psychological changes. However, in the absence of disease (and of course, even with illness a confidant would be important for the individual), a stable intimate relationship seems to be a profound asset for the aging person. Women are somewhat more likely to have such a confidant than men (69 percent and 57 percent, respectively); married persons are more likely to have one than widows, who are more likely to have a confidant than single persons; and the confidant is about equally likely to be a spouse, a child, or a friend. They suggest that this sex difference may be related to the greater longevity of women, the lower rate of suicide (which increases rapidly with age for white men), and the lower rate of mental illness following widowhood among women as compared with men.

Although the practical implications of these findings are apparent—that aged persons who have intimate relationships benefit from maintaining close ties and the loss of a confidant has a more negative effect on morale than any other social losses—there are three important related points. First, some persons have maintained adequate levels of functioning with relative isolation over a long period of time; they seem no more prone to mental illness than nonisolates (Lowenthal, 1964). These isolates may also have high morale, but the majority of those who had and lost a confidant are depressed. Second, loss of a confidant may result from a general dislocation (such as moving into a smaller home or into a nursing home) that represents a double loss—a loss of social interactions and roles as well as loss of the confidant. Several studies have found an increased rate of death following major relocation, particularly among institutionalized aged (e.g., Aldrich and Mendkoff, 1963); thus, when a confidant is needed most, he may be unavailable. Third, gaining a confidant may help some, but the importance of a stable relationship seems most significant. These are important practical points we will recall in Chapter 10 where we will discuss the "no deposit, no return" treatment of the aged.

Conclusion

Taken together, these data on personality changes, successful aging, and the importance of a confidant indicate that there is an important shift in the interaction of the personality and the social world as one moves from middle to old age. Neugarten (1964) has described this change as a "centripetal" movement, with an increasing focus on inner processes that begins in the middle years of life. Later, as social roles and social interaction begin to decrease, the personality structure comes to be laid bare, as it were, and the individual comes to rely more heavily on the supports he has built up for himself. For some, an important support seems to be a confidant. In general, however, life satisfaction does not decline markedly with age and ability to function or general adaptation does not seem to be related to age. Disease, important social losses (such as a confidant), and long-standing personality characteristics seem to be more important than age per se in causing depression or, for some, mental illness. In the final section of this chapter we will discuss mental illness, especially in terms of the later years of adulthood.

PSYCHOPATHOLOGY IN ADULTHOOD

It becomes immediately apparent in discussing psychopathology in the context of adult development that we have suddenly entered an entire field of psychology—the field of psychopathology. Although that field is sometimes divided into "child," "adult," and perhaps "geriatric" psychopathology, most of the content of an introductory course in the area concerns adulthood. For obvious reasons, we cannot survey that entire area; however, we can suggest that our interdisciplinary and developmental framework seems to pull together a number of such areas (including "personality," "social psychology," and "social deviance") in a somewhat new way. For example, we tend to be more interested in age differences in the incidence of mental illness and in the specific factors that link psychological dysfunction with developmental changes (such as identity issues, occupational reevaluation, or depression following retirement or widowhood) rather than with the general causes of schizophrenia, depression, or suicide (and so on). In addition, this discussion will be relatively brief since we cannot review all the work that has been done in this large and complex area. Instead, we will present a framework for viewing psychological dysfunction (a term we prefer to mental illness) that hopefully will be useful in sensitizing us to the complex interactional nature of dysfunction and will suggest some ways of helping those who cannot quite seem to "get their heads together" but maybe have something to teach us.

An important and obvious first point is that the "mentally ill" are people rather similar to the rest of us but who are different in some ways, too. However, the point is that in interacting, helping, or relating to someone who seems "peculiar" or "crazy" they are, above all, human, social persons, and individuals who need to be understood and interacted with just as we all do. Put another way, our model of personality should be as applicable to persons who are up against something they cannot handle as it is for others who function fairly smoothly; the "mentally ill" are *not* possessed by demons (although that view may be useful in some sense, just as saying they are "sick" may be useful in some sense), nor are they deposited here from Mars. Instead, they have a self with an *I* and a set of *me*s; they have memories, internal experiences, and physiological responses; they have personality characteristics, expectations about future consequences, and motivations for competence and for self-actualization; and they exist in social situations—at least in our view. The difficulty seems to be best expressed by the phrase "dysfunction"—that is, all of these interrelated factors that all of us have, we argue, do not seem to process and interact functionally.

For some (who may be somewhat like typical "neurotics"), their *me*s or inner experiences are not acceptable to the *I*; that is, their self-concept is highly divergent from their ideal self-concept and their inner experiencing is often characterized by a kind of dis-ease or anxiety. It may be that a part of the self (a *me* or a group of feelings) was not accepted by a significant other at some time or the *I* could not integrate everything together so something important was left out. It may be that some feelings were too threatening to really experience, so the processing was stopped and the interacting *I-me* system became hung up at that point. There are many views regarding the cause of the dysfunction—it might be an attempt to cope with a larger social dysfunction such as a family dysfunction—but the general sense we are suggesting is one of a "stopped process" (Gendlin, 1964).

For other individuals (who resemble classical "psychotics"), the dysfunction may be characterized as a near-total breakdown of the *I-me* interaction. That is, the *I* may experience something that is poles apart from the message given off by the *me*—as in a classic catatonic schizophrenic who stands motionless for hours while internally being very aware of everything that is going on around him. Or the *me* may be seen by others in one way, but not seen the same way by the *I*—the extreme case of a psychotic delusion such as "Napoleon" will serve here. And the *me* may be so totally unacceptable that part of it is severed off from the rest as a "not me" (Sullivan, 1953)—such as the schizophrenic who hears voices. Sometimes there is an extreme variation in inner experience from deep depression to hyperexcitement that gets translated almost directly into *me*s with the *I* playing almost no role in synthesizing and integrating these experiences and with little "reflexive role taking" (taking the attitude of others toward oneself).

While this brief description can hardly be an adequate view of the phenomenon of psychological dysfunction, we expect that it will serve as a framework for making the jump from "normal" personality to psychopathology. For example, most of us probably experience such phenomena as we noted above—such as rejecting a *me* as not acceptable, or experiencing something with the *I* that is not expressed as a *me*. Yet we are usually able to continue processing our inner and outer experiencing as individuals whose *I-me* interaction seems highly dysfunctional are unable to do. For them, the process seems to be stopped in some sense. Perhaps it is stopped for a very good reason (it usually is, once one begins to see the world through their eyes)—such as they are "up against" something that is really a block. Frequently we identify the problem as the block—and sometimes it is (like a family mess, a rat-infested apartment, or a lousy job), but often it is not. Often the "problem" is the stopped process and that is why "giving advice" is usually not very helpful—after all, if they could not solve the problem after all the thought they have given to it, how could someone who just learned of the problem solve it? Instead, a helpful approach would be to help the *I-me* processing get moving again. One way of doing this (in a client-centered therapy approach) is to listen, try to understand, and feed back the understanding (that is, present their *me* back to them so that their *I* may react to it) while valuing the person who may be giving off rather confusing and upsetting *me*s. In short, listening and understanding and accepting the person would seem to be particularly helpful for increasing the *I-me* functioning. This would be the role played by an ideal confidant, in our view.

Another approach suggested by the symbolic interaction approach would be viewing the "problem" as a larger dysfunction than just a dysfunction in the *I-me* interaction. For example, the dysfunction may be in the complex *I-me-me-I* kinds of interactions among persons in groups such as families. As we suggested in Chapter 5, family functioning may be dysfunctional to the point where one member adopts a *me* at his own expense in order to salvage the functioning of the family unit. Thus, it is often useful to gather the entire functioning unit together to explore and facilitate *I-me* interaction within each member within the group. In this view, "pathology" is seen as an interpersonal phenomenon and the implication for helping is to involve the significant others in the therapy.

In general, then, facilitation of *I-me* functioning, interpersonal *I-me* interaction with significant others, and carefully understanding what the person is "up against" are useful steps. Often, a particularly helpful technique is simply listening, understanding, and checking out the understanding with the person in a context in which the person is accepted.

Finally, physiological factors—and particularly chronic disease—play an important part in mental illness, especially among the aged. A number of factors are involved. Decreasing hearing, sight, or physical mobility affect the kind of interactions one can have with others and also affect the inner experience of sensory stimulation. In addition a general "slowing down" of reaction time (which, as we will discuss in Chapter 8, seems to be associated with *aging* itself rather than disease) makes it difficult to think and respond quite as fast as younger people. Sometimes these physiological changes make one less sure of oneself, more isolated from stimulation, and more likely to be confused and slow at daily cognitive tasks (such as counting out the change for purchases in a fast-moving supermarket). Taken together, and combined with feelings of decreased status, such changes can lead to some feelings of "persecution" that, in extreme form, could resemble psychopathology. One example of this perhaps common experience in old age is from a fictional story:

> ...They were all squabbles of one kind or another. The milkman had begun counting out the wrong change for me. The postman had held back my mail. The paper boy had delivered my newspaper or not, as the inclination struck him. And the clerks at the grocery store had amused themselves by playing petty tricks on me, breaking a few of my eggs as they packed the carton in a bag, or speaking so softly I could not hear them. The milkman wanted money, the postman and the newspaper boy convenience, the clerks amusement. To keep me from insisting on justice and courtesy, they relied on the precariousness of an old person's reputation, on the skepticism with which the word of the old is regarded, on my fear and feebleness. But I caught each of them up, and I did insist (Webber, 1963).

It is, of course, impossible to determine how much of these "persecutions" were actual (and related to the negative status of the aged) or were exaggerated because of some hearing loss, social isolation, and slower cognitive processes. However, more marked physical impairment can lead to a high degree of social isolation and also to mental illness. Lowenthal (1964) reported that a sample of aged respondents in a mental hospital were "considerably sicker physically" than a community sample of respondents of the same age (three-fourths reported "physical illness" as a major life-change since age 50). She also found that although life-long extreme isolation did not seem to be conducive to mental illness in old age, late-developing isolation and physical illness seemed to be related to mental illness, which suggests that physical illness may precede and cause both relative isolation and mental illness in old age. Butler (1963a)

reported a relationship between "contemporaneous environmental deficits" (largely losses of significant persons), response time to psychomotor tasks, and "depression" rated by psychiatrists. It seems that there
is an important interaction between physiological, psychological, and
social variables—even in the absence of such extreme cerebral diseases
as senility and cerebral arteriosclerosis (hardening of the arteries resulting in decreased oxygen flow to the brain)—in the development of
mental illness in the aged.

In the remainder of this chapter we will discuss some of the more
common manifestations of psychological dysfunction in the aged, emphasizing particularly the higher rate of suicide and depression and the
chronic organic disorders (senility and cerebral arteriosclerosis).

Psychological Dysfunctions and Age

First impressions of mental hospital wards and their outpatient services
suggest that the aged comprise a relatively large number of mental
patients. There are two factors involved: (1) some patients are hospitalized for a period of years and literally grow old in the hospital or are
maintained in the community through outpatient medication and therapy; and (2) a large percentage of first admissions to mental hospitals
are aged 60 or over, largely because of cerebral arteriosclerosis or senility—Busse (1959) reports that 27 percent of new admissions are for
cerebral or senile diseases and 38 percent of new admissions are 60 or
older. Nonetheless, only a tiny fraction (1 or 2 percent) of the population is ever hospitalized for mental disorders, and many hospitals are
currently attempting to maintain and treat potential patients in the
community and to decrease the length of hospitalization through such
community facilities as "halfway houses." Also, with the federal support
provided by Medicare, many aged hospital patients have been placed in
private facilities when physical care was the primary reason for hospitalization. Such changes have both positive and negative aspects for individual patients. In general, reducing the length of hospitalization seems
useful in preventing "institutionalization" of the patient (so that he is
never able to function outside the hospital); and it allows the continuing interaction of the person and his community. However, in practice,
community maintenance (as well as hospital life) is too often just maintenance, dependency on medications, and subsistence; yet it at least
offers the possibility of involvement in the community.

In general, aged persons seem to be subject to the same range of
psychopathology as young and middle-aged adults, and there does not
seem to be much difference in the incidence of neuroses and psychoses
with age. Although it is a bit difficult to conceive of childhood factors
leading to a psychotic episode or the onset of major neuroses in old age.

certainly physical illness and social trauma in the adult years would be relevant precipitating events for pathology in late life. Also, marital difficulties or identity problems can be important issues for young, middle-aged, and old adults. It is important, we feel, not only to try to understand what the person is "up against" regardless of his age but also to be sensitized to particular crisis points from a developmental perspective as well. It may be true that different forms of therapy are useful for different types of issues and at different ages, but the general forms of psychopathology seem to be generally unrelated to age. However, there are three exceptions: cerebral disease, depression, and suicide.

Cerebral Disease

Arteriosclerosis is currently thought to be related to the amount of cholesterol that accumulates in arteries, particularly in middle age when a certain type of fat (saturated—that typically solidifies at room temperature) is eaten in large quantities but is not burned off in exercise (eggs, whole milk, and cheese also contains cholesterol). This accumlation of cholesterol leads to "hardening of the arteries" that not only decreases blood circulation but also increases blood pressure. Heart attacks and strokes, common causes of death, may result. When the blood flow to the brain is affected, less oxygen is carried to the brain tissues. If the oxygen supply is disrupted in part of the brain, there is an abrupt onset of the symptoms of cerebral arteriosclerosis, which is commonly called a "stroke." A stroke is characterized by a sudden loss of movement and sensation caused by a brain hemorrhage or a blood clot in the brain that disrupts the blood (and oxygen) supply to a part of the brain. Typically it turns out that the stroke is only the latest symptom in the progressive development of cerebral arteriosclerosis. That is, the patient frequently has noted some loss of memory for some time; and he may have suffered headaches, blackouts, and palpitations of the heart before the onset of the stroke. Gradually the effects of the disease affect habitual behaviors, memory loss will become more marked, and he will become unable to grasp the meaning of social situations. The patient's range of interests narrows, and his emotional reactions are changed. In general, the disease destroys the "more complex and subtle features of the personality, though judgements based on experience, and the more salient personality traits, may remain relatively intact" (Bromley, 1966, p. 133).

The abrupt onset of marked symptoms disrupting the person's compensations for a gradual loss of memory and the fluctuating nature of the subseuent deterioration of memory are generally seen as indicators of cerebral arteriosclerosis. Busse (1959) reports that it is more common in men than in women, which suggests that female sex hormones may play somewhat of a preventative role. However, the best prevention is probably education about the causes of arteriosclerosis in general.

Senile Brain Syndrome, which Busse (1959) reports is more common in women, is characterized by a gradual decay of memory. The *Diagnostic and Statistical Manual of Mental Disorders* (American Psychiatric Association, 1952) defines these symptoms:

> These cases vary from mild organic brain syndrome with self-centering of interest, difficulty in assimilating new experiences, and "childish" emotionality, up to and including those so severely affected by senile brain disease as to require institutional care. Deterioration may be minimal or it may progress to a state of vegetative existence, with or without superimposed psychotic, neurotic, or behavioral reactions (p. 22).

Postmortem examinations of senile brains indicate atrophy, changes in the convolutions, thickening of the arteries, and a reduction in neurons. Those neurons remaining are discolored and shrunken (Bromley, 1966). Bromley suggests that genetic factors are probably involved, although we have little understanding of the causes of senility. Birren (1964) points out that senile and arteriosclerotic changes may occur separately or together, and that the type of brain deterioration is related to the kind of symptoms shown; however, the studies on healthy aged men (Butler, 1963a) clearly emphasize the distinction between aging and disease—that is, senility is a disease that may or may not occur with advancing age.

Depression and Suicide

Although depression and suicide are not necessarily related, many suicides in old age result from severe depression sometimes in association with other psychotic symptoms such as delusions. In some cases, suicide may be seen as a solution to an intolerable social situation or physical illness; that is, suicide may be attempted when the depression seems intolerable and there is no chance for improvement resulting from a decreased ability to function or compensate for the losses. Mild depression seems to be fairly common in old age; for example, Butler (1963a) reports that about one-fifth of his healthy aged respondents were rated "mild reactive depression" by psychiatrists, and this diagnosis was the largest single pathology. There are, of course, many physical and social losses that occur in old age, which may lead to some degree of depression. Retirement may lead to a transitory depression, but severe depressions usually result from multiple stresses; widowhood usually involves a period of depression also, and it seems to be more severe for men than women (at least in the Lowenthal, 1964 study). Busse (1959) suggests that depression in old age differs from young adult depression in that it results from a loss of self-esteem directly related to aging rather than from a turning inward of hostility.

Suicide death rates increase steadily with age for white males (Figure 7.5). Although there is a marked difference between the rates for men and women as well as between the rates for white and nonwhite persons, the reasons for the differences are not clear. Birren (1964) notes that older men frequently choose violent means of committing suicide, which leaves little doubt that the intent is death and is not a gesture calling attention to one's suffering. Bromley (1966) points out that suicide threats greatly outnumber, but also frequently precede actual suicide attempts, and that both suicide and mental illness are higher in lower socioeconomic classes and in areas that are rundown and disorganized (findings that were first

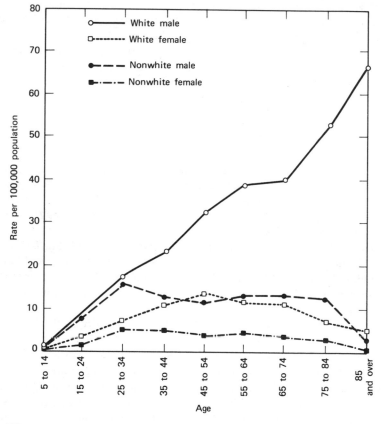

Figure 7.5
Suicide rates by age and color in the United States, 1964. (Source. Adapted from National Center for Health Statistics. Vital and Health Statistics, *Series 20, No. 5. Washington, D.C.: U.S. Government Printing Office, 1967, p. 5.)*

discovered by Durkheim). It seems that with regard to both suicide and psychological dysfunction in general, psychological factors (coping styles, personality integration, and past experiences), social factors (losses of roles, status, and significant others), and physical factors (illness, loss of hearing or sight, and loss of mobility) may combine and interact in differing ways for each individual case.

This overview of psychopathology in adulthood has been quite brief, but it points out the importance of considering the personality as an interacting system involving psychological, physiological, and social factors. With advancing age the environmental niche in which the individual lives typically changes; this brings a shift in the fit between the individual and his environment. At the same time, physiological changes typically occur that may place additional stress on the personality system as it seeks to maintain the fit with the environmental niche. Sometimes these internal and external stresses overwhelm the system, and a dysfunction occurs. In the next chapter we will discuss these physiological changes in detail. But first, we will pause for another interlude—a 67-year-old grandmother whose personality seems to be functioning very competently despite some disease and a reduction in some social roles.

References

*Aldrich, C. Knight, and Mendkoff, Ethel. 1963. Relocation of the Aged and Disabled: A Mortality Study. *Journal of the American Geriatrics Society, 11*(3), 401–408.

Allport, Gordon W. 1962. Psychological Models for Guidance. *Harvard Educational Review, 32*(4), 373–381.

American Psychiatric Association. 1952. *Diagnostic and Statistical Manual: Mental Disorders.* Washington, D.C.: American Psychiatric Association.

Bardwick, Judith M. 1971. *Psychology of Women.* New York: Harper & Row.

Birren, James E. 1964. *The Psychology of Aging.* Englewood Cliffs, N.J.: Prentice-Hall.

Broadhurst, P. L., and Eysenck, H. J. 1965. Emotionality in the Rat: A Problem of Response Specificity. In C. Banks and P. L. Broadhurst (Eds.), *Studies in Psychology.* Aylesbury, Bucks, England: Hazell, Watson and Viney, Ltd.

Bromley, D. B. 1966. *The Psychology of Human Ageing.* Baltimore: Penguin.

Busse, Ewald W. 1959. Psychopathology. In James E. Birren (Ed.), *Handbook of Aging and the Individual.* Chicago: University of Chicago Press.

*Butler, Robert N. 1963a. The Facade of Chronological Age: An Interpretive Summary. *American Journal of Psychiatry, 119*(8), 721–728.

*Butler, Robert N. 1963b. The Life Review: An Interpretation of Reminiscence in the Aged. *Psychiatry, 26*(1), 65–76.

Byrne, Donn. 1966. *An Introduction to Personality.* Englewood Cliffs, N.J.: Prentice-Hall.

Carson, Robert C. 1969. *Interaction Concepts of Personality.* Chicago: Aldine.

Cumming, Elaine, and Henry, William E. 1961. *Growing Old: The Process of Disengagement.* New York: Basic Books.

Ellefson, John O. 1968. Personality and the Biological Nature of Man. In Edward Norbeck, Douglass Price-Williams, and William M. McCord (Eds.), *The Study of Personality: An Interdisciplinary Appraisal.* New York: Holt, Rinehart and Winston.

Freedman, Daniel G. 1958. Constitutional and Environmental Interactions in Rearing Four Breeds of Dogs. *Science, 127*(3298), 585–586.

Gendlin, Eugene T. 1964. A Theory of Personality Change. In Philip Worchel and Donn Byrne (Eds.), *Personality Change.* New York: Wiley.

Gottschaldt, K. 1960. Das Problem der Phanogenetick der Personlichkeit. In P. Lersh and H. Thomas (Eds.), *Personlichkeits forschung und Personlichkeits theorie, Handbuch der Psychologie.* Vol. 4. Gottingen: Hofgrefie. Cited in Thompson (1968).

Gutmann, David L. 1964. An Exploration of Ego Configurations in Middle and Late Life. In Bernice L. Neugarten and Associates (Eds.), *Personality in Middle and Late Life.* New York: Atherton Press.

*Gutmann, David L. 1967. Aging Among the Highland Maya: A Comparative Study. *Journal of Personality and Social Psychology, 7*(1), 28–35.

*Havighurst, Robert J.; Neugarten, Bernice L.; and Tobin, Sheldon S. 1963. Disengagement and Patterns of Aging. Unpublished paper presented at the meeting of the International Association of Gerontology, Copenhagen, August, 1963.

Heine, Patricke Johns. 1971. *Personality in Social Theory.* Chicago: Aldine.

Jung, Carl G. 1933. The Stages of Life. (Translated by R. F. C. Hull.) In Joseph Campbell (Ed.), *The Portable Jung.* New York: Viking, 1971.

Kagan, Jerome, and Moss, Howard A. 1962. *Birth to Maturity: A Study in Psychological Development.* New York: Wiley.

Kelly, E. Lowell. 1955. Consistency of the Adult Personality. *American Psychologist, 10*(9), 659–681.

Kolodny, Robert C.; Masters, William H.; Hendryx, Julie; and Toro, Gelson. 1971. Plasma Testosterone and Semen Analysis in Male Homosexuals. *New England Journal of Medicine, 285,* 1170–1174.

Krohn, Alan, and Gutmann, David. 1971. Changes in Mastery Styles with Age: A Study of Navajo Dreams. *Psychiatry, 34*(3), 289–300.

Kroll, Arthur M.; Dinklage, Lillian N.; Lee, Jennifer; Morley, Eileen D.; and Wilson, Eugene H. 1970. *Career Development.* New York: Wiley.

*Kuhlen, Raymond G. 1964. Developmental Changes in Motivation During the Adult Years. In James E. Birren (Ed.), *Relations of Development and Aging.* Springfield, Ill.: Charles C Thomas.

Lewin, Kurt. 1935. *A Dynamic Theory of Personality.* New York: McGraw-Hill.

*Lowenthal, Marjorie Fiske. 1964.** Social Isolation and Mental Illness in Old Age. *American Sociological Review, 29*(1), 54–70.

*Lowenthal, Marjorie Fiske, and Haven, Clayton. 1968.** Interaction and Adaptation: Intimacy as a Critical Variable. *American Sociological Review, 33*(1), 20–30.

Lubin, Marc. 1964. Addendum to Chapter 4. In Bernice L. Neugarten and Associates (Eds.), *Personality in Middle and Late Life.* New York: Atherton Press.

Luce, Gay. 1971. *Body Time.* New York: Pantheon.

Maddox, George L. 1963. Activity and Morale: A Longitudinal Study of Selected Elderly Subjects. *Social Forces, 42*(2), 195–204.

*Maddox, George L. 1966.** Persistence of Life Style Among the Elderly: A Longitudinal Study of Patterns of Social Activity in Relation to Life Satisfaction. *Proceedings of the 7th International Congress of Gerontology,* Vienna, *6,* 309–311.

Maddox, George L. 1970. Themes and Issues in Sociological Theories of Human Aging. *Human Development, 13,* 17–27.

Maslow, Abraham H. 1950. Self-Actualizing People: A Study of Psychological Health. In W. Wolff (Ed.), *Personality Symposium.* No. 1. New York: Grune and Stratton.

Mischel, Walter. 1968. *Personality and Assessment.* New York: Wiley.

Mischel, Walter. 1969. Continuity and Change in Personality. *American Psychologist, 24*(11), 1012–1018.

Murphy, Gardner. 1968. Psychological Views of Personality and Contributions to its Study. In Edward Norbeck, Douglass Price-Williams, and William M. McCord (Eds.), *The Study of Personality: An Interdisciplinary Appraisal.* New York: Holt, Rinehart and Winston.

Neugarten, Bernice L. 1964. Summary and Implications. In Bernice L. Neugarten and Associates (Eds.), *Personality in Middle and Late Life.* New York: Atherton Press.

*Neugarten, Bernice L. 1968.** Adult Personality: Toward a Psychology of the Life Cycle. In Edgar Vinacke (Ed.), *Readings in General Psychology.* New York: American Book Co.

Neugarten, Bernice L., and Associates, 1964. *Personality in Middle and Late Life.* New York: Atherton Press.

Neugarten, Bernice L., and Gutmann, David L. 1958. Age-Sex Roles and Personality in Middle Age: A Thematic Apperception Study. *Psychological Monographs, 72*(17, Whole No. 470).

*Neugarten, Bernice L.; Havighurst, Robert J.; and Tobin, Sheldon S. 1965.** Personality and Patterns of Aging. *Gawein: Tijdschrift van de Psychologische Kring aan de Nijmessgse Universitiet,* Jrg. 13, Afl. (May, 1965), 249–256.

Reichard, Suzanne; Livson, Florine; and Peterson, Paul G. 1962. *Aging and Personality.* New York: Wiley.

Riley, Matilda White; Foner, Anne; and Associates. 1968. *Aging and Society.* Vol. 1. *An Inventory of Research Findings.* New York: Russell Sage Foundation.

Rogers, Carl R. 1959. A Theory of Therapy, Personality, and Interpersonal Relationships as Developed in the Client-Centered Framework. In S. Koch (Ed.), *Psychology: A Study of a Science.* Vol. 2. *Formulation of the Person and the Social Context.* New York: McGraw-Hill.

Rosen, Jacqueline L., and Neugarten, Bernice L. 1964. Ego Functions in the Middle and Late Years: A Thematic Apperception Study. In Bernice L. Neugarten and Associates (Eds.), *Personality in Middle and Late Life.* New York: Atherton Press.

Singer, Margaret T. 1963. Personality Measurements in the Aged. In James E. Birren, Robert N. Butler, Samuel W. Greenhouse, Louis Sokoloff, and Marian R. Yarrow (Eds.), *Human Aging: A Biological and Behavioral Study.* Publication No. (HSM) 71-9051. Washington, D.C.: U.S. Government Printing Office.

Skolnick, Arlene. 1966a. Motivational Imagery and Behavior Over 20 Years. *Journal of Consulting Psychology, 30*(6), 463–478.

Skolnick, Arlene. 1966b. Stability and Interrelations of Thematic Test Imagery Over 20 Years. *Child Development, 37*(2), 389–396.

Sullivan, Harry Stack. 1953. *The Interpersonal Theory of Psychiatry.* New York: W. W. Norton.

Thompson, William R. 1968. Genetics and Personality. In Edward Norbeck, Douglass Price-Williams, and William M. McCord (Eds.), *The Study of Personality: An Interdisciplinary Appraisal.* New York: Holt, Rinehart and Winston.

*Webber, Howard. 1963. Games. *The New Yorker,* March 30, 1963, 42–46.

White, Robert. 1959. Motivation Reconsidered: The Concept of Competence. *Psychological Review, 66,* 297–333.

Witkin, Herman A.; Goodenough, Donald R.; and Karp, Stephen A. 1967. Stability of Cognitive Style from Childhood to Young Adulthood. *Journal of Personality and Social Psychology, 7*(3), 291–300.

Woodruff, Diana S., and Birren, James E. 1972. Age Changes and Cohort Differences in Personality. *Developmental Psychology, 6*(2), 252–259.

* References marked with an asterisk appear in Bernice L. Neugarten (Ed.), *Middle Age and Aging.* Chicago: University of Chicago Press, 1968.

** References marked with a double asterisk have relevant selections in *Middle Age and Aging.*

Interlude
Joan, Age 67

Joan is a 67-year-old black grandmother who lives in Harlem in New York City. She is one of 16 children; her mother was born during slavery in Georgia; she eventually moved to New York and brought Joan to the city as a young girl. Both Joan and her mother worked as "domestics" for a single family for 37 years, and Joan still works for them one day a week. Her mother died nearly 20 years ago at the grand age of 93, and Joan has five grandchildren; the oldest are in high school. Her proudest moment was the graduation of her two children from high school. She has some health problems now but works one day a week at a local Senior Center helping prepare the luncheon that is served daily.

Why did the milestones that she chose to discuss stand out in her memory? Does she choose different milestones from those a man might choose? What are some of the "timing events" in her life? In what sense are they "timing events"? What effect has her health had on her? Is there a sense of "increased interiority" or "disengagement" in her life style? What are her feelings about death? How does living in Harlem affect her? In what ways has being black affected her developmental milestones and course of life? In what ways has poverty affected her? Are there any practical ways in which a Senior Center or the community might increase her opportunities for fulfillment? Do her many assets and strengths make her an atypical "senior citizen"?

As you look back over your life, what are some of the milestones that stand out? The education of my son and daughter; that's very hard if you're black. My son is 18 years in the Navy, and my daughter is 17 years with the telephone company, and I have five grandchildren. I'm 67 now. I was born January 1, 1906 in Georgia. I came to New York City as a young girl, attended school here, and then I started to work. And then I married and had my family. I never had any sickness until I reached my sixties. The doctor explained to me it comes with age—high blood pressure. He said high blood pressure gives me a blockage of the heart. When I feel so bad I go to the hospital and they give me treatments, you know; and he also discovered that I had sugar [diabetes] and I've been watching that. I have a diet that I don't really stick to, but I go in between—like if I eat bread one day, the next day I don't eat bread. He allows me three slices of bread a day, and no sodas, no beer, no alcoholic beverages, no jams and jellies. Plenty of fresh fruit and so far I think that I'm in pretty good health excepting the high blood pressure. *Does that hinder you getting around at all?* No indeed. I can get out every day. He told me to walk 20 blocks a day, but walk slow. Don't walk against the wind. Stay in the bed two hours in the mornin' and one hour in the afternoon when I find myself getting dizzy. But other than that I get up, walk around the house, and do the shopping. Don't climb no subway stairs, no kind of stairs. And he says if I want to catch a bus, if I miss that one, just wait; no hurrying at all and no emotional upsets. And I find out it really pays off. I do an awful lot of reading, so that way it quiets my nerves.

What were some of the big events in your life? Well, the marriage of my two children; that was a very big event. And I had my son come home from Vietnam. He was in Vietnam for two years and when he came back I was very happy. And...I don't know.... *You have one son?* Yeah, and one daughter. They were born in the same year. I had two kids in one year; my son was born January 21, 1937, my daughter was born December 8, 1937. I had quite a time convincing the insurance company that I had two babies in the one year. That was quite an event in my life. With my first child I was in the hospital 21 days because I was in my thirties when he was born. The doctor explained to me that my pelvis didn't expand like a younger girl. But my daughter came in the ambulance. On December the eighth I went to the hospital and they said they didn't have a bed, so they put me in the ambulance and were taking me to _____ hospital and before we got there she was born; and I was ready to come home. They made me stay 10 days, but I was ready to come home. I came home and went right back to work and never had a sick day until I got in my sixties, you know the blood pressure and overweight.

What kind of work did you do? Domestic work; I cooked. You see, my mother came up before and she was a cook and then when I came up to public school, on the weekends I would go out to Long Island and cook there and then when the family moved back to New York City I continued to cook for them. Now I go in one day a week. But I just do ironing, or maybe they ask me to prepare a roast, a leg of lamb, you know, make something like that and leave it for them, 'cause all their kids are married now and it's just the two of them. So I run the wash through the machine and press his shirts, make a leg of lamb or something like that. I go one day a week, every Thursday. *You've worked with this same family for...* Over 37 years. My mother was in their family; so I go now. Sometime when they have somethin' special on the weekend I go and help them serve or cook. But they stopped entertainin' now because food is goin' up so high. They said no more entertainin' now (laughs). So I just take it easy; and I go to the [Senior] Center and I cook Wednesdays and Fridays there [the Center serves lunch daily]. We finish about 2:00 or 2:30 and I come home, look at my stories [on TV], and that's it.

I don't go out at night no more, because ... well, you know the reason why that is. *Why don't you go out at night?* I'm afraid of being mugged; and don't have anyone to go out with me, so I stay home and do my entertainin' in the house; the neighbors come visit one another and that's it. We don't go out in the night, that's all. Because you can't get a cab half the time; and there's no shows that I would like to go to downtown and pay taxi fare all the way back here. So nighttime I'm in the house; definitely! There's no way I'm goin' out. Sometimes I have friends that have cars; they come and get me and they take me back. Then if I go to my daughter, I get a cab in front of my house, get out in front of her door, and then she and her friend bring me back. That's the way we have to travel—but never just to catch a bus or walk out at night. It took me a long time to get it through my head not to go out at night (she laughs). *Why is that; did something happen once?* Not only once. I've been very fortunate in that, you know. I went out one Saturday night and they told me to take a taxi home. So I stood on the corner and hollered "Taxi, taxi"; so I said I'll walk over to Eighth Avenue and get the bus. And I saw these two fellas and I got to the corner of Eighth Avenue and 23rd Street and one fellow asked me if I had a cigarette or somethin' and I said I don't smoke and he grabbed me and said, "Yes, you do," but when he went to grab at me I screamed and there's a hotel right across the street. There was a lady looking out the window and she started to scream; so when they turned around to see where the noise was comin' from—there's a restaurant right down there—and I ran into that. So I asked the cashier would he come out so I could get a cab. So he got a cab and I came home and that was all right. Then, another time, I was comin' home and got off the Eighth Avenue bus and a fellow ran up to me; I had a pocketbook. I don't know why I pulled back 'cause there was nothin' in it at all. My keys was in my coat pocket and I just had tissues and a compact and comb—stuff like that. So, when he grabbed at the pocketbook, I hauled off and hit at him. He was so young! It was unbelievable to think that a young kid like that could do somethin' like that. So when I saw him I said this is nothin' but a little kid. He was pullin' and I gave him a shove and he fell backwards. Naturally, I ran, screaming as usual, you know. Well, he didn't follow me; and I got to the corner; a couple of people was on the corner and they were laughin'. They said, "I don't think he'll snatch a pocketbook any more" (she laughs). I looked back and he was still layin' down. Another time too; so my daughter said, "That's it!" That's why I tell you I don't go out at night no more. You don't push your luck too far. That's why I said when you're comin', push my buzzer; if I didn't know you was comin' I wouldn't answer that buzzer.

Oh, then in 1960—that's another happy event—I was picked as a delegate to go to San Francisco, California with my Eastern Star. So, my son and daughter tricked me into taking a flight; instead of taking an ordinary flight, I took a jet. I was in San Francisco before my daughter could get from Kennedy Airport to the Bronx. *Sounds like a big trip.* A wonderful trip! Six weeks. I was a delegate. From San Francisco we went to Tijuana. You see, we flew there, but I wouldn't get back on, so they made arrangements to come back through the country, which was beautiful. Anywhere I go now, I travel on a Greyhound bus; no plane. I haven't had a trip since 1960, besides ordinary ones to [New] Jersey and Atlantic City, like that.

Were there any other big moments in your life? The biggest one was when my son came home from Vietnam. When he was 17 years old he enlisted in the Marines; he was in high school and decided he wanted to be a pilot; when he graduated in June, he changed over to the Navy and when he was 18 years old he was in Capetown, Africa. Really, he had never been away from home and he wasn't 18 years old then when he was sent overseas. Then I started readin' about Formosa, those different little straits and islands.... So then I didn't hear from him in a long time and a letter came. He had came down with pneumonia; but he got well and everything and he went right back. He came home after a year. "I'm goin' back overseas," he said; he loved it. Well, he came back the third time and he got married. Then he was stationed in Rhode Island and New Jersey and his first kid was born in Rhode Island; his second kid was born in Florida; the third kid was born in California. From then on he left from San Diego for Vietnam. After he came back from Vietnam—he served two years—he was up for promotion; so now he has his office here in New York City. So it worked out beautifully.

How does it feel to become a grandmother? Well, it's a thrill! The first grandchild, I'm tellin' you. My birthday is January the first and he was born on December the thirty-first. So I had this big party to serve, and I said my daughter was goin' to the hospital, and I said if everything is all right then I'll serve the party. So I had her under the doctor's care and he said she will definitely deliver the latter part of December. She started her pains the thirtieth of December and I rushed her to the hospital, so the next morning at 3:28, she delivered. And they called me from the hospital. I was a nervous mother, believe it or not. I called the people who wanted me and said, "Go ahead, have the party; I'm a grandmother now." Oh, that was a happy evenin'. That was a happy time. Yessiree, that was a happy evenin'.

She was married one week, my son was married the next week. My first grandchild was born in December; my second grandchild was born that March. They married together, they started havin' their families together, so I started becomin' a grandmother in December and then in March. I went up to visit my daughter-in-law with my second grandchild; the third one was born in Florida and I went down there; and I said, "Look, the next grandchild you have, I'm not comin' out." *Why was it such a special event?* That was a very happy occasion. I thank God I had lived to be a grandmother and to see my kids married, grown, and have their own family. And believe me, you will never have a lonely moment. Never, I could never tell anyone I'm lonely, because they're here with their records and their rock 'n' roll, they keep me up to date on everything and I do an awful lot of readin' myself, you know. And then with their homework, believe it or not, I'm being reeducated. Because when I was goin' to school, we didn't have the things that they have. And now, I'm really reeducatin' myself on their homework, you know, which is very good. It keeps me very young and very happy, I can truthfully say [two of her grandchildren live with her during the week so they can live closer to their high school].

How old were you when you came from Georgia? I was in my teens when I came. World War I ended in November, 1918 and I came here the very next year in September, 1919. And then I went to public school and after that I went to high school for two years, but I didn't graduate. I had to work with my mother, 'cause times was very hard then. Then I was supposed to go to school at night, and I went for a while, but it was gettin' me, you know, so my mother said, "No, I won't punish you like this." So we had to go to work to help support the family.

This is why I say a happy event is when my son graduated from high school and when my daughter graduated from high school; and then my son went to college on Uncle Sam [G. I. benefits]. My daughter went to _____ College, which I helped her pay for that. So, the education of my two kids is a really happy event in my life, 'cause that's what counts today, education. The work that I had to do, they don't have to do. Oh yes, that was a very happy event. He graduated one year and she graduated the next year. I don't know about other people, but that's a very happy thing; and they done it in three years.

What about some of the sadder points; have there been any crisis points in your life? The crisis points, well, when my mother had a stroke. She was in her nineties when she died. I had brought her to live with me then. She had her own apartment, but by workin' all day it was too hard for me to go to her apartment, cook, wash and iron, clean up and ask the neighbor to look in on her, 'cause she didn't want to go in the hospital. So I brought her here to live with me, and she had her first stroke here. She was ninety in January, and in October she had her first stroke. Naturally, I had an ambulance come and take her to the hospital, and the doctor said that she was not able to be by herself any more, and I put her in a nursing home. She was out there, and she was able to get around a bit, not too much, in a wheel chair, and they worked on her. She was a wonderful musician; and she was born in slavery time too. So she was able to play for the Christmas carols and entertainment. The third year, she was 93, and in September she had her third stroke. It was on a Tuesday at 1:30 and on Wednesday at 2:30 she passed. That was sad because being close to your parents, you know, and my father went away when I was quite young. So, she was a mother and father to us.

And then I had a brother, who was in the service also; he was in Italy with World War II; and he had a murmur of the heart, and he came back and his hair had turned snow white. He always said, "I guess it was those bullets that frightened me." He had had pneumonia twice, and while he was up my mother passed, and he came down with lobar pneumonia the third time, and he went in the hospital on a Friday, and he passed the next Wednesday. It was so quick, you know, it was a shock to us, 'cause we thought he'd pull through that, but he didn't. So that was another sad time. So now it's only three girls left.

My mother had 16 children. *Sixteen children!* But see, my mother was born in slavery. She was married when she was 13, she said; you see, my grandmother was a "house slave," and my mother married what you called a "yard slave." You see, they had different kinds of slaves then. And she married at the age of 13; she had 14 children by him. After he died my grandmother brought her and some of her kids—'cause some of them had died when they were quite young—to _____ Georgia. And she met my father, and she had two kids by my father, which is me and my brother. She raised us, and my sisters got married; one went to Chicago; one came to Baltimore; and then my mother used to go back and forth to Florida to work, go to Virginia to work. You know, she was a cook, so she worked seasonal, you know. So she finally decided she'd get us out of the South. *You went with her when she went to these different places?* No, you see, my older sister was takin' care of us. We had to go to school; and then somethin' happened—we had a lynchin' down there; it was frightening with the Klan and all. So my mother got me up here, then the next year she got my brother up here. Then my sisters got married and my brother got married up here. We had plots here in the cemetery and she said, "When I pass don't ever bring me back there; we got plots up here and bury me up here." So she never went back. But I went back. My brother wouldn't go back, but I went back (laughs), I certainly did. Yeah, my mother was 93 when she passed; and she had all her facilities 'til she was 90. She used to forget, but you know she never used a walkin' cane. *How old were you when she passed?* Oh, let's see now. She's been dead now about 19 years.

You said you did get back to Georgia once? Yeah, I went back in 1949 but I didn't know it. I wanted my kids to see my home and their father's home, so I carried them to Savannah and I went to_____, Georgia, but I didn't know my home. It was changed around. But my son, when we got on the buses, it said, "White to the front and Colored to the rear." My son was takin' a picture so he could bring it back to show and he said, "Momma, I'll never come back here any more" (she laughs). So I said, "Well Johnny honey, things will change in years to come." We went into a souvenir store 'cause I wanted to get some cards to send home. The girl refused to wait on me, a little white girl, you know. I went over to the manager and I said, "Mister, I would like to get some souvenir cards to send back to New York and the young lady won't give them to me." He goes over to her and says, "Look, if you don't want to work, you can go to the office and get your pay. This lady wants to buy some cards and you refused to wait on her." So the man waited on us.

Is your husband still alive? Yes. We separated over 20 years ago. *Twenty years ago?* When people try to stay together in New York, you know, I was considered to be very old-fashioned, bein' from the South. So we agreed to disagree. That's why I say when my son and daughter came out of high school I was very happy 'cause I worked very hard. I worked night and day; I used to cater parties at night and cook in the day. So when I saw them come up that aisle and get their diploma, believe me, my chest was out this big.

This question of welfare was....I didn't go for that at all. *You didn't want any welfare?* No, no. Nobody in my family ever had any. Why should I have it? There's work here; there's work enough! If my heart wasn't bad now, I could probably do two or three hours work every day. But now Friday we serve 175 people every day for lunch. *At the Senior Center?* At the Center. Boy was I tired Friday afternoon. No, I could never work every day no more! 'Cause my breath is very short. I have my pills for my heart, you know, and I had an electrocardiogram not so long ago, and the doctor told me not to do strenuous...you know. He wanted to put me in the hospital and I said, "Oh, no. I'll take your advice." I come back here at 2:00 every afternoon and watch my stories on TV.

How long were you and your husband together? We were married in 1941. We married for the convenience of keeping him from going into the Army (she laughs); that's what I told him. We went together for three years and never got married; and when World War II broke out he said, "Oh, yes, we're goin' to get married," to my mother. They put him in 4E [classification for the draft] (laughs). *Was that a big day in your life when you got married, or not?* Yeah, we just went to City Hall. Got married and came back to my mother's house; we had presents and my mother baked a couple cakes and different friends came in. Now if you get married in a church you got to pay; I don't go in for things like that.

I don't like a whole lot of fancy things. This is why people say, "You're still staying in that dump [referring to the apartment]?" I say, "Look, the way they raise the rent, any apartment you move in now you're gonna pay over a hundred dollars." I've been here since February, 1933, so now why should I move? The landlord can't raise the rent, you know [some apartments in New York have their rent controlled by law so it cannot be raised while the same tenant keeps the apartment]. And I'm a Senior Citizen so I got [rent] exemption, 'cause my Social Security's only $103. So now I have to take my rent out of there and my telephone and gas and electric. *$103 a month?* Yeah. My daughter takes care of the kids [who stay with her during the week] and the food and all like that, but as I say, I'm not well enough to work every day, and when I go in on a Thursday, they give me $12, so that helps out. And I don't need a whole lot of clothes 'cause I don't go nowhere. My daughter says, "Now, Momma!" I say I don't need it. I don't need a pocketbook 'cause they're gonna snatch it from me, right? What do I need all those clothes to put in the closet? They're gonna come in here and rob me and take your things, you know. She's always sayin', "Momma, you need . . ." and I say, "You shut up! I know what I want." *So you have managed to stay off welfare so far?* Yeah, thank God. *You'd really hate to go on welfare if you had to?* At my age I wouldn't. None of my family ever been on it. And we're makin' out. My son is in the service; my daughter is workin'. I say I don't need clothes, and Social Security can pay my rent, and my telephone is for my comfort, for my health too. My daughter says, "Momma, come give me your gas and electric bill." When my son comes home he says, "Momma, give me your telephone bill." He says, "You got money to last you?" I say yeah, you know. So I budget myself. I got a Medicaid card; so I go to Harlem Hospital. For my eyeglasses I go to the eyeglass place; so now why should I go on welfare. I'm not goin' in and lay my life on the line for a few dollars.

Were there a lot of crisis points in your marriage? Was that a pretty difficult time? Yes it was. It was a problem trying to get him to come home with the salary; sittin' down and trying to budget ourselves, you know. I was workin' and meetin' the bills. Also, my mother used to help me too. And when his sister first got married, she and her husband were roomin' in the back room there. They was young and didn't have enough money, so they couldn't pay no rent. So we had to carry the rent, and feed them, you know. After five years, that's long enough. That was a terrible family problem, you know. *There were a lot of arguments about that?* Don't ever shack up with your in-laws! Take it from me. I'm tellin' you. That's what I went through; that's my problems! *That really destroyed your marriage?* That, and then after that, well you know, New York get a lot of glamor girls and he used to go to the bar. That was all right, but I couldn't go into the bar; but then they got a little too bold. I didn't want the kids to see that. Right now his son and daughter respects him, but they tell him, "Daddy, you know what you did to momma." They don't like that, you know.

You said that you worked with this one family for 37 years; have there been any crisis points in your job there? No, a wonderful family! I am one of their family, and my mother was one of the family, and my children and grand-children are part of the family. When the older girl got married I served at the party and my grandson helped me; my granddaughter helped me; my daughter helped. We were just one of his family. *It sounds like you're going to continue working there as long as you want.* I only work there one day a week now. I'm my own boss. I have my keys. When they first bought a house in Fire Island I used to go every weekend. So I've had a happy life. Poor, but happy. As I say, I don't go for welfare. I'm not against anybody gettin' it, espe-cially some elderly people that we know. They really deserve it because some people they used to work for didn't pay Social Security for them and that's really unfair. I know I talked to one lady and she said that she worked 47 years for one family, and all the time they told her they were payin' Social Security, and they didn't pay. Now that's unfair to her. My people paid it. So when I got sick when I was 62 years old they said why don't you wait until you're 65 and you'll get more. I said there was no guarantee that I'm gonna live 'til I'm 65.

I was sick, really sick then. And two years ago I was takin' cancer tests. The doctor didn't tell me, but every test he would give me I would look it up, or ask my friends who are doctors or nurses and they told me what it was. I went and the last test I had was all the X rays. I was X-rayed a whole day; all differ-ent angles. And I came home; it was in July, I'll never forget it. I had a chill 'cause the hospital was air-conditioned and the metal tables that you lay on, you know. So I put on my clothes and got a cab and came home. Now I was in a terrible state for two weeks, waitin' for the hospital to send for me or get a letter. So I went back for a check-up, and they said my X ray hadn't come back, and the nurse told me not to worry. She said the X rays must have come back negative, otherwise they would have sent for you in a hurry. Well, that didn't satisfy me. In September I went back again. I said to the doctor, "Where's my X rays?" So he said, "Don't worry. How did you feel?" I said, "All right—Doctor, do I have cancer?" He said, "Get that out of your mind! Now go on home and enjoy yourself and if we need you we'll send for you." They never sent for me, so, I go to the clinic for my weight and blood pressure now. *It must have been a pretty frightening time, though, waiting and not knowing....* Yeah, this is the frightening part. In the meantime I had lost two friends that had cancer of the rectum.

Would you say that you've changed very much in the last few years? My reflexes—I could walk in the kitchen and forget what I go in there for, somethin' like that. I spoke to the doctor and he said, "Well, you realize...." I said, "Don't you say that I'm gettin' old!" He said, "Do you want to stay like you were when you were 16?" So he said to stop worryin' about my reflexes. You know, I have to make a list to go to the supermarket. I have that list in my hand with the shoppin' cart, and I forget I have the list. But this comes with age.

Do you sometimes look back over your life and kind of review and think about the things that have happened? Well, I look back over the good times that I had, you know. I look back on my family life. You see, we was a big happy family. Every Thanksgiving my mother had us over to her house and she served everything from soup to nuts. And then Christmas we all would be together. And after my son went in the service and my daughter got married, well, I was here alone, and then my mother passed. So then after my daughter had children, it kind of gave me a second hold on life, you know. 'Cause I sat here by myself after the children got married; I couldn't expect them to stay here, you know. And then my mother was gone and my brother was gone. I used to get up 5:30 in the mornin' for work, but on the weekend I'd get lonesome, and I didn't want to go up to my daughter's house all the time. But after they had kids I always have a crowd here. You see, my Thanksgiving's gonna be here now. I carried on after my mother; and my sister have Christmas dinner; and then my daughter have me for New Year's. So, it's happy moments in my life. I can truthfully say I'm happy. *As you look back over your life, are you satisfied?* I'm very satisfied! I don't have no regrets. The one regret, I couldn't get the education that I wanted; but it was hard on my mother, so I had to come and start workin' with her. But I saw that my kids and my grandchildren are gettin' it. But I tell you one thing, a lot of peoples that know me they say, "Well, I don't know where you cut yourself short of education, 'cause you got a lot of mother wit." They say I think fast, you know. And if you keep your head above water in New York City, you're doin' pretty good, believe me.

Do you feel like you've left your mark here someplace? Yes, I have no regrets at all. I have a happy life. I have grandchildren. I have a son and daughter. So, you know, I'm happy.

Do you sometimes think about death? No. I had a pain in my chest last week. I was in the bed. I got up and said, "Oh, Lord, I'm not ready" (she laughs). It was pressin' down, you know. I said, "Oh, Lord, I'm not ready." So I called my sister. She burst out laughin'. She said, "What are you doing?" I said, "I'm sittin' up!" When I got up I took a small glass of 7-Up for the gas. The doctor told me don't let it worry me as long as I abide by his rules. *So you don't think about it very much at all?* No. That's why I stay in the house (laughs). No, I don't think about it. *You're not ready for it yet?* No, these are my golden years. I can truthfully say, I am happy, 'cause I can lay down in the bed, I have money to pay my rent, gas, and electric—things like that—when before it was a struggle. But it's not a struggle at all. It's just contentment. That's why I can sit in this house seven days a week and have no worries, no worries at all. When I was young I had them. I don't think about death.

How does the future look to you? It looks rosy for me, if Nixon don't cut off our Social Security. 'Cause if Nixon cut off mine, I would be right on his doorstep in Washington, D. C., 'cause I work very hard. A dollar's taken out of this and out of that. Now if you go back to work your Social Security check is goin' to stop. I think that's very unfair! It's not like money that they have to give you. That's money that the people had to pay in! Now why take that from us? I think it's ridiculous, things like this. So these are my happy years. I'm 67, and I don't have to work hard. When I was younger I had to work very hard. Now if I wake up in the mornin' and it's rainin' or snowin' I don't have to go to the Center or to work. I can stay in the house all day, 'cause as I said, the rent will be paid and that means a lot. I can make it.

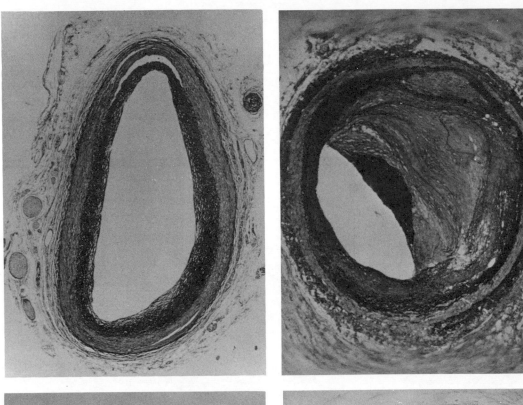
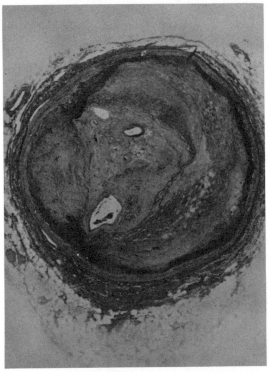
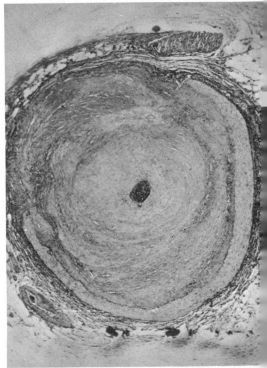

eight

Biological and Intellectual Aspects of Aging

What does it mean to "grow old?" Why do humans and many domestic animals age and eventually die while other forms of life such as trees or single-celled organisms are able to live indefinitely? What causes human aging? And what changes occur in this period of biological aging and decline—that is, in the period of *senescence*?

Such questions are indeed puzzling, since we have not yet found satisfying answers to them. A great deal of research on aging today is delving into the nucleus of the cell in an attempt to find some of the basic causes of aging; other research is attempting to produce temporary symptoms of aging in young subjects; and much research is exploring aging in various animals. In addition, considerable research is focusing on the most prevalent causes of death—cancer, stroke, and heart disease. However, despite the medical progress of the last century, the life expectancy of individuals who survive to the age of 80 is no greater today than it was 100 years ago, and there is no evidence that the maximum length of human life is any longer today than it has ever been. Thus it seems clear that the length of human life is, in general, determined by biological factors that are related to the age of the organism. However, the nature of this relationship—that is, the actual causes of biological aging—are not yet clear; but we will discuss several theories of aging as well as some of the social implications of the increased longevity that may eventually result from this intensive research into the nature of human aging.

In addition to considering the biological processes of aging, this chapter also shifts our focus to the later years of the life span, since with advancing age physiological aspects play an important role in the characteristics and changes in adulthood and interact with psychological and social factors in important ways. For example, with increased age, susceptibility to disease (especially chronic disease) increases dramatically;

Photo at left:
Cross sections of coronary arteries showing increasing blockage by atherosclerotic plaques. Left top: a near-normal artery; right bottom: a totally blocked artery from a patient who died of a heart attack. Courtesy of National Institutes of Health: Dr. William C. Roberts, Dr. L. Maximilian Buja, Dr. Bernadine Healy Bulkley.

and even in the absence of disease, there is a general slowing down in many aspects of functioning involving the central nervous system (CNS). Thus, intellectual processes in particular, and all systems of the organism in general, are affected by the physiological changes of senescence. However, there is a crucial distinction between the physiological changes resulting from *aging* and changes resulting from *disease*. That is, while aging (if there is a process that is pure change with age) typically occurs along with disease in the ordinary population, disease itself has marked consequences for the total functioning of the organism. Thus, in order to understand the effects of aging per se, the effects of disease must be separated from those changes that occur with age in the absence of disease. Otherwise, the effects of aging are confounded with the effects of disease.

We begin with some of the major theories of aging, leaving the discussion of disease and its effects for the second section of the chapter. In the third section we will consider some of the important physiological changes with age (probably resulting from a combination of aging and disease) and will then discuss the changes in intellectual processes with advancing age.

THEORIES OF AGING AND MORTALITY

There are many different types of aging noted by biologists: bacteria are able to continue living indefinitely, limited only by the supply of food and physical space; annual plants complete their life cycle in one year of well-defined, genetically programmed stages; trees continue to grow until they can no longer transmit the sap to the upper branches or the lower branches no longer receive adequate sunlight; and animals in the wild generally do not grow old but are killed by predators or starve when their physical strength declines. Also, the various mammals have characteristic life-spans, many exceeding their reproductive life only slightly, if at all; however, African elephants and perhaps Indian elephants live long enough after becoming infertile to rear their young (Sacher, personal communication: cf. Laws, 1971).

However, the human life span, while clearly characteristic of the species, lasts long beyond the end of reproductive capabilities (menopause occurs around the age of 50, while the average woman lives 20 years longer and lives 35 to 40 years beyond the birth of her last child) and involves a period of senescence atypical among animals in their natural habitat. The oldest man in the United States is currently 130 (authenticated by the American Medical Association and the Social Security Administration), and there were 7000 U. S. citizens over the age of 100 in 1972—an increase from 5200 in 1971 (*Newsweek*, 1972). In a region of the USSR there is a group of people called Abkhasians who appear to typically live to be very old (Benet, 1971; Leaf, 1973); the possible reasons for their long lives are currently being studied by an international team of gerontologists.

Currently, the field of gerontology has been unable to determine whether aging results from an evolutionary necessity related to the survival of the species, from the accumulated effects of "wear and tear," or from a natural process of physiological change. In general, aging leads to a growing inability of the organism to adapt to the environment and thus to survive. We will discuss several aspects of this aging process, beginning with hereditary and external factors, and then we will consider physiological theories of aging. While none of these theories seems adequate to explain the process of aging at present, each makes a valuable contribution to our understanding of this elusive process.

Hereditary Factors

Clearly there is an hereditary component involved in the length of life characteristic of a particular species. However, man's life span exceeds the length that would be expected for a mammal of his size, and he is the longest-lived species of mammal. Comfort (1964) reports that Indian elephants are known to reach 60 years, and the horse, hippopotamus, and probably the ass are the only other mammals known to reach or exceed 50 years of age. Baboons, chimpanzees, and other primates (as well as large cats, bears, and the African elephant) may reach or exceed 30 years. The life span of whales and dolphins is probably between 30 and 50 years. In general, the length of life among various species of mammals is related to the size of the animal, with man as the marked exception. This is not the case for birds (some owls, cockatoos, eagles, parrots, condors, and pelicans have been found to live more than 50 years) or among reptiles (tortoises have been reported to live from 70 to over 152 years). Sacher (1959) has proposed that it is the ratio of brain weight to body weight that is best related to the longevity of mammals, including man. That is, the much larger size of man's brain (largely because of the cerebrum) may be an important biological asset contributing to his longevity (as body size alone contributes to the longevity of other mammals).

From these observations it appears that the life span of a species is relatively set by genetic or hereditary characteristics that, according to the theory of evolution, have evolved over countless years. Sacher's observations suggest that man's thinking capacities may be a primary factor in the evolution of his long life span. However, it is not clear what evolutionary function might have been played by man's long postreproductive life. That is, what function could this have played for the survival of his species? Indeed, it would seem that the characteristics of man's senescence (i.e., postreproductive aging) could not have been under evolutionary control since survival into old age would not directly lead to more offspring or greater viability of the offspring. However, it has been argued, notably by Weissman (1891), that man's long period of aging, which is typically not characteristic of other species, may *socially* increase the survival value of the human species. That is, the aging process may have evolved as a means to promote the survival of the children and grandchildren since the aged would remember, for example, where food and water were found during the drought many years ago (Mead, 1972). Others have argued that senescence results only from the "running out" of the genetic program and is not specifically developed through evolution. Instead, man's thinking may simply have allowed him to live longer so that aging is a kind of "exhaustion of program"; in that sense, man's later years may be analogous to a rocket that was programmed to place a satellite in orbit and simply continues on for a time after accomplishing this programmed task until pulled back into the atmosphere by the earth's gravity (Comfort, 1964). Another evolutionary model of aging is proposed by Birren (1960) in the *counterpart theory* of aging. This suggests that human senescence is affected by the later manifestation of negative characteristics that had their primary adaptive importance earlier (prior to the end of reproductive ability when they would directly enhance species survival). Their negative effects in senescence would then be counterparts or by-products of those characteristics. For example, the nonreplacement of cells in the human nervous system may be highly adaptive for species survival (e.g., enhancing memory and learning abilities) but may also prevent indefinite functioning and life.

Thus, it is unclear whether man's long life (and consequent period of aging) evolved directly because of its importance for his survival as a species (perhaps because the elderly provided leadership and wisdom) or whether it results simply from man's success as an evolved species in. coping with the environment and in prolonging his life because of his advanced cognitive powers.

Another type of evidence of an hereditary component in longevity is found in the studies of identical twins (Kallmann and Jarvik, 1959). One-egg twins tend to have more similar lengths of life than two-egg twins; this indicates that even within the species, genetic factors play a role in an individual's length of life. This study also found striking physical similarities between identical twins well into old age, indicating the persistence of genetic influence even to changes in appearance during aging (Figures 8.1 and 8.2). In addition, many studies have found that offspring whose parents and grandparents were long lived are also likely to live longer. However, while such data indicate a genetic component in longevity, it may not be a directly transmitted genetic trait; for example,

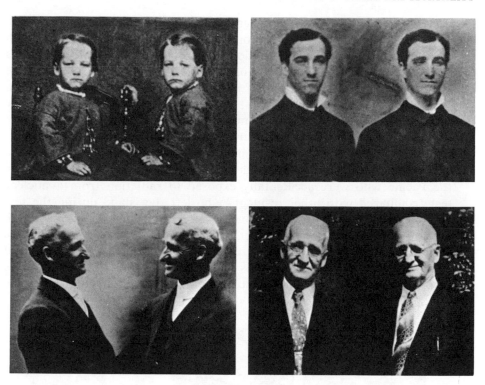

Figure 8.1
One-egg twins at the ages of 5, 20, 55, and 86 years. (Source. Kallmann and Jarvik, 1959, Figure 8. Reprinted with permission.)

increased vigor and resistance to disease may be the genetically transmitted potentials that also lead to a longer life. Also, hybrids (rather than inbred animals), individuals with younger mothers (father's age does not seem to be relevant), and females generally live longer (Comfort, 1964).

External Factors

These hereditary factors are probably best seen as *potentials* that may only be realized to their greatest extent in a particular environment. Obviously, an accident may terminate one's life regardless of genetic potentials, as may disease or starvation or lightning. For example, Jones (1959) estimates that external factors such as rural living or marriage increase the average length of life by five years while being overweight decreases the average life by 4 to 15 years (Table 8.1). It is important to note that the control of childhood and infectious diseases has been the major factor to date in prolonging life; it has added an estimated 15 years to the overall length of life (since fewer persons die in childhood).

Radiation has received some attention as a possible cause of aging since everyone is exposed to a small amount of cosmic radiation daily. Although only much higher levels of radiation damage the nucleus of cells, Curtis (1966) reports that the amount of damage to cells (measured by the amount of chromosomal damage) is related to the amount of life shortening produced. This suggests that more rapid aging occurs because the chromosomes were destroyed. Numerous studies have reported a connection between radiation and decreased life span caused by an acceleration of all forms of disease in animals (Lindop and Rotblat, 1961). And a 15-year longitudinal study of residents of one of the Marshall Islands in the Pacific who were accidentally exposed to radiation from a nuclear test (compared with other residents who left the island during the test and returned) found evidence of increased chromosome loss among individuals exposed to the radiation; this suggests that radiation exposure "is related to and possibly accelerates the aging process" (Demoise and Conrad, 1972). However, there is evidence of a kind of spontaneous recovery process within the cell so that the effects of radiation decrease

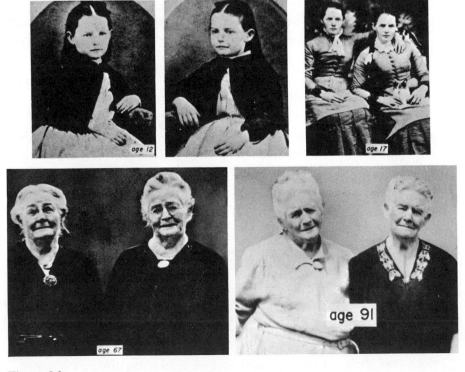

Figure 8.2
One-egg twins before and after long separations (between the ages of 18 and 65). (Source. Kallmann and Jarvik, 1959, Figure 9. Reprinted with permission.)

Table 8.1 Effect of External and Physiological Factors on Length of Life

Reversible		Permanent	
Comparison	Years	Comparison	Years
Country versus city dwelling	+ 5	Female versus male sex	+ 3
Married status versus single,		Familial constitutions	
widowed, divorced	+ 5	2 grandparents lived to 80	
Overweight		years	+ 2
25 percent overweight group	− 3.6	4 grandparents lived to 80	
35 percent overweight group	− 4.3	years	+ 4
45 percent overweight group	− 6.6	Mother lived to age 90 years	+ 3
55 percent overweight group	−11.4	Father lived to age 90 years	+ 4.4
67 percent overweight group	−15.1	Both mother and father lived	
Or: an average effect of 1 per-		to age 90 years	+ 7.4
cent overweight	− 0.17	Mother lived to age 80 years	+ 1.5
Smoking		Father lived to age 80 years	+ 2.2
1 package cigarettes per day	− 7	Both mother and father lived	
2 packages cigarettes per day	−12	to age 80 years	+ 3.7
Atherosclerosis		Mother died at 60 years	− 0.7
Fat metabolism		Father died at 60 years	− 1.1
In 25th percentile of popula-		Both mother and father died	
tion having "ideal" lipo-		at age 60 years	− 1.8
protein concentrations	+10	Recession of childhood and in-	
Having average lipoprotein		fectious disease over past cen-	
concentrations	0	tury in Western countries	+15
In 25th percentile of popu-		Life Insurance *Impairment Study*	
lation having elevated li-		Rheumatic heart disease, evi-	
poproteins	− 7	denced by:	
In 5th percentile of popula-		Heart murmur	−11
tion having highest ele-		Heart murmur + tonsillitis	−18
vation of lipoproteins	−15	Heart murmur + streptococcal	
Diabetes		infection	−13
Uncontrolled, before insulin,		Rapid pulse	− 3.5
1900	−35	Phlebitis	− 3.5
Controlled with insulin		Varicose veins	− 0.2
1920 Joslin Clinic record	−20	Epilepsy	−20.0
1940 Joslin Clinic record	−15	Skull fracture	− 2.9
1950 Joslin Clinic record	−10	Tuberculosis	− 1.8
		Nephrectomy	− 2.0
		Trace of albumin in urine	− 5.0
		Moderate albumin in urine	−13.5

Source. Jones, Hardin B. A Special Consideration of the Aging Process, Disease and Life Expectancy. In J. H. Lawrence and C. A. Tobias (Eds.), *Advances in Biological and Medical Physics.* Vol. 4. New York: Academic Press, 1956. Reprinted with permission.

with time (Curtis, Tilley, and Crowley, 1964). Thus, the effects of chromosomal mutations may reflect not only the amount of damage done but also the efficiency of the repair mechanism of the cell. Spiegel (1972), on the basis of an examination of the available experimental evidence, concludes that "radiation does not seem to play a major role in accelerating the aging process" (p. 570). Thus, it is not at all clear whether radiation is associated with aging.

Viruses may also be implicated in the changes that occur with age (Hotcin and Sikora, 1970) and have been recently receiving attention in the etiology of cancers and diseases previously thought to be genetic in origin (Gajdusek and Brown, 1970).

For man as a species, however, the *force of mortality* (i.e., the risk of mortality) is clearly related to age. Gompertz (1825) is credited with giving a mathematical representation to the exponential increase in the probability of death with advancing age—a relationship that differs by constant parameters for different species (resulting from a differential length of life)—but that is relatively accurate for many different species. From his mathematical relationship one obtains an exponential increase in the risk of mortality with age; and it is on this basis that life insurance tables are devised. It may be seen that medical advances (for example in Sweden where the population has benefited relatively completely from medical technology) have markedly decreased the mortality for the younger age groups (mentioned above), while the older age groups have been little affected (Figure 8.3). That is, the increase in average life span has had little effect on the force of mortality in the later years. It has been estimated that if all cardiovascular and kidney diseases were eliminated, only about 7.5 years would be added to the average life span; and if all cancer were eliminated only 1.5 years would be added to the average length of life (Dublin, Lotka, and Spiegelman, 1949; Kohn, 1963; Myers and Pitts, 1972).

Thus, it seems that while both hereditary and external factors (such as marital status, disease, and possibly radiation and viruses) may be related to longevity, these factors do not provide very satisfying answers to the puzzle of aging. What does aging mean? Why do people age? Indeed, so far we may have discovered some clues, but the questions remain unanswered. Let us search for some more clues (for there really are no answers . . . yet) by looking "inside" the organism.

Physiological Theories of Aging

Aging may be defined as ". . . a decline in physiologic competence that inevitably increases the incidence and intensifies the effects of accidents, disease, and other forms of environmental stress (Timiras, 1972, p. 465)." Thus, with the passage of time, there is a greater probability of dying (the Gompertz curve); and an individual's death by "natural causes" means that enough important life-maintaining processes degenerate so that death results. Presently it is not clear whether there is a specific cause of aging, whether several potential causes operate together, or even if aging is

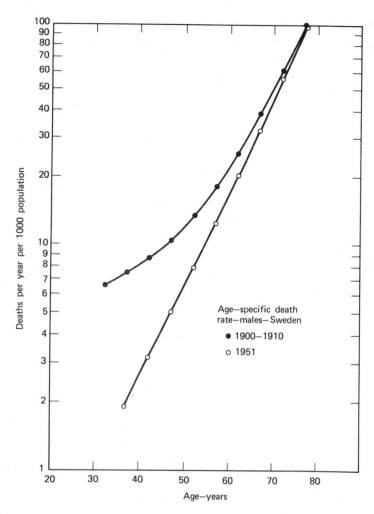

Figure 8.3

Log age-specific death rate versus age (Gompertz plot) for Swedish males before and after the advent of modern medicine. This shows the striking decrease in the death rate for young men but the lack of change for old men. (Source. Curtis, 1966, p. 7. Reprinted with permission of Charles C Thomas, Publisher.)

simply an accumulation of physiologic deficits. The various physiological theories of aging we will present below may be equally valid, although some may be found to be more basic causes of aging than others. Actually, at this time we may be in a better position to apply our practical knowledge (gained from animal studies) to lengthen life by slowing the aging process than we are to understand the nature of the aging process itself (Comfort, 1972); it may be that we will develop the technology to extend life before we have an adequate theory of aging.

Wear and Tear Theory. Perhaps the most common-sense theory of aging is that the organism simply wears out, similar to a machine. In this view, aging is the result of the gradual deterioration of the various organs necessary for life and has currently given rise to an interest in the replacement of organs such as heart and kidney transplants. However, there is no conclusive evidence that either hard work or increased stress alone is responsible for shortening an individual's life span (Curtis, 1966). To a large extent, the effects of hard work and stress are removed by a period of rest, and even the effects of a severe chemical stress, once removed, leave the animal with as long a life expectancy as before as long as these stresses do not overwhelm the physiological capacity to adapt to the stress. Nonetheless, the total rate of metabolism seems to be a factor in aging; for example, underfed animals and cold-blooded animals living at lower than usual temperatures tend to live longer than usual. Thus, lower rates of metabolism may postpone some of the consequences of aging. However, the interrelation of the various systems in the body is probably more implicated in aging than is the failure of any particular organ; thus, while transplants of organs may be particularly helpful when a single organ is diseased, it is not likely that "spare-parts replacement" will lengthen the human life span to an appreciable degree since the declining efficiency of complex homeostatic mechanisms and the process of cellular aging (to be discussed below) would not be corrected by such transplants.

Homeostatic Imbalance. Comfort (1964) has proposed that the efficiency of crucial homeostatic mechanisms that maintain vital physiologic balances in the body (such as the pH and sugar levels of the blood) is central to the process of aging. Thus, in his view, "... aging is characteristically an increase in homeostatic faults" (p. 178). Although there is little change in these mechanisms of self-regulating equilibrium between young and old persons under *resting conditions*, Shock (1960) has demonstrated that the rate of readjustment to normal equilibrium after stress is slower in old subjects than in young. For example, the capacity of the kidneys for maintaining homeostasis, the ability to maintain body temperature during exposure to heat or cold, and the efficiency of blood sugar regulation decrease with age[1] (cf. Timiras, 1972, pp. 558-561). Thus, the self-regulating feedback mechanisms decrease in efficiency with age so that when they are no longer able to maintain the necessary equilibrium, the organism dies (Figure 8.4). Thus, strains on the homeostatic mechanisms, easily tolerated in young persons, may threaten the survival of the aged. The stress that may disrupt these processes can be physical (such as exercise or glucose intake), or it may result from changes in the

---

[1] Because of such changes, especially in the kidneys, the medication prescribed for the elderly should typically be lower than the level tolerated by young adults.

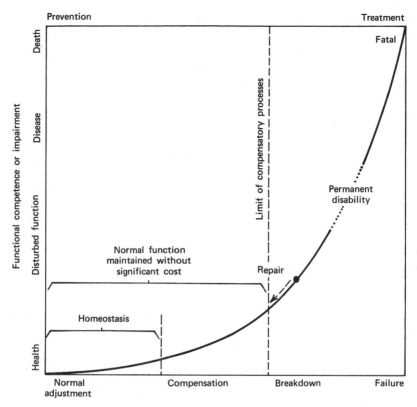

Figure 8.4

Progressive stages of homeostasis from adjustment (health) to failure (death). In the healthy adult, homeostatic processes ensure adequate adjustment in response to stress, and even for a period beyond this stage compensatory processes are capable of maintaining overall function without serious disability. When stress is exerted beyond compensatory capacities of the organism, disability ensues in rapidly increasing increments to severe illness, permanent disability, and death. When this model is viewed in terms of homeostatic responses to stress imposed on the aged and to aging itself, a period when the body can be regarded as at the point of "limit of compensatory processes," it is evident that even minor stresses are not tolerable, and the individual moves rapidly into stages of breakdown and failure. (Source. Timiras, 1972, Figure 28–1. Reprinted with permission of Macmillan Publishing Co., Inc. Copyright © 1972 by Paola S. Timiras.)

physical or social environment. Hence, the emotional stresses that accompany the aging process (loss of spouse, environmental changes, and so on) are more likely to increase the risk of death for the aged than for the young because of this homeostatic inefficiency (cf. Selye, 1950; Selye and Prioreschi, 1960). This lessened efficiency of the physiologic response to stress is perhaps the most general theory of aging and provides the clearest link between physiological, social, and psychological aspects of aging. Hormonal balance is probably also disrupted with aging and the endocrinic response to stress is markedly impaired; certainly the gonads become less responsive with age (as discussed in Chapter 4). However, the causes and effects of these age-related endocrine changes (for example on the interrelation of the central nervous system (CNS) and endocrine production) are not yet understood.

Accumulation of Metabolic Waste. Although it has been suggested for some time that organisms age because their cells are slowly poisoned or hampered in their function by the waste products of metabolism, Curtis (1966) argues that these waste products are more likely a symptom than a cause of aging. Yet, waste products clearly accumulate with age, may have an important role in the changes associated with aging, and have received a great deal of study. For example, *collagen*, a fibrous protein, is formed in some tissues at a rather slow rate and is eliminated only very slowly if at all; in time these fibers tend to shrink and choke off the tissues. These strands of protein have also been found to change with age because of changes in their cross-linkages between the intertwined strands of protein. This building up of collagen and its change with age is involved in the wrinkled skin and slowness of wound healing characteristic of old age. Another group of substances, *lipofuscins*, build up in some nerve cells with age and give rise to pigments in these cells. Again, while they may be an important cause of a decline in function of those nerve cells, Curtis feels that they are primarily important as a symptom of aging, rather than a cause. A third type of increase in waste material results from a defect in calcium metabolism that Selye and Prioreschi (1960) argue leads to a shift of calcium from bone to soft tissues (such as cataracts in the eye, calcification in the arteries, or wrinkled skin with consequent brittleness of bones). While such a shift in calcium deposits seems to occur for some aged persons, the calcification seen typically in old persons suggest that defects in calcium metabolism are not necessarily so severe as to be a dominant cause of aging (Strehler, 1962). Perhaps it is another aspect of a breakdown in homeostasis or one of the many interrelated consequences of cellular aging.

Autoimmunity. The frequency with which the immune systems of animals reject their own tissues through the production of autoimmune antibodies increases with age and is involved in several diseases that increase with age, such as rheumatoid arthritis. Some leading causes of death (cancer, diabetes, vascular diseases, and hypertension) have also been linked to autoimmune reactions, and Blumenthal and Berns (1964) have postulated a link between this process and aging on the basis that those causes of death fit the Gompertz formula for the force of mortality. However, although the data presented by Walford (1969) supporting the concept that aging is a generalized, prolonged type of autoimmune reaction forms an attractive hypothesis of aging, these reactions may be related to other, more basic causes of aging and, like the other factors described in this section, may be more of a symptom rather than a general cause of aging. Nonetheless, recent data on the inability of cells to reproduce suggest that this age-related phenomenon may be related to an excessive immune reaction (Gelfant and Smith, 1972).

Cellular Aging. A common misconception of aging is that cells of the body begin dying at a faster rate than they are produced some time in young adulthood, and that this decline continues until there are no longer enough cells to function and death results. The situation is hardly this simple. Although some cells seldom or never reproduce (notably cells in the brain, nervous system, and muscles), most cells continue to reproduce themselves and theoretically allow the organism to live indefinitely. However, cells may age in the sense that they reproduce only a finite number of times, or that they reproduce imperfectly because of age or a random accumulation of chance mutations. Hayflick (1965, 1966, 1970) has found that cells grown in cultures ("aging under glass") undergo a finite number of doublings (about 50), which suggests that a finite growth potential of cells might be a mechanism of aging. Whether this inability to reproduce occurs in the organism as well as "under glass" in the laboratory is an unanswered question, although Gelfant and Smith (1972) report blockage of cell division in living animals (which can be reversed by drugs that suppress the immune reaction). In addition, the doubling capacity of cells in cultures does decrease with the age of the organism from which they were taken (about 45 at birth to age 10; about 30 by 80 to 90 years of age). Another line of evidence suggests that an impairment of RNA synthesis (Cristofalo, 1970) or faulty transcription of information from DNA leads to a "catastrophe of errors" (Orgel, 1963) which impairs or diverts cell function and cell division. Recent data (Johnson and Strehler, 1972) indicate a selective loss of DNA from the cells of aging animals that would impair the production of RNA by DNA and would impair the functioning of the cells. To be sure, the cell's ability to function would be affected by changes in this genetic material within the cell since DNA (deoxyribonucleic acid) leads to the formation of RNA (ribonucleic acid) that produces the enzymes required for cellular functioning. Yet it is not clear whether these changes are genetically programmed in the sense that when the program is exhausted the cells break down, or whether these errors are essentially random events that accumulate with age until the cell becomes defective. All of these data suggest that the differentiation of cells, presumably evolved characteristics of the human species, may in some way interfere with the ability of those cells to reproduce indefinitely. More specifically, those highly differentiated cells that do not divide (such as in the CNS) may have developed that ability through evolution in order to provide continuity and regularity (of performance and experience) important for the survival of the younger individual. But, in old age, these same characteristics may be implicated in their greater susceptibility to the effects of mutations or cross-linkages or loss of DNA, which brings about eventual cellular death. This may be an example of Birren's (1960) counterpart theory of aging in that evolutionary adaptations that grant positive survival value to young organisms bring about negative results in old animals. One of the important results of these changes may be an increase in the *chemical noise* within the cell, since it functions less effectively as an information system (Comfort, 1968). As we will discuss in the section on intellectual functioning, such an increase in chemical noise may account for a number of the age-related changes that occur.

Implications

As may be apparent from the preceding discussion, there is a great deal of complex research currently investigating the nature of aging and particularly the physiological changes that occur with advancing age. It appears that the secret of the "fountain of youth" may lie in the cellular processes of aging and perhaps equally in the other aspects we have discussed. It apparently does not lie in the prevention of disease alone, as important as this factor clearly is, because there seems to be some kind of limit set by some unknown mechanism to the length of human life. However, as noted above, Comfort (1972), who describes himself as an "optimistic gerontologist," predicts that soon we will be able to extend life by 10 to 20 percent if the sort of techniques that work on laboratory animals can be made to work on humans. This may occur before we have gained a complete understanding of the causes of aging; and if we can modify the aging process, then we may come to understand it.

There are profound social issues raised by the possibility of a marked increase in life span. One is overpopulation, since more people would be living longer. A related issue would be the increased number of people who would be aged and living in retirement (or swelling the proportion unemployed). Although the problems of the aged in our society as well as the population problem will probably have to be solved regardless of increased life spans, serious problems remain. For example, will this "pill" (or whatever) be available to all, or will it be so expensive as to be used only by the rich? Who will support these aged persons? Will we have to choose between having children and living indefinitely? If so, who will decide who lives and who has how many children? And, most important of all, will this involve not only adding years to life but also adding life to years? Currently our medical technology has provided greater freedom from disease for more years. Probably attempts to lengthen life will increase this trend so that diseases that occur during the sixties now may occur during the seventies. This will be an important advance, but it must be matched by economic and social advances for the elderly also if these added years are to be fully beneficial.

DISEASE: A MOST IMPORTANT CONSIDERATION

In the preceding section we discussed the major theories of aging in an attempt to uncover some of the basic biological processes that change with age in the absence of disease. However, the effects of these two processes—aging and disease—are complexly intertwined, and it is difficult to disentangle them. That is, some of the age-related changes in biological processes may be involved in some diseases. For example, mutations in cells in the arterial wall may be involved in circulatory disease; and perhaps what now seem to be "normal age-changes" may eventually be found to be disease processes (such as if viral infections are, in some way, implicated in aging). Indeed, one additional theory of normal aging is that deficits such as disease accumulate over time so that disease itself is a cause of aging (Selye, 1970).

In general, it is very difficult to separate the physiological, social, and psychological effects of aging from the effects of disease since aging and disease are highly correlated. That is, as individuals age they generally become more troubled by chronic diseases (such as arthritis, heart conditions, or high blood pressure). And the effects of aging and disease compound one another. For example, aged persons tend to experience growing effects of disease, more social losses, and lessened hearing and visual acuity. As a result, accidents are more prevalent and bones break more easily and take longer to heal for the aged person.

Nonetheless, it is important to attempt to distinguish between the changes that result from aging per se, from disease, and from other social, psychological, and physiological factors. Otherwise, if these different variables are not disentangled, we are easily misled into equating aging with disease (for the aged very often are also chronically ill), as if sick old people are the only kind of old people there are. If we make that error, then we not only overlook the old people who are quite healthy but also we do not know whether the characteristics of the sick old people result from their advanced age, their illness, or from the interaction of both. One example is that while religious feelings and beliefs do not decline with age, church attendance does decrease with advanced age (Moberg, 1965). In a sense, this change might be seen to reflect the increased interiority of the personality in that religion is more internal and less externally practiced in old age. However, a very important factor may be simply that the aged have more chronic illnesses that make attendance at such activities more and more difficult.

In this section we will describe the prevalence and effects of disease among the aged; and then we will discuss a study that attempted to separate the effects of aging from the effects of disease. In general, disease is a very potent factor in aging; in the absence of disease, the effects of aging are relatively minor; but when even a mild amount of chronic (i.e., irreversible and incurable) disease is present, a wide range of effects results.

Prevalence of Disease Among the Aged

Riley, Foner, and Associates (1968), in their review of the research on aging, point out that older persons are less often afflicted with *acute* diseases (such as infectious diseases) and are more often afflicted with *chronic* diseases. They are also more likely to suffer disability restrictions because of their health than young persons.

Acute Diseases. Temporary illnesses are much more common in childhood than at any other age, and their prevalence decreases with age for both men and women (Table 8.2). Since acute conditions, by definition,

Table 8.2 Number of Acute Conditions per 100 Persons per Year, by Age, Sex, and Condition: July 1969–June 1970

Sex and Condition Group	All Ages	Under 6 Years	6-16 Years	17-44 Years	& Over 45 Years
Male					
All acute conditions	196.9	352.1	261.6	176.0	106.4
Infective and parasitic diseases	24.6	53.5	40.3	17.0	9.1
Respiratory conditions	107.1	205.7	134.6	97.3	56.7
Upper respiratory conditions	61.4	140.7	79.5	48.5	30.2
Influenza	39.1	44.3	48.0	44.4	23.2
Other respiratory conditions	6.7	20.7	7.2	4.4	3.3
Digestive system conditions	10.2	10.9	15.2	9.9	6.3
Injuries	33.5	35.7	45.7	35.0	20.7
All other acute conditions	21.5	46.3	25.8	16.9	13.6
Female					
All acute conditions	212.2	340.8	264.5	208.6	138.0
Infective and parasitic diseases	24.3	57.5	34.8	22.0	9.0
Respiratory conditions	118.5	193.3	155.2	111.9	76.3
Upper respiratory conditions	69.9	135.5	105.2	57.6	38.5
Influenza	43.0	43.3	45.1	49.5	33.8
Other respiratory conditions	5.5	14.5	4.9	4.8	3.9
Digestive system conditions	11.8	14.9	16.0	11.9	7.7
Injuries	22.3	21.4	25.6	22.5	20.0
All other acute conditions	35.3	53.8	32.8	40.4	25.0

Note. Excluded from these statistics are those conditions that do not involve restricted activity or medical attention.
Source. National Center for Health Statistics. Acute Conditions: Incidence and Associated Disability, United States, July, 1969–June, 1970. *Vital and Health Statistics*, Series 10, No. 77. Washington, D.C.: U.S. Government Printing Office, 1972.

only include those diseases that restrict one's activity or involve medical attention, the number of days of restricted activity because of acute conditions also decrease with age. Thus it is apparent that the control of acute illness with vaccines, antibiotics, and improved health conditions have primarily affected young children and have had much less impact on either adults or the aged—on the average. This is the primary reason for the sharp increase in life expectancy at birth, while there has been only a very modest increase for persons who have already survived to age 65.

Chronic Diseases. In contrast, long-term (or incurable) diseases are much more common in adulthood and old age than among young people. Arthritis and rheumatism, heart conditions, and high blood pressure are the most prevalent chronic diseases afflicting persons over age 45, and they increase in prevalence with age. Other chronic conditions such as asthma, hayfever, and diabetes show little consistent increase after age 45 (Figure 8.5). It is apparent that these chronic diseases may lead to restricted activity, and heart conditions as well as high blood pressure are associated with the leading causes of death.

Chronic Impairments. Blindness, visual impairment, hearing impairment (in particular), or impairment of some part of the body increase in prevalence with age during the adult years. For example, 25 percent of all persons over 75 reported a hearing impairment in 1958 (Riley et al., 1968). Various kinds of injuries, especially accidental falls, are an important cause of chronic impairment. In addition, loss of teeth is common; two out of three persons over age 75 had lost all of their natural teeth in 1960 (ibid.). When these impairments are combined with chronic diseases, fully three-fourths of all persons over 65 in a national health survey reported one or more chronic conditions in 1958, and about half of the persons over 65 reported two or more (Spiegelman, 1964).

Restricted Activity. As a result of this rise in chronic disease and chronic impairment with age, the days of restricted activity increase with age after 25 for both men and women. That is, the increase in chronic conditions offsets the decrease in acute conditions so that, over all, days of restricted activity increase with age. Days of restricted activity also reflect family income, however, so that persons with higher income have fewer days of disability a year (Table 8.3). At first glance it appears that persons of lower income suffer more chronic conditions than persons of higher income; but also, chronic conditions might be a cause of the lower income as well as a consequence of it. Socioeconomic status was also found to be more related to the extent of physical disability than age or race among a sample of 256 volunteer (i.e., probably healthier than average), non-home-bound community residents over age 60 in the Duke Study of Aging (Dovenmuehle, Busse, and Newman, 1961). Persons in the higher socioeconomic group showed lower levels of disability than persons in the lower socioeconomic group. Several chronic conditions

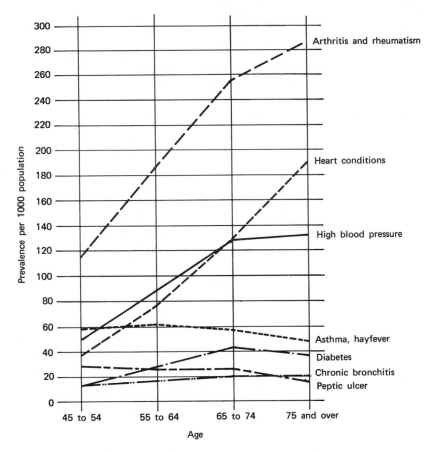

Figure 8.5
*Prevalence of selected chronic illnesses among persons 45 and over in the United States,
1957 to 1959. (Source. United States Health Survey. Health Statistics, Series C, No. 4. Washington, D.C.: U.S. Government Printing Office, 1960, pp. 31, 35.)*

also occurred more often among the lower socioeconomic respondents:
impairment of vision, arteriosclerosis, cardiovascular disease, high blood
pressure, and lung disease. Arthritis was a prevalent condition reported
by 35 percent of the respondents, but there was no significant social
class difference in its prevalence. Dovenmuehle (1970) also found a significant increase in disability among the 180 surviving respondents 22 to 65
months later. Yet while 53 percent of the respondents suffered disability
and there was a dramatic drop in respondents with no disability, 12 percent became *less* disabled over this period.

Taken together, these data indicate that while physical disabilities are
certainly more common among the aged than among the young or
middle-aged adult, there is great individual variation; and socioeconomic
factors probably both affect and result from these impairments. How-

Table 8.3   Days of Restricted Activity per Person per Year, by Family Income, Sex, and Age (United States, 1968)

Sex and Age	All Incomes[a]	Family Income					
		Less than $3000	$3000–$4999	$5000–$6999	$7000–$9999	$10,000–$14,999	$15,000 or More
Male							
All ages	14.3	28.6	18.9	12.8	12.1	10.3	10.0
Under 5 years	10.9	12.6	12.4	11.3	8.5	10.6	9.0
5–14 years	9.8	11.0	8.9	9.6	10.7	9.4	9.3
15–24 years	9.7	13.3	10.3	8.8	9.7	9.2	7.9
25–44 years	11.1	24.3	18.3	11.8	10.2	7.6	9.5
45–64 years	20.6	54.9	33.4	17.1	17.7	14.5	11.0
65–74 years	31.2	42.8	31.0	25.7	27.8	16.4	18.3
75 years and over	35.0	40.9	30.9	31.8	36.9	26.1	20.4
Female							
All ages	16.3	30.6	16.9	14.5	13.1	12.9	11.4
Under 5 years	10.8	13.4	8.6	11.1	10.5	11.5	9.6
5–14 years	9.5	11.2	9.1	9.0	10.1	9.0	9.0
15–24 years	11.3	13.2	10.2	13.0	9.9	11.0	10.4
25–44 years	14.5	27.4	17.9	12.8	13.7	12.9	11.1
45–64 years	20.9	38.7	22.9	19.3	17.1	16.7	13.3
65–74 years	30.3	40.5	23.5	23.4	20.0	26.0	11.7
75 years and over	47.6	50.2	46.1	47.4	45.7	41.1	32.4

[a] Includes unknown income.

Source. National Center for Health Statistics. Disability Days, United States, 1968. *Vital and Health Statistics*, Series 10, No. 67. Washington, D.C.: U.S. Government Printing Office, 1972.

ever, only a minority of aged persons suffer severe restrictions in their ability to get around in the community. According to the 1970 census, 95 percent of persons over 65 live in the community—only 5 percent live in nursing homes or other institutions. Of the community residents, 81 percent have no impairment that limits their ability to get around (including 14 percent with no chronic impairment at all). Only 5 percent are confined to their homes because of disability; 8 percent have difficulty but manage on their own; and 6 percent need help to get around (Brotman, 1972).

Causes of Death. About 80 percent of deaths after age 65 are attributed to cardiovascular diseases (such as heart attacks and strokes), cancerous neoplasms, or accidents. However, the proportion of deaths from these causes varies by age and sex (Figure 8.6). In 1968 the eight leading causes

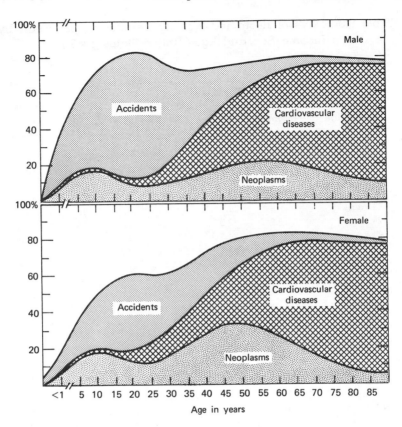

Figure 8.6
Mortality from malignant neoplasms (cancer), cardiovascular diseases (heart disease and cerebrovascular disease), and accidents in the United States, 1969. Expressed as a percentage of total mortality by age group and sex. (Source. Timiras, 1972, Figure 24–6. Reprinted with permission of Macmillan Publishing Co., Inc. Copyright © 1972 by Paola S. Timiras.)

of death were: (1) diseases of the heart; (2) malignant neoplasms (cancer); (3) cerebrovascular diseases (strokes); (4) influenza and pneumonia; (5) arteriosclerosis; (6) accidents; (7) diabetes; and (8) bronchitis, emphysema, and asthma. Each other cause accounted for less than one death per thousand population. Death rates for heart disease were three times as great as the rate for any other cause (U. S. Bureau of the Census, 1973). Men had higher rates than women for nearly all causes of death. Their rates were much higher than women for (in order) bronchitis, emphysema, and asthma; motor vehicle accidents; malignant neoplasms; influenza and pneumonia; and heart disease. Racial differences in causes of death are also apparent. For persons 65 to 74, the ratio of persons of "Negro and other races" is about twice as high as for white persons for cerebrovascular diseases, diabetes mellitus, influenza and pneumonia, and arteriosclerosis (ibid.).

Health of Poor Old Persons. The interaction of aging, disease, social class, and leading causes of death can be vividly illustrated by a study of the health among welfare recipients over age 65 (Ostfeld, 1966). Although few of the respondents perceived themselves as sick, the health status as determined by physicians found only one out of five or six to be in "good" health. About half were rated to be in "fair" health; and about one-third were in "poor" health or were so gravely ill that death was felt to be imminent (Table 8.4). Negro men were slightly more healthy in general, while Caucasian men and women were the least healthy (sex differences were slight). Perhaps since life expectancy is lower for Negro persons (especially men), the survivors over age 65 are more robust than their white counterparts. The most prevalent disease was hypertensive heart disease (high blood pressure); it was more common among Negro men and women (34.8 and 21.5 percent, respectively), while Caucasian women and men were lower (13.0 and 9.3 percent); an additional 10 percent of the respondents had some other heart disease, and 5 percent were so troubled by heart disease that they were not able to walk across the room without getting out of breath and had badly swollen ankles indicating poor circulation. Strokes, Parkinson's disease, chronic bronchitis, and neurological gait disturbance (difficulty in walking, which may be an important cause of death or injury in accidental falls or pedestrian accidents) were other major illnesses in this sample. When standards applicable for younger subjects were used, one-half of the respondents had symptoms of diabetes (indicating that these standards may not be wholly appropriate for older persons). Many respondents had symptoms of thyroid problems and showed high cholesterol levels (leading the physicians to anticipate that 2.5 percent of the respondents would experience

Table 8.4 Health Status of Old Age Assistance Recipients Over 65 as Determined by Physicians (Percentages)

Categories	Male Caucasian	Male Negro	Female Caucasian	Female Negro
Good	16.0	21.5	16.3	18.2
Fair	45.6	49.7	46.7	48.2
Poor	33.5	24.7	31.9	30.0
Gravely ill	3.9	2.2	4.6	2.2
Unknown	1.0	1.9	.5	1.4
Total	100.0	100.0	100.0	100.0
Subjects	331	372	392	407

Source. Ostfeld (1966), p. 88.

strokes in the future). One out of four subjects manifested a hearing loss (which may lead to withdrawal from social interaction); and 30 percent had cataracts, although 95 percent of the subjects had vision within correctable limits. As a group, three-fourths of these respondents should have been taking daily medication, according to Ostfeld, but most did not take any medication. Clearly, old people living in poverty are likely to be in poor health.

Medical Care. Recent advances in medical technology and its availability for all persons are likely to result in persons reaching old age with better health and fewer consequences of earlier acute disease than has been true in the past. However, it also allows persons with weaker health to survive to old age, which may lead to a less-healthy population of old people (Riley et al., 1968). Not surprisingly, in view of the data on the health of older persons, the number of visits to a physician increases with age as does the extent of hospital care. Women over 65 average one more physician visit a year than men of the same age, but women are less likely to be hospitalized than men. When hospitalized, the old person is likely to stay considerably longer than a younger person. And, on the average, persons over 65 spend three times as much for medicines as persons under 65. In 1970 health expenses for medical care were three and one-half times higher for persons over 65 than for persons under 65 ($791 compared to $226 on the average); two-thirds of this cost for the elderly was paid by public programs although medicines, eyeglasses, and other needs are not covered by Medicare or Medicaid programs at present.[2] Clearly, Medicare (federally funded) and Medicaid (state and federal funds) programs have had a significant impact; in 1971, 42 percent of health care expense for the aged was paid by Medicare, 36 percent by Medicaid, 6 percent was paid by private insurance, and the remaining 26 percent was paid by the person himself (Ball, 1972). However, even the 26 percent can be a severe burden, for health expenses begin to rise dramatically about the same time that one's income is cut dramatically by retirement.

Implications. One of the major concomitants of growing old is the growing susceptibility to chronic disease. While many old persons retain good health, many more may be expected to manifest the symptoms of one or more chronic impairments and possibly to be disabled to some degree as a result. And even when there is little apparent disability, decreased hearing, impaired vision, or the pain and reduced mobility resulting from arthritis can isolate the old person from social and psychological stimulation. These social and psychological isolations may enforce some disengagement from social activities and roles. Thus, aging, confounded as it

[2] In New York State, for example, Medicaid pays for eyeglasses and prescription drugs only if the person is on, or eligible for, public assistance.

typically is by disease and the consequences of disease, is often thought to bring about a wide range of changes that, in fact, probably result more from disease and its consequences than from aging per se. In the next section we will discuss one important study that attempted to separate the effects of aging from those of disease by studying very healthy old men. But before concluding here, let us call attention to the importance of good health care for the elderly—that is, health care that not only is adequate and economically available but care that recognizes the differences between the elderly and the young (for example, in the tolerance for medications that is lower in the elderly, and thus poses problems to the physician who may want to prescribe several medications for the various diseases).

Another important aspect of geriatric medical care is that, unlike treating the young, many old persons cannot be restored to optimal health; while this may diminish the motivation of some physicians who seek to "cure" the patient, it does not diminish the importance of high-quality care, medical interest, and continuing research on ways of treating chronic disease. In addition, the extent of disease and its consequences are important to note in the design of nursing homes, retirement homes, or community housing for the aged. Simple architectural and environmental considerations such as a minimal number of stairs, adequate fire protection devices, hand rails along the walls, signs printed larger than usual, amplification attachments for telephones, nonskid floors or carpets, special slow-crossing lights for busy streets, and hand rails alongside toilets and bath tubs are some of the simple conveniences that make life easier for the elderly person. Transportation is typically a problem and, in particular, inexpensive transportation to allow frequent visits to a physician is of great importance. Similarly, water fountains should be provided with disposable cups to facilitate taking medications. And, of course, maximum dignity, self-respect, and independence should be of paramount importance in designing housing for the elderly.

Aging and Disease among Healthy Elderly Subjects

While aging and disease typically occur together, the theories of biological aging presented earlier in this chapter suggest changes in cellular or homeostatic functioning that are a consequence of age alone and do not necessarily involve disease. Thus, in order to uncover the physiological changes which occur with age alone, it is necessary to separate out those changes which are primarily caused by disease. Put another way, what changes occur with aging in the absence of disease? The data we will present make two important points in this regard: (1) many of the changes usually attributed to aging are better seen as the result of disease; and (2) even in the absence of disease there are important changes in physiological functioning with age, although there is far less impairment than is commonly observed among the aged.

This classic study was carried out by Birren, Butler, Greenhouse, Sokoloff, and Yarrow (1963), and the subjects were restudied 11 years later (Granick and Patterson, 1971). Birren and his associates obtained a sample of 47 men between the ages of 65 and 91 who were extremely healthy on the basis of clinical examination. These subjects were given lengthy and extended examinations on a wide range of medical, physiological, psychological, and social variables. The first important (and serendipitous) finding was that this group of very healthy men actually consisted of two different groups: Group 1, whose subjects were in optimal health in every regard, and Group 2, whose subjects were without clinical symptoms of disease but who were found to have mild diseases that were discovered only through intensive medical examination. As will be clear from their data, this difference between those in optimum health ($N = 27$) and those with asymptomatic (subclinical) disease ($N = 20$) proved to be one of the most important differences in the study—on nearly all of the subsequent tests, the healthy group differed from the subclinical disease group in a positive direction. These findings make it abundantly clear that the presence of even a mild degree of chronic disease has major consequences for the aged on a wide variety of functions.

Medical Data. A considerable number of variables showed no difference between the optimally healthy aged men and standards for young men. For example, measures of cerebral blood flow and oxygen consumption during exercise did not differ and the elderly subjects (mean age 71 years) were as vigorous and capable of exercise as young men (mean age 21 years). However, the important measure of cerebral blood flow differed between the young and the Group 2 subjects, suggesting that even their subclinical degree of disease may affect the efficiency of brain functioning.

Electroencephalogram. Even among the most healthy old people, the EEG was found to change with age, although all the patterns of electrical activity in the brain were within the normal range for younger persons. In general, the average frequency spectrum of these old subjects was approximately one cycle slower than the comparable young-adult rate. The EEG of the Group 2 subjects differed from Group 1 in the same direction as the general-age trend. Thus, there was some evidence of slowing down of the electrical activity of the brain with age, and disease seemed to increase this trend.

Psychometric Data. Scores obtained by the subjects in Group 2 were poorer than scores obtained by the optimally healthy group on 21 out of 23 tests of intellectual performance. Thus, one central finding is the negative effect of even mild disease on cognitive performance, particularly on the processes involved in the retrieval of stored information. However, the performance of the elderly subjects (both groups) was superior to the norms for young subjects on measures of verbal intelligence (such as vocabulary) and was also superior to previously studied aged samples (perhaps related to the superior health of both groups of subjects in this study). Nonetheless, both groups were significantly slower in psychomotor speed than young adults, and intelligence measures that involved fast responses were impaired for both groups. Thus, age was found to be most important in measures of the speed of response, such as reaction time, while health was more important than age on verbal measures that involved the retrieval of stored information. These data indicate that one effect of aging (in the absence of disease) is a *slowing down* of reaction time, regardless of the sensory modality (auditory or visual) and regardless of the muscle used for the response (foot, jaw, finger, speech, and so on). This change, since it occurred equally in both Group 1 and 2, seems to be related to aging rather than to disease (and it may be related to the slowing down of the EEG pattern noted above). This general slowing down was also found to be greater when there was a history of greater social and environmental losses; and it was more marked for respondents who were rated as "depressed" in psychiatric terms. Thus, this age-related change is apparently independent of mild disease but is modulated by social and psychological factors.

Personality and Psychosocial Data. The less-healthy group performed consistently less well on several personality tests than the optimally healthy group. That is, even this slight degree of illness affected the degree to which they terminated responses appropriately, adhered to the task goal, and showed an ordered sequence of thought. However, the optimally healthy respondents did not differ noticeably from young adequately functioning persons. The amount of loss suffered by the respondent in his personal environment was also related to psychological and psychiatric functioning. That is, persons who had suffered marked losses, especially the loss of significant persons, tended to perform less adequately on the psychometric and personality tests and to be more likely to have been rated as depressed. In addition, slowing down (on psychometric tests) was related to less adequate daily functioning (i.e., the planful aspects of daily behavior and the nature of social interaction). Perhaps individuals who showed greater slowing down were, in a sense, physiologically "older." Finally, case analysis of personality styles suggested that some individuals adapted more easily to the crises that are associated with aging, while other personality styles (such as the "paranoid reaction") made the adjustment more difficult.

Implications. One of the major findings of this study is the integrated interrelations of various systems (medical, cerebral, psychological, social-psychological, and psychiatric) in the aging person. That is, while no single factor of aging was found, the pattern is one of interacting factors reinforcing or canceling the effects of other factors in a complex interdependency. However, three aspects of the aging process (in the absence of disease) also were particularly striking: (1) the slowing down, or decrease in speed on psychological tests, on reaction time measures, and perhaps related to depression and EEG frequencies through a general decline in cortical excitation; (2) the effect of personality style and the degree of social loss on psychosocial and cognitive performance, depression, self-perceptions, and adaptive responses to aging; and (3) the widespread effects of a mild degree of disease (especially the development of a kind of condition that may precede senility). Overall, the major finding was that for the aged, the presence of even asymptomatic disease increases the statistical dependency of the psychological capacities on the physiological status of the organism; that is, moderate disease leads to a greater correlation between psychological capacities and physiological status, compared with relatively low correlation in the absence of disease. Perhaps, as the discussion of the homeostatic imbalance theories of aging suggested, with advancing age the organism's ability to function becomes more marginal so that it is less able to adapt to stress; thus, even a small amount of disease may upset the balance and many functions suffer.

Eleven-year Follow-up Study. These same subjects were retested after 11 years by a different team of investigators (Granick and Patterson, 1971)—one of the difficulties of longitudinal research. Two major findings stand out from this study of actual age changes. *First,* about half of the original sample had died; most (70 percent) of the Group 2 subjects did not survive, but most (63 percent) of the very healthy Group 1 subjects did survive. Clearly, the mild degree of disease that differentiated these two groups was important in terms of eventual mortality; and most of the differences initially found between the two groups were also related to survival (higher intelligence, faster reaction time, better personality adaptation, and lower social loss). In general, two measures—greater organization of daily behavior (organized, planned living and gratifying pursuits in the living pattern) and not smoking cigarettes—taken together, correctly predicted 80 percent of both the survivors and the nonsurvivors! While it is difficult to be certain whether both of these variables are related to physical health, they seem to indicate the harmful effects of cigarettes as well as the importance of psychosocial factors. Could this indicate a marked psychosomatic factor in mortality? *Second,* among the surviving subjects there was a "remarkably limited amount of change" (p. 132) with age; average age at that point was 81. However, the increased correlation between psychological and physiological functioning was even more marked than previously and there was, in general, a gradual decline in "reserve capacities" of energy and of general physical status (such as a greater vulnerability to psychosocial stresses). Also, the decline in the speed of functioning was, again, found to be related to age. Thus, on the one hand, changes with aging alone seem to be relatively minor (in the absence of disease); but on the other hand, these changes may have wide-reaching effects insofar as they involve increased vulnerability to stress and to disease.

PHYSIOLOGICAL CHANGES WITH AGING

To be sure, some of the most obvious changes with aging are in such physical characteristics as graying or loss of hair, wrinkling of the skin, decrease in height, and loss of teeth; in such sensory modalities as decreased vision and hearing; and the slowing of CNS functioning. Some of these changes have major effects on the concept of self; others, especially decreased perceptual acuity and CNS slowing, have more widespread effects on psychosocial adjustment. There is much individual variation in the extent of these changes since they probably reflect the effects of both disease and aging combined. Also, nutrition, heredity, health care, and variations in wear and tear are each important factors related to the extent of these physical changes in any particular individual. Yet, in general, these changes are age related in the sense that they affect more and more individuals as they age.

Since these changes are typically associated with aging, they tend to be seen as negative changes in our society. However, it may be noted that smooth, unwrinkled, clear skin *could* be negatively valued since it may indicate inexperience, unfamiliarity with life's pain and pleasures, and irresponsibility. And it is fascinating to study an old face and to try to imagine what history might be written in those wrinkles and folds that are so uniquely individual to that face.

Physical Characteristics

Bromley (1966) reports that the skeleton is fully formed by the early twenties and there is no change in individual bones after that time. Yet there may be a slight loss in stature in old age because of changes in the discs between the spinal vertebrae caused by changes in collagen with age. This loss of stature may be exaggerated by stooping from muscular weakness; and it is also exaggerated by the population trend toward increased stature among younger persons. Also, with advancing age, the chemical composition of the bones changes, perhaps because of changes in calcium metabolism, so that the risk of breakage increases in later life. And, of course, the skeleton of old persons reflects previous damage or disease. Diseases of the joints (such as arthritis) probably are the result of wear and the age-related changes in collagen.

Loss of teeth is a frequent mark of entry into old age and, undoubtedly, the surgery required and the adjustment to dentures may be a time of crisis or at least readjustment of the self-concept. Although advances in dentistry have been marked in the prevention and treatment of decay, which may decrease the proportion of elderly persons who have lost all or most of their teeth, these advances have often meant that adults lose fewer teeth to decay so that they will lose them later to the other major dental disease, *periodontal* (gum) *disease.* Unfortunately, little mass education is currently being devoted to informing young and middle-aged adults about the prevention and treatment of this major cause of tooth loss. When it begins, and it generally does to some degree in all adults, surgical treatment may be required to prevent tooth loss. Certainly, natural teeth are far more effective than dentures for chewing, but sound teeth in old age require lifetime care, proper diet, and occasional repair. Perhaps the failure of teeth is basically because of their evolutionary selection under different dietary conditions and when the average life span was much shorter. They may have evolved to last through the child-bearing years, but now we want them to last twice as long!

One of the most apparent changes in old age is the increased paleness, change in texture, loss of elasticity, dryness, and appearance of spots of pigmentation on the skin; many of these changes are attributed to changes in collagen with age. As noted earlier in the chapter, these age changes in this fibrous protein are important symptoms of aging, but it is not clear to what degree they are a basic cause of aging; certainly, they are a cause of many of the signs of aging however. *Collagen* is one of the components of connective tissue and is found throughout the body; connective tissues function in many important ways, such as mechanical support of the body and in repair of injury. Collagen undergoes continuous change with age and has received much research attention; although its changes remain irreversible, the nature of those changes is slowly becoming understood. In addition to its effects on stature, joint diseases, and skin changes, collagen aging also causes wounds to heal less quickly.

Compounding the loss of elasticity of the skin, the amount of subcutaneous fat and some of the muscle bulk built up during middle age (unless one cuts back the intake of food to match the reduced exercise and work of typical middle-age life) begins to decline, so that in old age the skin is left hanging in folds and wrinkles. Although older persons tend to need less food because of decreased exercise, adequate amounts of necessary nutritional requirements are important to prevent excessive weight loss, especially when the person is living in some degree of social isolation as in widowhood. Much of the function of eating is social, and eating alone is not only likely to be lonely but also to be ignored or avoided. Thus, an important service to the aged person who lives alone are hot lunches at Senior Centers or programs such as "Meals on Wheels," which bring one hot meal a day and a bit of companionship.

These changes in body image certainly affect one's self-concept, confidence, and sense of value. In addition, changes in the voice, changes in hair color or the loss of hair may affect one's self-image and mark oneself as "old." Bromley (1966) suggests that the gradual decline in secretion of the adrenal glands after the late twenties may be related to the loss of hair, although blood circulation in the scalp may also be involved. Gray hair results from the absence of pigment in the hair, presumably because the melanocytes that provide the pigment granules for the hair eventually run out of these granules. Genetic factors have long been recognized to determine hair pigmentation and loss of hair in men. Changes in the voice, which is often less powerful and more restricted in range in old age, seem to result from gradual bodily senescence that may limit the capacity and control of expelled air, from upper respiratory congestion, or from atrophy of the muscles of the larynx (Timiras, 1972). Speech may also slow down somewhat, probably as a result of the general slowing down of the CNS.

The digestive system is the system least affected by ordinary aging (Bromley, 1966), although an age-related decline in sensitivity to smell or taste may decrease the appetite. In particular, there is no evidence of an increase in constipation with age, despite the impression (and stereotypes supported by TV commercials) that old people may complain more about it. These complaints may reflect cohort factors of rigid toilet habits stressed during their childhood rather than actual constipation, since there are marked individual differences in bowel function. Also, Bromley reports an increase in red blood cells and hemoglobin in later life, suggesting little general need for "iron" tonics for the aging.

Changes have been found in sleep patterns with age, although sleep time as well as the proportion of REM (rapid eye movement) and non-REM sleep is fairly constant to age 60. Spontaneous interruption of sleep, relatively infrequent through adolescence, increases with age and the amount of time spent awake in bed increases after the fourth decade; thus the aged often compensate by spending more time in bed. Also, Stage 4 sleep, the deepest, is virtually absent and the amount of REM sleep begins to decline in old age (Timiras, 1972).

Sense Organs

Older persons are more likely than younger persons to show decrements in at least four of the five senses. While it is not clear how much of this decrement is from aging alone, the change is at least partly the result of higher thresholds of stimulation required for perception, suggesting that the sense receptors become less efficient with age. Thus in general, the aged require higher levels of stimulation in vision, audition, taste, and smell for the sense receptors to perform with acuity equal to a young person's senses. These decrements, especially in vision and hearing, are important to note since they influence not only the individual's ability to function in the physical environment but also may create a kind of sensory deprivation and social isolation that may have important psychological and social effects.

Vision. Several aspects of vision decline with age. Visual *acuity* (the ability to see clearly at a distance) typically reaches its maximum in the late teens, remains fairly constant until 45-50, then declines gradually; less than 10 percent of persons under 45 have vision poorer than 20/70, while 40 percent of the men and 60 percent of the women over 65 have poorer vision than 20/70 (National Center for Health Statistics, 1964). In addition, the threshold for *adaptation to darkness* rises with age, indicating a decline in the ability to see clearly when illumination is low (as in night driving) and, in general, the ability of light to penetrate the lens, cornea, and vitreous humor of the eye declines with age (and is markedly affected by the presence of cataracts, a change in the lens making it opaque to light). Also, *accommodation* of the lens of the eye to focus on near objects decreases from age 5 to age 60 at a constant rate (Hofstetter, 1944); this is commonly noted in the growing necessity for bifocal glasses or reading glasses in middle age—as some individuals describe it, "My arms seemed to grow shorter so that I couldn't hold the newspaper far enough away to read it!"

Hearing. Several studies report a marked loss of hearing among older persons, especially in the highest frequencies; also the auditory threshold declines regularly with age (Weiss, 1959). Long-term exposure to noise is probably a factor in addition to probable lowered sensitivity of the auditory receptors. It has also been found that the ability to understand speech decreases with age in a manner that implies some loss in auditory perception by the CNS, rather than just changes in auditory thresholds (Melrose, Welsh, and Luterman, 1963).

Taste and Smell. Although Bromley (1966) reports that there are degenerative changes in smell and taste receptors, Riley, Foner, and Associates' (1968) review of the data found conflicting evidence but suggests that there is an increase in the *threshold* for taste and smell, similar to the threshold found for vision and hearing. That is, sensory perception generally becomes less efficient, requiring higher levels of stimulation in old age than is the case for younger persons. This may be partly responsible for the clinically noted increase in complaints about food among the elderly.

Pain. The clinical impression is that sensitivity to pain may decrease with age, partly because many older persons experience more frequent pain from chronic disease (such as arthritis) than do younger persons and because the threshold for other kinds of stimulation increases with age. However, empirical studies have not validated this impression. Perhaps the (expected) higher threshold for pain sensitivity is offset by an actual lowered tolerance of pain—at least in the laboratory.

Central Nervous System (CNS)

Several neurophysiological changes are found with age. As we noted above, the speed of CNS functioning slows with age, and this change is one of the few age-related changes that seem to occur independently of (but are exaggerated by) disease. Also, since cells in the CNS do not reproduce themselves, it is widely accepted that when neurons are lost they are not replaced; thus, cell death, lack of oxygen, and changes within the cells could reduce the efficiency of the brain's functioning. There is evidence that the weight of the brain decreases with age (Himwich and Himwich, 1959) and that the number of cells in the cortical layers of the cerebral cortex decreases with age (Brody, 1955); however, adequate measurement from a representative sample is obviously difficult to obtain, and these observations remain open to question.

The slowing of the CNS with age is most apparent in tests of *reaction time*. That is, the time between a signal and the subject's response has been consistently found by many investigators to increase slightly with age (Welford, 1959); we noted this earlier in the study by Birren et al. (1963). Clearly, reaction time involves a number of aspects of CNS functioning (e.g., perception, attention, short-term memory, and transmission of neural impulse), but it is not clear whether all of these processes slow with age or whether the slowing occurs only in some of the processes. For example, the *pupillary reflex* to light stimulation slows with age; Feinberg and Podolak (1965) report a slowing of .040 second between subjects aged 15 and 65. Such a slowing of an autonomic reflex indicates that at least some of this slowing may occur in the transmission of the neural impulse—perhaps caused by physical-chemical changes at the synapse (the juncture between two neurons), by reduced neural excitability, by fewer functioning neural cells, or by changes in subcortical centers (Birren, 1964).

A provocative hypothesis about the change in the CNS with age is that there is a disturbance of the signal resulting from interfering "noise" in the neural transmission; that is, a decrease in the ratio of signal-to-noise. This may be caused by a weakening of the signal strength (as suggested by the heightened threshold of sense receptors noted above) or by an increase in the amount of random background activity ("noise"). This decrease in signal-to-noise ratio might result from fewer functioning cells, from lower signal strength (decreasing the signal aspect of the ratio); and it might result from greater random activity, or from longer after-effects of neural activity (increasing the noise in the system). Currently, the precise nature of the changes in neural activity is not known, but one day it might be possible to treat these changes by some sort of drugs to reduce the neurological effects of aging.

There are several additional factors which may affect the functioning of the CNS with advancing age, although they are too complex for discussion here (cf. Timiras, 1972). For example, changes in hormones that affect the level of brain excitability, or changes with age in such cell components as nucleic acids (RNA and DNA), amino acids, proteins, and enzymes have been suggested as possible factors affecting the efficiency of the central nervous system. Another important factor is *oxygen deficiency* (hypoxia) resulting from impaired circulation of the blood (resulting from arteriosclerosis and the accumulation of collagen in the cerebral blood vessels). It has been suggested that the changes involved in adaptation to high altitudes resemble aging changes in some respects; and experimental administration of oxygen to senile subjects seems to improve their performance on several psychometric tests (Jacobs, Winter, Alvis, and Small, 1969).

Certainly, the effects of CNS changes are likely to be widespread and to influence a range of behaviors from intelligence test performance to driving skills. And, in general, regardless of the basic cause of CNS changes with age, all behavior mediated by the central nervous system can be expected to show the characteristic slowing with advancing age.

Sensorimotor Skills

Since only part of the increased reaction time has been explained by the slowing of the CNS, an increase in *movement time* (the time required to physically respond) may also occur. And indeed, studies reviewed by Riley et al. 1968) indicate that, in general, there is a larger age-related increase in the time required for complex sensorimotor tasks (such as tracking a moving target or adjusting dials) than in reaction time alone. One important practical example of this increase in reaction and movement time may be automobile driving. Drivers over 65 are involved in a higher percentage of accidents and are in more accidents per miles driven than middle-aged drivers; they are also more likely to be found at fault (Figure 8.7); however, young drivers have the highest accident rate of all (McFarland, Tune, and Welford, 1964). In terms of accidents on the job, Bromley (1966) suggests that the cause may often be inexperience for the younger worker but slowness to respond for the older person. And Birren (1964) points out that with age there are more accidents resulting from rapid evasive movements or falls and fewer resulting from poor judgment; however, he reports little change in occupational performance in general up to age 60 or 65. Of course, many successful workers are likely to move into jobs with less time-pressure and more emphasis on past experience or personal contacts so that slowness in reaction and movement time would be of little consequence to their job.

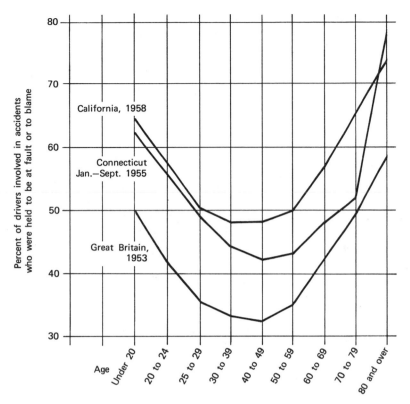

Figure 8.7
Drivers held to be at fault or to blame in accidents. (Source. McFarland et al., 1964, p. 191. Reprinted with permission.)

Other factors that might slow performance on sensorimotor tasks in the laboratory include cautiousness and avoidance of unnecessary risks; and it may be that these strategies tend to be adopted by the elderly as an effective means of coping with decrements of perceptual ability and response time in their daily environment. Thus, these coping strategies may hinder performance on laboratory tests while they allow the person to deal effectively with his real environment at the same time.

Summary and Implications

In sum, these data indicate that with advanced age the body becomes less efficient in perceiving, processing, and responding to external stimuli. While it is not clear to what degree these changes may be caused by aging per se or by the greater incidence of chronic disease among the aged, these findings clearly suggest important differences between the typical old person and the typical young or middle-aged person. Certainly it is important to note these changes in terms of the kind of physical environments that are better suited to the slightly slowed pace and heightened threshold for perceiving stimuli than the fast-paced, stimulus-overload world of young adults. And perhaps as the pace of life continues to speed up, especially in urban areas, the elderly may find life more and more difficult because of the conflict between the rapid pace of change and the slowing of speed and behavior. Perhaps this conflict is somehow involved in the trend toward "increased interiority" discussed in Chapter 7. However, because of a lack of experience, skill, and status, the younger person is likely to be working near the limit of his physiological capacities, while the aged person (with less reserve capacities and greater vulnerability to stress) is likely to have developed compensations to function effectively within the limits of his decreased physiological capabilities. Also, these capacities typically decline so gradually that the compensations are largely automatic except when disease or injury brings a sudden and drastic change.

In the concluding section of this chapter we will consider the cognitive changes that occur with advancing age. Some of these changes will follow from the physiological changes we have discussed up to this point; others will shed some additional light on the nature of the physiological changes that occur within the aging human organism.

CHANGES IN INTELLECTUAL PROCESSES WITH AGING

We used an example of intellectual change in the first chapter to illustrate the difficulties involved in research in adulthood. Specifically, the example demonstrated the kind of error that may result from cross-sectional studies of age differences in intelligence (which confound age and cohort effects) and the kind of error involved in longitudinal studies (which confound age with selective dropout and other experimental factors). It may be recalled from that example that cross-sectional studies have found a decline in scores on intelligence tests with age after about age 30, but that differences in the amount of education received by subjects of different ages may largely explain this decline in intelligence test scores. Also, longitudinal studies have found little or no decline in intelligence test scores up to at least age 50; subjects who were initially above average tend to improve slightly with age, while those of average intelligence or below tend to decline somewhat in performance with age. Thus, the data on age changes in intelligence are far from definitive; and, as we discussed in Chapter 1, they point up a central difficulty in obtaining empirical data on age differences in adulthood.

However, we are now interested in a more detailed discussion of the specific nature of intellectual changes with age. That is, we are interested in the effects of the physiological changes we have discussed in this chapter on such intellectual processes as IQ test performance, memory, learning, thinking, and creativity. Do these processes change in predictable ways with advancing age? If so, what are some of the plausible explanations of the origin of these changes?

Individual differences in intellectual functioning are, of course, marked; and with age, these individual differences tend to become more pronounced as initially more-able subjects tend to improve slightly while less-able subjects tend to decline faster. In addition, the effects of disease and other noncognitive factors such as education, social class, personal losses, and even nearness to death act to add to the differences between individuals since persons close to death, persons suffering disease, or persons surviving psychosocial losses tend to decline in IQ performance while others remain higher. However, with the onset of senility (which may be seen as a chronic disease) individual differences tend to vanish; memory (especially recent memory) declines markedly, cognitive ability drops sharply, and creativity may be almost nonexistent. Thus the findings we will discuss do not apply to persons who are senile since they are regarded as a different population from the "normal" aged in studies of intellectual functioning.

Simplifying considerably, there are two types of intelligence tests: one, typically used in the United States, measures the "quantity" of intelligence (IQ) and is useful in predicting school performance, for example; we will discuss this measure in some detail. The other type of test measures the process of thinking, and Piaget has developed a series of tasks that children solve in differing ways as they grow older. Little attention has been given to possible changes in these processes of thinking with aging until recently; but the data so far are quite interesting. For example, Papalia, True, and Salverson (1972) report that aged persons tend to "regress" with age to less-advanced thinking processes (i.e., "concrete operations" characteristic of school-age children) on these tasks. Piaget (1972) has reported that his laboratory has found similar "regression" from "formal" to "concrete operations." This observation is highly suggestive and deserves much further research as to what lies behind it.

Age and Intelligence

While the "classic aging pattern" of IQ test performance is a decline with advancing age, several of the subtests on the standard IQ test that measure *verbal* abilities show little or no change with age; and much of the decline is accounted for by declines on the subtests that measure *performance* aspects of intelligence. "Verbal" scores are based on tests that require the subject to verbally answer questions such as defining a series of words (the "vocabulary" subtest), solving arithmetic story problems ("arithmetic"), or determining elements that two objects have in common ("similarities"). "Performance" scores are based on those subtests where the subject is asked to physically do something—such as to demonstrate psychomotor skill by filling in symbols that he is instructed correspond to numbers ("digit symbol") or to perform perceptual integrative tasks such as putting pieces of a puzzle together ("object assembly"). The performance subtests differ from the verbal ones in another important way than the verbal-performance distinction; the performance tests are scored on the basis of the amount of *time* required to perform the task so that a rapid performance is given a higher score than one with a slower time.

Thus, the general decline in intellectual functioning is largely a result of the declines in performance aspects of the standard intelligence tests, which may result from *slower* performances. That is, the slowing down of reaction time and other CNS functions with age may account for much of the decline in intellectual *performance* noted among elderly subjects.

Verbal subtests generally do not show a marked decline with age and, for superior subjects, often increase with age. In particular, "vocabulary" functions are noted for their stability with age (in nonsenile samples). That is, stored information that is recalled with no direct time-pressure seems to be least affected with age. Other aspects of verbal intelligence are not quite as stable, however, and the pattern of age changes is rather complex. One important distinction, proposed by Reed and Reitan (1963) and supported by their data, is that *stored information* is relatively unaffected by advancing age, while *problem solving ability* does show age changes. This suggests that there are changes in thinking processes to the point where finding solutions to new problems where past experience is no help becomes more difficult for older subjects—at least on IQ tests.

In sum, age changes in intelligence have received considerable empirical study that has clarified the initial findings of intellectual decline with age. Much of that decline is a result of a slowing down of performance speed, which seems to be a relatively pure age-related change; and much of the remaining decline is probably the result of changes in solving new and unfamiliar problems for which accumulated experience is little help. This implies that the typical elderly person is likely to be somewhat "slow" at intellectual tasks, somewhat impaired at mastering new problems in his daily life (such as Medicare forms), but relatively unimpaired in many aspects of his ordinary intellectual functioning. Certainly, these changes would be unlikely to affect a typical person's occupational functioning at least up to age 60 (Birren, 1964, p. 148). In general, the older person would be likely to select situations and tasks where accumulated experience and knowledge is important instead of tasks that involve time pressures and the development of new approaches; thus his performance might be more effective than a young person's performance. However, health factors and, as we will discuss in the next chapter, nearness to death (perhaps because CNS functions are highly sensitive to physiological changes leading to death) often bring a sharp decline in intellectual abilities. Thus, the aged population would consist of persons who are quite healthy (showing little or no intellectual decline) and persons who are suffering disease or nearing death (showing marked intellectual decline); this combination of two different aged populations in any cross-sectional sample may well account for much of the decline in intellectual performance in the later years (Riegel and Riegel, 1972). Nonetheless, slowing down seems to clearly affect intellectual performance, although it is not specifically a cognitive change. Let us now turn to a discussion of memory and learning (and later to thinking and creativity) since these processes may also be affected not only by the slowing down but also by the older person's lessened ability to solve new unfamiliar problems.

Memory and Learning Changes with Age

As Botwinick (1970) points out, it is impossible to separate memory and learning skills since most tests of learning involve memory and memories nearly always involve learning. For example, memory may be thought of in three phases: acquisition, retention, and retrieval. Acquisition involves the stimulus registering on a sense receptor and registering in memory, which is essentially a learning process. Conversely, a learning test involves that memory being retained and retrieved upon command. Thus, changes in memory with age are likely to affect learning; and changes in learning with age are likely to affect recent memories (although not necessarily old memories). Further complicating studies in this area is the observation that a decline in performance ability (specifically a slowing down in movement time) may impair an old person's functioning on learning or memory experiments.

Memory. Two types of memory need to be distinguished since age affects them differently: *long-term memory* and *immediate recall*. Long-term memory is generally found to be highly resistant to the effects of aging (except, of course, senility); "vocabulary" skills on IQ tests, as well as one's personal history, past experience, and knowledge tend not to be lost with age. And even when senility causes memory loss, the old "rehearsed" memories that are often recalled and reviewed are the last memories to be lost. Based on his review of the data, Botwinick (1967) points out that it is not correct to conclude that with advancing age there is a progressive loss of memory; instead, the data indicate that *memory decline describes more and more persons as they get older* since many persons retain a sound memory regardless of their age. There are several theories about memory loss: that memories are lost through *disuse*; that memories are lost through the *interference* of other memories in the large store of memories that is accumulated with age; and that *neurochemical change* or loss of cells in the CNS is responsible for memory loss. Currently, the interference theory in combination with neurochemical factors seems to be favored; that is, the amount of stored information increases with age while the neural changes (loss of cells, increased chemical noise, and general slowing down) leads to slower and less-efficient processing of the stored information with age. However, we know almost nothing about the way in which memories are "stored" or "recalled" so that, at best, theories of either memory or forgetting are only plausible hypotheses. It seems that memory results from some kind of chemical changes in cells that may involve RNA and DNA molecules; and DNA molecules have recently been found to be selectively lost from brain cells of 10-year-old dogs; such a loss of genetic material would be likely to impair brain function (Johnson and Strehler, 1972). However, the mechanism behind the prevalence of memory loss with advancing age is unknown; certainly health factors are important and even a mild degree of vascular disease has been found to be related to a decline in memory ability (Klonoff and Kennedy, 1966; Spieth, 1964).

Acquisition or Retrieval of Memory? While the preceding discussion dealt with memory loss at the storage and recall stages, a great amount of data has also been collected on *short-term memory* of recently learned material. These laboratory experiments deal primarily with the acquisition and registration stage of memory, although retention and retrieval are also involved. In general, these studies have found a decline in immediate recall with advancing age; but it is not clear whether this decline is a result of impairment in the *acquisition* of the memory or in the *retention* and *retrieval* of the memory. Several studies of acquisition in elderly persons and a series of studies on rats (in which the acquisition of learning was hindered or facilitated using chemical agents) suggest that interference with the acquisition process may be much of the cause of the decline in short-term memory with advancing age (Botwinick, 1970). That is, the older person may have more trouble remembering tasks in a psychology laboratory because he has more difficulty getting the memory into storage than a young person has. However, three recent studies have independently concluded that the age-related decline in memory is a problem of retrieval rather than a problem of acquisition (Johnson, 1972; Thomas, 1972; Waugh, 1972). For example, Johnson found that young subjects perform better than old subjects on "free recall," but there is no difference on "cued recall" or "recognition." Thus, remembering (retrieving) the words was easier for the young person than the old when no cues were given to aid in the recall, but both groups did equally well (and better) when cues were given; this indicates that the memory was equally well acquired but was harder to retrieve for the older subjects. Yet these data do not deny that the acquisition process may not be more easily interfered with (by faster stimulus exposure rate or alternating visual and auditory inputs, for example) in older subjects, although optimally acquisition may work as well in old as in young persons.

Learning. This decline in short-term memory seems rather clearly to indicate learning deficiencies with advancing age. However, pure learning deficits with old age are not particularly clear. Instead, performance factors seem to be of major importance in describing the declining ability of the aged in learning experiments. For example, many studies have found a decline in paired-associate learning with age. In such experiments the subject is to learn which response is associated with each stimulus as in the random pairing of nonsense syllables on a "memory drum"—the decline is in the speed with which he learns a predetermined number of such pairings. Other studies have found a similar slowness in acquiring a conditioned response among elderly subjects; and once acquired, the conditioned response is readily extinguished. In both cases, the slowing with age would impair the performance of the elderly subject and thus the decline in learning ability may reflect a decline in performance ability instead of learning. In response to this critique of the early studies on learning among the elderly, more sophisticated methodology has been used (such as self-pacing, which allows the subject to select the speed at which he must respond in order for the answer to be correct). These studies have suggested that there may be some learning deficit, although the results place more emphasis on the performance deficit than on the learning deficit (Botwinick, 1970).

Implications. By this time it may be clear that the age-related slowing of the CNS is a major change since its implications are legion. Indeed, many of the social, psychological, and physiological changes with aging may be understood as reflecting this change, which probably has its origin in the physical-chemical functioning of neural cells. For example, the slowing of tempo in activities and the tendency to rely on one's own speed rather than an external pace reminds us of the disengagement process and the increased interiority of the personality discussed in Chapter 7. At the same time, it points out the importance of the adaptive qualities of the person in compensating for these varied physiological changes. One practical implication of these findings is that health, education, and individual differences are more important than age alone in the ability (and interest) for continued learning. To be sure, comfortable, rehearsed skills may be more attractive than learning a new set of skills (for example, on the job); but if retraining and continuing education occur during the early and middle-adult years (such as during leisure time or during sabbatical leaves from the job), there is little reason an elderly person could not learn as well as a young person. Certainly up to age 60-65, there is little decline in learning or memory ability; factors of motivation, interest, and lack of recent educational experience are probably more important in learning complex knowledge than age per se. Learning may just take a bit longer for the elderly and occur more at the individual's own speed instead of at an external and fast pace. Of course, the presence of cerebral vascular disease, and especially senility, may bring marked changes in these abilities.

Thinking, Creativity, and Age

In this final section we will build upon the previous discussions of general changes in intellectual functioning and of changes in learning and memory as they culminate in thinking processes and creativity. It is apparent that major impairment of either learning or memory would have consequences for the ability to think or to create; however, older persons would be likely to have developed ways to counteract the slight loss of memory or difficulty in learning new material so that their daily functioning would be impaired only slightly if at all. In fact, some of these compensating strategies may be a partial explanation for the findings we have described; for instance, well-established approaches to problems may serve the individual quite well in daily life but interfere with finding novel solutions to the kind of laboratory tests devised by psychologists.

This introduction helps to provide the perspective for describing the experimental data on changes in thinking with age since these changes may be considerably more apparent inside the laboratory than outside it; yet they also help to understand the changes in intellectual processes with age. Thus, elderly subjects have been found to show decrements in *concept attainment* that are similar to those for nonverbal measures of intelligence. For example, Wetherick (1965) found that elderly subjects tended to take less advantage of negative information and were less likely to change concepts that were not adequate. Problem-solving ability, as noted earlier, has also been found to show declines among elderly subjects. Redundancy, difficulty in handling new concepts, and inability to make use of efficient strategies in problem-solving are other aspects of thinking processes that have been found to characterize elderly subjects (Botwinick, 1970).

Two other characteristics of thought processes of elderly persons that are commonly thought to be apparent from daily observations of aged individuals—rigidity and concreteness—are somewhat more difficult to observe in the laboratory, however. For example, elderly persons are sometimes described as being more rigid or more cautious in their thinking than young persons. One interpretation of these changes is that the old person sacrifices speed for accuracy ("rigidity"?) and sacrifices abstraction for functional conceptualizations ("concreteness"?). That is, when faced with various learning or memory experiments, the old person's adaptive strategies prove somewhat dysfunctional; this is not to deny greater rigidity among old persons but, instead, is an attempt to put this finding in some perspective. However, it may even be incorrect to say that older persons become more cautious and avoid taking risks because the situation seems to be more complex. Botwinick (1969) found that old subjects will take a "no risk" option more frequently than young subjects on a questionnaire; but when there is no "no risk" option available, they will take the same extent of risk as younger subjects. This suggests that the "cautiousness" may be a tendency to avoid risky decisions (perhaps because of a fear of failure), but when a decision cannot be avoided, the elderly are as likely to take a "high risk" solution to a problem as young respondents.

Conceptualization ability would seem to be clearly associated with creativity; and insofar as conceptualization ability declines in old age, we would expect a similar decline in creativity. However, the definition of creativity, let alone the measurement of it, is a very difficult task. What is *creativity*? How can it be measured? If we were to give a lump of clay to an old person would he make less creative use of it than a young person? Are not some of the most brilliant creative works produced late in life; and are not some of the most brilliant minds a result of extensive experience, years of wrestling with ideas in search of an answer and a vast amount of slowly accumulated knowledge? For example, philosophers who had long lives reached their peak of creativity, on the average, between the ages of 60 and 64 (Lehman, 1953). However, other kinds of creativity, such as Einstein's, seem to be a result of discovering a new conceptualization and a new way of viewing an old problem—abilities that may benefit from relatively little experience with old ways of seeing the problem. And, of course, some creative individuals are more creative in their ordinary works than most of us will be in our greatest work. Can there then be a generalized description of changes in creativity with age; and if so, how can creativity be measured?

Two divergent approaches to this problem have been formulated and, as might be expected, these different definitions have led to divergent findings about the age changes in creativity. The pioneering work in this area was done by Lehman (1953) who measured "creativity" by the percentage of *high-quality output* produced by great men during each year of their lives. He found that for most fields the rate of production of superior work occurred during the decade of the thirties (Figure 8.8). The rate then declines gradually with age so that about 80 percent of their superior work is completed by age 50—leaving 20 percent to be produced after age 50. The rate for worthy but less-superior work was found to peak somewhat later, and the decline through the later years of life was more gradual than for high-quality work. More recently, Lehman (1962) has examined the creative rates for high-quality productions of a variety of scientists (medicine, atomic energy, astronomy, mathematics, and botany)

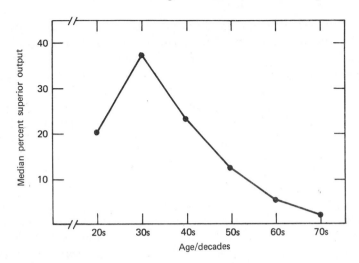

Figure 8.8
Percentage of superior output as a function of age. This is a generalized curve representing a combination of various fields of endeavor and various estimates of quality. Data are from Lehman (1953), Table 34. (Source. Botwinick, 1967, Figure 20. Reprinted with permission from Cognitive Processes in Maturity and Old Age, copyright © 1967 by Springer Publishing Company, Inc.)

—and even psychologists (1966)—with similar results: a peak in the early years followed by a decline with age. He suggests that this decline with age is probably the result of a number of interacting factors, including

> . . . a decrement in physical vigor and sensory capacity, more illness, glandular changes, more preoccupation with practical concerns, less favorable conditions for concentration, weakened intellectual curiosity, more mental disorders, and an accumulation of unfavorable habits. . . . Moreover, the individual who already has achieved prestige and recognition may try less hard thereafter to achieve further success (Lehman, 1962).

In contrast, Dennis (1966) has studied the *total productivity* (not just the "high quality" works) of creative persons in the sciences, the arts, and other scholars. He found the decade of the forties was the most productive, or only slightly less than most productive, period of life. For scholars in the humanities, the decade of the seventies was as productive as the decade of the forties. Scientists showed a significant decline in the decade of the seventies, while the decade from 20-29 was the least productive. For artists, the decline was even sharper; and only for this group was the decade of the twenties more productive than the seventies (Figure 8.9). It would appear that a number of factors other than intellectual ability are involved in these trends. For example, the amount of time required to produce a creative work is probably much longer in a scholarly field

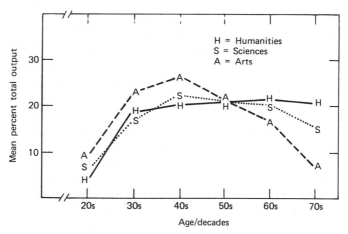

Figure 8.9

Percentage of total output as a function of age. The humanities, sciences, and arts are represented by the means of several specific disciplines. Data are from Dennis (1966), Table 1. (Source. Botwinick, 1967, Figure 21. Reprinted with permission from Cognitive Processes in Maturity and Old Age, copyright © 1967 by Springer Publishing Company Inc.)

than in the arts; also the amount of study required for scholarly or scientific fields may be considerably longer than for the arts; in addition, the contributions of assistants may greatly benefit the creative productivity of middle-aged scientists and scholars, but be of little importance to the creative productions of artists.

Thus, depending on whether one defines creativity as a person's major and most superior works (Lehman), or as a person's total productivity (Dennis), the graphs for creativity differ considerably; also whether one examines creativity in one field or another, the peaks and changes in the graphs differ. For example, Manniche and Falk's (1957) study of the age during which Nobel prizewinners (1901-1950) did their work corresponds to Lehman's findings for physics and chemistry but averages in the forties for medicine.

However, regardless of the way in which creativity is defined, the peaks and declines are, perhaps, more the result of noncognitive factors than intellectual changes. That is, following some major creative work, the scientist would be likely to be given greater responsibilities (department chairman or director of research, for instance), to become more involved in more scientific and governmental committees, and to find that there is less time and energy left over for creative productivity (Bjorksten, 1946). Nonetheless, there may also be some significant cognitive factors involved that incline the younger person toward more unique or novel solutions to problems—not necessarily because his mind works differently (although that may be a factor also) but because he has a fresh perspective and has not learned to think about the field in conventional ways. At the same time, the older person might benefit from his accumulated knowledge and perspective (as well as from research grants and assistants).

Undoubtedly, as with all of the changes we have detailed in this chapter on intellectual processes, health is perhaps a paramount consideration. For example, not only is one's potential creativity cut short by incapacitating disease or death before old age (that in itself tends to push the creativity graph toward the young ages when *all* creative persons are alive), but also failing health can reduce the time and energy, as well as the cognitive abilities, that may be devoted to creativity. Nonetheless, these data on creativity reaching its peak in young adulthood (or the decade of the thirties) imply that if one began work at an earlier age, more creative production might result (assuming that sufficient knowledge could be accumulated to produce a creative work). However, the current trend in our society is toward an *increase* in the age of entry into careers, raising the probability that some of the potentially most creative years might be passed during the training preparatory to independent creative work. Perhaps this is inevitable in a rapidly advancing technological society, but many students wonder how creative they might be if they were not spending so much time in school learning the necessary skills for their profession.

References

Ball, Robert M. 1972. Living With Social Security. *Geriatrics/1972.* (Published by *Medical World News.*)

Benet, Sula. 1971. Why They Live to be 100, or Even Older, in Abkhasia. *New York Times Magazine,* December 26, 1971, 3ff.

Birren, James E. 1960. Behavioral Theories of Aging. In Nathan W. Shock (Ed.), *Aging: Some Social and Biological Aspects.* Publication No. 65. Washington, D.C.: American Association for the Advancement of Science.

Birren, James E. 1964. *The Psychology of Aging.* Englewood Cliffs, N.J.: Prentice-Hall.

Birren, James E.; Butler, Robert N.; Greenhouse, Samuel W.; Sokoloff, Louis; and Yarrow, Marian R. (Eds.) **1963.** *Human Aging: A Biological and Behavioral Study.* Publication No. (HSM) 71-9051. Washington, D.C.: U.S. Government Printing Office.

Bjorksten, J. 1946. The Limitation of Creative Years. *Scientific Monthly, 62,* 94.

Blumenthal, Herman T., and Berns, Aline W. 1964. Autoimmunity In Aging. In Bernard L. Strehler (Ed.), *Advances in Gerontological Research.* Vol. 1. New York: Academic Press.

Botwinick, Jack. 1967. *Cognitive Processes in Maturity and Old Age.* New York: Springer.

Botwinick, Jack. 1969. Disinclination to Venture Response versus Cautiousness in Responding: Age Differences. *Journal of Genetic Psychology, 115,* 55–62.

Botwinick, Jack. 1970. Geropsychology. *Annual Review of Psychology, 21,* 239–272.

Brody, Harold. 1955. Organization of the Cerebral Cortex. III. A Study of Aging in the Human Cerebral Cortex. *Journal of Comparative Neurology, 102,* 511–556.

Bromley, D. B. 1966. *The Psychology of Human Ageing.* Baltimore: Penguin.

Brotman, Herman B. 1972. One in Ten: A Statistical Portrait. *Geriatrics/1972.* (Published by *Medical World News.*)

Comfort, Alex. 1964. *Ageing: The Biology of Senescence.* New York: Holt, Rinehart and Winston.

Comfort, Alex. 1968. Feasibility in Age Research. *Nature, 217,* 320–322.

Comfort, Alex. 1972. The Prospects of Longevity. Paper presented at the meeting of the Gerontological Society, San Juan, Puerto Rico, December, 1972.

Cristofalo, V. J. 1970. Metabolic Aspects of Aging in Diploid Human Cells. In E. Holečková and V. J. Cristofalo (Eds.), *Aging in Cell and Tissue Culture.* New York: Plenum Press.

Curtis, Howard J. 1966. *Biological Mechanisms of Aging.* Springfield, Ill.: Charles C Thomas.

Curtis, Howard J.; Tilley, John; and Crowley, Cathryn. 1964. The Elimination of Chromosome Aberrations in Liver Cells by Cell Division. *Radiation Research, 22,* 730–734.

Demoise, Charles F., and Conrad, Robert A. 1972. Effects of Age and Radiation Exposure on Chromosomes in a Marshall Island Population. *Journal of Gerontology, 27*(2), 197–201.

*****Dennis, Wayne. 1966.** Creative Productivity Between the Ages of 20 and 80 Years. *Journal of Gerontology, 21*(1), 1–8.

Dovenmuehle, Robert H. 1970. Aging versus Illness. In Erdman Palmore (Ed.), *Normal Aging.* Durham, N.C.: Duke University Press.

Dovenmuehle, Robert H.; Busse, Ewald W.; and Newman, Gustave. 1961. Physical Problems of Older People. *Journal of the American Geriatrics Society, 9,* 208–217.

Dublin, Louis I.; Lotka, Alfred J.; and Spiegelman, Mortimer. 1949. *Length of Life: A Study of the Life Table.* New York: Ronald Press.

Feinberg, Richard, and Podolak, Edward. 1965. Latency of Pupillary Reflex to Light Stimulation and its Relationship to Aging. In A. T. Welford and James E. Birren (Eds.), *Behavior, Aging, and the Nervous System.* Springfield, Ill.: Charles C Thomas.

Gajdusek, D. Carleton, and Brown, Paul. (Eds.) 1970. Isolated and Migratory Population Groups: Health Problems and Epidemiologic Studies. I: Introduction. *American Journal of Tropical Medicine and Hygiene, 19,* 127–129.

Gelfant, Seymour, and Smith, J. Graham, Jr. 1972. Aging: Noncycling Cells—an Explanation. *Science, 178*(4059), 357–361.

Gompertz, B. 1825. On the Nature of the Function Expressive of the Law of Human Mortality on a New Mode of Determining Life Contingencies. *Philosophical Transactions of the Royal Society (London),* Series A, *115,* 513–585.

Granick, Samuel, and Patterson, Robert D. (Eds.) **1971.** *Human Aging II: An Eleven-Year Followup Biomedical and Behavioral Study.* Publication No. (HSM) 71–9037. Washington, D.C.: U.S. Government Printing Office.

Hayflick, Leonard. 1965. The Limited *in vitro* Lifetime of Human Diploid Cell Strains. *Experimental Cell Research, 37,* 614–636.

Hayflick, Leonard. 1966. Senescence in Cultured Cells. In Nathan W. Shock (Ed.), *Perspectives in Experimental Gerontology.* Springfield, Ill.: Charles C Thomas.

Hayflick, Leonard. 1970. Aging Under Glass. *Experimental Gerontology, 5,* 291–303.

Himwich, Williamina A., and Himwich, Harold E. 1959. Neurochemistry of Aging. In James E. Birren (Ed.), *Handbook of Aging and the Individual.* Chicago: University of Chicago Press.

Hofstetter, H. W. 1944. A Comparison of Duane's and Donders' Tables of the Amplitude of Accommodation. *American Journal of Optometry and Archives of American Academy of Optometry, 21,* 345–363.

Hotcin, John, and Sikora, Edward. 1970. Long-Term Effects of Virus Infection on Behavior and Aging in Mice. *Proceedings of the Society for Experimental Biology and Medicine, 134*(1), 204–209.

Jacobs, E. A.; Winter, P. M.; Alvis, H. J.; and Small, S. M. 1969. Hyperoxygenation Effect on Cognitive Functioning in the Aged. *New England Journal of Medicine, 281,* 753–757.

Johnson, L. K. 1972. Memory Loss With Age: A Storage or Retrieval Problem? Paper presented at the meeting of the Gerontological Society, San Juan, Puerto Rico, December, 1972.

Johnson, Roger, and Strehler, Bernard L. 1972. Loss of Genes Coding for Ribosomal RNA in Ageing Brain Cells. *Nature, 240,* 412–414.

Jones, Hardin B. 1959. The Relation of Human Health to Age, Place and Time. In James E. Birren (Ed.), *Handbook of Aging and the Individual.* Chicago: University of Chicago Press.

Kallmann, Franz J., and Jarvik, Lissy F. 1959. Individual Differences in Constitution and Genetic Background. In James E. Birren (Ed.), *Handbook of Aging and the Individual.* Chicago: University of Chicago Press.

Klonoff, Harry, and Kennedy, Margaret. 1966. A Comparative Study of Cognitive Functioning in Old Age. *Journal of Gerontology, 21*(2), 239–243.

Kohn, R. R. 1963. Human Aging and Disease. *Journal of Chronic Disease, 16,* 5–21.

Laws, R. M. 1971. Patterns of Reproductive and Somatic Aging in Large Mammals. In George A. Sacher (Ed.), *Aging in Relation to Development and Reproduction.* Argonne, Ill.: Argonne National Laboratory.

Leaf, Alexander. 1973. Every Day Is a Gift When You Are Over 100. *National Geographic, 143*(1), 93ff.

Lehman, Harvey C. 1953. *Age and Achievement.* Princeton, N.J.: Princeton University Press.

*Lehman, Harvey C. 1962. The Creative Production Rates of Present Versus Past Generations of Scientists. *Journal of Gerontology, 17*(4), 409–417.

Lehman, Harvey C. 1966. The Psychologist's Most Creative Years. *American Psychologist, 21,* 363–369.

Lindop, Patricia J., and Rotblat, J. 1961. Long-Term Effects of a Single Whole-Body Exposure of Mice to Ionizing Radiations. *Proceedings of the Royal Society (London),* Series B, *154*(956), 332–349.

Manniche, E., and Falk, G. 1957. Age and the Nobel Prize. *Behavioral Science, 2,* 301–307.

McFarland, Ross A.; Tune, G. Sidney; and Welford, Alan T. 1964. On the Driving of Automobiles by Older People. *Journal of Gerontology, 19,* 190–197.

Mead, Margaret. 1972. Long Living in Cross-Cultural Perspective. Paper presented at the meeting of the Gerontological Society, San Juan, Puerto Rico, December, 1972.

Melrose, Jay; Welsh, Oliver L.; and Luterman, David M. 1963. Auditory Responses in Selected Elderly Men. *Journal of Gerontology, 18,* 267–270.

*Moberg, David O. 1965. Religiosity in Old Age. *Gerontologist, 5*(2), 78–87.

Myers, G. C., and Pitts, A. M. 1972. The Demographic Effects of Mortality Reduction on the Aged Population of the U.S.: Some Baseline Projections. Paper presented at the meeting of the Gerontological Society, San Juan, Puerto Rico, December, 1972.

National Center for Health Statistics. 1964. Binocular Visual Acuity of Adults, United States, 1960–1962. *Vital and Health Statistics,* Series 11, No. 3. Washington, D.C.: U.S. Government Printing Office.

Newsweek. 1972. The 130-Year-Old Man. October 2, 1972, 74.

Orgel, L. E. 1963. The Maintenance of the Accuracy of Protein Synthesis and its Relevance to Ageing. *Proceedings of the National Academy of Sciences, U. S. A., 49*(4), 517–521.

Ostfeld, Adrian M. 1966. Frequency and Nature of Health Problems of Retired Persons. In Frances M. Carp (Ed.), *The Retirement Process.* PHS Publication No. 1778. Washington, D.C.: U.S. Government Printing Office.

Papalia, D. E.; True, M.; and Salverson, S. 1972. The Status of Mass, Weight, and Volume Conservation Ability During Old Age. Paper presented at the meeting of the Gerontological Society, San Juan, Puerto Rico, December, 1972.

Piaget, Jean. 1972. Roundtable Discussion at the Graduate Center of the City University of New York, October, 1972.

Reed, Homer B. C., Jr., and Reitan, Ralph M. 1963. Changes in Psychological Test Performance Associated with the Normal Aging Process. *Journal of Gerontology, 18,* 271–274.

Riegel, Klaus F., and Riegel, Ruth M. 1972. Development, Drop, and Death. *Developmental Psychology, 6*(2), 306–319.

Riley, Matilda White; Foner, Anne; and Associates, 1968. *Aging and Society.*

Vol. 1. *An Inventory of Research Findings*. New York: Russell Sage Foundation.

Sacher, George A. 1959. Relation of Lifespan to Brain Weight and Body Weight in Mammals. In E. W. Wolstenholme and Maeve O'Connor (Eds.), *Ciba Foundation Symposium on the Life Span of Animals*. London: Churchill.

Selye, Hans. 1950. *The Physiology and Pathology of Exposure to Stress*. Montreal: Acta, Inc., Medical Publishers.

Selye, Hans. 1970. Stress and Aging. *Journal of the American Geriatrics Society*, *18*(9), 669–680.

Selyle, Hans, and Prioreschi, P. 1960. Stress Theory of Aging. In Nathan W. Shock (Ed.), *Aging: Some Social and Biological Aspects*. Washington, D.C.: American Association for the Advancement of Science.

Shock, Nathan W. 1960. Some of the Facts of Aging. In Nathan W. Shock (Ed.), *Aging: Some Social and Biological Aspects*. Washington, D.C.: American Association for the Advancement of Science.

Spiegel, Paul Martin. 1972. Theories of Aging. In P. S. Timiras, *Developmental Physiology and Aging*. New York: Macmillan.

Spiegelman, Mortimer. 1964. *Significant Mortality and Morbidity Trends in the United States Since 1900*. Bryn Mawr, Pa.: The American College of Life Underwriters.

Spieth, Walter. 1964. Cardiovascular Health Status, Age, and Psychological Performance. *Journal of Gerontology*, *19*, 277–284.

Strehler, Bernard L. 1962. *Time, Cells, and Aging*. New York: Academic Press.

Thomas, J. C. 1972. Remembering the Names of Pictured Objects. Paper presented at the meeting of the Gerontological Society, San Juan, Puerto Rico, December, 1972.

Timiras, P. S. 1972. *Developmental Physiology and Aging*. New York: Macmillan.

U.S. Bureau of the Census. 1973. Some Demographic Aspects of Aging in the United States. *Current Population Reports*, Series P-23, No. 43. Washington, D.C.: U.S. Government Printing Office.

Walford, Roy L. 1969. *The Immunologic Theory of Aging*. Baltimore: Williams and Wilkins.

Waugh, N. C. 1972. Age-Related Differences in Primary and Secondary Memory. Paper presented at the meeting of the Gerontological Society, San Juan, Puerto Rico, December, 1972.

Weiss, Alfred D. 1959. Sensory Functions. In James E. Birren (Ed.), *Handbook of Aging and the Individual*. Chicago: University of Chicago Press.

Weissman, August. 1891. *Essays on Heredity*. Oxford: Clarendon Press.

Welford, Alan T. 1959. Psychomotor Performance. In James E. Birren (Ed.), *Handbook of Aging and the Individual*. Chicago: University of Chicago Press.

Wetherick, N. E. 1965. Changing an Established Concept: A Comparison of the Ability of Young, Middle-Aged, and Old Subjects. *Gerontologia*, *11*, 82–95.

* References marked with an asterisk appear in Bernice L. Neugarten (Ed.), *Middle Age and Aging*. Chicago: University of Chicago Press, 1968.

Henry, Age 75 and Mrs. K., Age 89

Both Henry and Mrs. K. immigrated to the United States about 50 years ago; for them America was the land of opportunity, but life was also very difficult. Both respondents are exceptionally hardy persons who have out-lived their spouses and most of their contemporaries, and they remain in reasonably good health although their health is failing. Both continued working well past age 65—Henry had to continue working in order to support himself and his wife; Mrs. K. seems to have worked as long as possible because there was nothing else she considered doing. These exam-ples are atypical old persons in many respects, yet they also point out many of the problems which are shared by most old people.

Henry is a 75-year-old man who recently suffered the death of his wife of 52 years. He has continued to work because he could not manage on Social Security alone and because he will soon be eligible for a small pension from his union; he would have received a pension earlier, but he was unable to work for a time and lost the pension payments that he had built up; now he must work two more months in order to fulfill 15 con-tinuous years work and receive his pension. He works as a waiter in a small restaurant, but when he was interviewed his feet were "burning" with arthritis after finishing his day's work, so our interview was ended prematurely. He is also suffering an increasing loss of hearing, which may reflect a general decline in health. He does not see how he will be able to continue working. And, with the death of his wife, he has suffered a severe emotional upset.

What will the future hold for him; what resources might he have to offset the loss of his wife and confidant? In what ways does he seem typical of old people in this country today? In what ways is he atypical? Why did he choose to talk about the milestones he picked—is there a sex difference in the milestones that men and women seem to choose to discuss? Is his difficulty in getting a pension a frequent problem for old people today? If he is no longer able to work, what do you think he will do? What could a social worker or a friend do to help?

What are some of the milestones that stand out in your life as you look back? What do you mean by "milestones"? *Some of the important events?* Was very important when I was married and had a nice son, a school teacher, a very nice man. And I was very happy 'til 1972 when my wife passed away; I lived with her 52 years. *She just passed away?* Yeah, in November the 21st. *That must have been a very sad time for you.* That was very sad, a very sad time for me. And now life is not so much interested where it used to be. *How is your life different now?* Well, for a senior citizen, it's a very great difference when you lose your wife and you lose your companion; it is not so easy. When you're young you don't mind so much, but when you get old, it's pretty tough. *In what way is it so tough for you?* Tough in every way. In general, in life and everything. You've got no companionship; in everything. When I go home now I'm all by myself. Just coming into the house...making a little dinner for myself, and straighten out the house; see everything should be in order; and watch television, read a book. Don't sleep so good no more. *You were married 53 years ago now?* It's going on 53. I was married in 1920, October the 24th, 1920. *Was that a big event in your life?* Oh yeah. I had a beautiful wife, good looking, smart woman in every way; and I enjoyed life even though I wasn't a rich man. I was a poor man, but I enjoyed my life.

Were you born in this country? No, no. I was born in Russia. *How old were you when you came to this country?* I was about 18 years. *Was that a big event for you?* It was very surprising for me. I was studying, I don't know how they call it in English, not a rabbi, [the man] who kills the cattle—kosher, and all that. That's what I was supposed to be, but they drag me to the army because my brother and me was twins. One remain home, the other go because my father needed him for work, and I went to the army. I was in the army six months and I came to this country. Oh, it wasn't so easy. *Tell me about it.* When I came to the Russian Army, I was there six months, and then after six months when you take the second oath, they let you go in the city. Before I went to the city I wrote a letter home to my sister that I hate to be in the army. It's very tough to be in the Russian Army. So she said, "All right, I'll try to get together a few dollars and get an agent and we'll take you out of there." But it's very dangerous, because God forbid if you get caught—no court-martial, nothing; they shoot you right there on the spot. But finally I take the chance. I took that chance and came to the city. She wrote me where, and the agent was waiting for me, and he took me over and took off my uniform and everything, and he sent me away to a different city. Even if they should catch me without the clothes they would shoot me right away. Yes, martial law. *And then you came to America?* Yes, then I came here. It took me a long time. I came here with the boat. I was sailing about 26 days and nights and I lost...I weighed 160 pounds when I left; when I came here I weighed 120 pounds. I lost on the boat, because I couldn't eat and I couldn't drink nothing. I was vomiting. I couldn't take the sea. Seasick.

And what did you do when you came here? So when I came here I got a little job, you know, in the grocery store, because I couldn't speak. I got sick after that. I got a tumor and I lost my speech. That's why I become the counterman in the waiter business; my buddy who was singing in the Hebrew College, I learned with him, he was the sexton in the temple. I couldn't make it [as a cantor] on account of my voice. Finally I had an operation. At that time years ago they did not know so much about cancer, and Dr. B. operated on me and took out that growth; and it took me three years to get back my voice and my speech, and then I was off my track. It was too late already to go again.

Then I worked as a grocer for three-and-a-half dollars a week, but 12 hours a day or more, six-and-a-half days a week; no, no, too many hours. It was very tough, very tough. And then I bought myself a suit for two dollars. An old one, secondhand; you could put two like me in there [it was so big]. I went to the man and I paid him a quarter a week; eight quarters; in eight weeks I paid him off for the suit and then I bought myself a pair of secondhand shoes. You shouldn't wear no secondhand shoes. I didn't have the money. What can I do? I slept by a shoemaker on the floor for a dollar a week. *Could you speak English?* No, I went to night school to learn a little; but I was so tired. As soon as I came into school I fell asleep right away. So the teacher say it's no good for you; you come to school, you sleep, you don't learn. So I says to her I try to learn by myself, and I did. I used to get books and learn by myself little by little; it take me a long time, but I learned. Well, of course, I speak a little bit an accent, you know.

Then my brother came along from Russia too, so after a few years we work together. He was a carpenter, and I went with him to help him bring the lumber. So we saved a little money and then we opened up a candy store. And I was in the candy store and he was working as a carpenter. So I was making a little money. I was making that time about nine, ten dollars in the candy store and it was a tough life. Used to get up five o'clock in the morning and work 'til two o'clock in the morning. Oh, it was very tough.

When did you get married? I got married about eight years later. I met the girl in the candy store. She was a nice girl; she came to buy a piece of candy so I got acquainted with her and she brought another friend. So the friend my brother took...he should rest in peace, he's dead already...and I took this one here. So that's how it is. *Was it a big moment when your children were born?* I have only son. Of course I was very surprised. It was a boy. And my wife said, "Well, once you sell the candy store you buy another candy store, you fix up the candy store, you can't have too many children because you're moving around; one is enough." So we had one child.

Were there any other big moments in your life? Yes, I remember some. Three ... (he counts on his fingers) ... three years and eight months [ago] I went to Russia to see my brother, the youngest one. I had a very nice time. I was in Moscow, in Kiev, and Leningrad. And I met my brother and I enjoyed myself very nicely because I haven't seen him close to 60 years. And he remained alive. All the other family, my sisters and brothers, Hitler killed them. There was about 220 people from the family; everybody was killed. But this trip I enjoyed very very much. That was a great surprise in my life.

Do you have any grandchildren? Yes, one grandson. He goes to college. Oh, a beautiful boy; he was on the hockey team; a powerful kid, very nice boy. And I got my daughter-in-law; she is a manager in a department store; very nice person.

How about crisis points; were there any very difficult points for you? Difficult? Oh, yeah; was plenty of problems. When my son was drafted I felt very very bad. He was drafted and he was sent away on the other side and I didn't hear from him about six months. And I felt very bad and I got from loneliness—I figured that maybe I lose my son—I got like a paralytic stroke on my right side. Oh, was terrible! It took me about a year to get better. One day I was downstairs with a cane and I see under the door there's a telegram laying for me. I was so upset I couldn't take out the telegram, so I had the next door neighbor come over. So she took out the telegram, she says okay, your son is in the hospital. Thank God, you know, my son was in the hospital, he isn't killed. But he was very sick; he was there with malaria, very bad sickness.

What happened with your paralysis? I went to a chiropractor. And he takes my leg and brings it over here to my head in the back and I fainted. He went over and got a pitcher of cold water and washed me down and I came to and he said, "Don't worry, you wouldn't die." And he take the same leg and bring it here. Finally he gave me about 25 adjustments. Every day I supposed to come there and I couldn't ride a taxi because I couldn't take the shaking; that was terrible. *Did he cure you?* He did! *You weren't able to work then, were you?* No, I couldn't bend! I couldn't walk! No, I didn't work. Was no financial money; my brother-in-law helped me a little, but that time was no union, nothing to help you. So [one day] when I came home my wife wasn't home so she prepared me something to eat and I walked into the house; instead of eating the sleep went on me. I couldn't keep my eyes open. So I crept into the bed with my clothes and I laid down and I fell asleep and I slept maybe five, six hours. And then when I get up, I get off the bed like a new man. I got off the bed and I started walking. I could walk! *And that was it?* So, I called the doctor and he said, "Go to work! And come to me once a week and then I'll massage you." And then I went to work.

What kind of job did you go to then? I worked in a restaurant. I worked there quite a number of years. Then the restaurant went under, and I went to work for a man on Broadway, and I'm working for him 28 years already. And to him it's just like I came today. He don't give a damn! No pension, no nothing.

No pension? No pension, because I'm in the union not even 15 years. I worked without a union. And I can't work; I got to retire. I can't work. Impossible for my legs. Don't forget, I'm 75 years old. I can't work, and I've got no pension. *Why don't you have a pension at 75?* I'm trying to finish up yet; another couple weeks maybe, to pay into the union, to the pension. It's got to be paid in $160 and I haven't got the money to pay. *How long do you have to work before you get a pension?* You got to work at least 15 years in the union. *How much longer do you have to go?* The union says another couple months. And I can't do it. Here I'm sitting now. My feet are really burning like fire. *So you're just living on Social Security now?* Yeah, I get $165.20 a month. *Is that enough?* No. I need what I make here. I make here a couple dollars. But if I wouldn't work, then it would be tough for me. And from the union I could get, if I do get a pension, I get $52.75 a month. *That's not much.* Sure not. Especial the way, oh years ago—about 30 years ago—it would be fine, because the rent is very high. My rent is $150 a month. *So that's almost all your Social Security right there for rent.* Yeah, and then you got electric, telephone! And lodge money, insurance. Big expense! *What do you think is going to happen?* I have to go on welfare. They wouldn't take me. They wouldn't give me welfare. *Have you applied for welfare?* Yeah, they wouldn't give me. *How would you feel about going on welfare if you have to?* I don't want to; I don't want to; I hate that. Maybe Medicare would be better for me—the medicines and doctor bills, because it's a lot of medications. It costs a lot of money. I'm trying this (he stands up)—maybe this way it should be better circulation; oh, it [his feet] feels burning. Okay Professor, we're going to go!

Mrs. K. is an 89-year-old woman who lives in a nursing home; she has been in the home 11 years and is remarkably vigorous and independent. Her bed was covered with handcrafts she had made and she apparently works in her own private room. She is one of the longest residents in the home, living first in the small building next door (which she calls her "white house") until the new modern building was built a few years ago. The home seems close to an ideal nursing home; but like most of the patients in this private (proprietary) nursing home, she depends on Medicare and Medicaid to pay her expenses. Mrs. K. (no one called her by her first name) came to the United States 43 years ago and learned English on her own. She seems to have been quite independent and on her own for most of her life, although some of this independence may reflect the personality shift in the later years described in Chapter 7. She has outlived her husband by many years and has no children. After working until the age of 70 she had to "retire" and give up her apartment a few years later when her health failed.

This example raises important questions not only about her life but also about the problems of the aged in our society. If she were not living in a nursing home, where would she live? How could she pay the expensive rates for such excellent care without government help? Turning to her life, we wonder whether she married "late" for her time and if so, why? Why did she and her husband (Karl) not have children? Was their marriage satisfying for her? Might her strong personality be related to her ability to cope with the several traumatic events in her later years (the death of her husband, her illness, giving up her apartment, and moving from the old nursing home to the new building)—and possibly with her longevity? Has she worked through her feelings about death? Does she have a sense of meaningfulness in her life?

As you look back over your life, what milestones stand out? What milestones; let me think. I think there are many things where I am really interested and was always interested since a child. I was a child more reserved.

I don't know why. That time when I was young I didn't know what's what. But later when I knew more, then I knew I was—I can say—a special girl, special child. I always wanted to learn something. We lived that time in the country for several years because father was transferred from the city to the country; then after [that] we came to the city again. . . .

What things stand out in your memory of your life? What should I say? What kind of things stand out? . . . Having a job; of course this took most of my time; and then getting married is something different too; and then, the biggest moment was when we came to America. *That was really a big moment for you?* This was. This was an unexpected big moment, because my husband knew a gentleman from the German-American Consulate. And he asked my husband, "What do you do for a living? Would you like to go to America?" "No," my husband said, "this is not for us," because we made out good, you know. But then was the war [World War I]. We lost everything, so we couldn't make out anymore; and through that gentleman my husband came here in three weeks. Because my husband was in agriculture, diplomas he has, you know, he can work in big estates and everything. He comes himself from a big estate in Germany. He was always interested in horses; he raised horses and trained them. He was here in three weeks; I came here 10 months later, because I had to sell my household, you know. And this took me a little time. And then [I] came right away over too, and then I was working because I could not fulfill that job what I used [to] be, so I was sitting in the workroom and make dresses, and then after that . . . the worsest part was we couldn't speak English. That was the hindrance for me. Then, when I knew a little bit [of] English, and I came higher up, and then I started as a fitter, you know . . . ladies' body dresses. I pinned them up . . . and all of them had girls sitting in the workroom and then I was all right. This I did until I was 70 years [old]. *You did that until you were 70 years old!* I'm older now. Naturally. (she laughs). I'm 89. *Are you really! I never would have guessed.*

The last few years I grew older very much on account of my sickness, you know . . . swollen . . . (gestures to her legs) and it goes down and gets all flabby. Anyway . . . once we have to take something and I know this very well, so that's that. They leave me all alone; I can do just as I want. Of course, I don't do wrong things. I am very satisfied here and have a few nice, nice friends; and this makes me happy too. And I think I make them happy too, because they all look for me to talk with me. This makes me proud. Yesterday I received a card from a lady again. I met her in the hospital. She went to another residence; and through her I met her sister. Ever since then the sister comes and visits me and sends me always money. She's good off. So I have two other wonderful friends I met here and this makes me happy. You know, they come always once in a while and [it] is happy. So, I can say I'm never lonesome. I'm always occupied and happy so-called, you know. And that's the main thing, you know. And when I can have people I always try my best. This is not much, but . . .

You've lived here for 15 years? No, 11; I'm here in this room 11 years. Only, I'm here 43 years in the United States. So, now I keep on as long as I can.

Do you have any children? No, I have no children. My husband is dead 26 years already. *I see.*

Then, I was still working, working, working, 'til I got sick and then I came here. I was very much crying when [I was] told in the hospital I come to the home. I had my apartment, but I couldn't go. So, they couldn't let me go home and I cried. And the social worker said to me, "You are a citizen. You must receive everything that other people get. It's coming to you." I said, "No, I cannot do it; I had so much saved I could live to 90 years old with my Social Security." And now came all different, took sick. Was laying down and they brought me to hospital. You see, unexpected comes, you know. *It was a very sad time for you when you had to leave your apartment.* Yah, I didn't see it any more. They brought me back here from the hospital and I never saw my apartment again. *You just went to the hospital and then came here.* Yah, it was two months. I was two months in hospital and then they sent me here [to the old building]. I call it my "white house." *Your "white house."* And then I make always about [it] little poems or little essays, you know. It's nothing much but I do the best.... And it comes here in the paper—we have a monthly paper here, we write everything. So I put it in there for Christmas and for holidays and so on...little poems. So I always occupy myself. I must have something which, you know, I must create this myself (she laughs).

Your husband, did he live on some kind of an agricultural farm? No, my husband was in the academy when he came...in the riding academy in _____ [town in Germany]. He taught ladies and children riding. And then after... there was not enough money...then I came over and my husband was there with his horses. We rode out with the lady here, there, and everywhere on the big estate and all that kind of things. Then he took off; it was not enough money. When I came over I made some myself, but it was very little because we couldn't speak English. And then my husband met a man; he was a painter ...inside; he was German. He said, "Why don't you take [up] painting? You can make money." He learned my husband painting and my husband liked it very much and he made the nicest color, made everything nice and fine and even. We lived on _____ Street for 25 years until I took sick. We were always in New York.

Was getting married a big event for you? I married very late. I didn't want to get married at all because I had a wonderful position in Germany since 1910 and I could support myself. And I didn't want to take from a man money. I had plenty of opportunities to marry, but I said to my mother, "Nothing doing. I want to learn something. I want to make my own money. I don't want to take from a man. I just take what I want and do what I want, and that's good." So I did. I was 39 years old already. And I would have shoved him over also, but he was persistent. And I thank God for this, because through him I came to America; otherwise I would be destroyed in the Second World War. We came here in '29. See, when Hitler came, then we would have finished, you know. We didn't know him. But I have relatives over there and these [we] supported very much. I supported many many. I've never been [back] in Germany because, I say this cost a few thousand dollars and I'd rather give it to them because people need that more than....

What kind of a profession were you in? I was in dressmaking. I was a directress in the best places in _____ [large German city] since 1910. And had girls sitting, eight girls apart more or less, in the workroom. I cut the dresses;

I made the patterns; I fitted the dresses; and the girls would finish the dresses after that. It was a very good life. We had a few countesses; we had a few baronesses; we had one princess even, from Germany; this one I didn't fit because I was not a fitter. "Directress" we called it. I had a wonderful position for money. I didn't need to marry for money. Then when my husband was dead I was still working, always. Sure, I miss this, but as I say, I got sick and couldn't come [fit] in shoes; I get swollen. That was the hindrance.

So you had to stop working at 70? Yah, then I was sitting home. Seven years I was constantly in doctor's care; then he said, "I cannot help you anymore Mrs. K. You must go into hospital; they have facilities which I am not allowed to use." So, then I was sitting seven years in my house not going...I didn't want to go in hospital. Then I fall together several times; then they picked me up and brought me to hospital and that was that. So this was the end and then I came here. Since then I was always happy here and worked, worked, worked.

Do you sometimes look back over your life and think about the things that happened? I think back and look back constantly, from a little child on...how it happened, why it happened. Yes, I do, but I do not regret. I'm alone, have nobody. Even if I would have children I wouldn't live with them. I would leave them alone. They should be happy. I wanted that too when I was young. I would leave them too. I would go in a home. *Do you wish that you did have children sometimes?* No, on account of the war [World War I], you know. We losed every penny; then, how can you get children? I had to work. And at least you want your children raised like you are raised, you know. And especial you would want a little decent, and this we couldn't do. Then was the big moment when we came here, you know. That was the biggest moment for me in the later years. I was glad to be here, and still am, you know.

Why was that such a big moment for you? You know, I never thought we could come to America! Imagine! We had a nice income and a flat [apartment], but through the war we lose everything; no work, no nothing. We had debts by my parents and this couldn't go on anymore. So, finally my husband met this man and through him he came here; and then, of course, he sent the fare back to my mother. Then, months later I came, and I made my own money too. We saved a little. This was the biggest, the nicest moment. That's what I must say. I loved here when we came how cheap everything was. In Germany, it cost a pound of butter, two dollars—marks, we say; and here, we bought four pounds of butter from dollar. I say, "You bring it right back." He said, "You are a funny woman. Why don't you taste?" "It can't be good; you know how much cream you need for a pound of butter." He was an agricultural man, you know. Then he was stunned and thought it over. He said, "Taste it," and I tasted; it was the good butter. So, everything was so cheap here. Food! Oh, I love food. I always ate food, food, food. Every Saturday we bought food. Everything for the whole week. I like food still, all my life. *You still like food.* Oh, crazy about it! I cannot do without food.

How was your marriage? My marriage was fairly good. You know, there's always a little smoke in every kitchen; but this was overcome, you know. You must give in. My husband had his own mind and I had my own mind; but I always helped him. When something happened I always told him in advance what can happen and he didn't believe me. "Can't do nothing with that woman!

Can't do nothing with that woman! Can't do nothing with that woman!" he always said. When sometimes trouble came, for instance, he wanted to participate with a partner. He wanted to make a little business. We had a little money saved. Not much, but a little. I say, "Karl, you do not do that. We are strange in this country. We don't have the language exactly right and we don't know the rules and everything. We leave our hands off! You lose the money." Twice we lose and I say, "No; now I keep my money and you keep yours. You can do with it what you want, and I keep my money." And that's why sometimes we get trouble. We had a few troubles and I balled him out in the right place in the right way. That's why he always said, "You're a smart woman!" But I said, "You don't listen when I tell you in advance, 'don't do it!'" That was really the idea, because I had the feeling in me, you know . . . I have the house of Cancer ruling me, you know. I made all the horoscopes. We learned to make all the horoscopes—a hell of a work. You need charts of the stars, where they are at this and that moment, and all the tables and all that. This I wouldn't want anymore, but that's why I said I feel. There are people who see, not directly, but they see. I feel; I feel in advance something is wrong, not coming right. And that's really true. I advised people and helped people. You think they did it? They didn't do it, see! You must always work, work and improve more and more and more; but they have not that ambition in them. That's what I believe . . . in the stars and how they stand in nature of the almighty universe. That is my special, how you say, work. If I could write very good as a writer I would make a nice book, but I'm not so intelligent so I can write. I make little things.

I get up in the morning [at] quarter to five. Bathe myself down every morning; nobody is up then. Then I'm finished; make my bed; pick everything up and then I sit here 'til seven and then get breakfast; and then we start working (she laughs). That's my life. *You work down in the craft shop?* No, I do not, because I'm on my own. *You work up here* [*in her private room*]? Yah, I'm all my own, because I could be the instructor of everything. I don't want to be under. They wanted me under them to show the others. But, I must say, I'm never—how should you say—high-headed. But this is what I worked out for myself, and this I keep. I didn't work under other people. I'm a creator in everything. What I do is all my own. *I get the feeling you've always been that way.* When I was a child already. But then I didn't know what's what. I had to learn first how to go, what is what. And then I figured out how, why, and so. Then I was able. So, no, I worked for things, but all on my own. I made recently for Mrs. D. a suit—crocheted suit with skirt and jacket, and she wears it once or two times, three times, four times. She's very pleased. I made very, very many things for Mrs. D., for her daughter, for her daughter-in-law; all sorts of dresses and outfits. Everything I make, everything. Other people cannot do that, you know. There are a few now [who can make] a little something, yes sure, but when they want really something now, then they ask me. And I gladly advise when I can help, sure.

Were you and your husband very close to one another? Oh yah. I loved my husband very much. And he loved me too. Because, what should I say, he was an educated man, came from a good family; he was also in the war and he had nice position there and he kept this. Yah, I loved my husband; we were happy, but as I said, sometimes was smoke in the kitchen (she laughs). *You had your arguments too?* Oh sure, sure. For instance, I tell you what was the biggest argument we had. When that damn, excuse me, Hitler was ... and he heard from other German men on 86th Street ... Saturdays he usually went there, or Sundays. And then he talked about everything, and he listened and listened. Now my husband was from a big estate, and he was the oldest son. He would have inherited it if he stayed. I said, "Karl, you leave the hands from it. We have no children; we are both alone. We have good work. We are satisfied and we want peace now." "No, no" he said. "I understand you stay in your house or you lose it, but imagine what you have to pay. You pay the trip over and you have to pay the man to look out for it. What is left for you—only work," I said. "Don't do it." No, he didn't want it [her advice]. And there was that Bund [club or association] from Hitler, and he would like to join that too, those meetings. [The German-American Volksbund, or Bund, was a pro-Nazi organization in the United States during the 1930s and 40s.] I said, "You leave the hands from this," I said. "We are new in America. We do not participate in anything." "He promised you get back what you losed." I said, "Karl, don't you believe that!" "Yah, yah, yah, yah," he said. "I go over to Germany," he said. I said, "You go over from here to Germany? No!" And I talked with him over that often, very often. He insisted that he wanted to get his estate back. I told him everything as it comes and how it is away. I never believed in Hitler. I know. He said, "Yes, yes, yes." And I said, "No, Karl, let's make it here. You go over to Germany. I don't keep you. You know, I don't need you. I make my own money. I never needed no husband for making money. You go over. I don't keep you away. But once I tell you now in advance. I know you wouldn't like it. It won't come out as you think. You will be glad to come back here, but I don't give you a penny to come back. Stay there!" That was the biggest moment in all. Otherwise was nothing. *That was a big fight?* Oh yah, always fighting. And then finally when it came out what Hitler was and that Bund was, then he said, "I know you are a smart woman." I said, "Don't say that. You don't do when I tell you in advance." That was ... oh ... we had many fights. I would have let him go if he really wanted to go, but then find out a little bit before; so he stood here. Oh, yah, we had big fights. Now, how could we [have gone back to Germany?] ... I was glad to be here, you know. Oh, I never liked that man [Hitler]. I didn't know him personally.... We were here already in '29 and he was there I think '33, you know, he started. No, I said, "Nothing doing." Otherwise, I said this was a very big moment—coming to America and having this event with him; he wanted to go.

Were sexual relations very important between the two of you? Oh, we were both [on] in years, you know, and—how should I say ... I said to my husband before we were married, "One thing, think it over; when we marry don't go with other woman. If you cannot do this, we don't get married then." We never talked about this later ... I don't think so. No, that's all right. That was not my main thing, you know. My main thing was working and learning. *Sexual relations weren't very important in your relationship then?* No, not so, not so. I could not say that. He was a very nice man with manners and so, and that's all.

Was his death quite a shock for you? Yes, very, yah, sure; because I was all alone here, and I just came from work and he was before me in the house, and we always had little dogs and they were always with him. They sat outside in the street and waited for me. So I came home and I wanted to go to the doctor because I get injection for my sickness. And I had the feeling that I don't like to go today. I'd rather go home. I went home, you know. Then I came, he was sitting in the sofa in the front, and sick. I said, "What's the matter, Karl?" He said, "Now I am finished." I said, "What's the matter?" "I have all here these things. It hurts me here, here, here. I have double pneumonia," he said. But I said, "It is not pneumonia." I said, "Come in the kitchen just the same," and I made him a wet pack and I knew this was not pneumonia; but I didn't know either what it was. So I did this and bedded him on the couch, and then he said, "Give me a little drink," and I gave him ginger ale. He drank that and I turned my back and wanted to set it on the table and then there was (she makes gasping, choking sounds) and I look back and I say, "Karl! You are not dying!" And then . . . he was finished. He had the heart, how you say, blood clot on the heart. That was quite a . . . that was, of course, big moment. This was very . . . I was all alone then, but I was used to things. I could manage. I was courage person, you know. Of course, was a long time 'til you get over that, but I worked and a lady called me from the shop and said, "Mrs. K. you better come and work; you'll overcome the things better." I had everything regulated so far in advance back in my shop. Then after . . . little by little. You know how it is. Yes, this was hard moment. Since then I am all alone. Nothing was too much for me. Day and night I would work and everything. So now we sit here . . . and we see how long (she laughs). *We see how long we stay here.* Oh, here we stay; but when the death comes, you know.

Do you sometimes think about death? I often think and I pray always. There is nothing what I do without praying. Nothing. When I take something and do something, I always pray, pray, pray, pray. So, of course, I think often on the death; and . . . I always think about this; I always say, "If I die, I would wish to die nicely, quietly, without pain." That is my only wish, my last wish, nothing else. But this we don't know. *Right; but we can pray.* I hope, I hope. Yah, we hope the best. I do nothing without praying to God . . . nothing. People don't know. I say when the minister comes, you know. Those things I know, of course, I should do it and did it Sunday morning [go to services in the home], but usually not, because I know how I act, what I do, and that's enough. I think so at least. Maybe I'm wrong. I could be wrong, but that's all right.

Do you feel you left your mark here somewhere; that your life has been meaningful and productive? I think, if I understood right, I think . . . I was from child on already dedicated to help people. Now in my age I still do. I always helped, I always did, and nothing was too much for me. And still I'm this way; and I think I was a person who was so-called dedicated to do those things, otherwise you couldn't do. *So helping people has been very important for you; and you've done that?* Yes, I did plenty. Not with money so much, because I had to make my own living, but whatever I could help . . . helping them . . . doing things for them. I never took money from anybody, not a penny, not a penny. As long as I had what I needed. I'm not crazy for money. So I need a little—a certain amount to have this and this and that and many things that you do too, but not overdoing. It's not necessary. But give a poor old man something, a little bit; help poor people.

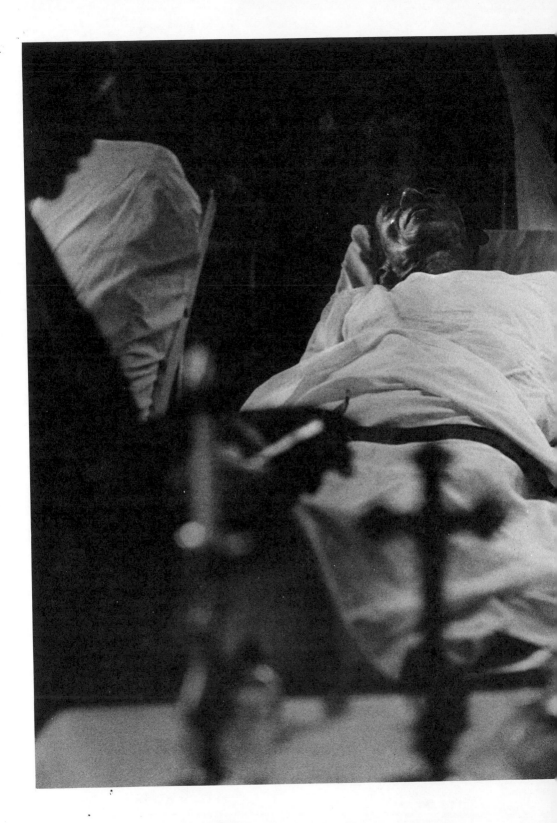

nine
Dying
and
Bereavement

The discussion of death is not an easy one to begin because it is a topic not readily discussed in free and relaxed conversation in our society. In many ways, death is a "taboo" subject that may be both frightening and of deep interest at the same time. Perhaps the topic of death is a more sensitive and avoided topic than sexuality is today; in that sense, death may have replaced sex as the taboo topic in our culture. Interestingly, the two most popular courses at one Eastern university are on sexuality and on death (*Newsweek*, 1972). Yet the instructor (who happened to teach both courses) not only asserted that death is the more taboo subject of our times but also admitted that he uses the usual defense mechanism: "It ain't going to happen to me."

So it is probably realistic to begin the discussion somewhat slowly and to recognize from the outset that we typically avoid thinking about death, the dying, and hence the aged or terminally ill person. We probably (and perhaps necessarily, at least in our "unconscious") feel that *we* shall surely never die—accidents, heart attacks, and fatal illnesses happen to others, but not to me. Yet death is obviously inevitable and we will undoubtedly experience the death of persons close to us during the course of our lives. Perhaps, then, this discussion of death will lead us to a more humane perspective toward the dying while only partially lifting the mystery and fear of death. One result of the fear of death (and consequent avoidance of the topic) is to avoid and sometimes to dehumanize those who are dying otherwise very human deaths.

He may cry for rest, peace, and dignity, but he will get infusions, transfusions, a heart machine, or tracheostomy if necessary. He may want one single person to stop for one single minute so that he can ask one single question—but he will get a dozen people around the

clock, all busily preoccupied with his heart rate, pulse, electrocardiogram or pulmonary functions, his secretions or excretions but not
with him as a human being. He may wish to fight it all but it is going
to be a useless fight since all this is done in the fight for his life, and
if they can save his life they can consider the person afterwards.
Those who consider the person first may lose precious time to save
his life! At least this seems to be the rationale or justification behind
all this—or is it? Is the reason for this increasingly mechanical, depersonalized approach our own defensiveness? Is this approach our own
way to cope with and repress the anxieties that a terminally or critically ill patient evokes in us? Is our concentration on equipment, on
blood pressure our desperate attempt to deny the impending death
which is so frightening and discomforting to us that we displace all
our knowledge onto machines, since they are less close to us than the
suffering face of another human being which would remind us once
more of our lack of omnipotence, our own limits and failures, and
last but not least perhaps our own mortality? (Kübler-Ross, 1969,
p. 9).[1]

This view of the critically ill patient in modern hospitals and the provocative questions which it raises was written by Elisabeth Kübler-Ross
in the introduction to her report on a seminar she conducted on death
and dying with terminally ill patients, students from a theological sem-
inary, and hospital staff. Her concern was to learn from the dying patients
themselves about the process of dying and simultaneously to learn ways
of helping persons with terminal illnesses resolve this very salient milestone of adult life in the most positive and human way possible. We will
discuss her work in considerable detail in the middle section of this chapter, for it has increased our awareness and understanding of the dying
process and has shaken and opened to discussion a wide range of assumptions about dying in our culture; by implication it has also called attention to the assumptions and values about life in our society.

In reality, is the dying process any less important or meaningful an
aspect of life than the birth process? Have we not typically turned away
from the actual process of birth in much the same way as we turn away
from the process of dying? Do we not favor birth in a hospital with
anesthetics, with the husband separated from the wife, and with the
actual birth behind closed doors? Perhaps there may be a parallel between the growing popularity of "natural childbirth"—still in a hospital,
but with the parents jointly sharing this important event and hearing the
first cries of the child—and the perspective Kübler-Ross might call "natural dying"—in a hospital, but with the humanness of the patient not oblit-

[1] All quotations from Kübler-Ross (1969) are reprinted with permission of Macmillan
Publishing Co., Inc. and Tavistock Publications, Ltd. from *On Death and Dying*, copyright © 1969 by Elisabeth Kübler-Ross.

erated by the machines and tubes and technology that seem almost to turn him into an extension of the machine. She does not, of course, advocate a denial of medical technology but, instead, affirms the dignity and humanness of the dying person who may need psychological, religious, and family support and the chance to resolve the issues involved in this final important event in his own meaningful ways.

Indeed, if we come to humanize the dying process and to deal somewhat with our own fears of death (at least at a conscious level), perhaps we may also come to more fully humanize living. From the existential point of view, the reality of death is necessary for life to be meaningful; if death is denied, life is also denied. Yet we are inundated by statistics of death—on the highways, in Vietnam, and in the cities—and are exposed to countless TV deaths. If death has lost its sting, where is the value of living? In one particularly provocative section, Kübler-Ross suggests, "Is war perhaps nothing else but a need to face death, to conquer and master it, to come out of it alive—a peculiar form of denial of our own mortality?" (ibid., p. 13). As she suggests, perhaps an understanding of death in all its reality, rather than its denial, may bring with it "a chance for peace" and that "perhaps there could be less destructiveness around us" (ibid.).

In this chapter we will discuss three aspects of the stage of life that precedes death. We will begin with the psychological issues and changes that appear to precede the actual dying process and that seem best understood as developmental changes timed by the approach of death. Next we will present Kübler-Ross's insights and understanding of the dying process itself, which she sees as consisting of five stages progressing from denial of death to acceptance of death. In the last section we will discuss the process of mourning and the issues faced by the survivors and conclude with a brief discussion of the social view of death as a status passage for the dying person and also for his survivors. From time to time we will quote from the classic short story by Leo Tolstoy (1828-1910), *The Death of Ivan Ilych*, which is an exceptional example of the parallel between the insight of the artist and the insight of the social scientist.

DEVELOPMENTAL CHANGES PRECEDING DEATH

Up to this point we have been discussing developmental changes, milestones, and sequential issues of adulthood with reference to the length of time the person has been alive—that is, *timed by the years since birth* (his age). However, the data available so far suggest that the changes or developmental progression in the late years of life may not be timed primarily by chronological age, but rather they may be set in motion or *timed by the nearness of the individual to death*. For example, the Erikson stage of Integrity versus Despair, the last of his eight ages of man, would seem to be most descriptive of persons who are nearing death and in the later years of their lives, although they might be as young as 40 or as old as 90. Thus, his theory implies that the beginning of the final stage may be triggered by the realization of one's impending death. This is to say that a *future event* (death) may be a salient marker replacing, to some degree, the importance of the number of years since birth as a timing factor in the later years.

In the case of Erikson's theory, it is implied that the integrity crisis is triggered by the anticipation of dying and by the recognition that it is too late to change one's life in major ways for the time is too short to start over. Cues such as illness, advanced age itself, the death of one's cohorts, and perhaps inner cues of the approaching end of life would be likely to be involved in triggering this final turning point posited by Erikson. In addition, some psychological processes (such as ego energy) have been found to decrease markedly as death approaches, and it is this empirical data that most clearly suggests that the nearness to death itself brings developmental changes. Moreover, some of Neugarten's (1967) data on middle-aged persons also points to a shift in time perspective during the middle years from "time lived" to "time left to live" as an important marker for timing and for regulating one's internal social clock.

> Both sexes, although men more than women, talked of the new difference in the way time is perceived. Life is restructured in terms of time-left-to-live rather than time-since-birth. Not only the reversal in directionality but the awareness that time is finite is a particularly conspicuous feature of middle age. . . .
>
> The recognition that there is "only so much time left" was a frequent theme in the interviews. In referring to the death of a contemporary, one man said, "There is now the realization that death is very real. Those things don't quite penetrate when you're in your twenties and you think that life is all ahead of you. Now you know that death will come to you, too" (Neugarten, 1967).

Erikson's Eighth Stage: Integrity versus Despair

The last stage in Erikson's theory is perhaps his least well-defined turning point; however, he sees this stage as the fruition of the previous seven stages and involves ". . . the acceptance of one's one and only life cycle and of the people who have become significant to it as something that had to be and that, by necessity, permitted of no substitutions" (Erikson, 1968, p. 139). Thus, in this framework, one would look back over one's life and deal with the question of the meaningfulness of one's life, the intersection of one's life with history, and the degree to which one's life was a worthwhile venture. He sees old age as providing the link between past heritage and future generations and thus giving perspective to the life cycle. The positive resolution of this stage, *integrity*, involves *wisdom* —"ripened 'wits' ... accumulated knowledge, mature judgment, and inclusive understanding" (ibid., p. 140)—and the essence of wisdom which is often provided by *tradition*, and consideration of *ultimate concerns* about transcending the limitations of one's identity. The opposite polarity in this stage is *despair*: "Time is short, too short for the attempt to start another life and to try out alternate roads to integrity" (ibid.).

In Tolstoy's short story, *The Death of Ivan Ilych*, Ivan Ilych is slowly dying from the effects of an injury; he was (as a fictional character) a judge in Russia in the late nineteenth century. There are political and religious themes written into the story, but Erikson's concept of despair— as the negative resolution of this last stage of life—is clearly portrayed in Ivan Ilych's psychological suffering.

> Ivan Ilych saw that he was dying, and he was in continual despair.
>
> In the depth of his heart he knew he was dying, but not only was he not accustomed to the thought, he simply did not and could not grasp it (Tolstoy, 1886, p. 131).
>
> It occurred to him that what had appeared perfectly impossible before, namely that he had not spent his life as he should have done, might after all be true. It occurred to him that his scarcely perceptible attempts to struggle against what was considered good by the most highly placed people, those scarcely noticeable impulses which he had immediately suppressed, might have been the real thing, and all the rest false. And his professional duties and the whole arrangement of his life and of his family, and all his social and official interests, might all have been false. He tried to defend all those things to himself and suddenly felt the weakness of what he was defending. There was nothing to defend.
>
> "But if that is so," he said to himself, "and I am leaving this life with the consciousness that I have lost all that was given to me and it is impossible to rectify it—what then?" (ibid., p. 152).

Existential Anxiety and Death. This view of man's final struggle to resolve the meaning of his life (in terms of integrity versus despair) seems similar to the existential argument that mankind strives to find meaning in their great or mundane lives, and that the absence of a sense of meaning leads to despair. However, in the existential view, death is an ever possible choice that provides man ultimate freedom—he is always walking along the edge of the abyss and is free to jump or to continue walking— and this ultimate freedom is at the core of the meaning of existence. Put another way, "... one finds meaning in life when one is committed to something for which one is willing to accept death" (Barnes, 1959, p. 81).

Similarly, "... the confronting of death gives the most positive reality to life itself. It makes the individual existence real, absolute, and concrete" (May, 1958, p. 49). But death also represents the threat of nonbeing and thus brings existential anxiety as an essential characteristic of man who, after all, is perhaps the only animal which can be aware of its own impending death. May defines this anxiety as: "... the subjective state of the individual's becoming aware that his existence can become destroyed, that he can lose himself and his world, that he can become 'nothing'" (ibid., p. 50).

As profound as these insights may be into the basic nature of the human condition, we wonder if they do not pertain to the contemplation of death by those for whom death is not actually imminent; that is, how could existential anxiety about death have the same impact on an aged, suffering, cancer patient as it would have on a healthy young person or a powerful middle-aged person who is not facing his own death? Do these views imply that patients in hospitals for the chronically ill (where nearly all of the patients do not leave until they die) are actively contemplating the meaning of their lives and attempting to resolve their anxiety about becoming no-thing? Beauvoir (1972), in her treatise on old age, points out that death for the aged may not be feared because it is an acceptable alternative to a life that has become meaningless.

> ... Even if the old person is struck by no particular misfortune [physical suffering, outliving all those one loves], he has usually either lost his reasons for living or he has discovered their absence. The reason why death fills us with anxiety is that it is the inescapable reverse of our projects: when a man is no longer active in any way, when he has ceased all undertakings, all plans, then there remains nothing that death can destroy. It is usual to put forward wearing-out and fatigue as an explanation for the way some old people resign themselves to death; but if all a man needed was to vegetate he could put up with this life in slow motion. But for man living means self-transcendence. A consequence of biological decay is the impossibility of surpassing oneself and of becoming passionately concerned with anything; it kills all projects, and it is by this expedient that it renders death acceptable (Beauvoir, 1972, p. 443).

Thus, it may be that anxiety about nonbeing, introspection about the meaning of one's life, and concern with the issue of integrity versus despair—in sum, resolution of the "death issue"—may not be highly salient *immediately* before death in old age (although it may occur when death seems imminent among younger persons). Instead, these issues may be more salient when death is not at the doorstep (so to speak), and our interest in life is high—for example, in late middle-age when the imminence of death is not upon us, but its inevitability becomes apparent as parents, friends, and loved ones begin to die one by one. So while the integrity versus despair issue may be triggered by the realization of one's eventual death, we need not assume that the final days of a person's life (especially in old age) are spent in coming to a resolution of that crisis— it may occur a decade or two earlier.

Data on Acceptance of Death. One nationwide sample of 1500 adults found that most old people (over age 60) say quite openly that death is an important issue (Riley, 1963); the increase in percentage reporting they "often" think about death is marked in the oldest group among those with at least a high school education (Table 9.1). This study also found that, at all ages, the attitude is more one of acceptance ("death is sometimes a blessing" or "death is not tragic for the person who dies, only for the survivors") than of fear ("death always comes too soon" or "to die is to suffer"). Negative views of death are much less prevalent among those with higher education (Table 9.2). Interestingly, in line with the hypothesis that resolution of the death issue may occur in late middle-age (proposed by Lieberman and Coplan, 1969), the data in Table 9.2 indicate a slightly lower percentage of older respondents who feel death always comes too soon, compared to the higher percentages in the ages 41-60. Over 60 percent of the respondents described death as "a long sleep" and only about one-third indicated a spiritual orientation toward death. Swenson (1961) found that acceptance of death was higher among the religious, however, and highest among those who live with others (family,

Table 9.1   Percent Who Think Often About the Uncertainty of Their Own Life or the Death of Someone Close to Them by Age and Education ($N = 1500$)

	Education			
Age	Junior High School or Less	High School	College	"Effect" of Higher Education
30 and under	47	28	18	−29
31–40	41	23	18	−23
41–50	36	37	20	−16
51–60	41	32	22	−19
61+	46	50	40	− 6
"Effect" of older age	− 1	+22	+22	

Note. The smallest base for any percentage is 45.
Source. Riley (1963). Exhibit 14.15 reprinted with permission from *Aging and Society,* Vol. I, by Matilda White Riley, Anne Foner, and Associates, copyright © 1968 by Russell Sage Foundation.

Table 9.2   Percent Who Agree with Two Negative Views of Death by Age
and Education ($N = 1500$)

Age	Education			"Effect" of Higher Education
	Junior High School or Less	High School	College	
(a) Death always comes too soon.				
30 and under	65	53	40	−25
31–40	58	50	24	−34
41–50	75	64	49	−26
51–60	70	50	53	−17
61+	58	59	29	−29
"Effect" of older age	− 7	+ 6	−11	
(b) To die is to suffer.				
30 and under	31	13	5	−26
31–40	23	5	7	−16
41–50	18	11	10	− 8
51–60	28	8	9	−19
61+	24	13	8	−16
"Effect" of older age	− 7		+ 3	

Note. The smallest base for any percentage is 45.
Source. Riley (1963). Exhibit 14.17 reprinted with permission from *Aging and Society*, Vol. I,
by Matilda White Riley, Anne Foner, and Associates, copyright © 1968 by Russell Sage
Foundation.

friends, or in an institution) than among those who live alone. Not surprisingly, fear of death was found to be higher among those in poor
health (Richardson and Freeman, 1964). Nonetheless, Kastenbaum (1963)
found that most references to death are positive among old persons who
were dying in a geriatric hospital. And Lieberman (1966) found that
thoughts of death are no more frequent as death approaches. Riley (1963)
also reports that most old people make plans for their death. The extent
of this preparation rises consistently with age and with education (Table
9.3). However, plans for death were found to be more common among
whites than among Negroes, regardless of education (Lipman and
Marden, 1966).

   These data suggest that thoughts about death and preparation for it
tend to rise (among those with higher education) during the later years,
but do not necessarily indicate that the "death issue" is a major focus of
the final decade or two of life. Instead, it may be that this period is one

Table 9.3   Percent with High Degree of Preparation for Death[a] by Age and Education (N = 1500)

Age	Education			"Effect" of Higher Education
	Junior High School or Less	High School	College	
30 and under	0	1	3	+ 3
31–40	2	4	8	+ 6
41–50	8	14	22	+14
51–60	8	25	40	+32
61+	20	30	44	+24
"Effect" of older age	+20	+29	+41	

[a] Based on positive answers to questions about whether it is best in general to make any plans about death, and whether specific actions have been taken (discussing with those closest, making funeral or cemetery arrangements, making a will).
Note. The smallest base for any percentage is 45.
Source. Riley (1963). Exhibit 14.20 reprinted with permission from *Aging and Society*, Vol. I, by Matilda White Riley, Anne Foner, and Associates, copyright © 1968 by Russell Sage Foundation.

of occasional anticipation of the inevitable and a kind of anticipatory socialization for the final period of life. Lieberman and Coplan (1969) found that many of their aged respondents living in a nursing home or in the community had "worked out the meaning of death for themselves and most have developed a personal viewpoint toward their own death" (p. 83). These respondents were willing to talk openly about death; and most anxiety or disruption about death was related to the stability of the socioenvironmental conditions. That is, those respondents who (as it later turned out) were near to death and were living in the home or in stable environments in the community seemed to be dealing with the task of facing death without storminess or reactivity or disruptiveness; "it was as if they were dealing with a developmental task that they were coping with adequately" (ibid., p. 82). Persons who were waiting to enter the home or had only recently entered, however, "... experienced disruption and anxiety about death. Many lacked an articulate personal philosophy to deal with death. ... Individuals in this crisis state may have been anxious over impending death, not because their approaching death was of such great concern to them, but because life again had impinged on them, forcing them to make new adjustments and face anew previously solved problems (including, perhaps, a previous resolution of the death issue)" (ibid). They suggest that although nearness to death seems to clearly bring psychological changes (which we will discuss in a later section), the crucial resolution of the meaning of death may come considerably earlier, perhaps in late middle-age. The psychosomatic changes that occur within a year or two of death may then have less to do with resolving the issues of death (and of life) than with coping and responding to the physiological changes preceding death itself. Thus, while it may be that the resolution of questions about the meaning of life and acceptance of death are typical tasks one undertakes as one nears the end of one's life, it is not apparent that they dominate the last decade or two of life, nor that they dominate one's thoughts on the deathbed (Lieberman and Coplan report that respondents near death typically avoid introspection). Instead, the sense of integrity may be gradually developed over several decades; and fear of death during the last months of life may result from a crisis in the social environment disrupting one's previous acceptance or resignation.

Life Review Process

A second concept of the psychological tasks preceding death and triggered by one's closeness to death is the process of the life review, suggested by Butler (1963). The life review is defined as a "...naturally occurring, universal mental process...prompted by the realization of approaching dissolution and death, and the inability to maintain one's sense of personal invulnerability." It potentially proceeds toward personality reorganization, including the achievement of such characteristics as wisdom and serenity in the aged; thus it is a potential force toward increased self-awareness. However, it may also lead to some pathological manifestations as well, such as depression, guilt, or obsessional ruminations about past events. The process consists of reminiscence, thinking about oneself, reconsideration of previous experiences and their meanings, and "mirror gazing" (which may serve as one of the best indications that the process is taking place). One example of mirror gazing (i.e., pausing to look into a mirror, perhaps for several moments and perhaps with some verbal comments intended for one's self) is given by Butler: "I was passing by my mirror. I noticed how old I was. My appearance, well, it prompted me to think of death—and of my past—what I hadn't done, what I had done wrong" (ibid.). A similar episode is described in the Tolstoy story of Ivan Ilych:

> Ivan Ilych locked the door and began to examine himself in the glass, first full face, then in profile. He took up a portrait of himself taken with his wife, and compared it with what he saw in the glass. The change in him was immense. Then he bared his arms to the elbow, looked at them, drew the sleeves down again, sat down on an ottoman, and grew blacker than night (Tolstoy, 1886, p. 127).

The symbolic interaction interpretation of this process would be that the person is actively working to integrate his new (physical) *me* into his relatively continuous sense of self and is, in a sense, attempting to gain mastery and integration from his changed physical *me* and his internal experiencings. His *I* is striving for a new integration based on this different *me*, memory of past *me*s, and current bodily experiencings. Possibly, the body *me* is changing as rapidly as it ever did (for example, at adolescence), and these changes may require a reintegration of rather massive proportions. Thus, the past is reviewed as one attempts to sense the consistency between past *me*s, present *me*s and future *me*s in the light of current reality and future potential. Perhaps the feedback from others (such as a "confidant" discussed in Chapter 7) would be important in this process. That is, just as when one's sense of identity is the crucial issue during adolescence and young adulthood and feedback from others is significant, so also it may be that such symbolic feedback is important for this later, potentially massive reorganization of the self in preparation for death.

However, Butler's concept of the life review emphasizes not only the potential reorganization of the self but also emphasizes the adaptive aspects of reminiscence among the aged. Often this reminiscence might be seen as beyond the older person's control, or as an escape from the present, or as simply filling up empty time; but he sees the life review as an important and characteristic step for those, whether old or young, who expect death (and it may be a general response to other types of crises as well). Although Butler does not draw the parallel between this life review process and Erikson's stage of integrity versus despair, it seems clear that a central aspect of the integrity issue might involve looking back over one's life; that is, this psychological reorganization, which might also ignore or selectively recall old memories in the search for meaning or despair, would be deeply involved in the eventual resolution of the integrity versus despair crisis. Tolstoy (1886) also illustrates the life review quite explicitly; and it is one major source of Ivan Ilych's despair.

He lay on his back and began to pass his life in review . . . (p. 152).

And in imagination he began to recall the best moments of his pleasant life. But strange to say none of those best moments of his pleasant life now seemed at all what they had then seemed—none of them except the first recollections of childhood. There, in childhood, there had been something really pleasant with which it would be possible to live if it could return. But the child who had experienced that happiness existed no longer, it was like a reminiscence of somebody else.

As soon as the period began which had produced the present Ivan

Ilych, all that had then seemed joys now melted before his sight and turned into something trivial and often nasty.

And the further he departed from childhood and the nearer he came to the present the more worthless and doubtful were the joys (p. 147).

Although the phenomenon of reminiscence is typically thought to occur among the aged, we must insert a note of caution. Just as the existential search for meaning and the resolution of the integrity issues *may* strongly reflect the expectations comparatively young people have about death and may not be borne out by empirical studies into the reality of the matter, so also, reminiscence and the life review among the aged tends to be more widely assumed than demonstrated, according to Cameron (1972). He interviewed three groups of respondents by interrupting them and asking them what they were just thinking about, the topic of their thoughts, and whether they were thinking about the past, present, or future. He interviewed three different groups varying in age from 18 to 65+ at their home, at work, or on a beach. At all ages the most frequent orientation was present, followed by the future and then the past. That is, Cameron found no evidence that old people think about the past more than the present or the future or that they think about the past more than young people do. While it might be argued that this measure of time orientation does not adequately tap reminiscence, Riley, Foner, and Associates (1968), in a review of research on aging, observed that old people appear to be oriented more toward the future than toward the past (although there is relatively little data available). However, when there is memory loss (as often occurs among the aged as a result of disease such as senility), immediate and short-term memory is most affected, while rehearsed memories (such as those one would reminisce about) tend to be retained almost indefinitely. Thus reminiscence may be characteristic of only some aged persons—or characteristic of aged persons only some of the time, while present and future orientations are also maintained.

Psychological Changes Preceding Imminent Death

Although the study of psychosocial aspects of the dying process is fairly new, there is a rapidly growing body of data indicating that there are important changes associated with nearness to death—that is, changes that are brought on not by age or illness but are brought about by the imminence of death. These data are particularly interesting since they suggest (on the basis of careful empirical studies of respondents who subsequently died within a few months after the data were gathered) that developmental changes occur in the last year or two of life and are apparently timed by impending natural death. In addition, these data indicate that in many cases these psychological changes may serve as better predictors of the nearness to death than medical or physical factors alone.

Lieberman has conducted some central studies in this area. He reported (1965) that he became interested in possible psychological changes preceding death when one of the nurses in a nursing home where he was working displayed a "remarkable accuracy" in predicting the death of residents several months in advance and before there were any pronounced physical changes. She was unable to identify what led to her predictions except that a person approaching death "just seemed to act differently."

To explore this phenomenon, he used several psychological tests that required the subject to perform a series of tasks; two tests that were later found to be related to the imminence of death were the Bender-Gestalt test (where the subject is asked to draw free-hand copies of geometric figures presented on cards) and the Draw-A-Person test (where the subject is asked to draw a human figure). These tests were administered to a group of 30 elderly volunteer subjects every three or four weeks over a period of two-and-a-half years; potential subjects who had any "incapacitating physical illness or gross neurological or psychiatric disorders" were not included in the subjects selected for the study; five of the subjects dropped out or died before the study was completed.

The variables used in the study (and which were found to be related to the imminence of death) were *ego energy* (based on the size of the free-hand drawings of the Bender-Gestalt figures), *ego sufficiency* (based on the complexity of the human figure drawn), and *organization-disorganization* (based on the adequacy of reproduction of the Bender-Gestalt figures). These tests were administered to all subjects at least five times. Subjects who died less than three months after completing these five trials were placed in the "death imminent" (DI) group ($N=8$); subjects who were still living one year after completing at least ten trials were considered in the "death delayed" (DD) group ($N=17$).

If we think about the design of this study, one possible hypothesis would be that the DI group would be lower on all the measures than the DD group; that is, those who died shortly after completing five trials would be lower on ego energy, ego sufficiency, and organization than those subjects who remained alive one year after the study was completed. However, this was found not to be the case (except for ego energy, which was lower for the DI group than for the DD group). Instead, there was a great deal of individual variation reflecting such extraneous variables as the ability to draw figures, manual dexterity, and so on.

However, and perhaps even more interesting, the differences between the DD group and the DI group were in the *changes* in individual scores on each of the three variables over the repeated administration of the tests. As would be expected, many subjects showed a gradual improvement on these tests with repeated trials; those subjects who improved their level of performance over time turned out to be in the DD group. The responses of the DI group, as it turned out, were considerably different—they showed a pattern of declining or poorer performance over time on these variables (Figures 9.1-9.3). Thus, for the DI group, there was a decline in these measures of ego energy, ego sufficiency, and organization over time. However, three other variables also measured in the study (amount of activity, number of emotions felt, and ability to estimate time) did not show any change.

Lieberman concluded that the DD and DI groups could be distinguished by changes in the tasks reflecting the "adequacy of ego functioning" and

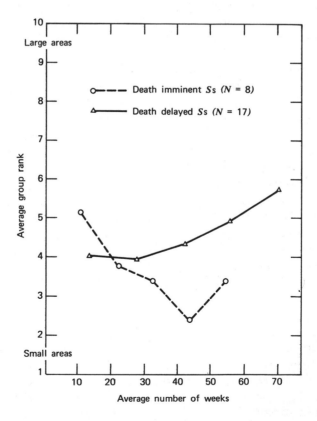

Figure 9.1
Trends in Bender-Gestalt area ("ego energy") scores over time for the DI and DD groups. Each point is an average of group rank. High ranks indicate large drawings; low ranks indicate small drawings. (Source. Lieberman, 1965. Reprinted with permission.)

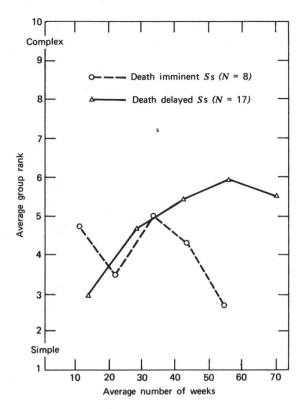

Figure 9.2
Trends in Draw-A-Person complexity ("ego sufficiency") scores over time for the DI and DD groups. Each point is an average group rank. High ranks indicate complex drawings; low ranks indicate simple drawings. (Source. Lieberman, 1965. Reprinted with permission.)

noted that the occurrence of a major illness requiring hospitalization among the DD subjects (that is, among those who recovered from the illness) did *not* result in a drop in the scores on any of the measures; and the average performance level was similar before and after the illness. Thus, illness alone does not seem to be the factor that brought the decline on these measures for the DI group. Instead, he speculates that the imminence of death may bring a "general system decline" and perhaps involve a withdrawal of energy from the outer world to cope with the inner experience of upheaval and disintegration. It is as if the nearness of death brings a marked increase in the amount of psychic energy directed inward in an effort to cope with the changes brought by impending death. Perhaps the individual withdraws his energy and ego investment from the outer world (and the psychologist's tasks) into more important issues in order to retain an integration in the face of the psychological and physiological decline and disintegration preceding

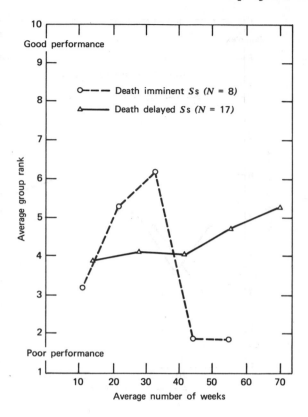

Figure 9.3
Trends in Bender-Gestalt Pascal ("organization") scores over time for the DI and DD groups.
Each point is an average group rank. High ranks indicate good performance; low ranks
indicate poor performance. (Source. Lieberman, 1965. Reprinted with permission.)

death. It is speculated that this shift is a kind of final step in the personality trend toward "increased interiority," which begins at about the age of
50 (as we discussed in Chapter 7).

Two subsequent studies (Lieberman, 1966; Lieberman and Coplan,
1969) found similar differences in a range of psychological realms (both
cognitive and affective) among larger numbers of aged subjects between
persons who were a year or less away from death and persons who were
at least three years away from death. In both studies subjects were
"matched" so that all comparisons could be made between similar subjects in the death-near and death-far groups. For example, they found
(1969) a decline in various measures of cognitive functioning, in affective
complexity, in introspection, and in several aspects of self-image among
the death-near subjects, compared to their matched death-far "control."
These results support the hypothesis that *distance from death*, rather
than chronological age, is the most useful time dimension for organizing

changes in psychological functioning in the aged. And this implies that general changes in these psychological aspects among the aged may involve marked individual changes brought about as each individual moves closer to death; in other words, psychological changes among the aged may reflect nearness to death (rather than, or in addition to, aging alone) and individual differences would be expected to be large, reflecting the nearness of each individual to his own death (the cross-sectional versus longitudinal problem, again).

A study of intellectual test performance among aged male veterans who died within a year, compared to veterans who remained alive longer (Reimanis and Green, 1971), found a similar decline in IQ performance among the subjects who died within a year of the testing, but not for those who died over a year after the testing. For their sample the mean decline for the group that died was 15.5 IQ points—more than twice the decline in full-scale IQ score for either the group who did not die within one year or the group who were still living after two years (Table 9.4). Since intellectual processes are intertwined with physiological and personality processes, it would seem that the imminence of death may disrupt the entire personality system described in Chapter 7. And indeed, Lieberman and Coplan (1969) see these psychological changes reflecting a *psychosomatic* interaction in which the bodily decline and progression toward death affects the psychological processes.

THE DYING PROCESS

Elisabeth Kübler-Ross (1969), who described herself as "a country doctor," was a psychiatrist at the University of Chicago (which operates a teaching-research hospital) when she was approached by some gradu-

Table 9.4 Comparison of Average Decrement in Verbal, Performance, and Full Scale IQ for Aged Men by Length of Survival Following Second Testing ($N = 187$)

Group	Verbal	Performance	Full Scale	N
Died within 12 months	7.4*	8.10*	15.50*	10
Died within 12–24 months	4.5	4.90	9.00	10
Died after 24 months	4.16	5.28	9.75	32
Still living after 1 year	2.81	3.59	6.60	177
Still living after 2 years	2.37	3.09	5.67	135

* $p < .05$ between group that died within 12 months and both still living groups.
Source. Adapted from Reimanis and Green (1971), Table 2. Reprinted with permission from *Developmental Psychology*, copyright © 1971 by the American Psychological Association.

ate students in theology for help on a paper on terminally ill patients. Her approach was: "If you really wish to share and experience what it is like to have a very limited time to live, sit with your dying patients and listen" (Kübler-Ross, 1970). A seminar on death and dying developed from this idea, as dying patients were invited to talk with her or other participants, sometimes observed through a viewing window by various members of the "helping profession" (doctors, nurses, chaplains, rabbis, priests, social workers, and so on). If necessary the patient was interviewed in his bed with whatever medical attention was needed (transfusions, infusions, and so on).

Initially the project met with a great deal of resistance since it seems to be generally assumed, as another pioneer in studying death was asked, "Isn't it cruel, sadistic, and traumatic to discuss death with seriously ill and terminally ill people?" (Feifel, 1963, p. 9). Kübler-Ross reported initially insurmountable difficulties and hostility:

> Suddenly, this big teaching hospital did not have a single dying patient!
> During the first year of this undertaking it required an average of ten hours per week to search for a patient—and to get permission from a physician. . . .
> In general, the very young physicians or the very old ones were more amenable to our requests, the nurses and nurses' aides the most interested, and the patients themselves the most enthusiastic. With few exceptions, the patients were surprised, amazed, and grateful. Some were plain curious and others expressed their disbelief that "a young, healthy doctor would sit with a dying old woman and really care to know what it is like." In the majority of cases the initial outcome was similar to opening floodgates. It was hard to stop them once the conversation was initiated and the patients responded with great relief to sharing some of their last concerns, expressing their feelings without fear of repercussions (Kübler-Ross, 1970, pp. 157-158).

Much of Kübler-Ross's work can be seen as an attempt to humanize the dying process, to counteract the current tendency in America of depersonalizing the dying person, and to reinstate the process of dying back into the full course of human life. Part of the difficulty, she argues, is that death is feared and denied in our unconscious: "In simple terms, in our unconscious mind we can only be killed; it is inconceivable to die of a natural cause or of old age. Therefore death in itself is associated with a bad act, a frightening happening, something that in itself calls for retribution and punishment" (Kübler-Ross, 1969, p. 2). But also, this anxiety about death is aided by our highly developed technology that attempts to find a "solution" for every "problem"—so that, too often while attempting to preserve life, we tend to turn the patient into a "thing" in which something has "gone wrong" and that needs to be "fixed." Often someone else makes the decision that the person needs to be hospitalized; he is then rushed to the hospital, endures the siren and hectic rush in an ambulance and is subjected to busy hospital staff, tests, X rays, cardiograms, and so forth. He may overhear discussions of his "case" but have no real chance to participate in the discussion; he is the "case," the "object." And once in the hospital, he must learn the rules and regulations of that institution and, in short, becomes resocialized into the role of a patient—especially in chronic or geriatric hospitals.

She reports (1969) one extreme and memorable case of a woman who seemingly had to resort to a "psychotic break" in order to prevent one last operation that might prolong her life although she was prepared to die and wanted only to die in peace. Questions of "mercy killing," relations between physician and patient, between nurse and patient, and between family and patient all come to be provocative and unanswered issues. Perhaps medical schools might do more to train physicians to deal with the incurably ill and dying patient; currently, the emphasis is often—understandably—on preserving life and on maintaining health; in a sense, death is a medical failure. Perhaps nurses, clergy, aides, and orderlies should be given some opportunity to work through their own feelings about dying patients so that they might be more helpful. Perhaps psychologists, psychiatrists, and hospital staffs might be better able to facilitate the final communication between the patient and the family. And Kübler-Ross argues that while hope of recovery needs to be maintained, the patient often would be aided by being told he is dying (he usually knows it anyway) in a manner that respects the person's dignity yet allows him to complete his life without being forced into deceptions and lies. Tolstoy has Ivan Ilych making this point quite eloquently.

What tormented Ivan Ilych most was the deception, the lie, which for some reason they all accepted, that he was not dying but was simply ill, and that he only need keep quiet and undergo a treatment and then something very good would result. He however knew that do what they would nothing would come of it, only still more agonizing suffering and death. This deception tortured him—their not wishing to admit what they all knew and what he knew, but wanting to lie to him concerning his terrible condition, and wishing and forcing him to participate in that lie. Those lies—lies enacted over him on the eve of his death and destined to degrade this awful, solemn act to the level of their visitings, their curtains, their sturgeon for dinner—were a terrible agony for Ivan Ilych. . . . He saw that no one felt for him, because no one even wished to grasp his position. Only Gerasim recognized it and pitied him. And so Ivan Ilych felt at ease only with him. . . . Once when Ivan Ilych was sending him away he even said straight out: "We shall all of us die, so why should I grudge a little trouble?"—expressing the fact that he did not think his work burdensome, because he was doing it for a dying man and hoped someone would do the same for him when his time came (Tolstoy, 1886, pp. 137-138).

Kübler-Ross reminds me considerably of Gerasim (Ivan's servant) in the story; but this aspect of her work is only a part of her contribution to our understanding of death and dying. She also described five "stages" of the dying process that help us to understand the process of dying as she discovered it from her interviews with dying patients. We will discuss those stages now.

Stages in the Dying Process

From the interviews with over 200 dying patients, Kübler-Ross (1969) has distilled five characteristic aspects of the dying process that she calls stages. She implies that these stages occur in a regular sequence, although it is not clear why the stages would be necessarily sequential or why a person might not alternately express some or all of the stages within a few hours. Hence, we prefer to view these five stages as characteristic aspects of the dying process and perhaps crucial issues that increase our understanding of the experience of the dying patient. These stages are (1) *denial and isolation*, (2) *anger*, (3) *bargaining*, (4) *depression*, and (5) *acceptance*; through all the stages, Kübler-Ross sees *hope* as a central theme. We will present each of these stages in summary form, and we will use short quotations from *The Death of Ivan Ilych* to illustrate the issues (Kübler-Ross's book, *On Death and Dying*, is a most useful and interesting primary source; she uses excerpts from interviews with dying patients to illustrate the various stages).

Denial and Isolation. The first response made by most of the patients she interviewed was: "No, not me, it cannot be true." Some felt a mistake had been made (the X ray or lab tests had been confused with someone else—and we know of one case where this did occur); others would find another physician or go to many doctors or to faith healers in an attempt to obtain a more positive diagnosis (of course, seeking a second opinion would be a realistic response but a manifestation of denial nonetheless). This denial is seen as a healthy manner of coping with shocking, unpleasant news; it functions as a buffer in the short term, allowing the patient to develop less-radical defenses to cope with long-term suffering and the reality of his impending death. Only 3 of her 200 respondents maintained denial to the very end; most replaced it with "partial acceptance" after the central buffering function of denial had served its purpose. Clearly, when a patient is heavily invested in denial of the seriousness of his case, attempting to discuss his feelings about death would be threatening; hence, the patient's willingness to discuss dying may be the best indicator of his readiness to begin dealing with the issue. Other patients may not yet be diagnosed as terminally ill, but they may wish to deal with the possibility of death before it becomes an immediate reality. Also, the sensitive listener will note the times when the patient needs to occasionally deny the reality of his impending death and to psychologically *isolate* that reality from his awareness; but after the initial shock gives way to partial acceptance, the periods of denial are usually transient. Examples of this type of denial are prevalent in the story of Ivan Ilych; for example:

> The progress of his disease was so gradual that he could deceive himself when comparing one day with another—the difference was so slight. But when he consulted the doctors it seemed to him that he was getting worse, and even very rapidly. Yet despite this he was continually consulting them.
>
> That month he went to see another celebrity, who told him almost the same as the first had done but put his questions rather differently. . . . A friend of a friend of his, a very good doctor, diagnosed his illness again quite differently from the others. . . . A homoeopathist diagnosed the disease in yet another way, and prescribed medicine which Ivan Ilych took secretly for a week. . . . One day a lady acquaintance mentioned a cure effected by a wonder-working icon. Ivan Ilych caught himself listening attentively and beginning to believe that it had occurred (Tolstoy, 1886, p. 124).
>
> The syllogism he had learnt from Kiezewetter's Logic: "Caius is a man, men are mortal, therefore Caius is mortal," had always seemed to him correct as applied to Caius, but certainly not as applied to himself (ibid., p. 131).

Anger. Once the fact that the illness is fatal begins to register, and the patient gains some beginning acceptance of that fact—that is, as denial becomes less complete—the response is often "Why me?" The central feeling comes to be one of anger, envy (at those who are healthy), and resentment. This anger is often very difficult to cope with for the family or the staff, yet from the patient's point of view it is quite understandable. It tends to be anger directed at anyone who happens to be available— doctors, nurses, staff, family, and visitors. And perhaps, as Kübler-Ross states, all of us might well be angry if our lives were interrupted prematurely, we were confined to a hospital bed, and others rushed around doing things to and for us that indicated our helplessness and dependency. Perhaps part of the message of anger is: "I am alive, don't forget that. You can hear my voice, I am not dead yet!" (Kübler-Ross, 1969, p. 52). Her suggestion to deal with this difficult situation is to provide some respect and understanding to the patient instead of taking the anger as a personal message (which it frequently is not) and avoiding the patient. Instead, he needs to feel cared for and to feel that he will be visited not because he rings the bell or is angry but because he is valued and it is a pleasure to drop in for a short visit—especially when the result of such attention and visits is a reduction in his anger. Ivan Ilych shows considerable anger and rage when he begins to accept the reality of his dying and, as noted above, his servant Gerasim comforts him and relieves the anger and bitterness because he values Ivan as a human being.

"Death. Yes, death. And none of them know or wish to know it, and they have no pity for me. Now they are playing." (He heard through the door the distant sound of a song and its accompaniment.) "It's all the same to them, but they will die too! Fools! I first, and they later, but it will be the same for them. And now they are merry . . . the beasts!"

Anger choked him and he was agonizingly, unbearably miserable. "It is impossible that all men have been doomed to suffer this awful horror!" (Tolstoy, 1886, p. 130).

After that Ivan Ilych would sometimes call Gerasim and get him to hold his legs on his shoulders, and he liked talking to him. Gerasim did it all easily, willingly, simply, and with a good nature that touched Ivan Ilych. Health, strength, and vitality in other people were offensive to him, but Gerasim's strength and vitality did not mortify but soothed him (ibid., p. 137).

Bargaining. Kübler-Ross suggests that this stage is helpful to the patient for brief periods of time after the anger subsides somewhat. It is as if the child, learning that he cannot get what he wants by demanding (in anger), now turns to "asking nicely" and trying to strike a bargain—with God, or the staff, or with the illness itself. The notion is akin to "time off for good behavior"—but is successful for only short periods of time since the illness tends to quickly invalidate the "bargain." She gives a poignant example of a patient who wished to live long enough to attend the marriage of her oldest and favorite son. By efforts from several staff, she was taught self-hypnosis and could control the pain for several hours and left the hospital to attend the wedding "an elegant lady." "I will never forget the moment when she returned to the hospital. She looked tired and somewhat exhausted and—before I could say hello—said, 'Now don't forget I have another son!'" (Kübler-Ross, 1969, p. 83). Examples of bargaining do not seem to be as obvious as the other stages; and possibly not all patients attempt to cope with dying in this way, or if they do, their bargains are relatively subtle. Yet, such attempts, although rather short-term, may be seen as positive attempts to cope with death and, insofar as they are appropriate, need not be discouraged. One possible instance of bargaining in Ivan Ilych indicates some of the forms it may take and also the subtlety of this stage.

> He would say to himself: "I will take up my duties again—after all I used to live by them." And banishing all doubts he would go to the law courts, enter into conversation with his colleagues, and sit carelessly as was his wont, scanning the crowd with a thoughtful look and leaning both his emaciated arms on the arms of his oak chair. . . . But suddenly in the midst of those proceedings the pain in his side, regardless of the stage the proceedings had reached, would begin its own gnawing work. . . . He would shake himself, try to pull himself together, manage somehow to bring the sitting to a close, and return home with the sorrowful consciousness that his judicial labours could not as formerly hide from him what he wanted them to hide, and could not deliver him from *It* (Tolstoy, 1886, pp. 132-133).

Depression. The next stage in this framework is one of a great sense of loss, which Kübler-Ross differentiates into a *reactive depression* (that is, one that results from past losses and may be accompanied by guilt or shame at the loss—such as a woman who has her breast removed due to cancer or whose teeth have been removed or whose body is disfigured by the illness) and a *preparatory depression*. This latter type involves the "preparatory grief" that is involved in giving up the things of the world and in preparing oneself for the final separation from the world. "The patient is in the process of losing everything and everybody he loves. If he is allowed to express his sorrow he will find a final acceptance much easier, and he will be grateful to those who can sit with him during this stage of depression without constantly telling him not to be sad" (Kübler-Ross, 1969, p. 87). This type of depression is often "a silent one" and frequently silent gestures and mutual expression of feelings and tenderness can be quite helpful. In contrast, the reactive depression may require some intervention, some "cheering up" and some support for the patient's self-esteem. Thus, it seems useful to distinguish between these types of depression. Kübler-Ross suggests that members of the helping professions and patients' family members should realize that this preparatory type of depression "is necessary and beneficial if the patient is to die in a stage of acceptance and peace" (ibid., p. 88).

Although most of Ivan Ilych's depression was more typically seen as despair (the negative of Erikson's Integrity versus Despair crisis) resulting from his meaningless life and his inability to find any semblance of integrity until the very end, there are also some examples of preparatory grief.

> . . . No one pitied him as he wished to be pitied. At certain moments after prolonged suffering he wished most of all (though he

would have been ashamed to confess it) for someone to pity him as a sick child is pitied. He longed to be petted and comforted.... Ivan Ilych wanted to weep, wanted to be petted and cried over.... (Tolstoy, 1886, p. 138).

But Ivan remained in continual despair, and made little progress in working through this preparatory grief. Finally, near the end, "... the screaming began that continued for three days, and was so terrible that one could not hear it through two closed doors without horror" (ibid., p. 154). It is thus somewhat questionable whether he made it into the fifth and final stage of acceptance—perhaps partly because of the inability to accept his life (that is, despair rather than a sense of integrity) and partly because of his inability to work through his grief about dying and his terrible isolation from all those in his family except his son, Vasya, and his servant, Gerasim. Of course, Tolstoy is making political, religious, and literary points in the way he constructed the story; but the illustration for our purposes here seems useful as well.

Acceptance. This last stage in the Kübler-Ross scheme is a quiet culmination of the previous trials and preceding stages. Here the patient, if he has sufficient time to work through the denial, anger, depression, and general fear/anxiety about death, comes to "... contemplate his coming end with a certain degree of quiet expectation. He will be tired and, in most cases, quite weak" (Kübler-Ross, 1969, p. 112). The stage is described as "almost void of feelings" and a period, as one of her respondents phrased it, of "the final rest before the long journey" (ibid., p. 113). This is the time, she suggests, when short visits, often in silence, sometimes holding the patient's hand, are the most helpful. She preferred to visit such patients at the end of the day when she too was tired and enjoyed a few minutes of peaceful silence. Visits with such patients (in the acceptance stage) are meaningful for the visitor also, "as it will show him that dying is not such a frightening, horrible thing that so many want to avoid" (ibid., p. 114). It is also a time when the wishes and feelings of the patient may be more acceptant of death than is true for the family. She cites one case we noted above in which the husband wished one last operation to save his wife, who had accepted death and wished to be left in peace; her only recourse was to develop a gross psychotic episode in the operating room that effectively prevented the operation. The next day she told Dr. Kübler-Ross in reference to her husband, "Talk to this man and make him understand" (ibid., p. 117).

Despite Ivan's three days of agonized screaming, there is some indication of his acceptance of death:

This occurred at the end of the third day, two hours before his death. Just then his schoolboy son had crept softly in and gone up to the bedside. The dying man was still screaming desperately and waving his arms. His hand fell on the boy's head, and the boy caught it, pressed it to his lips, and began to cry.

At that very moment Ivan Ilych fell through and caught sight of the light, and it was revealed to him that though his life had not been what it should have been, this could still be rectified. . . .

And suddenly it grew clear to him that what had been oppressing him and would not leave him was all dropping away at once from two sides, from ten sides, and from all sides. He was sorry for them, he must act so as to not hurt them: release them and free himself from these sufferings. "How good and how simple!" he thought. "And the pain?" he asked himself. "What has become of it? Where are you, pain?" . . .

He sought his former accustomed fear of death and did not find it. "Where is it? What death?" There was no fear because there was no death.

In place of death there was light.

"So that's what it is!" he suddenly exclaimed aloud. "What joy!" (Tolstoy, 1886, pp. 155-156).

Hope. Through all of the five stages that, as indicated before, perhaps do not follow one another in an invariant sequence but instead may come and go as successively more complete acceptance of death is achieved, Kübler-Ross sees hope as an important, continuing factor. She suggests that it is the hope of eventual recovery (a new drug, a last-minute success in a research project, or some kind of cure—which, of course, *has* occurred; for example, in the discovery of insulin or penicillin) that maintains the patient through the weeks and months of suffering. She notes that patients showed greatest confidence in doctors who allowed some hope to remain; and also a majority of her respondents made a "comeback" in some way or another—often from talking about the seriousness of their illness and from regaining that glimpse of hope that they are not forgotten or rejected. And certainly this hope is not only for a recovery, but also the hope that one may die in acceptance of death and with the important issues worked through with family and loved ones. If the last bit of life can be valued and meaningfully comprehended by those left behind, and if there can be some real communication between the dying and the bereaved while there is still time for it to occur, she argues very persuasively that both the dying and the bereavement are made both more humane and more meaningful.

If this book serves no other purpose but to sensitize family members of terminally ill patients and hospital personnel to the implicit communications of dying patients, then it has fulfilled its task. If we, as members of the helping professions, can help the patient and his family to get "in tune" to each other's needs and come to an acceptance of an unavoidable reality together, we can help to avoid much unnecessary agony and suffering on the part of the dying and even more so on the part of the family that is left behind (Kübler-Ross, 1969, p. 142).

The Psychological Autopsy

Weisman and Kastenbaum (1968) describe a procedure that they have developed in a geriatric hospital that they call a "psychological autopsy" in which the staff analyzes the psychosocial aspects of an individual patient's death with the aim of improving the psychosocial support that they might have provided to the patient during his hospitalization. Despite Kübler-Ross' important work, it is apparent that individuals do not all progress calmly through the five stages and do not die in the same manner. Hinton (1967) reports that about one-quarter of the persons dying in a general hospital showed a high degree of acceptance and composure; but circumstances surrounding the illness and hospitalization play an important role. He suggests that about half of the patients eventually come to acknowledge openly and to accept the end of their life (and it is more common among the elderly); a quarter express distress; and another quarter say little about it. Weisman and Kastenbaum (1968) reviewed the data on fear of death and offer a few tentative conclusions: "Only a few elderly subjects express fear of death ... fear of death is more likely to be found among elderly people who are suffering from acute emotional or psychiatric disturbances ... elderly people manifest a variety of orientations toward death, not a uniform pattern" (p. 35). They suggest two distinct patterns of dying among their chronic patients—the ones who seemed to be aware of and to accept impending death who slipped into withdrawal and inactivity until the final illness, and the ones who remained actively engaged in hospital activities until they were interrupted by death.

Weisman and Kastenbaum suggest that little attention has been paid to dying patients, especially during the "preterminal" period, largely because little attention is given to the aged in general. And their psychological autopsy indicates five principal objectives: adequate medical care, encouragement of competent behavior, preservation of rewarding relationships, maintenance of a dignified self-image, and attainment of an acceptable and, if possible, appropriate death. In sum, the person in the hospital is likely to become "a patient" (a social role), and attention needs to be given to the other roles the person maintains (parent, spouse, and so on) and to the social situation within the hospital so that his identity is not diminished to that of only "patient in bed number 14" or worse, that he becomes a "thing." They point out, "Many aged people suffer from devaluation, not disease" (ibid., p. 37).

BEREAVEMENT AND GRIEF

Much of Kübler-Ross's work on dying is aimed at helping the dying patient to resolve the last issues and weeks of life with dignity and psychological integrity. However, her approach clearly involves the family; a central theme in her interaction with the patients is the importance of relatively open and honest communication between the hospital staff, the patient, and the family (at least to the extent that the patient is open and responsive to such honesty). Such communication, she feels, aids the patient and also aids the family in saying good-bye to one another for the last time. Such a farewell involves many deep, complex, and sometimes conflicting emotions within each person; and the interaction of these deep feelings between the dying and the bereaved is even more complex. For example, as the patient progresses through the stages she describes, his reactions may confuse, confound, and conflict with those of his family. He may express denial, anger, depression, and acceptance intermittently over a few days while the family may be seeking acknowledgement that they are not being rejected and have behaved properly toward the person. Also the patient may move into such phases as preparatory depression and acceptance while his closest relatives may still be denying the imminence of his death. Perhaps the bereaved also go through stages similar to those of the dying person, and it would be helpful if the family and patient could assist one another through these reactions. Yet, often the anger (aimed in reality at the disease or at death) is misinterpreted as directed at the patient or at the family; or it may be choked back by feelings of guilt at being angry. Such guilt—at this anger, at the inability to prolong the life, at the inability to pay for some famous specialist, or at some real or imagined "wrong" that may have been done —can be a particularly heavy burden for the bereaved, and it would often be helpful for this kind of feeling to be worked through while the patient can still participate. Thus, one therapeutic task might be to facilitate the discussion of such dysfunctional, conflicted, and uncompleted feelings between the family and the patient while there is still time. If that is possible, the burden may be less for both the patient and for the family. Somehow, helping the bereaved and the dying say farewell to one another —even though that farewell may involve some anger or resentment as well as sadness, grief, and loneliness—would seem to be a primary goal from a psychological point of view for the sake of both the dying and the bereaved. Also important would be the family's understanding of the dying process; for example, anger may be expressed by the patient and may be felt by the family, or the dying person may need to say good-bye to some persons earlier than others so that he may focus his fading energy on saying farewell to those very few whom he has saved until last. But even these persons may erroneously feel rejected when he focuses nearly all of his energy inward in coping with oncoming death or has moved into the final acceptance and has so little energy left he does not even squeeze the hand or acknowledge the kiss. The bereaved are often overly sensitive to clues from the dying about their value to him and may leave the hospital feeling rejected, guilty, or depressed because their need for acceptance was not met; when, in reality, the dying person clearly has important internal issues to deal with and often little energy left.

A similarly important task during this period of final farewell is to begin the expression of grief before death actually occurs. That is, once some of the guilt, anger, and resentment have been resolved by the patient and by the family, they may then share together some of the preparatory grief, supporting one another in that process, and sharing this deep emotion with the one whose absence will be so keenly felt. We all know, for example, that pretense and facade that cover up honest feelings frequently block communication, require a great deal of effort, and make a close relationship more difficult. Perhaps then, during the last few days when a relationship with the dying person is possible, these facades (which the patient can probably see through anyway) may interfere with that relationship and might best give way to the genuine sadness and preparatory grief.

Psychological Reactions to Bereavement

We would expect that the reactions to bereavement would be related to the kinds of interactions discussed above; that is, when relatively open and honest relations are maintained until the end and when both the patient and bereaved have been able to mutually share the preparatory grief and have gained some degree of acceptance of the death, then the reaction to the loss would be less severe. Crane (1970) suggests that adjustment to the death of a family member would be related to the conflicts that preceded it, particularly feelings of uncertainty about decisions that were made regarding the dying person. She also points out the lack of systematic research about the relationship of events preceding death and the nature of the subsequent grief reaction, but that reports of the interaction between dying persons and their family often emphasize the difficulty relatives have in responding meaningfully to the fact of death before it occurs. Consequently, the severity of the grief reactions reported by several sources may be more extreme than would be the case if Kübler-Ross's suggestions could be utilized in practice.

The grief reactions that have been reported are sometimes of almost pathological intensity. Gorer (1965) reports that many of his respondents were unable to adjust to their loss and characterized the grieving of one-third of his respondents as "unlimited." An early study by Lindemann (1944) of persons bereaved by an accidental fire at the Cocoanut Grove nightclub in Boston found that somatic distress, preoccupation with the image of the deceased, a sense of unreality, guilt, hostile reactions, loss of patterns of conduct, and irritability were characteristic of the bereaved. It may be that these relatively extreme symptoms resulted in part from the accidental crisis that caused the deaths since other studies have found that these symptoms may be present but are not the most common ones. That is, a study by Clayton, Halikes, and Maurice (1971) based on interviews with 109 widowed persons during the first month of bereavement found that the most common symptoms were crying, depressed feelings, and difficulty in sleeping; difficulty in concentrating or poor memory, lack of appetite or weight loss, and reliance on sleeping pills or tranquilizers were also noted in more than half of the randomly selected subjects in the study (Figure 9.4). However, more pathological reactions were relatively infrequent in these samples. About one-third of the respondents complained about the physician or hospital—often that the physician did not indicate the severity of the illness, especially if it was short and unexpected; and 21 percent reported guilt feelings. They report that the bereaved indicated a benefit from reviewing the terminal illness during the study and suggest that reviewing the illness (perhaps with the physician) aids the bereaved by allowing him to express pent-up emotion and to confirm the reality of the death. Perhaps the funeral service provides a similar institutionalized setting for this process to occur. The respondents also reported that their children were the most helpful persons in their environment after the death, while the undertaker and the lawyer were also often viewed as helpful—perhaps because they aid the widowed person in the important task of making immediate decisions. Clayton et al. (1971) suggest that helping with immediate plans may be the most beneficial aid that can be given to the bereaved and that decisions about the future should be avoided, at least during the first month.

While these studies found a relatively low incidence of suicidal thoughts among the bereaved in the first month, other studies have reported that the incidence of death among the recently widowed is higher than among married persons of the same age (Hinton, 1967; Rees and Lutkins, 1967). For example, Clayton (1971) reported that surviving relatives have been found to have a higher death rate than expected during the first year; surviving spouses are more vulnerable than other relatives; the risk is greater for men than for women; and higher for younger than older spouses. However, the increased risk seems to be most pronounced in

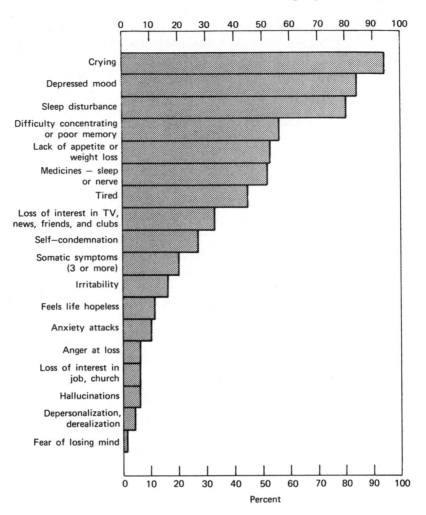

Figure 9.4
Percentage of randomly selected recently widowed persons reporting various symptoms of bereavement (N=109). Somatic symptoms include headaches, blurred vision, dyspnea, abdominal pain, constipation, urinary frequency, dysmenorrhea, and other body pains. (Source. Adapted from Clayton et al., 1971, Table 1. Reprinted with permission.)

the first six months after bereavement. Similarly, suicide rates are higher for the widowed (both male and female) especially in the first year after the death of the spouse and especially for older men. Rees and Lutkins (1967) found a higher risk of close relatives dying during the first year of bereavement if the death causing the bereavement occurred in a hospital compared with at home, perhaps because of the added stress of hospitalization.

Bowlby (1960) distinguished five phases of grief and mourning: (1) thought and behavior directed toward the lost loved object; (2) hostility toward the lost object or others; (3) appeals for help and support from others; (4) despair, withdrawal, regression, and disorganization; and (5) reorganization of behavior directed toward a new love object. He emphasizes the importance of mourning (the psychological processes set in motion by the loss of the loved object) and grief (subjective states that follow the loss and accompany the mourning) for the full resolution of the loss that leads to a reorganization of behavior. However, he maintains that a person may become fixated at any stage of the process; and Paul (1969) suggests that a person may reach a "pseudoreorganization" that is not sufficient for effective coping with the demands of living and that hides the incomplete working through of the mourning process. Bowlby indicates that for younger adults the reorganization directed toward a new love object may involve a period of promiscuity for both males and females; while this may be true for younger persons, the social pressures undoubtedly preclude promiscuity or a new love object for the aged and may indeed play an important role in addition to the grief. In addition to this inability to replace the spouse and the termination of a long love relationship, the weakened physical condition of the aged (perhaps compounded by anxiety and loss of sleep and proper food during and after the death) may be important factors contributing to the higher than expected mortality rates among aged widowed persons.

In sum, the psychological response to bereavement involves a period, often a year or two, of grief and mourning during which the person's ability to function is somewhat impaired but it does not generally involve overt pathological symptoms (unless previous symptoms were present). There seems to be an increase in the risk of a fatal illness, accident, or suicide among spouses of the deceased, perhaps resulting from physical exhaustion, loneliness, and grief itself. Reworking the events leading up to the death of the spouse may often be helpful, especially with someone (such as the physician) who knew the deceased up to the end. Perhaps one of the most traumatic aspects of the loss would be the loss of a confidant, as discussed in Chapter 7; such a confidant generally seems to buffer the aged against losses and even against bereavement as well as the general difficulties of aging. When such a confidant is lost it is often a severe loss indeed, for there is no longer anyone to provide the buffer to the loss. Kübler-Ross (1969) suggests that the worst time for the bereaved may come when the funeral is over and the relatives have left, and one is all alone for the first time. It would seem that visits by family and friends during this long period of mourning might aid as much, if not more, than immediate aid and company after death. Yet the lonely hours of evening and night, the quiet home, and the empty bed are often reported to be the worst of all.

Social Aspects of Bereavement

In concluding this chapter, we wish to briefly consider some of the social aspects of the dying process and of bereavement. Glaser and Strauss (1965) point out that death can be seen as a *status passage* that, like other institutionalized changes in status, involves a shift in social roles and presents some difficulties for the maintenance of the social system; for this reason, many aspects of the status passage are structured by society. For example, the complex legal process of inheritance and wills is institutionalized to insure the continuance of a stable social structure and to provide for an acceptable distribution of the deceased's economic assets. Similarly, the funeral is a socially structured event to commemorate this status passage and to provide a means for public expression of grief. Mandelbaum (1959) lists three social functions of the funeral: disposal of the body, aiding the bereaved in reorienting themselves (i.e., beginning the resocialization process into their new roles), and publicly acknowledging the death of the person and the viability of the social group. In addition, he suggests several latent functions beside these manifest functions of the funeral: to reaffirm the stability of the social order, to demonstrate family cohesion, to affirm extended family ties, and to reaffirm the social character of human experience. Certainly, although funeral services may be criticized on several counts, social necessity does require that the basic service be performed; and perhaps it *is* better to be charged an "all inclusive" charge for the casket, rather than for the bereaved to receive an itemized bill two weeks later! Nonetheless,

> There is a newer road which now leads from the pleasant resorts of Eastern Long Island into the city; a highway eight lanes wide over which one speeds through the city's brutal outskirts in a hermetic trance, interrupted from time to time by streams of headlights, incongruously glowing in the daylight. These are cars of mourners following the hearses that come out of the city each morning to the immense new graveyards that ring New York, perhaps thirty or forty miles from the center. There is no time on this road for stately travel. The hearses race along, sometimes two or even three abreast, at the speed of other traffic or even faster, past the roaring trucks and lines of casual travelers. One watches and wonders how often, in this frightful race, a car of mourners, falling behind, becomes detached from the proper object of its grief and follows a stranger to his grave. Perhaps it doesn't matter. You die here as you live, more or less irrelevantly, and you grow accustomed to losing your way (Epstein, 1966, pp. 15-16).

The death of a friend or relative leads to some degree of resocialization; that is, it leads to some adjustment in one's *self*. There is a new relationship with the deceased now, one located primarily in the memory of past experiences; there is a new social identity if one becomes widowed; there are some *mes* that, in some sense, are stored away—for the other to whom they were significant is no longer present; there are new feelings of grief and shock and loss that are slowly integrated into the self by the *I*. Some of these changes were discussed in Chapter 5; but these social and psychological shifts, changes, and reorientations are important to note again. Perhaps these "adjustments" (far too mechanistic a term for this process) begin with the death, perhaps during the period of preparatory grief with the dying person, perhaps with the funeral. They may be aided by the support of family and friends, and a confidant may be an important resource for those fortunate enough to maintain a close relationship. But these supports cannot satisfy the loneliness and the bereaved have to do their grief work alone, often with the increased realization of their own impending death. Clearly there is a place for persons whom Strauss and Glaser (1970) term "Grief-Workers" who are sympathetic listeners or comforters helping the bereaved to work through their long mourning process.

One final and curious note. This discussion, and the research we have examined on bereavement, has focused primarily on the death of a *spouse*. While the death of a spouse is clearly a potential crisis point, and while there is a reasonable amount of research on this topic and on the effect on young children of the death of their parents or grandparents, we were not able to find any research on the effect of the death of one's parents on middle-aged persons. Certainly this topic would be an important one for a study of adulthood. Perhaps this curious lack of research is an indication of the prevalence of a marked fear and taboo about death since the death of one's parents would be the most immediate way in which death would be likely to affect those who would be conducting the research. Of course, a great many other aspects of this important topic also require additional research and studies of dying and bereavement have increased rapidly in the last decade; but still, it is curious.

In the next chapter we turn toward the future. We will examine the conditions of the aged in our society and imagine how it will be when we get there. Since there is much we would probably like changed from this personal perspective, we will also discuss some of the ways in which we might have a hand in changing our own future, our parents' future, and the quality of life for all aged persons.

References

Barnes, Hazel E. 1959. *Humanistic Existentialism: The Literature of Possibility.* Lincoln: University of Nebraska Press.

Beauvoir, Simone de. 1972. *The Coming of Age.* (Translated by Patrick O'Brian.) New York: G. P. Putnam's Sons.

Bowlby, John. 1960. Grief and Mourning in Infancy and Early Childhood. *Psychoanalytic Study of the Child, 15,* 9-52.

*****Butler, Robert N. 1963.** The Life Review: An Interpretation of Reminiscence in the Aged. *Psychiatry, 26*(1), 65–76.

Cameron, Paul. 1972. The Generation Gap: Time Orientation. *Gerontologist, 12*(2), 117–119.

Clayton, Paula J. 1971. Bereavement: Concepts of Management. *Psychiatry.* (Published by *Medical World News.*)

Clayton, Paula J.; Halikes, James A.; and Maurice, William L. 1971. The Bereavement of the Widowed. *Diseases of the Nervous System, 32*(9), 597–604.

Crane, Diana. 1970. Dying and Its Dilemmas as a Field of Research. In Orville G. Brim, Jr., Howard E. Freeman, Sol Levine, and Norman A. Scotch (Eds.), *The Dying Patient.* New York: Russell Sage Foundation.

Epstein, Jason. 1966. Living in New York. *New York Review of Books, 5,* 14–16.

Erikson, Erik H. 1968. *Identity: Youth and Crisis.* New York: W. W. Norton.

Feifel, Herman. 1963. Death. In Norman L. Farberow (Ed.), *Taboo Topics.* New York: Atherton Press.

*****Glaser, Barney G., and Strauss, Anselm L. 1965.** Temporal Aspects of Dying as a Non-Scheduled Status Passage. *American Journal of Sociology, 71*(1), 48–59.

Gorer, Geoffrey. 1965. *Death, Grief and Mourning in Contemporary Britain.* London: Cresset.

Hinton, John. 1967. *Dying.* Baltimore: Penguin Books.

Kastenbaum, Robert. 1963. Cognitive and Personal Futurity in Later Life. *Journal of Individual Psychology, 19*(2), 216–222.

Kübler-Ross, Elisabeth. 1969. *On Death and Dying.* New York: Macmillan.

Kübler-Ross, Elisabeth. 1970. The Dying Patient's Point of View. In Orville G. Brim, Jr., Howard E. Freeman, Sol Levine, and Norman A. Scotch (Eds.), *The Dying Patient.* New York: Russell Sage Foundation.

*****Lieberman, Morton A. 1965.** Psychological Correlates of Impending Death: Some Preliminary Observations. *Journal of Gerontology, 20*(2), 181–190.

Lieberman, Morton A. 1966. Observations on Death and Dying. *Gerontologist, 6,* 70–73.

Lieberman, Morton A., and Coplan, Annie Siranne. 1969. Distance from Death as a Variable in the Study of Aging. *Developmental Psychology, 2*(1), 71–84.

Lindemann, Erich. 1944. Symptomatology and Management of Acute Grief. *American Journal of Psychiatry, 101*(2), 141–148.

Lipman, Aaron, and Marden, Philip W. 1966. Preparation for Death in Old Age. *Journal of Gerontology, 21*(3), 426–431.

Mandelbaum, D. G. 1959. Social Uses of Funeral Rites. In Herman Feifel (Ed.), *The Meaning of Death.* New York: McGraw-Hill.

May, Rollo. 1958. Contributions of Existential Psychotherapy. In Rollo May,

Ernest Angel, and Henri F. Ellenberger (Eds.), *Existence: A New Dimension in Psychiatry and Psychology*. New York: Basic Books.

*Neugarten, Bernice L. **1967**. The Awareness of Middle Age. In Roger Owen (Ed.), *Middle Age*. London: British Broadcasting Corporation.

Newsweek. **1972**. A Course on Death. May 8, 1972, 75.

Paul, Norman. **1969**. Psychiatry: Its Role in the Resolution of Grief. In Austin H. Kutscher (Ed.), *Death and Bereavement*. Springfield, Ill.: Charles C Thomas.

Rees, W. D., and Lutkins, S. G. **1967**. Mortality of Bereavement. *British Medical Journal, 4*, 13–16.

Reimanis, Gunars, and Green, Russel F. **1971**. Imminence of Death and Intellectual Decrement in the Aging. *Developmental Psychology, 5*(2), 270–272.

Richardson, Arthur H., and Freeman, Howard E. **1964**. Behavior, Attitudes and Disengagement Among the Very Old. Unpublished. Cited in Matilda White Riley, Anne Foner, and Associates. *Aging and Society*. Vol. 1. *An Inventory of Research Findings*. New York: Russell Sage Foundation, 1968.

Riley, John W., Jr. **1963**. Attitudes Toward Death. Unpublished. Cited in Matilda White Riley, Anne Foner, and Associates. *Aging and Society*. Vol. 1. *An Inventory of Research Findings*. New York: Russell Sage Foundation, 1968.

Riley, Matilda White; Foner, Anne; and Associates. **1968**. *Aging and Society*. Vol. 1. *An Inventory of Research Findings*. New York: Russell Sage Foundation.

Strauss, Anselm L., and Glaser, Barney G. **1970**. Patterns of Dying. In Orville G. Brim, Jr., Howard E. Freeman, Sol Levine, and Norman A. Scotch (Eds.), *The Dying Patient*. New York: Russell Sage Foundation.

Swenson, Wendell M. **1961**. Attitudes Toward Death in an Aged Population. *Journal of Gerontology, 16*(1), 49–52.

Tolstoy, Leo. **1886**. The Death of Ivan Ilych. In Leo Tolstoy, *The Death of Ivan Ilych and Other Stories*. New York: New American Library (Signet), 1960.

Weisman, Avery D., and Kastenbaum, Robert. **1968**. *The Psychological Autopsy: A Study of the Terminal Phase of Life*. Community Mental Health Journal Monograph No. 4. New York: Behavioral Publications, Inc.

* References marked with an asterisk appear in Bernice L. Neugarten (Ed.), *Middle Age and Aging*. Chicago: University of Chicago Press, 1968.

ten
Epilogue:
Toward
the
Future

New discoveries based on intensified research and refined methodology are likely to be some of the main characteristics of the field of adult development and aging for some time to come. Yet, perhaps the most significant change—and one of the most important—is likely to be in the economic and social conditions in which the aged live out the late fall and winter of their years. Not only will future generations of aged persons benefit from better health (because of longer and better medical care), more education, and longer length of life, but also, they (i.e., we) will benefit from whatever political and economic changes are made to improve the quality, dignity, and security of old age in this country. Few areas of social-economic-political change seem so necessary as the current status of the aged; and few areas offer such direct rewards to the legislators and the people because improved conditions for the aged today insure their (our) security in the future. Certainly, adequate health care and adequate incomes are obvious necessities for the aged; and the lack of these has, tragically, shaped and distorted the lives of many (if not most) aged persons in our society. To be sure, the length of life has been increasing and will probably continue to do so. But should not our goal be to add life to years as well as to add years to life? Indeed, future generations of senior citizens will be quite different from those currently receiving attention. We will have a pension that is secure (as too many are not today), we will have higher Social Security payments (for we will have paid into the system for longer years and now all jobs are covered, but today many aged persons do not receive full coverage because their low-skilled jobs were not covered), and we can rely on federal insurance for medical care (which only recently has lifted much of this burden from the aged). So, in important ways, the process of aging will change during our lifetime, unless we are foolishly shortsighted and incredibly calloused to the pleas of "senior power."

At the same time we look to the future, we must also look around us in the present because without knowing how it is today we are in no position to bring about the changes that are so desperately needed and that will insure the future for us as well. What is it like to be old; and especially, what is it like to be old and poor (which are too often synonomous today)? How must it be to live in a contemporary nursing home or in the only kind of home or apartment that we could afford on $100 a month from Social Security? What is the loneliness of a widow living in a high-crime area in a rundown apartment (because that is all she can afford) when to walk on the street means fear of mugging, flights of stairs to climb, fast-moving traffic and pedestrians, and everything priced too high to buy? How is it to be sick and not able to afford the cab fare to visit a doctor and, most of all, to fear dying alone in the apartment or home and not being found for days? We can only sketch in some of the parameters of these experiences since they can scarcely be expressed in words. Yet we will try—with words and statistics.

In 1971, 1 out of every 10 persons in the United States was over 65— about 20 million persons—twice the number of persons over the age of 65 in 1940. One out of every four of these persons lived in poverty in 1971 (under $1852 per year for an individual or $2328 per year for a couple). In contrast, 1 out of 9 younger persons was living in poverty (U.S. Senate Special Committee on Aging, 1971). Sixty percent of the elderly persons living alone or with non-relatives were living "in or near" poverty in 1967 (income under $2315 for an individual). The oldest man in the United States, Mr. Charlie Smith, was living on $78 a month from Social Security at the age of 130 in 1972 (this was probably raised in late 1972 to the new minimum of $84.50). He reportedly worked until he was 113 (*Newsweek*, 1972b), but probably because his farm occupation was not covered by Social Security until recently, he never paid into the system and thus receives only the minimum benefit despite 100 years of work!

It is apparent that old age is often a negative social position in our country. One way of conceptualizing this negative social position of the aged is to consider the compounding of negative statuses that may characterize the aged. First is the negative status of being old—bad enough by itself in our youth-oriented society characterized by what Butler (1969) terms *ageism*. Add to this the other negative statuses that may be present: poor, black (or Spanish speaking, or Indian, or other minority group), and woman (probably widowed). The result is a quadruple compounding of negative social positions that is typically intensified by sickness and loneliness.

In large cities there are the advantages of activities, programs, and some other old people around; but there is also the major disadvantage of crime and the constant vulnerability to mugging, robbery, and physical injury.

In rural areas, although the physical situation is rather different, the problems are no less severe—transportation, housing maintenance, lack of nearby medical care, absence of senior citizens centers, and physical as well as social isolation stand out as the major difficulties.

In short, there is a great deal about aging in our country that most of us have probably seen around us from time to time but certainly would not want to experience ourselves. Assuming that one of the goals of education is to increase the understanding and improve the quality of life, let us examine the social issues of aging more closely and systematically. In this discussion we will draw heavily from the reports of the professionals and the aged who participated in the 1971 White House Conference on Aging. We will then take a look at some of the problems and alternatives of nursing homes and will conclude this final chapter with the educational challenges presented by these major issues.

MAJOR SOCIAL PROBLEMS OF AGING PERSONS 🔶

Social workers, economists, politicians, and gerontologists who are concerned with issues of social policy, providing services, or planning programs for the aged typically divide the issues into five broad categories: *income, health, housing, transportation,* and *nutrition.* Less concrete but equally important issues are education, employment, postretirement roles, spiritual needs, legal aid, consumer protection, safety, and discrimination. In addition, the special problems of such groups of minority elderly as black, Spanish-speaking (e.g., Puerto Rican, Cuban, and Mexican American), Asian, and American-Indian persons are of great importance in our heterogeneous society. We will discuss each of the five broad categories, incorporating several of the other important issues in the discussions; then we will discuss other special concerns of the aged and will conclude with some of the unique problems of the various minority groups.

Income

Certainly, the basic and most central issue for aging persons in our society is the maintenance of an adequate income. After retirement, there is little income available (from part time jobs, odd jobs, gifts, and so on) except for one's own savings, Social Security, and private pensions. Inflation eats away at all of these items, because the dollars saved in 1940 or 1950 or 1960 buy much less in 1973. Social Security is literally a lifesaver but its payments, even after a total of 51 percent in increases from 1970 to 1972, average only $156 a month for an individual and $271 a month for a couple—above the officially defined poverty level, but clearly minimal. The amount of Social Security payments depends on the individual's age when payment was begun (62-65 for men; payments begin at age 62 for women), and the average income up to a maximum during the 38 highest years (for men born after 1929). The minimum payment was set at $84.50 a month for an individual and $126.80 for a couple in 1972 ($1010 and $1522 per year, respectively) with graduated increases built in to keep up with inflation. Since most aged persons who are currently among the aged poor worked in domestic, farm, or government occupations—which were not covered by Social Security until recently—their checks are little, if any, above this minimum. And in an urban area such as New York City with a high concentration of elderly persons (12 percent in 1970), these minimum incomes are about half of the income defined as poverty ($1840 for a single individual; $2400 for a couple in New York City, 1971). Since half of all elderly households in New York City in 1967 had an income of less than $3000 compared with only 9 percent of younger households (under age 65), it is likely that many of the elderly never experienced such poverty before they retired (New York City Office for the Aging, unpublished). In short, the major problem for many aged persons is basic economic *survival.*

Of course, persons in minority groups are the hardest hit, with many aged Negro, Puerto Rican, Asian, and Jewish persons suffering extreme poverty. But age tends to equalize discrimination somewhat, since nearly one-quarter of the aged poor were white in 1969. Older women are the hardest hit—51 percent of those living alone had incomes below the poverty line, and an incredible 77 percent of nonwhite women living alone suffered poverty (Kreps, 1970). Adding to the problem for women is that until recently widows received only 88½ percent of their husband's benefits; and that benefit could be reduced by as much as one half if they remarried—a financial inducement to "live in sin"! Beginning in 1973 a widow may receive up to 100 percent of her spouse's benefits and, if she remarries, she continues to collect either her widow's benefit or her wife's benefit, whichever is higher; she loses half her deceased husband's benefit only if she marries a man who is still working. In addition, women who worked are likely to receive lower benefits than men, since their typical preretirement income is lower than for men. But current employment trends also indicate a growing problem for men—about half of the benefits currently (1970) requested were by men at age 62 wishing to receive reduced benefits, and one in five of the men had not worked for the preceding 12 months; only about one-third of them reported any other pension income. Thus, easing older workers (often with sporadic work history and low lifetime-earnings) out of jobs prior to age 65 may be setting up a new group of elderly poor.

What are the answers? For an individual, savings might be one. But given the realities of inflation—for example, the cost of medical care increased by 30 percent, housing increased by 25 percent, and hospital charges jumped 64 percent from 1967 to 1971—savings, with interest, barely keep up with the cost of living. And, of course, medical expenses become a marked burden with advancing age (even with Medicare). Property taxes are another burden for the aged who have some assets such as a home because these taxes have been increasing markedly in recent years; and even increases in sales taxes can hit the aged harder than they do wage earners.

Another answer is a pension of some kind. Yet, these also have been a bitter disappointment for many of the aged. Most of the poor aged do not have any pension income—either because they did not work for an employer who offered one or could not afford one, or because they lost their pension because of what might seem to be a technicality. Many pensions do not have what is called "vesting rights" or "portability," which means that if the worker leaves the job or the union and moves to another, he does not own his pension and cannot take his investment with him. Thus, too often, the employee quit or was fired before the pension was to begin paying him and so he lost everything. Sometimes changing from one union to another at the same company meant losing the pension investment and having to start over again. Sometimes being "laid off" or sick for too long meant a loss of the pension, since the work may have to be "continuous" for 20 or 30 years in order to receive any pension. Other pensions were lost when the company went out of business or declared bankruptcy (as with the Studebaker Corporation several years ago). An analysis of 87 (out of the 1500) pension plans released by Senators Javits and Williams found that of the 51 plans with no vesting or 11 or more years of service for vesting, only 5 percent of the participants who left their jobs since 1950 received any benefits. Of the remaining 36 plans, requiring 10 years or less for vesting, only 16 percent of the participants who left after 1950 received any pension. Nearly 10 million workers had participated in these plans since 1950, and a substantial number of long-term employees had lost their benefits. In a subsequent study of 764 private pension plans, the senators reported that the median monthly payment was only $99 (U. S. Senate Special Committee on Aging, 1971).

The problem of retirement income is obviously complex, critical, and intertwined with the larger problem of poverty, welfare, and discrimination. Should there be, for example, a guaranteed minimum retirement income? If so, how should it be administered to protect the dignity and privacy of individuals? How can it be financed? Should elderly persons who wish to continue working full or part time receive full Social Security benefits? ($1 is lost for every $2 earned over $2100 per year.) Or will the recent improvements in Social Security, combined with adequate private pensions, eventually bring the needed improvements? If so, what should be done in the meantime? Currently the aged who receive less than poverty-level income may apply for Old Age Assistance (similar to welfare); but many do not, because, in part, they have never been on welfare before and have too much pride to go on welfare now. Other problems such as lack of information, bureaucratic complexity, and desire for privacy also hinder full use of the existing benefits.

It is apparent that the problem of income for aged persons is at the core of the social problems that confront them. Inadequate income has repercussions in the availability and maintenance of adequate housing, health, transportation, and a general varied life style. Consumer fraud, exposure to crime, and availability of legal services are all less-serious problems if one is able to retire with a comfortable income from some source. Indeed, the promise of a retirement community in a warm climate, with occasional trips to visit the children, and sound financial security is probably the aim of most middle-class Americans. But it is clear that this dream does not automatically come true even after 45 years of hard work, saving, and good health. Too often there was never the chance for that dream; and too often those dreams have been cruelly misleading.

Housing

Just as there is no substitute for an adequate income if a person is to be able to exercise his free choice about the style of his life, there is no substitute for a variety of alternate housing arrangements for him to exercise freedom of choice. The freedom of choice and the desire to extend the span of independent living in comfort and dignity are two central themes of the recommendations of the White House Conference on Aging. The participants (both professionals and senior citizens) agreed that a variety of housing is needed for the aged, corresponding to health, income, and free choice—both inside and outside of institutions such as nursing homes. The poor, minority groups, disabled, and rural aged are particularly in need of adequate and well-maintained housing. But it also needs to be the kind of housing that meets their health and aesthetic needs as well as being located where they want to live and where they can readily get to visit those places of interest for them.

For example, minority groups often have cultural attitudes about housing that are important. How acceptable is the design for Chinese, or Japanese, or Puerto Rican persons? How available are the preferred foods? How can family ties be maintained? Are there persons who speak the language? For these reasons, many old persons prefer to remain in their deteriorating family homes or apartments; others stay for senti-mental reasons or because the neighborhood is familiar. It may also be cheaper to stay. But in urban areas, this means that too often the neighborhood is decaying around them, crime is becoming a problem, and family and younger friends have moved away. Many Spanish-speaking elderly persons own their own homes, as do many other elderly persons; this may be their only "real property." But it is expensive to maintain a house, especially with property taxes and general inflation. Many rural elderly also own their homes but live in a community that is gradually migrating to the cities: the doctor and dentist may have left the town, as many as one out of five residents may also be old, and the town is slowly dying while property taxes spiral upward. Many urban elderly live in apartments sometimes paying very moderate rents but receiving less than adequate services because the building is not profitable for the landlord, or they are forced to move because the rents are increased or the apartment is turned into a "condominium" (where each tenant buys his apartment from the landlord and then pays a monthly "maintenance" fee) and they cannot afford the initial payment. What happens then? Where do they go?

Some public housing projects have apartments reserved for the aged. But often the noise, location, and fear of crime disincline the elderly to move in. Some housing projects have sought to serve only the elderly, but sometimes the community rejects having "all those old people around"; and not all old people would choose to live only with other old persons. In any such housing arrangements, architectural considerations are paramount. Are the spatial environment, the physical buildings, the interior design, and the approaches from the community designed with the aged in mind? Is it safe in case of fire? Are the necessary community, health, and cultural necessities available for the residents? Special cross-walks, complete absence of physical barriers (such as stairs, unguarded streets, and icy walks), efficient and safe elevators, and the most modern fire prevention devices in every room are some of the basic requirements. Appropriate research would indicate the design, the extent of window space, the presence of children and other aged persons, and other preferences that should be considered for the particular group of aged persons likely to live in the housing.

Certainly, the problems and the scope of the housing issue are very complex and few answers are available. One partial solution in New York and other cities is a special rent exemption for senior citizens to at least lighten the financial burden of housing costs. While this does not solve the basic question of how to insure free housing choice to the elderly, it does at least allow the elderly to pay the rent where they currently live. But this, like the other financial measures, involves red tape and is not fully utilized by the elderly. One recommendation of the delegates to the White House Conference was to provide tax incentives or rent reductions for young families to provide housing and care for their aged relatives.

More than adequate housing is required for the elderly to extend their length of independent living, however. Often the tasks of shopping for food, cooking, caring for household duties, laundry, and short errands become difficult, painful, and (if living alone) not very meaningful duties that are avoided as much as possible. If there is disease, or physical impairment, stairs to climb or cold to endure, and a sense of uselessness or depression, the aged person is likely to become almost a prisoner of his own home. Combined with more general social isolation and poverty, these difficulties compound one another—food delivered to the home costs more; not going out increases the social isolation; isolation and lack of adequate foods makes eating less enjoyable, and it tends to become more infrequent. The next step may be a lonely period of wasting away or being moved to an institution. Even in less-severe conditions, the absent mindedness of developing senile disease or lack of interest in food or lack of desire to continue cooking for one person can make independent living nearly impossible. One particular service is of great importance in situations like these—a homemaker or health aid. Such a person—carefully trained, screened, and supervised—may visit several times a week to cook a hot meal, provide necessary supplies, services, and information, and to provide some companionship. Other programs such as "Meals on Wheels" or other community meal programs can also meet many of these needs. The important service, however, is allowing the individuals to remain independent and in their own homes longer, instead of being moved to some kind of institution or nursing home. These homemakers could be young, middle aged, or older persons, perhaps providing a double benefit of added jobs for persons previously unable to support themselves. The delegates to the White House Conference recommended a tenfold increase in the number of such paraprofessional homemakers.

Finally, some attention might be paid to the needs of the aging family in terms of housing. For example, many more homes for the aged might be designed so that aged couples could live together in privacy and dignity. The separation of husband and wife during long periods of illness or chronic disease must be one of the most terrible aspects of the aging family; but when one partner of a 50-year union must move to a nursing home for the remainder of his life, the separation is surely unendurable! Also, for widowed or divorced aged persons, the White House Conference participants point out the need for "attractive social centers ... where older men and women could enjoy the formation of new friendships and relationships to take the place of those that they have lost, and all personnel should be taught to accord full respect and dignity to these" (White House Conference on Aging, 1971, p. 207).

Health

Until the fairly recent enactment of Medicare in 1965, aged persons had only the protection of their savings, private insurance, and charity to

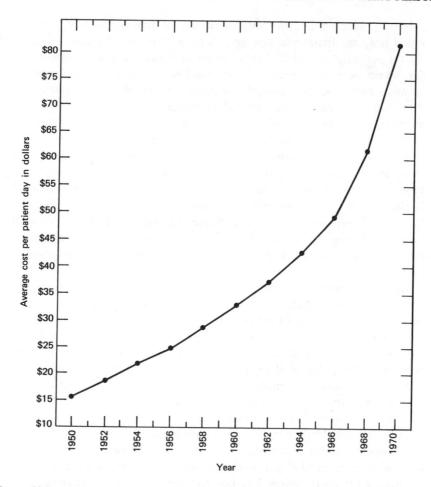

Figure 10.1
Average hospital cost per patient day, 1950–1970. (Source. *Data compiled from* Hospital
Statistics *and from* Hospitals, Journal of the American Hospital Association. *Reprinted with
permission.*)

buffer them against their increasing susceptibility to disease discussed
in Chapter 8. And the enormous increase in medical and hospital expenses
put these basic necessities out of the financial reach of most aged
Americans (Figure 10.1). There remains considerable doubt whether
Medicare provides adequate protection, however, since several important
items are omitted (such as prescription drugs; care of eyes, ears, teeth,
and feet; and eyeglasses, hearing aids, and dentures); and the individual
must often pay part of the fee. The delegates to the White House Conference recommended a comprehensive national health security program
serving not only the elderly but the entire population as the most meaningful solution to the health problems of the aged.

Briefly, Medicare, Title XVIII, Part A of the Social Security Act, provides hospital insurance for any person over age 65 who is entitled to Social Security or railroad retirement benefits; various options also exist for some persons under age 65 and surviving spouses or dependent spouses may also be covered. Generally, protection is provided for hospital inpatient care, posthospital extended care, and home health visits by nurses or other health workers; doctors' services or drugs are not covered. Funding is from federal Social Security funds. *However*, $68 of the hospital bill is deductible (paid by the individual—as of 1972; up from $40 in 1966); when the hospital stay exceeds 60 days, the individual pays $17 a day up to the ninetieth day and then $34 a day after 90 days. If the person goes to an "extended-care" facility, the cost is $8.50 per day after 20 days—larger than the Social Security check received by the average old person. All of these patient costs have gone up since 1966, and in 1973 proposed federal cuts threaten to raise them considerably higher.

Medicare, Part B, helps to pay for doctors' bills, outpatient hospital services, medical supplies and services, home health services, outpatient physical therapy, and other health care services. This insurance is *voluntary* and currently costs $6.60 per month (up from $3 in 1966). Usually this is subtracted from the Social Security check each month. Thus, even with Medicare, the aged person (with only half the income of younger individuals) still pays more than twice as much for health services as younger persons (U. S. Senate Special Committee on Aging, 1971). And the costs of Medicare are steadily rising.

There is also Medicaid. This is funded jointly by the federal and state governments and is available to all recipients of public assistance and to the "medically needy" (at a state's option)—that is, persons who have resources for daily living, but not for needed medical care, and all children under 21 whose parents cannot afford medical care. In New York State, for persons on public assistance, Medicaid covers costs for physicians, dentists, other professionals, hospitals, nursing homes, outpatient or clinic services, home care, drugs, eyeglasses, etc. Payment is directly to the medical person or service. In at least two states, New York and California, recipients are being charged a fixed fee for each prescription ($1 in California), for each doctor's visit ($1) and for each day in a hospital or nursing home ($3); although this is prohibited by federal law, it has been allowed as an "experiment" for 18 months beginning in 1972.

Recent cost-cutting cutbacks and regulations have saved money, but at the price of denying urgently needed health care to our older citizens. By placing limits on care available and by increasing costs, we have merely decreased the health and happiness of our older people. Too often, the choice for them must be made between food and medicine (Muskie, 1971).

Regardless of the politics involved in the administration and equitable funding of health care services, it is apparent that more is required for total physical and mental health care than financial resources, whatever their source. Health education is of primary importance and the related task of health assessment is crucial to increase the extent of good health among the aged—for example, hypertension is easily diagnosed and generally treatable, but individuals need to learn that it is important to have their blood pressure checked periodically. Such goals imply greatly expanded preventive and outreach services, such as mobile clinics that could visit rural as well as urban and suburban areas for education, assessment, and preventive medicine. Health care would also involve rehabilitation, including occupational rehabilitation that tends to be emphasized only for younger persons. And it involves not only maintenance or restoration of health but also long-term care if disability occurs. This suggests the need to explore alternative modes of extended care in addition to currently existing institutions, such as caring for the person in his own home with proper health services and possible subsidies to families for providing the needed care, or the use of senior citizen centers to provide some of this home health care or related services.

Transportation

There are three obvious facets to the problem of transportation for the elderly. First, whether it is available to their residence and is economical so that it is truly available; second, whether it is safe, convenient, and designed with the needs of the elderly in mind; and third, whether there is any place worth going on it. Certainly, the elderly, as all of us, depend on transportation to participate in spiritual, cultural, social, and recreational activities; and lack of transportation implicitly denies full participation in the community. Again, income issues are paramount since with limited income the elderly are often forced to live in areas that are not well served by mass transit, and they do not have resources for taxi fares or for private automobiles; even transit fares may be a large expense for the poor aged and rising fares combined with reduced service hit the aged and the poor hardest. Also, many aged persons living in deteriorating neighborhoods in urban areas face realistic fears of crime riding mass transit. Transportation is a significant problem in rural areas since there is often none at all available and distance is a major barrier to health care, social interaction, and community participation.

Several urban areas have experimented with "reduced fare" for senior citizens during nonrush hours; and indeed the experiment seems to be successful in New York City where the reduced-fare card has become as important as a student ID. Several theaters (including the Metropolitan Opera) have begun allowing certain types of discounts to senior citizens with their reduced-fare card (or other proof of age)—such as "student rush tickets" available 30 minutes before the performance. Such cultural benefits, at reduced prices and during hours when (movie) theaters are largely empty, not only provide some extra profit for the theater but provide a potentially positive place for the older person to go during the day while the streets are reasonably safe. However, there are still many steps to climb, closing doors to dodge, jerking trains or buses to keep one's footing in, and other problems such as finding one's way to a new place. In other cities, infrequent buses, slow travel, and long walks from the nearest bus stop to one's home or destination make the trip more difficult than it is for younger persons with available cars.

Since lack of transportation is most critical when it prevents easy access to one's doctor or clinic, one promising experiment is being carried out in New York City. The experiment is called "Dial-A-Ride" in which aged persons simply telephone for a taxi reservation one day in advance to take them to a destination within a prescribed area of the city. A taxi picks them up, probably picking others up along the way, and takes them to their destination (doctor's office or whatever); the cost is 75 cents per person for a single individual for a one-way trip—still a substantial expense on a limited budget but probably as cheap and certainly more convenient than a bus.

In sum, adequate transportation facilities are needed for *all* elderly persons (rural and urban) in order to effectively remove many of the physical and spatial barriers that separate the aged from their freely chosen activities in the community. Special consideration needs to be given to the needs of the rural elderly, the handicapped, and elderly persons in various minority groups whose life styles or cultural interests require more adequate transportation facilities. The availability of bilingual information about transit routes and service may also help reduce the barrier of fear and confusion and allow free access to the community by non-English-speaking aged persons. Other physical barriers, such as stairs, escalators, high steps, and cold waiting areas may prevent free access to transit for the aged and the handicapped; but architectural creativity may eliminate most or all of these barriers—as has been attempted on the Bay Area Rapid Transit (BART) system in San Francisco.

Nutrition

The fifth basic necessity for at least an adequate, hopefully a comfortable life in the aged years with maximum freedom of choice, dignity, and independence is adequate and proper food. Obviously, poor nutrition may result from inadequate income—as when food or medicine must be sacrificed because there is not enough money for both. But, as we suggested earlier, poor nutrition may also result from social isolation, physical inability to go out to eat or shop, or from loneliness and depression. After cooking for a family or a couple all of one's adult life, it is absolutely no fun to cook only for oneself and to eat alone. If one never cooked until widowed, the additional problem of having to learn how to cook compounds the nutrition problem. Buying and affording suitable and enjoyable foods is hindered by inflation, food packaging (in that small quantities typically cost more than large packages per unit), and the difficulty of finding food sold in portions for only one.

Several issues are interrelated in this nutrition problem. In addition to income, the aged need education about nutritional needs and sources; and consumer protection is also required to insure that the stores where the aged shop have small packages of necessary foods on sale, and ideally, priced at the same amount per unit as larger packages. Perhaps the frozen food and "TV dinner" products have been one of the greatest assets for meals for the elderly—but only recently has the Federal Food and Drug Administration begun to require identification of nutritional contents of packaged food. Clearly, shopping and feeding oneself properly is not a simple matter, especially on a small budget, and especially when the body has less tolerance for stress than the body of younger persons. Thus education—about nutrition, about food, about shopping, about food budgets, about price comparisons, and about food preparation—is likely to be quite important. How should this be done? Where? By whom? How can the local stores be involved? Obviously, it should be bilingual, if appropriate. Could this education be linked up with volunteers who would physically help with the shopping and cooking and be there to share the meal?

We briefly discussed some of the problems of buying food, shopping, cooking, and some of the suggestions that have been made for those problems earlier. We also mentioned the loneliness of eating alone and the importance of the social function of eating in our society. Because of its social importance, organizations of old persons have strongly recommended the establishment of community meals—perhaps in a church, or a school, or a senior center—some place where they could prepare food for one another, eat together, and share some important social interaction. The United States has long had a federally supported school lunch program for children, utilizing agricultural surplus food; why not for the aged too? Many programs such as these, in various settings, and with various funding, currently exist. Some senior centers have a daily luncheon that provides this double service—social contact and, perhaps, the only hot meal for that person all day. Another innovative program in New York City is sponsored by the city's largest private chain of cafeterias—in Woolworth stores; certain stores offer a special meal, planned by a nutritionist, ethnically matched to the neighborhood, for senior citizens at a current cost of 89 cents. Reportedly, one graduate student in a gerontology program earned her master's degree by designing and carrying out that program. In another context, we also mentioned the "Meals on Wheels" program, which also provides that important hot, nutritional meal to homebound elderly persons.

Although some inroads are being made, the problem of nutrition is still a major one for the elderly, especially for the poor and socially isolated person. As serious as this problem may be in some areas of the cities, however, consider the dimensions of the nutrition problem among the rural elderly who may live miles from the nearest store, and especially for elderly persons on American Indian reservations! We will discuss this a bit more later.

Special Concerns of the Elderly

The five issues we have discussed are the basic ones in terms of social policy and social service for the elderly. However, there are a great number of additional issues that are perhaps as important. Not the least of these issues are the multiple jeopardies of minority aged persons, which we will discuss in some detail in the next section. Now, however, we call attention to a number of special concerns expressed by the elderly at the 1971 White House Conference on Aging.

Employment and Retirement. Should persons have free choice whether to continue working or to retire? If continued employment is desired, where will the jobs come from, considering the current level of general unemployment? How can age discrimination be removed from areas where chronological age alone is not relevant, such as in performance of many jobs? What kind of volunteer or part-time paid jobs might be well suited to the elderly? In New York, for example, there is a group of retired business executives (called "Executive Volunteer Corps") who provide business advice to younger business men; the men are volunteers, and the program is supported by the city. Also, some "grandmothers" are working in elementary schools, schools for the retarded, and day-care centers as paid or nonpaid "paraprofessionals"; some "grandfathers" are working in kindergartens providing a unique male presence and generally delighting parents, teachers, and children. One nationwide program, the Foster Grandparents Program, has been in operation over six years, funded by federal poverty programs. Not only does it provide patience, love, and understanding—qualities that often come easily to grandparents —but also the program takes a number of persons off welfare rolls and provides much-needed service to the community; it is estimated that the program generates more in benefits than it costs (*Newsweek*, 1972a). What other creative and useful roles could the aged play in society?

Spiritual Needs. Do the aged have special spiritual needs? Are they living in places in the community and in institutions where spiritual counsel is readily available? Might special training of the clergy and other religious workers be beneficial for meeting these needs? What role might religious institutions play in affirming the reverence for life (even in old age and even in nursing homes) and the right to die with dignity? Can religious institutions play a role of advocacy, helping the elderly find ways to meet their varied needs?

Age Discrimination. Perhaps there are legitimate ways in which chrono-logical age may be used as a criterion—for example, in determining eligi-bility for Social Security or reduced transit fares. But is age a relevant criterion for determining eligibility for credit, insurance, or employment? Is chronological age alone a relevant criterion for revoking a driver's license? At the least, more specific research is needed to determine whether age is a relevant criterion for particular areas; and uniform na-tional guidlines might be established for such areas as driving or profes-sional practice. However, age discrimination may be considerably more subtle than overt discrimination; it may take the form of what has been called *ageism.*—"... moderately negative stereotypes about the aged, feel-ings of superiority among the non-aged, and simple exclusion or avoid-ance of the aged" (Palmore, 1972). As Butler (1969) pointed out when he coined the term, "Prejudice of the middle-aged against the old in this instance, and against the young in others, is a serious national problem. Age-ism reflects a deep seated uneasiness on the part of the young and middle-aged—a personal revulsion to and distaste for growing old, dis-ease, disability; and fear of powerlessness, 'uselessness,' and death" (p. 243). Such subtle ageism is probably present (or at least not directly counteracted) in most professional training programs (such as medicine, law, and psychology) as well as in most of the institutions that serve or have contact with the aged (hospitals, courts, police, businesses, and so on). Ageism is also easily compounded into a double jeopardy by racism.

Legal Services. The aged, like all citizens, are guaranteed full access to all legal services, including advocacy, administrative reform, litigation, and legislation. But does this exist in reality? Do they have special legal needs, such as protection from consumer fraud? Are there special considerations in helping them function as witnesses or plaintiffs in trials or in police investigations? How can they be provided better police protection? Do they need access to free legal advice and counsel? Are their constitutional rights to privacy, dignity, and freedom of association actually protected by legal, welfare, and police institutions (to name only a few)? Undoubt-edly, law schools, police academies, and the judicial system are not com-pletely free of ageism.

Crime. The aged are the most vulnerable persons in the community to muggings, robbery, and physical assault. They are physically incapable of escaping or resisting the attacker, and their slow pace makes them easy targets. In addition, since many urban aged remain in their old home or apartment, they are more likely to be living in deteriorating neighborhoods from which the more affluent and younger families have fled; if they are living in public housing—or, the New York tragedy, "welfare hotels"—they are exposed to crime, drugs, and violence inside the building as well as on the streets. Valerie Levy, director of the Harlem-East Harlem Office for the Aging in New York City, has pointed out the complexity of the problem since it reflects not only the many factors involved in urban crime, but also reflects the attitudes of the young toward the elderly. Perhaps, she suggests, if the country can mount a yearly public relations campaign to protect school children, there might be a similar effort to protect the elderly. One slogan that comes to mind is: "Was *YOUR* Grandmother Ripped Off Today?—Protect Our Elderly!"

Consumer Protection. There are a range of consumer services that are important to the elderly but that may be confusing and seductively attractive as well, thus setting the stage for fraud. Consumer protection for the elderly involves two interrelated aspects: education and legal protection. Both consumer education and adequate protection against fraud are important in such varied areas as budgeting, banking and lending, funeral plans, insurance, health foods, quack cures, nutrition, pricing practices, medical care and services, public assistance and services, real estate, retirement planning, safety, door-to-door selling, telephone or mail solicitation, and false advertising. Of particular importance are such concerns as unit pricing of consumer commodities (showing cost per standard unit), access to prices for prescription drugs (to allow comparison between stores), obvious dating of all perishable food products, and a "cooling off" period to allow cancellation of contracts sold door-to-door.

Mental Health. Because aged persons are likely to suffer a number of economic and social losses during their later years, the elderly require unrestricted access to adequate mental health care reflecting the variety of needs represented in the heterogeneous population of elderly persons. Adequate care does *not* mean "custodial care" because the old person is assumed to be "too old to change"; it means increased availability of knowledge and workers trained to deal with the emotional problems of the aged, and it means the continued development of innovative in-patient and community-based treatment programs.

Multiple Jeopardy: Minority Aging

In many ways the aged suffer the problems of minority group status comparable to racial and ethnic or cultural minority persons in this country. But these minority group problems are compounded when one is *both* aged and black or aged and an American Indian, for example. Typically, there has been little information available on such double minority persons until recently. Yet these minority aged not only have more severe struggles with the problems we have discussed but also have unique problems and needs as well as unique contributions that might otherwise be given to society; thus the social loss is also doubled. We will discuss several (but certainly not all) of the countless minority groups.

Elderly Blacks. About 7 percent of the Negro population in the United States is over age 65 (compared with 10 percent of the total U.S. population), reflecting the somewhat shorter life expectancy of black persons (which essentially disappears for individuals who survive to the later age periods). Strikingly, nearly half of the black persons over age 65 are below the poverty line (compared with 23 percent of elderly whites); and in 1969, one-third of elderly black persons who lived alone or with non-relatives had incomes below $1000, compared with only 14 percent of such white persons (U. S. Senate Special Committee on Aging, 1971). Life expectancy for black men is about seven years less than for white men (61 and 68), indicating that many do not live to be old enough to collect Social Security or Medicare (ibid.). However, many who survive to old age are likely to live as long as whites; and there is no significant difference between elderly blacks and whites on such characteristics as marital status, importance of family, religion, health, or activity in formal organizations (Jackson, 1970). One acute problem for the black elderly is *survival* on a less than subsistence income. Most black persons receive less than the average Social Security check because the jobs that were open to them during their working lives were domestic and farm jobs that were not covered by Social Security; they then receive only the minimum payment today and may be forced to degrade themselves after a life of hard work by applying for welfare (in the form of Old Age Assistance and food stamps). Another major problem, beyond the countless ones that this poverty income imposes, is the great difficulty in gaining admission to an old age home—"The greater problem for black aged is not [staying out but] ... *getting into nursing homes*" (White House Conference on Aging, 1971, p. 184). A 1967-1969 survey of nursing homes in Chicago found that homes with the largest number of resources for their residents were "more likely to care for only white residents, while blacks were cared for in institutions sparse in treatment resources" (Kosberg and Tobin, 1972, p. 216). Similarly, the homes with greater treatment resources were located in nonurban areas, and homes with sparse treatment resources cared for public aid recipients. Added to this double jeopardy is the combination of liabilities involving less education, poorer housing, and fewer choices of alternate styles of life. The recommendations of the participants at the White House Conference included lowering the age for

Social Security benefits for black persons, enhanced training of black students and staff for nursing homes, development of a wide range of alternate strategies for nursing home care, funding training programs at black colleges for working with the aged, abolition of Old Age Assistance in favor of a guaranteed retirement income, and greatly expanded funding of all services for the black aged. It is obvious that in this respect, as in most others, the problems of the aged are a magnified reflection of the problems faced by younger persons; and any change for the aged is likely to involve major changes throughout the entire society. Certainly, the general social plague of racism and poverty is extenuated for the aged, and the scourge for the aged cannot be solved without also attending to racism and poverty.

American Indians. Perhaps the most deprived group in the United States are the natives. Almost no data is available on the depth of their misery, but the per capita income of American Indians is about one-third that of the total population. Life expectancy is estimated at 46 years; and only about 6 percent or 45,000-50,000 Indians survive to age 65. Their life is characterized by dilapidated housing (63 percent have inadequate heating, 21 percent have no electric power), inadequate nutrition, insufficient medical services, and poor transportation (U. S. Senate Special Committee on Aging, 1971). There are almost no programs for the aged, and most services are noncoordinated and do not give much consideration to the cultural desires of the tribe. Clearly, the plight of the aged Indian (and, by implication, all Indians) demands immediate forceful intervention; indeed it raises the more basic social question of why the life-maintaining conditions have been allowed to exist at such a low level.

Asian Americans. According to the delegates at the White House Conference, aging Asian Americans are one of the most overlooked groups. No funds were earmarked for them during 1969-1971 and a study was reported that found one-third have never had a medical or dental examination; instead, they look only to their families for help. Clearly, research is needed to establish the extent and types of needs for this group of aged persons. Language barriers and the cultural diversity of Asian Americans are two of the obvious aspects that may present unique challenges to providing services that are meaningful for these aged persons. Also, the delegates recommended providing support services which recognize the salience of family and kin networks and which build upon these existing systems, rather than imposing a strange new bureaucratic system. Housing within the cultural environment seems obviously important. Bilingual staffing, ethnic foods, counseling, recreation, and leisure activities relevant for the person's cultural experience would be benefits in nursing home settings. Bilingual mobile health teams might be one creative way of providing meaningful medical services. Food stamps should be allowed to be used for the purchase of ethnic foods. Recognition should be given to the unique income-saving plans of Asian elderly and they might be legitimated and safeguarded. One other recommendation the delegates made is even more surprising than the others—that the time spent by the aged Japanese in concentration camps in the United States during World War II has not been, but should be counted toward Social Security benefits!

Spanish-Speaking Americans. Extreme poverty characterizes this group of elderly persons also. "For all Mexican-Americans, the likelihood of being poor is nearly three times as great as for Anglos" (U. S. Senate Special Committee on Aging, 1971); life expectancy is about 57 years; and most of the 3.3 percent (about 165,000) over age 65 worked in occupations that were not covered by Social Security until recently. Many are not aware of the benefits available, even if they are qualified to receive them. About 626,000 Cubans are living in the United States, and it is estimated that about 6 percent are over age 65, but large numbers of them are ineligible for Social Security because they did not work in this country long enough to qualify for benefits; hence 61 percent of all persons receiving welfare assistance under the Cuban Refugee Program are 65 or older (U. S. Senate Special Committee on Aging, 1971). One important issue for these two groups is the distinction between alien and citizen; benefits that are available to citizens are not always available to noncitizens; and voting power is clearly one unavailable resource for aliens. The twentieth century airborne migration of Puerto Ricans to the mainland of the United States has brought an estimated 811,000 persons born on the island of Puerto Rico; total Puerto Rican population on the mainland was estimated to be 1,454,000 in 1971; about two-thirds live in New York City. Four percent of these persons in New York City are over 65, compared with 6 percent on the Island (mortality patterns have changed drastically on the Island—life expectancy was 46 years in 1940; in 1960 it was 71 years!). Although little data is available nationwide, in New York City, the Puerto Rican population was the poorest in 1971—60 percent of the elderly and 35 percent in the age group from 45-64 had incomes below $3000 (compared with 55 percent and 15 percent for blacks and 50 percent and 5 percent for whites according to the N. Y. City Office for the Aging). In addition to these obvious income problems, Spanish-speaking aged also have language and cultural barriers that prevent full utilization of the community resources. As with other bilingual groups, the delegates to the White House Conference recommended training bilingual students for careers in aging, bilingual information from all agencies about programs and services available, and the involvement of these aged in the planning and development of all programs serving them. In addition, the delegates recommended emphasizing rehabilitation of housing, rather than urban renewal, since many Spanish-speaking elderly own their own homes and value this "real" property. Also, cultural considerations as well as bilingual staffing should be involved in nursing home facilities. And they recommended extending all programs on the mainland to the island of Puerto Rico and emphasized requiring Social Security payments to be made by migrant workers as well as by the farmers who employ them.

Implications

The goals and the problems of the aged in our country reflect our basic assumptions as a free society. That is, we assume every person is entitled to freedom of association and expression, the right to privacy, the right of individual choice, free access to the resources of the community, and independence and dignity. Ideally, such basic freedoms are taken away only under the most judicious and extreme circumstances. Yet, many elderly persons have effectively lost some of these basic human rights because there can be no freedom of choice if there are no viable alternatives. If one is to choose where to live out one's last days, there must be a range of alternatives. Thus, an important policy goal is to widen the range of positive alternatives for the aged person. As Britton and Britton (1972) concluded from their study of personality and aging:

> It seems quite imprudent to speak of a *single*, optimum environment for all people. Rather, we prefer a society that strives to provide a variety of behavioral settings which offer continued opportunities for individually satisfying involvement, for the possibility of new and stimulating experiences, and for varieties of behaviors which can be freely chosen. Recognition that growth and change in persons *of all ages* and characteristics may be possible is essential to a truly humanitarian and democratic society (Britton and Britton, 1972, p. 170).

Too often today this freedom to choose between viable alternatives is lacking in many areas of the aged person's life. Where is this freedom, for example, when all one can do is to struggle for survival in an urban (or rural) slum? And do these freedoms also imply that every person is entitled to education, health care, adequate food and housing regardless of age or sex or color?

Elderly persons have been relatively slow to take an active role in protesting their complaints and making their political power effective. However, they represent a sizable minority group—and a group who typically have a higher proportion of voters than other age groups. When they hold demonstrations—using the slogan "Senior Power"—their impact is often very significant. Old persons in wheelchairs or walking with a "walker" and carrying protest signs conveys a very effective message. And if senior citizens developed more political consensus and vote as a

power group, local, state, and federal politicians would take their complaints more seriously.

One encouraging development is the rapid growth of senior citizen
organizations. At a national level the most obvious example is the American Association of Retired Persons, whose membership has grown from
400,000 members in 1960 to 5,000,000 members in 1973. At the local level,
senior citizen centers and offices for the aging are developing; these often
provide a sense of community and identification for old people who
have common problems. The political—and moral—force of the collective
complaints, protests, and political power that may arise from this sense
of common problems is clearly an important positive force for improving
policies affecting the aged.

NURSING HOMES: A NATIONAL SCAPEGOAT

It is too easy to condemn nursing homes as an unmitigated evil that
brings terror to the minds of aging persons. Our society has been forced
to deal with the severe problems of caring for the sick and infirm old
person who either could not be cared for at home or was not wanted at
home. Thus, nursing homes developed. With Medicare and public assistance and a sense of social responsibility commingled with the motive for
profit, nursing homes or extended care facilities have turned into a major
business in our country (Table 10.1).

Some nursing homes probably make substantial profits; but most are
caught between the expense of providing the best possible care for the
relatively low amount of money that society (government, families, insurance—all of us) has seen fit to spend caring for the incapacitated and
dying old person. There have been flagrant abuses of old persons in every
regard—not the least of which are cases of food poisoning, fires, and
policies requiring the applicant to sign over his entire estate in return for
care, but when the money runs out before his life forces do, he is moved
to another home for public aid recipients.

Although only 4-5 percent of the aged live in nursing homes at any one
time, a study of "places of death" obtained from obituary notices or death
certificates found that 12 to 20 percent of the deaths had occurred in an
extended care facility (Kastenbaum and Candy, 1972). This implies that
while nearly all aged persons are community residents, a substantial
proportion spend their last days in a nursing home.

In general, there are very good nursing homes and very bad nursing
homes; and one usually gets what one pays for. Kosberg and Tobin (1972)
analyzed a survey of all 214 nursing homes serving aged persons in the
Chicago area from 1967 to 1969. They found marked variation in a wide
range of characteristics among the homes. For example, only 37 percent

Table 10.1   Characteristics of Nursing Homes in the United States, 1970

Number of nursing homes	23,000—doubled since 1960
Type of ownership	
Proprietary for profit	77 percent
Private nonprofit	15 percent
Type of support	
Government (state and local)	8 percent
Federal government	Over $1 billion
State and local government	$700 million
Private sources	$900 million
Total revenues	$2.6 billion (increased four times from 1960–1967)
Number of beds in nursing homes	1,100,000—tripled since 1960
Number of nursing home residents	894,500 (1969)
Proportion over age 65	90 percent
Proportion over age 85	33 percent
Average age	80 years
Nursing home personnel (total)	500,000

Source. U.S. Senate Special Committee on Aging (1971), p. 30; and U.S. Senate Special Committee on Aging. *Developments in Aging, 1970.* Report No. 92-46. Washington, D.C.: U.S. Government Printing Office, 1971, p. 42.

of the homes had physical therapy equipment. Two out of five homes did not employ physical therapists at all; three out of five did not have an occupational therapist; 85 percent did not employ a social worker at all.

From these findings, it is apparent that the nursing home field, *in toto*, is composed of institutions varying considerably in their ability to provide restorative care and treatment—as indicated by the extent of treatment resources. On one end of the continuum are nursing homes which have high proportions of nursing personnel . . . , contain medical and therapeutic equipment, and frequently have a variety of professionals available for the residents. On the other end of the resource continuum are those nursing homes which have few professionals available, low proportions of nurses to total staff and residents, and little equipment to meet the medical and therapeutic needs of the residents. This latter group of nursing homes can offer little more than custodial care to the elderly population (Kosberg and Tobin, 1972, p. 216).

Nursing homes that offered many treatment resources tended to be located in nonurban, usually suburban areas; they were likely to conform to licensing standards, to be accredited (by the Joint Commission on Hospital Accreditation), to be certified by Medicare, and to belong to nursing home associations. They were more likely to care only for white persons; their payments were from private sources or from Medicare; and their residents were likely to have referred themselves or to have been referred by a physician. Referrals by public aid or for public aid recipients were to homes with few treatment resources. The homes with few treatment resources tended to care for black persons and persons who had lived in other nursing homes, mental hospitals, and other long-term care facilities.

Although only a few of the homes were not privately owned, there was no relationship between extent of services and type of ownership, background of the owner or administrator, or ownership by a multiunit corporation. Instead, the larger the size of the home, the greater the resources; the greater the number of levels of care (e.g., intensive, intermediate, and basic), the better the resources; and the greater the expense, the better the resources. It was also found that the best homes in terms of treatment resources often charged extra for a number of care services (while homes with fewer resources did not)—"It could only be assumed that extra charges for care are necessary to allow a home to afford treatment resources" (ibid., p. 218).

Kosberg and Tobin conclude that upgrading nursing home standards, which are often taken to represent maximum extent of care, is an important means to improve the conditions of these homes combined with efficient formal and informal surveillance (e.g., by family, friends, and the physician). But the worst homes were those that cared for the poor, indicating a "cycle of indifference" that reflects not only the inadequacy of national policy and social welfare but also wider social values and attitudes about the aged and the poor.

 Upgrading nursing homes is only one aspect of a possible solution, however. Much innovative exploration needs to be done on the alternatives to institutional care such as home health services, outpatient occupational and physical therapy, meals on wheels, day centers, short "recuperative holidays" in the nursing home (perhaps while the family takes a planned vacation), and intermittent short admissions. After all, much of the worst part of nursing homes is the "No Deposit, No Return" attitude of the community and the family.

In 1970 a small group of students under the direction of Ralph Nader investigated the entire area of nursing home care for the aged (Townsend, 1971); their report is valuable reading because it contains not only a wide range of information, but also includes personal reactions of the students to working in several homes. It also presents a stinging critique as well as many suggestions for improvement—not the least of which is an "Old People's Liberation Movement." One of its most useful contributions is a list of questions to ask and areas to explore when considering a nursing home for an aged person. Some of these questions include:

> Does the home offer progressive stages of care? ... Does the home require a complete physical before entrance, or immediately upon arrival? Is there also a questionnaire to be filled out dealing with the patient's hobbies, favorite pastimes, etc.? ... Does the owner require entrance contracts that fail to promise a return of property if a patient leaves the home? (Always get an entrance contract checked by a lawyer.) ... How many patients are bedridden? (If large numbers are confined to their beds, it might indicate a lack of staff.) ... Is there an in-service training program ... ? (This shows a willingness on the part of the home to improve the quality of care.) ... Is there a good rapport between the staff and the patients? ... Are the patients clean? Is their hair neat, clean, and combed? Are their finger- and toenails clean and cut? Is there an extra charge for washing hair or for cutting nails? ... Are the bedrooms neat and clean? ... Are the emergency buzzers within reach of the patients? Do the nurses respond to these calls quickly? ... Is there any urine smell in the home? Or a heavy cover-up smell? ... Does the home have a regular dietician? (Ask to see the kitchen.) ... Are there different diets for patients who require them? ... Does the staff eat the same food as the residents? ... How many residents use the dining room? Do they seem to enjoy their meals? ... Do the bedridden patients receive hot food? ... At what hours are the meals served? (Some homes serve all the meals within one shift to save money.) ... Does the home charge extra for hand feeding? (This is ridiculous, since the need for being fed may well be the reason for institutionalization in the first place.) ... Are the surroundings cold, impersonal, hard to adjust to? ... Is there a sprinkler system and fire extinguishers? Is there a heat and smoke sensor system, with an automatic direct alarm line hooked up with the local fire station? [Does the staff have regular fire drills so they know what to do in case of fire?] ... Are there handrails along the halls? Guardrails in the bathrooms? ... Does the home provide occupational therapy? Physical therapy? Recreational therapy? ... Is there a therapist who works often enough to fulfill the patients' needs? ... Are visitors encouraged to come? (If visiting hours are restricted at all, perhaps the nursing home is trying to hide something.) ... Do the patients seem happy? Would *you* feel happy leaving your mother there? (Townsend, 1971, pp. 207-209).[1]

---

[1] Reprinted with permission of Grossman Publishers from *Old Age: The Last Segregation*, copyright © 1970, 1971 by The Center for Study of Responsive Law.

It may be obvious that if one explores the home carefully and asks these questions as well as the others suggested by Townsend and her coworkers, there is enough care and interest already expressed to insure that the old person whom one is trying to place will find a rather good home and that the family will continue to be involved, thereby maintaining surveillance of the home. This degree of interest is probably the key to not only finding a good home for a loved old person who requires one but also helps to improve the quality of care. However, good homes are also likely to be expensive and to have waiting lists—which brings us back to the basic social issues involved. If the old person is to have freedom of choice, then a range of desirable alternatives is essential. How can these be provided and maintained?

EDUCATION FOR THE FUTURE

There is scarcely a profession that is not directly or indirectly connected with the needs of aging persons. In the fields of psychology, sociology, social work, medicine, nursing, and psychiatry there are specialities in gerontology or geriatrics that train persons to provide direct service to the aged. In biology and physiology there is a great need for research on the basic mechanisms of aging. In anthropology there is a need for research on the effects of cultural variations on the aging process—both in different cultures and in different subcultures within a society. In fields such as architecture and engineering there are great challenges for designing barrier-free environments, housing, and transportation for the elderly. In political science, history, literature, drama, and the arts (to mention some less obvious examples) there are fascinating studies or applications waiting to be made concerning aging—one example may suffice: how have films portrayed aging and how is it portrayed presently; what symbols are used and what is its symbolism?

The past decade has seen the emergence of a number of training programs in adult development and aging, or human development, or gerontology. They have been established in a number of universities across the nation and have emerged in a variety of settings—both in established academic disciplines such as sociology, psychology, and social work as well as in interdisciplinary programs that draw faculty and students from a range of specialities. It is obvious that these training and research programs are important for advancing our understanding of the aging process and for equipping professionals to work with the aged. However, since the federal government has been the only governmental agency in the past that has been effective in advancing research and innovative programs for the elderly, these training programs—as well as a range of direct services for the aged—are directly dependent on federal funding.

Hence, the political power of the aged and the political question of national spending priorities directly affect research, training, and services concerning the elderly. Currently (1973), federal funds are being cut back and these programs—and the aged—are directly threatened. What are the national spending priorities that we want for the future?

The past decade has also seen an increase in the membership of professional organizations concerned with the aged such as the Gerontological Society. This organization is made up of persons in a wide range of professions concerned with research in the natural and social sciences and with planning and services concerning the aged. It has been deeply involved in training programs and serves as an important forum for the exchange of research and ideas about the field of gerontology. It also serves as a major clearinghouse and center for information about this rapidly growing field.

Thus, the field of adulthood and aging is one that offers a range of professional training opportunities; and since the field is relatively new, it offers one the possibility of playing an important part in its growth.

However, there are also a number of occupations that serve the aged directly in various contexts, but do not specifically involve gerontology. For example, administration, accounting, clerical work, and computer science are all fields that are important in hospital or nursing home management, in city and state and federal offices for the aging, and in organizations for the aged (such as the American Association of Retired Persons). And lawyers, accountants (especially for taxes), dentists, podiatrists, chiropractors, optometrists, and clergymen all serve the aged professionally and might even specialize in the aged or volunteer their services for the poor aged. In addition, several occupations are involved with the aged in hospitals and nursing homes. These occupations include, in addition to the ones we have already mentioned, physical therapists, occupational therapists, recreational therapists, music or dance therapists, and speech therapists. Dietitians, pharmacists, laboratory technicians, radiologists and, indeed, the entire health services field are represented in some of the best hospitals and homes for the aged. In many of these fields there are excellent opportunities for employment and advancement as well as for personal satisfaction.

Thus, there are countless ways in which students may be trained to work with the aging (or with adults generally). There are also countless paraprofessional jobs and roles being developed for persons with less than a bachelor's degree. Some of these include work in the community to improve the quality of community life and to maximize the freedom of aged persons. And nearly every senior citizen center and home or hospital for the aged or chronically ill appreciates volunteers for a variety of roles. Actually, there is little better way to gain an understanding of an area such as adulthood and aging than by directly experiencing it;

and volunteer roles provide this opportunity as well as an important additional benefit—they allow a young person to test out some of the jobs that are interesting and to talk with persons who are actually doing that kind of work. This is an important resource for vocational choice!

Since one of the keys to aiding the minority aged person is having trained minority persons (often bilingual) who can provide direct services to the aged and can serve as resource persons on ways to improve the condition of the aged they know best, it is clear that minority students need to be attracted into these fields. A heterogeneous group of aged persons demands a heterogeneous supply of trained professionals and paraprofessionals.

But education of young persons is only one aspect of the educational needs in this area. Middle-aged and older persons can also benefit from greatly expanded educational opportunities—in reality, throughout one's life—not only to fulfill themselves, but also to acquire new skills to aid others. Certainly, one significant resource for service to the aged are the aged themselves; and the range of skills needed to serve as representative members of groups being served on governmental boards setting priorities, establishing policies, and providing funding—or to provide direct services to the aged themselves—may require new education in a variety of fields. Some colleges, such as the City University of New York, have recently opened their doors to persons over 65, and the impact of this concept might revolutionize thinking about the place and function of education in life and in our society.

As we look toward the future and imagine what kind of lives we want to have for ourselves in a diversified society that is faced with serious social problems and a fast pace of technological change, the opportunities and challenges are truly astounding! As years are added to life, will life be added to (our) years? How quickly will the inequities faced by the aged and all of the other minority groups be adjusted? What will we do with these opportunities and challenges? Perhaps the place to begin is with that lonely old person who reminds us of what might happen to us if nothing changes but ourselves as we grow old.

References

Britton, Joseph H., and Britton, Jean O. 1972. *Personality Changes in Aging.* New York: Springer.

Butler, Robert N. 1969. Age-Ism: Another Form of Bigotry. *Gerontologist, 9*(4, Part 1), 243–246.

Jackson, Jacquelyne Johnson. 1970. Aged Negroes: Their Cultural Departures from Statistical Stereotypes and Rural-Urban Differences. *Gerontologist, 10*(2), 140–145.

Kastenbaum, Robert, and Candy, Sandra. 1972. The 4% Fallacy: A Methodological and Empirical Critique of Extended Care Facility Population Statistics. Paper presented at the meeting of the Gerontological Society, San Juan, Puerto Rico, December, 1972.

Kosberg, Jordan I., and Tobin, Sheldon S. 1972. Variability Among Nursing Homes. *Gerontologist, 12*(3, Part 1), 214–219.

Kreps, Juanita. 1970. Statement released by the White House Conference on Aging, December 31, 1970. Cited in U.S. Senate Special Committee on Aging. *Developments in Aging, 1970.* Report No. 92–46. Washington, D.C.: U.S. Government Printing Office, 1971.

Muskie, Edmund S. 1971. Hearings of the Subcommittee on Health of the Elderly, May 10, 1971. Cited in U.S. Senate Special Committee on Aging. *A Pre-White House Conference on Aging: Summary of Development and Data.* Washington, D.C.: U.S. Government Printing Office, 1971.

Newsweek. **1972a.** A Visit from Grandmother. October 30, 1972, 94.

Newsweek. **1972b.** The 130-Year-Old Man. October 2, 1972, 74.

Palmore, Erdman. 1972. Gerontophobia versus Ageism. *Gerontologist, 12*(3, Part 1), 213.

Townsend, Claire. 1971. *Old Age: The Last Segregation.* New York: Grossman Publishers (Bantam).

U.S. Senate Special Committee on Aging. 1971. *A Pre-White House Conference on Aging: Summary of Development and Data.* Washington, D.C.: U.S. Government Printing Office.

White House Conference on Aging. 1971. *Toward a National Policy on Aging.* Vol. 2. Stock No. 1762-0069. Washington, D.C.: U.S. Government Printing Office.

Author/Citation Index

*Pages in *italics* refer to citations in figures and tables. Pages in **boldface** refer to references.

Lewin, Arie Y.
    Lewin and Duchan (1971), 172, **174**
Lewin, Kurt (1935), 295, **329**
Lewis, C. S. (1943), 260, **272**
Lieberman, Morton A.
    Lieberman (1965), 15, **41**, 415-418, **436**
    Lieberman (1966), 410, 418, **436**
    Lieberman and Coplan (1969), 409, 411-
        412, 418-419, **436**
Lieberman, Seymour (1956), 72, **74**
Lief, Harold (1972), 103, **113**
Lindemann, Erich (1944), 431, **436**
Lindop, Patricia J.
    Lindop and Rotblat (1961), 348, **389**
Lipman, Aaron
    Lipman and Marden (1966), 410, **436**
Litwak, Eugene (1960), 191, **238**
Livson, Florine
    Reichard, Livson, and Peterson (1962),
        262-263, **272**, 308, **330**
Locke, Ben Z.
    Locke, Kramer, and Pasamanick (1960),
        225, **238**
Locke, Harvey J. (1951), 224, **238**
Loomis, Barbara
    Neugarten, Wood, Kraines, and Loomis
        (1963), 141-144, 146, **175**
Lotka, Alfred J.
    Dublin, Lotka, and Spiegelman (1949), 350,
        387
Lowe, John C.
    Neugarten, Moore, and Lowe (1965), 13,
        41, 62-65, **75**, **78**, **114**
Lowell, E. L.
    McClelland, Atkinson, Clark, and Lowell
        (1953), 161, **174**
Lowenthal, Marjorie Fiske
    Lowenthal (1964), 257, **272**, 319, 323,
        326, **330**
    Lowenthal and Haven (1968), 317-319,
        330
Lubin, Marc (1964), 310, **330**
Luce, Gay (1971), 297, **330**
Ludvigson, H. W.
    Kantor, Michael, Boulas, Shore, and
        Ludvigson (1966), 141, **174**
Luterman, David M.
    Melrose, Welsh, and Luterman (1963), 372,
        389
Lutkins, S. G.
    Rees and Lutkins (1967), 431, 432, **437**

MacBrayer, Caroline T. (1960), 159, **174**
Maccoby, Eleanor E. (1966), 152, 163, **174**

Maddox, George L.
    Maddox (1963), 315, **330**
    Maddox (1966)[a], 315, **330**
    Maddox (1966)[b], 215, **238**, 255, 256,
        272
    Maddox (1970), 315, **330**
Malcolm, Andrew H. (1972), 234, **238**
Mandelbaum, D. G. (1959), 434, **436**
Mannheim, Karl (1952), 30, **41**
Manniche, E.
    Manniche and Falk (1957), 385, **389**
Marden, Philip W.
    Lipman and Marden (1966), 410, **436**
Martin, Clyde E.
    Kinsey, Pomeroy, and Martin (1948), 103,
        113, 205, **238**
    Kinsey, Pomeroy, Martin, Gebhard, and As-
        sociates (1953), 104, **113**, 148, **174**, 204,
        206, **238**
Maslow, Abraham H.
    Maslow (1950), 298, **330**
    Maslow (1955), 202, **238**
Masters, William H.
    Kolodny, Masters, Hendryx, and Toro
        (1971), 134-135, **174**, 296, **329**
    Masters and Johnson (1961), 147, **174**
    Masters and Johnson (1963), 146, **174**
    Masters and Johnson (1966), 146, **174**,
        216-217, **238**
    Masters and Johnson (1970), 141, 146, **174**,
        212, 217, **238**
Maurice, William L.
    Clayton, Halikes, and Maurice (1971), 431,
        432, **436**
May, Rollo (1958), 408, **436**
McClelland, D. C.
    McClelland, Atkinson, Clark, and Lowell
        (1953), 161, **174**
McClemont, W. F.
    Price, Strong, Whatmore, and McClemont
        (1966), 133, **175**
McCurdy, Harold G. (1961), 202, **239**
McFarland, Ross A.
    McFarland, Tune, and Welford (1964), 374,
        375, **389**
Mead, George Herbert (1934), 44, 45-54, **74**,
    109, **113**
Mead Margaret
    Mead (1949), 151-152, **174**
    Mead (1970), 31, **41**, 82, **113**
    Mead (1971), 194, **239**
    Mead (1972), 346, **389**
Melrose, Jay
    Melrose, Welsh, and Luterman

Subject Index